AF400666

A HISTORY OF THE WESTERN ART MARKET

A HISTORY OF THE WESTERN ART MARKET

A HISTORY OF THE WESTERN ART MARKET

A Sourcebook of Writings on Artists, Dealers, and Markets

Edited by TITIA HULST

UNIVERSITY OF CALIFORNIA PRESS

University of California Press, one of the most distinguished university presses in the United States, enriches lives around the world by advancing scholarship in the humanities, social sciences, and natural sciences. Its activities are supported by the UC Press Foundation and by philanthropic contributions from individuals and institutions. For more information, visit www.ucpress.edu.

University of California Press
Oakland, California

© 2017 by The Regents of the University of California

Every effort has been made to trace copyright holders and to obtain their permission for the use of copyright material. The publisher apologizes for any errors or omissions and would be grateful if notified of any corrections or proper credits that should be incorporated in future reprints or editions of this book.

Library of Congress Cataloging-in-Publication Data

Names: Hulst, Titia, editor.
Title: A history of the western art market : a sourcebook of writings on
    artists, dealers, and markets / edited by Titia Hulst.
Description: Oakland, California : University of California Press, [2017] |
    Includes bibliographical references and index.
Identifiers: LCCN 2017024258| ISBN 9780520290624 (cloth : alk. paper) |
    ISBN 9780520290631 (pbk. : alk. paper)
Subjects: LCSH: Art—Marketing—History. | Art—Economic aspects—History. |
    Art—Collectors and collecting—History. | Artists—Europe, Western. | Art
    dealers.
Classification: LCC N8600 .H57 2017 | DDC 700.74—dc23
LC record available at https://lccn.loc.gov/2017024258

24   23   22   21   20   19   18   17
10   9   8   7   6   5   4   3   2   1

To Paul

CONTENTS

A NOTE TO READERS

The aim of this reader is to present a wide-ranging set of texts from a variety of academic perspectives on the art market and its participants. For this reason, the texts have been excerpted—with the gracious permission of all authors and rights holders—from published work. Section titles are sometimes a shortened or edited version of the original to more clearly convey the excerpt's content. Readers are encouraged to consult the original sources, listed with each excerpt, for the complete texts. Due to space restraints, footnotes, illustrations, tables, and other general references have been omitted, except for direct quotes from academic sources, which are cited within the texts and refer to the bibliography.

Within the excerpts the following punctuation conventions are followed: Ellipses (. . .) within a sentence indicate that a word or words were omitted. Bracketed ellipses [. . .] indicate omissions extending from a complete sentence to a paragraph or two, or several paragraphs when followed by a linespace. Ellipses and bracketed ellipses at the beginning of a paragraph indicate that the excerpt begins mid-sentence or mid-paragraph in the original source.

INTRODUCTION

The study of art markets has emerged as a promising new field within art history, a natural outgrowth of the renewed interest of art historians in the social and economic contexts in which artworks are produced. In the preface to his pioneering 1973 study of the social changes that took place in the mid-nineteenth century and their influence on the painter Gustave Courbet, the art historian T. J. Clark called for this change in focus. Instead of linking artworks and artists to the general history of the time studied, assuming that "the artist's point of reference as a social being is, a priori, the artistic community," and depending on "intuitive analogies" between form and content alone, Clark argued that art historians should focus on the *audience* for art, which, he maintained, is not the same as the public at large (1999, 9–10). He suggested that this audience (which necessarily includes dealers, collectors, and critics) needs to be examined empirically if we want to truly understand any major shift in the production of art in a society.

One of the best-known examples of such a market-driven shift was uncovered by Yale University economist Michael Montias in 1982. By combining traditional art historical analysis with his expertise in economics, Montias was able to shed light on the dynamics of the seventeenth-century art market in Delft and their influence on artistic production. Montias based his analysis on market data gleaned from the extensive Delft guild archives instead of relying on biographical materials or on the traditional source of art historical knowledge, the information contained within works of art (Haverkamp-Begemann 2006, 14). His analysis of interactions among dealers, artists, and art collectors permanently changed the art historical narrative of Dutch seventeenth-century art.

Traditionally, the practice of art history focused on the aesthetic value of artworks and the function of art in society without considering the impact of the economic value (or lack thereof) the art market assigns to the objects under study. Paradoxically, art historians themselves have long played an important role in the art market. As specialists, they not only offer aesthetic judgments about existing works of art—judgments that are valued by market participants—but also serve the market by authenticating works of art that have a doubtful provenance. They are called upon to evaluate whether a particular painting or sculpture is authentic—that is, was made by the artist to whom it is attributed—or whether the work is a copy, or worse, a fake. As Marcia Pointon has argued, by ignoring the impact of their discipline on the art market, art historians have developed an extraordinary blind spot, especially because "to be an art historian is to deal in a knowledge field that is mapped by price tags" (1997a, 17). As this volume makes clear, art market history, by bringing into the conversation not only economics but also a wealth of contributions from across the academic disciplines, expands the field of art history in new and sometimes provocative ways.

MARKET BASICS

By medieval times, the Old English word *market*, originating in the Latin *mercatus*, had cognates in all other spoken languages throughout northern Europe, including Old French, Old Frisian, Old High German, and even Old Norse. It described a central place in a town or city where farmers and merchants would bring produce, livestock, and other goods for exchange. In the parlance of today, the term *market* does not necessarily refer to a physical space. It is a more abstract concept: simply speaking, a market for goods or services exists when there are people who want to buy them and people who want to sell them (McMillan 2002, 6). When we speak of the oil market, for example, we refer to the activities of a multitude of oil producers, middlemen, and retailers, and millions of consumers. A key feature of Western capitalist markets is that participation is voluntary. Market participants control their own resources and are free to decide how to allocate these resources.

Economists have long concerned themselves with how value is established in markets. Karl Marx, for example, ascribed two types of values to goods produced for the market (which he called commodities). The first of these is use value, which is unrelated to price and instead focuses on the buyer's perceived usefulness of goods (utility). The second value that is embedded in all commodities is exchange value. This value is more closely related to price. It refers to a highly abstract concept: the labor time that is embedded in the goods that are produced. According to classic Marxist theory, no commodity is brought to market without having attained exchange value.

This concept is closely related to what is known as the labor theory of value, formulated in the nineteenth century, which holds that the value of a commodity increases in proportion to the duration and intensity of labor performed on average for its production.

Workers who labor with greater skill or more productivity than others produce more value through the production of greater quantities of the finished commodity. Adam Smith recognized that certain commodities may have an exchange value without containing use value (for example, diamonds), while a commodity with very high use value may have a very low exchange value (for example, water).

Alfred Marshall, who is widely considered the founding father of modern economics, combined the labor theory of value with the marginal utility theory in his *Principles of Economics* (1890). Marshall believed that it is impossible to tell whether value is governed by utility or cost of production, proposing instead that prices are established by supply and demand. But he, like most nineteenth-century economists, realized that the value of works of art cannot easily be explained using this model. Rather than reflecting the quantity of labor that produced the work of art, prices appeared to be more related to the wealth and taste of those who desire to purchase art. Thus Marshall argued that prices for art are resistant to economic analysis exactly because "the price at which each is sold, will depend much on whether any rich persons with a fancy for it happen to be present at its sale" (Velthuis 2007, 97–98).

Today it is widely accepted that in markets, decisions regarding investment, production, and distribution are based on both the supply of and the demand for goods. The price of a good or service is determined when an equilibrium between supply and demand is achieved. Sellers of goods generate a so-called supply curve: how much of the product they would be willing to sell at any given price. This is developed through an analysis of input costs and economic profit (which implicitly includes a normal profit margin). Each market participant has a unique supply or demand curve, which may or may not align with the overall market, and each must assess how he or she values a particular good versus how the market is valuing it.

Contemporary economists who focus on the market for art are exploring whether an analysis of the aggregate price data now available from auction houses can reveal how particular features embedded in a work of art can account for the price it obtains. A number of studies have focused on whether price can be related to characteristics such as size, the style of the work, the technique used, the age of the work, the reputation of the artist, or the piece's provenance (the history of ownership). As Federico Etro and Laura Pagani showed in their paper (included in this volume), this approach can yield new insights. However, as Olav Velthuis has pointed out, the shortcoming of this type of analysis is that it does not explain whether these price-determining factors are related to the demand or supply side of the market (2007, 99).

ANOMALIES IN THE ART MARKET

Certain anomalies in the market for fine art are revealed when we compare it to a durable goods market, such as the market for luxury cars. Those looking to purchase a luxury car construct, technically speaking, a demand curve based on the needs, priorities, and desires that inform their decision to purchase a particular brand of car. Consumers might be motivated by changes in circumstances, such as new commuting requirements for work, or by a desire for social recognition. Purchasing a Lexus or a BMW might reflect a buyer's desire to "show" his or her success in life. By choosing a Volvo or a Subaru, consumers might signal a desire to belong to a community that shares concerns about safety and longevity. At the same time, buyers also are limited by how much they are willing or able to spend to satisfy these needs. Producers of luxury cars take all of this into account when designing their products and developing supply curves.

It is an article of faith for most art lovers that the producers of art—artists—behave differently than automobile manufacturers. Artists are imagined to work alone, their products the result of their creative genius, and the form and subject matter of the work are believed to be unrelated to the desires of collectors. The texts in this volume will show that artists have, in fact, a much more complex relationship to the art market. As Michael Baxandall has argued, works of art are, among other things, "fossils of economic life" (1988, 2). Kevin Murphy (in this volume) has shown that the artist Winslow Homer was in effect utilizing a supply curve in the pricing of his paintings. Professional artists cannot operate outside the system of commerce—despite the rhetoric disclaiming such association. This is illustrated by the economists Victor Ginsburgh and A. F. Penders, whose paper (included in this volume) tracks the works of Land artists traded in the auction market of the late 1960s despite the anti-market rhetoric that surrounded their work.

Nevertheless, there is truth to the observation that the market for art is different from any other market. The artist-producer possesses less information about the art market, than, say, the maker of Mercedes-Benz does about the market for luxury cars. Since art galleries and dealers are privately held enterprises that are not required to report sales and profits, the size of the art market cannot be known. Moreover, unlike other producers, artists today generally do not compute the price of a new work by adding the cost of materials, the hours of labor invested, and a reasonable profit. The value of artistic labor (the creative process) is intangible. The legendary painter Pablo Picasso could produce a drawing on ink and paper in record time—creating a value that far exceeded the cost of his materials and labor. Calculating the use value or utility of the work of art for the consumer is likewise not practicable for establishing price. As Andy Warhol, whose iconic Pop works of the 1960s were produced in the studio he pointedly called the Factory, once remarked: an artist is "somebody who produces things that people don't need to have" (1977, 146).

Calculating the price for which a work of fine art is offered for sale in the market is thus not simply a matter of finding an equilibrium price between the demand (what the consumer is willing to pay) and the supply of works of art. Moreover, because art is produced by individuals, some of whom are able endow their works with distinctive qualities, the ability of consumers to judge the fairness of the price is similarly compromised. Since most works of art are considered unique, there are no perfect "comparables." But even if there were, pricing information is difficult to obtain. Both the volume of sales and prices paid for works of art are kept private by market participants, especially for works by artists new to the market. This makes production and purchasing decisions infinitely more complex for artists (how will my work be received?), middlemen such as galleries and dealers (will this sell?), and for consumers (is it worth this price?). The last complication in the market for art is that, unlike any other goods, exceptional artworks collectively represent a region's cultural heritage. Most of the art objects that are produced today will not reach that exalted status, but some works may eventually sell at extraordinary prices once their cultural value is universally recognized.

THE STRUCTURE OF THE ART MARKET

The art market actually encompasses two different markets for works of art: the primary market and the secondary market. In the primary market only *new* works of art are sold. Artists supply new works to dealers, who offer the works for sale. Dealers publicly exhibit the works and promote their artists through advertising and word-of-mouth campaigns. In return, they usually retain a substantial percentage of the selling price (their commission) when the works are sold. In the secondary market *previously purchased* works of art are bought and sold by consumers, either at auction or through art dealers. The original producers, the artists, are no longer party to those transactions and do not benefit from the profits of the sale. This was as true in seventeenth-century Italy, when Guido Reni complained about the success of his pictures in the secondary market (see Richard E. Spear in this volume), as it was in 1974, when the artist Robert Rauschenberg famously punched Robert Scull after the collector successfully auctioned Rauschenberg's works and pocketed the very substantial gain (Merryman 1993, 109).

The secondary market is more transparent than the primary market. The public nature of auctions, where the prices offered in the bidding process are instantly revealed to the public, helps to establish a benchmark for prices paid for works by individual artists—essential information for art market participants. However, in comparison to the primary market, the number of works sold at auction is relatively small. Major art centers with hundreds of art galleries, such as London or New York, are served by just two or three major auction houses. The primary and secondary art markets act as funnels: in an active art market, many more artists are producing work than its gallery system can absorb. Dealers select only a handful of artists whom they believe can be successful in the primary market and will not necessarily be able to sell all of the work their artists produce. The funnel further narrows in the secondary market, since the number of living artists whose works are traded at auction is even smaller. An artist's reputation needs to be firmly established before a public value (price) can be attached to his or her works.

The interaction between the primary and secondary art markets has yet to be studied in detail. Broadly speaking, however, the observation that a "hot" auction market tends to stimulate demand in the primary market appears to hold currency. Increased interest in purchasing new art in the primary market may result from the publicity that surrounds booming auction markets and more opportunistic behavior on the part of collectors ("getting in on the ground floor"). Successful auctions of art, such as the London sale of the Bicknell collection in 1863 or the 1914 Paris auction of the collection of the investment consortium La Peau de l'Ours, for example, established market values for works by contemporary artists, which in turn legitimized the value of their work in the primary market (see Dianne Sachko MacLeod's and Michael Cowan Fitzgerald's articles included in this volume).

The first public auctions of significant artworks took place in Amsterdam in the early seventeenth century. The extensive art collection of the Dutch merchant Lucas Van Uffelen was auctioned in 1637 and 1639, but information about the contents and purchasers is scant. No traces exist of the 1637 sale, but the auction of 1639 featured at least two Italian masterworks (Golahny 2013). The Van Uffelen sales reportedly attracted international attention partly as a result of the high prices that were obtained. Indeed, the taste for Italian art was spreading rapidly throughout Europe in the seventeenth century. Richard E. Spear and Philip Sohm report that Italy exported more Old Masters than contemporary paintings at this time (2010, 7). Sales of Italian aristocratic collections to foreign collectors at the beginning of the century undoubtedly helped set this secondary market in motion. The Amsterdam and London art auction markets continued to develop over the seventeenth and eighteenth centuries to become very significant. To this day London is regarded as the main auction market for Old Master paintings.

CONTINUITIES OVER TIME AND SPACE

The reader of this anthology will find that, in spite of the hyperbolic rhetoric that surrounds the twenty-first-century international art market, its manifestation of wealth and conspicuous consumption is a continuation of rather than a departure from the historical precedents. Similarly, the texts collected in this volume show that the production and consumption of art have always been conducted at an international level. In fact, history shows a consistent consumer preference for luxury goods that come from afar. The dictum that "the farther goods travel, the more value they obtain" was as true for fifteenth-century Florentines as it is for international collectors today. It explains why seventeenth-century English collectors purchased pictures in Italy rather than in London, why eighteenth-century French collectors swooned over shells and other exotica, why Americans and Russians flocked to Paris in the late nineteenth and early twentieth centuries to purchase the newest art, and why wealthy German and Dutch collectors had become great collectors of American Pop, Minimalist, and Conceptual artworks by the end of the 1960s. This phenomenon can still be observed today, as collectors travel the world to purchase pictures at art fairs—works that often could just as easily have been purchased at home, as Alain Quemin showed in his analysis of the participating artists in biennials and fairs and their collectors (included in this volume).

By focusing on the long history of the art market rather than its singular moments, this volume aims to enhance our understanding of the economic and social forces that have been consistently at play since the early days of Florence. The long-term trends and fundamental structures that emerge in the readings mark a departure from the traditional, narrower focus on art as objects. Generalist historians working today no longer subscribe to the idea that the dominant position of Europe and the United States in the modern period was the result of their exceptional nature. Instead, these scholars are now eager to study the commonalities among societies. Studies of household items that are common across all continents (salt, for example) have provided new insights into the global nature of our world (Tracy 1993). In similar fashion, the study of art markets as they emerged worldwide will offer art historians new and rich veins to explore art and artists within this global context rather than as expressions of singular cultures.

Yet, to a striking degree, artists, collectors, and many art historians, especially in the United States, have remained reluctant to discuss art and art production in the context of the market economy that creates the excess wealth that spurs artistic production. The impact of this dynamic was understood as early as 1604, when the Dutch art critic and historian Karel van Mander wrote, "Art follows wealth for its rich rewards." Van Mander came to this conclusion after he observed that the great wealth created by trade in the city of Bruges had attracted two remarkable master painters, the brothers Jan and Hubert van Eyck, whose works are now considered among the finest paintings produced in Renaissance Europe.

THE HISTORY OF CAPITALISM

The history of the art market can be squarely situated within the history of market capitalism. Capitalist markets started to emerge in fifteenth-century Western Europe when the economy evolved from a feudal system, where goods were produced for known consumers—the landowning nobility—to a market system in which goods were offered in a marketplace for purchase by any consumer. This change in the Western European economy and the subsequent development of the capitalist market economy was traced in great detail by the eminent French historian Fernand Braudel in his seminal three-volume study *Civilization and Capitalism, 15th–18th Century* (1992). Braudel did not focus exclusively on Europe—his study encompassed capitalist development around the world—but he framed his world history by examining the different capitalist "world-economies" that emerged around the globe between the fifteenth and the eighteenth centuries. He defined world-economies as geographical areas with clear boundaries (such as oceans or mountain ranges) that mark their identity. While one central city typically dominates each world-economy, the world-economy itself is comprised of the individual economies in its geographical area, which share a similar culture but stand in a hierarchical relationship to one another (1992, 3:24).

Western Europe's world-economy was the first to develop capitalist markets, according to Braudel—a phenomenon he ascribed to the decimation of its population by the plague in the mid-fourteenth century. Landowners started to trade in the agricultural surplus that resulted from the drastic decline in population, thus developing a new source of wealth. The movement of these goods was facilitated by significant improvements in transportation. Regular overland and maritime trade routes were established, and cities at the crossroads of those trade routes prospered. Regional trading fairs, seasonally held, started popping up around Europe. Although the fairs were open to the public, and most transactions involved perishable and cheap local goods, the economic significance of these markets was tied to the trade in luxury goods, which were expensive and usually came from far away (silk, for example). Most importantly, the fairs served also as money markets, where credit was issued and accounts were settled (1992, 2:90–91). Therefore, cities that hosted these fairs attracted tradespeople and merchants from all over Europe.

In combination, these factors resulted in a new cultural dynamic: social mobility. Those merchants who were able to build great trading fortunes—the new bourgeoisie—naturally aspired to join the ranks of the nobility, society's ruling class. To signal their new, elevated status, the merchants adopted the ostentatious luxury of the old aristocracy, which had long depended on demonstrations of wealth to signify its position of power in society. This new demand for conspicuously high-status goods, combined with the excess wealth generated by the luxury trade, attracted artists from far and wide to ply their wares. Over time, owing to economic competition and political maneuverings within the European world-economy, trading dominance shifted from city to city, and artists and markets would follow. While Italian city-states were the dominant center in the early fifteenth century, this position was taken over by Antwerp in the late fifteenth century, by Amsterdam in the late sixteenth century, by London in the eighteenth century, and ultimately by New York in the course of the twentieth century.

ARTISTIC COMMUNITIES AND INNOVATION

As Michael Montias has pointed out, innovation in any field of production, whether it is art or software, relies on a concentration of people, a critical mass, who are working on similar things. A recent example of this phenomenon is Silicon Valley, where software entrepreneurs have congregated, software development training programs have started up, and innovations and new products are created on an almost daily basis. Similarly, a dense community of skilled artists, with new schools and training methods, is likely to foster new and innovative artistic practices. This process took place in each major artistic center covered in this volume. Late fifteenth-century Florence, for example, counted more woodcarvers than butchers. In 1472, the city boasted fifty-four workshops for marble and stone; it employed forty-four master gold- and silversmiths, and at least thirty master painters. The number of painters registered in the Antwerp Guild of Saint Luke doubled, from 250 to 500, between 1500 and 1559. Jan de Vries estimates that in the Dutch northern provinces 700 to 800 master painters were at work by 1650 (1996, 264). By the end of the nineteenth century, more than 4,200 artists were working in Paris, according to the official 1886 census. The influx of hundreds of European artists in New York before and during World War II helped to establish the same critical mass that was needed for innovation in American painting.

The presence of dense artistic communities in major economic centers thus helps explain innovations such as the rapid improvements of the fifteenth-century Florentine painters in depicting the human body in space, the development of special genres in Antwerp and Holland over the course of the sixteenth and seventeenth centuries, the painterly innovations introduced by the Impressionists in Paris in the nineteenth century, and the new approaches in painting that developed in postwar New York in the twentieth century. The clustering of artists appears to add value to their works in the secondary market. Christiane Hellmanzik found a cluster premium in the auction market for paintings produced in Paris and New York of 11 percent and 43 percent, respectively, and argues that artists working in clusters reach a peak in prices for their work significantly earlier than artists working elsewhere (2010). Similarly, the absence of a critical mass of artists will have a detrimental effect on artistic innovation and quality. The drop in German demand for art in the wake of the Reformation that Carl C. Christensen identified in his study of the German art market (in this volume), for example, had significant consequences for artistic development in the centuries that followed.

THE ORGANIZATION OF THE TEXTS IN THIS VOLUME

The first and second chapters of this book establish a theoretical groundwork to assist readers in identifying and tracking key issues and concepts across the chapters that follow. Chapter 1 situates art in relation to the commercial world, drawing together key texts about the role and value of art in a society, as conceived by different academic disciplines. Chapter 2 looks at ways in which the behaviors of art market participants are informed by the forces of supply and demand and by anomalous features of art markets. Subsequent chapters are organized around the chronological succession of the major Western European trading centers Fernand Braudel first identified in his discussion of the shifting centers of the European world-economy, in which he included New York as well (1992, 3:76). The excerpts selected for each of these geographical market chapters reflect the viewpoints of art market participants—artists, dealers, collectors, experts—and describe local marketplaces at the time, such as galleries and auction houses. Each chapter includes at least one primary-source text.

The selections are intended to provide an overview of developments in the art market over time. Important nuances to this broader picture will inevitably emerge as future scholarship focuses on the roles of historically underrepresented groups, such as female artists and artists of color. The organization of the chapters by the dominant city in each art market makes intuitive sense. Art markets have always been identified by their exact geographic locations (Paris, London, New York) rather than by the corresponding nation-state. We are as likely to refer to local art markets by city today as artists, collectors, and dealers did in the seventeenth century. While this emphasis on individual cities is often seen as a side effect of a new globalized world in which nation-states have diminished stature, historians believe differently. As this volume shows, cities have always played privileged roles as centers of cultural and economic activity and have demonstrated a capacity for generating culture as well as commerce (Scott 1997, 323–24).

As soon as cities emerged as dominant trading centers in the modern world-economies, groups of foreign merchants would settle in to conduct business. These traders and their compatriots clustered in particular neighborhoods within these cities and operated autonomously within the commercial system—unhampered by guilds or other restrictions (Mauro 1993, 260–61). With the influx of merchants, new ideas and business methods spread throughout Europe. Major merchant cities became clearinghouses for information. Publishers responded by locating their presses in major cities and publishing, in addition to religious and political tracts, newspapers with lists of goods for sale, stocks and their trading prices, upcoming events such as lectures by philosophers, and advertisements for new books (Stewart 2001, 331). In seventeenth-century Amsterdam, for example, well over one hundred thousand titles were published, many destined for foreign markets (Hoftijzer 2008, 249).

The high level of literacy among merchants stimulated book consumption and interest in culture, general scholarship, and applied science (especially mathematics). While a systematic overview of the development of centers of learning is outside the purview of this book, cities with flourishing art markets, such as Florence, Antwerp, Amsterdam, London, and Paris, also took on leading roles in scholastic endeavors.

The historical narrative of the art market begins in chapter 3 with the city-states in Italy, where secular demand for paintings first emerged. The texts collected in chapter 4 describe the emergence of the first true anonymous marketplace in the cities of Bruges and Antwerp in Flanders. The selections in chapter 5 focus on market-oriented art production in Amsterdam and its neighboring towns in the northern provinces of Holland. Chapter 6 briefly addresses developments in Germany and Spain, wealthy countries that did not achieve a dominant cultural or market position in the European world-economy due to geographical, indigenous political, and religious factors. Chapter 7 explores the slow emergence of artistic talent in London despite Britain's dominant position as a maritime and trading power in the eighteenth century. Chapter 8 is dedicated to Paris, which became the dominant cultural capital of the European world-economy over the course of the nineteenth century. The texts gathered in chapter 9 focus on the development of artists and collectors in the United States, while chapter 10 covers the ascent of New York in the second half of the twentieth century as the new center of the Western European world-economy and the Western art market. The final chapter briefly touches on the market for art in the twenty-first century and the rhetoric of globalization that has surrounded it.

1

ART IN A COMMERCIAL WORLD

This chapter presents an overview of contributions from different academic disciplines that have been investigating the special role of art in our society. The excerpts highlight some recurrent themes and issues manifested throughout the larger narrative framework of this volume. Taken together, these multidisciplinary perspectives yield important new insights, enriching our understanding of a topic traditionally considered to be the purview of art historians: the production of art.

The excerpts included in section I condense long-standing philosophical arguments about art's essentially disinterested nature and its relation to the market. The art historical tendency to study art outside of the marketplace can be traced to the man who is widely considered the father of the discipline, Johann Joachim Winckelmann, in the eighteenth century. In his *Reflections on the Imitation of Greek Works in Painting and Sculpture* (1755), Winckelmann argued that a money-oriented society distorts artistic practice. This argument was continued by the German philosopher Immanuel Kant in 1790. Kant insisted that only art that has been created freely—that is, through play—can be considered art. Art that is the product of labor and made for monetary considerations he relegated to the category of craft: mercenary art. Generally speaking, Kant maintained, the creation of beautiful things can only take place in an aristocratic realm as opposed to a commercial realm. A similar argument was made by the German philosopher Friedrich Schiller a few years later. Schiller too believed that true art can only result from the innate drive to play and that the artist should refrain from any focus on fortune or the needs of daily life. As Paul Mattick points out in "Illusions of Disinterest," it was Schiller who firmly established the notion that art's production differs from all other production in its freedom from the market.

The need for "true" art to be the product of play, not work, is expressed in Karl Marx's writings on art as well, limited as they were. The art historian O. K. Werckmeister, teasing out Marx's convictions from various passages, shows that Marx believed that true art can only be created using an individual's innate talent. He deplored the professionalization of artists. In a communist society, Marx wrote, there will be no painters, but at most individuals who, among other things, paint.

Clement Greenberg, the influential mid-twentieth-century Marxist American writer and art critic, builds on Kant's ideas and further theorizes the distinction between art produced for a market and the art of the twentieth-century avant-garde in his 1939 essay "Avant-Garde and Kitsch." Arthur Danto introduces a new way to define the art of the twentieth century within the realm of aesthetic theory and philosophy, recognizing that much of the art produced by the avant-garde did not fit traditional aesthetic criteria. Last, Theodor Adorno explores the threat mass-produced culture poses to societal well-being and high art.

The excerpts in section II tackle the thorny issue of what endows art with value. The anthropologist Igor Kopytoff uses his observations across different cultures to show how societies assign exceptional value to certain objects, whether they hold intrinsic value or not, such as artworks. Walter Benjamin conjectures that the value of the original work of art lies in its particular location in both time and space and defined it as aura. The cultural economist Michael Hutter and the philosopher Richard Shusterman enumerate the values that aesthetic theories have assigned to art outside of the commercial realm. The sociologists Pierre Bourdieu, Raymonde Moulin, and Olav Velthuis use observations from the field to theorize how value is established in a work of art and communicated. Jean Baudrillard, the philosopher and sociologist, offers a critique of art in a postmodern society from a poststructuralist perspective, highlighting its increasing insistence on uselessness.

I. ART IN SOCIETY

PAUL MATTICK, *Illusions of Disinterest*

Excerpt (pp. 40–45) from "Illusions of Disinterest," in *Art in Its Time: Theories and Practices of Modern Aesthetics* (London: Routledge, 2003), 39–46. Copyright © 2003 Routledge. Reproduced with permission of Taylor & Francis Books UK.

In Winckelmann's *Reflections on the Imitation of Greek Works* (1755/1987), the historical distance between ancient and modern appears intermittently as a fall from grace, in which the corrupting effect of a commercial economy plays a central role. Explaining the special access of the ancient Greeks to "good taste," for instance, Winckelmann emphasizes the role played by the classical gymnasium as a school of art, where (thanks to the absence of "our present-day criteria of respectability") "natural beauty revealed itself naked for the instruction of the artist":

> The nude body in its most beautiful form was exhibited there in so many different, authentic, and noble positions and poses not obtainable today by the hired models in our academies.
>
> Truth springs from inner sentiment, and the draughtsman who wants to impart truth to his academy studies cannot preserve even a shadow of it unless he himself is able to replace that which the unmoved and indifferent soul of his model does not feel or is unable to express by actions appropriate to a given sentiment or passion. (13)

Here authenticity and nobility, embodied (ideally, at least) in the "inner sentiment" of the artist, are opposed to the gracelessness of the hired model, whose movements reflect not the free spirit of his personality but the requirements of his drawing-master employer. But the artist too suffers the distortions of the money-oriented society, for "an artist of our times . . . feels compelled to work more for bread than for honor" (55). Not only is his product at the mercy of its purchaser, who may choose to place it in positions quite unsuitable for proper viewing (61–69), but he is more or less required by the pressures of earning a livelihood to depend on the practical techniques he has picked up in his apprenticeship rather than engaging in the rigorous research into the principles of formal truth that allowed Michelangelo to come so near to the achievement of antiquity.

Winckelmann's account of art is, to say the least, philosophically naive in comparison with Kant's, but themes present in his work reappear in the *Third Critique*. For Kant (1790/1987) taste is not just ennobling and art not just an education in natural grace; the experience of beauty is in his system an essential element of the spiritual progress of humankind toward the realization of our rational nature. But the features in Kant's eyes essential to the fine arts (as opposed to the merely "agreeable" arts, like table conversation and games) involve the familiar oppositions, not only to the "mechanical" or manual but also to effort performed for a monetary reward. The basic principle is that "we should not call anything art except a production through freedom, i.e. through a power of choice that bases its acts on reason" (170).

Kant also clearly distinguishes art from science, as it had not been distinguished two and even one hundred years earlier. Freedom implies, on the one hand, the absence of governance by rules, characteristic of science. Art is the product of the creative genius, for whom technical training and the imitation of the ancients serve to shape a soul that will spontaneously generate new forms. For "genius is the exemplary originality of a subject's natural endowment in the free use of his cognitive powers" (186). The emphasis on an exercise of reason specific to the arts establishes their autonomy: they are to be guided not by demands external to their own formal natures but by principles internal to the sphere of art (Kant distinguishes "paintings properly so called," which are "there merely to be looked at" from those "intended to teach us, e.g. history or natural science") (193). On the other hand,

Art is likewise to be distinguished from *craft*. The first is also called *free art*, the second could be called *mercenary art*. We regard free art [as an art] that could only turn out purposive (i.e. succeed) if it is play, in other words, an occupation that is agreeable on its own account; mercenary art we regard as labor, i.e. as an occupation that on its own account is disagreeable (burdensome) and that attracts us only through its effect (e.g. pay) so that people can be coerced into it. (170–71)

This passage, not unrelated to the status preoccupations of eighteenth-century artists, evokes elements basic to Kant's theory of taste as "the ability to judge an object, or a way of presenting it, by means of liking or disliking *devoid of all interest*" (53). The experience of beauty is the experience of an object as "purposive"—as having, we might say, the character of design—but without actually having a defined purpose for the viewer, who is caught up in no relation of action (including that of scientific cognizing) with it. Hence the object is a "free beauty," exemplifying design in the abstract and in principle representing nothing under a determinate concept; given Kant's (inter-) subjective conception of beauty, this reflects the fact that the viewer's judgment of taste can be considered free of any idea of functions which the object might serve for him or her and therefore involves "no concept [as to] what the object is [meant] to represent; our imagination is playing, as it were, while it contemplates the shape, and such a concept would only restrict its freedom" (77).

The concept of "interest" at work here includes both morality (we have an interest in the good) and the common eighteenth-century sense of that word which "centered on economic advantage as its core meaning" (Hirschman 1977, 32). The contemplative realm of the aesthetic is contrasted, therefore, with realms of action: that of the good, object of the Practical Reason, and that of the "agreeable" (pleasing to the senses) and of those things answering to "material" needs. (In the case of cooking, "only when their need has been satisfied can we tell who in a multitude of people has taste and who does not") (Kant 1790/1987, 52). Freedom, at least of the will, is essential to morality; the freedom of aesthetic play signifies the bracketing of material desire and so of the economic domain to which those desires look for satisfaction. Aesthetic appreciation requires neither ownership nor consumption, but only perception.

Kant's treatment of the nature of art involves a complex drawing together of many conceptual strands in the idea of freedom. The production of beautiful things must have an aristocratic character opposed to *labor*: "anything studied and painstaking must be avoided in art." The idea of "play" is central because it is the opposite of "work." And the concept of labor involved here is that of wage labor: art must be free in a double sense, including that "of not being a mercenary occupation and hence a kind of labor, whose magnitude can be judged, exacted, or paid for according to a determinate standard" and "the sense that, though the mind is occupying itself, yet it feels satisfied and aroused (independently of any pay) without looking to some other purpose" (190).

The aristocratic flavor of aesthetic experience is if anything more pronounced in Kant's doctrine of the sublime, the experience of the superiority of the reason to the imagination, bound to the representation of empirical material. Like the experience of the beautiful, that of the sublime presupposes the satisfaction of material needs, in this case that for physical safety: "just as we cannot pass judgment on the beautiful if we are seized by inclination and appetite, so we cannot pass judgment at all on the sublime in nature if we are afraid." But paradoxically physical safety allows us to respond (aesthetically, not practically) to the thrill of danger viewed and therefore "to regard as small the [objects] of our [natural] concerns: property, health, and life." This appreciation of human response to aestheticized peril reflects the esteem given by society to a person "who does not yield to danger but promptly sets to work with vigor and full deliberation." This character is best exemplified by the warrior, so that "no matter how much people may dispute, when they compare the statesman with the general, as to which one deserves the superior respect, an aesthetic judgment decides in favor of the general." For "even war has something sublime about it," whereas peace, in contrast, "tends to make prevalent a mere[ly] commercial spirit," which brings with it "base selfishness, cowardice, and softness" (121–22). In such a passage we may recognize, in this student of Hume and Rousseau, the discourse of civic virtue and its decline under the influence of commerce—here to be countered by the transmutation of aristocratic (military) values into a spiritual principle.

Since work, as wage labor, is marked by the anti-artistic character of mercenary culture, it is not surprising that play will appear to incarnate the aesthetic impulse. It was in Schiller's *Aesthetic Education of Man* (1794/1986) that this theme received its fullest development at the end of the eighteenth century. For Schiller too "the character of our age" is established by way of "an astonishing contrast between contemporary forms of humanity and earlier ones, especially the Greek." With the development of the division of labor, the unified human personality of the ancients has been split into fragments, so that "we see not merely individuals, but whole classes of men, developing but one part of their potentialities, while of the rest, as in stunted growths, only vestigial traces remain" (31, 33). When a society "insists on special skills being developed with a degree of intensity which is only commensurate with its readiness to absolve the individual citizen from developing himself in extensity—can we wonder that the remaining aptitudes of the psyche are neglected in order to give undivided attention to the one which will bring honor and profit?" (37). It is the task of art, expression of the drive to play, to reconstitute the fragmented human person, "to restore by means of a higher art the totality of our nature which the arts themselves have destroyed" (43).

If art is to be the instrument of humankind's education and elevation to a more advanced order of social being, it must resist the characteristic forces of the present age. The artist must protect himself from the corruption of modernity: "Let him direct his gaze upwards, to the dignity of his calling and the universal Law, not downwards towards Fortune and the needs of daily life." And he must seek an audience among people of similar temperament: "Those who know no other criterion of value than the effort of earning or the tangible profit, how should they be capable of appreciating the unobtrusive effect of taste on the outward appearance and on the mind and character of men?"

(57, 65). Taste, by fostering harmony in the individual, will bring harmony to society. Providing a spiritual experience of the physical world, it opens a realm of experience in which the interests of reason are reconciled with the interests of the senses. Art thus holds out the promise of a future happiness for humankind, but even under current conditions it provides "an ideal semblance which ennobles the reality of common day." Taste, that is,

> throws a veil of decorum over those physical desires which, in their naked form, affront the dignity of free beings; and by a delightful illusion of freedom, conceals from us our degrading kinship with matter. On the wings of taste even that art which must cringe for payment can lift itself out of the dust. (201, 219)

With these words, nearly the concluding ones of Schiller's book, a conflict at the heart of the modern practice of art—that the commodity status of artworks hinges on their representation of an interest superior to that of mundane commerce—has achieved frank expression, if only in the form of the wistful hope that it can be overcome. Fundamental to this practice is the idea that art's production differs from all other production in its freedom from the market. Hence art is like play, not work; hence, considered as work, it engages the whole person, not the fragmented laborer of today; hence it is a fully creative effort, not constrained by a mechanical process; hence it is "disinterested," not aiming at the satisfaction of material needs. In reality, however, art's rise to autonomous status itself involved the replacement of artistic work to the order of premodern patronage by production for the market. It is therefore not surprising that the "delightful illusion" of art's separateness from the commercial culture which in fact produced it in its modern form has proved impossible to sustain, and that the history of this institution to the present day has seen artists alternate between claims to a higher calling and complaints of insufficient payment for their practice of it.

From the side of the consumer, the worship of art has expressed the claim of capitalist society's higher orders to rise above the confines of commerce as worthy inheritors of the aristocratic culture of the past. Here, involvement with the autonomous artwork represents detachment from the claims of practical life, even while its ownership and enjoyment require both money and the time made possible by money and so signify financial success along with cultural superiority. It is indeed the new uses made of images, music, writing, and the rest—notably for the construction of a mode of sensibility characterized by distance from material necessity and so free to cultivate responsiveness to experience—that appear as the autonomy of art. Essential to this concept is not just the liberation of the arts from their former social functions but their conceptual separation from the everyday life under the sway of economic interest that the bourgeoisie in reality shares with its social inferiors, apart from those moments devoted to the detachment essential to the aesthetic attitude. In fact, the acquisition of the aesthetic attitude derives from and marks a position of privilege in the very realm of economics from which that attitude officially declares its independence. And although the conception of art as transcendent of social reality provides a naturalist disguise for the actual historical process within which it came into existence and for the socio-economic prerequisites—leisure and education—of its enjoyment, the truth, as we have seen, will out. If Baudelaire was moved by the Salon of 1859 to compare poetry and progress to "two ambitious men who hate one another with an instinctive hatred," it was the same poet who had addressed his criticism of the Salon of 1846 "To the Bourgeois": "for as not one of you today can do without power, so not one of you has the right to do without poetry."

O. K. WERCKMEISTER, *Marx on Ideology and Art*

Excerpt (pp. 501–9) from "Marx on Ideology and Art," *New Literary History* 4, no. 3 (1973): 501–19. Reprinted by kind permission of the author.

Marx concerned himself with the history and theory of art only at the beginning of his career. In 1841 and 1842 he wrote short polemical treatises on art directed against Hegel, which are now lost. He never wrote a theoretical or historical text that dealt with art as an issue after that. Neither did Engels. Both repeatedly commented on questions of literature, but not on the visual arts and architecture, or on art as a generalized concept of philosophical aesthetics. Hence the place of art in later Marxist theory of history and society remains uncertain. Official Soviet scholarship has tried to fill the gap by abstracting any one of Marx's and Engels' scattered and casual remarks on art and literature from the context of their numerous writings, and systematically compiling them into two huge volumes entitled *On Art and Literature*. [. . .] On the other hand, scholars in capitalist states have concluded that if Marx, in his sustained effort to substantiate his theory of history and society through decades of methodical research, never returned to his early interest in aesthetics, he must have considered that art did not form any part of the primary material in which the historical progress towards a socialist future could be traced. [. . .]

The discussion is inevitably thrown back at the few short text passages, quoted and interpreted time and again, where Marx directly comments about art, referring to historical examples. Two apparently contradictory notions of art, one idealistic–utopian, the other historical–deterministic, seem to emerge from them. Are they just aspects of a dialectically ambivalent conception which is consistent in the final analysis, as official communist aesthetics maintains, or are they in fact so irreconcilable as to defy the formation of a coherent aesthetic theory?

The idealistic notion of art in Marx's thought may be deduced from the famous passage on the art of the Greeks, contained in the draft for the *Critique of Political Economics* (1857–58).

It is known that certain heydays of art are not at all related to the general development of society, and neither, therefore, to the skeleton, as it were, of its organization. For example the Greeks, compared to the moderns, or also Shakespeare. Of certain art forms, the epics for example, it has even been recognized that they can never be produced in their epochal, classical shape when art production as such occurs; and that consequently within the realm of art itself certain important creations are only possible on the basis of an undeveloped stage in the development of art. If this is the case with regard to the relationship of the various art genres within the realm of art itself, it is already less striking that it should be the case with regard to the relationship of the realm of art as a whole to the general development of society. The difficulty consists only in the generalization of these contradictions. As soon as they are specified, they are already explained.

Marx then poses the notorious problem that past works of art like those of the Greeks continue to be appreciated with immediacy under social conditions that are advanced beyond those under which they themselves were made:

> . . . the difficulty is not to understand that Greek art and epics are tied to certain stages in the development of society. The difficulty is that they still yield artistic pleasure to us, and in a certain way count for a norm and for unattainable models.

Marx proposes to solve the difficulty with an analogy between the organic development of the human individual and the history of mankind as a whole, which he similarly conceives of as a straightforward "evolution." In this scheme, the historical epoch of the Greeks takes the place of infancy, and their works of art express this stage.

> Why should the historical infancy of mankind where it is unfolded most beautifully, not exert an eternal fascination, as a stage that will never return? There are rude children and precocious children. Many of the ancient peoples belong in this category. The Greeks were normal children. The fascination of their art for us does not stand in contradiction with the undeveloped stage of society from which it grew. On the contrary, it is the result of this stage and is inseparably linked to the fact that the immature social conditions under which it came about, and only could come about, can never return.

It is well known that Marx derived this notion of Greek art as "epochal" and "classical" from German idealist philosophy, especially from Hegel. The idea of classical art, which implies that the ideal of artistic perfection has once been realized at a historical moment of the past, comes into conflict with Marx's emphatically evolutionary view of history. Man's production of his life, his dominion over nature through the social organization of his work, inexorably progresses towards higher stages, but in art the highest stage was reached early, and has never been attained again. On the contrary, in the more developed stages of society it can no longer be made to perfection. Then, there is only "art production," that is, art produced in accordance with organized, feudally repressed or capitalistically alienated conditions of life. "Art," which is opposed to "art production," is related to that notion of humanity which, far from being perfected in the progressing social organization of production, is on the contrary debased by it. Thus, "art production" is no longer true to human nature. Yet the art of the Greeks is perfect, although their society was far from being so. Communist commentators recognize that this thesis would contradict Marx's and Engels' general assumption that the cultural "superstructure" is determined by the economic "base." They try to reconcile the contradiction by upgrading the Greek city of antiquity with its plebiscitary democracy as an analogous political ideal which could not be maintained in later stages of history. But for Marx the material basis resides in economic production, not in political organization. He never declares the "slaveholder" society of ancient Greece as anything of an ideal for human society in general, the way he here declares Greek art as an ideal for art in general. The point of his text is to state that such a correlation does not appear to exist, either in the historical situation of Greek art, or in the theoretical notion of a perfect art that can be derived from it.

Already in the notes and excerpts which Marx prepared for his article "On Religious Art" (1842), now lost, he implicitly defines the realism of Greek art as a true expression of human nature. He opposes it to religion, thereby radicalizing Hegel's distinction of both as parallel if subsequent forms of human consciousness. Those excerpts from the writings of idealist art historians elaborate on the theory that art in the service of religion is alienated from its ideal quality, which is human realism; religious art of ancient and medieval civilizations, they say, distorts human images into those of fictitious gods, deforming their natural features into the terrorizing expression of idols by which submission of believers is enforced. The essential quality of art appears to be sacrificed to its religious function, which in turn is nothing but a means for kings and priests to maintain authority over their people. The insincere relationship of religious art to its manifest contents in these early excerpts is the same as that of ideology to its contents in Marx's later writings. On the basis of his readings, the young Marx must have thought that such a relationship contradicts the basic definition of art, which for him meant the undistorted revelation of true human nature. This contradiction is carried over into the opposition between "art" and "art production" in the later text of 1858.

Marx's early confrontation between art and religion hinges on the term "fetishism." It denotes the use of human images contrary to their true meaning, as fictitious deities, tools for dominating men. In Marx's later economic theory, the same term denotes the transformation of the products of human labor into commodity form, contrary to their genuine purpose of serving the needs of men's lives. Art, according to Marx's original conception, is by implication free of any social purpose, an object of contemplation or enjoyment, perhaps in line with Kant's definition of disinterested aesthetic experience. On this assumption, any art which becomes part of culture and is thereby ultimately produced by and for society, runs the danger of being estranged from its essence. Marx sustained this conception in his later philosophical writings, where he set out to demonstrate that any and all products of culture are dependent on the socially organized "base" of material production. Now he subsumed art, together with "morals, religion, metaphysics," under the term "ideology," as one of the "fog formations in the brains of men." All of them are made to appear autonomous in relation to the primary, material production of life, while in fact serving its social organization. Marx's still later text on the art of the Greeks is consistent with this view, yet sets art apart from the other products of ideology. Whereas religion, law, and philosophy in its traditional understanding, are exclusively and adequately defined by the socially conditioned dependence of ideology on its material base, art maintains an essence of its own, from which it appears perennially estranged by its recurrent ideological functions throughout history. The art of the Greeks is the one historical example where this essence can be contemplated in its purity, since it appears exempt from the normal ideological relationship to its economic base. It thus provides an Archimedean point from which to judge most later art as untrue to its own essence. The most extreme judgment is to denounce capitalist society as a whole as detrimental to art. If man's estranged relationship to nature under capitalism is given as a reason for this verdict, it becomes clear how much it depends on the idealist conception of an art that captures the essence of nature.

The text presents obvious difficulties for purposes of formulating a "Marxist" theory of art. It projects the essence of art back into a past historical ideal which cannot be recaptured, and thus keeps it apart from the ideal of human emancipation as a task of conscious historical progress towards the future. The ideal of art also cannot easily be projected into an emancipated society of the future if its definition implies that it should not be affected by social organization and function. As for the "art production" of the past, it completely escapes the correlation of art and truth, the ultimate aim of any philosophical aesthetics. It can only be subjected to a historical critique.

A text from *The German Ideology* (1845) shows that Marx could project the Archimedean point, from which to criticize "art production" with its ideological dependence on organized society, into the utopian future as well as into the classical past.

Raphael, as well as any other artist, was conditioned by the technical advances of art which had been made before him, by the organization of society and the division of labor in his locality, and finally, by the division of labor in all the countries with which his locality was in communication. Whether an individual like Raphael develops his talent depends entirely upon demand, which in turn depends upon the division of labor and the educational conditions of men which result from it. . . . The exclusive concentration of artistic talent in single individuals and its suppression in the broad mass of people which this entails is a consequence of the division of labor. . . . With a communist organization of society, there ceases, in any event, the subsumption of the artist under local and national limitations, which ensues solely from the division of labor, and there ceases the subsumption of the individual under one determined art, whereby he is exclusively a painter, a sculptor, etc., and already his designation sufficiently expresses the limitation of his commercial career and his dependence on the division of labor. In a communist society, there are no painters, but at most men who, among other things, also paint.

The close relationship of this text to the much later one on the art of the Greeks is an indication of how consistent Marx's conception of art remained. Already here, professional "art production" is denounced as a deviation from the human potential of art itself, because it is adapted to the needs and conditions of a working society whose organization is detrimental to the nature of man. It is opposed to "talent" as a natural human capacity, which has to be emancipated from professionalization in order to be practiced according to its essence. This amounts to an emancipation from social organization as such.

In the later text, Marx acclaims Greek art as a classical ideal for similar reasons: because it is not limited by its social base, and because it directly expresses human nature. Both these texts, spanning thirteen years of Marx's writing, are the idealistic and the utopian versions of the same sweeping judgment on art as socially motivated and organized work. By implication they declare the entire past history of European art an alienated activity. This is in line with other, even more sweeping statements about art as just another brand of ideology. With regard to the socialist society of the future, the text from *The German Ideology* virtually calls for the cancellation of "art production," along with alienated work in general. Art as a basic human activity, free from any socially determined function, and according to the freely developed potential of human nature, will continue to be practiced. But its content, its purpose, and the conditions of its existence are difficult to envisage in terms of any art we know, with its inevitable integration into society. Conditions under which virtually everyone can become active as an artist, yet no one will be limited to artistic activity alone, are reminiscent of that generalized aesthetic state of being which according to Kant and Schiller is to characterize the behavior of emancipated man whose nature and freedom coincide. Marx converts this anthropological construction of idealist aesthetics into a materialist if utopian perspective for the historical future. It is so radical that it cannot but invoke the idea of the end of art according to its past definition, with its inevitable aspect of socially useful work. That idea had already been formulated by Hegel when he conceived of a stage of human intellectual emancipation for which art is no longer an adequate means of objective communication. It is an idea incessantly pondered and finally rejected by contemporary German dialectical philosophers who follow Hegel and Marx.

Looking back on the art that did and does exist, the philosopher's task, according to Marx, will be to point out its constant estrangement from its ideal or utopian perfection. He will demonstrate that the "semblance of autonomy" projected into ideological products is by definition a fictitious one. As an exception, the notion of an autonomy of art is not fictitious; on the contrary, it is fundamental for both the art of the Greeks and the art spontaneously created by the emancipated individuals of the future. But history shows art tangled in ideological concerns. Time and again, it can be shown how the semblance of its autonomy under these conditions was in fact contrived to serve particular interests of socially organized material production. This is the historian's task. "We know only a single science, the science of history," wrote Marx and Engels in *The German Ideology*. It is an all-comprehensive science which will endeavor to relate every human activity or product to the socially organized material conditions of men's lives. The historical investigation of art, like that of any other human product, is bound to go beyond its confines and to reach the basis of these conditions. Taken by itself, art has not even a history of its own. Marx and Engels insist that the only viable method of demonstrating the all-embracing historical context is "empirical observation." They oppose it to philosophy, which "through the historical representation of reality loses its medium of existence" as an autonomous discipline. Theory is thus reduced to "a synthesis of the most general results . . . which may be abstracted from the observation of man's historical development." However justified such a radical confidence in empirical knowledge of reality may be, taken on its own terms it leads only to one conclusion: there can be no science which explains human products in any other than a historical way, much less an autonomous philosophical discipline about such products. As far as art is concerned, there can be no aesthetics. Abstraction is Marx's and Engels' negative antithesis to empirical knowledge. They admit it only as a way of devising auxiliary constructions for the incomplete progress of historical experience. Abstract terms and concepts are merely functional, subordinate to the actual results which they recapitulate or generalize, but they have "no value at all if taken by themselves, severed from real history." To construct from them schemes and systems with a claim to independent meaning is the fallacy of philosophy. Since such constructions obscure the historical basis of human conditions, they tend to become themselves ideological, for the semblance of intellectual autonomy is tantamount to ideology. As a result, consistent historical research, as it is bound to destroy any such semblance, converges with the critique of ideology.

CLEMENT GREENBERG, *Avant-Garde and Kitsch*

Excerpt (pp. 10–14) from "Avant-Garde and Kitsch," in *The Collected Essays and Criticism*, vol. 1, *Perceptions and Judgments, 1939–1944*, ed. John O'Brian (Chicago: University of Chicago Press, 1986), 5–22. © 1939 Clement Greenberg. All rights reserved. Reprinted by permission of the University of Chicago Press.

The avant-garde's specialization of itself, the fact that its best artists are artists' artists, its best poets, poets' poets, has estranged a great many of those who were capable formerly of enjoying and appreciating ambitious art and literature, but who are now unwilling or unable to acquire an initiation into their craft secrets. The masses have always remained more or less indifferent to culture in the process of development. But today such culture is being abandoned by those to whom it actually belongs—our ruling class. For it is to the latter that the avant-garde belongs. No culture can develop without a social basis, without a source of stable income. And in the case of the avant-garde this was provided by an elite among the ruling class of that society from which it assumed itself to be cut off, but to which it has always remained attached by an umbilical cord of gold. The paradox is real.

And now this elite is rapidly shrinking. Since the avant-garde forms the only living culture we now have, the survival in the near future of culture in general is thus threatened.

We must not be deceived by superficial phenomena and local successes. Picasso's shows still draw crowds, and T. S. Eliot is taught in the universities; the dealers in modernist art are still in business, and the publishers still publish some "difficult" poetry. But the avant-garde itself, already sensing the danger, is becoming more and more timid every day that passes. Academicism and commercialism are appearing in the strangest places. This can mean only one thing: that the avant-garde is becoming unsure of the audience it depends on—the rich and the cultivated.

Is it the nature itself of avant-garde culture that is alone responsible for the danger it finds itself in? Or is that only a dangerous liability? Are there other, and perhaps more important, factors involved?

Where there is an avant-garde, generally we also find a rear-guard. True enough—simultaneously with the entrance of the avant-garde, a second new cultural phenomenon appeared in the industrial West: that thing to which the Germans give the wonderful name of *Kitsch*: popular, commercial art and literature with their chromeotypes, magazine covers, illustrations, ads, slick and pulp fiction, comics, Tin Pan Alley music, tap dancing, Hollywood movies, etc., etc. For some reason this gigantic apparition has always been taken for granted. It is time we looked into its whys and wherefores.

Kitsch is a product of the industrial revolution which urbanized the masses of Western Europe and America and established what is called universal literacy.

Previous to this the only market for formal culture, as distinguished from folk culture, had been among those who in addition to being able to read and write could command the leisure and comfort that always goes hand in hand with cultivation of some sort. This until then had been inextricably associated with literacy. But with the introduction of universal literacy, the ability to read and write became almost a minor skill like driving a car, and it no longer served to distinguish an individual's cultural inclinations, since it was no longer the exclusive concomitant of refined tastes. The peasants who settled in the cities as proletariat and petty bourgeois learned to read and write for the sake of efficiency, but they did not win the leisure and comfort necessary for the enjoyment of the city's traditional culture. Losing, nevertheless, their taste for the folk culture whose background was the countryside, and discovering a new capacity for boredom at the same time, the new urban masses set up a pressure on society to provide them with a kind of culture fit for their own consumption. To fill the demand of the new market a new commodity was devised: ersatz culture, kitsch, destined for those who, insensible to the values of genuine culture, are hungry nevertheless for the diversion that only culture of some sort can provide.

Kitsch, using for raw material the debased and academicized simulacra of genuine culture, welcomes and cultivates this insensibility. It is the source of its profits. Kitsch is mechanical and operates by formulas. Kitsch is vicarious experience and faked sensations. Kitsch changes according to style, but remains always the same. Kitsch is the epitome of all that is spurious in the life of our times. Kitsch pretends to demand nothing of its customers except their money—not even their time.

The pre-condition for kitsch, a condition without which kitsch would be impossible, is the availability close at hand of a fully matured cultural tradition, whose discoveries, acquisitions and perfected self-consciousness kitsch can take advantage of for its own ends. It borrows from it devices, tricks, stratagems, rules of thumb, themes, converts them into a system and discards the rest. It draws its life blood, so to speak, from this reservoir of accumulated experience. This is what is really meant when it is said that the popular art and literature of today were once the daring, esoteric art and literature of yesterday. Of course, no such thing is true. What is meant is that when enough time has elapsed the new is looted for new "twists," which are then watered down and served up as kitsch. Self-evidently, all kitsch is academic, and conversely, all that's academic is kitsch. For what is called the academic as such no longer has an independent existence, but has become the stuffed-shirt "front" for kitsch. The methods of industrialism displace the handicrafts.

Because it can be turned out mechanically, kitsch has become an integral part of our productive system in a way in which true culture could never be except accidentally. It has been capitalized at a tremendous investment which must show commensurate returns; it is compelled to extend as well as to keep its markets. While it is essentially its own salesman, a great sales apparatus has nevertheless been created for it, which brings pressure to bear on every member of society. Traps are laid even in those areas, so to speak, that are the preserves of genuine culture. It is not enough today, in a country like ours, to have an inclination towards the latter; one must have a true passion for it that will give him the power to resist the faked article that surrounds and presses in on him from the moment he is old enough to look at the funny papers. Kitsch is deceptive. It has many different levels, and some of them are high enough to be dangerous to the naive seeker of true light. A magazine like the *New Yorker*, which is fundamentally high-class kitsch for the luxury trade, converts and waters down a great deal of avant-garde material for its own uses. Nor is every single item of kitsch altogether worthless. Now and then it produces something of merit, something that has an authentic folk flavor; and these accidental and isolated instances have fooled people who should know better.

Kitsch's enormous profits are a source of temptation to the avant-garde itself, and its members have not always resisted this temptation. Ambitious writers and artists will modify their work under the pressure of kitsch, if they do not succumb to it entirely. And then those puzzling borderline cases appear, such as the popular novelist, Simenon, in France, and Steinbeck in this country. The net result is always to the detriment of true culture, in any case.

Kitsch has not been confined to the cities in which it was born, but has flowed out over the countryside, wiping out folk culture. Nor has it shown any regard for geographical and national cultural boundaries. Another mass product of Western industrialism, it has gone on a triumphal tour of the world, crowding out and defacing native cultures in one colonial country after another, so that it is now by way of becoming a universal culture, the first universal culture ever beheld. Today the Chinaman, no less than the South American Indian, the Hindu, no less than the Polynesian, have come to prefer to the products of their native art magazine covers, rotogravure sections, and calendar girls. How is this virulence of kitsch, this irresistible attractiveness, to be explained? Naturally, machine-made kitsch can undersell the native handmade article, and the prestige of the West also helps, but why is kitsch a so much more profitable export article than Rembrandt? One, after all, can be reproduced as cheaply as the other.

ARTHUR DANTO, *The Artworld*

Excerpt (pp. 571–74) from "The Artworld," *Journal of Philosophy* 61, no. 19 (1964): 571–84. Estate of Arthur Danto. Reprinted by kind permission of the *Journal of Philosophy.*

Hamlet and Socrates, though in praise and deprecation respectively, spoke of art as a mirror held up to nature. As with many disagreements in attitude, this one has a factual basis. Socrates saw mirrors as but reflecting what we can already see; so art, insofar as mirrorlike, yields idle accurate duplications of the appearances of things, and is of no cognitive benefit whatever. Hamlet, more acutely, recognized a remarkable feature of reflecting surfaces, namely that they show us what we could not otherwise perceive—our own face and form—and so art, insofar as it is mirrorlike, reveals us to ourselves, and is, even by socratic criteria, of some cognitive utility after all. As a philosopher, however, I find Socrates' discussion defective on other, perhaps less profound grounds than these. If a mirror-image of *o* is indeed an imitation of *o*, then, if art is imitation, mirror-images are art. But in fact mirroring objects no more is art than returning weapons to a madman is justice; and reference to mirrorings would be just the sly sort of counterinstance we would expect Socrates to bring forward in rebuttal of the theory he instead uses them to illustrate. If that theory requires us to class *these* as art, it thereby shows its inadequacy: "is an imitation" will not do as a sufficient condition for "is art." Yet, perhaps because artists were engaged in imitation, in Socrates' time and after, the insufficiency of the theory was not noticed until the invention of photography. Once rejected as a sufficient condition, mimesis was quickly discarded as even a necessary one; and since the achievement of Kandinsky, mimetic features have been relegated to the periphery of critical concern, so much so that some works survive in spite of possessing those virtues, excellence in which was once celebrated as the essence of art, narrowly escaping demotion to mere illustrations.

It is, of course, indispensable in socratic discussion that all participants be masters of the concept up for analysis, since the aim is to match a real defining expression to a term in active use, and the test for adequacy presumably consists in showing that the former analyzes and applies to all and only those things of which the latter is true. The popular disclaimer notwithstanding, then, Socrates' auditors purportedly knew what art was as well as what they liked; and a theory of art, regarded here as a real definition of 'Art', is accordingly not to be of great use in helping men to recognize instances of its application. Their antecedent ability to do this is precisely what the adequacy of the theory is to be tested against, the problem being only to make explicit what they already know. It is *our* use of the term that the theory allegedly means to capture, but we are supposed able, in the words of a recent writer, "to separate those objects which are works of art from those which are not, because . . . we know how correctly to use the word 'art' and to apply the phrase 'work of art'." Theories, on this account, are somewhat like mirror-images on Socrates' account, showing forth what we already know, wordy reflections of the actual linguistic practice we are masters in. But telling artworks from other things is not so simple a matter, even for native speakers, and these days one might not be aware he was on artistic terrain without an artistic theory to tell him so. And part of the reason for this lies in the fact that terrain is constituted artistic in virtue of artistic theories, so that one use of theories, in addition to helping us discriminate art from the rest, consists in making art possible. Glaucon and the others could hardly have known what was art and what not: otherwise they would never have been taken in by mirror-images.

Suppose one thinks of the discovery of a whole new class of artworks as something analogous to the discovery of a whole new class of facts anywhere, viz., as something for theoreticians to explain. In science, as elsewhere, we often accommodate new facts to old theories via auxiliary hypotheses, a pardonable enough conservatism when the theory in question is deemed too valuable to be jettisoned all at once. Now the Imitation Theory of Art (IT) is, if one but thinks it through, an exceedingly powerful theory, explaining a great many phenomena connected with the causation and evaluation of artworks, bringing a surprising unity into a complex domain. Moreover, it is a simple matter to shore it up against many purported counterinstances by such auxiliary hypotheses as that the artist who deviates from mimeticity is perverse, inept, or mad. Ineptitude, chicanery, or folly are, in fact, testable predications. Suppose, then, tests reveal that these hypotheses fail to hold, that the theory, now beyond repair, must be replaced. And a new theory is worked out, capturing what it can of the old theory's competence, together with the heretofore recalcitrant facts. One might, thinking along these lines, represent certain episodes in the history of art as not dissimilar to certain episodes in the history of science, where a conceptual revolution is being effected and where refusal to countenance certain facts, while in part due to prejudice, inertia, and self-interest, is due also to the fact that a well-established, or at least widely credited theory is being threatened in such a way that all coherence goes.

Some such episode transpired with the advent of post-impressionist paintings. In terms of the prevailing artistic theory (IT), it was impossible to accept these as art unless inept art: otherwise they could be discounted as hoaxes, self-advertisements, or the visual counterparts of madmen's ravings. So to get them accepted *as* art, on a footing with the *Transfiguration* (not to speak of a Landseer stag), required not so much a revolution in taste as a theoretical revision of rather considerable proportions, involving not only the artistic enfranchisement of these objects, but an emphasis upon newly significant features of accepted artworks, so that quite different accounts of their status as artworks would now have to be given. As a result of the new theory's acceptance, not only were post-impressionist paintings taken up as art, but numbers of objects (masks, weapons, etc.) were transferred from anthropological museums (and heterogeneous other places) to *musées des beaux arts*, though, as we would expect from the fact that a criterion for the acceptance of a new theory is that it account for whatever the older one did, nothing had to be transferred out of the *musée des beaux arts*—even if there were internal rearrangements as between storage rooms and exhibition space. Countless native speakers hung upon suburban mantelpieces innumerable replicas of paradigm cases for teaching the expression 'work of art' that would have sent their Edwardian forebears into linguistic apoplexy.

To be sure, I distort by speaking of a theory: historically, there were several, all, interestingly enough, more or less defined in terms of the IT. Art-historical complexities must yield before the exigencies of logical exposition, and I shall speak as though there were one replacing theory, partially compensating for historical falsity by choosing one which was actually enunciated. According to it, the artists in question were to be understood not as unsuccessfully imitating real forms but as successfully creating new ones, quite as real as the forms which the older art had been thought, in its best examples, to be creditably imitating. Art, after all, had long since been thought of as creative (Vasari says that God was the first artist), and the post-impressionists were to be explained as genuinely creative, aiming, in Roger Fry's words, "not at illusion but reality." This theory (RT) furnished a whole new mode of looking at painting, old and new. Indeed, one might almost interpret the crude drawing in Van Gogh and Cézanne, the dislocation of form from contour in Rouault and Dufy, the arbitrary use of color planes in Gauguin and the Fauves, as so many ways of drawing attention to the fact that these were *non-imitations*, specifically intended not to deceive. Logically, this would be roughly like printing "Not Legal Tender" across a brilliantly counterfeited dollar bill, the resulting object (counterfeit *cum* inscription) rendered incapable of deceiving anyone. It is not an illusory dollar bill, but then, just because it is non-illusory it does not automatically become a real dollar bill either. It rather occupies a freshly opened area between real objects and real facsimiles of real objects: it is a non-facsimile, if one requires a word, and a new contribution to the world. Thus, Van Gogh's *Potato Eaters*, as a consequence of certain unmistakable distortions, turns out to be a non-facsimile of real-life potato eaters; and inasmuch as these are not facsimiles of potato eaters, Van Gogh's picture, as a non-imitation, had as much right to be called a real object as did its putative subjects. By means of this theory (RT), artworks re-entered the thick of things from which socratic theory (IT) had sought to evict them: if no *more* real than what carpenters wrought, they were at least no *less* real. The Post-Impressionist won a victory in ontology.

THEODOR W. ADORNO, *Culture Industry Reconsidered*

Excerpt (pp. 98–102) from "Culture Industry Reconsidered" (1975), in *The Culture Industry: Selected Essays on Mass Culture* (London: Routledge, 2001), 98–106. Copyright © 2001 Routledge. Reproduced with permission of Taylor & Francis Books UK.

The term culture industry was perhaps used for the first time in the book *Dialectic of Enlightenment*, which Horkheimer and I published in Amsterdam in 1947. In our drafts we spoke of 'mass culture'. We replaced that expression with 'culture industry' in order to exclude from the outset the interpretation agreeable to its advocates: that it is a matter of something like a culture that arises spontaneously from the masses themselves, the contemporary form of popular art. From the latter the culture industry must be distinguished in the extreme. The culture industry fuses the old and familiar into a new quality. In all its branches, products which are tailored for consumption by masses, and which to a great extent determine the nature of that consumption, are manufactured more or less according to plan. The individual branches are similar in structure or at least fit into each other, ordering themselves into a system almost without a gap. This is made possible by contemporary technical capabilities as well as by economic and administrative concentration. The culture industry intentionally integrates its consumers from above. To the detriment of both it forces together the spheres of high and low art, separated for thousands of years. The seriousness of high art is destroyed in speculation about its efficacy; the seriousness of the lower perishes with the civilizational constraints imposed on the rebellious resistance inherent within it as long as social control was not yet total. Thus, although the culture industry undeniably speculates on the conscious and unconscious state of the millions towards which it is directed, the masses are not primary, but secondary, they are an object of calculation; an appendage of the machinery. The customer is not king, as the culture industry would have us believe, not its subject but its object. The very word mass-media, specially honed for the culture industry, already shifts the accent onto harmless terrain. Neither is it a question of primary concern for the masses, nor of the techniques of communication as such, but of the spirit which sufflates them, their master's voice. The culture industry misuses its concern for the masses in order to duplicate, reinforce and strengthen their mentality, which it presumes is given and unchangeable. How this mentality might be changed is excluded throughout. The masses are not the measure but the ideology of the culture industry, even though the culture industry itself could scarcely exist without adapting to the masses.

The cultural commodities of the industry are governed . . . by the principle of their realization as value, and not by their own specific content and harmonious formation. The entire practice of the culture industry transfers the profit motive naked onto cultural forms. Ever since these cultural forms first began to earn a living for their creators as commodities in the marketplace they had already possessed something of this quality. But then they sought after profit only indirectly, over and above their autonomous essence. New on the part of the culture industry is the direct and undisguised primacy of a precisely and thoroughly calculated efficacy in its most typical products. The autonomy of works of art, which of course rarely ever predominated in an entirely pure form, and was always permeated by a constellation of effects, is tendentially eliminated by the culture industry, with or without the conscious will of those in control. [. . .] Cultural entities typical of the culture industry are no longer *also* commodities, they are commodities through and through. This quantitative shift is so great that it calls forth entirely new phenomena. Ultimately, the culture industry no longer even needs to directly pursue everywhere the profit interests from which it originated. These interests have become objectified in its ideology and have even made themselves independent of the compulsion to sell the cultural commodities which must be swallowed anyway. The culture industry turns into public relations, the manufacturing of 'goodwill' per se, without regard for particular firms or saleable objects. Brought to bear is a general uncritical consensus, advertisements produced for the world, so that each product of the culture industry becomes its own advertisement. [. . .]

. . . The expression 'industry' is not to be taken literally. It refers to the standardization of the thing itself—such as that of the Western, familiar to every movie-goer—and to the rationalization of distribution techniques, but not strictly to the production process. Although in film, the central sector of the culture industry, the production process resembles technical modes of operation in the extensive division of labor, the employment of machines and the separation of the laborers from the means of production—expressed in the perennial conflict between artists active in the culture industry and those who control it—individual forms of production are nevertheless maintained. Each product affects an individual air; individuality itself serves to reinforce ideology, in so far as the illusion is conjured up that the completely reified and mediated is a sanctuary from immediacy and life. Now, as ever, the culture industry exists in the 'service' of third persons, maintaining its affinity to the declining circulation process of capital, to the commerce from which it came into being. Its ideology above all makes use of the star system, borrowed from individualistic art and its commercial exploitation. The more dehumanized its methods of operation and content, the more diligently and successfully the culture industry propagates supposedly great personalities and operates with heart-throbs. It is industrial more in a sociological sense, in the incorporation of industrial forms of organization even when nothing is manufactured—as in the rationalization of office work—rather than in the sense of anything really and actually produced by technological rationality. Accordingly, the misinvestments of the culture industry are considerable, throwing those branches rendered obsolete by new techniques into crises, which seldom lead to changes for the better.

The concept of technique in the culture industry is only in name identical with technique in works of art. In the latter, technique is concerned with the internal organization of the object itself, with its inner logic. In contrast, the technique of the culture industry is, from the beginning, one of distribution and mechanical reproduction, and therefore always remains external to its object. The culture industry finds ideological support precisely in so far as it carefully shields itself from the full potential of the techniques contained in its products. It lives parasitically from the extra-artistic technique of the material production of goods, without regard for the obligation to the internal artistic whole implied by its functionality (*Sachlichkeit*), but also without concern for the laws of form demanded by aesthetic autonomy. The result for the physiognomy of the culture industry is essentially a mixture of streamlining, photographic hardness and precision on the one hand, and individualistic residues, sentimentality and an already rationally disposed and adapted romanticism on the other. Adopting Benjamin's designation of the traditional work of art by the concept of aura, the presence of that which is not present, the culture industry is defined by the fact that it does not strictly counterpose another principle to that of aura, but rather by the fact that it conserves the decaying aura as a foggy mist. By this means the culture industry betrays its own ideological abuses.

It has recently become customary among cultural officials as well as sociologists to warn against underestimating the culture industry while pointing to its great importance for the development of the consciousness of its consumers. It is to be taken seriously, without cultured snobbism. In actuality the culture industry is important as a moment of the spirit which dominates today. Whoever ignores its influence out of skepticism for what it stuffs into people would be naive. Yet there is a deceptive glitter about the admonition to take it seriously. Because of its social role, disturbing questions about its quality, about truth or untruth, and about the aesthetic niveau of the culture industry's emissions are repressed, or at least excluded from the so-called sociology of communications. The critic is accused of taking refuge in arrogant esoterica. It would be advisable first to indicate the double meaning of importance that slowly worms its way in unnoticed. Even if it touches the lives of innumerable people, the function of something is no guarantee of its particular quality. The blending of aesthetics with its residual communicative aspects leads art, as a social phenomenon, not to its rightful position in opposition to alleged artistic snobbism, but rather in a variety of ways to the defense of its baneful social consequences. The importance of the culture industry in the spiritual constitution of the masses is no dispensation for reflection on its objective legitimation, its essential being, least of all by a science which thinks itself pragmatic. On the contrary: such reflection becomes necessary precisely for this reason. To take the culture industry as seriously as its unquestioned role demands, means to take it seriously critically, and not to cower in the face of its monopolistic character.

II. THE VALUE OF ART

IGOR KOPYTOFF, *The Cultural Biography of Things*

Excerpts (pp. 66–76, 80, 82–83) from "The Cultural Biography of Things: Commoditization as Process," in *The Social Life of Things: Commodities in Cultural Perspective*, ed. A. Appadurai (Cambridge, England: Cambridge University Press, 1986), 64–91. Copyright © 1986 Cambridge University Press. Reprinted with permission of Cambridge University Press.

In doing the biography of a thing, one would ask questions similar to those one asks about people: What, sociologically, are the biographical possibilities inherent in its "status" and in the period and culture, and how are these possibilities realized? Where does the thing come from and who made it? What has been its career so far, and what do people consider to be an ideal career for such things? What are the recognized "ages" or periods in the thing's "life," and what are the cultural markers for them? How does the thing's use change with its age, and what happens to it when it reaches the end of its usefulness? [. . .]

[. . .] We have . . . biographical expectations of things. To us, a biography of a painting by Renoir that ends up in an incinerator is as tragic, in its way, as the biography of a person who ends up murdered. That is obvious. But there are other events in the biography of objects that convey more subtle meanings. What of a Renoir ending up in a private and inaccessible collection? Of one lying neglected in a museum basement? How should we feel about yet another Renoir leaving France for the United States? Or for Nigeria? The cultural responses to such biographical details reveal a tangled mass of aesthetic, historical, and even political judgments, and of convictions and values that shape our attitudes to objects labeled "art."

Biographies of things can make salient what might otherwise remain obscure. For example, in situations of culture contact, they can show what anthropologists have so often stressed: that what is significant about the adoption of alien objects—as of alien ideas—is not the fact that they are adopted, but the way they are culturally redefined and put to use. The biography of a car in Africa would reveal a wealth of cultural data: the way it was acquired, how and from whom the money was assembled to pay for it, the relationship of the seller to the buyer, the uses to which the car is regularly put, the identity of its most frequent passengers and of those who borrow it, the frequency of borrowing, the garages to which it is taken and the owner's relation to the mechanics, the movement of the car from hand to hand over the years, and in the end, when the car collapses, the final disposition of its remains. All of these details would reveal an entirely different biography from that of a middle-class American, or Navajo, or French peasant car. [. . .]

But . . . such biographies—economic, technical, social—may or may not be culturally informed. What would make a biography cultural is not what it deals with, but how and from what perspective. A culturally informed economic biography of an object would look at it as a culturally constructed entity, endowed with culturally specific meanings, and classified and reclassified into culturally constituted categories. It is from this point of view that I should like to propose a framework for looking at commodities—or rather, speaking processually, at commoditization. But first, what is a commodity? [. . .]

I assume commodities to be a universal cultural phenomenon. Their existence is a concomitant of the existence of transactions that involve the exchange of things (objects and services), exchange being a universal feature of human social life and, according to some theorists, at the very core of it. Where societies differ is in the ways commoditization as a special expression of exchange is structured and related to the social system, in the factors that encourage or contain it, in the long-term tendencies for it to expand or stabilize, and in the cultural and ideological premises that suffuse its workings.

What, then, makes a thing a commodity? A commodity is a thing that has use value and that can be exchanged in a discrete transaction for a counterpart, the very fact of exchange indicating that the counterpart has, in the immediate context, an equivalent value. The counterpart is by the same token also a commodity at the time of exchange. The exchange can be direct or it can be achieved indirectly by way of money, one of whose functions is as a means of exchange. Hence, anything that can be bought for money is at that point a commodity, whatever the fate that is reserved for it after the transaction has been made (it may, thereafter, be decommoditized). Hence, in the West, as a matter of cultural shorthand, we usually take saleability to be the unmistakable indicator of commodity status, while non-saleability imparts to a thing a special aura of apartness from the mundane and the common. In fact, of course, salability for money is not a necessary feature of commodity status, given the existence of commodity exchange in non-monetary economies. [. . .]

To be saleable for money or to be exchangeable for a wide array of other things is to have something in common with a large number of exchangeable things that, taken together, partake of a single universe of comparable values. To use an appropriately loaded even if archaic term, to be saleable or widely exchangeable is to be "common"—the opposite of being uncommon, incomparable, unique, singular, and therefore not exchangeable for anything else. The perfect commodity would be one that is exchangeable with anything and everything else, as the perfectly commoditized world would be one in which everything is exchangeable or for sale. By the same token, the perfectly decommoditized world would be one in which everything is singular, unique, and unexchangeable.

The two situations are ideal polar types, and no real economic system could conform to either. In no system is everything so singular as to preclude even the hint of exchange. And in no system, except in some extravagant Marxian image of an utterly commoditized capitalism, is everything a commodity and exchangeable for everything else within a unitary sphere of exchange. Such a construction of the world—in the first case as totally heterogeneous in terms of valuation and, in the second, as totally homogeneous—would be humanly and culturally impossible. But they are two extremes between which every real economy occupies its own peculiar place. [. . .]

In the realm of exchange values, this means that the natural world of singular things must be arranged into several manageable value classes—that is, different things must be selected and made cognitively similar when put together within each category and dissimilar when put into different categories. This is the basis for a well-known economic phenomenon—that of several spheres of exchange values, which operate more or less independently of one another. The phenomenon is found in every society, though Westerners are most apt to perceive it in uncommercialized and unmonetized economies. The nature and structure of these spheres of exchange varies among societies because . . . the cultural systems of classification reflect the structure and the cultural resources of the societies in question. And beyond that . . . there's also some tendency to impose a hierarchy upon the categories. [. . .]

The problem of value and value equivalence has always been a philosophical conundrum in economics. It involves the mysterious process by which things that are patently unlike are somehow made to be alike with respect to value, making yams, for example, somehow comparable to and exchangeable with a mortar or a pot. In the terms we have been using here, this involves taking the patently singular and inserting it into a uniform category of value with other patently singular things. For all the difficulties that the labor theory of value presents, it at least suggests that while yams and pots can conceivably be compared by the labor required to produce them (even while allowing for the different investment in training that the labor represents in each case), no such common standard is available in comparing yams to ritual offices or pots to wives and offspring. Hence, the immense difficulty, indeed impossibility, of lumping all such disparate items into a single commodity sphere. This difficulty provides the natural basis for the cultural construction of separate spheres of exchange. The culture takes on the less sweeping task of making value equivalence by creating several discrete commodity spheres. [. . .]

Commoditization, then, is best looked upon as a process of becoming rather than as an all-or-none state of being. Its expansion takes place in two ways: (a) with respect to each thing, by making it exchangeable for more and more other things, and (b) with respect to the system as a whole, by making more and more different things more widely exchangeable. [. . .]

The counterdrive to this potential onrush of commoditization is culture. In the sense that commoditization homogenizes value, while the essence of culture is discrimination, excessive commoditization is anti-cultural—as indeed so many have perceived it or sensed it to be. And if, as Durkheim (1912/1915) saw it, societies need to set apart a certain portion of their environment, marking it as "sacred," singularization is one means to this end. Culture ensures that some things remain unambiguously singular, it resists the commoditization of others; and it sometimes resingularizes what has been commoditized.

In every society, there are things that are publicly precluded from being commoditized. Some of the prohibitions are cultural and upheld collectively. In state societies, many of these prohibitions are the handwork of the state, with the usual intertwining between what serves the society at large, what serves the state, and what serves the specific groups in control. This applies to much of what one thinks of as the symbolic inventory of a society: public lands, monuments, state art collections, the paraphernalia of political power, royal residences, chiefly insignia, ritual objects, and so on. Power often asserts itself symbolically precisely by insisting on its right to singularize an object, or a set or class of objects. [. . .]

Such singularization is sometimes extended to things that are normally commodities—in effect, commodities are singularized by being pulled out of their usual commodity sphere. Thus, in the ritual paraphernalia of the British monarchy, we find a Star of India that, contrary to what would normally have happened, was prevented from becoming a commodity and eventually singularized into a "crown jewel." [. . .]

If sacralization can be achieved by singularity, singularity does not guarantee sacralization. Being a non-commodity does not by itself assure high regard, and many singular things (that is, non-exchangeable things) may be worth very little. [. . .] To be a non-commodity is to be "priceless" in the full possible sense of the term, ranging from the uniquely valuable to the uniquely worthless.

In addition to things being classified as more or less singular, there is also what might be called terminal commoditization, in which further exchange is precluded by fiat. In many societies, medicines are so treated: the medicine man makes and sells a medicine that is utterly singular since it is efficacious only for the intended patient. Terminal commoditization also marked the sale of indulgences in the Roman Catholic Church of half a millennium ago: the sinner could buy them but not resell them. In modern Western medicine, such terminal commoditization is achieved legally; it rests on the prohibition against reselling a prescribed drug and against selling any medicine without proper licensing. [. . .]

Other factors besides legal or cultural fiat may create terminal commodities. Most consumer goods are, after all, destined to be terminal or so, at least, it is hoped by the manufacturer. The expectation is easily enough fulfilled with such things as canned peas, though even here external circumstances can intrude; in times of war shortages, all sorts of normally consumable goods begin to serve as a store of wealth and, instead of being consumed, circulate endlessly in the market. With durable goods, a second-hand market normally develops, and the idea that it does may be fostered by the sellers. There is an area of our economy in which the selling strategy rests on stressing that the commoditization of goods bought for consumption need not be terminal: thus, the promise that oriental carpets, though bought for use, are a "good investment," or that certain expensive cars have a "high resale value."

The existence of terminal commoditization raises a point that is central to the analysis of slavery, where the fact that a person has been bought does not in itself tell us anything about the uses to which the person may then be put (Kopytoff 1982, 223ff). Some purchased people ended up in the mines, on plantations, or on galleys; others became Grand Viziers or Imperial Roman Admirals. In the same way, the fact that an object is bought or exchanged says nothing about its subsequent status and whether it will remain a commodity or not. But unless formally decommoditized, commoditized things remain potential commodities—they continue to have an exchange value, even if they have been effectively withdrawn from their exchange sphere and deactivated, so to speak, as commodities. This deactivation leaves them open not only to the various kinds of singularization I have mentioned so far, but also to individual, as opposed to collective, redefinitions. [. . .]

There is clearly a yearning for singularization in complex societies. Much of it is satisfied individually, by private singularization, often on principles as mundane as the one that governs the fate of heirlooms and old slippers alike—the longevity of the relation assimilates them in some sense to the person and makes parting from them unthinkable.

Sometimes the yearning assumes the proportions of a collective hunger, apparent in the widespread response to ever-new kinds of singularizations. Old beer cans, matchbooks, and comic books suddenly become worthy of being collected, moved from the sphere of the singularly worthless to that of the expensive singular. And there is a continuing appeal in stamp collecting—where, one may note, the stamps are preferably cancelled ones so there is no doubt about their worthlessness in the circle of commodities for which they were originally intended. As among individuals, much of the collective singularization is achieved by reference to the passage of time. Cars as commodities lose value as they age, but at about the age of thirty they begin to move into the category of antiques and rise in value with every receding year. [. . .]

Most of the conflict, however, between commoditization and singularization in complex societies takes place within individuals, leading to what appear to be anomalies in cognition, inconsistencies in values, and uncertainties in action. People in these societies all maintain some private vision of a hierarchy of exchange sphere, but the justification for this hierarchy is not . . . integrally tied to the exchange structure itself; rather, the justification must be imported from outside the system of exchange, from such autonomous and usually parochial systems as that of aesthetics, or morality, or religion, or specialized professional concerns. When we feel that selling a Rembrandt or an heirloom is trading downward, the explanation for our attitude is that things called "art" or "historical objects" are superior to the world of commerce. This is the reason why the high value of the singular in complex societies becomes so easily embroiled in snobbery. The high value does not visibly reside in the exchange system itself. . . . In a complex society the absence of . . . visible confirmation[s] of prestige, of what exactly is an "upward" conversion, makes it necessary to attribute high but nonmonetary value to aesthetic, stylistic, ethnic, class, or genealogical esoterica.

When things participate simultaneously in cognitively distinct yet effectively intermeshed exchange spheres, one is constantly confronted with seeming paradoxes of value. A Picasso, though possessing a monetary value, is priceless in another, higher scheme. Hence, we feel uneasy, even offended, when a newspaper declares the Picasso to be worth $690,000, for one should not be pricing the priceless. But in a pluralistic society, the "objective" pricelessness of the Picasso can only be unambiguously confirmed to us by its immense market price. Yet, the pricelessness still makes the Picasso in some sense more valuable than the pile of dollars it can fetch—as will be duly pointed out by the newspapers if the Picasso is stolen. Singularity, in brief, is confirmed not by the object's structural position in an exchange system, but by intermittent forays into the commodity sphere, quickly followed by reentries into the closed sphere of singular "art." But the two worlds cannot be kept separate for very long; for one thing, museums must insure their holdings. So museums and art dealers will name prices, be accused of the sin of transforming art into a commodity, and, in response, defend themselves by blaming each other for creating and maintaining a commodity market. It would, however, be missing the point of this analysis to conclude that the talk about singular art is merely an ideological camouflage for an interest in merchandising. What is culturally significant here is precisely that there is an inner compulsion to defend oneself, to others and to oneself, against the charge of "merchandising" art.

The only time when the commodity status of a thing is beyond question is the moment of actual exchange. Most of the time, when the commodity is effectively out of the commodity sphere, its status is inevitably ambiguous and open to the push and pull of events and desires, as it is shuffled about in the flux of social life. This is the time when it is exposed to the well-nigh-infinite variety of attempts to singularize it. Thus, singularizations of various kinds, many of them fleeting, are a constant accompaniment of commoditization, all the more so when it becomes excessive. There is a kind of singularizing black market here that is the mirror-image of, and as inevitable as, the more familiar commoditizing black market that accompanies regulated singularizing economies. Thus, even things that unambiguously carry an exchange value—formally speaking, therefore, commodities—do absorb the other kind of worth, one that is nonmonetary and goes beyond exchange worth. We may take this to be the missing non-economic side of what Marx called commodity fetishism. For Marx, the worth of commodities is determined by the social relations of their production; but the existence of the exchange system makes the production process remote and misperceived, and it "masks" the commodity's true worth (as, say, in the case of diamonds). This allows the commodity to be socially endowed with a fetishlike "power" that is unrelated to its true worth. Our analysis suggests, however, that some of that power is attributed to commodities after they are produced, and this by way of an autonomous cognitive and cultural process of singularization.

WALTER BENJAMIN, *Aura*

Excerpt (pp. 220–21) from "The Work of Art in the Age of Mechanical Reproduction" (1935), in *Illuminations: Essays and Reflections*, ed. H. Arendt, trans. Harry Zohn (New York: Schocken, 1969), 217–51. Copyright © 1955 by Suhrkamp Verlag, Frankfurt A.M.; English translation copyright © 1968/1996 by Houghton Mifflin Harcourt Publishing Company. Reprinted by permission of Houghton Mifflin Harcourt Publishing Company, all rights reserved; and Writers House LLC acting as agent for the author.

Even the most perfect reproduction of a work of art is lacking in one element: its presence in time and space, its unique existence at the place where it happens to be. This unique existence of the work of art determined the history to which it was subject throughout the time of its existence. This includes the changes which it may have suffered in physical condition over the years as well as the various changes in its ownership. The traces of the first can be revealed only by chemical or physical analyses which it is impossible to perform on a reproduction; changes of ownership are subject to a tradition which must be traced from the situation of the original.

The presence of the original is the prerequisite to the concept of authenticity. Chemical analyses of the patina of a bronze can help to establish this, as does the proof that a given manuscript of the Middle Ages stems from an archive of the fifteenth century. The whole sphere of authenticity is outside technical—and, of course, not only technical—reproducibility. Confronted with its manual reproduction, which was usually branded as a forgery, the original preserved all its authority; not so *vis-à-vis* technical reproduction. The reason is twofold. First, process reproduction is more independent of the original than manual reproduction. For example, in photography, process reproduction can bring out those aspects of the original that are unattainable to the naked eye yet accessible to the lens, which is adjustable and chooses its angle at will. And photographic reproduction, with the aid of certain processes, such as enlargement or slow motion, can capture images which escape natural vision. Secondly, technical reproduction can put the copy of the original into situations which would be out of reach for the original itself. Above all, it enables the original to meet the beholder halfway, be it in the form of a photograph or a phonograph record. The cathedral leaves its locale to be received in the studio of a lover of art; the choral production, performed in an auditorium or in the open air, resounds in the drawing room.

The situations into which the product of mechanical reproduction can be brought may not touch the actual work of art, yet the quality of its presence is always depreciated. This holds not only for the art work but also, for instance, for a landscape which passes in review before the spectator in a movie. In the case of the art object, a most sensitive nucleus—namely, its authenticity—is interfered with whereas no natural object is vulnerable on that score. The authenticity of a thing is the essence of all that is transmissible from its beginning, ranging from its substantive duration to its testimony to the history which it has experienced. Since the historical testimony rests on the authenticity, the former, too, is jeopardized by reproduction when substantive duration ceases to matter. And what is really jeopardized when the historical testimony is affected is the authority of the object.

One might subsume the eliminated element in the term 'aura' and go on to say: that which withers in the age of mechanical reproduction is the aura of the work of art. This is a symptomatic process whose significance points beyond the realm of art. One might generalize by saying: the technique of reproduction detaches the reproduced object from the domain of tradition. By making many reproductions it substitutes a plurality of copies for a unique existence. And in permitting the reproduction to meet the beholder or listener in his own particular situation, it reactivates the object reproduced. These two processes lead to a tremendous shattering of tradition which is the obverse of the contemporary crisis and renewal of mankind.

MICHAEL HUTTER AND RICHARD SHUSTERMAN, *Varieties of Artistic
Value in Contemporary Aesthetics*

Excerpt (pp. 197–200) from "Value and the Valuation of Art in Economic and Aesthetic
Theory," in *Handbook of the Economics of Art and Culture*, vol. 1, ed. V. A. Ginsburgh and
D. Throsby (Amsterdam: Elsevier, 2006), 171–208. Copyright © 2006 Elsevier BV.
Reprinted with permission of Elsevier.

In the vague concept of artistic value, different kinds of value seem to be nested. We
distinguish ten kinds which have been to some extent suggested in [aesthetic theories].
[. . .] It is hard to imagine how all these types of value could be organized into one accepted
calculus for ranking the value of all works of art, not least because the relative weighting
of these different types would be much contested. Yet, to distinguish them could enable
us to be more precise about what we are in fact valuing when, with respect to particular
artworks, we speak of artistic value.

(1) Art's *moral or religious vision*, its power to edify and spiritually uplift, can still form
part of a work's artistic value, while the appeal to low human drives and the toleration of
morally condemned behavior diminishes the value of an artwork. Form cannot be adequately isolated from content. The moral or religious vision expressed in a work forms
part of the work's content and structure, and as such its valuation can be legitimately
included in our appraisal of the work's value. [. . .]

(2) Art has long been valued for its deep *expressiveness*. Expression, it is argued,
requires a medium through which the self can be expressed, and the various media of
art, rich with perceptual and semantic potential, provide a superb matrix for such expression. Advocates of expression theories of art . . . argue that the artist begins with an
unclear feeling or sense of what she wishes to express, and it is only through art that the
expression acquires clarity and distinction. Apart from this transitive sense of expression,
where an artwork's expression is the expression of something anterior—a specific emotion, idea, etc.—there is an intransitive sense of artistic expressiveness that is valued. It
makes sense to say of a painting or a piece of music that it is expressive without our being
able to specify what exactly it expresses. Here expressiveness connotes the degree of
power and impact which is suggestive of artistic value.

(3) Art's *communicative power* for the sharing of feelings and ideas between artists and
their public is part of artistic value. Art's emotional quality, direct experiential appeal, and
link to pleasure give it a penetrating, pervasive infectiousness that promotes easy, rapid,
powerful, and widespread communication. Kant located the grounds of aesthetic judgment in the "sensus communis" of human nature. Schiller argued that only "the aesthetic mode of communication unites society because it relates that which is common to
all" (1986, 217). [. . .]

(4) Communicative power is also essential to art's *social and political* value. Artworks
typically embody the meanings and ideals of the society in which they are created; even

works that have a revolutionary message must rely to some extent on shared meanings and values or else they would be unintelligible and totally rejected. Art thus provides an attractive repository of ideas and ideals that build social unity and stability, while enabling their transmission over generations. [. . .]

(5) Plato's condemnation of art as a deceptive purveyor of falsehood has been frequently countered by affirming art's *cognitive* value. Even if we dismiss the notion of a special form of truth that is accessible only through artistic means, art has undeniable value in effectively communicating a wide variety of truths and in honing our symbolic skills of conveying and processing very subtle forms of information. Because emotion has a strong bodily dimension, art's emotional power makes the truths it expresses more powerful and convincing, because as emotionally grasped truths they become more deeply embodied and impressed in our consciousness and memory. The very appreciation of form and meaning is an exercise whose practice enhances our cognitive skills and our proficiency in symbolic processing.

(6) Many theorists . . . locate art's value largely in the special, directly satisfying or pleasurable experience it gives. We call this art's *experiential* value. It includes art's entertainment value—the entertaining pleasure and distraction it provides as a pastime. But art also has experiential rewards that are not primarily pleasurable. Avant-garde works, for example, may produce experiences of shock, intensity or outrage that we recognize as valuable without their being pleasant or enjoyable. [. . .]

(7) Aesthetics has long emphasized certain formal or design values embodied in art: unity, harmony, complexity, balance, intensity, dramatic tension, etc. Such formal values are sometimes distinguished by philosophers as distinctively *aesthetic* values in contrast to artistic values. This is because these formal values clearly seem applicable to objects other than artworks (a flower or sunset or ocean storm) and do not seem to require historical knowledge of art in the ways demanded by assessments of art-historical value, art-technical value, or cult value. Nor do these values demand for their appreciation the sort of external, non-aesthetic knowledge we need for assessing the cognitive, moral, religious or communicative value of artworks. [. . .]

Expressiveness, in the intransitive sense of evocative suggestiveness, can also be included under specifically aesthetic properties of artworks. We can appreciate an artwork as expressive without external art-historical knowledge about what its creator wanted to express and without even assuming that there was a distinct idea the work aims to express. [. . .]

(8) A specific kind of artistic value could be called *art-technical* value. Such value relates to the skill, technique, or technical innovation displayed by an artwork. We can, for example, regard the content or form of an artwork as not particularly worthy of appreciation but still value the virtuosity of technique or invention that the work or its performance displays.

(9) *Art-historical* value concerns the value an artwork has for art's history, either by its providing evidence of historical innovation or influence, whether technical, stylistic, or

in terms of new content, or by simply being a crucial historical artifact for art history. Though some viewers find Picasso's *Demoiselles d'Avignon* a very unattractive painting, its artistic value in terms of art-historical value (as the harbinger of cubism) cannot be denied. Physical rarity, because very few other surviving exemplars of its period or style have been found, adds to appreciation.

(10) Related to art-historical value is *artistic cult* value. Through a history of appreciation and dissemination, a particular artwork, for example, Leonardo da Vinci's *La Gioconda*, becomes identified as a hallowed locus of artistic genius and a paradigm of self-representation. The strength of the aura, to which Benjamin refers, gives value to the reproduced versions of the image, and the volume of reproductions, in turn, increases the cult value of the original.

Some of the works of art created also have economic value. Economic value is a property which all works can attain, irrespective of the kind of artistic value attributed to a particular work. Money is paid in exchange for original works, copies of originals (books, prints and disks), and performances of musical or theatrical scores. Certain patterns of demand and supply are directly connected to some of the artistic values sketched above.

PIERRE BOURDIEU, *The Production of Belief*

Excerpts (pp. 74–81, 103) from "The Production of Belief" (1980), in *The Field of Cultural Production*, ed. R. Johnson (New York: Columbia University Press, 1993), 74–111. Copyright © 1993 Columbia University Press. Reprinted by permission of Columbia University Press and Polity Press, Cambridge.

The art business, a trade in things that have no price, belongs to the class of practices in which the logic of the pre-capitalist economy lives on. . . . These practices, functioning as practical *negations*, can only work by pretending not to be doing what they are doing. Defying ordinary logic, they lend themselves to two opposed readings, both equally false, which each undo their essential duality and duplicity by reducing them either to the disavowal or to what is disavowed—to disinterestedness or self-interest. The challenge which economies based on disavowal of the 'economic' present to all forms of economism lies precisely in the fact that they function, and can function, in practice—and not merely in the agents' representations—only by virtue of a constant, collective repression of narrowly 'economic' interest and of the real nature of the practices revealed by 'economic' analysis.

In this economic universe, whose very functioning is defined by a 'refusal' of the 'commercial' which is in fact a collective disavowal of commercial interests and profits, the most 'anti-economic' and most visibly 'disinterested' behaviours, which in an 'economic' universe would be those most ruthlessly condemned, contain a form of economic rationality (even in the restricted sense) and in no way exclude their authors from even the 'economic' profits awaiting those who conform to the law of this universe. In other words, alongside the pursuit of 'economic' profit, which treats the cultural goods business as a business like any other, and not the *most* profitable, 'economically' speaking (as the best-informed, i.e. the most 'disinterested', art dealers point out) and merely adapts itself to the demand of an already converted clientele, there is also room for the *accumulation of symbolic capital*. 'Symbolic capital' is to be understood as economic or political capital that is disavowed, misrecognized and thereby recognized, hence legitimate, a 'credit' which, under certain conditions, and always in the long run, guarantees 'economic' profits. Producers and vendors of cultural goods who 'go commercial' condemn themselves, and not only from an ethical or aesthetic point of view, because they deprive themselves of the opportunities open to those who can *recognize* the specific demands of this universe and who, by concealing from themselves and others the interests at stake in their practice, obtain the means of deriving profits from disinterestedness. In short, when the only usable, effective capital is the (mis)recognized, legitimate capital called 'prestige' or 'authority', the economic capital that cultural undertakings generally require cannot secure the specific profits produced by the field—not the 'economic' profits they always imply—unless it is reconverted into symbolic capital. For the author, the critic, the art dealer, the publisher or the theatre manager, the only legitimate accumulation consists in making a name for oneself, a known, recognized name, a capital of consecration implying a power to consecrate objects (with a trademark or signature) or persons (through publication, exhibition, etc.) and therefore to give value, and to appropriate the profits from this operation.

[. . .] The disavowed economic enterprise of art dealers or publishers, 'cultural bankers' in whom art and business meet in practice—which predisposes them for the role of scapegoat—cannot succeed, even in 'economic' terms, unless it is guided by a practical mastery of the laws of the functioning of the field in which cultural goods are produced and circulate, i.e. by an entirely improbable, and in any case rarely achieved, combination of the realism implying minor concessions to 'economic' necessities that are disavowed but not denied and the conviction which excludes them. The fact that the disavowal of the 'economy' is neither a simple ideological mask nor a complete repudiation of economic interest explains why, on the one hand, new producers whose only capital is their conviction can establish themselves in the market by appealing to the values whereby the dominant figures accumulated their symbolic capital, and why, on the other hand, only those who can come to terms with the 'economic' constraints inscribed in this bad-faith economy can reap the full 'economic' profits of their symbolic capital.

WHO CREATES THE 'CREATOR'?

The 'charismatic' ideology which is the ultimate basis of belief in the value of a work of art and which is therefore the basis of functioning of the field of production and circulation of cultural commodities, is undoubtedly the main obstacle to a rigorous science of the production of the value of cultural goods. It is this ideology which directs attention to the *apparent producer*, the painter, writer or composer, in short, the 'author', suppressing

art value based
on the artist, not
production costs

the question of what authorizes the author, what creates the authority with which authors authorize. If it is all too obvious that the price of a picture is not determined by the sum of the production costs—the raw material and the painter's labour time—and if works of art provide a golden example for those who seek to refute Marx's labour theory of value (which anyway gives a special status to artistic production), this is perhaps because we wrongly define the unit of production or, which amounts to the same thing, the process of production.

dealer creates
a product
dealer announces
value & prestige

The question can be asked in its most concrete form . . . : who is the true producer of the value of the work—the painter or the dealer . . . ? The ideology of creation, which makes the author the first and last source of the value of his work, conceals the fact that the cultural businessman (art dealer, publisher, etc.) is at one and the same time the person who exploits the labour of the 'creator' by trading in the 'sacred' and the person who, by putting it on the market, by exhibiting, publishing or staging it, consecrates a product which he has 'discovered' and which would otherwise remain a mere natural resource; and the more consecrated he personally is, the more strongly he consecrates the work. The art trader is not just the agent who gives the work a commercial value by bringing it into a market; he is not just the representative, the impresario, who 'defends the authors he loves'. He is the person who can proclaim the value of the author he defends (cf. the fiction of the catalogue or blurb) and above all 'invests his prestige' in the author's cause, acting as a 'symbolic banker' who offers as security all the symbolic capital he has accumulated (which he is liable to forfeit if he backs a 'loser'). This investment, of which the accompanying 'economic' investments are themselves only a guarantee, is what brings the producer into the cycle of consecration. Entering the field of literature is not so much like going into religion as getting into a select club. . . . Even clearer is the role of the art dealer,

less publicity
compared to
commercial
market

who literally has to 'introduce' the artist and his work into ever more select company (group exhibitions, one-man shows, prestigious collections, museums) and ever more sought-after places. But the law of this universe, whereby the less visible the investment, the more productive it is symbolically, means that promotion exercises, which in the business world take the overt form of publicity, must here be euphemized. The art trader cannot serve his 'discovery' unless he applies all his conviction, which rules out 'sordidly commercial' manoeuvres, manipulation and the 'hard sell', in favour of the softer, more discreet forms of 'public relations' (which are themselves a highly euphemized form of publicity)—receptions, society gatherings, and judiciously placed confidences.

THE CIRCLE OF BELIEF

[. . .] We still have to determine the source of the art-businessman's acknowledged power to consecrate. The charismatic ideology has a ready-made answer: the 'great' dealers, the 'great' publishers, are inspired talent-spotters who, guided by their disinterested, unreasoning passion for a work of art, have 'made' the painter or writer, or have helped him make himself, by encouraging him in difficult moments with the faith they had in him, guiding him with their advice and freeing him from material worries. To avoid an endless regress in the chain of causes, perhaps it is necessary to cease thinking in the logic, which a whole tradition encourages, of the 'first beginning', which inevitably leads to faith in the 'creator'. [. . .] His 'authority' is itself a credit-based value, which only exists in the relationship with the field of production as a whole, i.e. with the artists or writers who belong to his 'stable' . . . and with those who do not and would or would not like to; in the relationship with the other dealers or publishers who do or do not envy him his painters or writers and are or are not capable of taking them from him; in the relationship with the critics, who do or do not believe in his judgement, and speak of his 'products' with varying degrees of respect; in the relationship with his clients and customers, who perceive his 'trademark' with greater or lesser clarity and do or do not place their trust in it. This 'authority' is nothing other than 'credit' with a set of agents who constitute 'connections' whose value is proportionate to the credit they themselves command. It is all too obvious that critics also collaborate with the art trader in the effort of consecration which makes the reputation and, at least in the long term, the monetary value of works. 'Discovering' the 'new talents', they guide buyers' and sellers' choices by their writings or advice . . . and by their verdicts, which, though offered as purely aesthetic, entail significant economic effects (juries for artistic prizes). Among the makers of the work of art, we must finally include the public, which helps to make its value by appropriating it materially (collectors) or symbolically (audiences, readers), and by objectively or subjectively identifying part of its own value with these appropriations. In short, what 'makes reputations' is not . . . this or that 'influential' person, this or that institution, review, magazine, academy, coterie, dealer or publisher; it is not even the whole set of what are sometimes called 'personalities of the world of arts and letters'; it is the field of production, understood as the system of objective relations between these agents or institutions and as the site of the struggles for the monopoly of the power to consecrate, in which the value of works of art and belief in that value are continuously generated.

FAITH AND BAD FAITH

The source of the efficacy of all acts of consecration is the field itself, the locus of the accumulated social energy which the agents and institutions help to reproduce through the struggles in which they try to appropriate it and into which they put what they have acquired from it in previous struggles. The value of works of art in general—the basis of the value of each particular work—and the belief which underlies it, are generated in the incessant, innumerable struggles to establish the value of this or that particular work, i.e. not only in the competition between agents (authors, actors, writers, critics, directors, publishers, dealers, etc.) whose interests (in the broadest sense) are linked to different cultural goods, . . . 'established' painting or avant-garde painting, 'mainstream' literature or 'advanced' literature, but also in the conflicts between agents occupying different positions in the production of products of the same type: painters and dealers, authors and publishers, writers and critics, etc. Even if these struggles never clearly set the 'commercial' against the 'non-commercial', 'disinterestedness' against 'cynicism', they almost always involve recognition of the ultimate values of 'disinterestedness' through the denunciation of the mercenary compromises or calculating manoeuvres of the adversary, so that disavowal of the 'economy' is placed at the very heart of the field, as the principle governing its functioning and transformation.

This is why the dual reality of the ambivalent painter-dealer or writer-publisher relationship is most clearly revealed in moments of crisis, when the objective reality of each of the positions and their relationship is unveiled and the values which do the veiling are reaffirmed. No one is better placed than art dealers to know the interests of the makers of works and the strategies they use to defend their interests or to conceal their strategies. Although dealers form a protective screen between the artist and the market, they are also what link them to the market and so provoke, by their very existence, cruel unmaskings of the truth of artistic practice. [. . .] The makers and marketers of works of art are adversaries in collusion, who each abide by the same law which demands the repression of direct manifestations of personal interest, at least in its overtly 'economic' form, and which has every appearance of transcendence although it is only the product of the cross-censorship weighing more or less equally on each of those who impose it on all the others.

A similar mechanism operates when an unknown artist, without credit or credibility, is turned into a known and recognized artist. The struggle to impose the dominant definition of art, i.e. to impose a style, embodied in a particular producer or group of producers, gives the work of art a value by putting it at stake, inside and outside the field of production. Everyone can challenge his or her adversaries' claim to distinguish art from non-art without ever calling into question this fundamental claim. Precisely because of the conviction that good and bad painting exist, competitors can exclude each other from the field of painting, thereby giving it the stakes and the motor without which it could not function. And nothing better conceals the objective collusion which is the matrix of specifically artistic value than the conflicts through which it operates. [. . .]

COLLECTIVE MISRECOGNITION

[. . .] The artist who puts her name on a ready-made article and produces an object whose market price is incommensurate with its cost of production is collectively mandated to perform a magic act which would be nothing without the whole tradition leading up to her gesture, and without the universe of celebrants and believers who give it meaning and value in terms of that tradition. The source of 'creative' power, the ineffable *mana* or charisma celebrated by the tradition, need not be sought anywhere other than in the field, i.e. in the system of objective relations which constitute it, in the struggles of which it is the site and in the specific form of energy or capital which is generated there. So it is both true and untrue to say that the commercial value of a work of art is incommensurate with its cost of production. It is true if one only takes account of the manufacture of the material object; it is not true if one is referring to the production of the work of art as a sacred, consecrated object, the product of a vast operation of *social alchemy* jointly conducted with equal conviction and very unequal profits, by all the agents involved in the field of production, i.e. obscure artists and writers as well as 'consecrated' masters, critics and publishers as well as authors, enthusiastic clients as well as convinced vendors. These are contributions, including the most obscure, which the partial materialism of economism ignores, and which only have to be taken into account in order to see that the production of the work of art, i.e. of the artist, is no exception to the law of the conservation of social energy. [. . .]

Without entering into a systematic analysis of the field of the galleries . . . we may simply observe that . . . the differences which separate the galleries according to their seniority (and their celebrity), and therefore according to the degree of consecration and the market value of the works they own, are replicated by differences in their relation to the 'economy'. The 'sales galleries' (e.g. Beaubourg), having no 'stable' of their own, exhibit in relatively eclectic fashion painters of very different periods, schools and ages (abstracts as well as post-surrealists, a few European hyper-realists, some new realists), i.e. works whose greater 'accessibility' (owing to their more classic status or their 'decorative' potential) can find purchasers outside the circle of professional and semi-professional collectors (among the 'jet-set executives' and 'trendy industrialists', as an informant put it). This enables them to pick out and attract a fraction of the avant-garde painters who have already been 'noticed' by offering them a slightly compromising form of consecration, i.e. a market in which the prices are much higher than in the avant-garde galleries. By contrast, galleries like Sonnabend, Denise René or Durand-Ruel, which mark dates in the history of painting because they have been able in their time to assemble a 'school', are characterized by a *systematic slant*. Thus in the succession of painters presented by the Sonnabend gallery one can see the logic of an artistic development which leads from the 'new American painting' and pop art, with painters such as Rauschenberg, Jasper Johns, Jim Dine, to Oldenburg, Lichtenstein, Wesselmann, Rosenquist, Warhol, sometimes classified under the label minimal art, and to the most recent innovations of *art pauvre*, conceptual art and art by correspondence. Likewise, there is a clear connection between the geometric abstraction which made the name of the Denise René gallery (founded in 1945 and inaugurated with a Vasarely exhibition) and kinetic art, with artists such as Max Bill and Vasarely forming a sort of link between the visual experiments of the inter-war years (especially the Bauhaus) and the optical and technological experiments of the new generation.

RAYMONDE MOULIN, *The Paradox of Rarity: Photography*

Excerpts (pp. 457–63) from "The Genesis of the Rarity of Art," *Art in Translation* 3, no. 4 (2011): 441–71. Reprinted by permission of Taylor & Francis, Ltd. London, tandfonline .com.

At its outset, photography was placed in a context of rarity due to technology, but at the same time found itself in a position of artistic ignominy—again due precisely to its technical mode of operation. [. . .]

The controversy over photography's status, and whether it pertained to the categories of "industrial arts" or "fine arts," was a subject of great debate in the nineteenth century (and is as yet, we feel, to be fully explored) that had a bearing on the relationship between art and industry. It is not possible here to retrace the complete history of debate over the status of photography from the nineteenth century to the present day. We will . . . simply make one or two remarks, with the particular aim of stating that the recognition of photography as a work of art, even if it was not unanimous, nor without ambiguity, is nonetheless a nineteenth-century legacy—despite Baudelaire's famous diatribe against naturalism and photography, and the idiotic confusion between art and industry. [. . .]

Independent of the photography sold by "photo shops," the photography market currently comprises two sectors. These cannot be compared in terms of transaction figures, but the second sector offers considerable interest in our present context. The first market is that of reproduction rights: the photographer sells the photography reproduction rights, which is to say, according to the law of March 11, 1957, on artistic ownership, the royalties. The second market is that of prints: the photographer sells objects, which are the photographic prints. [. . .]

The intermediaries are the paint galleries, photograph galleries, brokers, and those in charge of public sales (auctioneers). The major prizes are those of the United States, where distribution and specialized marketing systems were first set in place. If one considers and compares the number of columns relating to photography in the major newspapers, the number of specialist magazines, the number of exhibitions (200 in 1972), the sum of public sales, and the significance of the buyers (in particular museums and universities), the United States is first in the list and is the top place for international validation. In a market of an international nature like that of painting, it is clear that many places have seen photograph galleries multiply and art galleries with dedicated photography areas increase; these include London, Rome, Paris, the large German towns, Japan, and South America.

All leaders of the photographic print market, together with a small number of photographers (those who, belonging to the generation of under-40s, would like there to be no other photographic practice than that which leads to the print as work of art), a small number of curators and museum directors (those who benefit reciprocally from the highest recognition as connoisseurs), dealers and gallery directors (the last conferring more importance than the first on what they call "cultural engagement"; that is to say, exhibitions), and finally, collectors (of greatest to smallest means, "passionate" art lovers and/ or potential speculators), all support the theory of effective rarity, which is imposed by the means of production of the original print.

Industry intervenes both before (with the photographic industry of instruments and films) and sometimes after, with industrial printing techniques. Between these two moments, the photographic print is the result of an artisan process consisting of three stages: the taking of the shot, the development of the negative, and the printing. Photographers who hold art to be the product of individual work carry out all three operations. The product of such actions may or may not be recognized as artistic beyond the studio: the verdict comes from the international community of connoisseurs, whose authority will impact on the market.

In the micro-sphere of the print market, reference to the unique print is constant. Metaphors inspired by artistic practices such as painting, engraving, and sculpture also occur: "light is the photographer's clay." Printing is held to be a long and difficult operation that in certain cases involves physical or chemical treatments reminiscent of painters' "mixing"; as Paul Strand, whose printing contributed to his success, said, "every photo is unique." Market regulars like to say that the difficulty arises more out of the excessive rarity of original print-runs: print-runs, numbered on the model of the engraving and usually fixed at twenty-five or thirty copies, are imaginary in the sense that it would be almost impossible to obtain several original print-runs from those new fanatics of the unique that certain photographers have now become.

By far the most important criterion for a plastic work of art's originality (1957 law) is its individual execution, which precisely expresses the dominating artistic ideology. Some variations are accepted with respect to a photographic print or an engraving, but this is as long as everything possible is done to protect the principle. The definition of an authorized edition, such as given in fiscal legislation, does not concern photography. And if the custom of restricted editions is now becoming established, it is nonetheless not exclusive. Many very well-known photographers do not undertake to print their photographs, yet as soon as they are signed, they are considered to be original. In signing a photograph, the person who took the shot acknowledges it as being in conformity with his idea. Restricting the print-runs of prints sold as originals was not usual practice within the generation of the great photographers such as Brassaï, Cartier-Bresson, and Doisneau.

We should add that the distinction between an original work and its reproduction is particularly difficult to establish in the area of photography. A photograph of a painting or an engraving is a reproduction, but is no longer an engraving, whereas the photograph of a photograph is a reproduction of the same nature as the original: a duplicate—negative taken from a negative or a print—is a copy, but remains a photograph. One example is enough to justify, in monetary terms, the differences between types of practice. A photograph by Imogen Cunningham, printed by herself, was in 1977 worth approximately $400; when it was printed by a laboratory, but signed, it was worth $200, when it was printed after her death, it was valued at $150.

The definition of an original print, in usual market terms, carries certain ambiguities due to the fact that its very nature is analogous. By analogy with the plastic work of art (painting, sculpture, or engraving), originality assumes that the work is personally executed by the artist, in all its stages; and by analogy with engraving, has a limited number of copies. As we have seen, infractions of one or the other of these principles occur frequently among well-known artists, but only on condition that the print is signed. Fame itself is the result of a complex system whereby two different kinds of photograph market interact. As a result of photography's elevation in the hierarchy of cultural legitimacy and its recognition both within and outside the area of artistic production, a community of experts has emerged (historians of photography, directors and curators of museums and libraries) and contributes to the establishment of a hierarchy of quality.

As in the painting market, one may already observe that photography—despite its relative youth—has two sectors in the print market. The old prints market combines several effects of rarity: original rarity (in particular in the case of the daguerreotype), residual rarity, rarity or uniqueness of the represented subject, and rarity of the artistic excellence as defined by photographic historians and museum directors—in particular, for France, those in the *Cabinet des Estampes* at the National Library in Paris. When all criteria of rarity are met (or at the very least, a large number of them), the price nears the absolute limit and the factors determining it are comparable to those applied to pre-modern paintings—on the condition that the possibility of reproducibility is overlooked. In the old print market, prices are more and more elevated, although they remain beneath those of pre-modern paintings. [. . .]

When the price is not fixed objectively, as it is after the death of a work's author, many factors intervene, which can contribute to the "launch" of a photographer, to methods of recognition, and to a rise in price. The main difference with respect to the contemporary painting market (other than reproducibility) rests with the dual photography market and to the various positions one photographer can occupy, on the one hand, in the press, illustration, and publishing market and in the print market, on the other. The reader should bear in mind that the development of the print market is not the sole product of a conscious or unconscious quest by market players with rarity as their objective. The lack of outlets in the market for large print-runs (given the crisis in the illustrated press) has been one of several favorable conditions that together have contributed to the rapid growth of the print market.

At a time when technical innovations enable huge print-runs and where photography is practiced by all social classes and age groups among the public, we are now witnessing a revival, in one of the photography markets, of the rarity of beginning. However, in no way is the process the same. Photography in its early stages was frustrated by being the prisoner of faltering techniques, whereas today's photography is in revolt against a technology that overwhelms. And the question has to be raised as to whether the celebration of photographic rarity does not represent an unconscious quest for the ultimate "artistic certificate." Photographic prints belong to the category of reproducible goods. Because of their technical production, they are multiples, and as merchandise cannot be assimilated either to unique works of art, produced by artisanship, or to pre-industrial forms of reproduction such as engraving. As soon as the photographic print market began to structure itself according to the model of the artworks market—in the accepted sense of the term—the contradiction between uniqueness and multiplicity, rarity and abundance, and art and industry, exploded. To drive the photographic print, as merchandise, into the category of artworks, one must firstly cleanse it of its original sin of reproducibility. If the photograph currently appears to be winning its case before the tribunal of art (on the economic grounds that the art market represents), it is at the cost of a massive techno-logical Malthusianism and a cult-like regression. But what significance and what influence might a victory have that is gained before a tribunal that the very invention of photography disqualified? In the artistic world of the avant-garde, artists can turn to photography to strengthen a step that is anti-art. The photographic print, on the contrary, in refusing the stigma of reproduction and the "mark" of industry (although large companies do figure on the list of silent partners who intervene in the market), holds itself up as being in accordance with the inherited definition of a work of art. Nevertheless, an original print signed by a professional photographer is positioned at a lower price than the most self-proclaimed-as-ordinary-photograph signed by a painter-artist. In these complicated games where rarity is the issue, the rarity of the artist's signature remains more socially valuable than the photographer's.

OLAV VELTHUIS, *Symbolic Meanings of Prices*

Excerpts (pp. 158–64) from "Symbolic Meanings of Prices," in *Talking Prices: Symbolic Meanings of Prices on the Market for Contemporary Art* (Princeton, NJ: Princeton University Press, 2007), 158–78. Copyright © 2007 by Princeton University Press. Reprinted by permission.

Pricing . . . is not just an economic, but also a signifying act: by distinguishing different types of prices or by identifying auction and gallery prices with different sets of values, art dealers turn pricing into a meaningful activity. [. . .] The purpose of [this] chapter is to address two major anomalies of the price mechanism with the meaningful, symbolic, or expressive dimension of prices in mind. The first anomaly is the existence of a strong taboo on price decreases. This taboo has been widely recognized in academic literature on the art market, it appears in artists' guides to the market, and it is universally acknowledged by the dealers I interviewed. [. . .] In fact, art dealers and artists seem to behave more like *price* than *profit* maximizers. In their everyday models of the art market, the concept of price elasticity, which is so important in academic economic thinking, plays a subordinate role. From an economic perspective this may make sense as far as the negative effect of price decreases on the investment potential of art is concerned. The finding must also be puzzling for neoclassical economists, however, since it inhibits the movement of the market into equilibrium: if lowering prices is really impossible, the market cannot be cleared in case of excess supply. [. . .]

The second anomaly [. . .] is the fact that artworks of the same size, within the oeuvre of one artist, almost invariably have the same market price. [. . .]

The rule of pricing according to size is anomalous, since it implies that art dealers miss out on a price premium on works they expect to sell more easily; they fail to exploit excess demand for some works, in other words. This is indeed acknowledged by the dealers I interviewed. As one of them put it: "there is always somebody's favorite piece in the show that you can sell ten times over." . . . If dealers claim to be concerned about quality, why do they refrain from expressing those concerns in the prices they set? Why do they say, as one of my respondents did, that "[i]t is a code in the gallery circuit to conceal which artworks you value higher than others"? In fact, the same dealers who distinguished themselves sharply from the immorality of the secondary market had to acknowledge that secondary market dealers *do* price according to quality. [. . .]

How does the price mechanism contribute to the audience's valuation of an artwork? When setting prices, dealers take into account that collectors make inferences about the quality of the work from its relative price or from a price change. First of all, the danger of low prices, dealers think, is that collectors do not take the work seriously. If a work is priced lower than the conventional or expected price level, collectors may be pleased, but at the same time it incites distrust about the quality of the work. As an American dealer said: "Sometimes you can find work that is greatly undervalued, and people say 'wow, is that only that price?' [Confidential tone:] That makes them nervous, they think it should be a higher price. It is a psychological factor."

The second manifestation of the constructive, meaningful role of prices is encapsulated in the script of pricing according to size. The rationale to avoid pricing works of the same size differently is that by allowing for price differences, dealers would convey implicit messages about differences in quality of the works exhibited. Such messages are avoided for a number of reasons. To begin with, they would create a sense of disorder in a market where uncertainty already reigns. As one dealer put it: "Let me miss out on that upper part of the price I am not able to ask. Stability is more important than that extra bit of money." Also, many dealers question whether their own value judgments are similar to those of their customers; they said that they cannot predict how collectors will evaluate individual pieces in a show. By pricing all artworks equally, dealers seek to let buyers decide themselves what they like. [. . .] Finally, a straightforward economic rationale for the size script is that attaching a higher price to one work may complicate selling the lower-priced works in a show. One of my respondents, for instance, admitted that pricing according to size rather than quality means that "the real hits" are less expensive than they could be, but, he continued, "you violate another system if you would comply with that. You will have a more difficult time selling the rest. In fact, you reconfirm that the rest is less desirable."

The third contribution of prices to the construction of value is related to price changes rather than price differences or absolute price levels. Contrary to other markets, including those for cultural products such as literature or music, success on the art market is measured in terms of rising prices rather than rising sales. An increase in the price level of an artist's work therefore conveys the message that her career is developing or that her art is being accepted in the art world; simultaneously, it makes collectors feel secure about the acquisitions which they have made in the past or which they intend to make in the future.

The positive meanings of increases encourage dealers to be price rather than profit maximizers: since high prices are perceived as a sign of success, dealers and artists have an incentive to actively produce scarcity. This provides a tentative explanation for the fact that galleries, both in the past and in the present, deliberately restrict the number of works they hang in an exhibition (Grampp 1989, 86–87; Gee 1981); for the fact that even highly successful artists like Mark Rothko, Francis Bacon, or Picasso left a large number of works when they died; and for the fact that art dealers are eager to restrict the edition size of photographs and prints. All these practices suggest that artists and their dealers aim at maximizing prices.

The opposite argument applies to price decreases. Price decreases affect more than just the return on investing in art. In fact, such a direct economic effect was not even mentioned in the interviews. Instead, dealers were concerned about the meanings which those decreases convey to both artists and collectors. However strong the economic logic of a price decrease may be, by lowering the price an art dealer conveys a message about the worth of an artist's work and thereby affects her self-esteem. Says an *éminence grise* of the New York gallery scene: "[A price decrease] has a caustic reverberation. If the artist goes down, it means the gallery has lost confidence in him, or the collectors have lost confidence, or he lost his audience. Those are the implications, and you must never allow for those implications, because if you continue to exhibit him, it means that you continue to have faith in him. And if you continue to have faith in him, that means you believe that the artist's progress is ongoing. It is injurious to an artist if he finds that he cannot sustain his price level. That is a blow to his self-esteem." Indeed, even the most well-known dealers I interviewed, representing famous artists who sell their work to museums for prices well over $100,000, confirmed that prices are a "personality issue": they seriously affect the pride of artists.

Price decreases generate comparable meanings for collectors. They create "suspicion in the audience," as one dealer put it; as a result, collectors will "distrust your instincts" and will "lose faith." If the collectors' belief in the artistic value of the work is harmed because of a price decrease, the consequences can be dramatic. One dealer said that "if [the price] is going down, they will start asking what's wrong with it. That can have a backlash and can destroy a career at the beginning." Another dealer confirmed with regret that, when an artist has hardly been selling for a considerable amount of time, "[y]ou drop the artist, because you cannot drop the price." Art dealers are particularly reluctant to decrease prices, since they expect that information about such decreases spreads fast in the art world.

The dramatic consequences of price decreases on the collector's appraisal, combined with the effect they have on the artist's self-esteem, shed light on the script of starting low which I discussed before. Cultural economists have argued that dealers "underprice" artworks, since it is difficult to attract the one buyer willing to pay the exact equilibrium price on a thin market like the art market. The alternative explanation which my interviews suggest is that the taboo on decreasing prices generates an incentive for galleries to underprice from the outset, and increase prices as slowly as possible. Nevertheless, in the unfortunate case of prices that are higher than the market "bears," there is a repertoire of strategies to decrease prices less visibly. The repertoire lacks the legitimacy of most other pricing decisions, which means that dealers only make use of it in emergency situations. First of all, the size of the work which the artist and the dealer select for an exhibition can be increased while keeping prices on the same level; *de facto* this reduces the selling price per unit of size, albeit in a concealed way. The second strategy is to "restructure" the prices of an artist's work once he changes gallery. If an artist, either voluntarily or involuntarily, leaves a gallery and finds representation at another one, the taboo on price decreases is temporarily annulled, which makes it legitimate to start from scratch with prices. [. . .]

The third component of the emergency repertoire which I encountered is to decrease prices when an artist experiments with a new technique or develops a new body of work. Finally, the most frequently used technique to achieve price decreases is to award discounts. Indeed, whereas courtesy and museum discounts serve a relational purpose . . . flexibility discounts are given in order to make sales. Although such flexibility discounts are only given when the market dictates it, they provide dealers the best of both worlds: on the one hand, they can maintain high prices that signal quality, while on the other hand, dealers reaffirm social ties to collectors.

JEAN BAUDRILLARD, *Art . . . Contemporary of Itself*

Excerpt (pp. 94–97) from "Art . . . Contemporary of Itself" (2004), in *The Conspiracy of Art*, ed. S. Lotringer, trans. A. Hodges (New York and Los Angeles: Semiotext(e), 2003/2005), 89–97. Reprinted by permission of Semiotext(e).

Interface and performance: the two leitmotifs of today.

In performance, all forms of expression are combined: the plastic arts, photography, videos, installations, interactive screens. This vertical and horizontal, aesthetic and commercial diversification is now part of the work, and the work's original core is beyond repair.

A (non-) event like *The Matrix* serves as a perfect example: it is the very model of a global installation, of a total world event. Not only the film, which is only an excuse to some extent, but the spin-off products, the simultaneous projection at all points of the globe and the millions of spectators themselves who are inextricably part of it. We are all, from a global and interactive point of view, actors in this total world event.

Photography has the same problem when we decide to make it multimedia by adding to it all the resources of montage, collage, digital effects, computer generated imagery, etc. This opening onto the infinite, this deregulation leads precisely to the death of photography by raising it to the level of performance.

In this universal mixture, each register loses its specificity—just as every individual loses his or her sovereignty in networks and interaction—like reality and image, art and reality lose their respective force when they cease to be differential poles.

Ever since the 19th century, art has wanted to be useless. It turned this uselessness into a reason for praise (which was not true of classical art where, in a world that was not yet real or objective, usefulness was not even considered).

By extension of this principle, making any object useless would be enough to make it a work of art. This is precisely what the readymade does when it merely divests an object of its function, without changing anything about it, to turn it into a museum piece. It is sufficient to make reality itself a useless function to turn it into an art object, prey to the all-consuming aesthetic of banality.

By the same token, older things, coming from the past and therefore useless, automatically acquire an aesthetic aura. Their displacement in time is the equivalent of Duchamp's gesture; they become readymades as well, nostalgic vestiges resuscitated in our museum universe.

One could extrapolate this aesthetic transformation to material production as a whole. As soon as it reaches a level where it can no longer be exchanged in terms of social wealth, it becomes a giant surrealist object, seized by an all-consuming aesthetic and is included everywhere in a sort of virtual museum. Like for the readymade, an in-situ museification in the form of dormant industry for every technical waste land.

The logic of uselessness could only lead contemporary art to a predilection for waste—that which is useless by definition. Through refuse, the figuration of refuse, the obsession with refuse, art strives to display its own uselessness. It presents its non-use value, its non-exchange value—while still being sold at very high prices.

There is a contradiction here. *Uselessness has no value in itself.* It is a secondary symptom. And by sacrificing its implications to this negative quality, art goes astray in a useless gratuitousness. The scenario is similar for nullity, the claim of nonsense, insignificance, banality, all a sign of elevated aesthetic pretense.

Anti-art in all its forms attempts to escape the aesthetic dimension. But ever since the readymade annexed banality, all that is finished. The innocence of nonsense, of the non-figurative, abjection and dissidence is over.

Everything that contemporary art would like to be or become again only reinforces the inevitably aesthetic character of this anti-art.

Art has always denied itself. But it did it before out of excess, exalting in the play of its disappearance. Today, it denies itself by default—worse yet, it denies its own death.

Art immerses itself in reality instead of becoming the agent symbolically assassinating reality, instead of being the magical agent of its disappearance.

The paradox is that the closer it comes to this phenomenal confusion, to this nullity as art, the more it is overvalued and credited. To such an extent that, to paraphrase Elias Canetti, we have reached the point where nothing is beautiful or ugly, we have crossed this point without realizing it, and if we are unable to find this blind spot again, we will continue to pursue the current destruction of art.

What is this useless function good for in the end?

What does it deliver us from with its very uselessness?

Like politicians, who relieve us of the bothersome responsibility of power, contemporary art, with its incoherent artifice, relieves us of the grasp of meaning through the spectacle of nonsense. This explains its proliferation: independent of any aesthetic value, it is ensured of prospering in function of its insignificance and vanity. Just as politicians persist despite the absence of any representation or credibility. Art and the art market therefore flourish to the extent that they decay: they are the modern charnel houses of culture and simulacra.

It is therefore absurd to say that contemporary art is null and that all of this is worthless since that is its vital function: to illustrate our uselessness and our absurdity. Or even better: to use this decay as its capital while at the same time exorcising it as a spectacle.

If, as some propose, the function of art was to make life more interesting than art, then we must lose this illusion. I have the impression that a good portion of art today is conspiring in a process of deterrence, a work of mourning the image and the imaginary, a work of aesthetic mourning. This work usually fails, leading to the general melancholy of the artistic sphere, which seems to survive by recycling its history and its vestiges.

Yet art and aesthetics are not the only ones doomed to this melancholy destiny of living, not above their means, but beyond their ends.

2

ARTISTS AND COLLECTORS
IN THE MARKET FOR ART

Markets are where demand and supply meet. While this principle is easily envisioned when thinking of, say, the market for luxury handbags, its relevance to the market for art is less evident. The first section of this chapter is designed to clarify how artists and collectors behave as economic agents in the art market. The economist Xavier Greffe describes the variety of practices that define artists and art. Economists James Heilbrun and Charles M. Gray offer a detailed explanation of how supply and demand operate in the art market.

The motivations of collectors who purchase highly valued (read: expensive) works of art are explored in section II. The French historian Fernand Braudel describes the effects of upward social mobility on the development of luxury markets in the sixteenth and seventeenth centuries. Georg Simmel and Thorstein Veblen, the former a German sociologist and philosopher, the latter an American sociologist and economist, explain and theorize the motivations of the new—wealthy—consumers who emerged at the end of the nineteenth century. Business marketing expert Russell Belk examines collectors' motivations at the end of the twentieth century using a consumer behavior perspective. Last, the art historian Jonathan Brown traces the development of the role of the expert in ascertaining value in works considered for purchase or that are present in major existing collections.

The excerpts collected in section III focus on how individual artists have operated in the market over time. The art historians Elizabeth Honig and Eric Jan Sluijter focus on issues surrounding original art production, copying, and artistic collaboration by examining the market behavior of artists in the sixteenth and seventeenth centuries. Similarly, Griselda Pollock explores the market tactics and strategies of an avant-garde painter in late nineteenth-century Paris. Writings by conceptual artist and philosopher Adrian Piper, legal expert Barbara Hoffman, and cultural historian Ulrich Lehmann elucidate twentieth- and twenty-first-century artistic practices and market approaches.

The final section of the chapter focuses on the art market itself. Cultural economist Walter Santagata details two significant anomalies in the market for art, while finance expert William Goetzmann explores the informational (in)efficiencies and price risks in the art market using historical data. In the final excerpt, James Pesando debunks some established assumptions held by art market participants after analyzing the market for contemporary prints.

I. THE SUPPLY OF AND DEMAND FOR WORKS OF ART

XAVIER GREFFE, *Two Paradigms of Artistic Activity*

Excerpt (pp. 109–12) from "The Artist as an Entrepreneur of His Talents," in *Arts and Artists from an Economic Perspective* (London: Unesco, 2002), 107–35. Reprinted by kind permission of the author.

How does one define the work of an artist? Is it the creation of a product or participation in an activity? The first answer seems obvious, but the second is not without significance because aesthetic and artistic criteria are unstable and do not suffice to define the areas of artistic activity. Besides, artists are now identifying themselves in terms of the environment or the network to which they belong rather than in terms of artistic reference: 'communication within the sphere of activity and co-operation in specific situations try to compensate for the decline in the membership of artistic groups'. In the absence of other obvious benchmarks, the artist's identity is determined on the basis of his activities within the network, as some of his products will become works of art even if they do not gain recognition. This does not mean that the artist does not strive to create works of art; it only means that he needs time to establish himself as an artist. Being recognized depends as much on his role as a producer as on his function as a creator, as much on his activity as on his work. This change of attitude has grave consequences—instead of basing ourselves on the idealization of the artist's creative function, we base ourselves on activities and practices. We thus contribute to the much-touted disenchantment of art, but at the same time we gain in terms of pertinence.

Artistic activity covers a variety of disciplines, opinions, sensibilities and social positions. It sustains itself by denying that it belongs to a single group and by denying that it indulges in diverting techniques or in overstepping references. The main principle underlying the understanding of artistic activity has less to do with its result than with the heterogeneous association of its components. The method of co-ordinating the activities and persons involved is more important than the work that they produce. By approaching the artist in this manner, we can no longer think of him in terms of his gifts, his precociousness, his Bohemianism, his talents or as an unchangeable and invincible person. These concepts are deeply rooted in the artistic environment and they make it easier to understand his psychodynamics than the functioning of the art market. Too often, the notion of vocation has been used to justify, rather than explain, the years of suffering and underpay and to sidestep the role of talent and socio-political factors. As a matter of fact, this view of the artist as a creator is gradually disappearing and people are beginning to realize that it is no longer necessary to depend on natural aptitudes and talents. . . . The artist is a hybrid who lives by the logic of income (talent, creation and reputation) and by the logic of insurance (acquisition of skills, use of spouse's resources, etc.). So the artist has now become socialized, whereas earlier he was idealized.

Since artistic activity involves groups of actors, practices and references, it is bound to be compared to a network. Since the artist's knowledge is mobilized within the network of knowledge, he is in a better position to innovate by the linking of knowledge than by living in isolation or by being different from other members of the network. The production of a work of art is not so much the accomplishment of an individual as that of a professional group. When artists form a group, they do not necessarily work together, but each of them works independently within the group. This brings to the fore a plethora of creative impulses and references that do not merge into a standard pattern, which would be quite unproductive.

This multiplicity of practices and procedures, leading to the creation of a work of art, is responsible for a variety of cultural professions, also called 'applied intellectuality'. There is a continuum of activities with numerous poles, so that a creation is not independent and also it cannot be assimilated with another. As H. S. Becker (1988, 110) writes, 'In the world of art, every function can be considered artistic, anything that an artist does, even his most undisputed action, can be an encouragement for someone else.' Artistic activity thus progresses through successive accumulation. 'New concepts are being constantly added to earlier ones: design to the plastic arts, industrial design to design, industrial packaging to industrial design . . .' . Artists move from one activity to another, from collective activities like staging shows to more individual activities like teaching art. Actually, these networks may be in the form of an association or they may have a hierarchical structure. They could be specialized bodies, e.g. artistic, technical, management, etc., having corresponding positions. A cultural institution brings these poles and positions together in a single structure and gives them a definite form. The only danger is that these diverse elements, which are supposed to work together, may start working only for themselves. Subsequently, conflicts become inevitable and this underscores the formalism of these institutions. The ultimate imbalance is reached when works of art become products of the institution.

If we admit that artistic activity has precedence over the artist as a creative force that shapes the material world, we must envisage the possibility of an artist who does not produce any work of art. Several interpretations are possible. Some artists think that by crystallizing their creativity in a work of art they come into conflict with themselves since it arrests their artistic activity, which, by definition, is an open and unending process. It is true that the work freezes their creativity at a particular point of time, but this makes it easier for the user to understand the work. Some artists opt quite openly for non-creation, as they do not want to be compelled to give proof of their artistic status and prefer to live for themselves and the people around them. Still others claim to defend an open and evolving art and are not interested in the promotion and diffusion of their works. But if you cannot associate a work with an artist, how can you assess his contribution, his creativity or even his productivity? As Nicolas Le Strat says (1999, 115), 'How can one break away from the overpowering and structured view of the artistic product? How can one avoid the excessively conclusive role of creative work?'. One solution is to allow artistic activity complete freedom without trying to arrest its development and to let other artists give it a meaning and a value. The unity of the work no longer lies in the artist's intention or in the object's unitary nature but in the conclusion of a work of art. The viewer's active participation is needed, since it helps to make news, to complete the process and to inspire a work of art. Artistic activity thus leads to a situation where the viewer's intrusion can give shape to what was only a glimmer in the mind.

These two paradigms of art—art as a creation and art as an activity—should be considered permanent features. These two dimensions are to be found in different measures in every artist and this explains the difference between his profession and status.

JAMES HEILBRUN AND CHARLES M. GRAY, *Arts Markets*

Excerpts (pp. 169–82) from "Arts Markets," in *The Economics of Art and Culture*, 2nd ed. (Cambridge, England: Cambridge University Press, 2006), 165–86. Copyright © 2001 James Heilbrun and Charles M. Gray. Reprinted by permission of Cambridge University Press.

THE PRIMARY MARKET

The primary market is one in which original works are sold for the first time. As is the case in any other market, the resulting price reflects the operation of the forces of supply and demand. This market includes artists' studios, art fairs and festivals, galleries, and similar outlets. As might be expected, participants in the primary market are hampered by imperfect information and encounter considerable transactions costs. The works of new artists—the "unknowns"—and the new works of more established painters are traded in this market. Purchases of art via primary market participation may entail a fair amount of risk, largely because the intellectual appeal is uncertain for many people (I may not know art, but . . .), even though the decorativeness attributes may be more widely recognized and understood (. . . I know what I like). Neophyte buyers may not know what works are being offered for sale, whether they are of high quality, or where the works are available without considerable expenditure of time and effort.

The process by which the primary market in paintings operates is much like that of other markets. The prospective buyer goes to the point of sale, perhaps a studio or gallery where works are displayed, often—but not always—with prices attached. In a typical scenario, an artist may have established an exclusive relationship with a dealer who arranges an exhibition of the artist's work. Under such an arrangement, the artist provides the creative work, and the dealer contributes market knowledge and experience. The prices that they attach to the works reflect the "reserve price" of the artist plus a best guess of what the work can command over the reserve price. The reserve price is the minimum the artist is willing to accept in bringing a work to the market. Setting the price is tricky; it should exceed the reserve price without being too high for buyers.

To the extent that the artist and her representative may be uncertain of the price that a given work can command, they may rely on a "feel for the market" or use such rule-of-thumb practices as "markup pricing." The feel for the market is based on experience in selling the artist's work in the past, the prices of similar works at the present, and knowledge of trends in buyer preferences. For new artists who have yet to establish themselves, a dealer may keep prices low in the first show. A sellout encourages slightly higher prices for a subsequent show. Markup pricing in most markets is a standard percentage of increase—say, 50 percent—above the costs of production. Usage in this market is necessarily less precise, since a very large component of the production costs consists of the opportunity cost of the artist's time, and this value itself may be unclear. [. . .]

New works of well-known artists may also be sold through dealers who have represented them historically. However, auction houses, which are described more fully in the next section, are increasingly active in the sale of these works. Some of the reasons for this evolution are presented below.

THE SECONDARY MARKET

The exchange of existing works of art constitutes the secondary market, and in contrast with the primary market, participants are likely to have very good information about artists and their "seasoned" works. Acquisition of recognized work in this market is not so risky as the purchase of unknowns. "News about the art world can be had at the corner newsstand. More than 100 magazines are dedicated to reporting on and explaining art, and most big-city dailies have a section devoted to art happenings." In this instance, attributes of both decorativeness and intellectual appeal are likely to be well known.

Information costs in secondary art markets have fallen in recent years. Not too long ago, dealer markups were routinely two to four times the wholesale price. Auction house commissions, by contrast, may total no more than 20 percent of the sale price. Another innovation is that galleries more frequently post prices of exhibited works. Newcomers to these markets may be surprised to learn that prices have not always been posted. By keeping prices private, dealers could size up potential buyers and quote a price in keeping with a subjective estimate of willingness to pay. Posted prices are felt by some to protect potential buyers from possible "gouging." The fact remains, however, that so long as purchase is voluntary, the buyer may be regarded as willing to pay the price if the transaction occurs. [. . .]

[. . .] Auctions are used when markets have neither breadth (numerous buyers and sellers) nor depth (a number of closely related products that can be considered substitutes, even if imperfectly). Under such circumstances, market interaction does not produce a standard valuation reflected in a market price. As we show below, sale at auction may gain the maximum price for the seller.

Works of art typically are sold via what is known as an "English auction," where the price is raised until only a single bidder remains. One feature of such a process is that all bidders know the current high bid for a work. The most famous auction houses are the British firms of Christie's and Sotheby's, each of which has offices and auction rooms in many countries, including the United States. [. . .]

THE SUPPLY OF ART

[. . .] Artistic products can be regarded as either commissioned or speculative. Commissioned works are those that are specifically requested by a client who is familiar with the artist's technique, such familiarity having been gained from previous exposure. Portraits typically are commissioned, and established artists are more likely to secure commissions. William Grampp (1989, 46–51) recounts numerous examples even of old masters acquiescing to specific expressions of consumer preference. More often than the lay public may realize, paintings have in the past been made to order, altered, and updated, adding a new child to a family portrait or more luxuriant growth to a landscape. Speculative works are those produced by the artist with no guarantee of sale. The artist invests time, talent, and materials in producing art that may—or may not—subsequently be purchased for an acceptable price. As already described, these works are offered in the primary market. Schneider and Pommerehne (1983, 42) view the supply of works of art in the primary market as dependent on two factors, the costs of production and the expected selling price. The higher the production cost, the less willing is the artist to produce a work, while the higher the expected selling price, the more likely is the artist to bring a work to market. In the case of unique works, this boils down to an either/or decision. Either the market conditions support a supply decision, or they do not.

A painter may offer his or her works to the market sparingly, seeking to avoid an oversupply that may depress the price. [. . .] Works produced at a rapid pace may also be retained in the artist's own inventory as a hedge against unexpected price increases. This is one means by which an artist can take advantage of being "discovered." Another means is through a resale right, or *droit de suite*, which is a legal entitlement in the European Union and in the state of California. This right entitles an artist to a fixed percentage of the sale price of a work whenever it changes hands. The California law provides for payment to the artist or heirs of 5 percent of the sale price, and the EU rate is 3 percent. [. . .]

The demand side of the market includes a number of participants, including collectors, dealers, museums, corporations, and anyone else with a desire to possess a work of art. [. . .] Although the other market participants [other than museums] may differ in size, awareness, and taste, they share enough characteristics for us to lump them together and simplify the discussion a bit. We refer to buyers of paintings as "households," but our analysis can easily be extended to all of the other purchasers.

Households must make a number of decisions regarding the disposition of their income. The first decision is how much to spend and how much to save. The amount spent must then be allocated among a very large number of consumer goods and services. The amount saved will be divided among a number of assets, both real and financial. Although the U.S. Department of Commerce classifies acquisitions of works of art as consumption expenditure, they might more properly be regarded as additions to a household's asset portfolio. In that regard, they are akin to savings.

When households are considering the acquisition of assets, they weigh, at least implicitly, a number of attributes of those assets. According to the theory of asset demand, the decision to acquire art depends on the following: wealth, or the total resources available to the household; expected return on the asset relative to the return on all potential substitutes; expected risk, or the degree of uncertainty associated with the return on the asset relative to that of other assets; liquidity, or how quickly and easily the asset can be converted to cash; and tastes and preferences. Although usually taken as given, here we mention them explicitly because of their importance in arts markets.

A change in any of these elements can cause the demand curve for paintings to shift, and a favorable shift will result in a price increase and an increase in earnings for those currently offering the paintings for sale (as well as a potential increase in earnings for other current owners). [. . .]

WEALTH

Households that are wealthy can buy more assets, including art, than those that are not wealthy. Accordingly, we would expect purchases of most types of art to increase as household wealth increases. Among the exceptions to this general rule are so-called inferior goods, purchases of which may actually decline as wealth rises. Examples from the art world might include reproductions or art posters, which in many households are relegated to the basement or storage closets in response to growing affluence. The degree to which asset demand responds to wealth changes is known as the wealth elasticity of demand, similar in concept to the price and income elasticities of demand. [. . .] In an approximation of this measure, Michael Bryan (1985, 4) found the value of the "real economic growth elasticity" for paintings to be about 1.35. This supports the contention that paintings, in general, can be considered luxury goods. This may help to explain the recent and substantial Japanese entry into the art market. As Japanese wealth has grown, one would expect increased purchases of luxury goods and acquisition of assets. [. . .]

RISK

The amount of risk associated with an asset affects the quantity demanded. [. . .]

[. . .] To summarize, if we are confident that a work of art—say, a Picasso—will increase in value we are more likely to acquire it. If we are far less certain about the future course of the asset's price, we are less likely to be interested in purchasing it. Most contemporary paintings actually depreciate in value, rather like automobiles. According to one knowledgeable gallery owner, "The percentage of contemporary paintings that are resold at a profit is minuscule" (Lee 1988, 67).

LIQUIDITY

An asset that can be readily converted to cash—sold in a secondary market—is likely to be more attractive, and hence command a higher price, than one that is not so liquid. The work of a master can be resold; that of a novice may or may not be resold. The former is more liquid than the latter.

In general the development of arts markets has made many works more liquid. Not too many years ago, Robert Anderson was able to say:

> The vast majority of collectors and most domestic museums give little or no thought to resale possibilities when buying art works. Even in private collections holding periods typically span generations; paintings are usually sold only to settle estates. (1974, 15)

[. . .] Works of art may, in the past, have been owned for forty years and more; now they more typically reappear on the market within five to seven years. A collector can quickly sell a painting through the major auction houses.

TASTES AND PREFERENCES

In considering most markets, economists take tastes and preferences as given. We choose to vary from that practice because of the unique nature of arts markets. Most consumers are able to recognize the quality of, say, tomatoes, and we can be fairly certain of the quality and usefulness of items that are widely advertised. We have a lot of information and/or experience in consumption.

To the extent that the arts are a luxury good, however, many possible buyers by definition do not enter the market until they are sufficiently wealthy. Hence, they are less likely to have experience in purchasing and face the prospect of investing a great deal of their time and energy in learning about the market. But the fact that they have become wealthier may also indicate that the value of their time has increased. This creates a potential conflict that may be resolved in different ways. Some collectors may rely on "experts," the art gallery owners, and others who may be in a position to divine (shape?) current public taste. Others can economize on information costs by purchasing, and then reselling, only recognized works, thereby reinforcing the superstar phenomenon in the art world, where the works of the most recognized creators, whether living or dead, often command extraordinary sums, while new talent encounters ever higher hurdles.

II. THE NATURE OF THE DEMAND FOR WORKS OF ART

FERNAND BRAUDEL, *The Synchronization of Social Change in Europe*

Excerpts (pp. 477–79, 482–85, 487–93) from "Society: 'A Set of Sets,'" in *Civilization and Capitalism, 15th–18th Century*, vol. 2, *The Wheels of Commerce*, trans. S. Reynolds (Berkeley: University of California Press, 1992), 458–99. Copyright © Armand Colin, Paris, 1986. English translation copyright © 1981 by William Collins and Sons & Co. Ltd. and Harper & Row, Publishers, Inc. Reprinted by permission of HarperCollins Publishers.

No one will be surprised that the economy played some part in social mobility. What is more surprising is that despite the obvious time-lags between one country and another, social developments, like the familiar economic developments they coincided with or expressed, had a tendency to be synchronized throughout Europe.

The headiest days of the sixteenth century, for example, from as early as 1470 until say 1580, were, to my mind, an age of accelerated social promotion throughout Europe. . . . A bourgeoisie emerging from the background of trade was climbing by its own efforts to the highest place in contemporary society. The vigour of the economy created great trading fortunes, sometimes almost overnight, and the doorway to social advancement stood wide open. During the last years of the century by contrast, with the reversal of the secular trend, or at any rate a prolonged intercyclical depression, the societies of continental Europe put up the barriers once more. In France, Spain and Italy, one has the impression that after a period of substantial renewal of the establishment, with a series of newly-created titles as compensation for losses, the door to social advancement was in effect slammed shut, the ladder pulled up. This also seems to have happened in Burgundy, in Rome, and in Spain . . . [and] Naples. . . .

The process seems to have been general then; and it was twofold—in the course of this long century, a section of the nobility disappeared and was immediately replaced, but once the gaps had been made good, the door swung to behind the newcomers. [. . .] And the process took place all over Europe. Throughout the sixteenth century, the social and economic circumstances were the same, and they called the tune. The situation was similar in the eighteenth century, when social mobility was once more widespread in Europe. [. . .]

The word *gentry* is here used to describe that upper section of the French bourgeoisie, enriched by trade but having forsaken shop and business one or two generations back; having, that is, shed the stigma of being 'in trade', and sustained in its wealth and comfort by farming huge country estates, by continued financial dealings and by the purchase of royal office which had gradually become part of the heritage of these prudent, thrifty and conservative families. The term *gentry* will certainly cause a shudder among specialists in this period of French history. But this provocative word can stimulate a useful debate: it suggests the problem with which one must come to grips at the outset: the definition of a class, or group, or category making its way slowly towards nobility and traditional social success; a discreet and complicated class having nothing in common with the luxurious court aristocracy, or with the shabby gentility of the rural nobility—a class which was in short moving towards its own concept of nobility and a way of life peculiar to itself. [. . .]

The word *bourgeoisie* has shared the fortunes of the word *bourgeois*: both were probably in use as early as the twelfth century. A bourgeois was a privileged citizen of a town. But depending on the region or the town in France, the word did not become really widespread until the late sixteenth or even the late seventeenth century. It was in the eighteenth century that it gained greatest currency, and the Revolution launched it for good. Where we would expect to find the word 'bourgeois' . . . the usual expression was '*honorable homme*,' a term which can serve as a kind of test: it unmistakably denotes the first rung on the ladder of social advancement, the difficult first step up from the 'condition of the earth', i.e. the peasantry, to that of the so-called liberal professions. [. . .] In the ranks of the *honorables hommes*, although not practising a liberal profession, merchants had their legitimate place ('merchants' preferably but not exclusively in the sense of wholesale merchants, *négociants*). [. . .]

But a profession alone was not sufficient to create *honorabilité*: the privileged person had to own a certain amount of wealth, to live in dignity and comparative prosperity, to have bought a few estates near the town and—a vital condition—to have a house with 'a gable on the street'. [. . .]

[. . .] Let me emphasize the ordinary conditions of entry to the nobility at this time. After 1520, such moves became easier and more frequent, visible and widespread. I am not referring to the granting of letters of nobility by the king, which was very rare, nor to the purchase of ennobling offices, nor to the exercise of aldermanic functions which conferred a kind of nobility (known disrespectfully as *noblesse de cloche*). The threshold of nobility was crossed most frequently by a judicial inquiry, after taking statements from witnesses who could testify that the applicant 'lived nobly', i.e. that he lived off his income without labouring, and that his parents and grand-parents had also 'lived nobly' in the sight of all. These ennoblements were only possible to the extent that the growing wealth of the privileged enabled them to live in 'gentlemanly style', that the rising classes enjoyed the sympathy of the judges who were often their kinsmen; and lastly that in the sixteenth century as we have seen, the aristocracy had not closed ranks. [. . .]

An extra complication was that this new nobility did not always feel the desire to merge into the ranks of the traditional nobility. [. . .] That social vanity informed their behaviour there can be little doubt—but it did not drive them to share the tastes or the prejudices of the *noblesse d'épee*, the nobility of the sword; they showed no enthusiasm for prowess in arms, hunting or duels; on the contrary, they expressed some scorn for the way of life of people whom they considered lacking in wisdom and culture. [. . .]

[. . .] These *grands bourgeois* who became nobles in fact carried on living, as before, sensible balanced lives, divided between their splendid town houses and their chateaux or country residences. Their pride and joy was their humanist culture; they took their greatest delight in their libraries, where the better part of their leisure was spent. The cultural frontier which marked them out and effectively identified them was their passion for Greek and Latin, law, ancient and national history. They were behind the founding of countless lay schools, in towns and even in villages. The only feature they had in common with the authentic nobility was their rejection of trade or labour, their taste for idleness or rather leisure, which was for them synonymous with reading and learned discussions with their peers. This way of life required a degree of affluence, and in general these nobles were more than comfortably off, possessing solid fortunes drawn from three chief sources: land, methodically farmed; usury, practised primarily at the expense of peasants and gentlemen; and lastly offices in the judiciary or in the royal finances, which had become hereditary and transmittable. . . . But most of their fortunes were inherited rather than constructed: they consolidated and extended them, it is true, for money begat money and made social breakthroughs and triumphs possible. But the launching of the dynasty was invariably the same: the gentry had sprung from trade, something it sought to hide from prying eyes and kept as dark as possible. [. . .]

[. . .] After 1600, things were different—the social atmosphere, the economy, politics, culture. It was no longer possible to attain noble rank by means of a few witnesses testifying before a sympathetic judge: one had to produce genealogical tables and submit to searching investigations—and even rank already acquired was not safe from scrutiny. The social mobility which had brought so many recruits to the French gentry was now less a matter of course, and above all less widespread. Was this because the economy was less thriving than in the previous century? The monarchy, restored to strength by Henri IV, Richelieu and Louis XIV, became oppressive, showing it was determined to exact obedience from its officers, starting with the members of the *parlements*. Moreover the king had revived the court aristocracy, allowing it to thrive and prosper occupying the limelight around the Sun King. . . . This court nobility closed ranks against the '*noblesse de robe*'. The latter had to face not only this obstacle but also the monarchy which simultaneously conferred upon it both its powers and its limitations. The would-be nobles were in an equivocal situation both politically and socially. And as the last straw, the Counter-Reformation was unleashed in part against this class, against its ideas and its intellectual positions. Our 'gentry' foreshadowed the Enlightenment: it was informed by a certain rationalism, and on the point of inventing a 'scientific' form of history. [. . .]

It was in the course of these difficulties and this series of upheavals that the gentry gradually turned into what would be known as the *noblesse de robe*: that second-class nobility always contested by the first, and never merging fully with it. From now on, there would be a distinct hierarchy between the two nobilities, which the monarchy played off against each other the better to rule. It is surely no accident that the expression *noblesse de robe* appears only at the beginning of the seventeenth century [. . .]

In Europe, there was . . . a visible distinction between two broad categories: urban socie-ties on one hand, that is the societies of the merchant cities of Italy, Holland and even Germany, with their precocious wealth; and the more extended societies of the territorial states, slowly emerging (not always completely) from a medieval past, and sometimes bearing the marks of their origins down to modern times. It is barely a century since Proudhon wrote: 'in the economic organism as in the real body politic, in the administra-tion of justice and in education, feudalism is still stifling us'.

That there were marked differences between these two worlds has been pointed out many times. One could produce a hundred versions, ancient and modern, of the remark made in a French memorandum of 1702: 'In monarchical States, the merchants cannot attain the same degree of consideration as in Republican States, where it is usually the men of business who rule.' [. . .] In short a city ruled by merchants will live very differ-ently from a city ruled by a prince. [. . .]

In the Italian city-states which had been taken over early by the merchants (Milan in 1229, Florence in 1289, Venice in 1297 at latest), money was an effective and discreet cement of the social order, 'the strongest glue' as the Parisian printers used to say in the eighteenth century. The patriciate did not need to dazzle and fascinate its subjects in order to rule—it simply controlled the purse-strings and that was enough. Not that luxury was unknown to the rulers, but they were discreet not to say secretive about it. In Venice, the nobleman wore a long black gown which was not even a sign of rank. [. . .] In Genoa, the *nobili* dressed rather severely. Feasts were held discreetly in country houses or urban palaces, not on the streets or in public squares. [. . .] Even in this period life in Florence seemed simple, almost bourgeois to a visiting Spaniard. What made Amsterdam the last *polis* of Europe was, among other things, the deliberate modesty of its wealthy citizens, which struck even Venetian visitors. Who could pick out the Grand Pensionary of Hol-land from any other bourgeois he might meet in an Amsterdam street?

To move from Amsterdam or one of the long-established city-states of Italy to the capital of a modern state or a princely court, is to move into a completely different atmosphere. Here modesty and discretion were never the order of the day. The nobility of the front rank allowed itself to be dazzled by the magnificence of princes and wished to dazzle in its turn. It was obliged to parade and display itself. To shine at court meant standing out from the common run of mortals, to demonstrate in almost ritual fashion that one was of another race, and to keep others at a distance. Unlike the privilege conferred by money, which was self-evident and could be held in the hand, the privilege conferred by birth or rank was only of value when it was appreciated by other people. [. . .]

In short then, there were two ways of living and facing the world: display or discretion. Wherever a society based on money was slow appearing, ostentatious luxury, an old-fashioned policy, was forced upon the ruling class, since it could not rely too much on the silent support of money. Ostentation could of course creep in anywhere: it was never entirely absent wherever men had the time and the inclination to keep comparing themselves with others, to watch like hawks for the detail, the way of dressing or eating, of behaviour or speech that would give away respective social positions. [. . .]

It is tempting to say that the reverse was happening in England; but things were more complicated. The seventeenth century was an age when luxury glittered everywhere. There was the court and the extravagance of the nobility. [. . .] In the eighteenth century, it is true, and especially during the long reign of George III (1738–1820) the rich and powerful families of England preferred luxury in the form of comfort to display. [. . .] The English nobility or rather the peerage, having on the whole reached the pinnacle of the social hierarchy since the Reformation, was of recent origin. But for a number of reasons, including self-interest, it gave itself the airs of an ancient landed aristocracy. A great English family had to have a great estate, and in the centre of the estate the symbol of success was a stately home, often of princely dimensions. This was an aristocracy 'both plutocratic and feudal'. As a feudal group, it was virtually obliged to do things on the grand scale, somewhat theatrically. [. . .] But such extravagance did not eliminate the taste for, or practice of business. Already in Elizabeth's reign it was the peerage, the highest in the realm, which was most readily investing in long-distance trade.

A different picture emerged from Holland, where the Regents of the towns . . . reached the top of the hierarchy. They formed a bourgeois aristocracy.

In France, the picture is, as in England, rather complicated. The capital city, dominated by the court, developed rather differently from the big merchant cities which were just becoming aware of their growing strength and originality. Rich merchants in Toulouse, Lyons or Bordeaux made little display of their luxury, keeping it for the domestic interiors of their elegant town houses and even more for their 'country residences, pleasure houses scattered around the town at a radius of a day's ride'. In Paris on the contrary, the plutocrats of the eighteenth century were bent on imitating and outdoing the luxury around them and copied the way of life of the highest aristocracy.

GEORG SIMMEL, *Economic Value as the Objectification*
of Subjective Values

Excerpt (pp. 75–78) from "Economic Value as the Objectification of Subjective Values,"
in *The Philosophy of Money*, 3rd ed. (London and New York: Routledge, 2004), 61–139.
Copyright © 2004 Routledge. Reproduced with permission of Taylor & Francis
Books UK.

It may be said . . . that the value of an object does indeed depend upon the demand for
it, but upon a demand that is no longer purely instinctive. On the other hand, if the object
is to remain an economic value, its value must not be raised so greatly that it becomes
an absolute. The distance between the self and the object of demand could become so
large—through the difficulties of procuring it, through its exorbitant price, through moral
or other misgivings that counter the striving after it—that the act of volition does not
develop, and the desire is extinguished or becomes only a vague wish. The distance
between subject and object that establishes value, at least in the economic sense, has a
lower and an upper limit; the formula that the amount of value equals the degree of
resistance to the acquisition of objects, in relation to natural, productive and social opportunities, is not correct. Certainly, iron would not be an economic value if its acquisition
encountered no greater difficulty than the acquisition of air for breathing; but these difficulties had to remain within certain limits if the tools were to be manufactured which
made iron valuable. To take another example: it has been suggested that the pictures of
a very productive painter would be less valuable than those of one who was less productive, assuming equal artistic talent. But this is true only above a certain quantitative level.
A painter, in order to acquire the fame that raises the price of his pictures, is obliged to
produce a certain number of works. [. . .]

[. . .] If an object of any kind provides us with great pleasure or advantage we experience
a feeling of joy at every later viewing of this object, even if any use or enjoyment is now
out of the question. This joy, which resembles an echo, has a unique psychological character determined by the fact that we no longer want anything from the object. In place of
the former concrete relationship with the object, it is now mere contemplation that is the
source of enjoyable sensation; we leave the being of the object untouched, and our sentiment is attached only to its appearance, not to that which in any sense may be consumed.
[. . .] Th[is] whole development of objects from utility value to aesthetic value is a process
of objectification. When I call an object beautiful, its quality and significance become
much more independent of the arrangements and the needs of the subject than if it is
merely useful. So long as objects are merely useful they are interchangeable and everything can be replaced by anything else that performs the same service. But when they are
beautiful they have a unique individual existence and the value of one cannot be replaced
by another even though it may be just as beautiful in its own way. We need not pursue . . .
remarks on the origin of aesthetic value into a discussion of all the ramifications of the

subject in order to recognize that the objectification of value originates in the relative distance that emerges between the direct subjective origin of the valuation of the object and our momentary feeling concerning the object. The more remote for the species is the utility of the object that first created an interest and a value and is now forgotten, the purer is the aesthetic satisfaction derived from the mere form and appearance of the object. The more it stands before us in its own dignity, the more we attribute to it a significance that is not exhausted by haphazard subjective enjoyment, and the more the relationship of valuing the objects merely as means is replaced by a feeling of their independent value.

THORSTEIN VEBLEN, *Conspicuous Consumption and Pecuniary Canons of Taste*

Excerpts (pp. 73–75, 85, 116, 126–28, 159–60) from "Conspicuous Consumption" and "Pecuniary Canons of Taste," in *The Theory of the Leisure Class: An Economic Study of Institutions* (New York and London: Macmillan, 1912), 68–101, 115–67. This edition is available at Archive.org.

During the earlier stages of economic development, consumption of goods without stint, especially consumption of the better grades of goods,—ideally all consumption in excess of the subsistence minimum,—pertains normally to the leisure class. This restriction tends to disappear, at least formally, after the later peaceable stage has been reached, with private ownership of goods and an industrial system based on wage labour or on the petty household economy. But during the earlier quasi-peaceable stage, when so many of the traditions through which the institution of a leisure class has affected the economic life of later times were taking form and consistency, this principle has had the force of a conventional law. It has served as the norm to which consumption has tended to conform, and any appreciable departure from it is to be regarded as an aberrant form, sure to be eliminated sooner or later in the further course of development.

The quasi-peaceable gentleman of leisure, then, not only consumes of the staff of life beyond the minimum required for subsistence and physical efficiency, but his consumption also undergoes a specialisation as regards the quality of the goods consumed. He consumes freely and of the best, in food, drink, narcotics, shelter, services, ornaments, apparel, weapons and accoutrements, amusements, amulets, and idols or divinities. In the process of gradual amelioration which takes place in the articles of his consumption, the motive principle and the proximate aim of innovation is no doubt the higher efficiency of the improved and more elaborate products for personal comfort and well-being. But that does not remain the sole purpose of their consumption. The canon of reputability is at hand and seizes upon such innovations as are, according to its standard, fit to survive. Since the consumption of these more excellent goods is an evidence of wealth, it becomes honorific; and conversely, the failure to consume in due quantity and quality becomes a mark of inferiority and demerit.

This growth of punctilious discrimination as to qualitative excellence in eating, drinking, etc., presently affects not only the manner of life, but also the training and intellectual activity of the gentleman of leisure. He is no longer simply the successful, aggressive male,—the man of strength, resource, and intrepidity. In order to avoid stultification he must also cultivate his tastes, for it now becomes incumbent on him to discriminate with some nicety between the noble and the ignoble in consumable goods. He becomes a connoisseur in creditable viands of various degrees of merit, in manly beverages and trinkets, in seemly apparel and architecture, in weapons, games, dancers, and the narcotics. This cultivation of the aesthetic faculty requires time and application, and the demands made upon the gentleman in this direction therefore tend to change his life of leisure into a more or less arduous application to the business of learning how to live a life of ostensible leisure in a becoming way. Closely related to the requirement that the gentleman must consume freely and of the right kind of goods, there is the requirement that he must know how to consume them in a seemly manner. His life of leisure must be conducted in due form. Hence arise good manners. . . . High-bred manners and ways of living are items of conformity to the norm of conspicuous leisure and conspicuous consumption.

Conspicuous consumption of valuable goods is a means of reputability to the gentleman of leisure. As wealth accumulates on his hands, his own unaided effort will not avail to sufficiently put his opulence in evidence by this method. The aid of friends and competitors is therefore brought in by resorting to the giving of valuable presents and expensive feasts and entertainments. Presents and feasts had probably another origin than that of naive ostentation, but they acquired their utility for this purpose very early, and they have retained that character to the present; so that their utility in this respect has now long been the substantial ground on which these usages rest. Costly entertainments, such as the potlatch or the ball, are peculiarly adapted to serve this end. The competitor with whom the entertainer wishes to institute a comparison is, by this method, made to serve as a means to the end. He consumes vicariously for his host at the same time that he is a witness to the consumption of that excess of good things which his host is unable to dispose of single-handed, and he is also made to witness his host's facility in etiquette. [. . .]

From the foregoing survey of the growth of conspicuous leisure and consumption, it appears that the utility of both alike for the purposes of reputability lies in the element of waste that is common to both. In the one case it is the waste of time and effort, in the other it is a waste of goods. Both are methods of demonstrating the possession of wealth, and the two are conventionally accepted as equivalents. [. . .]

Under the selective surveillance of the law of conspicuous waste there grows up a code of accredited canons of consumption, the effect of which is to hold the consumer up to a standard of expensiveness and wastefulness in his consumption of goods and in his employment of time and effort. This growth of prescriptive usage has an immediate effect upon economic life, but it has also an indirect and remoter effect upon conduct in other respects as well. [. . .]

The utility of articles valued for their beauty depends closely upon the expensiveness of the articles. A homely illustration will bring out this dependence. A hand-wrought silver spoon, of a commercial value of some ten to twenty dollars, is not ordinarily more serviceable—in the first sense of the word—than a machine-made spoon of the same material. It may not even be more serviceable than a machine-made spoon of some "base" metal, such as aluminum, the value of which may be no more than some ten to twenty cents. The former of the two utensils is, in fact, commonly a less effective contrivance for its ostensible purpose than the latter. The objection is of course ready to hand that, in taking this view of the matter, one of the chief uses, if not the chief use, of the costlier spoon is ignored; the hand-wrought spoon gratifies our taste, our sense of the beautiful, while that made by machinery out of the base metal has no useful office beyond a brute efficiency. The facts are no doubt as the objection states them, but it will be evident on reflection that the objection is after all more plausible than conclusive. It appears (1) that while the different materials of which the two spoons are made each possesses beauty and serviceability for the purpose for which it is used, the material of the hand-wrought spoon is some one hundred times more valuable than the baser metal, without very greatly excelling the latter in intrinsic beauty of grain or colour, and without being in any appreciable degree superior in point of mechanical serviceability; (2) if a close inspection should show that the supposed hand-wrought spoon were in reality only a very clever imitation of hand-wrought goods, but an imitation so cleverly wrought as to give the same impression of line and surface to any but a minute examination by a trained eye, the utility of the article, including the gratification which the user derives from its contemplation as an object of beauty, would immediately decline by some eighty or ninety per cent, or even more; (3) if the two spoons are, to a fairly close observer, so nearly identical in appearance that the lighter weight of the spurious article alone betrays it, this identity of form and colour will scarcely add to the value of the machine-made spoon, nor appreciably enhance the gratification of the user's "sense of beauty" in contemplating it, so long as the cheaper spoon is not a novelty, and so long as it can be procured at a nominal cost.

The case of the spoons is typical. The superior gratification derived from the use and contemplation of costly and supposedly beautiful products is, commonly, in great measure a gratification of our sense of costliness masquerading under the name of beauty. Our higher appreciation of the superior article is an appreciation of its superior honorific character, much more frequently than it is an unsophisticated appreciation of its beauty. The requirement of conspicuous wastefulness is not commonly present, consciously, in our canons of taste, but it is none the less present as a constraining norm selectively shaping and sustaining our sense of what is beautiful, and guiding our discrimination with respect to what may legitimately be approved as beautiful and what may not. [. . .]

It is to be added that a large share of those features of consumable goods which figure in popular apprehension as marks of serviceability, and to which reference is here had as elements of conspicuous waste, commend themselves to the consumer also on other grounds than that of expensiveness alone. They usually give evidence of skill and effective workmanship, even if they do not contribute to the substantial serviceability of the goods; and it is no doubt largely on some such ground that any particular mark of honorific serviceability first comes into vogue and afterward maintains its footing as a normal constituent element of the worth of an article. A display of efficient workmanship is pleasing simply as such, even where its remoter, for the time unconsidered outcome is futile. There is a gratification of the artistic sense in the contemplation of skilful work. But it is also to be added that no such evidence of skilful workmanship, or of ingenious and effective adaptation of means to end, will, in the long run, enjoy the approbation of the modern civilised consumer unless it has the sanction of the canon of conspicuous waste.

The position here taken is enforced in a felicitous manner by the place assigned in the economy of consumption to machine products. The point of material difference between machine-made goods and the hand-wrought goods which serve the same purposes is, ordinarily, that the former serve their primary purpose more adequately. They are a more perfect product—show a more perfect adaptation of means to end. This does not save them from disesteem and depreciation, for they fall short under the test of honorific waste. Hand labour is a more wasteful method of production; hence the goods turned out by this method are more serviceable for the purpose of pecuniary reputability; hence the marks of hand labour come to be honorific, and the goods which exhibit these marks take rank as of higher grade than the corresponding machine product. Commonly; if not invariably, the honorific marks of hand labour are certain imperfections and irregularities in the lines of the hand-wrought article, showing where the workman has fallen short in the execution of the design. The ground of the superiority of hand-wrought goods, therefore, is a certain margin of crudeness. This margin must never be so wide as to show bungling workmanship, since that would be evidence of low cost, nor so narrow as to suggest the ideal precision attained only by the machine, for that would be evidence of low cost.

The appreciation of those evidences of honorific crudeness to which hand-wrought goods owe their superior worth and charm in the eyes of well-bred people is a matter of nice discrimination. It requires training and the formation of right habits of thought with respect to what may be called the physiognomy of goods. Machine-made goods of daily use are often admired and preferred precisely on account of their excessive perfection by the vulgar and the underbred who have not given due thought to the punctilios of elegant consumption. The ceremonial inferiority of machine products goes to show that the perfection of skill and workmanship embodied in any costly innovations in the finish of goods is not sufficient of itself to secure them acceptance and permanent favour. The innovation must have the support of the canon of conspicuous waste. Any feature in the physiognomy of goods, however pleasing in itself, and however well it may approve itself to the taste for effective work, will not be tolerated if it proves obnoxious to this norm of pecuniary reputability.

RUSSELL W. BELK, *Collectors and Collecting*

Excerpt (pp. 317–23) from "Collectors and Collecting" (1988), in *Interpreting Objects and Collections*, ed. S. M. Pearce (London: Routledge, 1994), 317–26. Copyright © 1994 Routledge. Reproduced with permission of Taylor & Francis Books UK.

By one estimate, one out of every three Americans collects something. Collecting is a common, intensely involving form of consumption. Yet it has been the subject of almost no prior work in the field of consumer research. This paper defines collecting and presents some initial findings from qualitative research on collectors. Propositions are derived for further investigation concerning the appearance and nature of collecting in contemporary American society. [. . .]

PROPOSITIONS ABOUT COLLECTING

Collections seldom begin purposefully   Contrary to traditional wisdom, our findings . . . indicate that collections of a particular type of item often begin with an incidental or accidental start. [. . .] A survey of 215 collectors . . . found that, for many, fascination with a single item that had been acquired led to a quest to acquire similar items. This desire to find replicable material pleasures is consistent with our interpretation of collecting as a materialistic activity.

In a sense, many collections are 'discovered' by their creators long after the materials have been gathered. Among our informants, one had amassed a number of paintings, wall hangings and other artefacts representing animals. This 'collection' did not register as such in his consciousness, but was rendered apparent upon reflection.

In some instances a collector began with inherited 'seed' objects or an intact 'starter' collection that primed the adoption of a collector role. For instance one informant had received such a 'starter' set of Christmas plates. [. . .]

Addiction and compulsive aspects pervade collecting   Collecting is often likened by the collector, and perhaps more frequently by his or her family and friends, to an addiction, while search behaviour is frequently described as both an obsession and a compulsion. Both our interviews and others' examinations of collecting have suggested that collecting is addictive. Despite their incidental start, many collections are seen as becoming an addictive activity in which adding items to the collection constitutes a 'fix'. As with other addictions, the object of the addiction is relatively unimportant; it could be almost anything and acts only as the focus of release from other fears or feelings of inadequacy. [. . .] The fact that many collectors readily admit to being addicted indicates the power of the attraction or of the social sanction bestowed upon compulsive activity when it is legitimized with the label 'collecting'. Association with other compulsive collectors further supports this feeling of positive addiction.

The altered states of consciousness produced through the collector's search and acquisition are commonly described as mood swings resembling the euphoria and depression induced by chemicals. Collectors frequently experience a holistic, autotelic sensation described as 'flow'. The search process is clearly a thrill-seeking experience for many collectors, which may engender distress as well as eustress. Collectors often report feeling both a craving and a loss of control with respect to their acquisition habits, and occasionally experience negative consequences in other spheres of their personal and social activity as a result of their chronic collecting. The coincidence of collecting and chemical dependency, or the incidence of symptom substitution or displacement (from chemicals to collectables) is sufficiently high as to warrant extended investigation. [. . .]

Collection legitimizes acquisitiveness as art or science   For the collector (and perhaps the hoarder to a lesser degree), the recognition of the collection by others as being 'worthwhile' legitimizes what is otherwise seen as abnormal acquisitiveness. This can give the collector not only a sense of purpose, but a sense of *noble* purpose in supposedly generating knowledge, preserving fragile art, or providing those who see it with a richer sense of history. Having one's collection accepted into a museum collection or in some instances even having it *become* a museum is the ultimate in legitimization of the activity. Having items *like* those that one collects appear in a museum is a less direct means of legitimizing one's collecting activities.

The distinction between art and science in collecting seems to appear in the two (pure) types of collectors detected by Danet and Katriel (1986). Their 'Type A' collector employs affective criteria to choose items for the collection. Such collectors try to improve their collections, but have no sense of a series needing completion. The 'Type B' collector uses cognitive criteria to choose items that add to a series and help improve their knowledge rather than the beauty of the collection. We agree that these two types, while sometimes mixed, represent the two distinct approaches of art and science as ways of legitimizing a collection. In either case, a halo effect of sorts occurs, such that search and acquisition are ennobled through association with the collection itself. In turn, the effort invested in search and acquisition further legitimizes the collection. This effort raises these activities in the eyes of the collector to the level of art, if not science. Collecting is not mere stockpiling or warehousing, mean acquisition or sheer accumulation. [. . .] The ardour and passion driving search behaviour is nurtured by a sense of purpose and worth.

Profane to sacred conversions occur when an item enters a collection   This legitimization and sanctioning of acquisitiveness is related to another phenomenon that occurs in collecting—the transformation of ordinary profane commodities into sacred icons. The terms 'sacred' and 'profane' are not used here in a vernacular religious sense. Instead profane is taken to mean mundane, ordinary and common, while sacred is taken to be extraordinary, special and capable of generating reverence. Collectors 'singularize' (Kopytoff 1986) items enshrined in collections when they remove an item from the secular, profane, undifferentiated realm of the commodity, and ritually transform it into a personally and socially significant object. The sacralized item becomes a vehicle of transcendent experience which exceeds its utilitarian and aesthetic endowment.

Sacred conversions are accomplished in a number of ways. The sheer bringing together of items under the rubric of 'collection' is the most basic transformation. By metonymic association, the sacrality of each item is enhanced. The container (whether it be envelope, box or room) chosen to house the collection defines a sacred space. Conventions for handling the collection and schedules for interacting with it provide the ritual grounding for maintaining its sacredness. As Kopytoff notes, the function of the collection in sacralizing formerly ordinary objects is aided by these objects being removed from the sphere of commodity exchange and also from their ordinary utilitarian roles. Thus collected automobiles or furniture must be sufficiently old that they are not merely seen as 'used' rather than rare antiques. . . . Collectors of automobiles, if they drove them at all, drove them sparingly and only on special occasions because they were regarded as primarily non-utilitarian icons. [. . .]

Another means of sacralizing a collectable object is by its having been 'contaminated' (in a positive sense) by contact with prominent persons. [. . .] An item can . . . gain sacred significance by having been a part of a famous collector's collection. Thus collectors may refer to a Walferdin Boucher, a Weil-Picard Fragonard, or a Gangnat Renoir. For this reason, an auction house such as Sotheby Parke Bernet or Christie's carefully explains the price-inflating provenance of an item for sale when it has a famous history. This contamination of property is also why collections are devalued and desacralized by the discovery of a forged work. If the utilitarian or aesthetic qualities of the item were paramount, the forgery would not matter. But because a collection depends instead upon other qualities for its sacredness, the forgery loses its value for the collection upon discovery. [. . .]

Collections serve as extensions of self   Our self-definition is often highly dependent upon our possessions. The collection is especially implicated in the extended self because it is often visible and undeniably represents the collector's judgements and taste. In addition, the time and effort spent in assembling a collection means that the collector has literally put a part of self into the collection. [. . .]

Because collections are seen as extensions of self, to lose one's collection is to experience a diminished sense of self. [. . .] In the sense that nations are also collectors of art and artefacts, concern with loss of national pride results in efforts to repatriate such objects when they are in the hands of other nations and to prevent further loss of national heritage in this way. [. . .]

Just as a personal collection serves to shape the self-definition of a collector, so do museum collections serve to define the identity of a region or historical period. As with personal collections, a part of this identity is grounded in reality, and a part in fantasy and myth. This extension of the proposition was derived from instances like a museum of pioneer farm life in the Midwest which attempted to create a regional identity by displaying such household items as Limoges china, ornate parlour tables, pianos and sideboards, china cupboards with leaded glass fronts, and lace dresses. Such items may have been found in the town banker's house, but are certainly not representative of the area lifestyle at the turn of the century. Yet, through the collection, a nostalgic image of life is constructed as the identity of the region's past.

Collections tend towards specialization   While collections may begin broadly, there has been a trend towards specialization in the West since the eighteenth century. This has helped the collector define a more manageable collecting task and narrow the competition so one's chances of being unique are improved.

JONATHAN BROWN, *Connoisseurs and Experts*

Excerpts (pp. 232–33, 235–38) from "The Prestige of Painting," in *Kings and Connoisseurs: Collecting Art in Seventeenth-Century Europe* (Princeton, NJ: Princeton University Press, 1995), 227–53. Copyright © 1995 the Trustees of the National Gallery of Art, Washington, DC. Published by Princeton University Press. Reprinted by permission.

[In the seventeenth century] the ebullient demand for fine paintings was proving irresistible to forgers and fakers. Even in the absence of skulduggery, there was the problem of distinguishing between the creations of the masters and those of their assistants, pupils and followers. As more collectors and greater amounts of money entered the market, and as pride of ownership swelled in the heat of competition, the demand for certain knowledge of authorship became ever more urgent.

In response to these circumstances the expert, armed with the tools of connoisseurship, became crucial in determining attribution and hence value. This function had long been performed by painters, who were not only skilled in the practice of art but who, as part of their training, closely studied the work of the great masters. It is a piquant irony of art history that the pioneers of the discipline of connoisseurship were later to become its most conspicuous victims. Many collectors and agents consulted a painter when considering a major purchase, and all the princes employed a practitioner of the art as the keeper or curator of their collections. Thus, Velázquez served in this capacity for Philip IV; Teniers for Leopold William; Le Brun for Louis XIV; Abraham van der Doort for Charles I. At the same time, individual collectors—Brienne and Jabach are good examples—honed their skills as experts in furtherance of their collecting pursuits. For that matter, some of the rulers became renowned for their discernment. In 1636 an intermediary in the proposed sale to Charles I of a painting supposedly by Raphael warned a dealer in Perugia not to send a dubious work. The Italians, he said, should no longer presume that the English were ignorant about painting because "His Majesty himself and the other gentlemen of the court so exquisitely understand it."

A sure sign of the increasing importance of authenticity are the attempts to codify the principles and practice of connoisseurship. The history of connoisseurship, like the history of picture collecting itself, passed through a transitional phase in the seventeenth century. The issue of authenticity had, of course, been a live one during the 1500s, and is implicit throughout the text of Vasari's *Lives*. However, the question of determining authenticity was systematically explored only in books on ancient coins, such as Enea Vico's *Discorsi* (1555), which applied the critical methods of humanist inquiry to the detection of fakes and forgeries. Ancient writers, notably Plato, had established a higher moral value for the original versus the copy, laying the groundwork for the privileged status of the authentic work of art, and ultimately for its increased economic value. [. . .]

Credit for the first publication on connoisseurship belongs to the French engraver Abraham Bosse, whose short, somewhat disorganized work *Sentimens sur la distinction des diverse manières de peinture, dessein et gravures, et des originaux d'avec leurs copies* was published in Paris in 1649. Bosse's text, which appeared at about the time the term *connoisseur* was introduced into the French language, is clearly a response to the heightened interest in picture collecting at the French court. *Amateurs* needed expert guidance, although they were also a threat to the hegemony of the painter as expert, and Bosse's treatise moves uncomfortably between altruism and self-defense.

For Bosse, the "distinction of the diverse manners of painting, drawing and engraving, and of originals from copies," was not terribly challenging. Like Mancini, he identified the dexterity of brushwork as the most revealing element of authorship, and this quality, as he saw it, was largely self-evident to the expert connoisseur. Thus, Bosse did not perceive great problems in detecting copies. [. . .]

In contrast to Bosse's pragmatic connoisseurship are the essays of Roger de Piles (1635–1709), one of the most important French writers on art. De Piles' approach to the subject, set forth in *L'Idée du peintre parfait* and *Abrégé de la vie des peintres*, published together in 1699, is only incidentally concerned with the problems of attribution, which were of distinctly secondary importance to him. Writing as a theorist and aesthete, de Piles extended the purview of connoisseurship to the question of quality in painting, by which he meant quality of the intellect and spirit, and not of execution. Therefore the connoisseur had to study long and think hard about the art of painting, as opposed to Bosse's instinctual approach to the pursuit. As a guide to connoisseurship in the more narrow sense, de Piles' writings are neither innovative nor important. His true significance lies elsewhere, particularly in the elevation of the amateur over the practitioner as the best judge of painting. However, this idea would not bear fruit until the eighteenth century, nor would thoroughly systematic treatises on the methods of attribution appear until that time.

De Piles' dismissive attitude toward the study of making attributions would have been hard to sell in the cutthroat world of collectors and dealers, where high-minded conceptions about artistic judgment were quickly routed by greed and pride. Attribution is not to be taken lightly when money is on the line, and collectors, merely as a matter of self-defense, did their best to become good connoisseurs. Then as now, however, there was an insuperable problem—connoisseurship is not an exact science, no matter how carefully its procedures may be described. At the core of the enterprise is human judgment, the progenitor of human error. Collectors and dealers sometimes sought insurance policies in the form of certificates of authenticity, but, as every serious student knows, they are usually not worth the paper they are written on. Still, the hope of gaining a foothold in the quagmire of connoisseurship was irresistible, and sometimes it seemed within the reach of a pen. Writing in August 1637 Viscount Feilding informed his brother-in-law, the duke of Hamilton, that a painting of St. Peter (now Vienna), attributed to Guido Reni, had been guaranteed as authentic by the seller, who "promis'd a certificat thereof from Guido Rheno, and that it is of his most fierce and best way." With any luck, Reni, then living in Bologna, obliged. [. . .]

It has never been easy to assemble a great collection of pictures, and the princes of seventeenth-century Europe were justifiably proud of their accomplishments. Distinguished visitors were always taken to the galleries and could be relied on to return home with tales of the wonders they had seen. Another vehicle for advertising their treasures and arousing the admiration and envy of rivals was the illustrated book, which still proves expedient for stroking the egos of vain collectors. The idea of publishing a book devoted to a single collection seems to date to the 1620s. (Reproductive prints of single paintings have a separate and longer history.) One of the early examples was produced by Cardinal Federico Borromeo, under the title of *Museum Bibliothecae Ambrosianae* (Milan, 1625), a guide to the archbishop's collection which lacks, however, the key element of illustrations. Four years later the earl of Arundel published an illustrated book of antique sculpture, *Marmora Arundeliana*, and around 1637 started to plan a comparable anthology of selected paintings and drawings in his collection, to be illustrated by the Bohemian printmaker Wenceslaus Hollar. Hollar made drawings of numerous paintings but produced only four prints before fleeing to Antwerp as the Civil War broke out. During his stay in the Netherlands, he independently published a number of prints after pictures in the Arundel collection to help him to earn a living. Inspired by these and other examples, Everhard Jabach in 1656 launched an effort to produce engravings of selections from his collection of paintings and drawings, although they were never published in book form.

It was not until *Theatrum Pictorium* (1660), organized by David Teniers, that the first illustrated book on a single picture collection appeared. . . . *Theatrum Pictorium* communicates several messages concerning the nobility of painting and painters as well as the glory of the collector, which distinguishes it from other efforts of this kind. A more focused instance of the collection book was produced in the 1660s by the heirs of Gerard (1599–1658) and Jan Reynst (1601–46), two Dutch merchants who had made a modest but interesting collection of Italian painting and antique sculpture. [. . .]

The most ambitious publication of a collection in the seventeenth century was executed at the court of Louis XIV and is known by the misleading term of the *Cabinet du Roi*. Far from reproducing the contents of a collector's cabinet in any of the established ways, it is a huge *mélange* of prints; eventually over 950 were produced, representing a wide variety of activities sponsored by the king. [. . .] [In 1663] the newly founded Academy of Science commissioned engraved plates of plants and animals as well as a translation of Vitruvius, which were incorporated in the project.

In December 1667 Colbert took control, and in 1670 he decided to print the plates . . . and to publish them in thematic series. [. . .] These volumes were distributed to other European courts via the French ambassadors and are known to have reached such places as Holland, Bavaria, Poland, Sweden and Rome. Eventually the costs of the *Cabinet du Roi* became excessive, and in 1679 the volumes were offered for public sale. Despite unending financial problems, production continued until 1712, and when it was done the *Cabinet* was the largest, if least coherent, collection book published in its time.

The place of the picture collection in this publication is admittedly small, although the quality of the prints is superb. Over the years a mere thirty-eight paintings from the royal collection were engraved. However, the proportion is a consequence of the universal ambitions of the French royal collection, on the one hand, and the relative indifference of the king to the art of painting, on the other.

III. THE ARTIST: HOMO ECONOMICUS / FEMINA ECONOMICA
ELIZABETH HONIG, *Art, Honor, and Excellence*

Excerpts (pp. 89, 91–95, 98–99) from "Art, Honor, and Excellence in Early Modern Europe," in *Beyond Price: Value in Culture, Economics, and the Arts*, ed. M. Hutter and D. Throsby (Cambridge, England: Cambridge University Press, 2008), 89–105. Copyright © 2008 Cambridge University Press. Reprinted with permission of Cambridge University Press.

In all my doings, spendings, sales, and other dealings in the Netherlands, in all my affairs high and low, I have suffered loss, and Lady Margaret in particular gave me nothing for what I gave her and did for her.

ALBRECHT DÜRER, JOURNAL, MAY 1521

For one evaluates pictures differently from tapestries. The latter are purchased by measure, while the former are valued according to their excellence, their subject, and number of figures.

PETER PAUL RUBENS, LETTER TO SIR
DUDLEY CARLETON, JUNE 1, 1618

By 1521, when being feted by admiring colleagues on his journey through the Netherlands, Albrecht Dürer had good cause to think of himself as a bit of a superstar in the European art world. A century later, when Peter Paul Rubens was bargaining with a potential client in England over what would be an immensely lucrative deal for him, he had even better reason to be secure in his status as one of Europe's greatest cultural figures. The hundred years that separate these famed artists and their business transactions is a century during which, by most accounts, paintings and prints—the art forms produced by these two— were consolidated in the status of being products for a market. [. . .] No longer produced on commission by a craftsman for a patron, or by privileged makers allied with a court, the work of art is by Dürer's time becoming an object whose worth is primarily determined in market terms, and has by Rubens's time become a commodity whose market value can be described and assessed by a definite calculus. Or so Rubens seems to think. [. . .]

So what was Dürer's problem in the Netherlands? The journal of his trip there is a good place to start this inquiry, for in it he recorded with great precision all of his business dealings. . . . The social side of the journal is inextricable from the business side, for Dürer's new acquaintances, landlords, dinner companions, and all their families are all his potential partners in trade. That trade does not simply consist in selling the generous supply of his prints that he had taken along. Dürer's personal economy is still very much one of barter and of gifts. He receives many gifts from admirers: works of art, naturalia, curiosa from exotic lands; textiles and wine and candies; a parrot. And he gives gifts, constantly, prolifically—whole books of prints, series and single leaves, woodcuts and engravings. He even makes paintings and gives them away. Transactions that we would probably call simple sales are also described in terms of the exchange of gifts: "I presented a 'St. Nicolaes' to the largest and richest guild of merchants at Antwerp, for which they have made me a present of 3 Philip's florins."

But to operate in a "gift economy" is a long way from being Santa Claus; Dürer is a calculating giver. He is often well aware of the monetary value of what he gives: A statue and a bundle of prints for the Portuguese factor are worth five florins, while a painting of Veronica and a group of prints for Herr Bannisis are worth seven florins. [. . .] And like all gifts in such an economy, Dürer's demand reciprocation. [. . .]

The more important the recipient of Dürer's gifts, the higher the stakes of reciproca- tion become, and the more urgent his interest in establishing some claim to return. A key recipient of these more coercive gifts is the regent of the Netherlands, Margaret of Austria. To her, Dürer gives first a copy of his engraved *Passion* and then a full set of all his printed works. On top of that he bestows upon her two fine drawings on parchment, probably watercolors that would have been elegant collectors' items. All of this, he calcu- lates, is worth fully 30 florins. But no return gift is forthcoming from Lady Margaret. Finally some months later, when she is showing him her own collection, Dürer gets up the nerve to ask her for a book by Jacopo de' Barbari. She replies that it has been promised to "her" painter, presumably one associated with her court. Hence his complaint, cited at the beginning of this essay, about his losses in the Netherlands, with the chief of these caused by the regent herself, who gave nothing in return for all his uninvited presents to her.

Dürer has been trying to play between two systems for the valuation of artworks and by his own estimation has ended up the loser. There is the market system, one that he understands and is accustomed to—as a printmaker, especially, he already considers the market the natural site where his products receive their worth, the one by which he also privately values his wares. But there is a second system, which he expects will offer him rewards that are in some sense greater than those the market has offered. This is a system in which he is not a seller but a giver, not a recipient of any "just price" but the recipient of fine gifts. This is a system in which his artworks are not commodities but rather are reifications of social relationships. And even though somehow this system is not working for him and does not give him the return on his labor that he would anticipate from the market, he nonetheless insists upon performing within it and is frustrated by its refusal to operate as he wishes.

This second site of value-creation, which I will call the honor system, is akin to what Martin Warnke (1993) has portrayed as the "court system," but it is broader than what he describes and endures long after artists have stopped looking to the court as their main source of patronage. It comes to encompass forms of discourse that evolve in the Renaissance to validate the status of the artist, but it also incorporates complex modes of social behavior that are in themselves means of negotiating status. The objects that circulate in this system cannot and indeed must not be translatable into a purely monetary value, for they are signifiers of power, honor, and obligation to those who exchange them. They are exchanged by all members of the society, but the person who makes valued objects may claim thereby a special place as the creator of socially crucial signs, the inventor of things that have immense social value. The honor system needs to be preserved and protected as a locus of value because within its compass artists of outstanding talent and ingenuity can receive recognition of a type not easily generated by the market: personal esteem, social elevation, acknowledgment of aesthetic achievements.

In the honor system, even when money is used as a means of compensating a maker for his product, it will not register what we would term the "price" of his work. Rather the money will represent a balance between a notion of the maker's personal worth or honor as an artist and the honor of the work's recipient as a generous patron, prince, or friend. Inflecting these dual claims to personal honor in establishing the "value" of an exchanged object will be the particular nature of the relationship between the two parties, a relationship that may alter as a result of the gift exchange. The artist makes his bid for honor by presenting a work that is artful and excellent and will reflect well upon the taste and glory of its recipient; the prince or client makes his or her bid for honor by demonstrating liberality in bestowing upon the artist a gift of sufficient munificence to impress the rest of the court, or simply a more extended group of friends. Ideally, there will be a significant and positive difference between the gift and the object's potential market value (not part of the calculus, but now extant); the degree of that difference will depend not only upon pure liberality, but upon the relationship that has been or is being established between the two parties in the transaction. A gift exchange may initiate a patron–artist relationship but it may also enact and refine an ongoing established relationship. The exchange also has the potential to elevate the artist into a relationship with his social superior that is something approaching friendship. At the very least, it establishes connections and obligations that are not the distanced, quantifiable ones of the market, but are all the more enduring and valuable for being social. [. . .]

Perhaps Dürer loses out with Lady Margaret because he has failed to establish that preliminary social relationship (which she enjoys with another artist) that would enable him to practice the negotiations that the honor system necessitates. The deployment of gift giving as a means to social positioning and the acquisition of wealth was not a straightforward matter; it demanded a specific form of discourse. That is why George Puttenham covers courtly gift etiquette in his *Arte of English Poesie*. . . . In his section on decency and decorum, a point where the conformity of behavior to social status is addressed, Puttenham mentions the possibility that a philosopher at court (for whom we may substitute any liberal artist) may be given a massive gift by the king. Is this proper? It is a problem: The king may give the gift without impoverishing himself (so it is proper) but the philosopher-artist will be excessively enriched by receiving it (which is improper). Gifts, in other words, have the potential to alter financial status radically beyond what social status allows.

But the situation is more complicated than this. For of course the artist cannot refuse a gift, since refusal would be "some empeachement of the kings abilitie or wisedome." Nor should we in fact think of the transaction in terms of the exchange of wealth, "since Princes liberalities are not measured by merite nor by other mens estimations, but by their owne appetits and according to their greatnesse." So in this ritually de-economized transaction, immense wealth may be bestowed upon the artist, but (Puttenham adds) with one huge caveat: that he not ask for it. What will be called for will be a hint but not a supplication, a gesture of refusal (perhaps a protest of unworthiness) but eventual acceptance. Vasari, in an aside in his *Lives*, offers similar tips to painters on how to handle patrons known for their liberality (discreetly) or those who are "miserly, unthankful, and discourteous" (a bit more bluntly). If the artist plays his cards right, the eventual gift will be massive in size. And it will be entirely detached from the value of anything its recipient has produced, which is why we can so easily substitute "artist" for Puttenham's philosopher: The gift-reward is not about objects, but about persons. [. . .]

In an honor system transaction, then, worthiness is added to persons through the correct operations of gift exchange. The object that is created and then exchanged does not have a "value" that can be in any way separated from its social situation. Because its meaning and worth are entirely bound to the status being formulated by its maker, it is not truly alienable and can never be considered a commodity. Therefore, according to the tales of art writers, the best patrons—those with the most money and the greatest appreciation of art—have no idea of the value of objects. Instead of knowing the value of things, they understand the *worth* of Art and its makers. This is the ideal to which the Portuguese writer Francesco da Hollanda is appealing when he criticizes Spaniards as lacking in true understanding of art: They will sing a picture's praises "but press them further and they have not the spirit to order or pay for the slightest work; and what I consider viler still, they are amazed if you tell them of the great sums given in Italy for works of painting, for they do not seem to me in this to act up to their boasted nobility."

Hollanda comes from a society where both the honor system and the market system had singularly failed to establish a high value for art-objects, an elevated appreciation for artists, or a sense of the worth of Art in general. Because he wishes to remedy this situation, prices and market values are discussed quite a lot in his text and are interwoven in unusual ways with appeals to gentlemanliness and liberality. At one point he asks Michelangelo, with whom he is ostensibly conversing throughout the book, to explain to him how works of art should be valued. The ploy here is, of course, to co-opt the voice of an artist widely recognized as "divine" and to have him explain value to the clueless Iberians. Michelangelo replies:

> What do you mean by valuing? . . . Would you have the painting of which you and I speak valued in terms of money or that any one should be able so to value it? For, as for me, I value as of the highest price the work done by a great painter, even if he have spent little time over it; for if he has spent much, who is there who could tell its worth? And I value very little that which an unskillful painter has painted in many years of work . . . for works are not to be judged by the amount of useless labor spent on them, but by the worth of the skill and mastery of their author.

Michelangelo wants us to keep price and value separate. A valuation of fine art by the common market is, he implies, quite inappropriate—not just anyone can truly "value" art, and measuring that value in money is a somewhat unnatural thing. In other words, art should not acquire value as other commodities do. Hollanda's Michelangelo then makes a further argument, that it is not labor that determines value in artworks but rather "the worth of the skill and mastery" of the artist. Artists need protection from a standard economic means of assigning value to objects, the cost of the labor involved in their production. *The object* is not, in Michelangelo's calculus, what the notion of "value" should focus on: Value should remain with the person of the artist, and in particular with his possession of skill or talent. When pressed to detail the determination of price, Michelangelo returns to the principles of the honor system instead.

ERIC JAN SLUIJTER, *Determining Value on the Art Market in the Golden Age*

Excerpts (pp. 7–12) from "Determining Value on the Art Market in the Golden Age: An Introduction," in *Art Market and Connoisseurship: A Closer Look at Paintings by Rembrandt, Rubens and Their Contemporaries*, ed. A. Tummers and K. Jonckheere (Amsterdam: Amsterdam University Press, 2008), 7–28. Reprinted by kind permission of the author.

An art historian who assesses the attributions of particular paintings in a scholarly publication knows that this will have consequences for the art market. The art historian in question, however, usually prefers to ignore this because he sees his work as a value-free analysis of certain qualities of the artwork in the service of constructing art historical categorizations. However, the owner of the work will have a different opinion. What a painting is valued at on the art market—especially paintings dating from the last five centuries—mainly depends on the fact whether or not it is considered an autograph work of a certain artist. A *communis opinio* among experts about authorship guarantees a basic market value. The process of canon formation establishes a relative value: X is on average more expensive than Y, but cheaper than Z. These values may vary hugely, depending on the position of the master in the 'ranking', while other factors such as subject matter, condition, rarity, provenance, place of an individual work within the oeuvre of a master and temporary phenomena like fashions and trends add to the many imponderables that make the prices of works of art vary tremendously. But when a work loses its aura of being by a certain artist's hand, it is robbed of its identity and becomes an outcast, even if none of the physical qualities and appearance of the work have changed; the value plummets and becomes even more difficult to assess than an 'authentic' work. [. . .]

Giulio Mancini [wrote] between 1617 and 1621 . . . 'a painting in itself cannot have a definite price' because its value in part 'is linked to the quality of the patron who owns it and the artist who makes it'. Thus, the price depends 'mainly on the taste and wealth of the buyer, and the need of the owner [which might be the artist] to dispose of the work'. But these are the words of a Roman art lover. Were opinions regarding the assessing of the value of a work of art different in the Netherlands? What were the accepted seventeenth-century practices? Which roles were played by the artists themselves, by connoisseurs, art lovers or art dealers? How was value related to artistic qualities, name and authorship? [. . .]

The 'craftsmanlike' way of calculating [the price of a painting], largely determined by labor, in other words, the time spent producing a work of art, must have been used by many artists. In a few cases—and these are all 'fine painters'—we are certain they operated in this manner. The best paid artists of the Dutch Golden Age, Gerrit Dou and Frans van Mieris, were among them. Joachim von Sandrart informs us that Dou daily noted the exact number of hours he devoted to a painting and charged 'ein Pfund Flemsch' (a Flemish pound = 6 guilders) an hour, while Houbraken noted that Van Mieris calculated one gold ducat (5 guilders) per hour. Considering the practice recorded in the surviving account books of Adriaen van der Werff, undoubtedly the best paid artist of the following generation, as well as his pupil Hendrick van Limborch, it is entirely plausible that Dou and Van Mieris indeed determined a minimum price in this way, although the figures reported seem exaggerated. That Dou and Van Mieris were able to pocket excessive sums, however, is revealed by the fact that Dou received 4,000 guilders from the States of Holland for *The Young Mother*, as part of the Dutch Gift to Charles II, and that Van Mieris was paid 2,500 guilders by Cosimo III the Medici for a *Family Concert*. In these cases, it seems that the status and wealth of the client—which was also mentioned by modern artists, as we have already seen—figures into the equation to a considerable degree.

Adriaen van der Werff and Hendrick van Limborch's account books show that they continued with this method, offering accurate information about how [an] artist calculated the price based on hours worked on a painting. Van Limborch noted with great precision every half a day he spent on an artwork (for history paintings the total number of days could vary between 45 and 160 days; portraits took much less time); regrettably he neither mentions the price for which a painting ultimately sold, nor the sum he charged per day. Based on circumstantial evidence, Guido Jansen assumed that the latter must have been approximately 10 guilders per day. However, we do know Van der Werff's rates. Marten Jan Bok demonstrated that, whatever his subject, van der Werff would charge a basic rate of 25 guilders a day; the total number of days would determine the minimum asking price, which served more or less as a bottom line for price negotiations with his patrons. To this he would add additional costs such as the frame, packing and transportation costs. 'Then he would take a good look at the painting and decide what the market would bear. . . . In this way, he would arrive at a target figure for his negotiations. Sometimes he settled for less, but there were occasions when he received more. Moreover, Van der Werff made a distinction—not for the customer, but for his own calculations—between his own labor and that of his brother and close collaborator Pieter. He calculated Pieter's labor, who did the groundwork for most of his paintings, at 25 guilders a day as well, which means that Adriaen did not differentiate between the price of a picture he painted all by himself—which he rarely did—and a painting he did with Pieter, even if the latter did the largest portion of the work. However, according to Johan van Gool, Adriaen paid his brother only one ducat (5 guilders) a day, which means that Adriaen made an extraordinary profit on Pieter's labor. The above demonstrates that ultimately Adriaen van der Werff guaranteed the quality of all the works that left his studio, pricing them on the basis of his personal reputation, regardless of the contribution made by his brother Pieter. [. . .]

Bok (1998, 104) . . . tested the relationship between size and labor and it appeared that three-quarters of the difference in invested labor can be explained by the difference in size of the panels. This must have often been the case. For example, we find a landscape by Herman Saftleven in the inventory of baron Willem Vincent van Wyttenhorst for which, according to his own notes, Van Wyttenhorst paid 120 guilders; for a landscape *'halff soo groot als de bovenstaende'* (half the size of the one mentioned above), Saftleven was paid exactly half that sum: 60 guilders. A painter like Cornelis van Poelenburch probably used a similar method. Van Wyttenhorst's inventory, which was drawn up between 1651 and 1659, contains a large number of paintings by Van Poelenburch (57), most of which were purchased directly from the artist. The prices Van Wyttenhorst recorded having paid vary greatly, from 36 to 464 guilders. The inexpensive ones are recorded as being small landscapes. . . . The most expensive piece is indeed described as being 'large'. That the price varies more than the difference in size would warrant, is due to the fact that it was a history painting. All the costly works by Van Poelenburch in this inventory are history paintings with numerous figures, such as 'a piece representing the Passion' or 'the martyrdom of St. Lawrence', which took a great deal more time to paint than a landscape containing only a few small figures.

Concerning calculations of monetary value, we do not have information about painters who used a rapid technique, but it seems likely that an artist like Jan van Goyen calculated the price in the same 'craftsmanlike' manner. These painters used a method of working that was geared towards high levels of production while saving labor, which resulted in lower prices per painting and—at least initially—higher profit margins. As far as we can gather from various sources, the prices of a painting by Van Goyen—who, Van Hoogstraten recounts, could produce a painting in one day—would have been approximately 10 guilders for a small painting and 60 for a large one.

His artistry and incredible virtuosity must have been greatly admired by connoisseurs; Huygens mentions Van Goyen in the same breath as Van Poelenburch, while Orlers pays even more attention to him as to Rembrandt and emphasises that his work was greatly valued. Van Poelenburch and Van Goyen could probably charge more or less the same daily rate. It seems reasonable to assume that Van Poelenburch, whose paintings appear to be on average about ten times more costly than Van Goyen's, indeed worked about ten times as long on a painting. Guessing from the prices and the time they presumably spent on a painting, I estimate that both calculated approximately eight to 10 guilders a day. This is more or less the same amount that, according to Houbraken, Nicolaes Berchem earned at the time he worked in the service of a certain patron.

But what does it mean that the daily rates varied considerably between different artists when using this method of calculating monetary value? With this obvious question we arrive at the cost of the reputation of an artist. How was this reputation determined and how was it translated into hard cash? Also in the seventeenth century it was a matter of 'trial and error'. . . . Whenever there was a conflict, appraisers could be appointed by the guild, which means there must have been a certain level of consensus among professionals about the ranking according to reputation and the reflection of this in the daily rates they could charge.

Excerpts (pp. 12–17, 20, 28, 31) from "Reference, Deference and Difference," in
Avant-Garde Gambits 1888–1893: Gender and the Color of Art History (New York:
Thames and Hudson, 1993), 12–35. Copyright © 1992 Griselda Pollock. Reproduced
by permission of Thames & Hudson, London.

Paul Gauguin left France on 1 April 1891 amid considerable publicity equipped with letters from the Ministry of Public Education and the Fine Arts commissioning him to 'study
and ultimately to paint the customs and landscapes of Tahiti'. On this French colony he
hoped to be able to live cheaply and paint enough to support the intended resumption of
his marriage to Mette Gauguin ... with whom he had not lived since 1887. Almost
immediately disappointed by Tahiti, Gauguin nevertheless spent two years there before
he managed to persuade the French government to repatriate him. He landed in Mar-
seilles—now penniless—on 30 August 1893.

By unexpected good fortune, he soon inherited from an uncle a small amount
of money which enabled him to settle in a studio in Paris and prepare for a one-
man show at the prestigious galleries of Paul Durand-Ruel. On 9 November 1893
the exhibition opened with forty-one canvases and two sculptures from his two years
in Tahiti plus a few from his time in Brittany. The Durand-Ruel exhibition was not
a financial success, since Gauguin demanded over-high prices. As a critical event, however, it was strategically important for him. Gauguin needed to regain a foothold in that
fraction of the Parisian art world which we, in retrospect, call 'the avant-garde'. In his
calculated career strategies, Gauguin was paradigmatic of avant-gardism of the
1880s/90s.

Avant-gardism involves a series of gambits for intervening in the interrelated spaces
of representation, publicity, professional competition and critical recognition. By the
1890s, the spaces of avant-garde practice were wide-ranging, from the exhibition sites of
the recently formed Salon des Indépendants in Paris and the Salon des XX in Brussels
to the galleries of selected dealers and *ad hoc* exhibitions mounted in cafés and other
places of entertainment, to the offices of specialist journals, to the discursive spaces in
daily newspapers and art magazines which advertised, reviewed and gossiped. These
provided an informal network which was both fluid and yet sufficiently coordinated to
provide a field of representation for the decisive character of avant-gardism: the play of
reference, deference and difference.

This trilogy proposes a specific way of understanding avant-gardism as a kind of
game-play. In contrast to conventional histories of modern art, which tell its story through
heroic individuals, each 'inventing' his (usually) novel style as an expression of individual
genius, I propose my three terms. To make your mark in the avant-garde community,
you had to relate your work to what was going on: *reference*. Then you had to defer to the
existing leader, to the work or project which represented the latest move, the last word,

or what was considered the definitive statement of shared concerns: *deference*. Finally your own move involved establishing a *difference* which had to be both legible in terms of current aesthetics and criticism, and also a definitive advance on that current position. Reference ensured recognition that what you were doing was part of the avant-garde project. Deference and difference had to be finely calibrated so that the ambition and claim of your work was measured by its difference from the artist or artistic statement whose status you both acknowledged (deference) *and* displaced. [. . .]

In the 1880s and 1890s the term avant-garde was not used. From our perspective, however, I think we need the concept. It is not a synonym for new or modern art. It defines a subculture. Furthermore, it is a structure for the production of art based on a series of chess-like moves: reference, deference and difference. It is a framework which generates and contains intense competitiveness, antagonism and ambition under a shared rubric. [. . .]

It was not until the late 1880s that the institutional conditions for this game-play were in place. The informal arrangements of tentative and often irregular exhibition strategies associated with the loose confederation organizing the Impressionist exhibitions of 1874 to 1886 were formalized with the founding in 1884 of the Salon des Indépendants as a regular and less cliquish exhibition space for those involved in the new art. The Impressionist initiative made the break with the obligation or desire to exhibit exclusively, or indeed at all, at the official Salon. Such independence was, moreover, entirely in keeping with the cultural policies of the Third Republic, in which independent enterprise was encouraged by republican cultural managers. The Republic's liberalism, namely *laissez-faire*, meant distaste for government interference and the government applauded artists' attempts to make new circuits of exchange and distribution independent of the state.

These new strategies are not only typical of their political moment but also symptomatic of the economic modernization of artistic practice by capitalist forms of production which are based on private producers making commodities for exchange on a market. In the case of cultural practice, product identification and validation took place through the expansion of circulation and publicity systems. To become cultural capital and make cultural profit, the art work as product must be incorporated into a public discourse through recognition by a critical framework within which both the particular character of the product (the *difference* achieved by this gambit) can be named and its relation to an already valorized context of meanings can be identified (its *reference*).

This complex process increasingly involved the manufacture of a public identity for the artist/producer which would stabilize and secure additional value for the product/art. The promotion of the self—the artist as author—was a specific effect of the processes of commodification which this stress on personality and individuality might seem to belie. The relations between the product and producer invert the typical ideological formation under capitalism—namely, the fetishism of the commodity—by creating an excessive mystique for, and overvaluation of, artistic personality. Gauguin was typical of this process, his oeuvre a specific narrative of it. [. . .]

The spectator in Durand-Ruel's gallery in Paris in 1893 was positioned in front of a very famous avant-garde bed [depicted in Gauguin's *Manao Tupapau*], which has been transported from the Rue Bréda in Paris's red light district to the South Seas where it acquired some more colourful bed-linen. Now it is back in Paris. It is, of course, Olympia's bed. . . . Executed by Manet in 1863 and exhibited at the Salon of 1865, [*Olympia*] had entered the public domain again in 1889 when it was shown at . . . the Exposition Universelle in Paris. In 1890 Monet had raised a subscription to buy it for the nation and it was placed in the Luxembourg Museum, the national home for contemporary art (and not in the Louvre, as intended). In February 1891 Gauguin had made a copy of the painting, and the copy was in fact on show in Paris in the autumn of 1893. . . . He also had a photograph of *Olympia* which he had taken with him to Tahiti. [. . .]

[In *Manao Tupapau*] the reference to Manet's *Olympia* . . . was quite obvious to the public in 1893. Gauguin's gambit is exemplary of the avant-garde strategies of reference, deference and difference which appear to stage a typically Oedipal formation: reference to the Father (that is, the artist who currently dominates the selected scene or group), deference to his coveted place, and difference, the deadly blow by which his place is appropriated or usurped. Several contemporary critics in 1893 noted the connection between *Manao Tupapau* and *Olympia*. [. . .]

Despite the apparent differences, Parisian critics confidently established continuities between *Olympia* and *Manao Tupapau*, between Manet and Gauguin, between 1863 and 1893. [. . .] An avant-garde gambit works only if you can evoke a reference text, and rework it so that its status is overcome and its place occupied. If the work is too different, reference will be stymied; if it is too close, deference will overwhelm its separate identity and it will seem merely derivative or, worse, banal and hackneyed. [. . .]

Gauguin's gambit after 1888 . . . involved a decisive geographical shift, from city to country, through which he effected a cultural translation of the avant-garde as well as the creation of a distinct facture, a style. This involved the most extensive appropriation to date of the treasury of non-Western art, Egypt, Java, Japan, whose cultures provided the syntax for an otherness, an unfamiliarity, a distance, which is too casually called the exotic in tourist literature and 'synthetist' in art historical literature. Gauguin probably hoped that a synthesis of exoticism would help him really achieve the necessary *difference* from those avant-garde leaders he had to refer to, in order to be recognized as a contender.

ULRICH LEHMANN, *The Trademark Tracey Emin*

Excerpts (pp. 60–61, 63–67, 75–76) from "The Trademark Tracey Emin," in *The Art of Tracey Emin*, ed. M. Merck and C. Townsend (London: Thames and Hudson, 2002),

60–78. Copyright © 2002 Thames & Hudson, Ltd., London. Reproduced by permission of Thames & Hudson.

'Créer un poncif, c'est du génie. Je dois créer un poncif,' exclaimed Charles Baudelaire halfway through the nineteenth century. 'To create a trademark, that's genius. I must create a trademark.' A clichéd trademark that is at once recognizable and which identifies the artist as the creator of a work emerging through and existing within its subjectivity. Not a work of art for the sake of art, but for the sake of its progenitor, a testimony as much to creative will as to the aesthetic experience that is propagated for its reception. The subjectivity that makes the work of art come alive also determines to some degree its survival. It binds the artistic object to the creative subject and assures their mutual existence within the art world. The *poncif* therefore is an intimate part of the artist, a personal mannerism and aesthetic marker that distinguishes his work.

However, *poncif* literally translates also as a 'pattern' in a commodified world; a recognizable formal trait that distinguishes the artist's output from works by other artists competing in the market. The recurrence of the pattern curiously individualizes the work of art by tying it repeatedly to the artist, and thereby constructing a serial reference to his subjectivity. The pattern needs to repeat itself for its effect to be noticed. Its first occurrence is an invention, its second an artistic strategy, the third a gesture no longer to the viewer but to the market. The *poncif* here becomes, in today's parlance, a logo. It is reified and separated from its creation and cast into the realm of commerce. It is at this point that Baudelaire's double coinage of the *poncif* emerges as both commonplace trademark and commodified logo, as idea and reified appearance. It becomes an epistemological *Kippfigur*, an image that can be turned around to be read as a different image altogether. These *Kippfiguren*, very popular in Baudelaire's time, present us with readable figures (a young woman in a feathered hat, for instance) that we have to invert to reveal their counterparts or opposites—in this well-known example it is the gnarled face of an old woman. The *Kippfigur* is meant to innocently amuse, yet it is, more often than not, morally charged, because the secondary image reminds the spectator of the first image's uncanny potential. [. . .]

The *poncif* can be understood as a semantic *Kippfigur*, for it draws its potential from a metaphorical pairing of its secondary meaning, the pattern that occupies the surface of the image, with its primary effect. The underlying trademark stands for the subject that created it. So, on the one hand, there is the trademark-*poncif* as a substantial trait, an (at times clichéd) characteristic of the artist; on the other hand, there exists the pattern-*poncif* as formal stylistics, ephemeral elements of fashion that have to constantly rejuvenate themselves. No doubt, artistic autonomy—the will to let subjectivity distinguish the work, as opposed to an expressive religious, political or even artistic programme—is embedded in the *poncif*. [. . .] However, the *poncif* is also responsible for a formal objectivity, it works towards its application to the marketplace and its significance in positioning the artefact within a commodified art world. The more memorable the pattern, the quicker the viewer's transposition from object to subject, the closer the connection of the work of art to its creator. When one is able to instantly determine the object as being 'made by so-and-so', then one can adjust one's aesthetic experience accordingly and forsake any imperative in one's possible interpretation in favour of simply arranging the work as part of the oeuvre of a particular artist. [. . .]

. . . It is important to emphasize that the creation of a *poncif* is not simply a marketing strategy. It is not about selling the artist, it is about making his subjectivity recognizable in his work and subsequently creating a pattern that will allow for easy identification. It might seem therefore that the *poncif* would work best when the epistemological *Kippfigur* dissolves itself, that is, when the trademark becomes a pattern or, better still, the pattern becomes the trademark. This confluence, however, can be problematic, as we will see in contemporary art. For when pattern or logo equals trademark, the artist's subjectivity is consumed in artifice and the autonomy that is necessary for progressive artistic creation is lost in the constant hurrying after fashion rather than instigating trends. For the male modern artist the subjectivity that might serve as his trademark could be separated quite easily from his person, since his own body, subjectivity *per se*, was not thematized as a consumable object. Traditional mores that shaped a commonplace view of the body, and of sexuality, positioned the male as active subject in contrast to the female as passive object. The dominant action of socially sanctioned desire therefore had to be directed outwards, away from the male body, and did not permit a self-reflective investigation through the male artist's creativity. [. . .]

For the female artist, in contrast, subjectivity invariably meant dealing intimately with her own eroticized and even sexually objectified body, its shifting shape and its objectification through morals, customs and rapidly changing sartorial fashions. [. . .] *In extremis*, for the modern female artist the *Kippfigur* of the *poncif* tilts away from the dialectics of trademark and pattern and establishes subjectivity as the pattern itself. The female subject is caught between articulating subjectivity as necessary for the creation of works of art and the anxiety of seeing such subjectivity consumed as a pattern that becomes representative for the work itself. Her work is commonly interpreted as dealing with the juxtaposition of being a (receptive) woman and a (creative) artist; it has to be seen to debate her body, her sexuality in particular; only then does it appear to become truly marketable and materially successful. Thereby it slips into the process that is commonplace in many parts of Western culture (from opera to Hollywood), where the female body is objectified for consumption and her subjectivity is reduced to emotive residue rather than maintained as a genuine structural force.

In April 2001 the British edition of *Vogue* opened a feature on Tracey Emin with a photograph of the artist in the bathroom of her East End studio. The space is easily identifiable as the artist's own because the bathtub in the background had featured prominently in Emin's photographic work *Sometimes I Feel Beautiful* a year earlier. [. . .] What initially appears as an incidental observation quickly shifts to become part of an extended artistic strategy that makes each public representation as subjective and personal as possible, homing in on the privacy of the artist and her immediate environment. The trademark is here 'made by Emin' as the spectator expects to be privy to the artist's most intimate surroundings and her exposure within it. [. . .]

The clothes in the image are chosen not merely for their appropriate 'chic' within a fashion magazine, but to complement Emin's establishment of a trademark-*poncif*. The artist is wearing a silk-brocade dress and high-heeled shoes by the British designer Vivi- enne Westwood. Professional make-up and hair-styling complement the fashionable rep- resentation in the portrait, while Emin's day-to-day attire of jeans and sweater is decora- tively tossed at her feet and she hitches up the dress over her thigh as if to provide an erotic frisson reminiscent of the much more daring revelation of the female body in her artwork. The portrait is a careful construct of pictorial journalism and calculated artistic *poncif*. It functions not so much as a deliberate marketing strategy (she is selling neither the dress nor, directly, her art), but rather as a controlled self-image of the artist's trademark-*poncif*. [. . .] One can assume that the outfit has perhaps been chosen by the artist herself and therefore constitutes an integral part of the creative strategy of the *poncif*, the cliché that renders the artist's subjective taste part of a recognizable commodity. Indeed, it could be argued that this is very much the case: Emin wears Westwood because her audience expects it. [. . .] To successfully underscore her *poncif*, Emin wears Westwood: because Westwood is the Emin of the fashion industry, or perhaps because Emin is the Westwood of the art world. [. . .] Both raise subjectivity to a highly sublimated and artistically relevant methodology, both create an instantly recognizable *poncif* of anarchic protest through thematizing their own bodies: Westwood in creating risqué female clothes which she wears herself, Emin by creating an infinite variation of revelatory self-portraits. [. . .]

The original direction of the move within the series from brand name to artistic trade- mark, however, demonstrates the realization by the artist that the use of the *poncif* has to be underscored by artistic integrity of some sort. [. . .] For the contemporary artist, a conceptual switch occurs from the use of commodified images for fine art to positioning the fine artist as a commodifiable persona. In the monoprints, the trademark intimacy of the nude figure with open legs is more significant than the use of any logo, even if it is one representing a congenial designer like Westwood. [. . .]

[. . .] In the present cultural climate, redolent with unfettered artistic enthusiasm for brand names and logos, the artist can only share the success of her *poncif* if it appears as calculated, if the commodification of the self is knowingly tongue-in-cheek. [. . .] In Emin, one *poncif* is her depiction of the open legs which also occurs in the central part of the 'Westwood' monoprints. This motif—if one can reduce such a charged image to a formal element—is repeatedly figured throughout Emin's work. The pattern-*poncif* of the open legs is essentially Emin and can be varied, in a similar way to Offenbach's cancan sequences, according to the context in which it appears. In Emin's oeuvre, with its con- stantly changing media, the open legs can be seen in different material contexts and with different art-historical references: as a painted 'Erich Heckel' in her student work, . . . an engineered 'Bruce Nauman' in the neon wall pieces, . . . or as a written 'Charles

Bukowski' in the opening lines of a poem. Once the *poncif*-pattern is repeated a certain number of times and becomes exposed in the media, an interpretive framework is established into which any subsequent artwork can neatly slip. This framing is a significant strategy for contemporary art because it permits a controlled reception of the work, in contrast to the exhaustive need for manifestoes, proclamations or performances to influence critics and audience, as was the case with the modernist avant-garde. An aesthetic logo, in Emin's case an image of female sexuality, is created which originates from the critical *poncif* of the artist's subjectivity. Of course, one must add that such a motif is Emin's very own *poncif* because the artist imbues it with a profound sensibility, notwithstanding its critical perception as merely feminine or outspokenly feminist. In this artistic pattern one part of the *poncif* glides into the other, the stylistic logo and conceptual trademark are almost indistinguishable, since the creation of a public reception, as well as commercial success, is built into the variants of the motif. The success of the recognizable pattern prompts the artist's repeated investigation over time in different media, in different contexts.

ADRIAN PIPER, *Notes on the Mythic Being I–III*

Reprint from "Notes on the Mythic Being I–III 1974–1976," in *Out of Order, Out of Sight*, vol. 1, *Selected Writings in Meta-Art 1968–1992* (Cambridge, MA: MIT Press, 1999), 120–21. Copyright © 1999 MIT Press. Reprinted by kind permission.

1. I don't make concrete, spatiotemporally unique, discrete objects that cannot be multiply reproduced or assimilated to any type or space.

2. I don't rely on discrete, spatially unique art contexts for presentation of the work. It can be done or shown anywhere; but I specifically eschew art contexts as such (galleries, performances).

3. The exchange value of the work is equal to its production value. Like all art, its economic value is an intrinsic element in its aesthetic value.

4. I utilize art contexts only in their information-disseminating capacities. I have used them only to the extent of making available information about work or works that can be cheaply distributed on request.

One intentional consequence of these constraints is that my work has no investment value, because its exchange value is an economic constant, that is, a function of its production value at the time of its production. So it may or may not be good art, but it can't be a good investment. My early performances were done in public spaces, freely accessible to whomever was around at the time. I also considered making these performances available to particular people on a weekly basis: For $125.00 per week, I would give one performance a day in a public space of my own choosing, for the period of time during which I was hired. I say I considered this idea because, after broaching it to a few people,

I got the general impression that no one particularly wanted to pay for something they couldn't own, at least temporarily. More recently, the work has had more to do with visual imagery and written information. My practice here has been to distribute the work as widely as possible by utilizing the public media . . . or by employing cheap and easily available means of reproduction, such as photostats, offset printing, posters, etc.

This is desirable to me because I don't think aesthetic value has anything to do with investment value. But a confusion between the two is primarily responsible for the hierarchical power structure of the art world, to which all participants in this confusion implicitly contribute. At one end, there are dealers and collectors who explicitly regard good art as little more than a good investment: The monetary value of a work increases with the gallery-generated publicity accorded to the artist, time, the death of the artist (very important), the critical response to the work, the artist's circle of friends, etc. Although one of these separately is innocuous, their combination can be insidious. At the other end of the spectrum, there are artists who justifiably wish compensation for their labor but for whom a gradually increasing and inflated overcompensation soon becomes a necessary index of personal and artistic worth, power, and success.

BARBARA HOFFMAN, *Whose Image Is It?*

Reprint from "Whose Image Is It?" *College Art Association News* 15, no. 5 (1990): 5–6. Copyright © 1990 College Art Association, Inc. Reprinted with kind permission of the author.

Contemporary artists often use appropriation—the copying of existing imagery—as the basis of their artistic expression. Such use of preexisting images as a source for new artwork has created conflicts with the owners of the rights to the existing material under federal copyright and trademark law. Several artists have been sued for copyright and trademark infringement for the use of appropriated images—but since the cases were settled out of court, no judicial opinions have considered appropriation per se. Two cases, however, both against New York–based artist Jeff Koons, are presently being argued in the federal district court in New York.

In *Art Rogers v. Jeff Koons and Sonnabend Gallery, Inc.,* Art Rogers, a professional California-based photographer and artist, created and copyrighted a photograph titled *Puppies.* During 1988 and 1989 Koons created wood polychrome sculptures titled *String of Puppies* that Rogers claims infringed on the copyrighted *Puppies* and represent a false designation of origin of the goods.

In another case, *United Feature Syndicate v. Jeff Koons,* United Feature, the owner of the copyright in the "Garfield" comic strip and the character Odie, who has been featured continually in the strip, sued Koons for violation of federal copyright law, among other claims.

United Feature claims that Koons infringed on its copyright by creating and selling a sculpture that pictures a dog that is copied from and bears a substantial similarity to the character Odie.

The Copyright Act of 1976 provides in section 106 that the owner of copyright has the exclusive right to reproduce the copyrighted work and to prepare derivative works; it also provides that the copyright owner has the exclusive right of publication, performance, and display.

To prove copyright infringement, a copyright holder (plaintiff) must show that the alleged infringer (defendant) copied the work. Copying may consist of a defendant's admission that he copied or circumstantial evidence, usually access, which permits an inference of copying. The plaintiff must prove that the copying went so far as to constitute improper appropriation. To this end, the copyright owner must demonstrate substantial similarity relating to protected material. Substantial similarity must go to copyrightable expression and not to the idea or facts that are noncopyrightable elements. The line, however, between idea and expression is often elusive. The real battleground is which factors and what test go into a finding of substantial similarity.

For example, in the 1987 case of *Kisch v. Ammirati and Paris, Inc.*, the plaintiff had made a photograph of a woman seated in the Village Vanguard; the woman was holding a concertina and behind her was a large mural on the wall. The defendant was a photographer hired by an ad agency who had made a photograph of a man seated in front of the same mural in the Village Vanguard, holding a saxophone, with a bottle of lime juice on a table nearby. The defendants conceded access. The court in refusing to dismiss the claim for copyright infringement on a motion for summary judgment noted that camera angle, lighting, etc., might be protected elements. The court stated: "... with respect to the issue of unlawful appropriation under the ordinary observer test, the court is unable to conclude that a rational trier of fact would not be permitted to find substantial similarity relating to the protected material. Significantly, a rational trier of fact would be permitted to find that the underlying tone or mood in the defendant's photograph was similar to the original conception in the plaintiff's work."

The basic defenses to infringement are fair use and freedom of expression. In 1976 Congress enacted the doctrine of fair use, which had been a judicial creation, as part of the copyright law. Section 107 provides that reproductions of copyrighted work for the purpose of criticism, comment, news reporting, and teaching shall be fair use. In addition, the report that accompanied the copyright law specifically included the example of parody. The section further provides that in any determination, the court shall consider the following factors, summarized as: (1) the purpose and character of the secondary use, (2) the nature of the copyrighted work, (3) amount and substantiality, and (4) the effect on the market or value. Judges do not have a consensus on the meaning of fair use, and judicial opinions reflect widely different notions. Thus, despite the listing of the four factors, no clear guidelines have developed.

Koons argues that no infringement has taken place. Relying on the proposition that facts and ideas are not copyrightable, he argues that even though a person might witness an event and record that event, this does not give that person any proprietary rights to it.

As applied to the *Rogers* case, the argument is that Koons has taken the image of the nonprotected event and thus does not infringe on Rogers's copyright. Since the expression and the fact converge, the photograph is entitled only to limited protection. By selecting a different medium of expression, most of the "photographic" and thus protected elements are gone. (Normally, the change in the medium of expression does not preclude infringement, i.e., a photograph of a painting.)

Evidently this argument is difficult to apply in the *United Feature* case, where the source of the image is not fact but the imagination. John Koegel, Koons's lawyer, has previously argued that the appropriate test is "whether an ordinary lay observer would regard the *aesthetic appeal* of the two works to be the same." Koons has also raised other defenses including fair use and the First Amendment.

In *Harper and Row Publishers v. Nation Enterprises*, the Supreme Court instructed that the effect upon the potential market for the work is "undoubtedly the single most important element of fair use." Koons no doubt will rely on the fact that his sculptures were not in competition with the plaintiff's works.

While Koons's argument with respect to the test for substantial similarity offers almost no protection to the photographer, reliance on an "appropriation" or "concept and feel" test may result in protecting noncopyrightable ideas. On the other hand, this may suggest only that the defendant has gone beyond mere style to utilize elements that are "expressive." Whatever one thinks of Koons's art, should the concept of fair use incorporate the "appropriation" concept?

There are no simple answers to resolve potential conflicts that result from artistic appropriation, and the space considerations of this newsletter preclude any complex answer or substantial analysis.

Suffice it to say that wherever the line is drawn (and my instinct is that, if at all, it should be within fair use) it should take account of the goal of the copyright law: to stimulate activity and progress in the arts for the intellectual enrichment of the public by permitting authors to reap the rewards of their creative efforts.

IV. THE ART MARKET

WALTER SANTAGATA, *Property and Exhibition Rights*

Excerpts (pp. 187–93) from "Institutional Anomalies in the Contemporary Art Market," *Journal of Cultural Economics* 19, no. 2 (1995): 187–97. Copyright © 1995 Kluwer Academic Publishers. With permission of Springer.

The market for contemporary paintings, like any other market, is created by institutions (the "rules of the game") and organisations (the "players"). Without organisations, such as studios for artistic production and art galleries, there can be no art market. Without institutions, such as conventions (confidence and reputation) and formal rules (contracts and property rights), transactions would be difficult and it is unlikely that the art market, *per se*, would exist.

Institutions, by creating incentives and constraints to individual action, and organisations, by taking advantage of the related opportunities, cause the emergence of an "artistic field", where artists struggle for their autonomy and assert their social role. In the artistic field we can see which institutions are created and how. We can also go back to the origin and special features of the property rights system in the contemporary art market.

Not all institutions develop to the point where they attain efficiency and equity. Sometime during the history of human evolution or somewhere in the world they reflect the power of private interests, rent seeking and privileges. In this case they do not develop efficiently or fairly. This leads to anomalies, like those that exist in the market for contemporary paintings. [. . .]

The first anomaly concerns the acknowledgement of property rights. As far as the acknowledgement and the allocation of property rights are concerned, the art market is not homogeneous. To illustrate this point let us have a look at a paradox typical of the market of paintings.

Consider the case of Giulio Paolini, a leading artist of the *Arte Povera* movement. The manager of a world-renowned company in Turin visited Paolini's studio to see his work. At the end of the visit, he asked to buy an exceptionally valuable work. He and Paolini agreed on a price, and Paolini signed a contract giving up his property rights. The buyer wanted to associate the image of his company with an important venture in the cultural field. So the Paolini work was exhibited—and entrance tickets were sold—at company headquarters. It was a success. Every day many people bought tickets to see Paolini's work and the ticket sales guaranteed that a substantial flow of money entered the company's coffers.

In a case such as this, the exclusion of the artist from the wealth produced by his work was unfair, at least from a Kantian ethical point of view. On the other hand, from the point of view of efficiency, if we lived in a world in which all phenomena were predictable, including artistic success, and information was costless, then a contract contingent on all the future states of the world could have been signed and the price would have included all future benefits. But the future is instead uncertain, and in a highly controlled contemporary art market the artist could be discriminated against with regard to his right to the product of his work, skill, or investment. The paradox lies in the legal acceptance of a prejudice to Paolini's right to future income yielded by his work.

To solve the Giulio Paolini paradox according to an ethical idea of fairness, the artist should share in the income produced by his intellectual work. He should be given the opportunity to choose between selling his complete bundle of property rights or exploiting an exhibition right, alternatives that exist in other art markets. If the royalties are not acknowledged, the artist, under the pressure of necessity, could be driven to take illegal action. We can cite the case of Giorgio De Chirico, who illegally dated his works back to the period 1910–1915 in order to take advantage of the higher market value for his meta-physical works of art. We can imagine a successful artist, a *maestro*, compelled by personal circumstances to stop painting altogether; while the collectors of his works are well off thanks to steady capital gains, he himself is starving.

The same result in terms of Kantian fairness could be interpreted according to the neo-classical theory of property. The aim of this theory is to add a legal and institutional dimension to the analysis of efficient markets. This leads to an analysis of the maximising behaviour of artists and dealers, *given their initial constraints*. The principal constraints in the Paolini paradox are the acknowledgement and the allocation of the property rights in the presence of high transaction costs. When an artist sells a painting, we observe that he/she can sell the complete bundle of rights, private and transferable, pertaining to the use of the painting, to its destruction, to the income the painting yields in the future and to the exchange (resale) of the painting. *Ex post* the price reflects the composition of the bundle of rights being exchanged, in the sense that the greater the number of rights sold the higher, *ceteris paribus*, the price. *Ex ante*, however, what matters are the constraints (which are not given). These include not only the endowment and the bargaining power of the individuals that take part in the exchange, but more generally the institutional setting, the "rules of the game", the culture and the "civicness" of a particular place or historical period. The property rights approach seems to take for granted what must be ascertained: that is, what are the actual contents of the bundle of property rights in the current market for contemporary paintings. For instance, is the right to use without limitation? Is the right to the destruction of the work included in the bundle? And what about the exhibition right? A non-dogmatic definition of law stresses that its essence is the attempt to realize the idea of justice in a *given social environment*. Then the bundle of property rights is historically determined and we cannot postulate an absolute *complete* bundle, linked to prices changing according to the number and the quality of rights sold. We cannot sell rights that do not *exist*.

The first anomaly of the market of contemporary paintings thus concerns an evolution of the institutional setting that does not acknowledge an equivalence of copyrights. Is this evolution a consequence of the special nature of the artistic goods, or does it depend on the way the art market is organised? [. . .]

Allocation of property rights to the prejudice of the artist seems to be a special characteristic of the market of contemporary paintings. In order to go into the subject more deeply, I will draw an analogy and a comparison between the art market and the markets for music, films and books. As a general rule the author's property rights to his work must be acknowledged. These rights have not enjoyed a non-conflictual enforcement in the past.

Given this preliminary caveat, we can see that the composer and the writer can choose between two main courses of action: selling the complete bundle of acknowledged property rights; or selling the bundle of acknowledged property rights, except for the copyright to sound or written reproduction.

In the *film* market as well—which is more complex, due to the presence of a film producer—the author/director can either sell the property rights or exploit the copyright. [. . .]

On the other hand, in the international contemporary art market, the painter exercises only one choice: whether or not to sell all his property rights. Why? It could be said that the bundle of property rights is complete, in the sense that it specifies all the possible uses of ownership. In this case the lack of enforcement of the copyright system could be a result of high transaction costs. The argument, given what it presupposes, is apparently acceptable, but in comparative terms it fails to explain why, for instance, the high transaction costs involved in detecting the reproduction of music, even when performed by a small orchestra in a remote village, can be afforded by the music market and analogous or even smaller transaction costs cannot instead be afforded by the market of paintings. [. . .] While these markets have generated a system of reproduction and distribution of the original work, the market for paintings is organized as a widespread network of art galleries selling and buying the absolute ownership of original works without any acknowledgement of a copyright system. [. . .]

[. . .] Let us examine some objections to the feasibility (acknowledgement) of a copyright system in the market of contemporary paintings. At first sight they seem to be crucial, but on deeper analysis they disappear.

The first of these objections concerns consumption. We could say that paintings are original works and that consuming them implies the ownership of the original. On the contrary, a person who experiences and enjoys music or a novel is not necessarily interested in owning scores or manuscripts: a compact disk or a book is enough. This argument, however, is contingent on existing consumer preferences or styles and on the current market structure. In principle it is possible to rent a painting or to consume it by buying the ticket of an exhibition.

The second objection concerns demand. Art collectors want the exclusive ownership of a work of art and there is no room for a different market structure. But the behaviour of art consumers is changing. For example, consider the recent success of temporary exhibitions: the art market is not made up of collectors and buyers alone. A large demand for "consuming" art exhibitions is a recent phenomenon that has been readily satisfied by a new market structure. We must recognize however that this currently holds true for classical paintings, not yet for contemporary art. In any case, this does not prevent us from observing two kinds of demand in the contemporary art market: the demand for the original works of art and the demand for visual consumption.

The third objection states that in the music market copyrights are a rational answer. Musical compositions are considered a public good, and there is inefficient production in the music market because of "free riding" and pirate recordings. So the artistic production of music is below its efficiency level. Protecting creators from illegal consumption is, then, a way of restoring an efficient level of production. However if this holds true for musical works, why could it not be true for paintings? If a painting is publicly exhibited, it can be considered a public congested good (not rival consumption, but with congestion costs) and accordingly, if the exhibition right is unacknowledged, the same inefficiencies can be found.

Finally, it is said that a masterpiece is the only extant example, i.e., there are no copyrights sold and consumed over different units. This too could be falsified. The consumption of a masterpiece is reproducible. For example, the exhibition of a painting in a public space: paying for a ticket could mean an acknowledgement of an exhibition right. [. . .]

Summing up, there are no obvious justifications for differences among art market structures, even though differences in the nature of artistic goods do exist. This analogical argument also seems to hold true with reference to the specification of rights. I refer here to the *droit de suite* and to an exhibition right.

The *droit de suite*, a particular specification of an artist's right to the yields of his work, was the first institutional measure in place in many bodies of legislation . . . but on the whole neither enforced nor claimed by the artists. The *droit de suite* gives painters a little share in the value that their works may attain in a sale following the first one. Although intended to correct inefficient rights allocations, the *droit de suite* has some serious drawbacks.

First of all, the existence of this right depends on a hypothetical future resale. If there is no resale, there is no such right! This contradicts the process of valorization of the work of art, a continuous process which evolves independently of the resale of the painting. As a right that depends on the action of a third person, it does not seem to offer the artist adequate protection.

The *droit de suite* does not seem to protect the artist from the economic point of view either. If a painter were to sell the complete bundle of property rights, except the *droit de suite*, the price of the work would have been lower by an amount equal to the expected future income from the valorisation process. [. . .]

If the *droit de suite* were enforced in one country only, the art dealers and sellers could move to other countries, thus avoiding the cost of royalties. In this case the country introducing the *droit de suite* would be exposed to a sort of unfair competition and an impoverishment of the national market. [. . .]

Because of its serious failures, a substitute of the *droit de suite* must be examined, such as an exhibition right.

In the copyright system an exhibition right, if acknowledged, seems to be a preferable choice. And it also seems to be feasible. Consumers tend to enjoy a commodity or a service, so for example, the visit of 300,000 visitors to the famous Van Gogh exhibition in Rome corresponds to the reproduction of a musical composition on 300,000 compact disks or the printing of 300,000 copies of a book. From a logical and technical point of view, there do not seem to be any major objections or impediments to the acknowledgement and enforcement of an exhibition right. It seems to be a classic patrimonial right, such as the *droit de suite* or the copyright. Its moral justification is self-evident. Consider the case of a museum of contemporary art and the Giulio Paolini paradox. One might wonder why artists have no right to share the revenue from the box office, especially if it can be shown that the visitors are attracted specifically by their works of art. If the art work is exhibited in museums and public halls where exclusion is possible, an exhibition right, like the copyright, is a contribution to the efficient market.

This prospect indicates that the art market may be expected to evolve a new organisation. In order to demonstrate this, let us imagine that selling property rights is forbidden and that artists can only exploit an exhibition right. To satisfy demand, private and public spaces are required. There will be public museums of contemporary art paying an exhibition right to the authors. There will be private entrepreneurs renting galleries, selling tickets; there will be companies renting paintings; there will be authors' associations regulating the enforcement of their rights. The market will be segmented: from the avant-garde that interests a limited number of amateurs to the more popular artists. On Saturday and Sunday, people will visit galleries, just as they visit museums or cinemas today and just as they once did in the United Kingdom during the 19th century.

WILLIAM N. GOETZMANN, *Informational Efficiency of the Art Market*

Excerpts (pp. 25–26, 30–32) from "The Informational Efficiency of the Art Market," *Managerial Finance* 21, no. 6 (1995): 25–34. Copyright © 1995 Emerald Group Publishing Limited; reprinted with permission.

Paintings are like stocks and a dealer is like a broker. Someone makes money, then there is someone else who's really good at investing in stocks, and he tells the investor what to buy. If someone tells you to go to a good gallery rather than one that's not so good, you'll get a painting that might turn out to be worth something, a painting you like that's also a good investment. It's like having a broker tell you what stocks to buy.

ANDY WARHOL

The parallels that Pop master Andy Warhol drew between the stock market and the painting market provide an insider's insight into the issue of art market efficiency. If the art market were a perfect "informationally efficient" market, then Andy Warhol would have been wrong—no art expert or gallery could help predict which paintings would appreciate in value and which would decline. In other words, if information about the future prospects of painting prices were common knowledge, then these prospects would already be reflected in *current* price levels. No dealer or gallery, no matter how clever, would know when the art market was poised for a boom or a bust, nor would they know which artist was "undervalued." The efficient market hypothesis has long dominated research in the stock market—Warhol's observations to the contrary. While the efficient market hypothesis may logically apply to the stock market where differences of opinion about asset values play out in the continuous double-auction of the New York Stock Exchange every day, it is *examines Predictability*

Prices should be random & unpredictable

not clear that the hypothesis should apply to the art market, where purchase decisions are based on taste as much as upon discounted expectations of future price appreciation.

A logical consequence of the efficient market hypothesis . . . is that asset prices should follow a random walk. In other words, past returns should not predict future returns. In fact, this implication is valid only to the extent that profitable timing strategies are allowed by transactions costs, and if superior returns may be obtained on alternative investments. In this paper, I examine the predictability of an index of art returns. I find that "weak form" efficiency, that is, predictions using past price level, cannot be rejected for the art market. Despite this, there is some evidence of persistence in market returns, and consequently the profitability of timing strategies by knowledgeable market participants cannot be ruled out.

is this why that hypothesis doesn't work for the art market?

Another implication of an efficient market is that the immediate resale value of an asset will yield approximately what an investor paid for it. For instance, the purchaser of a share of stock on the NYSE should be able to immediately re-sell it for approximately the cost of the bid–ask spread. . . . This is a function of the high liquidity of the stock market, and the broad availability of financial information about share values. [Using transaction data to estimate the uncertainty surrounding an immediate resale of a painting, I found,] in contrast to the stock market . . . the re-sale uncertainty for art to be extraordinarily high. This large "price-risk" suggests that there may be great value to art dealers who, like specialists on the NYSE, can match buyers and sellers. When taken as a metric for art market efficiency, the price risk for paintings suggests that the art market has tended towards greater efficiency over its history. I attribute this trend to the increasing availability of auction information to prospective art buyers and sellers. [. . .]

no guaranteed higher resell value

[The test results are strongly indicative of the tendency of the market to move in trends.] One explanation for the persistence pattern [I found] in art returns is that they may be correlated to inflation, which is itself positively auto-correlated. This possibility is particularly pertinent to the issue of whether the persistence in returns may be exploited. For instance, if the auto-regression model predicts that art returns will fall, then an investor may not be able to exploit the decrease, because disinflation will cause the prices of alternative investments to fall as well.

trends! dealers know!! what will be trendy

inflation affects resell

The results [. . .] suggest that the market displays some long-term serial dependency. This may be due to trends in inflation, or it may be due to slowly changing expected returns to art investment. Neither of these two possibilities may be exploited by trading rules, but, given the high transactions costs associated with art investment, it is unlikely that an investor would attempt a market timing strategy with art. None-the-less, the [results] suggest that a dealer or market maker with access to past transactions information may be able to forecast the long-term future direction of the art market. Whether or not, as Andy Warhol suggested, this forecast can be exploited by judicious purchases and sales is an open question. [. . .]

there is more risk than chance of reward !!!

transactions could be predicted, but can they also be exploited?

Recall from the introduction that another implication of efficient market theory is that price information in the market is broadly available. Thus, the purchase price and the immediate resale price should not vary dramatically from each other. The price risk associated with immediate resale has been studied in the U.S. housing markets. [. . .] Studies find that price risk for housing ranges between 5% and 10% of value. In other words, the price obtained in an immediate turn-around sale of a property may vary around the purchase price by 5 to 10%. . . . We are able to estimate price risk for the art market. [. . .] The estimate [of price risk] over the entire 271 year period suggests that the standard deviation of an immediate resale of a painting would be as much as 100%. [. . .]

[. . .] [The results also show that] the price risk spread has decreased steadily through time. It is unlikely that this pattern is due to errors in the exchange rate estimates, since exchange rates were fixed for most of the pre-20th century prices. By conditioning on our measure of the price risk upon the purchase date of the painting, we find evidence that, even though the basic institutions of the art market may have evolved as early as the 18th century, it appears to have steadily tended towards greater efficiency as a mechanism for processing information and matching buyers and sellers. Part of this increase in efficiency may be due to the increase in quality and quantity of public information about auction prices. Comprehensive international art auction records have been available in printed form since 1970. Since the mid-1980s, interested buyers and sellers have been able to access online databases such as ArtQuest, Inc. to search for auction transactions by artist, medium, size and subject matter of painting. This type of information will inevitably reduce the uncertainty about the current value of a work of art. Another source of increase in efficiency is the development of art historical research. Despite a long history of active art scholarship, it has only been in the twentieth century that many painters have *catalogues raisonné*, or comprehensive accountings of their *oeuvre*. Art historical publications "level the field" for owners and prospective buyers of art, by identifying the range of styles, characteristic signatures and major collections of an artist. Neither good auction information, nor a good library are substitutes for market experience. A dealer specializing in the work of a single artist will [possess] information about the quantity and location of the artist's works, as well as about the prices for which that work has sold. In addition, a dealer will also know who is in the market for a particular artist's work. Until the price risk of owning a painting drops to much narrower range, this market information will continue to provide substantial rewards.

The large spread between the "true" value and the market value of a painting has broader implications beyond the evolution towards efficiency of the art market. Even if one were unaware of the extensive network of dealers and valuation experts in the art market, the results of our price risk analysis would suggest their existence. Dealers profit by having superior information about the paintings, or about the collectors interested in the paintings. A gap of 50% in the going rate for a particular work of art suggests that profits may be high for a market-maker. The high price risk represents a considerable motivation for a dealer to develop superior information about the assets, and about the market demand for them. For example, if the price variation in the auction market were similar in magnitude to the price variation in the dealer market, then an art dealer who is attempting to purchase low and sell high might expect to mark prices up by 50%. [. . .]

The art market is considerably less liquid than the financial markets. This illiquidity may be a cause of an effect of the mechanisms by which information is processed by the structure of collectors, dealers, agents and auction houses that currently make up the market. [. . .] Estimates indicate that the art market has five to ten times more price risk than the U.S. housing market. This is bad news for art investors seeking to liquidate their properties at a profit. They appear to expose themselves to more than a 50% standard deviation in the realized price when they take a painting to auction. This transaction risk implies that there are large potential rewards to art dealers who can match buyers and sellers. The 50% price risk estimate may translate into a potential 50% dealer markup. The emergence of information vendors and the growth of art historical scholarship may have contributed to the decrease in price risk over the history of the art market. If so, then I would anticipate such a trend to continue.

JAMES E. PESANDO, *The Market for Modern Prints*

Excerpts (pp. 1075, 1081–87) from "Art as an Investment: The Market for Modern Prints," *American Economic Review* 83, no. 5 (1993): 1075–89. Reprinted by kind permission of the author.

A major obstacle to testing the economic efficiency of the art market is the difficulty in tracking prices of individual works of art over time. Since multiple sales of unique art objects occur infrequently, it is difficult to construct data on returns to art that are readily aligned with data on the periodic returns to traditional financial assets.

The present paper circumvents this problem by focusing on the auction market for modern prints. Because prints are multiples, often published in editions of 50–100 or more, several impressions of the same print may be offered for sale at auction in a single season. As a result, the increase in the number of repeat sales is quite dramatic. [. . .]

Art dealers traditionally advise clients to buy the most expensive artworks they can afford, on the presumption that the top works of the most established artists will outperform the market. The proposition appears to be that the cumulative return on a masterpiece port-folio will exceed that on the market as a whole, for an unspecified holding period. It is frequently noted, as well, that masterpieces are less susceptible to market downturns. If so, a masterpiece portfolio might have a higher expected return for a given level of risk, than middle-level and lower-level works of art. This cannot be true if the art market is efficient, since the desirable characteristics of masterpieces will simply be capitalized into their prices. While this result may seem self-evident to economists, it is clearly unfamiliar to those in the art trade. [. . .]

If the trade view is correct, the estimated price indexes [I created] for the masterpiece portfolios must lie uniformly above the estimated price indexes for the alternatives. [. . .]

[. . .] [My] results provide no support for the view that masterpieces outperform the market. [. . .]

The print prices used in this study are inclusive of the buyer's premium and thus reflect the final prices paid by purchasers. If an artist's prints are actively sold in two or more geographically distinct markets, the "law of one price" dictates that no significant price differences persist, in the absence of transactions costs. If systematic price differences exist, buyers would face an obvious incentive to undo them. In spite of this fact, the trade maintains that such systematic price differences do exist, at least for some artists.

Ideally, one would like to compare the prices of identical prints that are sold in different markets at the same moment in time. Unfortunately, this is not possible, since the major auctions are staggered in order to facilitate participation by potential buyers. The major fall sales at Christie's and Sotheby's in New York, for example, take place in mid-November, while the London sales take place at the beginning of December.

To compare prices realized in different markets, one must specify a window within which sales are deemed to be contemporaneous. There is an obvious trade-off. The wider the window, the greater will be the number of sales of identical prints in the sample; yet the more suspect will be the assumption that the sales are contemporaneous. For the period 1977–1992, I choose to focus on a 30-day window, that is, on the sale of identical prints in different markets which occur within 30 days of each other. [. . .]

Price comparisons for the German Expressionists, the School of Paris, and American artists, as well as for Picasso, Chagall, and Miro, are [made]. Prices realized in the United States are compared to prices realized in London and in Europe. To provide an additional benchmark, prices are compared across these three markets for all artists contained in the aggregate portfolio.

One is immediately struck by the substantial price variation that occurs in the contemporaneous sales of the same print. This price variation is seen in the ratio of the mean absolute price difference to the mean price in each comparison. For Picasso prints sold in the United States and in Europe, for example, this ratio equals 30 percent. In the full set of comparisons, this ratio ranges from 18 percent to 59 percent.

In part, price differences reflect unobserved variation in the quality and in the condition of prints. Nonetheless, much of the price variation is simply due to "noise" in the realization of prices at auction. This is readily apparent in an extreme example. An impression from the edition of 250 of *Le Repas Frugal*, Picasso's first published print, sold for $374,000 at Christie's, New York on November 19, 1990, against an estimate of

$160,000–$200,000. Two weeks later, at Christie's in London, an impression of this print sold for $189,980. The descriptions of the quality and the condition of these impressions in the respective auction catalogues are virtually identical. There is no apparent justification for this dramatic price discrepancy.

The results [. . .] indicate that, on average, prices during the period 1977–1992 are higher in the United States than in either London or Europe. (This is *not*, one should note, the essence of the trade proposition.) For all artists, the mean price of prints sold in the United States exceeds the mean price in London by 7 percent, and the mean price in Europe by 10 percent. The latter spread is statistically significant at the 5-percent level. The mean price difference is, of course, sensitive to extreme observations. For this reason it is also instructive to calculate the number of times that prints realize higher prices in one market than in the other. For all artists, realized prices for identical prints were higher in the United States than in London for 54 percent of the 661 matched sales, and higher in the United States than in Europe for 55 percent of the 685 matched sales.

The above result, however, is somewhat misleading. In an earlier version of this paper, I had access only to data for the period 1977–1988. In this shorter sample period, there is no tendency for auction prices in the United States to exceed prices realized in London or Europe. Additional tests for the subperiod 1989–1992 confirm that the reported excess of prices in the United States is confined to this later period. [. . .]

There are a number of other results that merit note. The mean price for German Expressionist prints is 14-percent higher in the United States than in West Germany. This finding is contrary to the trade suggestion that prices for these prints are systematically higher in German-speaking countries. For the American artists, however, prices are 30-percent higher in the United States than in Europe and London (combined). This difference is statistically significant. The results for the American artists are interesting on another account. [. . .] The only American artist whose prints are actively sold in Europe/London as well as in the United States is Whistler. For his prints, alone, there is a tendency for prices to be higher in the United States. For the others, there is *only* the U.S. market. This is, of course, consistent with the prediction of the "law of one price": if certain prints are likely to command higher prices in the United States, then sales should occur only in the United States.

There is also evidence that prices are systematically higher at certain auction houses than at others. For the 447 matched sales at Sotheby's and Christie's in New York, prices average 14 percent higher at Sotheby's, and this difference is statistically significant. Dividing the full sample into the 1977–1984 and 1985–1992 subperiods, there is no evidence that this spread is declining over time. In London, by contrast, there is essentially no difference in the prices realized at the two major auction houses. [. . .]

The results for the New York salesrooms of Sotheby's and Christie's are the most puzzling. Unlike price discrepancies that might emerge between the United States and either London or Europe, there is no geographical barrier to arbitrage. Since the buyer's commission at both houses was 10 percent and the seller's commission (for dealers) was 6 percent, the 14-percent spread between Sotheby's and Christie's in New York is not sufficient to allow a dealer to buy profitably at Christie's and sell at Sotheby's. A dealer would have to inventory such prints, while waiting (at the earliest) for the next major sale at Sotheby's. Further, as evidenced by the substantial price variation in the sale of identical prints, such arbitrage would not be risk-free. The obvious incentive for buyers to purchase at Christie's, until average prices are equalized, remains a puzzle.

During the sample period, the number of lots sold at Sotheby's was more than twice the number sold at Christie's. In the trade, the belief is that the larger number of lots in a typical sale at Sotheby's attracts a larger audience of out-of-town and foreign dealers who bid more aggressively in person than when leaving order bids. The larger audience, in turn, is due to the greater likelihood of acquiring inventory, in light of the larger number of prints for sale. From the economic analysis of auctions, it is known that increasing the number of bidders serves to increase the average price if bidders have independent private values. In common-value auctions, where bidders lack complete information about the item's true value, the auction price converges to the true price if the number of bidders is sufficiently large. If the audience were composed exclusively of dealers buying for resale, the common-value assumption might be more appropriate. If so, the greater number of bidders is less likely to explain the higher prices realized at Sotheby's, so long as the number of bidders at Christie's is sufficiently large. At both auction houses, however, there will be some collectors buying for their own use rather than for resale, and hence the private-value assumption may also be relevant. As noted previously, this could help explain the higher prices realized at Sotheby's. The puzzle, however, is just drawn back one step: why do private collectors not eschew Sotheby's in favor of Christie's?

3

THE ITALIAN CITY-STATES

The history of art production and trade in the Italian peninsula is intertwined with the rise of city-states such as Florence, Genoa, and Venice over the course of the fourteenth and fifteenth centuries. These city-states were the earliest centers of the European world-economy. Their wealth and power derived from their location at the crossroads of trade routes between Europe and the East and led to the flowering of culture and commerce known as the Renaissance. The influx of Greek scholars and texts following the fall of Constantinople in 1453 had a significant impact on the increasing sophistication of merchants and bankers. Italian banking families, for example, started to finance trading expeditions around the world, and networks of Italian traders were rapidly established throughout Europe.

At fairs, Italian merchants sold goods, exchanged money, and provided credit. Most importantly, the Italians started to issue bills of exchange, which circulated much like paper money and eliminated the need to travel with large amounts of coins. The most famous of the Florentine banking families, the Medici, achieved its legendary status and power not only by making their bank bigger and more diversified than any previous financial institution but also by becoming major patrons of the arts. The Medici became the model for non-aristocratic patronage that continues to influence collectors today. The Medici palace in Florence, filled with art and costly furnishings, was designed to create an image of dynastic (and Florentine) wealth and taste and to provide an impressive setting for prominent guests, such as the German emperor Frederick III and the Byzantine emperor John Paléologue, as well as other princes of church and state.

In the period between 1620 and 1650 a world economic crisis, the causes of which are still debated, hit Italy hard, and its effects were felt well into the eighteenth century. As a result of innovations in the design of merchant ships, maritime trade had rapidly expanded and privileged northern port cities such as Antwerp, which soon became the new center of all European trade. The reversal of fortune experienced by the city-states—followed by Napoleon's conquest in 1796—prompted large sales of art collections by the Italian aristocracy, and the Italian masterworks of the Renaissance were dispersed across Europe, where they found eager buyers among royalty and nobles as well as the newly prosperous Northern merchants.

RICHARD A. GOLDTHWAITE, *The Culture of Consumption*

Excerpts (pp. 213, 220–21, 229–30, 233, 236–37, 243–45, 252–53) from "The Culture of Consumption," in *Wealth and the Demand for Art in Italy, 1300–1600* (Baltimore: Johns Hopkins University Press, 1993), 212–55. Copyright © 1993 The Johns Hopkins University Press. Reprinted with permission of Johns Hopkins University Press.

Architecture was at the center of the model for secular consumption that emerged in Renaissance Italy. The secular culture of architecture, with its roots deep in medieval traditions of communal culture but also taking much of its nourishment from classical ideas resurrected in the fifteenth century by the humanists, was the foundation on which urban elites literally built their claims to status. More than anything else a palace, now embellished as never before, provided its builder with a focus for establishing a public identity. Although obviously a public art, architecture raises questions about the function of interior space. At the least, the heightened aesthetic appreciation of the public presence of one's home would seem to lead naturally to greater concern for interior arrangements, whatever they might be, to bring the interior up to the level of the architecture. Moreover, since Italians had a fixed residence in a single place, conditions were favorable for the accumulation of goods and for the evolution of furnishings as permanent fixtures, whereas in traditional feudal society furnishings were largely transportable to accommodate the itinerancy of great rural households. Finally, if the patrician palace with its great facade was a public assertion of the presence of its builder, his family, and his dynasty, it also closed off a vast inner world behind; and it would be surprising if the passion for palace building were not also related—as either cause or effect—to a concern for the quality of life people wanted to live within these places. [. . .]

The concept of magnificence was by far the most frequently cited rationale for building in fifteenth-century Italy. The point of departure was Aristotle's notion, found also in Aquinas, that the virtuous use of money consisted in expenditures for religious, public, and private things if they were permanent. [. . .] The humanists took full possession of this classical notion that buildings as permanent private monuments adorning public space assured the fame that great and worthy men seek. [. . .] Building . . . could be rationalized (always echoing classical authors) as the proper expression of one's inner qualities, a moral ace as the measure of a man: "the magnificence of a building," according to Alberti, "should be adapted to the dignity of the owner," and for Palmieri "he who would want . . . to build a house resembling the magnificent ones of noble citizens would deserve blame if first he has not reached or excelled their virtue." [. . .] Moreover, in emphasizing the architectural component of magnificence, [the writers] gave a distinctive Italian sense to a term that traditionally was associated with largess and hospitality; they appropriated a feudal virtue to the urban world. [. . .]

As the locus for a man's concentration of his most luxurious possessions, the [bed] chamber became in the course of the fifteenth century an elaborate decorative ensemble of furnishings, including some of the first secular art forms in a domestic setting. It was a relatively small space furnished with a few major pieces. The principal object was the bed, which consisted of a sleeping platform placed on a low pedestal which might contain storage spaces and served also as a seating bench. Another important piece of furniture was the *lettuccio*, a massive bench serving also as a bed and containing storage space below. Both the bed and the *lettuccio* were display pieces of great prestige, made of wood that could be elaborately carved and decorated in inlay by artists of the stature of Giuliano and Benedetto da Maiano. Other pieces of furniture were great chests and benches, massive forms that complemented the bed and *lettuccio* for their architectonic quality; and the total decorative ensemble of woodwork was rounded out by wainscoting on the walls against which these pieces were placed. There were hardly any smaller pieces of furniture—no chairs, for instance (in the whole of the Medici house in 1418 there were only six); and luxurious stuffs were not part of the permanent decorative ensemble but kept in storage, to be brought out only on an occasion appropriate to their display. [. . .]

[. . .] In the fifteenth century painting appears as decoration applied to chests and beds and inserted into wainscoting; and as decoration subordinated to furniture forms, one had to look downward to floor level to see much of it. When painting finally appeared as an independent decorative object hung on a wall, the frame began its own evolution as a richly carved and gilded condo or *cassetta* that could be made by artists as prominent as the painter himself and could cost almost as much as the picture. Along with its evolution as a physical form, the picture, once it emerged in a domestic setting, became subject to the influence of the entire range of secular culture and took on greater variety in its content and a more highly charged cultural meaning.

With the accumulation of pictures through the sixteenth century, they came to constitute a decorative ensemble in their very quantity, and accordingly the frame receded in importance to a more modest item, often simply painted black or gilded in gold. By the beginning of the seventeenth century many Florentine patricians had dozens and sometimes hundreds of pictures in their houses. A 1626 inventory of Piero Guicciardini lists a total of 230 paintings and 165 sculptures: two-thirds of all these items were collected together in only three rooms, which had little else in them, while the major living rooms had few of these kinds of art objects. [. . .]

The evolution of the Italian world of goods marked something new in the spending habits of the rich. In many respects Italians continued to spend money in the traditional ways. Clothing was still by far the largest category of expenditures; jewelry and plate became more conspicuous items with the passing of time; and expenses for servants, including feeding, clothing, and housing, mounted sharply with the enlargement of residences, the elaboration of furnishings, and (in the seventeenth century) the opening of stables to accommodate coach transport. In all this Italians followed a model the rich had always followed everywhere in Europe. In the course of the Renaissance, however, one distinct new area of material culture opened up—household furnishings; and its expansion included many new forms and a proliferation of varieties within traditional forms. By the beginning of the seventeenth century the house of the rich Italian was a far different place from what it had been three centuries earlier, in the age of Dante and Giotto and of the Bardi and Peruzzi. On the whole it was a much larger and more artistically conceived building, it certainly was filled with many more objects, and these furnishings defined the functions of space more precisely. Here we have the first manifestation of a new kind of consumption of durable goods in the economic history of the West. [. . .]

With the construction and furnishing of interior space from the fifteenth to the seventeenth century Italians created a world in which they could develop a different style of life and in which a new culture came to be defined. This is why so much was spent on objects, why so many new kinds of objects came into existence, why the arts flourished now in the domestic world as they had earlier in the ecclesiastical world. Consumption was a creative force to construct a cultural identity. In inventing all kinds of new furnishings ranging from pottery to paintings, in elaborating their forms, in refining their production, and in organizing them into new spatial arrangements within their homes, Italians discovered new values and pleasures for themselves, reordered their lives with new standards of comportment, communicated something about themselves to others— in short, generated culture, and in the process created identities for themselves. In this cultural development there was a dynamic for change that resulted from the interaction between people and physical objects.

The cultural development that resulted from this interaction is most evident in the process by which these objects acquired the attributes of secular art. The painted picture was probably the highest form of any of the household objects that evolved in the Renaissance. Already in the fourteenth century some religious pictures were transformed into something rightfully called works of art. [. . .]

Moreover, once household furnishings came to be considered as a decorative ensemble, worthy of greater attention and resources, room was made also for yet another transformation of the picture into a secular object, thus opening up an outlet for the visual expression of the expanding secular interests of the times. That the subject matter of much of this secular painting was classical in its inspiration is of secondary importance—had the same development occurred in the north of Europe, painting might have been predominantly chivalric in its subject matter and still had a stylistic development as original and vigorous as it had in Italy. The material conditions of the demand for painting were different in Italy: painting, having already taken on a conscious aesthetic identity in its religious and civic forms, now took on yet another identity that was no less complex than the entire range of secular culture it represented. This happened in Italy partly because the religious tradition in art had both aroused demand by conditioning people to a richer visual culture and stimulated productive forces ready to meet the new demand that arose in the secular world. The reasons this new secular demand arose with greater force in Italy are to be found in the new arrangements for the interior decoration of residences, be they patrician or princely.

The picture, in short, evolved into different things that were not always altogether distinct—a religious object, a household furnishing, a work of art, and a cultural statement; and as its meanings thus became more complex, involving people more intimately with the object, it achieved a cult status. [. . .] It had become a collectible thing sought for a variety of reasons, not the least of which was respect for the artist himself—as the best of contemporary artists (one of the principles of Isabella [d'Este]'s commissions), as one of the great artists of the past (a status first achieved in the later sixteenth century by Raphael and Andrea del Sarto, among others, whose works were sought also in copies), as a member of a school (for example, the Flemish painters collected by the Gonzaga duke of Mantua), as a painter of his own portrait (collected by the Medici), and as a draftsman (collected by Vasari and later by the Medici). A picture therefore came to be charged with a great variety of cultural meanings in the course of this evolution.

Painting was thus a physical object with which its owner established a special identity in the social world—hence, the social importance of patronage. Already in the early fifteenth century humanists—like Poggio, in his dialogue on nobility—cite the example of ancient patrons such as Lucullus and Alexander the Great to promote the patronage and possession of works of art as one way a person can lay a claim to fame. [. . .] By the mid-sixteenth century the proposition had become so much part of the cultural baggage of Italians that Cosimo I could utilize it in order to establish his credentials as a new prince by creating an elaborate myth about the historical mission of the Medici as patrons going back a century to Cosimo il Vecchio and Lorenzo the Magnificent. This political role of art is essential to understand much patronage in later Renaissance Italy. [. . .]

Another consumption habit generated by the accumulation of goods was collecting. Medieval princes, with their passion for displaying wealth as a symbol of power, collected gold and silver objects, jewels, reliquaries, and other luxury goods; and wealthy Italians did the same. In the course of the fifteenth century, however, Italian collections took on a different cast than medieval treasury hoards as the collecting instinct became informed by cultural values other than the traditional ones of wealth and religious piety. The humanists' interest in Roman culture gave rise to a flourishing market in antiquities . . . and the scientific and philosophic interests aroused the instinct to collect all those objects that filled up the virtuoso cabinet of curiosities in the sixteenth century. Such collections represented the humanist ideal of the universal man, with interests ranging from nature to art.

This new passion for collecting was itself an active force for generating demand for many new kinds of things, ranging from medals in imitation of ancient models to porcelain in the search for understanding the secrets of nature; and it was also directed to some of the very objects that now came into production for the first time—such as pictures, for instance, and other so-called artworks. Collecting, in short, followed the same process as consumption in general: an enlargement of the range of objects, refinement and specialization, and finally the reorganization of space into cabinets, studies, and galleries to accommodate it. The passion for collecting that was aroused in the Renaissance was itself a product of a new consumer mentality: it represented not just the objectification of cultural values but the rationalization of possessiveness in an expanding world of goods. [. . .]

The consumer-driven sector of the Italian economy during this period, however, did not take off as it later did in the north once demand began to well up from the lower ranks of society. In Italy the lower classes did not enter the market for household furnishings to the same extent as they later did in the north, although this subject has yet to be investigated. Inasmuch as many of these new consumer goods cost much less than traditional luxury objects, some of these things, such as painted pictures, found buyers correspondingly farther down in the social hierarchy. Inventories of more ordinary people from the fifteenth century onward document how their houses, too, slowly filled up with all kinds of durable goods. [. . .] Demand as it has been described here, however, was largely limited to luxury objects and too confined within a social structure where the enormous wealth of Italy was not widely enough distributed to permit expansion of the mass market for durable goods that began to open up in the eighteenth century.

The growth of consumerism in early modern Europe is not simply a matter of market expansion as measured on a quantitative scale. A veritable consumer culture also emerged in the conscious awareness of the economic potential of expanding consumer markets that surfaced both in government policies and in producer strategies. In Italy, however, such a culture was still inchoate. In the later sixteenth century the grand dukes of Tuscany anticipated mercantilist policy in their efforts to turn the Uffizi into a vast arts-and-crafts center for the production of everything from sculpture and painting to pottery and scientific instruments with the objective of capturing the market for such luxury goods, but otherwise Italian governments seem not to have recognized the possibility of exploiting growing consumer demand to promote economic development.

They did not anticipate the well-articulated economic policies developed by the northern European states in the course of the seventeenth century. The French monarchy took one approach in its effort to capture a new market for itself by establishing monopoly enterprises for production of luxury goods and at the same time promoting the court at Versailles as a consumer model for its products; and in the end it succeeded in setting high fashion throughout Europe. [. . .]

Italian artisans, of course, were not blind to the development of new market strategies. In engendering a proliferation of objects and an increase of their variety—indeed, redefining the very concept of luxury—the new dynamic that came into play in the Italian marketplace opened up incomparable opportunities for producers—from painters, sculptors, and architects to modest potters; and they took the initiative with new ideas to shape taste and so arouse demand yet further, thereby getting a certain control over demand. This is part of the dynamic behind the expanded production that created the Renaissance world of goods. Vasari incorporated these new market conditions in his concept of artistic progress, which he saw as arising out of the artist's struggle for a livelihood, the competition among artists, and the consequent sharpening of their critical faculties. The rise of the status of the artist and the extraordinary vitality of stylistic developments are marks of the success some producers had in seizing the initiative in the market for consumer goods to generate demand. Nevertheless, these strategies were confined to the luxury market.

MICHAEL BAXANDALL, *Conditions of Trade*

Excerpt (pp. 1–5) from "Conditions of Trade," in *Painting and Experience in Fifteenth-Century Italy*, 2nd ed. (Oxford: Oxford University Press, 1988), 1–28. Copyright © 1972/1988 Oxford University Press. By permission of Oxford University Press.

A fifteenth-century painting is the deposit of a social relationship. On one side there was a painter who made the picture, or at least supervised its making. On the other side there was somebody else who asked him to make it, provided funds for him to make it and, after he had made it, reckoned on using it in some way or other. Both parties worked within institutions and conventions—commercial, religious, perceptual, in the widest sense social—that were different from ours and influenced the forms of what they together made.

The man who asked for, paid for, and found a use for the painting might be called the *patron*, except that this is a term that carries many overtones from other and rather different situations. This second party is an active, determining and not necessarily benevolent agent in the transaction of which the painting is the result: we can fairly call him a *client*. The better sort of fifteenth-century painting was made on a bespoke basis, the client asking for a manufacture after his own specifications. Ready-made pictures were limited to such things as run-of-the-mill Madonnas and marriage chests painted by the less-sought-after artists in slack periods; the altar-pieces and frescoes that most interest us were done to order, and the client and the artist commonly entered into a legal agreement in which the latter committed himself to delivering what the former, with a greater or lesser amount of detail, had laid down.

The client paid for the work, then as now, but he allotted his funds in a fifteenth-century way and this could affect the character of the paintings. The relationship of which the painting is the deposit was among other things a commercial relationship, and some of the economic practices of the period are quite concretely embodied in the paintings. Money is very important in the history of art. It acts on painting not only in the matter of a client being willing to spend money on a work, but in the details of how he hands it over. A client like Borso d'Este, the Duke of Ferrara, who makes a point of paying for his paintings by the square foot—for the frescoes in the Palazzo Schifanoia Borso's rate was ten Bolognese *lire* for the square *pede*—will tend to get a different sort of painting from a commercially more refined man like the Florentine merchant Giovanni de' Bardi who pays the painter for his materials and his time. Fifteenth-century modes of costing manufactures, and fifteenth-century differential payments of masters and journeymen, are both deeply involved in the style of the paintings as we see them now: paintings are among other things fossils of economic life.

And again, pictures were designed for the client's use; it was not very profitable to speculate about individual clients' motives in commissioning pictures: each man's motives are mixed and the mixture is a little different in each case. One active employer of painters, the Florentine merchant Giovanni Rucellai, noted he had in his house works by Domenico Veneziano, Filippo Lippi, Verrocchio, Pollaiuolo, Andrea del Castagrio and Paolo Uccello—along with those of a number of goldsmiths and sculptors—'the best masters there have been for a long time not only in Florence but in Italy.' His satisfaction about personally owning what is good is obvious. Elsewhere, speaking now more of his very large expenditure on building and decorating churches and houses, Rucellai suggests three more motives: these things give him 'the greatest contentment and the greatest pleasure because they serve the glory of God, the honour of the city, and the commemoration of myself.' In varying degrees these must have been powerful motives in many painting commissions; an altarpiece in a church or a fresco cycle in a chapel certainly served all three. And then Rucellai introduces a fifth motive: buying such things is an outlet for the pleasure and virtue of spending money well, a pleasure greater than the admittedly substantial one of making money. It is a less whimsical remark than it seems at first. For a conspicuously wealthy man, particularly someone like Rucellai who had made money by charging interest, by usury indeed, spending money on such public amenities as churches and works of art was a necessary virtue and pleasure, an expected repayment to society, something between a charitable donation and the payment of taxes or church dues. As such gestures went, one is bound to say, a painting had the advantage of being both noticeable and cheap; bells, marble paving, brocade hangings or other such gifts to a church were more expensive. Finally, there is a sixth motive which Rucellai—a man whose descriptions of things and whose record as a builder are not those of a visually insensitive person—does not mention but which one is ready to attribute to him, an element of enjoyment in looking at good paintings; in another context he might not have been shy of speaking about this. [. . .]

[. . .] For the moment, the one general point to be insisted on is that in the fifteenth century painting was still too important to be left to the painters. The picture trade was a quite different thing from that in our own late romantic condition, in which painters paint what they think best and then look round for a buyer. We buy our pictures ready-made now; this need not be a matter of our having more respect for the artist's individual talent than fifteenth-century people like Giovanni Rucellai did, so much as of our living in a different sort of commercial society. The pattern of the picture trade tends to assimilate itself to that of more substantial manufactures: post-romantic is also post–Industrial Revolution and most of us now buy our furniture ready-made too. [. . .]

A distinction between 'public' and 'private' does not fit the functions of fifteenth-century painting very well. Private men's commissions often had very public roles, often in public places; an altarpiece or a fresco cycle in the side-chapel of a church is not private in any useful sense. A more relevant distinction is between commissions controlled by large corporate institutions like the offices of cathedral works and commissions from individual men or small groups of people: collective or communal undertakings on the one hand, personal initiatives on the other. The painter was typically, though not invariably, employed and controlled by an individual or small group.

It is important that this should have been so, because it means that he was usually exposed to a fairly direct relationship with a lay client—a private citizen, or the prior of a confraternity or monastery, or a prince, or a prince's officer; even in the most complex cases the painter normally worked for somebody identifiable, who had initiated the work, chosen an artist, had an end in view, and saw the picture through to completion. In this he differed from the sculptor, who often worked for large communal enterprises—as Donatello worked so long for the Wool Guild's administration of the Cathedral works in Florence—where lay control was less personal and probably very much less complete. The painter was more exposed than the sculptor, though in the nature of things clients' day-to-day interference is not usually recorded.

CINZIA MARIA SICCA, *Italian Artists in Sixteenth-Century England*

Excerpts (pp. 1–5, 9–10) from "Vasari's *Vite* and Italian Artists in Sixteenth-Century England," *Journal of Art Historiography* 9 (2013): 1–18. Reprinted by kind permission of the author.

References to works of art or individuals traveling to England are found in Vasari's lives of Benedetto da Maiano, Pietro Torrigiani, Benedetto da Rovezzano, Girolamo da Treviso,

Rosso Fiorentino, Perino del Vaga, Baccio Bandinelli, Bastiano 'Aristotile' da Sangallo, the brothers Davit and Benedetto del Ghirlandaio and their nephew Ridolfo (son of Domenico), Giovan Francesco Penni (il Fattore), as well as in a final, miscellaneous section in the Giuntina edition of 1568 entitled 'Di diversi artefici Italiani' (Of Several Different Italian Artists). This selection is striking for the density of Tuscan artists who . . . appear to have dominated the flux of artistic exchange between the two countries during the sixteenth century. [. . .]

The migration of artists to England, as well as to other European countries, is discussed by Vasari within the general framework of a far-ranging view of the movement of art through time and space, and serves the ultimate purpose of demonstrating the superiority of central Italian art. Writing about artists who had left their motherland and settled anywhere in Europe was, however, hugely problematic for Vasari who had no direct knowledge of the works produced abroad and was thus unable to discuss them in any detail. [. . .] Vasari compensated for his inability to resort to rhetorical descriptions of works of art with greater information about the functioning of the art market, weaving geographic notions about the diffusion of central Italian art into a complex fabric of ideas on the political and economic impact of art. Looking closely at the *Vite* it is therefore possible to discern the outlines of an economic and material history of art which can be verified with cross-references from the archives, and which provides us with a valuable interpretative model for the study of the migration of artists in the course of the fifteenth and sixteenth century. Furthermore, the analysis of the relevant passages in the *Vite* casts light on the sources of Vasari's information, confirming the increasingly received opinion that it is largely the result of collaborative work.

The notion that the arts, especially in Florence, contributed to the support and growth of the city and the state at large emerges from the very first chapter in the introduction to the *Vite*. . . . In the 1568 edition this introduction—whose authorship had not been claimed in the 1550 edition—is loudly announced as being by Vasari himself, though it would seem likely that he consulted with Vincenzio Borghini . . . who in 1550 had assisted him with the writing of the postscript. In a well-known letter of 24 January 1550 Borghini had provided a list of topics that should be emphasized, which included the usefulness of Vasari's efforts. In fact the political and propagandistic potential of Vasari's undertaking had by then been seized upon by Duke Cosimo and his literary advisors who intervened to give a theoretical twist to the *Vite*, turning them into one of the tools through which the Duke could promote the Florentine state.

In this first chapter, entitled 'Of the different kinds of stone that are used by architects for ornamental details, and in sculpture for statues', Vasari (1568, 1:16) described the types of stone used since ancient times and quarried in different regions around the Mediterranean. [. . .]

It is significant that Vasari focused not so much on the marble quarries of Carrara but rather on those of Pietrasanta, a territory conquered by the Florentines in 1484 and returned to them by Pope Leo X in 1513 after brief spells first in the hands of Charles VIII of France, and subsequently of the Republic of Lucca. Even before the promotion they received from Duke Cosimo in terms of protective legislation and technical development, iron-ore mines and the marble quarries found in this area played an important role in the Tuscan economy. Here the merchants from Florence and Lucca intervened to move, sell, and distribute not only the raw material but also the finished sculptures. It seems likely, in fact, that foreign interest in Tuscan Renaissance sculpture was nurtured by the merchant-venturers through the commercialization on the English and foreign markets of small-scale pieces circulated in marble as well as in bronze, so as to make evident the potentiality of reproduction in different materials. This would then have induced the demand for more such products, larger in scale and more easily and cheaply produced in situ rather than shipped all the way from Italy. The shipment of blocks of marble, as opposed to carved pieces, reduced the risk of damage to finished sculptures.

Similar marketing techniques were widespread and not exclusive to the Florentines, as transpires from the lives of other artists; in the 1550 Torrentiniana edition, for instance, Vasari (1568, 3:625) wrote of Simon Bianco, a Florentine sculptor who had moved to Venice, where he had a continuous production of works, such as marble busts that were sent to France by some Venetian merchants. The Milanese Tommaso della Porta, an excellent carver in marble, who counterfeited ancient marble heads sold as antiques, had made twelve very precious life-size heads of emperors, which, after having been retained by Pope Julius III for several months, were acquired for quite a high price by some merchants and sent to Spain (1568, 6:208). [. . .]

Painters . . . moved across Europe supported by merchants: Giovannantonio da Vercelli, known as Il Sodoma, was brought to Siena by some merchants who were agents of the Spannocchi firm (1568, 5:381). It is evident, therefore, that the migration of artists—be they painters or sculptors—could occur only with the backing of merchant-bankers who provided the financial means to undertake such costly and difficult trips, guaranteed a certain amount of work, and in many cases even provided housing in their own company lodgings. [. . .]

In the *Vite* Vasari singled out the types of sculptural works that enjoyed the widest currency in Europe at the time and that could not be supplied like any other luxury good but instead required the presence of skilled sculptors. Royal as well as aristocratic patrons demanded portrait busts and dynastic monuments, forms that both had strong Florentine connotations. The portrait bust in particular had been revived in Florence since the fifteenth century, and at the hands of Donatello, Antonio Rossellino, and Andrea del Verrocchio—to name but a few—it had reached levels of realism, as well as sophistication, that made it a veritable challenge to the achievements of the ancients.

LUKE SYSON, *Leonardo and Leonardism*

Excerpt (pp. 106–9) from "Leonardo and Leonardism in Sforza Milan," in *Artists at Court: Image-Making and Identity 1300–1550*, ed. S. J. Campbell (Boston: Isabella Stewart

Gardner Museum, 2007), 106–23. Reprinted by permission of the Isabella Stewart Gardner Museum, Boston.

Despite a revisionist approach to issues of artists and authorship that has led many art historians to question old myths, often carefully promoted by the artists themselves, of painters and sculptors as inspired and isolated geniuses, Leonardo da Vinci is still frequently discussed as sui generis. [. . .] Studies of his supposed pupils or followers are therefore mainly focused on establishing a distinction between fully autograph expressions of his brilliance and second-rate imitations of his style, for which, it is usually implied, he was never responsible. Such distinctions, however, are not always appropriate; on the contrary, an analysis of the way in which these two categories were, in fact, integrated will allow a better understanding of how Leonardo was employed during his eighteen-year period as court artist in Sforza Milan.

[The] designation—"court artist"—is problematic. . . . Evelyn Welch, for example, has challenged both the category and Leonardo's place within it, emphasizing the fact that Leonardo accepted commissions from outside the court as a means of supplementing his income. [. . .] Martin Kemp has rightly emphasized the fact that, though the duke housed him, there is no evidence for Leonardo as a courtier as such, as a daily member of Lodovico il Moro's entourage. On the other hand, Kemp has republished literary evidence . . . that explicitly posits Leonardo as an ornament of Lodovico's court, suggesting that the artist had developed a publically recognized, mutually rewarding pact with his employer of much the same kind that [Andrea] Mantegna had forged with the Gonzaga family. . . . The irregular payment of salary did not affect the general perception of a highly talented artist as the reflection of the talents of his employer. It can thus be argued that it is only by understanding Leonardo as a court artist—albeit one within the very specific circumstances of Milan—that one can explain his output in the 1480s and 1490s, and that of the many so-called "Leonardeschi."

How Leonardo might have worked within, or even exploited a very specific Milanese mode of art production needs to be understood. . . . Painters working for the Sforza—and for other patrons—traditionally formed ad hoc teams to undertake particular projects, for which they would bid as a team. One or two practitioners . . . may have had prized specializations, but all were expected to execute works that would form visually harmonious wholes; painters' individual styles were therefore apparently suppressed to create a kind of lavish "no-style." [. . .] Most of the artists employed on such projects survive only as names in documents. However, their resolute anonymity is again not necessarily a matter of chance. By eliminating the authorial voices of these individual painters, credit for the magnificence of these works would fall squarely on the shoulders of the patron. And, by working in these groups, one Lombard painter might adopt the motifs and working methods from another, without that latter artist having necessarily been his master, thus forging a common stylistic language—one that might be dubbed *alla Sforzesca*.

The adoption of this system by Duke Gian Galeazzo Sforza . . . is exemplified by the work of Bergognone and his *équipe* at the Certosa [monastery] of Pavia. Bergognone is first recorded there in 1489 and executed his first two chapel altarpieces in 1490 (dated) and 1491 (documented), one of which contains the initials of Gian Galeazzo Sforza (IO.G$_3$) on the throne of Saint Syrus. These paintings, and Bergognone's slightly later *pale*, were all made while Gian Galeazzo remained, at least nominally, duke, and while he was setting up with his consort, Isabella of Aragon, a rival court at Pavia to that of il Moro in Milan and Vigevano. This building therefore, was intended to present and represent both his individual and his familial glory; and indeed, in part because his role as patron has been much underestimated, it has gone unnoticed that his is the only sculpted portrait of a contemporary to adorn the facade. The paintings at the Certosa adhere to a long tradition of Lombard painting. It might legitimately be argued that their style was deliberately shaped to be continuous with the pan-peninsular courtly style associated with the regimes of Naples and North Italy before the midcentury. This stylistic conservatism can hardly be deemed surprising; it can be associated, for example, with the much longer use of the profile formula for portraits than elsewhere in Italy. It is well known that both Francesco Sforza and his eldest son and successor were keen to emphasize a dubious continuity with the earlier Visconti regime, and it seems that there was to be no major rejection of the style of, for instance, late Trecento and Quattrocento Visconti wall painting at the *castello* in Pavia. Indeed, there may even have been attempts to revive it. Gian Galeazzo, in the years around 1490, would have been equally keen to sustain his faltering claim to ducal power by stressing dynastic continuity.

At the Certosa, Bergognone's facial and figural types, developed from earlier generations of Lombard painters, become somewhat schematic, rather repetitive. And, in contrast to Bergognone's small devotional works in which his use of paint is gestural and vivid, his technique in the large-scale Certosa paintings is calculatedly smooth: the junctions between light and shade are less marked; individual highlights are painted with great care; the surfaces of the pictures have an enameled quality, the draperies harder and the color saturated. It is known that Bergognone was not working alone at the Certosa. His brother Bernardino was a constant collaborator, and other names appear in the documents as part of the Certosa company. Although a close examination of the pictures that remain there, altarpieces and frescoes, certainly reveals a variety of hands at work, similarity is much more evident than difference and none of the individual styles of Bergognone's collaborators can—or should—be properly defined. Bergognone's Certosa style was conceived deliberately to enable easier collaboration, developing motifs and a method of execution that could be copied more or less mechanically by others. [. . .]

This, then, was the context into which Leonardo arrived when he traveled to Milan in late 1482 or early the next year, following his eventually successful appeal to Lodovico il Moro for employment. In 1480, Lodovico had grabbed the regency of Milan from the mother of his nephew, Gian Galeazzo Sforza, and he made little secret of his political ambitions. With no legal right to succeed, he based his claim to the Milanese dukedom on his particular and individual virtues as a ruler. These were expressed in a variety of ways, not least, apparently, in his employment of painters. Lodovico il Moro as regent sought out artists with clearly defined and recognizably individual talents. He needed such artists, it might be argued, both to distinguish his activities as a patron from those of his nephew, Gian Galeazzo, and because he seems to have been adopting the model provided by earlier rulers of neighboring city-states, whereby the innate talents of an artist were to be identified with the singularity of the ruler himself.

The first years of the last decade of the Quattrocento saw the climax of the struggle for power between Lodovico and his nephew. In 1492 Lodovico defied the demand of the king of Naples, the father of Isabella of Aragon, to hand over the reins of government to Gian Galeazzo. [. . .] A now celebrated letter of ca. 1490, written by the Milanese ambassador in Florence to the regent, demonstrates [Lodovico's] unequivocal interest in the distinctive individuality of artists' styles: those of Sandro Botticelli, Filippino Lippi, Perugino, and Domenico Ghirlandaio. Perugino's altarpiece for the Certosa, the only one installed . . . by any of these painters, was clearly intended to stand out against the Bergognesque house style, a style that stood for Gian Galeazzo's emphasis on dynastic continuity. This can be read as a deliberate interpolation by Lodovico—a statement of his own individualism. And it is likely that at about this time he realized, albeit perhaps only gradually, that he could make much the same points using artists already in his employ. He had previously secured the services of Ambrogio Preda (or de Predis), who specialized in part as a portraitist, and by doing so he was equipping himself in the traditional mold of a Milanese ruler. However, it was upon Leonardo that he came to rely, a "star" who, partly in his service, had established an Italy-wide reputation.

The nature and extent of the relationship between this patron and his artist during the 1480s is not absolutely clear, and it seems likely that Leonardo was mostly employed in slow progress on the equestrian monument to Lodovico's father, Francesco: the famous *cavallo*. The traditional biography of Leonardo in Sforza service lays great stress on his great, individual virtuoso projects primarily from the 1490s; and indeed, from 1495 to 1497, he executed what can be regarded as almost a manifesto of his artistic philosophy in the *Last Supper* at Santa Maria delle Grazie. These individualist achievements justified Leonardo's place at the top of the Milanese artistic tree, and it should be remembered that the refectory at Santa Maria was treated as an extension of court space, decorated with Sforza arms, where Lodovico dined twice a week. Insufficient emphasis, however, has been laid on the other kinds of works that he did for the duke: great mural decorations at the *castello*, the planning of festivities, acting as an architectural adviser, all part of the established repertoire of a court artist. And two other primary activities appear to be missing. Where, it has been asked, are his portraits of il Moro and his family? And where is the evidence that he made designs for others to follow—in paint or other media?

Leonardo certainly painted portraits of Lodovico's mistresses, Cecilia Gallerani and Lucrezia Crivelli, the former correctly identified with the famous picture in Krakow, probably painted at the same time as the first, Louvre version of the *Virgin of the Rocks*, in the mid-to-late 1480s or very early in the 1490s. This image establishes a model for the Leonardesque portrait. His so-called *Belle Ferronière* in the Louvre, painted on the same wood as the portrait of Cecilia, has had, rather unreasonably, its share of doubters, and skeptics have questioned, again surely unnecessarily, the autograph status of his unfinished Ambrosiana *Musician*. The style and format of these pictures were much imitated, and they seem to have established a local idiom for the portrait in Milan. There survives a whole series of works in which elements of Leonardo's Milanese portraits were imitated by other artists to achieve a particular end result, pictures which, above all, set out to be convincing, both psychologically and, through the use of light and shade, volumetrically. However, it remains to be asked how actively Leonardo and his patron promoted this language of likeness. This question may be answered in part by the proposition that at least some of these portraits may have been regarded as the product of Leonardo. Indeed, in the years just before and after his usurpation of the dukedom, as his ultimate success became more assured, it appears that Lodovico il Moro was able to exploit the long-held expectation that Lombard artists should work together in teams so as to establish the Leonardesque as a new Sforza house style, one that could be identified with his rule and that could be adopted for works commissioned by his courtiers and supporters. Indeed it is at precisely this period, in the 1490s rather than the 1480s, that the Leonardesque takes off in Milan; an individual style was transformed into a collective one, and the artist himself became a kind of multiple.

RICHARD E. SPEAR, *Marketing*

Excerpts (pp. 211–13, 253–54) from "Marketing" and "Di Sua Mano," in *The "Divine" Guido: Religion, Sex, Money and Art in the World of Guido Reni* (New Haven, CT, and London: Yale University Press, 1997), 210–75. Copyright © 1997 Yale University Press.

As a mature artist, Reni clearly tried to avoid conventional contracts and to seek ways to increase his compensation, which, by around 1620, already was high enough to attract attention. Malvasia reports that "only with difficulty could [Reni] bring himself to transact an agreement in person, abhorring the mention of price in a profession in which, he said, it should be obligatory to negotiate on the basis of an honorarium or a gift." Indeed, in 1633 Alessandro Bentivogli advised Carlo de' Medici to give Reni a gold chain so he might work more speedily, since Reni did not . . . set prices for paintings. In principle, Reni agreed with Pino's position that the artist should value honor above payments, and abhor marketing as vile, mechanical, and unsuited to his profession.

To distance himself from transactions, Reni used a whole string of middlemen throughout his career. . . . "It was Guido's practice at times not to put a price on the works he painted for great personages and men of means but rather to give the paintings to them. In this way he received much more for them *than was the custom* or than he himself would have asked" (Malvasia 1841, 47). . . . Reni increasingly tried to rely on *valore di stima*, on estimation of value or worth, not determined by the artist but by the client, *after* the picture was completed. By doing so he was gambling on the *liberalitas* of the wealthy buyer. But unlike his Renaissance predecessors, Reni was not interested in appointing his own appraiser to look out for his interests. He wanted to take advantage of the situation that "a painting in itself cannot have a definitive price" because its value partly "is linked to the patron who owns it and the artist who makes it," to cite the earlier author most concerned with collecting, Mancini (1956–57, I:140). [. . .] Mancini praised this very method of "giving" works of art as ostensible gifts since, to him, it signaled good will, courtesy and honor, though he realized that the results could be inflationary: "through this [way of negotiating] one sees extravagant prices and compensation in the great generosity of some gracious person or prince."

Such a method of remuneration, in which the effect of a work on the client rather than the labor invested in making it decided its value, particularly suited Reni's "second manner" because a sketchy appearance could not easily justify high prices on the basis of time expended. [. . .]

In complete contrast, [Reni's contemporary] Guercino adopted a *prix-fixe*. He measured and determined cost in terms of labor, specified by the number of figures he painted, or by *valore fatica*, the value of the labor expended. His method of pricing privileged manual over mental achievement and reflects a reactionary view of painting that depreciates the importance of artistic invention. [. . .] The fixed-price was approximately 100 ducats for each full-length figure, 50 per half-figure, and 25 for heads. [. . .] Guercino is on record as having said that it *was* precisely the custom, meaning what others charged, that determined his prices. . . .

Reni's approach could not have been more different. He maximized chances for generous remuneration as he developed new ways to control and endanger the supply, which became unstable in a market where there were no real "substitutions" for a "Reni." In economic terms, he upset the supply and demand curves, making it difficult, if not impossible, to calculate prices when there was no inherent value or fungibility. Passeri observed that, far from discouraging demand, Reni's high prices actually increased it. Though Reni complained to Bernini how frustrated he was as he helplessly watched his own work appreciate on the secondary market without personally reaping profits, he still became one of the best paid artists of the century. [. . .]

From the modern perspective of what constitutes an "original" painting, [Reni's] activities . . . will seem puzzling at best, or duplicitous at worst, when the question is posed, "what is an original Reni?" [. . .] The most revealing incident concerns the Annunciation Chapel of the Quirinal Palace, the commission that caused Reni substantial grief with regard to payments and collaboration with Albani. A quite different problem arose when Pope Paul V arrived "at the work site one day after lunch, as he humbly deigned to do every day, and catching Lanfranco there painting the draperies of a certain figure, said that what he had always supposed was now clear: that Guido attached to the operation as much money as he did little work." Presumably Lanfranco told Reni what had happened, since,

> when he returned the next day, (Guido,) contrary to his usual custom, genuflected (which earlier he had been forbidden to do) and humbly requested permission to speak. '*Beatissimo Padre*,' he went on to say, 'the drawing, sketching and background painting are not the things that make up the work. They are just like a simple contract that, before you place your hand on it and sign it, is worthless. In addition to the ideas and designs that are mine, I go over, finish and redo everything in a way that, if a work given to me does not turn out to be by my hand, I will be content to incur your indignation, which would bring me as much grief as, so to speak, the loss of a thousand lives.'

As recounted by Malvasia (1841, II:15), Reni's response set the stage for his later practice given that, already by 1610, an "original" in his opinion was any work he designed and approved of, regardless whether retouchings were added to paintings that were not, literally, "by his own hand." [. . .] When Reni as a youngster copied a *Deposition* by Annibale, the master "was just waiting to be able to point out where it was lacking and to give it a general retouching." Reni's declaration to the pope is also quite like the assurance that Rubens later gave Dudley Carleton (1618) when Carleton complained that he wanted originals from his own hand, not retouched student works. The latter, Rubens insisted, "are not simple copies but are so well retouched by my hand that it would be difficult to tell them from originals."

Reni took a consistent stance. When Cardinal Spada "asked whether Guido would be willing to let him have a copy made of [the *Abduction of Helen*]," the artist responded . . . "I not only entreat Your Eminence to have a copy made of it, but I promise you that, without any profit, I will retouch and finish it all in such a way that it will not have to envy the original." Giacinto Campana made the copy, which still hangs in the Palazzo Spada as a quite pleasing replica, fully in the spirit of Reni. . . . Yet there was hyperbole in the master's guarantee since it, like many of Rubens' studio works, is dryer in brushwork, color, and expression, so it should indeed envy the original.

Reni nonetheless maintained that, through his retouching, pictures by Dinarelli, Sirani and others were transformed into works from his hand. [Here] "hand" has subtler and far more complex meanings than it does today when a painting is said to be from the hand of a modern artist, since now the issue usually is black and white: a work is, or is not, autograph, literally "self-written," at least insofar as it is unfitting to speak of a picture as being "Picasso workshop" or "from the studio of Jasper Johns." In Renaissance practice, however, as in Renaissance contracts, to say that something should be "*fatto di sua mano*"—made by one's hand—can be surprisingly equivocal in light of the apparent straightforwardness of the phrase. Charles Seymour in particular has argued that *fatto di ma mano* might imply moral responsibility equivalent to a notary's "hand" that draws up a contract, rather than signal autograph status. *Mano* in this understanding expresses personal obligation, authorial responsibility, and *fatto* means "to make or to have made," *fare o far fare*, as so many documents of the period read.

FEDERICO ETRO AND LAURA PAGANI, *The Market for Paintings in Italy*

Excerpts (pp. 426–42) from "The Market for Paintings in Italy During the Seventeenth Century," *Journal of Economic History* 72, no. 2 (2012), 423–47. Copyright © 2012 Economic History Association. All rights reserved. Reprinted with the permission of Cambridge University Press.

By the seventeenth century, the Italian market for paintings was characterized by a wide product differentiation: while most paintings from the previous centuries were figurative (mainly of religious, historical, or mythological subject), the raising demand from private buyers induced the production of new subjects (as landscapes, genre paintings, and still lifes beside portraits and battles . . .). Only the best painters were engaged in traditional paintings, especially altarpieces, whose more ambitious compositions could include many interacting human figures.

The market for oil paintings involved a form of price competition among painters. In the main art centers, as Rome, Florence, and Venice, artists were organized in guilds or academies that charged entry fees. A member of the guild could invest to open his own workshop and employ assistants to sell paintings under rules established by the guild. However, these guilds were not very effective at protecting the rents of their members. First, some low-quality or foreign artists did not join the guilds and sold their paintings without following the basic rules decided by the guild. Second, price competition was strong, with painters undercutting each other, adopting different forms of price discrimination, and heavily advertising their works.

Artists were extremely mobile. Italian and foreign artists could easily travel between the main art centers, and painters could receive commissions from distant locations, paint in their own workshop, and send the finished products to the final destination (especially when canvases replaced wood panels as support). Transport costs were low, and tariffs when in place were low enough not to constrain trade. Patrons were willing to hire painters from any provenance as long as they satisfied their tastes. Notice that there were substantial differences between the Venetian style (emphasizing *colore*) and the Central Italian style (emphasizing *disegno*) as pointed out by the art critic Vasari. Therefore, taking into account the mobility of painters and the differences in artistic style, one might conjecture that there were two highly integrated markets, one in the North around Venice and the other in Central Italy that included Rome, Bologna, Florence, and Naples. [. . .]

Large oil paintings required months or even years to complete, even though artists typically worked on several pieces at once with the help of assistants. Most commissions for figurative paintings were formalized in notarized contracts. These contracts, which were enforceable throughout Italy, stipulated the price and the responsibilities of the patron and of the artist. Of course, these contracts were largely incomplete because the main issue, the quality of the paintings, could be observed by the buyer, but it could be neither defined *ex ante* nor verified *ex post*. [. . .]

The price of paintings depended on a variety of factors; . . . those that reflect supply features, those that reflect demand features and those that relate to the incompleteness of the contracts. On the first level, prices should increase with the size of paintings, but in a less than proportional way because of likely economies of scale (any painting would require some time for thinking about the composition and for working on preparatory sketches independently from its size). Another obvious determinant of the price of a painting is the expected quality supplied by each painter, which translates in the aesthetic value as perceived by the contemporary audience: average prices clearly differ across painters.

Other important elements of a commission for a painting were related to the demand side. A crucial factor was the type of the buyers: differences in their willingness to pay may have affected the contracts in place and through them the prices. Another factor is the final position of the painting: the hierarchy of spaces within churches and buildings and the substitutability with competing decorations could affect the willingness to pay and therefore the prices. Finally, multiple commissions may have commanded lower unitary prices as a form of quantity discounts.

There are no deep artistic reasons for making prices depend on the number of human figures in a painting (after controlling for size). Spear and Sohm (2010) do not find wide contractual evidence of an explicit impact of the number of figures on prices. However, prices may have been decided on the basis of the number of figures in verbal agreements or separate notes, and from an economic point of view there could be an efficient rationale for the adoption of prices increasing in the number of figures.

More specifically, the patrons' payoff from a contract for a painting could be seen as the difference between the benefits obtained with the commission and the price paid to the artist. The benefits of the patrons were in terms of display of what was called "magnificence" in front of the contemporary audience, of the high-class elite and, in case of altarpieces, even in front of God. Clearly, the signaling benefits from these ostentatious commissions were positively related to the quality of the artworks. Hence, patrons cared for quality.

However, since quality was not directly negotiable (and verifiable) and it required also costly effort for the painter, moral hazard was a relevant issue in the artist–patron relationship, and patrons had to find ways to obtain high-quality artworks. The solution could be to include in the contract some verifiable and measurable feature of the painting correlated with effort and quality (according to the informativeness principle . . .).

A potential candidate for this was the number of human figures. This was not equivalent to the absolute quality of a painting, but was correlated with it for at least three main reasons. First of all, the subjects of the commissioned paintings were biblical or mythological stories where the variety and complexity of the composition, summarized by the number of players, had a positive, though partial, correlation with effort and final quality. Second, at the time there was a precise ranking in the aesthetic evaluation of subjects (genres), with figurative compositions at the top and landscapes, genre paintings, and still lifes in decreasing order of appreciation. A higher number of human figures was reducing on average the space available for subjects of lower perceived quality, as background landscapes or decorative still lifes, and this was automatically enhancing overall quality. Third, painters were often focusing their own effort on human figures and especially on difficult parts as the heads (where their own style was more easily recognized), delegating less relevant parts (including background decorations, landscapes, and still lifes) to their own assistants. Accordingly, a higher number of figures was a proxy for a wider direct intervention of the main painter in the overall execution, and consequently for higher quality.

However, if it can be taken as given that the number of figures affected quality positively, painting human figures required time and was costly for the painter. Hence, from an economic point of view, making the price of a painting depending on the number of human figures could be seen as a way for patrons to enhance quality by paying indirectly for it.

Indeed, there is evidence that even when a price per figure was not explicitly stated in the contracts, further agreements on the number of figures may have been established in separate notes, letters, or even verbal communications. Most important, we know that pricing by number of figures became a typical procedure during the early seventeenth century in the city of Bologna, where the leading painters Guercino and Guido Reni were able to maintain their high fees justifying them with a commitment to a high price per figure (again, rarely written in contracts but implicitly recognized in many agreements).

Finally, let us consider price differences between different destinations. According to Spear and Sohm (2010, 234–35), anecdotal evidence on the higher prices in richer cities is confirmed by the data on average prices for Venice and minor Venetian towns between the second half of the sixteenth century and the beginning of the eighteenth century. Similar anecdotal evidence emerges for price differentials between Rome and other Italian towns. The common view is that this phenomenon was general: large cities were perceived as paying better commissions and Rome better than all the other cities. However, the high mobility of painters suggests that we should be suspicious of this point of view. Indeed, high price differentials should have induced small town painters either to migrate to large urban centers, or to sell their art there. In any case, mobility should have led prices of similar paintings in different locations to converge. Given the high mobility of painters and paintings, we expect prices to have been similar throughout an integrated region as the Venetian Republic or as Central Italy. [. . .]

To examine the value of commissions for old masters' paintings in the Venetian Republic during the Baroque period, we follow the hedonic price literature, and regress the natural logarithm of the price of these paintings on a set of paintings' and artists' characteristics. The explanatory variables include the size of the painting and its number of figures. Squared size is also considered in order to test for economies of scale. Moreover, we include a set of indicator variables for the paintings' ultimate placement, for the type of patron, and for the final destination. Another regressor is the age of the artists when the work was produced. [. . .]

[. . .] Not surprisingly, larger paintings were more expensive: we find a premium of about 9 percent per square meter. Additionally, the negative and significant coefficient of squared size suggests that there were some scale economies over the range of painting's size. Each figure brought an increase in a painting's price of around 3 percent (we did not find indications of decreasing return to figures). [. . .]

Paintings' price also reflected where they were planned to be placed. Artworks produced for wall decorations in churches were paid much less than altarpieces. A potential explanation . . . is that a large number of substitutes for decorating lateral walls existed (for example statues, bronze decorations, tapestry, and stucco and wood works), especially in churches. Hence, the willingness to pay was lower for wall paintings than for both altarpieces and ceiling that, on the contrary, lacked feasible artistic substitutes (even frescoes were rare in Venice for problems of humidity). On the other hand, we do not find any statistically significant difference between prices of altarpieces and paintings for ceilings. . . . Multiple commissions were paid less, but not significantly so (partially because most were commissions of only a couple of works, rarely more than that). Finally, the final destination of the painting does not appear to affect prices.

SHEARER WEST, *The Gender and Internationalism of Rosalba Carriera*

Excerpt (pp. 46–47, 49–50, 52, 54–55, 62–66) from "Gender and Internationalism: The Case of Rosalba Carriera," in *Italian Culture in Northern Europe in the Eighteenth Century*, ed. S. West (Cambridge, England: Cambridge University Press, 2011), 46–66. Copyright © 1999 Cambridge University Press. Reprinted with the permission of Cambridge University Press.

Investigations of eighteenth-century Italian artists in their wider European context focus on the peregrinations of male painters such as Giovanni Antonio Pellegrini, Sebastiano Ricci, Canaletto and Bernardo Bellotto, rightly stressing their dependence on foreign taste and patronage for their livelihood. In glimpses of the international marketplace that characterised eighteenth-century Europe, the Venetian pastellist Rosalba Carriera (1675–1757) is generally represented as a contrast—a spinster dedicated to the care of her elderly mother; timidly clinging to her home on the Grand Canal; tenaciously producing skillful miniatures and sensuous pastels; yet despite the limitations of familial responsibility and exclusive dedication to 'minor' arts, achieving remarkable international success. [. . .] The reasons why she achieved European notoriety in a period unsympathetic to women practitioners concern not only her gender but a concatenation of social, economic and semiotic factors, which can be unpicked by an examination of her own writings and her art. The contradictions that characterise her private and public roles need to be tested: her international fame versus her domestic persona; her stoicism, spinsterhood and piety in the light of her often erotic pastels and miniatures; her role as an artisan whose output was compared to that of Correggio; her status as a bourgeois businesswoman whose public manner aped the etiquette of the aristocracy. Carriera's internationalism not only provides an insight into the social and commercial spaces of the eighteenth-century art world but also reveals much about the limits of representation and self-representation in a period of war, diplomacy and conspicuous consumption.

Even while Carriera was still alive, it was commonplace for observers to speak of her as someone whose dedication to her family prevented her from leaving her home in Venice. Certainly it is true that she did not settle with a court patron (like Antonio Bellucci), or travel frequently to fulfil large decorative commissions (like Pellegrini). However, it is important not to exaggerate her domesticity. In 1720–1 she spent a year in Paris, having first endured a fairly arduous trip via Livorno to get there; only two years after she returned to Venice, she left again for Modena to accept a major commission from Rinaldo d'Este; and in 1730 she travelled to Vienna to work for the imperial family. [. . .] However, her travels were only differentiated from those of her male contemporaries by the fact that she remained free of the ties of a court annuity, receiving commissions for individual works, or groups of works, rather than accepting a pension or any of the obligations that went with it. [. . .]

[Carriera had] some solid commercial reasons for remaining where she was, which contributed to her success, rather than detracting from it. Her presentation of herself as a weak-willed spinster dedicated to her family ironically allowed her certain freedoms that were outside the reach of her male counterparts. The advantages to staying in Venice were manifold. First of all, during the first half of the eighteenth century, a large proportion of Europe was a battleground with the War of Spanish Succession (1701–13), the Great Northern War (1700–21) and the War of Polish Succession (1733–5) bringing most of the major countries of Europe into a series of labyrinthine disputes about dynasty and territory. Although parts of Italy were spoils in these territorial struggles, Venice remained outside most of the major skirmishes. Carriera's correspondents gave frequent glimpses into the instability of their home cities or countries, occasionally lacing their letters with longing to return or revisit the relative calm of the Venetian lagoon. Secondly, as a centre of diplomacy and tourism, Venice was an attraction to both nobles and connoisseurs. Many of the most attentive and reliable patrons in Carriera's network—such as Crozat, Frederik I of Denmark and a number of English Grand Tourists—met her during their travels through Venice. Carriera's ability to produce small-scale pastels quickly was particularly convenient for visitors who often remained in Venice for only a short time but nevertheless wanted a portrait of themselves as a memento. Thirdly, Carriera's expertise as a miniaturist and pastellist enabled her to conduct much of her business via post and courier; this allowed her greater flexibility than decorative artists who were forced to work on large ceilings or wall paintings *in situ*, often for months at a time. Finally, and perhaps most significantly, Carriera used her Venetian base to construct a persona that helped contribute to her fame by stimulating curiosity about her appearance and character. By staying put, she drew her patrons to her, and those at a distance responded to her not so much as to a living woman, as to a legend or an icon. [. . .]

. . . [Carriera's] diaries are replete with details about payments and expenditure. Not only do they show a person concerned with how much she is receiving for her work, but they also reveal how carefully she invested her income, calculated the interest, passed money on to her sisters and worried about the price of purchasing necessities and luxuries for herself. While expenditure, savings, interest rates and value were of central concern to Carriera's private life, she chose, whenever possible, to avoid direct reference to these motives and preoccupations in her public correspondence. She thereby minimised her status as a money-earning woman, and gave herself instead the role of a paragon working for a higher purpose. [. . .]

To understand the fascination inspired by a spinster artist considered plain by her contemporaries, it is revealing to observe the pseudo-religious language used to describe her and her work. The words 'miracolo' and 'divino'—frequently applied to her skill—contributed to a tendency to allegorise her as a spiritual force, capable of more than an ordinary human being. Many of her correspondents cast their admiration of her work in the form of praise of her miraculous creative power. As one admirer wrote, 'Desiderava una figura dipinta e voi me mandate una conzella vivente,' and he went on to develop an elaborate conceit in which Carriera is brought before the Inquisition for her 'extraordinary heresy' because she 'assumes omnipotence' and creates 'like God with Adam'. The religious language of praise, coupled with the common knowledge of her spinsterhood and hence virginity, gave Carriera an almost saint-like status among her many Catholic admirers, who would have had an implicit belief in the sacred potential of celibate priests and nuns.

This implicit understanding of Carriera's creative force led people to view her as an abstraction, rather than a bourgeois businesswoman. Her iconic status allowed her clients to value her work (and thus their own taste) as something unique and worthy. Her spinsterhood—and by implication her virginity and spiritual power—was accepted as a source of her artistic skill, and it enabled her clients to maintain the fiction that the clearly sensuous and erotic objects she created were somehow untainted by any tincture of lust or desire. [. . .]

[. . .] Carriera was compared frequently to Correggio and Guido Reni, and more than one connoisseur singled out her work when it was hung in *cabinets* among old masters such as Rubens, Veronese and Carracci. In the face of traditions that worked against women artists, she was admitted into the Accademia di San Luca in 1706, and both the Accademia di Santa Clementina in Bologna and the French Royal Academy in 1720. These decisions were made despite the fact she had never travelled to Rome or Bologna, and although she was in Paris at the time of the French Academy's accolade, she was only told about it after the fact. Such accolades were unprecedented for a woman artisan, and they show that academic, social and professional codes could be and were freely subverted during the first part of the eighteenth century. The taste for rococo decoration, which was shared by the Regence bourgeoisie and the Electoral courts of Germany, could accommodate and extol works which were outside academic canons but could nevertheless be seen as equal to the best work of old masters. Carriera's ability to appeal to such a variety of clients drew strength from the consumerism that characterised the nascent commercialism of eighteenth-century Europe. [. . .]

Ironically, Carriera's European success was fuelled by the very instability of national and local economies during the decades of succession disputes. It has become a commonplace to talk of the economy of Europe as a polarised field: with England, France and some parts of Germany entering into a modern form of commercial capitalism, while Prussia, Poland and Russia remained court-based and relied on the caprices of local rulers and medieval taxation systems. [. . .] Carriera's relations with her clients took on this tenor of instability and drew strength from it. On one level she relied on personal contacts, introductions, word of mouth, and competition among courts for her commissions—all aspects of an age-old court patronage system. However, she did not enter into the protection of a single patron, and her dealings, even with her friends, revealed the pragmatic approach of an artist realising that she must compete in a 'free' market and set her prices and conduct her activities accordingly.

It is instructive to see the methods Carriera used to communicate with her clients, her use of middlemen and couriers, and her own occasional action as an agent or intermediary. Nearly all of her commissions for both German and French courts were made through secretaries or other delegates of the princes or electors for whom she worked. By this means, she had regular correspondence with men who had high administrative positions in their respective governments but were also generally respected as educated amateurs of the fine arts. Among these agents were the connoisseur Francesco Algarotti, who acted for Augustus III of Poland; the poet Rapparini for the Elector Palatine; the collector Crozat for the Regent and King of France, and many others. Their letters to her, and hers to them, give the impression of her feverish working pace and her ability to juggle the commissions of several clients at once. Not only did she work for remote princes and electors, but she punctuated longer term commissions by hastily produced pastels of Grand Tourists who passed through Venice. Occasionally, she would inform the member of one court of the work she was doing for a rival court, but even without her admission, it is clear that rival courts were competing to have her to themselves. The fact that she resisted any single association gave her a commercial freedom and forced clients to compete for her services on the open market. [. . .]

[. . .] Carriera usually charged a standard price of 50 zecchini for a miniature and, depending on the size, 20–30 zecchini for a pastel. However, to a certain extent, such a fixed price was meaningless in a fragmented international market, where there were as many currencies as there were princes. Payment was made to Carriera variously in louis d'or, pistoles, zecchini, lire, ungari and sequins. Although it was easy to exchange currencies in a commercial center such as Venice, the instability of exchange rates for such a plethora of currencies must have made Carriera's 'fixed prices' approximations rather than firm charges. There were also minor fluctuations, even within this band of charges: in one year, 1724, she was paid variously 10, 18, 22 and 30 zecchini for different commissions. By remaining where she was, Carriera had to contend with such variations in the currency of her payment, but the balance of strong and weak currencies must ultimately have been more beneficial to her than reliance on a single, fluctuating regional currency might have done. The unpredictable depreciation of regional currencies caused problems for other Italians who relied on a single court patron for their livelihood.

However, while Carriera's stable base allowed her to pool a variety of currencies into her various investments, it also forced her to make use of agents, middlemen and couriers, as well as a postal system disrupted by war and plague. The agents deputised to communicate with Carriera sometimes visited Venice and looked in on her to see how her work was progressing, but more frequently she and they relied on couriers to carry pastels, miniatures and money from place to place. Such a system worked surprisingly well but was inevitably disrupted by lost works of art, delayed payments and sluggishness in communication between artist and client. Such communications also added additional layers to otherwise simple business transactions, which Carriera experienced in a different light when she acted as an agent for the Elector Palatine's purchase of two pictures from the sale of the Gonzagas' picture collection. [. . .]

The systems in which she worked—informal and unstable as they were—contributed to her success, as she was able to capitalise on both the rivalries of court patrons and the full pockets of English Grand Tourists without the necessity for travelling herself. Her own dealings with money were shrewd but conducted informally, within the family and with the help of family friends such as Carlo and Gabriele Gabrieli, who oversaw some of her investments. [. . .] She undoubtedly used her unique position to her advantage. The lack of a clear taxation system for a woman in her position was only really questioned over a decade after her death, when Andrea Memmo, a government official, noted the need to investigate how women artists were taxed.

BERNARD BERENSON, *Letters to Isabella Stewart Gardner*

Excerpts (pp. 158, 288) from *The Letters of Bernard Berenson and Isabella Stewart Gardner, 1887–1924*, ed. R. van N. Hadley (Boston: Northeastern University Press, 1987). Copyright © 1987 by Rollin van N. Hadley. Reprinted with permission of University Press of New England, Hanover, New Hampshire.

5, Via Camerata, Florence   Nov. 3, 1898

Dear Mrs. Gardner,

I enclose a photograph of a panel whereon is painted the profile of a youth life size. The painter is no other than perhaps the very mightiest of all Florentine painters Masaccio. If you have my little book on the Florentines handy read what I have said about him there. As there is no public gallery in Europe except Berlin which has anything by him at all, and Berlin has unimportant things, you can imagine how priceless he is. Fortunately I am the first person with knowledge who has seen it. The owner has no precise idea of its value. Consequently a picture that under other circumstances one might be happy to pay four or five thousand pounds for can be had for 10,000 *Lire*: So, if you want it, please cable immediately Berenson, Fiesole YESACCIO. Then send shipping orders, and the cheque. If you don't mind please send a draft for £400 on London, for exchanges on Florence are a curse both to him who giveth and to him who receiveth. What is left over from this after deducting expenses, I will keep for you.

Yours in haste, B[ernard]. B[erenson].

.   .   .

[Interlaken]   May 31, 1902

Dear Mrs. Gardner,

[. . .] Just as I was leaving Italy the parliament of that noble land passed a law. Happily you have garnered in your treasures, so that you will not be greatly affected. The law is this: Every house shall be searched for works of art. These works of art shall be divided into two classes. The first class can under no circumstances be sold out of the country. The second only on payment of 20% of the value as export duty. No one may sell at all, even within the country, without first getting a permit from the government. Contravention will be treated as a penal offence, punished not only with fines but even imprisonment.

The result will be of course to raise enormously the price of Italian pictures that no longer are in Italy. But it is hard on people like myself who have put their savings into pictures and kept them in Italy. True, I have bought them to keep, but at the same time, felt that [at] a pinch I could sell. Now that has been rendered difficult or impossible.

But you see how wise you were to buy as you have done. Your Italian collection is nearly complete. It is now time to supplement it with a few great fifteenth-century Flemings and Germans. The difficulty however is to get hold of them. The Berlin people, both public and private, are always ready to pay any price for them. [. . .]

Yours ever devotedly, B[ernard]. B[erenson].

4

ANTWERP

Since the Middle Ages the cities of Antwerp and Bruges had already been centers of trade in fish, salt, and oats; in English wool; and in exchanges of all kinds with merchants throughout Europe. Then at the end of the fifteenth century, a series of fortuitous storms deepened the Scheldt River around the port of Antwerp, making the city accessible for increasingly large merchant ships coming from around the world. As a result, Antwerp took over from the Italian city-states as the new center of the European world-economy and soon attracted merchants from all over Europe, nearly doubling its population in the sixteenth century. Cargo ships arrived filled with merchandise and would set sail again laden with popular low-cost Netherlandish art produced in Antwerp's workshops. Visual evidence of this wide distribution of prints, paintings, and altarpieces can still be found in monasteries and museums in Spain and Latin America.

The production of movable works of art was as central to the development of markets in Antwerp as the conduits for selling these works of art—the major fairs and markets that sprang up around the lively port. By the mid-sixteenth century, Antwerp had become not only the largest center for trade and the exchange of capital north of the Alps, but also Europe's premier center for printing and publishing. The international merchant city—known for its tolerant religious climate—attracted printers from all over, including Christophe Plantin from Paris. In 1555 Plantin founded his press, Officina Plantiniana, in Antwerp, where he published 2,450 titles in multiple languages in just thirty-four years. For the art trade, Hieronymus Cock's publishing house, Aux Quatre Vents, played an important role in the spread of Italian High Renaissance art throughout northern

Europe by publishing engravings after the work of leading Italian painters. Cock published even greater numbers of prints made after paintings by artists from the Low Countries, which in turn were widely distributed across the world, informing a growing base of art collectors.

Antwerp's prosperity declined in the last three decades of the sixteenth century owing to the increasingly fractious relationship between the Spanish Habsburg Empire, of which it was part, and the northern Dutch provinces. In 1558, the Spanish took over the port of Antwerp. In the course of their war with Spain, the Dutch successfully and permanently blockaded the Scheldt in 1585, closing off the source of Antwerp's commercial and industrial greatness.

MARYAN W. AINSWORTH, *The Business of Art: Patrons, Clients, and Markets*

Excerpt (pp. 33–35) from "The Business of Art: Patrons, Clients, and Art Markets," in *From Van Eyck to Bruegel: Early Netherlandish Painting in the Metropolitan Museum of Art*, ed. M. W. Ainsworth and K. Christiansen (New York: Metropolitan Museum of Art, 1998), 23–37. Copyright © 1998 by the Metropolitan Museum of Art, New York. Reprinted by permission.

Over half the collection of early Netherlandish paintings at the Metropolitan Museum originated in either Bruges or Antwerp, the two principal centers of commerce and art of the Netherlands in the fifteenth and sixteenth centuries. Furthermore, the major artists of these cities are well represented in our holdings. Thus the museum collection provides numerous and key examples of works that reflect the changing relationships of clients, art markets, and artists in a period of transition. A brief look at the relationship of these artists to their clients and an examination of marketing strategies illuminates the development from a privileged ducal patronage to mass-market sales. [. . .]

One of the largest cities in Northwestern Europe and the most prominent commercial center of its day, Bruges by 1470 had some forty thousand inhabitants. Not only the active court life and the wealthy entourages of the dukes contributed to the city's economic health; it was nourished as well by the exceptionally prosperous and broad commercial middle class of Bruges together with an unusually large group of resident foreign merchants. The foreign community was extremely well established, with its own corporate buildings, chapels for regular religious services, and private living quarters. Its members were concentrated in three marketplaces north of the Groote Markt: the Italians lived around Beurze square, the Iberians at Biscay Square, the Scots and English in nearby streets, and the Hanse, or Germans, just beyond them. The clustering of these closely knit groups in one general area facilitated both trade and artistic exchange.

It is no wonder, then, that the city attracted artists from other regions. None of the succession of leading Bruges painters of the fifteenth and early sixteenth centuries—Jan van Eyck, Petrus Christus, Hans Memling, and Gerard David—was a native of the town. Except for Van Eyck, these émigré artists were not attached to the court or provided with a steady pension from the city, and, as a consequence, commissions from the growing and newly wealthy bourgeoisie were key to their economic success.

To a significant degree the regulations for the Corporation of Image Makers provided protective measures to help ensure the livelihoods of panel painters. It was necessary to have citizenship by birth or long residence or to purchase it to become a member of the guild, a requirement instituted for the purpose of controlling production. Bruges masters were allowed to exhibit and sell works only at the city's annual art fairs and one other place, usually their shops. Further restrictions were put in place to eliminate competition. For example, the cloth painters were ranked as separate from and inferior to the panel painters. (This held true even though painting on canvas was a major industry in Bruges, the chief center for its production until about 1530, where it was practiced by roughly 40 percent of artists in the fifteenth century.) In lawsuits between the two groups, the standing regulations that were challenged clearly favored the panel painters: cloth painters were not allowed to exhibit openly for sale, nor were they permitted to paint in oil. [. . .]

Within this tightly controlled guild system, how did individual artists secure their own share of the business of painting? A close look at the stylistic development of artists in Bruges and Antwerp reveals an important strategy, which has been little discussed: they catered to the clients whose patronage they sought by accommodating their presumed or stated aesthetic concerns and expectations. In Bruges, the prominence of foreign businessmen—especially Italians and Spaniards—who had a considerable amount of disposable income was a determining factor in the evolution of this strategy and, by extension, the style of panel painting.

The leading painter in Bruges in the mid-fifteenth century, after Jan van Eyck died and before Hans Memling arrived in the city, was Petrus Christus. Significantly, nearly half of his small oeuvre was commissioned by Italians, has an Italian or Spanish provenance, or was early on copied by southern painters and sculptors. It is not surprising to find that Christus appears to have appealed to the taste of his potential clients by adjusting his style to suit them. He moved toward implementing a one-point perspective scheme, a feature already fully in use in Italy and perhaps one that his Italian clients expected to see in his work. Christus also echoed Italian modes by employing the *sacra conversazione* format in at least one picture, *The Virgin Enthroned with Saints Jerome and Francis*, and attempting to reduce and monumentalize form in certain of his Virgin and Child paintings. In what could well have been an astute business move, Christus joined the Confraternity of Our Lady of the Snow by 1467–68 and the Confraternity of the Dry Tree by 1469. The former counted among its many members Charles the Bold and Isabella of Portugal, as well as numerous aristocrats; all the Burgundian dukes were honorary members of the latter, which also included individuals from Bruges's most important upper-class families and in particular a large group of notable foreign merchants (the Portinari, Tani, Altoviti, Ricasoli, Villani, Cavalcanti, Arnolfini, and Cenami from the

Italian community and the Gonsales, Loupes, de Castro, and Pardo families among the Spaniards).

Hans Memling received most of his commissions from native and Italian residents of Bruges, fewer from the Spanish community, and still fewer from the English and Germans who lived in the city. He effectively cornered the market in portraiture, which constituted a significant portion of the trade in paintings. . . . His ability to combine a striking verisimilitude with a certain idealization that conformed to the expectations of his sitters guaranteed Memling a prosperous business in this genre. This is an approach epitomized in his portraits of Tommaso Portinari and Maria Baroncelli, which convey the elegance of the courtly lifestyle to which his clients aspired. He seems to have attempted a pleasing conflation of northern and Italian modes of presentation in his portraits—juxtaposing an Italianate monumentality and simplification with a northern sense of atmosphere and light in a format that often placed his subjects before a charming, locally inspired landscape background. Perhaps in a further nod to Italian taste, Memling used decorative embellishments consisting of swags and putti to a number of his paintings of the Virgin and Child Enthroned. Commissions executed for major local patrons, in particular the altarpiece *Saint John the Baptist and Saint John the Evangelist* of 1479, made for the main altar of the Sint-Janshospitaal in Bruges, encouraged orders from other customers. Impressed by the grandeur of Memling's conception for the picture and by its prestigious location, they requested more modest variations, with the addition of their images as donors.

DAN EWING, *Marketing Art in Antwerp*

Excerpts (pp. 559–61, 563, 565, 574–75, 577–81) from "Marketing Art in Antwerp, 1460–1560: Our Lady's *Pand*," *Art Bulletin* 72, no. 4 (1990): 558–84. Copyright © 1990 by Dan Ewing. Reprinted by kind permission of the author.

The growth of the Antwerp art trade was a function of the city's expanding economy, especially during the sixteenth century. The sale and exportation of luxury goods was one of the distinguishing features of the Antwerp marketplace, which for about seven decades (1501–68) reigned as the commercial and financial capital of the European world economy, a position it had wrested from Venice. The basis of Antwerp's commercial life was its biannual fairs. . . . Typically, the fairs lasted six weeks each, though this sometimes varied greatly. Fairs were "free" markets used by foreign merchants and local and regional craftsmen, who displayed their goods at stalls set up in streets, squares, cloisters, *halles*, *panden*, and shops throughout town. Vendors selling the same goods customarily congregated in the same locations. *Pand* markets were the extension of this principle.

By the 1480s, the scale of Antwerp's fairs was so great that German merchants were claiming they had surpassed the fairs of Lyons, their chief rival. A more concrete indication of the fairs' growth was the constant pressure to prolong their duration and to practice flexibility in their scheduling. As early as 1465, the city announced its intention of becoming a permanent fair market, and between 1468 and 1520 it repeatedly extended fair times, over the loud objections of Bruges. By the second quarter of the sixteenth century, Antwerp had essentially become a permanent market. Although the fairs continued to be held, they were important mainly as times of payment for transactions occurring year-round.

One of the distinctive features of the Antwerp fairs was the proliferation of specialized markets. [. . .] Although today the medieval *pand* is often identified either as a monastic cloister or an arcaded courtyard . . . in Antwerp the term was applied to specialized salesrooms in a variety of types of buildings or spaces. A *pand* could be located as readily in an existing house, a new building, or a commercial exchange as in a cloister or courtyard. [. . .] Most *panden* were specialty markets serving the luxury trade.

The earliest reference to uncommissioned art being offered for sale at the Antwerp fairs comes from the *Chronicle of the New Church* in Delft, which records the visit of an out-of-town "artist and master" who stopped in Delft several years before 1411 while en route to the fairs of Antwerp and Bruges to market his works, one of which was a sculptured *Pietà*. [. . .] By the 1440s the Medici were instructing their agents in Bruges to go to the Antwerp fairs to buy paintings and tapestries, which they did and shipped to Florence in sacks of wool for protection. [. . .]

Aside from their precocity, what is so remarkable about the early Antwerp art outlets— Our Lady's *Pand* among them—is their demonstration of how fully the marketing of art preceded its making in Antwerp. The city did not begin to emerge as a major art center until the final decades of the fifteenth century, which is to say that Antwerp was already well established as the principal Netherlandish art market long before it was a significant center for art production. For most of the fifteenth century, Brussels was an important supplier of the art offered on the Antwerp market. [. . .] Braudel (1984, 34) reminds us that the priority of merchandizing over production was, in general, normative in the Antwerp marketplace, which he characterizes as a "bring and buy centre . . . to which everything came from the outside." [. . .]

. . . Our Lady's *Pand* was organized and operated by the Church, but unlike its predecessors, it was the first art market in postclassical Europe to be housed in a building specially constructed for the specific purpose of art exhibitions and sales. In that sense, Our Lady's *Pand* can be regarded as the first authentic art salesroom. Moreover, the construction of a large, new building involved expenditure and financial risk in a way that the adaptation of a cloister did not, making the erection of Our Lady's *Pand* a good indication of the economic significance and expected return on investment that the market for art had achieved in Antwerp by 1460. The *Pand* was further distinguished by being located physically apart from the structure of its sponsoring church. It stood autonomously, as an independent showroom, more like a secular *halle* than a monastic *pand*. Finally, it was the largest centralized art market of the period, exercising monopolistic control of sales, by the Antwerp and Brussels Painters' Guilds, at fair time. Until its eclipse in the 1540s by developments in Antwerp itself, Our Lady's *Pand* was the premier public art market in Europe. [. . .]

To the extent that [stall] rental income is an accurate index of the level of exhibition activity, [the] statistics indicate that art was the preeminent growth industry at the fair markets run by the church during the period 1465–1540. The quantitative data, especially the evidence they reveal of a dynamically expanding sixteenth-century market, complement the traditional qualitative appraisals of the growth and scale of the Antwerp art trade. Moreover, to a remarkable degree, the periods of growth and decline in *Pand* income coincide with periods of expansion and contraction in the Antwerp economy as a whole. [. . .] Interestingly, revenues at the church's other fair outlets show relatively little relation to the cycles of the larger economy. With only limited information available about these markets, it is not clear why this should be the case, but it seems safe to conclude that, in comparison to the products retailed at the church's non-*Pand* outlets (furs, gloves, parchment, animal skins, general merchandise), the demand for art goods was relatively robust. [. . .]

The range in quality and type of art exhibited at Our Lady's *Pand* is likely to have been great. Some vendors undoubtedly were minor craftsmen; others . . . were successful Antwerp artists of some standing. The one documented sale of a specific work at the *Pand*, the Keldermans' altarpiece purchased by Averbode monastery, was large—eight feet—and expensive. Its price of twenty-one and three-quarters Brabant pounds was the equivalent of half the purchase price of the painter Ambrosius Benson's house and garden in Bruges, or almost three years' salary for an Antwerp laborer. [. . .] Exhibited side by side with such works . . . were the crucifixes and small *Jhesusbeelden*—and, one assumes, cheap woodcuts and popular broadsides—that also constituted the offerings at the *Pand*. Many of the paintings may have been the less expensive (and more portable) works on fabric, if subsequent inventories at the New Bourse are any indication. Finally, it might be conjectured that part of the *Pand*'s retailing included the sale of copies and forgeries, at least by mid-sixteenth century. By the second half of the sixteenth century, the proliferation of forgeries of works by Quinten Metsys and other famous, deceased Netherlandish painters had become such a problem in Antwerp—the ironic success of producing for the market—that the city magistrates passed an ordinance prohibiting the forging of paintings. [. . .]

The gradual decay of Our Lady's *Pand* as an art salesroom . . . was due in part to a fundamental re-centering . . . then underway in the Antwerp marketplace. In 1532, in what proved to be a decisive event, the New Bourse opened. It was the first exchange in Europe to be truly international, built for the use of merchants of all nations. [. . .] It combined financial, wholesale commodity, and retail luxury markets under one roof. As a new kind of commercial and banking center, the Antwerp Exchange created an enormous sensation; indeed, subsequent exchanges in London (1566) and Amsterdam (1608) were modeled on it.

Erected just off the Meir, the Bourse was located outside the established city center—literally *extra muros*, although the fourteenth-century walls were no longer standing. In 1540 the city opened a Painters' *Pand* or *Schilderspand* in the second-floor gallery of the Bourse, and in 1553 a large new Tapestry *Pand* was constructed on the other side of the Meir in the Schuttershoven. Artists, dealers, and publishers settled in the newly prominent neighborhood, and by mid-century the Meir had become the new business center of gravity in Antwerp and the Meir-Schuttershoven axis had emerged as the new locus of Antwerp art marketing.

CHARLOTTE HOUGHTON, *Pieter Aertsen's* Meat Stall *as Contemporary Art*

Excerpts (pp. 277, 281–85, 290, 294) from "This Was Tomorrow: Pieter Aertsen's *Meat Stall* as Contemporary Art," *Art Bulletin* 86, no. 2 (2004): 277–300. Reprinted by kind permission of the author.

[With *The Meat Stall*, painted in Antwerp in 1551, Pieter Aertsen] turned a millennium of artistic convention inside out by bringing objects forward to dominate human actors: the picture's vivid display of freshly butchered meat (a subject unthinkable previously in panel painting) all but obscures a tiny background scene of the Flight into Egypt, and the largest person on view is smaller than a sausage. Art historians have granted *The Meat Stall* canonical status as the initiating work in not just one but several genres: market paintings, "inverted" morality pictures, paradoxical encomiums, and—ultimately—the entire field of modern still life, in which it enjoys a half page (color) in H. W. Janson's *History of Art*. This notoriety, however, carries disadvantages. [. . .] Indeed, it is impossible for a specialist to approach *The Meat Stall* today without an awareness of its niche in the tradition and the formal trajectories that proceed from it. [. . .] [Therefore] I will consider this picture when it was—emphatically—alone of its kind.

Aertsen's painting has generated many (often conflicting) art historical interpretations. Some have contended that its subject matter is resolutely secular, while others have read in it a sacred, indeed, Eucharistic message. While many have argued that its tone is moralizing, a few have described it as unabashedly festive, even Rabelaisian. Scholars have found sources for its imagery in authors as diverse as Pliny, Desiderius Erasmus, Saint Augustine, Martial, Juvenal, and Saint Luke. One reason that *The Meat Stall* can support such varying interpretations may be the total absence of surviving documentation concerning its original function or meaning. No records have come to light concerning its patronage. No inventories or eyewitness accounts offer the slightest clue about its initial location. On the other hand, visual evidence attests to the painting's immediate success: at least four virtually identical versions are extant, located today in Raleigh, North Carolina, Uppsala, Amsterdam, and Maastricht. While comparative scientific analysis may one day further clarify their relationship, visual examination indicates a similarity of facture suggesting near-contemporaneous production for at least three. *The Meat Stall* thus appears to have generated additional orders for Aertsen; in any case, it coincided with a turning point in his career. When he painted it, Aertsen was over forty and had been a guild member for sixteen years. Yet only four works can be securely situated in his oeuvre before *The Meat Stall*, while close to fifty are recorded or extant from after it.

The Meat Stall represented more than a new initiative in Aertsen's career; it was a radical departure in art making altogether. In an era when an artwork's valuation often hinged on the subtlety of its dialogue with convention, *The Meat Stall*'s reception was predicated instead on the way it broke the rules, confounded expectation, and even irreverently thumbed its nose at social and artistic pieties. At a time when artworks fulfilled a relatively definable array of functions, this picture correlated comfortably with none of them. For a work of its importance (a large-scale panel painting), its reference system appears singularly and explicitly topical. [. . .]

What first arrests attention in Aertsen's image is the meat. Great bloody hunks of it press outward from the picture plane, impinging on audience space with carcass parts and dripping viscera—a pig's body, cleaved in half and gutted; a marbled haunch; a lung strung up by a ragged windpipe. Just below, a freshly skinned ox head, looking chillingly alive, stares reproachfully at the viewer. The effect of abundant raw flesh is intensified by Aertsen's repeated use of red around the image: the painted post, the roof tiles and brick walls, the cloak on the bending figure's torso (itself eerily liver-shaped)—all conspire to heighten the presence of meat, even where it is absent. Aertsen portrayed the properties of the animal flesh itself in exquisite sensory detail: the translucence of tripe extruding slime; the soft, bloody muscle of a severed joint; the silken shimmer of cooling, just congealing animal fat, contrasted with the chalkiness of rendered suet. [. . .]

The Meat Stall is a synesthetic banquet that invokes not just vision but also taste, smell, and touch. To keep one's eyes on the picture is to feel one's skin implicated in the process as well, which may be why some viewers—professional as well as lay—are inclined so swiftly to look away. In savoring painting, it is one affair to submit oneself imaginatively to the tactile values of Gerard Terborch's satins and silks, to the velvety petals of Jan Brueghel's irises, or to the downy ermine that edges a Van Eyck cloak. It is quite another to probe the surfaces of Aertsen's display—the rubbery furrows and protuberances of gelatinous guts and organs, the clamminess (or worse, lingering warmth) of freshly butchered meat. These are not sensations that are normally aestheticized, or on which viewers would ordinarily linger. The longer one dwells on them, the more discomforts they evoke, moving beyond the physical to the psychological—from that unblinking

oxen eye, which seems to accuse the viewer (me, you) of complicity in its dismember-
ment, into an anthropomorphic territory of disturbing identification. It is far less threatening to study the memento mori in all manner of arcane languages than to be reminded,
somatically, of the death of the flesh before one's eyes.

Admittedly, meat stuffs in this form and profusion would have been a familiar sight
in sixteenth-century Antwerp, one of the northern epicenters of what nutritional historians call "carnivorous Europe" to describe a two-hundred-year period of highly elevated
(and virtually universal) urban meat consumption. Forthright display of body parts was
common practice in the stalls of early modern butchers, who placed heads, entrails, and
trotters on open view, for purchase by consenting consumers. In the butchers' hall, such
objects would be viewed without a second thought. It was neither this subject matter per
se nor the frankness of its exhibition that would have shocked an audience in 1551.
Rather, it was its utterly anomalous—indeed, unthinkable—locus: within a picture
frame. [. . .]

In 1551 . . . there was nothing to prepare Aertsen's audience for his exuberant, large-scale
portrayal of meat in all its bloody materiality. Moreover, Aertsen's viewers had never seen
an image that so relentlessly privileged *things*, while it so diminished the prominence of
human figures. For all the subsequent art histories that have proclaimed *The Meat Stall*
the first still life of modern times, this genre simply did not exist—was not a concept—in
1551, and this picture wasn't one.

It is important to note, too, that because the picture was not a still life, the items in it
retained their fullest specificity—in other words, they had not yet become generic
"objects," a class of inanimate articles that would become the subject matter for a definable branch of painting. It was not "a meat picture." The resonances that Aertsen's meat
evoked in his audience came not from the realm of art . . . but rather from other areas of
life. And in 1551, one set of associations this image offered Aertsen's viewers was
extremely topical. Meat was then at the center of a heated legal and economic contest,
which, in turn, exemplified broader civic tensions. These social and political resonances
therefore provided at least one starting point for the audience in parsing meaning from
the picture. [. . .]

From 1503 to 1551, while Antwerp's population doubled to 100,000, the number of butchers' stalls remained fixed. The Vleeschouwers' [Butchers' Guild] connection to the
emperor lent them prestige, and their modern hall advertised their success. With a closed
membership feeding a rapidly increasing (and meat-hungry) population, the butchers
might have anticipated a healthy share in Antwerp's growing prosperity. Instead, they
encountered unexpected problems. [. . .]

The Vleeschouwers' most implacable adversary . . . was not a cartel of suburban meat
cutters, nor even a potentially fickle ducal court. It was the deeper metamorphosis at work

in Antwerp's urban economy. This raised their predicament from the particular to the emblematic. [. . .]

Increasingly, the interests of individuals and groups with significant local investments, such as retail merchants and food producers . . . diverged from those of financiers and international merchants. The Vleeschouwers marketed goods for local consumption, based in an agrarian economy. The meat and animal byproducts they produced were perishable, unfit for long-distance trade; they were not among the items bought low and sold high in international markets. [. . .] The very growth that once had promised the Vleeschouwers increased prosperity gradually undermined their traditional civic status. [. . .]

If [these] topical references diminish *The Meat Stall*'s universality as a work of art, they in equal measure increase the aura of ingenuity that must have attended it in Antwerp in 1551. For the savvy viewer, the image's implications in its time and place offered multiple levels of pleasure. Aertsen presents in the work a series of signs requiring the application of the esoteric (in this case, local) knowledge . . . with its attendant sense of power. By invoking special knowledge, Aertsen also created and exploited a split between two potential viewing publics—one informed, the other not—thereby forging a sense of conspiracy and a knowing subculture of insiders, who, in turn, could enjoy their privileged position vis-à-vis the uninitiated. [. . .]

[. . .] Aertsen understood that Antwerp's artistic dynamism was itself a function of the city's rapid growth and transformation. Changing social and religious structures and an increasingly open market encouraged artistic experimentation and the development of new types of imagery. Capital accumulation, rapid circulation of wealth, the surge in population with its consequent home construction—all fueled painting consumption. The disruptive economic and social climate on which *The Meat Stall* commented also, in large measure, created the license for its own transgressive form and the precondition of its existence. Pushing the artistic envelope, Aertsen admitted full complicity in this process.

LARRY SILVER, *Second Bosch*

Excerpts (pp. 31–32, 43, 48–50) from "Second Bosch: Family Resemblance and the Marketing of Art," *Nederlands Kunsthistorisch Jaarboek* 50 (2000): 31–56. Reprinted by permission of Koninklijke Brill NV.

In his own century, Hieronymus Bosch continued to have great commercial success, even long after his death. Not only did his paintings attract the attention of avid collectors, led by King Philip II of Spain, but copies after his works and even forgeries flooded the art market, particularly in the busy port and commercial *pand* of sixteenth-century Antwerp. Much more research remains to be done into the quantitative aspects of this popularity, and the database of inventories from the sixteenth century is still in the process of being compiled, so most of the information we possess about Bosch collection and imitation remains largely anecdotal.

Yet the phenomenon of Bosch imitation, even by so noted an artist as Pieter Bruegel, has largely remained unanalyzed. The reasons for this are not difficult to understand. Once a work has been disqualified as a Bosch original, unless it is reattributed to an artist equally famous, like Bruegel, it is thereafter deemed 'unauthentic' and 'derivative' and confined to the dark basement of storage and neglect. Bosch copies are prized only to the extent that they are capable of being considered reliable traces of vanished originals; if the Bosch prototype happened to survive, then a copy of it usually has interest only insofar as it suggests where the original might have been located or how popular and visible it remained.

What I would like to do in this essay is to give more focused attention to the phenomenon and the character of Bosch copying over the course of the sixteenth century (and even beyond). I start with the premise that the very phenomenon of copying and varying the original inventions of Bosch points to a small industry of painted supply meeting consumer demand. In short, I assert that Boschian images, what we might call *diabelerien* after some of the inventory entries of the sixteenth century, served as the basis of its own genre of pictures, both in their forms (especially featuring the little hybrid demons) and in their favored themes (particularly divine judgments or temptations of hermit saints like St. Anthony).

This kind of re-production and sequel-mongering of a successful staple derives from the firm establishment of a recognized genre, composed of both formal qualities and consistent thematic material. A modern example would be the Hollywood horror film with all of its attendant stock characters and actors as well as its standard settings and plots. Such a process apparently shaped the phenomenon of Boschian pictures as a genre during the course of the sixteenth century in and around Antwerp. Indeed, one might almost compare the impresario decision-making by studio moguls of Hollywood to the pictorial production and distribution planning of print-publisher Hieronymus Cock, who included Boschian themes as only one of many diverse varieties of image for sale at his own trademarked studio, 'Aux Quatre Vents' in Antwerp.

Nomen est omen. To choose a name like 'At the Four Winds' suggests Cock's ambition for wide distribution and sales at the very outset of his printmaking enterprise. Moreover, the copycat aping of success in some other studio (whether modern film studios or rival printmaking studios in Cock's day) was something akin to the varieties of imitations of Bosch's imagery by both distinguished and less distinctive artists, including those working primarily in other genres, such as the landscape painters Joachim Patinir or Herri met de Bles, but also of the epigones and imitators (ranging from Mandyn and Huys downwards in quality and anonymity).

We can note a marked shift over time of the tone in horrific images of Last Judgments of saintly tribulations towards delight and even laughter or parody in comic variants on the Boschian models. We find the same kind of comically slanted sequels in the various Bosch followers, after the initial *frissons* occasioned by Bosch himself. In particular, what many of the Bosch imitators, including Bruegel, seem to have delighted in as the basis of their own works is the plethora of inventive and complicated monsters. [. . .]

[. . .] Instead of dismissing such a drawing or print produced by Cock as a pale imitation of what is usually regarded as the 'great and original' invention of a celebrated 'master,' in this case Bosch, I want to examine the sheer numbers of those imitations as evidence of an ongoing success story—a story abetted by the open art market in both paintings and prints. [. . .]

[. . .] Taken together, [the] latter-day Bosch imitators held more closely to the appreciation of his inventions, what the Italian visitor to Flanders, Ludovico Guicciardini, meant when in 1567 he called Bosch 'the most noble and marvelous inventor of fantastic and bizarre things,' even as he went on to call Bruegel a 'second Bosch.' From such praises of the forms rather than the chilling contents of these pictures, we realize that now—a half century after the 1516 death of Bosch himself—artworks are being prized for their aesthetic properties and for the recognizable, signature styles of their inventive creators. In fact, it is the foundation trademark style of inventive demonic combinations and unpredictable scales or hybrid settings that marked Bosch for a viewing public and provoked his imitators to follow his example. [. . .]

It is not too difficult to follow the commentators who praise Bruegel and liken him to Bosch, nor to understand their enthusiasm for Bosch himself, who has remained so popular in our own century. But there is an economic aspect of Bosch's success in the 16th century that I want to underscore by evoking his lesser imitators. That there were so many imitators is not only testimony to Bosch's popularity but also to his *marketability*, which is not the same thing. Bosch was unique and distinctive, but he was patently *imitable*. He was recognized as having brought a new kind of painting into the world, in the novel pictorial forms of his demons even when applied to traditional, late medieval concerns like the Last Judgment or the importance of an ascetic life as a spiritual model, such as St. Anthony. Hence the major Bosch imitators stayed with his demonic depictions of temptation, sinfulness, and Hell—in short, his *diabelerien*. [. . .]

Cock sold for the open market, and by selling prints directly without relying upon specifically commissioned work in the manner of painters, he quickly learned what would sell and what wouldn't. Demand by clients in turn stimulated new production, either in the form of literal copies or variations on proven successes or else with a clear consciousness of what kinds of figures and themes were appreciated by a succession of buyers.

It was the new phenomenon of the open market in Antwerp that brought about both the commodification of art and the resulting emphasis on replication and reformulation of successful models into pictorial genres of the kinds of pictures that were selling. One is tempted to make the biological analogy of a mold in a petri dish or some other energetic life form that multiplies when it finds a favorable environment. In this case, as we have seen, first Bosch and then Bruegel provided the basic material for a host of spinoff life forms, and it was the lively economic center of Antwerp that served as their nurturing environment. Prints after drawn or painted designs and literal copies in later paintings provide the surest index of this phenomenon. And an early by-product was the fame and success of an individual artist's signature style.

Yet we must remember that this early modern form of the art market is necessary but not sufficient to account specifically for the wild growth of Boschian—or, later Bruegelian—imitations. We need also to look—specifically in the case of Bosch demons—at the value systems and emotions conveyed by these images to their owners. For those ideological constructs in images were really the kinds of comforting—even when they were unsettling—messages brought into their homes by Antwerp's urban collectors of prints and paintings. Those owners found in their images precisely the kinds of self-confirming messages that merited purchase in the first place, messages that provided a shared community between producers and consumers, artists and audiences, in the crowded urban environment of early capitalist Antwerp. These images manifestly enjoyed long and widespread popularity as purchases.

A SIXTEENTH-CENTURY MASTER-PUPIL CONTRACT

Excerpt (pp. 6–7) from Dan Ewing, "Jan De Beer's Lifetime Reputation and Posthumous Fate," *Journal of Historians of Netherlandish Art* 7, no. 2 (2015): 1–23. Copyright © 2015 Dan Ewing. Reprinted by kind permission of Dan Ewing.

Original editor's note: What makes [the following] document so extraordinary is that two years earlier, on March 20, 1514, Lieven had already enrolled in the Ghent painters' guild as a free master. In 1516 . . . he was arranging for a "post-doc" in Antwerp.

Lieven van Male, son of Jan, apothecary, is 26 years old and himself a legal adult, [and together with] Lysbette vanden Beerghe, his mother and widow of the same deceased Jan, acknowledge that, with Martin and Michiele Bennins, brothers and the sons of Martin, both merchants, [they] have answered and pledged a guarantee before Lieven, each for the other and one for all, to Janne den Beer, painter of Antwerp, [for the] payment of the sum of 9 pounds groats of Flemish money, for which Lieven himself has drawn up the contract with Janne, made and done for Janne to teach him the art of painting for the time and term of two years' duration. [This agreement] was entered into the 21st day of June last, at which date he [Lieven] paid the ready money of 2 pounds 5 shillings. [The remaining amount is due as follows:] 2 pounds 5 shillings at the following Christmas Eve, 1516; 2 pounds 5 shillings at St. John's Mass [June 24]; and 2 pounds 5 shillings at Christmas Eve, both in 1517. In the second place, [should] Lieven require an exemption and exception,

[then] Lieven and the aforesaid Lysbetten, his mother, [and] the aforesaid brothers Martin and Michiele, [in] debt for the outstanding and overdue sum of 9 pounds groats of Flemish money, promise to pay and hand over the entire [amount] within three years of the initial [contract] date; or to pay and hand over the shortfall [from] the sum of 9 pounds groats of the aforesaid [debt] to pay the value of 10 shillings as an annual, hereditary annuity, [the interest on which is] 18 pennies [= 15 percent], due the first day of each hay month [July] in each year after the first payment, which falls on the first day of hay month in 1520, and commencing from then forth, year to year, on each consecutive day of hay month, 10 shillings in perpetuity and hereditary [payment] or until its discharge, from paying the aforesaid sum of 9 pounds groats [by] making up the shortfall through paying the annual rent. In addition, the [Bennins] brothers acknowledge and safeguard the 3 pounds 5 shillings groats that will be given up and paid if Lieven leaves his master during the two years of his instruction. The same Lieven and his mother and the brothers acknowledge and guarantee, on behalf of the contracting party [Lieven], and on behalf of the pledges, this surety for one and the other, above all. To insure [their] pledge, the aforenamed Lysbette, Lieven's mother, puts [up] her house and property, including the garden and rear house, plus all her belongings, from front to back, [located] near the house of Saint George at the Waal Bridge [Waelbrugghe, in Ghent], [between the house of] Jacop Vriendt, her nephew, on the [one] side, and Lieven Lievensz, baker, on the other. The tenant's rent, in service as rent, [is] worth [the value] or payment of the aforesaid 9 pounds groats. [This constitutes] a new assurance and counterpledge for the sum, [in which] the brothers [have] 10 days to pay the aforesaid sum or rent, which must be charged to them if they fail in payment. [This is based on the value of] her goods and the forenamed house and property which comprise the place. [Therefore,] in [this] other way, to be maintained according to the law of this city, from the same rent the payment of the aforesaid 9 pounds groats of principal can be discharged. [It will] cease [being paid as] rent on the day of discharging such money. [This contract is a legal] act [ratified on the] 1st [of] July 1516.

FILIP VERMEYLEN, *Exporting Art across the Globe*

Excerpt (pp. 18–20) from "Exporting Art across the Globe: The Antwerp Art Market in the Sixteenth Century," *Nederlands Kunsthistorisch Jaarboek* 50 (2000): 13–29. Reprinted by permission of Koninklijke Brill NV.

Produced for export were the works of the Antwerp Mannerists, a group of anonymous painters who were active during the first decades of the sixteenth century. They painted thousands of *Adorations of the Magi* which were unloaded on the international markets. These paintings were of varying quality and price—often dozens of cheap copies of one original existed. Renaissance paintings in the style of Quinten Metsijs were equally in demand, more specifically triptychs of limited size depicting scenes from the New Testament.

Antwerp paintings were exported across the globe. An analysis of the export registers of 1543–5 makes clear that the Iberian Peninsula was the most prominent importer of paintings from the Antwerp market, representing a third of all exports during that period. The Spanish and Portuguese appetite for Northern painting, however, was not a new phenomenon. Even before the 1440s, Flemish art had already found its way to the Iberian upper nobility and clergy, but was now distributed on a much larger scale including the Spanish monarchy and the middle classes who displayed a strong taste for Flemish art. As a result, the market for artistic goods expanded greatly, and paintings in the style of Van Eyck especially were in demand.

Portuguese businessmen bought vast numbers of religious paintings and etchings at the Antwerp fairs, Friday market or later at the painters' gallery in the new Bourse. The foundation for the strong cultural, economic and political ties between the Southern Netherlands and Portugal was laid in the 1430s, and demand for Flemish works appears to have reached its zenith during the first decade of the sixteenth century. Flemish styles were emphatically present in Portugal where they profoundly influenced the work of native artists, more specifically through the works of Jan Van Eyck and Quinten Metsijs.

Antwerp paintings even found their way to the New World via the port of Seville, the European gateway to the East and West Indies, where many Flemish artists such as Pieter de Kempeneer (Pedro de Campana) and Hernando Sturm lived and worked. Seville served as a meeting place for Flemish and Spanish trade throughout the sixteenth century. Today, many examples of Flemish paintings can still be admired in Latin American museums. These collections include works by Pieter Aertsen and Martin de Vos, the latter undoubtedly having been the most influential Antwerp painter in South America.

Italy was another great importer of Flemish paintings, and above all during the second half of the sixteenth century. Art exports seem to have been part of the regular transcontinental trade between Italy and the Southern Netherlands, and 10 shipments appear in the export registers to cities like Ancona, Genoa, Milan, Pavia, Rome and Venice. However, the presence of Flemish paintings in Italy was without a doubt much higher than the mere 9 percent of art exported according to the 100th penny tax. After all, many Netherlandish artists traveled to Italy to learn their profession, and in doing so, they may have produced substantial amounts of works of art for local patrons. The Italian gentleman and humanist Marcantonio Michiel wrote during the first half of the sixteenth century on a large number of paintings he was able to observe in Venice, and as much as 30 percent of them were of Northern origin. [John Michael] Montias argues that Michiel may have found equally high numbers of Northern paintings in Florence and Genoa. After all, these cities entertained the same intensity of commercial and cultural exchanges with Antwerp. In other words, Venice was certainly not an isolated case, which may indicate that the demand for Flemish painting in Italy was much higher than previously anticipated, even if Michiel's numbers turn out to be somewhat exaggerated.

Italian merchants turned to Antwerp art dealers rather than to the individual artists in order to supply themselves especially when large consignments were involved. Fascinating examples of this kind of trading can be found in the [export registers]. For instance, on December 7, 1576, the Antwerp merchant Peter Goetkint attested that he regularly sold sizable amounts of paintings and books to Jehan Bergami, a merchant from Florence *qu'il entend de mener dudit vers Italy pour les y vendre et ademirer.*

Exports of art work to France were virtually non-existent during the two years covered by the export registers. This should be no surprise as the export tax was conceived to pay for the war the Habsburgers were waging against France at this time. However, French imports of paintings did reach high volumes between 1570 and 1580 when Flemish works were exhibited in Paris at the *galerie de la conciergerie du Palais*. Here, interested buyers from the whole country could buy works from Antwerp masters. Evidence from the Antwerp archives underscores this assumption over and over again. For instance, the above mentioned Peter Goetkint was also heavily involved in the export of paintings and etchings to France: on one occasion he intended to sell 54 *couleurs et painctures* in Paris and other parts of France *pour gaigner sa vie*. In December 1576, he attested that he ordinarily travels to Paris twice a year to sell paintings and paint; he added that his wife and children remain in Antwerp when he is in France for business. The timing for heightened activities with France can perhaps be explained in the context of the erupting Dutch Revolt. In 1572, Protestant rebels [first] cut off the river Scheldt making it extremely difficult to export goods from Antwerp overseas. Merchants, therefore, may have sought out alternative markets and trade routes to sell their goods. France, Paris in particular, was without a doubt a viable alternative since it could be easily reached over land.

A surprising number of Flemish paintings were still shipped to England in the 1540s—25 shipments from Antwerp in 2 years, representing close to one fifth of the total exports. This is somewhat unexpected since religious paintings (the subject matter of the great majority of Antwerp paintings produced during these years) were particularly *non grata* in Britain after Henry VIII defied the Pope in the 1530s and launched the iconoclasm. The absence of a record of significant shipments of paintings in the London port books may suggest that these paintings were smuggled into the country, in which case the subject matter was almost certainly of a religious nature. Whatever the explanation might be, the fact remains that London remained an important destination for Flemish painting throughout the century. For instance, the English merchant Henry Pine purchased *two boxes of various sorts of paintings* to be sent to England in January of 1577. Nevertheless, the real boom occurred during the seventeenth century when the English nobility and royalty developed an insatiable appetite for Flemish landscapes, history paintings and portraits.

The German hinterland concludes the list of major importers of (in this case cheaper) paintings and prints. Cologne played a key role as the distribution center for the German market, for which ample proof is found in the [export registers].

ELIZABETH ALICE HONIG, *Trade and Art in Seventeenth-Century Antwerp*

Excerpt (pp. 111–14) from "Trade and Art in Seventeenth-Century Antwerp," in *Painting and the Market in Early Modern Antwerp* (New Haven, CT, and London: Yale University Press, 1998), 110–14. Copyright © 1998 Yale University Press.

Many dealers were . . . carrying out quite lucrative business in seventeenth-century Antwerp, and the market supported the city's painters at a relatively high standard of living. But there would seem to be a certain anomaly here, for if the city's economy was otherwise in decline one would not expect the luxury market to be so vigorous. It was, in fact, the dealers who were essential in maintaining a market for paintings in economically adverse conditions. Specialized full-time dealers were more able than professional painters to exploit the full potential of foreign markets, and they also found ways of both creating and supplying demand at the lower end of the local market. A Rubens or a Jan Brueghel could still pursue older channels of patronage and marketing, but lesser artists became ever more dependent upon markets formed and controlled by the art dealers.

The export market was an enormously important outlet for all Antwerp's luxury goods: art was in fact the only growth sector in the city's industrial production for export. Even though remarkably little foreign art seems to have entered Antwerp, the art produced there spread throughout Europe and farther afield. [. . .]

As examples of dealers operating within Antwerp we may take Suzanna Bernolie and Abraham Matthijs, whose death inventories were drawn up within a week of each other in September 1649. Bernolie, widow of the painter Philips III Liesaert, had 618 paintings in her possession. The vast majority were not even attributed; of those that were, most were by negligible masters, though she had a handful of slightly better cabinet paintings by artists like Frans II Francken and Louis de Caullery. Matthijs's inventory included only about half the number of paintings hers had—335—but a much higher proportion were attributed. He had multiple works not only by Rubens, Anthony van Dyck, and Paulus Bril but also by rare Italian masters like Raphael, Titian, Correggio, Annibale Carracci, and Domenichino. Clearly Bernolie and Matthijs each catered to a specific segment of the local market, she to the general public and he to a more cultivated audience. Such specialization was by now the rule among Antwerp dealers, some of whom limited their business much more precisely: Philips Liesaert's daughter Suzanna dealt solely in "small paintings painted on copper plates with ebony frames."

The boom time for high-level dealers like Matthijs was already passing by 1649, though; for as the local market in general shrunk from around midcentury, that for expensive new paintings became even more precarious. Cheaper art was a better business venture: profit margins were higher in this sector of the market, and many dealers, including even great ones like Musson, came to favor it. The preference for inexpensive works thus came about through a combination of demand patterns on the market and commercial expediency on the part of dealers; but it in turn had a profound effect on the nature of the art market and on painting itself. . . . Dealers in inferior works were what Michael Montias (1988, 245–46) has called "supply augmentors." They met a demand for simpler art by arranging to expand its supply, ordering cheap originals and copies after existing works. As a result, dealers gained control not only over the distribution of art but also over its very production so that, finally, much painting came to be directed at a fundamental level by people who formerly had been only intermediaries in the market structure.

It was not unknown even in the sixteenth century for artists to work on commission from dealers. [. . .] But during the seventeenth century the intervention of dealers in the manufacture of paintings expanded dramatically. Great families like the Forchondts and the Mussons were less brokers than mass employers, with scores of craftsmen at work on their commissions. A dealer might provide working space and equipment for his or her workers, so that the artist's studio was transformed into a workshop directed by its marketing manager, while others farmed out commissions among independent studios. Antonette Wael's inventory of 1627 suggests that she used both strategies: in her home was a studio containing twelve easels and scores of unfinished paintings, while the further list of her property included numerous panels that were with various artists waiting to be completed. But however a dealer arranged for production of paintings, he or she could retain strict control over the type of work produced, choosing artists and dictating subject matter based on knowledge of taste in the market being exploited.

An even less costly and more profitable means of supplying the demand for cheap paintings was to commission copies, either of existing works or of the originals then being commissioned. Dealers routinely ordered "doubly," asking an artist for both originals and copies at the same time. Alternatively, the third-rate artists working for a certain dealer might be set to copying one another's works. Payments for copy work could be remarkably low: for instance, in 1635 Crisostomo van Immerseel ordered seventy-five paintings from Adriaen van Stalbempt, in at least some of which the artist was only doing the *staffage*, or figure work. For these Immerseel paid, on average, about fl.10 each; but he also received copies of all seventy-five works, done in full by Stalbempt, who also provided the materials, and for those Immerseel paid only fl.31/2 each. By contrast, prices charged for finished copies—either by dealers or by independent painters—were relatively high, as much as three quarters and not less than a third of the cost of the original.

Hence the trade in copies, particularly in commissioned ones, must have seemed highly attractive to dealers, and their inventories are often quite full of them. Sometimes there are just stacks of paintings listed as "x number of copies"; in other cases, the authors of the originals and even the names of the copyists are noted. Even an elite dealer like Abraham Matthijs kept an ample stock of copies, including ones after Rubens, Bruegel, and Dürer, Raphael, Titian, Correggio, and Caravaggio. In some cases, the abundance of reasonably good copies available at such moderate prices had the effect of reducing market demand for originals, but dealers seem to have responded simply by increasing the supply of profitable copies. Thus when Immerseel ordered a double series of originals and copies from Jan II Brueghel, he specified that whereas the copies were to be sent directly to him in Spain, the originals should remain in Antwerp. There they would serve Immerseel's hired artists as models, "like a shoemaker is served by his last." Within this circuit, at least, the original painting has become nothing more than a pattern for infinite reproductions that will supply a hungry and, it would seem, rather uncritical low-level market.

The dealers were well aware of differences in skill among the artists for hire. Wages, whether calculated by the picture or by the day, were higher for more competent artists. But because their profit margins were better on cheaper works, which were also more saleable, dealers tended to favor less accomplished painters who were willing to work for lower wages. The painters' incomes did not necessarily suffer unduly from this system, for high levels of output could compensate for low per-painting wages, and working for a dealer saved the artist the cost of setting up a studio. What was severely reduced, however, was the artist's control over his output, both its content and, to some degree, its quality. Now more divorced than ever from real contact with the market, much less with individual members of the buying public, many artists produced works to meet an idea of demand dictated to them by their employers, the dealers.

These changes in production and marketing exacerbated the commodification of painting that had begun in the sixteenth century. Whereas then the painting that had entered the anonymous market had functioned as a kind of cipher of value between producer and consumer, the extent of dealer intervention now imposed a new barrier between making and beholding, creation and judgment. This split had significant implications for the creation of meaning in art—whether in intention or in reception—and for attitudes toward authorship, identity, and the calculation of value.

HANS VLIEGHE, *Rubens's Studio Practice*

Excerpts (pp. 636–40) from "Erasmus Quellinus and Rubens's Studio Practice," *Burlington Magazine* 119, no. 894 (1977): 636–43. Reprinted with kind permission of *Burlington Magazine.*

It is evident that Rubens's workshop practice was in keeping with a tradition which had originated in Italian High Renaissance conceptions. Following the example of a Raphael, a Giulio Romano, a Michelangelo or a Titian, Rubens's workshop also reflected the typical Renaissance dichotomy between the invention—the master's fundamental creative act—and the execution of the painting, which became partially entrusted to highly qualified collaborators who were perfectly capable of contributing to their master's projects. The task of Rubens's assistants was a twofold one. On the one hand they had a varying share in the execution of their master's paintings. On the other, some of them were used by Rubens in order to make preparatory drawings and oil-sketches, which served as *modelli* for the many engravings which had to be made either as reproductions of the painter's large-scale compositions, or as illustrations for the lavishly laid-out books which were printed and edited by his good friend Balthasar Moretus, the owner and manager of the world-famous Plantin Press.

Rubens had to be very careful and fastidious in the selection of his assistants, for we know from an often cited letter that already as early as 1611 he felt obliged to turn down more than 100 applicants. Rubens's severe standards were applied to those collaborators who had a specific share in the achievement of large-scale compositions, as well as to the engravers who had to 'translate' Rubens's ideas in copper or in wood and to make the preparatory drawings for these prints. It is due to this exactingness that such qualified painters as Van Dyck, Jordaens, Snyders, Wildens, Jan Brueghel and Paul de Vos, as well as such distinguished engravers as Vorsterman, Pontius, Bolswert and Jegher could link their names to Rubens's workshop.

Some of these collaborators however showed themselves skilful in both the main fields of activity of the studio. This was the case with Anthony van Dyck, who in the period between *c.*1616 and *c.*1621 was Rubens's first assistant. Not only had he an important share in the completion of an ever-growing number of compositions—especially the ceiling paintings of the Antwerp Jesuit Church and the Decius Mus cartoons—but he had also been employed by Rubens in making preparatory drawings for engravings which, in most cases, were executed by Lucas Vorsterman. The same double rôle, which Van Dyck had played in the earlier years of the foundation of Rubens's workshop, was afterwards assigned to Erasmus II Quellinus, who assisted his master in the last years of his career. [. . .]

Quellinus was an offspring of a family of artists. He was born in Antwerp, in 1607, the son of the Liège sculptor Erasmus I Quellinus who had settled in the city at the Scheldt in the earlier years of the seventeenth century. Nothing precise is known about Erasmus the Younger's apprenticeship. He became a master in the St Luke's guild of his native town, during the administrative year 1633–34. The name of his master, however, is not mentioned in the registers of the guild. It is not improbable that initially he followed in his father's footsteps. [. . .] He may, however, have also had a training in Rubens's studio. This may be deduced from the circumstance that Quellinus, immediately after having obtained his mastership, became closely involved in the execution of the latter's work. But again: there is no documentary evidence and furthermore, Rubens was allowed by privilege not to enroll his pupils.

Quellinus's rôle as the direct collaborator of Antwerp's leading artist is best known through his very personal contribution to the execution of the book-illustrations which Rubens had constantly to design for Balthasar Moretus's *Officina Plantiniana*. From at least 1637 onwards Rubens left Quellinus a free hand to draw the *modelli* for these prints. The master's part in the job was limited to instructions concerning iconography and layout. The style of these drawings was Quellinus's own. But he was also involved in designing from Rubens's inventions separate engravings which had nothing to do with the routine work for Moretus's editorial house.

It is quite understandable that a *peintre-graveur* like Quellinus also handled the etching needle. Thus he executed a representation of *Samson Fighting the Lion*, an etching with the following caption: *P. Paulus Rubbens inventor. E. Quellinus fecit in aqua forti.* Here Quellinus etched a rather sketchy draft by Rubens, which on sound grounds is datable after 1631. Quellinus's activity as a draughtsman in Rubens's workshop is further attested by some preparatory drawings he executed for the wood-carver Christoffel Jegher. Thus we know a full-length portrait of Cardinal-Infante Ferdinand of Spain, which is a partial copy in reverse of Rubens's similar representation of the Spanish governor, which in 1635 formed part of the decorations for the *Pompa Introitus Ferdinandi*. Although Rubens's name is not mentioned in the caption of the woodcut, it does not seem very likely that Quellinus would have drawn a *modello* for this woodcut without Rubens's knowledge and consent. [. . .]

Quellinus's part in the painting of large-scale canvases ordered from Rubens is best known by his share in 1636–38 in the execution of the Torre de la Parada paintings. For he was responsible for the execution of at least eight of the more than 100 mythological compositions of which this enormous series initially consisted. But already earlier he had contributed to the public decorations erected by the city of Antwerp, on the occasion of the State Entry of Cardinal-Infante Ferdinand in 1635. Then Quellinus painted from Rubens's *modello* an allegorical representation of *Plenty and Wealth*, a painting which was destined for the decoration of the so-called *Stage of Mercury*. However, unlike the paintings for the Torre de la Parada, this canvas has long been lost. Further there is a somewhat cryptic remark by the Cardinal-Infante which may prove that Quellinus was in any case playing an important role in the execution of Rubens's late works. The document here concerned is Ferdinand's letter to his brother, the Spanish King Philip IV, *d. d.* 10th June 1640. There the Spanish governor mentioned four paintings the King had ordered from Rubens and which, due to the painter's death which had occurred a few days earlier, remained incomplete in the studio. For that reason Ferdinand proposed to his brother that these paintings might be finished by '*su primer official*', i.e. Rubens's foremost collaborator. Rightly in my opinion this artist has been identified as Erasmus Quellinus, by Rooses and other authors. . . . As a matter of fact the collaboration between the two artists was very close in the field of graphic art and Quellinus, immediately after Rubens's death, took over the latter's role as Antwerp's first official painter so that, until his death, he remained responsible for all kinds of public decorations, in this way carrying on until the later decades of the century the tone set by Rubens's *Pompa Introitus Ferdinandi*.

5

AMSTERDAM

The permanent Dutch blockade of Antwerp's port on the Scheldt River in 1585 and the subsequent retreat of the Spanish army from the northern provinces brought about another shift in the European world-economy. In the early 1590s, Holland became the main entrepôt for international commodities. Its central location and connection to the large system of waterways in the north allowed for the efficient redistribution of goods brought in from Spain, Portugal, and the New World to a wide range of markets in northern Europe. Improvements in shipbuilding, such as further increases in the size of cargo holds, and in navigation, as well as the aggressive military protection of its shipping routes further cemented Dutch dominance in the north–south trade. By the start of the seventeenth century, the wealth generated by the expanded international trade led to the flowering of Dutch culture now known as the Dutch Golden Age.

Holland also benefited from a large migration of Flemish and Portuguese merchants and artisans in the wake of the fall of Antwerp to the northern cities. Amsterdam became a center for manufacture of luxury goods, as well as for printing and publishing, science and technology, and the arts. As Oscar Gelderblom (2012) has pointed out, the Dutch Republic was a country of entrepreneurs. They included not just merchants but also shipmasters, fishermen, printers, farmers, and shopkeepers. Their income depended on the profits and losses they made in the marketplace. Gelderblom correlated the number of active entrepreneurs with the high level of urbanization, which reached a seventeenth-century peak of 60 percent. This urban concentration of professionals accelerated the pace of innovation and helps to explain the rapid growth of the Dutch economy.

Holland's commercial culture extended to trading in works of art. The entrepreneurs, who undoubtedly regularly attended auctions of commodities, must have considered buying works of art at an auction a normal activity. Ever since the beginning of the sixteenth century, paintings had been sold at auction as part of the estates of deceased citizens, along with their clothes, furniture, and pots and pans. For those who were too busy to attend these mixed sales, specialized auctions of works of art had been held in Amsterdam at least as early as 1608 (Montias 2002).

The most extraordinary aspect of the Dutch Golden Age was the widespread ownership of paintings. Holland had become a mass market for works of art. John Michael Montias (1982, 220) has estimated that in the mid-seventeenth century, two thirds of the population of the town of Delft lived in households with paintings on the walls— eleven works on average. Montias found the occasional painting even among the few possessions of day laborers, and several small paintings were often listed in the inventories of simple artisans. Strong demand for pictures led to the emergence of numerous new subjects, such as still life, landscape, genre, and maritime scenes. The specialization of artists and the development of less labor-intensive painting techniques led to an unprecedented rise in the productivity of painters. This surge in both demand and supply created a dynamic Dutch art market that differed fundamentally from the art markets of previous periods, especially in Italy, which had been dominated by patronage. The final shift from patronage to the market system, which had started in Antwerp in the sixteenth century, took place in the Republic, where the iconoclast Protestant church ceased to be a patron of the arts and the aristocracy was much diminished. It is estimated that Dutch painters produced more than five million paintings in the seventeenth century. Ad van der Woude (1991) has calculated that some eighteen million paintings may have been present in Dutch households between 1580 and 1800.

ERIC JAN SLUIJTER, *On Brabant Rubbish, Economic Competition,*
Artistic Rivalry, and the Growth of the Market for Paintings

Excerpts from "On Brabant Rubbish, Economic Competition, Artistic Rivalry, and the Growth of the Market for Paintings in the First Decades of the Seventeenth Century," *Journal of Historians of Netherlandish Art* 1, no. 2 (2009): 1–32. Reprinted by kind permission of the author.

How did the art of painting come to occupy such an important place in the consciousness of well-to-do Dutch city dwellers, and why did they, from regents and wealthy merchants to trained craftsmen, fairly suddenly and in increasingly greater numbers begin to buy paintings by living masters to adorn the walls of their houses, paintings depicting a growing variety of subjects in different sizes, techniques, and prices? At times the figures are simply astounding. In the middle of the seventeenth century some interiors had thirty to fifty paintings per room, rooms which, it should be noted, were not all that spacious. In such a case, the number of paintings owned could total 150 to 250. The travelers' amazement at what they saw in the Netherlands is quite understandable. After all, in other European countries paintings were still largely produced for religious institutions, the aristocracy, and royal courts. Moreover, insofar as painters were employed in countries such as England, Germany, and Scandinavia, they were often recruited from the Netherlands. [. . .]

[. . .] When the number of painters did truly grow explosively from 1610 on, especially in Haarlem and Amsterdam, among this group were many children of immigrants with Southern Netherlandish roots who had opted to become painters and were indeed manifestly successful. Although some of these painters were born in the south, they were trained in Holland. Interestingly, within this generation the more traditional genres of the profession, the painting of histories and of portraits, remained largely in the hands of native painters, while the new specialities, particularly landscape and still-life painting, were primarily cultivated by the young southerners.

To better understand what happened, we must first concentrate on the public: the buyers of paintings. Amsterdam, Haarlem, and Leiden in particular had drawn a large number of immigrant merchants and highly trained artisans (many from Antwerp, especially in Amsterdam), whose purchasing power must have increased substantially in the two previous decades. They came from a culture in which it had become common for affluent burghers to buy paintings to embellish their homes as early as the second half of the sixteenth century. Moreover, they were accustomed to these decorations portraying profane subjects as well as being available in various price ranges, from exorbitantly expensive to extremely cheap. After all, vast quantities of landscapes, peasant scenes, and kitchen still lifes varying greatly in quality were already being produced in Antwerp and Malines in the second half of the sixteenth century.

For these immigrants there was probably not that much to buy just yet in the cities of their new homeland. In the late sixteenth century most of the painters in Holland seem to have primarily made fairly expensive history paintings destined for a select group of connoisseurs. Moreover, initially the immigrants will have had matters other than purchasing paintings on their minds. Presumably, as long as these refugees believed that their sojourn in Holland was temporary and their return to their former abodes imminent (a situation which must have lasted quite a long time), they elected not to spend their money on luxury articles to decorate their homes but rather on easily transportable valuables. Only when the hope or wish to return had vanished, and they had definitely resigned themselves to staying (which must have been around the time of the Twelve Years' Truce), will their desire to adorn their interiors have grown. And, as is revealed below, the immigrants were given the opportunity of doing so at just that moment.

As of 1608, and thus still shortly before the signing of the Twelve Years' Truce, a large number of paintings appears to have suddenly begun flowing from Antwerp to the

Republic, flooding the market in the Dutch cities. These were inexpensive works that—at least in the eyes of Dutch burghers—were sold in an unusual way. The established painters . . . responded vehemently. In Amsterdam and Leiden they demanded that the city councils immediately implement measures to contain this influx from Antwerp. They requested prohibitive orders for the sale of paintings by foreigners and wanted this laid down in new or revised guild regulations. In this period, the guilds, including that of the painters, were often dormant or no longer existed at all, as was the case in Leiden. All at once, however, steps to protect the local market were taken everywhere. [. . .]

Clearly, the inundation of the market with cheap paintings caused local artists to fear that their income would be eroded. But what actually happened? Precisely the opposite of what everyone had expected. With the swift growth in the number of painters as well as the number of works a painter produced, the market also embarked on what would be an extraordinary expansion. From the reactions of the Amsterdammers, who, after all, alleged that these sellers—encouraged by the profit they made—did everything in their power to amass whatever paintings they could in Antwerp and surroundings, it can be seen that the intruders were evidently successful and there was no shortage of buyers for the Antwerp imports. Although the guild members cited the inferior quality of the works as the main reason for their concern and capitalized on the customers' fear of buying a copy instead of an original (*principaal*), in my opinion their real objection (and panic) was that these paintings sold so readily for prices they felt were too high. In other words, they were in great demand—despite the disparaging judgment of the dean and headmen—by a public willing to pay more than they were worth, according to local painters. Most likely the buyers were primarily the Southern Netherlandish immigrants, who were now in a position and ready to purchase these, to them, familiar items.

The question is whether the quality of the imported paintings was, indeed, as inferior as their critics would have us think. They were very inexpensive compared to the paintings that the established painters tended to make, and undoubtedly that was threatening enough. The paintings were probably cheaper because they were made according to different production methods, for example by means of a less time-consuming and labor-intensive technique. And this afforded more than ample reason for labeling them as rubbish, apprentices' work, and copies; this was the most obvious vocabulary for expressing scathing censure. Moreover, when such works were sold for prices higher than the guild members deemed appropriate on the basis of technical execution and time investment, the traditional way in which they determined prices was entirely overturned. Furthermore, one wonders whether the buyers in fact mostly comprised burghers "who on the whole have little knowledge of paintings." [. . .]

The influx of cheap paintings from Antwerp seems to have functioned as a booster. The buying patterns of immigrants who began decorating the walls of their homes with these inexpensive paintings (the subject and style of which had hardly changed since they had fled) will have invited imitation on the part of indigenous citizens with the same social standing. After all, a large share of the new elite of affluent merchants and trained craftsmen was composed of immigrants. In several respects they also formed a cultural elite, although their culture was frequently mockingly stereotyped. This stereotyping must have derived primarily from a sense of inferiority and jealousy. As Briels described it, the ridicule almost always revolved around the cliché that the naturally sober Dutch were seduced by the finery, ostentation, and vanity introduced by the Brabanders. [. . .]

Because a group with equal purchasing power from the indigenous population began to adopt the Southern-Netherlandish custom of surrounding itself with paintings, the demand must have grown further still, while simultaneously—to the extent that this had not already taken place—measures were being instituted in virtually all of the cities to curtail the sale of imported paintings. I suspect that at that moment several established masters began to intensify their production by making less expensive works. Above all, however, ever more young men, including many children of immigrants, began to fill this hole in the market. Not only did they have to compete with their own masters from the older generation but also and chiefly with the cheap imports from Antwerp, which regardless of the illegal auctions (that were evidently still being held) must also have been available at annual and weekly markets and at kermisses and public sales held outside the city. [. . .]

The question of whether this "process innovation" was set in motion by artistic or economic impulses is irrelevant in my view. An obvious way of being able to compete in this new market of relatively inexpensive paintings was to supply higher quality—works that were more technically clever, appealing, interesting, and lifelike—while keeping the production costs low. As painters found themselves producing for a relatively broad public, which made its choices at auctions, at the market, or in the shop, artistic and economic rivalry became indelibly linked. As indicated above, to an ambitious young artist in this period, notions of artistic emulation would have been just as self-evident as the need for economic competition. And, given the various gradations of praise that [Karel] Van Mander, among others, lavished on specialists of all kinds—from Pieter Bruegel and Gillis van Coninxloo, to Jacob Grimmer, Pieter Baltens, Cornelis Molenaer, Hans Bol, and David Vinckboons, with emphasis being placed on how highly they were valued by art lovers—there could no longer be any doubt that landscapes and peasant scenes also afforded territory for artistic emulation and the opportunity of establishing one's reputation with the art lovers. The latter aspect was also—or perhaps precisely—of importance to painters who did not work on commission because they had to create their own demand. Should one want to be "held in great esteem"—which also meant being able to command higher prices—recognition was imperative.

Accordingly, a well-trained and ambitious young painter simply had to make his name by producing an identifiable, characteristic product of exceptional quality. He could elect to concentrate on one or more of the, for Holland still relatively new, specialities with which a substantial number of Southern Netherlanders had already found acclaim. In addition, he could try to keep the production costs per painting low by working fast and expanding his output to better counter the competition afforded by the inexpensive

Southern Netherlandish painters. Should he succeed in acquiring a good reputation with such paintings, then the profit margins became increasingly greater.

. . . Samuel van Hoogstraten pointed out much later in the seventeenth century that those artists who turned to "ras schilderen" (rapid painting) did this for profit as well as fame. From this comment, too, we see that economic and artistic preoccupations in this context appear to have been inextricably linked. Therefore, it should come as no surprise that this observation is followed by the mention of Jan Porcellis and Jan Van Goyen, two painters who were exceptionally successful in attaining high artistic standing with swiftly painted works. While their paintings were not expensive, they still commanded relatively high prices proportionate to their scant production costs.

JOHN MICHAEL MONTIAS, *Cost and Value in Dutch Art*

Excerpt (pp. 456–61) from "Cost and Value in Seventeenth-Century Dutch Art," *Art History* 10, no. 4 (1987): 455–66. © 1987 Association of Art Historians. Reproduced with permission of Blackwell Publishing, Ltd. and John-Luke Montias.

Students of the history of technology distinguish two basic types of innovation: product and process. Product innovations, as the name implies, generate either totally new products or products whose characteristics depart significantly from those known in the past. Process innovations lower the cost or otherwise improve the technology of making products that were already available or whose characteristics are essentially similar. [. . .] The process innovations in sixteenth- and seventeenth-century painting that I will be discussing also affected their visual characteristics. But they apparently did not detract from their attractiveness; or, if they did, the less expensive styles were still able to establish themselves in the market.

Consider, for example, the use of standardized patterns in paintings in Gerard David's workshops, which were brought into routine atelier practices by the Antwerp painter known as the Master of Frankfurt (1460–?1533) and his assistants. These patterns were applied chiefly to simulate the appearance of brocade materials but also in painting urban backgrounds and other routine parts. The technique, using templates of pounced patterns, cut down on the time, and therefore on the cost, of executing the shop's paintings. Such paintings were apparently sold on the open market rather than in carrying out commissions which might have had more demanding specifications. Whoever may have originated these mechanized devices, they were promptly and widely diffused, as we would expect a cost-cutting innovation to be since, in the absence of patents, the pressures of competition would force all the workshops competing for the same market to adopt them. According to Steven Goddard (1985), the mechanized transfer of complex brocade patterns appears to have been a commonplace in northern European art of the fifteenth and early sixteenth centuries. The importance for the diffusion of a process innovation of a wide competitive market cannot be overestimated.

The division of labor in producing a work of art is another classic way of increasing productivity and reducing costs. . . . Sixteenth- and seventeenth-century workshops, especially in Antwerp, were well known for the 'specialists' who contributed their separate skills in painting animals, landscapes, still-lifes, and pictures-within-pictures to integrated compositions. Rubens refined this technique to a high degree in the organization of his workshop. Collaboration among specialists could also flourish among independent masters. In the northern Netherlands in the seventeenth century, where there were fewer important workshops, paintings begun by one master would be completed by another. This practice was not confined to landscape painters and specialists in staffage. Bartholomeus van Bassen, who painted church interiors, frequently had the figures animating his works painted in by Esaias van de Velde, when both artists were living in The Hague.

Not all styles lent themselves to collaboration. The additive, mannerist style of building up a landscape or an interior was much more conducive to collaboration by two or more artists than tonal, atmospheric, or chiaroscuro painting. It is hard to imagine Jan van Goyen, in the 1640s or 1650s, parceling out to another master the task of filling in his figures. A process innovation must either leave the product unchanged or provide an acceptable substitute without a very perceptible decline in quality.

In any event, the division of labor may also develop without any collaboration at all. As the seventeenth century unfolded, an increasing number of artists in the North began to concentrate their output in a narrow specialty, such as the depiction of seascapes (Jan Porcellis), battle scenes (Palamedes Palamedesz.), fish (Jakob Gillig), barn interiors (Dirck Camphuyzen), and explosions and town figures (Egbert van der Poel). They too must have increased their productivity by honing their specialized skills. This deepening specialization was made possible by the growth of market demand, thereby illustrating Adam Smith's famous principle about the division of labor, 'which is determined by the extent of the market.'

Innovations of all sorts, whether in science, technology, or art tend to flourish when information flows freely and copiously between and among potential innovators. The critical mass needed for breakthroughs, so often cited in connection with the size of academic departments, hinges on the number of individuals interacting in a given milieu as well as on their access to external sources of information. Starting from this premise, it is obvious that the study of innovations in style and representation must take account not only of the few trend-setters but of the many, more modestly talented artists who contributed by their presence, by their teaching, and in lesser measure by their works, to the store of information available to the community. The mutual enrichment of artists residing in Delft in the late 1640s and 1650s—who included Pieter de Hooch, Carel Fabritius, Gerard Houckgeest, Johannes Vermeer, and Abraham van Beyeren—helped to create an influential 'school,' a group of individuals with a common interest in the representation of light, atmosphere and space. The group could not have been as successful as it was if Delft had been isolated. It profited from the influence of Nicholas Maes who was living in Dordrecht, of Gerard Dou and Frans van Mieris in Leiden, or

Gerard Ter Borch in Zwolle and The Hague, more indirectly, of Rembrandt in Amsterdam, and of various Caravaggist Utrecht painters. It is not always evident by precisely what conduits these influences were transmitted. Personal travel—of Delft painters to other towns and of 'foreigners' to Delft—must have played a role. Transportation by horse-drawn water coach on the canals linking Dutch towns from Dordrecht to Amsterdam and beyond was regular, swift and inexpensive. But many paintings were also imported into Delft from other centers, so that local artists who had access to Delft collections or who had contacts with local dealers could have an idea of what was being done in other parts of the Netherlands. Guild restrictions were fairly successful in preventing non-members from plying their trade in town; but they were either mild or ineffective in restricting imports. The best evidence of this is that 40–50 percent of the attributions I found in Delft inventories in different decades (based on a fairly systematic survey for the period 1610–80) were to out-of-town painters. In Amsterdam, which was a more open town than Delft and even less subject to guild restrictions, the percentage of attributions to out-of-town artists in my sample was very close to 50 percent in the period from 1620 to 1650 and then declined to 40 percent by the 1670s.

How critical a critical mass can be is best exemplified in the case of Delft, by the consequences of its loss. Starting in the mid-1650s, with an accelerating trend in the next decade, prominent artists including Pieter de Hooch, Emanuel de Witte, and Abraham van Beyeren left Delft, chiefly for The Hague and Amsterdam. Only one artist of any significance—Johannes Verkolje—joined the local guild from out of town. Probably by the mid-1660s but certainly by 1675, after the death of Johannes Vermeer—the last survivor and holdout of the great Pleiad of the 1650s—Delft had ceased to be a center of innovation. [. . .]

In the sixteenth century, the northern provinces lagged culturally behind the southern. In Antwerp specialized artists catered not only to church and municipal commissions but to a large anonymous market for standardized religious commodities. In the northern cities, artists were dependent on the church and on private patronage chiefly for portrait commissions. There was only a modest market demand on the part of private collectors and ecclesiastical institutions for religious 'histories' which were often copied after the more important commissions. Facing a narrow market, the more successful artists reduced risk by relying on patronage.

David Freedberg (1986) has recently argued that the religious debate over images and the iconoclastic disorders of 1566, which caused the destruction of countless works of religious art in churches, chapels, hospices and monasteries both in the Northern and the Southern provinces of the Netherlands in 1566, led to an 'imaginative reevaluation of the Dutch artistic tradition' and 'prepared the way for a magnificently inventive future.' As an alternative to this rather elusive dialectic process in the evolution of style, I would suggest an economic explanation bound up with demand factors. The destruction of works of art in ecclesiastic institutions is likely to have stimulated the private demand for art in the home as a substitute for the paintings and sculptures formerly on public display that had disappeared. For Roman Catholics this meant, quite straightforwardly, the erection of private tabernacles and altars, some of which may have come from erstwhile ecclesiastic institutions. Images were a natural complement to religious services, now conducted more or less in secret, at home. For Calvinists, the process of substitution was more subtle, and perhaps subconscious: they could collect religious 'histories' without fear of criticism by their pastors and satisfy a latent demand for art which their white-washed churches could no longer fulfill.

The economic expansion of the Republic, particularly after the truce in the war with Spain of 1609, also made it possible for more burghers to buy works of art. [. . .]

The main conjecture of this paper is that a combination of process and product innovations which occurred in the first quarter of the seventeenth century lowered the costs of producing paintings and enabled artists to penetrate new markets. This supply-cost reduction began with production of landscapes and gradually extended to the other subject categories. The innovation, pioneered by Esaias van de Velde and Jan Porcellis in the case of land- and seascapes and of Pieter Claesz, in the case of still-life, consisted in moving from linear depiction and additive composition toward a more painterly technique and a simplified composition integrated by the modulation of color and tone. [. . .]

This is not to say that the primary motivation of Esaias van de Velde or any of the innovators of the first half of the century was primarily to cut down on the time necessary to complete a painting and earn more money. The impulse may have been primarily artistic rather than mercenary. The rise of realistic landscape painting in Holland in the seventeenth century, viewed as a stylistic or product innovation, must surely be rooted in the culture of the period. However, if a painter's productivity—the number of paintings he could complete in a week or a month—rose, the economic effect was the same as if he had aimed at a reduction in per-unit costs.

Moreover, just as in the contemporary world of industrial Research and Development, after a process innovation occurs, it tends to be imitated, if not copied outright, unless it is protected by patents or secrecy. Competition compels rivals to adopt similar techniques that to a varying extent help them to cut down on costs and remain competitive. This competitive process eventually eliminates all the profits from the innovation. In a situation where product and process innovations were interwoven and the imitation of the product ('painterly' pictures) almost inevitably implied imitation of the process (a more rapid execution), the economic rents accruing to the innovators were soon dissipated. In the final reckoning, it was the consumer who benefited by paying lower prices for attractive paintings than he would have been obliged to pay in the absence of the innovation.

The wide diffusion of paintings by the main innovators in Netherlandish landscape and still-life painting and their frequent appearance in collections located in all the major cities of Holland suggest that they, as well as their less successful imitators, worked mainly for an anonymous market. Dealers, whose intermediary role in marketing works of art seems to have increased markedly from the 1630s on, bought the works of these artists directly from their studio and sold them to collectors all over the country.

Excerpts (pp. 245–47, 249, 252–53) from "Art Dealers in the Seventeenth-Century Netherlands," *Simiolus: Netherlands Quarterly for the History of Art* 18, no. 4 (1988): 244–56. Reprinted with kind permission of Stichting Simiolus and John-Luke Montias.

In general, I conjecture that the demand for dealers' services will depend positively both on *the degree of the artists' specialization* and on *the variegation of consumers' tastes* (the two variables themselves being interdependent). Dealers are needed to help consumers with sharply defined tastes find the suppliers they desire. The increasing attention paid to the authenticity and originality of works of art in the 1630s and 1640s and the rising percentage of attributed paintings in notarial inventories suggest that individual collectors' tastes were becoming more discriminating in this period, at least with respect to artistic style. Most consumers of art could not readily travel to other towns, let alone to other countries, in search of the things they liked. Dealers saved them time and monetary search costs by acting as their virtual agents, and by scouring markets on their behalf. Once a dealer had built up a stock-in-trade, he could invite his clients to examine and compare examples of the kind of works they might be interested in and help them make a more discriminating selection than they could by going around from one artist's studio to the next. The comparative advantage of dealers in economizing on search costs would lead us to expect that out-of-town artists would be better represented in dealers' stocks than local artists, from whom many collectors would be likely to buy directly or on the local *kermis* market. [. . .]

While some dealers specialized in mediating the demand for art works, others concentrated on increasing the supply of works available in the market. They did so either by setting artists to work at so much per day, per month or per year, or they bought paintings from a stable of artists at so many guilders each for a panel or a canvas of given dimensions. . . . These supply-augmenting dealers sold mainly less expensive paintings by run-of-the-mill artists, in contrast to the dealers facilitating the search of collectors who offered their clients works by well-known artists—both contemporary and "old masters"—at higher prices.

The artists willing to "sit in the galley," were often unknown, or so we can infer from the fact that their names only appear in dealers' inventories or only appeared in private inventories in later years, after they had acquired a reputation. A typical instance is the flower painter Elias van den Broeck who, in 1674, at the age of 21, painted for a year for the Antwerp dealer Bartholomeus Floquet for free board and lodging and a modest salary of 120 guilders. Pieter van den Bosch, when he first arrived in Amsterdam in 1645, signed a contract with Marten Kretzer, who must have been active as a dealer at the time, to paint "from sunrise to twilight in the winter and from 7 am to 7 pm in the summer . . . all such pieces as Kretzer would be pleased to order him," this for the rather grandiose sum of 1,200 guilders a year, at a time when ordinary journeymen carpenters earned less than a guilder a day and the manager of a Delft pottery was paid 800 guilders a year. Piece rates varied enormously. In 1641, Isaac van Ostade received only 27 guilders for thirteen pictures which the dealer Leendert Volmarijn had ordered from him, barely over two guilders apiece. This amount, however, was so low that Adriaen van Ostade sued Volmarijn on his brother's behalf. Following the judge's decision, Isaac was promised 6 guilders apiece for nine paintings. Herman van Swoll, who is chiefly known as a collector but must also have engaged in dealing from time to time, paid Nikolas Verkolje 12 guilders for every picture that he copied. [. . .] No doubt, the size of the paintings commissioned, the time an artist devoted to each picture (tight or loose brushwork), and his reputation helped determine these prices.

It is not obvious from the evidence at hand why artists chose to work for dealers rather than offer their works directly to the market. One possibility is that they were not guild members—because they had not completed their training, were not citizens of the town in which they worked, or had not paid their guild dues. This possibility cannot be checked for Amsterdam, because no guild lists have survived for the first 88 years of the century that would allow us to verify whether the artists who apparently painted for Cornelis Doeck and other Amsterdam dealers were or were not registered in the guild. A more likely possibility is that the dealers knew the market of the Netherlands as a whole much better than did the young artists in their employ: they were in a better position to meet consumers' demands than isolated artists were. Finally, the lack of working capital needed to pay for pigments, panels and canvases, and of paintings to build up an inventory, may have prevented less talented (or lucky) artists who had no resources at their disposal from striking out on their own. The role of the dealer in financing and controlling the "production" of paintings parallels that of the textile merchant who provided weavers with yarn and other necessary inputs and collected the finished cloth in the "putting out" system. The galley method, particularly in Amsterdam, seems to have been fairly widespread, but its importance in supplying the market for Dutch paintings lay mainly at the lower end of the quality spectrum, in copies and works-by-the-dozen. I doubt whether many of these inexpensive paintings survived. Dealers working the upper end of the market, such as Johannes de Renialme and Gerrit Uylenburgh, seem not to have employed low-paid artists to work for them. They and other prominent merchants bought the works in their stocks-in-trade from established masters or from other dealers, or accepted paintings on consignment. [. . .]

[. . .] My sample of dealers' inventories consists of ten inventories, seven from Amsterdam, two from Rotterdam and one from Middelburg, all of fairly large size, ranging from 42 attributions (in the inventory of Lambert Blaeuw) to 456 attributions (in that of Volmarijn). The earliest is the Balkeneynde inventory dated 1631, the latest, H. Meyeringh's, dated 1687. All were recorded after the death of the owner, except for the Uylenburgh inventory, which was drawn up by reason of his bankruptcy. [. . .]

From [the inventories] I draw the following conclusions. Renialme and Uylenburgh were oriented more or less exclusively to meeting the demand of a high-class clientele for quality paintings. They offered their clients different national styles (Dutch, Flemish, Italian) and periods (from the early sixteenth century on). They acquired paintings for the most part from artists working outside Amsterdam. They almost certainly did not have a stable of artists working for them on a regular basis. Their role, and their reward, lay in their search-and-find activities and in arbitrage—bringing works of art from places where their prices were relatively low to where they were higher. Balkeneynde, Blaeuw, Doeck, Volmarijn and Meyeringh made their living by buying or commissioning inexpensive pictures chiefly by obscure artists, some of whom probably sat for them "in the galley." A few of these artists appear nowhere else but in one or the other of these inventories (Jan Hermansz. Vinck, Pieter Vermeulen, Slort). Others appear in two or more dealers' inventories (Jacob Wynants, L. de Laeff), or are still known, albeit slightly, today (Hendrick de Meyer, Gerrit van Vucht, Pieter Cosijn). Some, like "den Haen" and "Vervries" were probably so familiar to the person who drew up the inventory that he felt no need to specify whether he was referring to Gerrit or Anthony de Haen in the former case or to Roelof, Michiel, or Jacob de Vries in the latter. The only direct evidence we have, however, that any of these dealers was employing or commissioning artists is the contract signed by Berneards and his fellow Middelburg dealer Abraham Buscare in 1671 . . . in which they agreed to share equally the profits from the sale of paintings and drawings they will have bought or that they will cause to have made as they may deem desirable.

Our last two dealers, Pieter van Meldert and Mathijs Hals, both of whom had numerous medium-priced Haarlem painters in their stock (Hendrick Mommers, Jan and Pieter Wouwerman, Gerrit and Jacob de Wet, Floris van Schooten), catered for a clientele somewhat superior to that of the dealers who had more or less unknown artists working for them, though far below the wealthy category of consumers to which Renialme and Uylenburgh were oriented. They contributed to the massive import into Amsterdam of "modern" landscapes, still lifes, and genre pictures from Haarlem.

From the evident lack of congruence between the incidence of the most frequently cited artists in the inventories of the Amsterdam dealers Blaeuw, Doeck and Meyeringh, who operated toward the lower end of wealth scale, on the one hand, and in the private collections in my sample on the other, we can draw another significant conclusion, provided we can assume, as I think we can, that these dealers sold their works chiefly to Amsterdam collectors. If any of the paintings by these obscure artists—or ones of a similar lack of renown—had appeared in the collections in my sample, then the chances are they would not have been recognized by the clerks or the assessors writing out the inventory. They would have remained unattributed. But they were attributed in dealers' inventories because they or their assistants, who knew their stock from first-hand contact with supplier-artists, were better able to make attributions to less well-known artists than were the clerks or the assessors drawing up inventories of private collectors, who had to rely on their connoisseurship.

BERT W. MEIJER, *Italian Paintings in Holland*

Excerpts (pp. 377–81, 384–86, 392–94) from "Italian Paintings in 17th Century Holland: Art Market, Art Works and Art Collections," in *L'Europa e l'arte italiana*, ed. M. Seidel (Venice: Marsilio Editori, 2000), 377–417. Reprinted with kind permission of the author.

Around 1630, the young Rembrandt and his friend Jan Lievens observed that it was easier to see Italian paintings north of the Alps than in Italy. However exaggerated this opinion may seem, it is true that the acquisition of Italian paintings increased enormously at the courts of England and Spain, and some decades later, through King Louis XIV, in France. During Holland's economic and artistic Golden Age, Dutch collectors, too, bought numerous Italian paintings. [. . .]

During the first decades of the 17th century, when, as far as we know, there were still relatively few Italian paintings in Amsterdam, most of the owners of such paintings . . . lived in the old part of the city, within the medieval walls. From then on, however, a growing number of the upper class—some of whom owned Italian paintings—built houses and resided in the so-called new town, an extension to the city, which was begun in the 1580s, with the still extant semi-crescent of canals laid around the old town. The growing strength of the Dutch economy and of Dutch cities, along with greater private wealth, were determining factors in the increasing refinement and sophistication of the Dutch life style. At the same time, the art market—including that of Italian paintings—was expanding.

Testimony of the deep appreciation of Italian painting is found in Dutch writing on Italian art during this period in inventories, in printed auction catalogues, and in prints after Italian paintings. As we can deduce from the sales catalogues listed in Lugt's *Répertoire des catalogues de ventes*, and from the number of sales advertisements in Dutch newspapers published in Amsterdam, Haarlem and Leiden from 1672 on, early printed auction catalogues in 17th century Holland were quite numerous and, in a way, unique. Although auction catalogues from the same years [could] be found elsewhere in Europe, particularly in Antwerp, London and Paris, in the latter cities the phenomenon seems to have been far less relevant than in Holland, and particularly in Amsterdam.

Dutch 17th century sale catalogues that included Italian paintings generally began with the Italian works, following with monumental Flemish paintings, then Dutch paintings, concluding with minor paintings from all countries. Italian paintings, then, belonged to the upper range of the market. The prices paid for these paintings were often much higher than those paid for Dutch religious or mythological paintings, for which the larger size of the Italian works is only a partial explanation.

Among the foreign visitors in Amsterdam during the first decades of the century was the chaplain Francesco Belli who, in the guise of secretary, accompanied the Venetian envoy Zorzo Zorzi on his embassy to Holland in 1626. Belli wrote in his diary "[. . .] I observed among others a piece of Reni, representing painting and drawing, held in singular value." [The painting Belli referred to was in] a monumental *palazzo* built five years earlier for Nicolas Sohier—a rich merchant of Flemish origin—along one of the new canals, the Keizersgracht. . . . Reni's *Painting and Drawing* . . . remained with Sohier at least until his death in 1642, and in Holland until the 1660s or later. In 1660 it was copied in a drawing by Jan de Bisschop. After the painting was acquired in the 1680s for the collection of Louis XIV, its rectangular format was changed into an oval.

Among the paintings owned by Nicolas Sohier that Belli does not explicitly mention, but which appear in the inventory compiled after Sohier's death in 1642, we find the well-known triple portrait of *A Man and a Woman Accompanied by a Second Woman*, now in Detroit, which in the Sohier collection was attributed to Giorgione, Titian and Sebastiano del Piombo together. After the death of Sohier's grandson . . . the painting passed to Marinus de Jeude (de Jode), bailiff of the Court of Holland in The Hague. Constantijn Huygens II, one of the sons of the great statesman and scholar, saw the painting in De Jeude's house in 1695, together with the *Annunciation to the Shepherds* by Bassano, also from the Sohier collection, as we know from Huygens' Diary. Huygens did not accept the triple-painter attribution. Subsequently the painting was bought by the Dutch *Stadhouder* and King of England, William III, along with other Italian paintings, to adorn the walls of his hunting-lodge Het Loo, near Apeldoorn. The paintings from Het Loo were put up for sale by the King's heirs in 1713, but not all of them were sold. In the sale, our painting figures as by Titian. The attribution was, and still is, a matter of controversy, and varies from all three painters together, to only one or another of them.

As documented by the same inventory of 1642, Sohier owned several other Italian paintings: A *Courtesan* by Palma il Vecchio; *St. Paul* by Paris Bordon; a *Madonna with Child and St. John* by Paolo Veronese; *St. John Preaching*, attributed to Parmigianino; a *Madonna and Child* by Titian; and, from a more recent generation—"i moderni" as Belli called them—"A Courtesan looking in the mirror and hanging a pearl in her ear" by Angelo Caroselli (1585–1652), which must have been rather similar to a painting now in the Fondazione Longhi. [. . .]

The brothers Gerard and Jan Reynst, successful partners in trade, must have started buying art works around 1625, when Jan transferred to Venice for reasons connected with business. He was to remain there until his death in 1646. Gerard lived in Amsterdam, where he held several high public offices. The brothers owned important art collections in Venice and Amsterdam. Their fundamental role in the world of Venetian art and collectors is clearly documented in the introduction to, and on the title page of, the first part of Carlo Ridolfi's *Le Maraviglie dell'arte* (1648), dedicated to the Reynst brothers. Ridolfi described their collections in Venice and Amsterdam, which comprised Egyptian archeological objects, naturalia, antique sculptures, and paintings by artists such as Raphael, Giovanni Bellini, Parmigianino, Titian, Tintoretto and Paolo Veronese, many of which had been bought by Jan and sent to Amsterdam. The future Grand Duke Cosimo III de' Medici visited the Reynst collection in Amsterdam on January 3, 1668. In the diary kept by Cosimo's secretary it was described as "una buona raccolta di pitture antiche e de' migliori maestri di Lombardia", that is to say mainly paintings from northern Italy, and not much from the central or southern part of the peninsula. From the same source we learn that Jan Reynst had acquired part of the collection of Andrea Vendramin (d. 1629), who had lived in Venice on the Canal Grande, near the church of San Gregorio. This collection, which was described in general terms by Scamozzi in 1615, in his *Idea della architettura universale*, was inventoried in detail in seventeen manuscript catalogues. One of these, *De picturis in museis Dni Andreae Vendrameni positis*, was illustrated with drawings made after the paintings, and finally published by Borenius in 1923. The Vendramin paintings and antique sculptures acquired by the Reynst brothers were shipped to Amsterdam and displayed in their house called "The Hope" on the Keizersgracht, which Gerard and Jan had bought in 1634. The house was praised by a visitor as being like "a Royal palace inside" with works of art valued at "three tons of gold or more". Other paintings owned by the Reynst brothers had come from the collections of Lord and Lady Arundel, and the Duke of Buckingham. [. . .]

For the admirers of Italian painting in Holland the arrival of the Arundel collection must have been a major event. It was one of the most important art collections in England and afterwards also in Holland. In 1642, Thomas Howard, Earl of Arundel, and his wife, Lady Aletheia, fled to the continent with the bulk of their fabulous collection of paintings and drawings and several antique sculptures. In 1644, Arundel went to Italy, where he died in 1646. Lady Aletheia, his universal heir, established herself in the Northern Netherlands. . . . She died in Amsterdam on July 3, 1654. Before her death, she had already started to sell off some of the best pieces of the collection—such as Paolo Veronese's large *Christ and the Centurion*, in the Prado—to Luis Méndez de Haro y Guzmán, Marqués del Carpio. Some of these paintings were intended for the Spanish King, Philip IV. After Lady Aletheia's death, much of the collection remained in Holland. In fact, many of the pieces stayed in Holland for longer than they had stayed in England. In, or shortly before, 1654 an inventory of more than 800 art works of the Arundel collection was compiled in Amsterdam, consisting mainly of paintings but also drawings, sculptures and *objets d'art*. Only half of the works listed were attributed. Moreover, the list is not complete. In addition to more than 40 Holbeins and paintings by German artists, there were also paintings by Dutch and Flemish artists, but the majority were by, or attributed to, the most important 16th century Italian masters: at least five works were attributed to Andrea del Sarto, thirteen to the Bassano, six to the Carracci, twelve paintings and drawings to Correggio, twenty-six to Parmigianino, sixteen to Giorgione, five to Leonardo, over fifteen to Raphael—but one of these is by Sebastiano del Piombo—ten to Andrea Schiavone, ten to Tintoretto, thirty-six to Titian, eighteen to Paolo Veronese, and so on. [. . .]

Some parts of the collection came up for sale on the Amsterdam art market over the next decades. Among those who succeeded in acquiring works from the Arundel collection in Amsterdam were the famous banker and collector, Eberhard von Jabach (Cologne 1618–Paris 1696) and his nephews, Franz and Bernhard Albert von Imstenraedt. [. . .] Several of the Arundel paintings bought by Jabach, including a number of Holbeins, were sold to Louis XIV in 1671 and are now in the Louvre.

SVETLANA ALPERS, *Freedom, Art, and Money*

Excerpt (pp. 99–105) from "Freedom, Art, and Money," in *Rembrandt's Enterprise: The Studio and the Market* (Chicago: University of Chicago Press, 1988), 88–122. Copyright © 1988 University of Chicago Press, Chicago and London.

Rembrandt was not only unwilling to play the social game with patrons, he was also unwilling to produce works that could be paid for, and hence valued, in the accustomed ways. What we described . . . as Rembrandt's "rough" studio mode can also be described in market terms. Contemporary remarks and complaints about the lack of finish of Rembrandt's paintings testify to the challenge he offered to the normal ways of calculating painterly value. Though clearly made by his hand, his works did not display the artist's labor in an expected and accepted sense. Rembrandt's characteristic working and reworking of the paint meant that the amount of time he spent was incalculable and the achievement of completion impossible to judge. Value in both senses in which the paintings by [Adriaen] Van der Werff were judged—time spent and perfection like that of Nature—was rejected by Rembrandt.

Because Rembrandt made paintings in the manner he did, the question of when a work was finished was open to dispute. It was all very well for him to say that a painting was finished when his intention was realized, as [Arnold] Houbraken reports, but that left judgment of finish, and hence the calculation of value, solely in the hands of the artist. A law suit taken up against him in 1654 shows the problems raised: a client named d'Andrada complained that Rembrandt's portrait of a young woman was not a likeness and demanded that he change it, or else return his advance of seventy-five guilders with interest. Rembrandt, unwilling as always to give an inch when challenged, replied as follows: he would not put his hand to the painting or finish it until he was paid the remainder of what was due; when it was finished, judgment as to the likeness would be left to the board of the Guild of St. Luke; if it must be changed again and still did not suit the client he would take it back, finish it in the course of time and sell it (presumably for a second, additional payment) the next time he held a sale of his paintings. [. . .]

It was normal workshop practice for a master to keep a number of unfinished or partially finished works in the studio for finishing to order. But Rembrandt worked this system to his own painterly and market ends. There were occasions on which Rembrandt told a client that if he did not think a work were finished it could be returned and he would, for a fee, paint at it some more. There is at least one occasion (the case of the [*Conspiracy of Claudius*] *Civilis*) on which Rembrandt must have calculated that he would be able to get more money by retouching a painting. A legal document records that one quarter of the payment, plus one quarter of the additional money he would be paid for retouching it, were destined for van Ludick, the dealer/creditor. . . . It would appear that the (to us) problematic return of the [*Civilis*] painting to Rembrandt for more work was anticipated, even desired, by the artist. [. . .] A less clear case is that of the *Homer*, which Rembrandt shipped to Ruffo in Sicily along with an *Alexander*. Ruffo liked the work but, referring to it as "*mezzo finito*" and disputing the price asked by the artist (which he pointed out was four times the price per head or per half-figure in Italy), he shipped it back to Rembrandt. Rembrandt, in response, held firm on the five-hundred-guilder price for the painting, which he referred to (in the Italian version which is all that we have of his letter) as "*il schizzo di Humerio*" [sic]. One wonders if Rembrandt had not hoped to get by with the *Homer* in the condition in which he sent it to Italy in the first place, and, failing that, counted on the fact that he could insist on the five-hundred-guilder fee when he put in some more work.

What seems odd in his practice as a painter is what brought Rembrandt fame and money as an etcher. His repeated reworkings of his plates and the resulting series of states were deployed as a marketing device which gained him great success. In Houbraken's words, "Thanks to his method of putting in slight changes or small additions so that his prints could be sold as new . . . no true connoisseur could be without the *Juno* . . . with or without the crown—or *Joseph* with his head in the light and with his head in shadow. . . ." In the case of his etchings, Rembrandt's long-drawn-out working procedure was made to pay off at each of several stages along the way in the working of a plate. By creating a demand for his works in progress, Rembrandt as an etcher established a remarkably successful marketing operation. It was preeminently through the sale and wide distribution of his etchings that Rembrandt's European reputation was made in his lifetime. He transformed a medium whose great distinction in other hands was its replicative nature into the most personal and individualized as well as the most widely circulated of commodities. What he treated as his most private preserve or property (in the sense that his assistants did not also etch), one that was labor-intensive, replicative in nature, and generally patron free, was his most successful mode of production.

What did Rembrandt have in mind in place of the patronage system? It seems to have been something a bit old but also rather new: a craftsman selling his products replaced by an entrepreneur, of sorts, working the market with pictures distinctive in manner or mode. Two terms deserve attention here: entrepreneur and market. I say "an entrepreneur of sorts." As far as production went, it was Rubens and not Rembrandt who was the prime innovator in the north of Europe at the time. Though Rembrandt's obsession with the intricacies of the market system permeated his life and his work, the organization of his shop— a master surrounded by student assistants each eventually producing paintings on their own for sale—was an established one. It was Rubens, by contrast, who promoted a division of labor. He developed a painting factory: assistants specialized in certain skills—landscapes, animals, and so on—and the master devised a mode of invention employing a clever combination of oil sketches and drawings. These permitted his inventions to be executed by others, sometimes with final touches to hands or faces by the master himself. It is in keeping with the logic of this factory procedure that Rubens, unlike Rembrandt, did not sign the works that were sold from his studio. Only five of the thousands of works produced were signed. On occasion, when challenged or pressed, Rubens agreed to make distinctions between hands. But the claim that all the works issuing forth from his studio were his was a claim about a commodity whose value was distinguishable from his own hand and which was capable of proliferation and replication. Rubens confirmed this expansive notion of authenticity and authentication when he sought and received copyright protection against the pirating of the engravings which his studio was in the business of producing after his paintings. Rembrandt imitated this mode in a brief experiment with essentially replicative etchings in the thirties, but he then gave it up. Modern attempts to separate works by Rubens's hand from those by others in the studio, and the taste for his *eigenhändig* oil sketches, intrude a notion of value inappropriate to his mode of production and to the commodity he produced. Though he was himself a brilliant wielder of both brush and pen, Rubens was a pioneer in encouraging the distribution and sales of his inventions through means that have come, in our age, to be called mechanical reproduction. For all its modernity in these terms, it did not prove to be a lasting model for art in our culture.

While Rubens's interest was in the work of art as a commodity distinct from himself personally, Rembrandt, despite the diffusion of his manner in his studio, was unwilling to make this separation. So far as we know he almost never collaborated on paintings with assistants. His merging of invention with execution, his distinctive handling of the paint (or of the etched line), his invention and use of his signature presented his works and those of his studio as an extension of himself. Related to this is the fact that, while Rubens's works benefited from and frankly displayed the fact that they did cleave to pictorial tradition, Rembrandt's, as we have seen, did not. But this was where Rembrandt's peculiarity and innovation lay. It was the commodity—the *Rembrandt*—that Rembrandt made that was new. And it is he, not Rubens, who invented the work of art most characteristic of our culture—a commodity distinguished among others by not being factory produced, but produced in limited numbers and creating its market, whose special claim to the aura of individuality and to high market value binds it to basic aspects of an entrepreneurial (capitalist) enterprise.

While other ambitious artists were defecting from the open market to patrons, Rembrandt maintained his freedom by choosing to make art for the new markets. This helps to explain certain accusations mounted against him in early lives. The charge that he chose to hobnob with the lower classes might well have been a reaction to Rembrandt's rejection of the social behavior or adaptation that the patronage system assumed. He was also said to have been overly interested in money: he was criticized for having charged stiff fees to his students and for making money from the sale of their work, though neither practice was at all unusual at the time. Since making money was not considered reprehensible in other artists—on the contrary it was one of the desiderata of the profession—some reflection must be being cast on the unacceptable way in which Rembrandt went about it. If one puts together the apparent contradiction between charges of hobnobbing with the poor on the one hand, and money-grabbing on the other, the common denominator would seem to be that of a man out for gain in a socially unacceptable, or what was considered a déclassé, way. The marketplace, not the dwelling places of the rich, they were saying, was his beat.

But was it simply gain or profit that drove Rembrandt? [. . .] His aim was less to get rich quick than to feed the mania for collecting or hoarding that he displayed throughout his life. Having frequented auctions starting in the mid-thirties, sometimes buying multiple copies of prints (eight copies of Dürer's *Life of the Virgin*, for example), he built up the huge collection of paintings (over seventy), works on paper (ninety albums), shells, statuary, and armor, only a part of which was inventoried when the famous bankruptcy sale was held. After having officially declared bankruptcy, Rembrandt began to collect again.

It appears that collecting came naturally to Rembrandt, but one must remember that this was a cultural phenomenon. I mean this not only in the sense that artists needed material for study in the studio, or that they were dealers on the side, or that the encyclopedic collection was the mark of the cultivated gentleman merchant at the time, but also in the sense that the storing up of goods, as assets for future dealings, was a remarkable and celebrated practice in the Amsterdam commercial and trading world. A feature of Amsterdam was the huge warehouses built to store grain, spices, wines, furs, sugar, cocoa—any goods the world wanted—in unprecedented quantities. This great abundance of goods was backed up by a banking system which assured sufficient credit for the most flexible possible scheduling of payments. The bulging depots were as fabled in the public world of commerce as the encyclopedic collections were in the private sphere, though they were not discussed in the same texts. [. . .] Warehouses and encyclopedic collections alike are evidence of an accumulating instinct endemic to a capitalist economy predicated on the existence of markets. Rembrandt was part of this.

Rembrandt entertained a number of different interests when he ventured forth to bid at auctions in Amsterdam. First, as we have seen, he was building up his own collection. But it appears that, contrary to what one would expect, Rembrandt was not necessarily after bargains. He bid excessively high prices (breaking all previous records, as one would say today) for certain works. The extravagant price of 79 guilders which he paid for a single copy of the so-called *Eulenspiegel* print of Lucas van Leyden was commented on at the time. One can chalk such extravagance up to artistic admiration as well as to scarcity: there is no question that Lucas was an artist for whose works Rembrandt had an affinity. But something else is also in play here, and Baldinucci recognized it when he explained that Rembrandt bid up the prices of works of art on the market in order to add credit to his profession, *per mettere in credito la professione*. The word *credito* has just the right historical inflection, since like the English "credit," *credito* engaged both reputation/ belief and the commercial/economic meaning which were conjoined in Rembrandt's market behavior on behalf of art. While other Dutch artists added to the esteem of their profession by forming clubs or academies to replace the craftsman's guild, and by serving courts and wealthy patrons, Rembrandt chose to do so by attending to the value of art on the market. For Rembrandt this was clearly an alternative way. He did not wish to establish value by personal association with those who had status or power through a taste in letters or through money, but rather in "free" market terms.

It is against this background that we should note the words "sold for 3,500 guilders" that Rembrandt jotted next to his quick, salesroom copy after Raphael's *Baldassare Castiglione*. . . . And this explains the story of how the Rembrandt etching known as "the hundred-guilder print" got its name. The eighteenth-century collector and amateur of the arts, Mariette, said that it was Rembrandt himself who bought up at a sale an impression of his *Christ Preaching* for this excessive price. It was not, Mariette wrote, that Rembrandt needed it. Not only had he kept the plate, but he had already bought up at any price he could every impression of it that he could find. What he wanted to do was to make his works rare, in order, the implication is, to add to their value. The specific value once established by reference to a print worth a hundred guilders has long since worn off—as has even the magic of the 2.3 million dollars paid for the *Aristotle*, when such paintings as a modest portrait of a woman certified to be by Rembrandt's hand are sold today for four times that amount. But the aura of the sobriquet "one-hundred guilder print," like that of the 2.3-million-dollar *Aristotle*, has stuck. It records not just a price, but a manner of indicating the worth of a work of art that has lasted.

From the point of view of the person who is doing the buying, Rembrandt's tactics were not money-making. If Rembrandt made it a practice to bid up and buy goods at high prices in order to establish their value on the market, it was a recipe for eventual bankruptcy. [. . .] Once again, as in most of his dealings (he was a true Amsterdam trader in this), it was less money in the bank than the promise of future returns that he was after. Rembrandt was using the marketplace to add honor to art. The term *honor* is not offered lightly. The nature of Rembrandt's dealings in the marketplace suggests a context in which to read the famous phrase "*eer voor goet*," or honor before goods or possessions, that he inscribed in the *album amicorum* of Burchard Grossman in 1634 on the eve of his marriage to Saskia.

REMBRANDT, *Letters to Constantijn Huygens, ca. 1639*

Excerpts from letters from Rembrandt to Constantijn Huygens, in *Die Urkunden über Rembrandt*, ed. C. Hofstede de Groot (The Hague: Martinus Nijhoff, 1906). Translation published by kind permission of Benjamin Binstock.

    My lord,

My most gracious lord Huygens, [I] hope that your lordship will please tell his Excellency that I am hard at work on and expertly completing the three passion paintings which his Excellency himself has commissioned from me, an entombment and a resurrection and an Ascension of Christ. These are companion pieces to a raising and a descent of Christ on the Cross. Of the three earlier named pieces one is finished, the one with Christ's ascension to Heaven, and the other two are about half done. And so if his Excellency prefers to have this finished piece first or the three together, [I] beg my lord let me know that I may best serve the desires of his Prince Excellency.

And [I] also can not resist, because of my readiness to serve, from honoring my lord with my latest work trusting that this will be taken in the best way Along with my greetings [I] commend all of yours to God in health.

My lord's ready and devoted servant Rembrandt

.   .   .

My lord,
After offering friendly greetings let me say I think it good that I follow directly to see how the piece fits in with the rest. As for the price of the piece, I have certainly earned 200 pounds with it but I will let myself be contented with whatever his excellence pays me. My lord if my lordship will not take my cheek amiss, I will not neglect to repay the favor.

Your Lordship's ready and devoted servant Rembrandt
In the gallery of His exc. it will show best as there is a strong light there.

.   .   .

My lord,
Because of the great pleasure and devotion that I have put into the execution of the two pieces which his Highness has had me make, being the one where the dead body of Christ is laid in the grave and the other one where Christ rises up from the dead to the great shock of the guards. These same two pieces are now complete as well due to studious diligence so that I am now also inclined to deliver these in order to please his Highness since in these two the greatest and the most natural movement is observed which is also the reason that I have had them so long in my hands.

I therefore would request if my lord could please tell his Highness of this and if my lord could please have the two pieces first delivered to your house as happened before. I will wait first for a short note to this effect.

And since my lord will be bothered with this business for the second time in recognition a piece 10 feet long and 8 feet high will be included as well which will do honor to my lord in his house. I wish you all happiness and the blessing of salvation, Amen.

Your Lordship, my lord's r. and devoted servant Rembrandt
the 12 January 1639

.   .   .

My lord,
It is then with the permission of your lordship that I send these two pieces which
I believe will be found sufficient that his Highness will now pay me no less than
a thousand guilders for each. Yet if his Highness thinks them not worth that and
will pay me less according to his own pleasure I rely on his Highness' knowledge
and discretion. I will thankfully let myself be contented with that and remain
along with my greetings his

    ready and devoted servant
    Rembrandt
    What I have advanced for the frames and the crate is 44 guilders

.   .   .

My lord,
I have read your lordship's agreeable missive of the 14th with particular pleasure.
[I] find there your lordship's good favor and disposition so that I remain with
heart-felt devotion obliged to repay your lordship with service and friendship.
Because of my inclination to do so I am sending the accompanying canvas
against my lord's wishes hoping that this will not be taken amiss by you as it is
the first token that I have presented my lord. The tax collector mr. wttenboogaert
paid me a visit as I was busy packing these two pieces. He wanted to see one
first. He said he could advance me the payments here from his office if it pleased
his Highness. Thus I would request of you my lord that whatever his Highness
grants me for the 2 pieces that I may receive this money here soon as it would be
particularly useful to me now. Awaiting your lordship's answer I wish your
lordship and your family all happiness and salvation along with my greetings.

    Your Lordship's r. and affectionate servant Rembrandt
    In haste this 27 January 1639
    My lord hang this piece in a strong light and such that one can stand far away so
    that it will sparkle at its best.

.   .   .

Honored Lord,
I have complete trust that everything will go well and in particular regarding my
compensation for these last 2 pieces trusting your lordship that if it had gone
according to of your lordship's favor and what is right there would have been no
objection to the agreed price. And as far as the pieces delivered earlier no more
than 600 carolus guilders were paid for each. And if his Highness can not be
moved to a higher price with good will although they are admittedly worth it,
I can be satisfied with 600 c. guilders each, as long as my outlay for the 2 ebony
frames and the crate, which is 44 guilders, can be included in the account.

So I would kindly request of my lord that I may now soon receive my payment
here in Amsterdam, trusting that due to the good favor shown me I will soon
enjoy my monies, while I remain grateful for all such friendship. And with my
heartfelt greetings to my lord and to all your lordship's nearest friends, all are
commended to God in long-lasting health.

> Your Lordship's r. and affectionate servant
> Rembrandt

. . .

> My Lord,

My noble Lord it is with scruples that I inflict my letter upon your lordship in
order to say that I complained to the collector Wttenbogaert concerning the delay
of my payment, although the treasurer Volbergen denies this as the dues were
claimed yearly. The collector Wttenbogaert responded to this last Wednesday that
Volbergen has claimed the same dues every half year up till now, so that more
than 4000 carolus guilders have once again appeared at the same office. And as
these are the true circumstances I beseech you my well-disposed Lord that my
warrant might be taken care of at once so that I might now at last receive
my well-earned 1244 guilders. And I will always seek to repay this to your
lordship with reverence, service and evidence of friendship. With this goes
my heart-felt greetings and wishes God keep your lordship in good health and
bless you

> Your Lordship's r. and affectionate servant
> Rembrandt

KOENRAAD JONCKHEERE, *Attributions in Auction Catalogs*

Excerpts (pp. 76–78, 82) from "Supply and Demand: Some Notes on the Economy of
Seventeenth Century Connoisseurship," in *A Closer Look at Paintings by Rembrandt,
Rubens and Their Contemporaries*, ed. K. Jonckheere and A. Tummers (Amsterdam:
Amsterdam University Press, 2008), 69–109. Reprinted by kind permission of the
author.

Jan Pietersz. Zomer was a renowned connoisseur in early eighteenth-century Amsterdam.
He was the most successful organizer of auctions and a very busy appraiser. He was thus
an obvious choice to study how connoisseurs dealt with painters' names at the end of
the seventeenth century in auction catalogues. Did they use a complex system of
attributions . . . or did they always attribute it to one painter or another, or even more
generally speaking, to one brand? [. . .]

[. . .] I took all the Zomer auction catalogues, annotated with prices and standardised
the painters' names to rank them alphabetically. [. . .] The results were as clear as they

were surprising. . . . Zomer always attributed the painting to the 'master', without bothering with any fine tuning. This means that all works in the manner of, for instance, Rubens were simply called Rubens. Zomer generally made a distinction between, for instance, fathers and sons if their styles were distinctly different (e.g., Pieter Brueghel and Jan Brueghel), but not between originals, studio copies or inferior copies (e.g., Jan Brueghel the Elder and Jan Brueghel the Younger) if they were of a similar nature. I only found a few exceptions to this rule in all of the lots in the sample. Zomer referred to just two paintings as 'copies after' out of a total of 1226, namely one after Rubens and one after Rembrandt. All of the other paintings were attributed to the masters themselves, without any reservations on the part of Zomer. This indicates that Zomer ranked the paintings in the style of the master under the master's brand name, without questioning their actual nature (copies, style of, etc.). A consequence could have been that Zomer sold many paintings as anonymous, but that was not the case at all. [. . .]

Even more stunning is the fact that Zomer never mentioned monograms or signatures, even though many of the thousands of paintings he handled during his career must have been signed or marked. Compilers of inventories and auctioneers like Zomer must have made use of the names and the monograms on the paintings for attributions. Nonetheless, he seldom referred to them as such. Zomer chose to keep this information a secret and thus worked against the idea of a transparent market, which is in sharp contrast with some eighteenth-century art dealers. . . . He apparently never considered a signature worth mentioning in his auction catalogues. It is therefore impossible to confirm the notion that an art dealer-connoisseur like Jan Pietersz. Zomer was interested in authenticity when attributing paintings, since he deliberately and almost systematically *denied* obvious evidence of authorship. However, Zomer was not unique in this respect. Seventeenth-century appraisers of probate inventories in Antwerp and Amsterdam seldom mentioned signatures or monograms. [. . .]

One cannot deny that Zomer was like most art dealer-connoisseurs in that he had little interest in the terms 'studio', 'pupil' or 'disciple'. . . . He used painters' names in his catalogues to divide the works of art into certain recognisable categories, rather than to define the precise, correct attributions. He used the names to sort out the vast number of paintings, to in effect 'catalogue' them. He never specifically mentioned whether any particular work was an original or a copy. In doing so, Zomer also dodged any possible legal actions. [. . .]

Zomer, like the other auctioneers, was paid a percentage of his turnover. If authorship and authenticity had been a primary concern of auctioneers, art dealers or appraisers, one would have expected them to systematically mention the signatures or monograms and to differentiate between copies and 'originals'. . . . Elite art lovers, who often purchased works at auctions, unlike the brokers, were interested in authenticity and thus a mark of authenticity increased a work's value. So why Zomer and the other appraisers systematically ignored issues of attribution must lie elsewhere. I believe that Zomer simply let the buyers figure it out for themselves. Zomer identified the type, the style, the brand of a particular work, but it was up to the buyers themselves to recognise the quality or lack of quality of a particular painting. [. . .] On some occasions [Zomer] would add 'quality labels' to the descriptions of paintings, calling them '*extraordinaer, vraei, konstig, kapitael*' (extraordinary, beautiful, artistic, important), etc. Did it help? It certainly did. Whenever Zomer added a 'quality label' to the description of the painting the prices rose to levels above the average prices paid for that particular painter's work. [. . .]

So, how did wealthy art collectors deal with the problem of attributions and connoisseurship? Did they place their recently purchased paintings on an easel, study the works in detail and then decide on the quality and attribution, as we can see on so many collector's cabinet paintings? They certainly did. . . . But did they base their final decisions completely on their own findings? I doubt it. I believe that connoisseurs at the top end of the art market rarely relied solely on their own good judgement. I will . . . argue that collector-connoisseurs used their own critical capacities to determine the quality and the monetary value of a piece of art. The mere pictorial quality was often as important as the artist's name as it appeared in the catalogues. . . . I will [also] argue that provenance and provenance research were also important in determining the value of an attribution for the elite art collector-connoisseurs in the early eighteenth century. Last, I will argue that collector-connoisseurs were dependent on each other. An implicit, widespread acceptance of an attribution seems to have been a key factor in determining authenticity. Contrary to the art dealer's connoisseurship, the art lover's connoisseurship was, foremost a matter of *falsification*: an attribution was considered correct if it was unchallenged. In other words, elite art collectors formed a closed community in which market transparency was quintessential and from which paintings with challenged attributions were systematically banned.

KOENRAAD JONCKHEERE, *The Solliciteur-Culturel*

Excerpt (pp. 162–70) from "The 'Solliciteur-Culturel': Some Notes on Dutch Agents and International Trade in Art and Applied Arts," *De Zeventiende Eeuw* 24 (2008): 162–80. Reprinted by kind permission of the author.

By the end of the seventeenth century and in the early eighteenth century, *solliciteurs-militaires* were leading Dutch merchant-bankers who provided short-term funds to finance the wars. During the War of the Spanish Succession in the early eighteenth century, they worked mainly for foreign princes who had sent in their troops as mercenaries. But this had not always been the case. The system of *solliciteurs-militaires* was . . . established in the Northern Netherlands during the Eighty Years War (1568–1648). After the Revolt the Northern Netherlands had no monarchy, but was ruled by stadholders. Always elected from the Orange-Nassau family, the stadholder was requested by the provinces to act as the military and political leader on their behalf. Unlike monarchs, stadholders had no steady tax income and depended entirely on the goodwill of the most powerful cities, such as Amsterdam, and several provinces. Occasionally, when a new phase in the war against Spain erupted, troops had to be raised swiftly, however, and money was needed instantly. As the stadholders were unable to provide this funding, several independent provinces had to do so instead. This was a time-consuming and ineffective process. Thus, around 1600, a group of intermediaries began arranging the financial transfers between some of the Dutch provinces and the captains of the troops. In fact, the *solliciteurs* acted as military bankers or 'brokers', immediately providing the money for the military wages to the captains and arranging the necessary forage. They subsequently requisitioned the funds from the provinces. For the financial risk they took, the *solliciteurs* received an *agio*, or a form of interest on the enormous loans.

Since the Dutch hired foreign troops—mostly German—during the Nine Years War and the War of the Spanish Succession, the *solliciteurs-militaires* often also became agents for foreign princes and aristocrats. As the primary financers of the hirelings, they established good contacts with their aristocratic captains, whom they helped not only with forage and other practical, political or military problems. For instance, when war ground to a halt in the winter months, *solliciteurs* guided their patrons around Holland and introduced them to its elite milieu and thus the best art collections. Obviously, *solliciteurs* had excellent networks in the Netherlands and abroad given that they had to raise enormous sums on very short notice. The crux of the system was the overlap of the diplomatic and the financial networks. *Haute finance* was never far off.

Although the system was subject to regulations and the number of official *solliciteurs* was limited after 1673, several of the system's aspects had proven their worth and were applied by most agents active in the Dutch Republic. [. . .] Agents became *solliciteurs* in everything, as the supply of art and other luxury goods was dependent on the instant availability of capital in a broadening and accelerating art market. [. . .]

Jacob Senserf met James Brydges [of Chandos] when the latter visited the Dutch Republic in the autumn of 1705. Brydges had just been appointed *Paymaster-General* by the English Parliament and travelled to Holland to establish a reliable network. [. . .]

From 1705 on, Brydges maintained a weekly correspondence with Jacob Senserf. In those letters they generally discussed the progress of the war, the political situation and financial details. Since he was sending letters regularly, Brydges seized the opportunity to prevail upon the Senserfs to also buy wine, all sorts of luxury items and paintings. As a 'gentleman', Senserf was simply expected to deliver everything his patron desired and moreover prove himself a man of good taste. Yet, it was not always Brydges who took the initiative. When the painting collection of Adriaen Paets came up for sale in 1713, Senserf informed Brydges of this unique occasion and sent over the catalogue.

Brydges was a British aristocrat who made an immense fortune by investing the war funds at the exchanges of Amsterdam, Paris and London before actually spending them on the war. Jacob Senserf, on the other hand, came from a rather more modest background. [. . .] Jacob became wealthy trading French wines and East-Indian spices. His fortune facilitated his entry into the Rotterdam city council and he became a so-called regent, or city administrator. This position brought him in contact with the Dutch political elite, and undoubtedly with the foreign elite as well. Besides James Brydges, Philip Ludwig Wenzel Count of Sinzendorf, Prince Eugene of Savoy, the Duke of Marlborough and many others frequently visited Senserf and probably also used his services.

Good personal contacts and confidentiality were essential to the relationship between an agent and his patron. The pre-financing of political, military, and cultural investments for the foreign princes and aristocrats by agents was a matter of trust. The sums were often so gigantic that a quick amortisation of the debts was necessary. Several agents found themselves in dire straits due to repayment delays. Agents such as Senserf often lent thousands of guilders themselves to satisfy the patron. What is more, *solliciteurs*, like Senserf, had to make decisions bearing on taste almost daily; the choices of such *solliciteurs* could influence or even significantly shape the 'taste' of the patron. The auction of the painting collection of Adriaen Paets in 1713 is a case in point. Senserf and his advisors had to make the choices. [. . .] In this instance, Brydges' taste in art was 'fashioned' by his agents abroad. [. . .]

Research on late seventeenth- and early eighteenth-century international art trade, thus, makes clear that war, diplomacy and cultural agency merged completely in that period. When Jacob Senserf was asked to buy paintings at the auction of Stadholder-King William III on 26 July 1713, the financial structure and the supporting network were in place. Senserf had learned the ropes when he first bought art for Chandos at the auction of Adriaen Paets' collection earlier that year. For the sale of King William's paintings, he set up a kind of joint venture. Matthew Decker, another confidant of Chandos and Senserf, was residing in the Netherlands in those months, as he was on a 'diplomatic' mission. Decker was actually a Dutchman who had left for England around 1700 and made a fortune there. He was personal banker to Brydges as well as a good part of the British aristocracy. One could call him an 'investment banker' and it was generally Senserf and Decker who sent letters of exchange to one another to settle Brydges' accounts in the end. The third party in the 'joint venture' was the Amsterdam banking firm Pels and Sons. The Pels's were considered to be the richest family in the Netherlands, and their firm made money in merchant banking as well. Naturally, they also acted as agents and residents for several foreign princes, including the Swedish crown. Pels and sons were Brydges' Amsterdam 'investment bankers'. The actual bidding at the auction of the collection of William III was left to Marcus Bavelaer, a broker from Amsterdam and Matthew Decker's nephew.

The reason for setting up this temporary 'consortium' had to do with the fact that Brydges, although he had shown a great interest in the collection, neglected his mail at this time. He had been occupied with 'the joys of a well chosen married state', as he excused himself later. He failed to send his agents clear instructions as to the finances and his artistic preferences. The agents had had to take the initiative and, as *solliciteurs* were wont to do, they raised the capital and invested the funds buying paintings at auction. The consortium was successful, acquiring nine pictures, worth 9,635 guilders.

Bavelaer placed the bids, the 'consortium' arranged the finances, and Chandos was honoured by the gift, for which he could pay whenever it suited him. Chandos obtained several paintings by Anthony van Dyck, by Peter Paul Rubens, by Gerard Dou and others. All of them were masterpieces.

This incident exemplifies the merging of *haute finance*, diplomacy and the elite art trade at the end of the seventeenth and early eighteenth century. Cultural investments in the Dutch Republic by foreign princes—be it buying paintings at auctions, silk stockings or pineapple plants—were primarily catered to by merchant bankers like Senserf. Those agent-financers functioned in most cases as *solliciteurs-militaires* and to the same extent as *solliciteurs-culturels*. They pre-invested in luxury items such as paintings, tapestry, porcelain, and so forth. They made the choices and eagerly awaited the patron's approval.

6

GERMANY AND SPAIN

Wealth alone is not a sufficient condition for a dominant art market to emerge in a major city. This chapter traces some early developments in Germany and Spain that may explain why neither country developed a strong local primary market for art with influential clusters of local artists—such as those observed in the Italian city-states, the port city of Antwerp, and the Dutch Republic.

I. GERMANY

Geography appears to play a major role. In the late medieval period a flourishing German merchant economy developed around the overland trade routes that had been established in conjunction with the fair system. The German city of Mainz, for example, reaped great wealth from the acceleration of trade in the fourteenth and fifteenth centuries, since it was located at the crossroads of the major trading routes that crossed Europe. It was a wealthy Mainz banker, Johann Fust, who financed Gutenberg's new printing press in 1450, which had a revolutionary impact on all sectors of society, including the information flow needed for efficient (art) markets. Gutenberg's technology and books spread rapidly: by the end of the fifteenth century, more than 250 cities across Europe had printing presses. Of the books printed between 1450 and 1500, about 30,000 editions can be identified in some 450,000 surviving copies.

The artist Albrecht Dürer, using his own printing press, managed to establish his reputation and influence across Europe while he was still in his twenties. His quick success can in large part be attributed to the location of his hometown, Nuremberg, at the major crossroads in the Holy Roman Empire (Germany). Dürer revolutionized printmaking, elevating it to the level of an independent art form by expanding the tonal and dramatic range of his prints and utilizing Gutenberg's movable type. His prints featured full-page illustrations on the recto and typeset text on the reverse of each sheet—instead of the brief inscriptions of biblical text that used to be cut in relief into the same woodblocks as the illustrations. Dürer was the first artist to act as his own publisher and found this to be much more profitable than painting commissions. Not only was he able to sell nearly unlimited numbers of prints at the fairs and markets around Nuremberg, his prints also served to promote his skill and his ideas about art on a large scale. His strategy was very successful: by 1497 he had hired an agent to handle all of his foreign print sales. He copyrighted his prints using his distinctive monogram and took copiers of his art to court. Dürer was undoubtedly an inspiration to all artists who desired to market their work internationally, including the Italian painters Raphael and Titian, and many started to collaborate with printmakers in order to promote and distribute their work (Hutchison 1990).

Because of their inland locations, Mainz and Nuremberg ultimately lost their economic advantage once the bulk of overland trade shifted to the Atlantic maritime trade. The German port city of Hamburg became a hub for international commerce but was located in an agricultural area that was neither a significant industrial production center nor an important consumer market (Lindberg 2008, 649). The shift to shipping benefited first Antwerp, and later Amsterdam, densely populated port cities that became the new loci for cultural activities, including fine-art printing. Furthermore, the Reformation curtailed the demand for art that would have allowed artistic life to flower in German cities. As Carl Christensen argues in his essay in this chapter, the larger force of the Reformation, set in motion in Germany by Martin Luther in 1517, dried up the traditional source of commissions, the Catholic Church. As a consequence, art production dwindled, and the remaining active patrons, chiefly the German courts, turned to artists and dealers in Italy, Flanders, and Holland to procure art for their collections. The demand attracted journeymen artists from Italy, Flanders, and Holland. The Bavarian court, as well as many other, smaller courts throughout the Holy Roman Empire, employed significant numbers of Italian and Netherlandish artists over the course of the sixteenth and seventeenth centuries. For example, in the early seventeenth century, Netherlandish (Dutch and Flemish) artists constituted nearly 20 percent of the population in Frankfurt am Main (Kaufmann 2004, 117).

CARL C. CHRISTENSEN, *The Reformation and the Decline of German Art*

Excerpts (pp. 215, 219–21, 223–24, 226) from "The Reformation and the Decline of German Art," *Central European History* 6, no. 3 (1973): 207–32. Copyright © 1973

Conference Group for Central European History of the American Historical Association. Reprinted with the permission of Cambridge University Press.

There is clear and abundant evidence of the loss of employment and financial hardship suffered by German painters and sculptors from the early years of the Reformation. But, as yet, there has not been confronted the question of how extensively the religious reforms themselves may have affected patronage. Did the coming of Protestantism really bring to an end the long-standing and close alliance between the church and the visual arts? The problem is an important one, also from the economic standpoint, for the simple reason that the great majority of art works commissioned or created in the immediate pre-Reformation period still drew their subject matter from the realm of Christian theology. With the exception of portraiture, painting and sculpture with a purely secular subject matter were as yet relatively undeveloped and no strong tradition of patronage for this type of art as yet existed. [. . .]

It is perhaps not without significance that Germany acquired a non-resident ruler, in the figure of the Emperor Charles V, just a few years before the crisis in the arts began to become apparent. Elected in 1519, Charles spent only eight of his fifty-eight years in the Empire, visiting it nine times, but never remaining as long as two years at a time on any visit until those of the 1540s and 1550s. It was in Spain and Italy that his major art commissions were given. [. . .] The result . . . was that there was no longer in the Empire any real center of "active patronage of the arts." [. . .]

Although the absence of large-scale royal sponsorship of the arts in Germany during this critical period must be considered significant, it remains true that, with the exception of the decline in demand for religious art, the overall structure of art patronage and the art market did not change radically during the 1520s and 1530s. Both princes and townsmen continued in their traditional capacity as commissioners and purchasers of painting and sculpture, while, on the other hand, the age of the great connoisseurs and secular art collections was not to dawn until the second half of the century.

Nor does the evidence suggest that the difficulties of the artists can be accounted for by any general economic decline in Germany at this time. Modern historians first speak of commercial and industrial stagnation in connection with the period following the middle of the sixteenth century. And, as has been pointed out by several scholars recently, the amount of money devoted by a society to artistic enterprises probably has less to do with overall economic affluence than with sociocultural considerations and the shape of political and tax structures. If economic recession does not bring an end to the concentration of funds in the hands of those few who are accustomed to patronize culture, it need not result in an immediate curtailment of aesthetic creativity. When economic decay did appear in Germany, families with great accumulated wealth apparently were able to preserve for a long time their traditionally high standard of living and costly habits of consumption.

Much the same thing can be said concerning the waning vitality of the German cities. [. . .] If painting and sculpture flourished in a particularly brilliant fashion in the late fifteenth and early sixteenth centuries, it was for a variety of reasons, among which the type of religious piety cultivated at the time played just as important a part as did socio-economic factors. Further, the slow erosion of the position of the towns came too late and was too gradual a process to account for the intense crisis of the arts in the 1520s and 1530s. About the most that can be said is that the eventual exhaustion of urban productive energies probably helped to inhibit a later revival of certain of the arts, such as occurred so spectacularly in the prosperous and Protestant Netherlands of the seventeenth century.

When one has assessed the various factors involved in the economics of art production in the early and mid-sixteenth century in Germany, it is difficult to avoid the impression that the financial and occupational distress suffered by the painters and sculptors was caused largely by the coming of the Reformation. [. . .]

The truth of the matter is that forces undermining the economic vitality of a trade or profession most likely do exert an adverse effect on the recruitment and training of that younger talent necessary to maintain quality of output. Where so many had (as in the decades preceding the Reformation) been encouraged by favorable employment opportunities to undertake the cultivation of skills related to various kinds of artistic production, it is not surprising that there should have arisen from their ranks at least a few with great talent. The sharp contraction in the market for art goods most likely brought an end to this favorable situation. And to this there might be added the observation that, within the thinned ranks of the remaining artists, there can no longer have been the same degree of invigorating competition and fruitful exchange of ideas that had existed earlier.

It would be a mistake, however, to focus attention too exclusively upon purely economic considerations, however important they may have been. The emotional and psychological effects of the Reformation must have been considerable. It has become almost an article of faith in modern times that the creative personality is a more than ordinarily sensitive individual, by whom the stresses and strains of life are especially acutely felt. The German artists, in particular, have often been characterized by art historians as highly emotional. [. . .] The theological controversies and political upheavals accompanying the religious reform must have affected the attitudes and outlook of artists in a variety of ways.

Iconoclastic destruction of religious art, though much less prevalent and severe in Lutheran areas than in the Zwinglian and Calvinistic regions of the South, must have had as its consequence, wherever it occurred, not only the loss of irreplaceable art works which could have served as models in the training up of new generations of artists, but also a damaging effect upon the morale of practicing painters and sculptors. One can easily imagine the anger and despair especially of those masters not themselves wholeheartedly committed to the eradication of image piety. [. . .]

The effect of these unsettled conditions upon artistic creativity cannot have been a beneficial one. In one recent book, an art historian comments that the political and religious troubles extending on into the years of the mid-century "were unfavourable to bigger projects, to the founding of workshops and local schools" (Osten and Vey 1969, 283). There was, he continues, "a lack of time and means to form new traditions. . . . Thus art in the Empire was extremely confused in style and had no definite points of reference or standard set up by the individual artists, who were always on the move."

THOMAS KETELSEN, *Art Auctions in Germany during*
the Eighteenth Century

Excerpts (pp. 143–47, 149–51) from "Art Auctions in Germany during the Eighteenth Century," in *Art Markets in Europe, 1400–1800*, ed. M. North and D. Ormrod (Aldershot, England: Ashgate, 1998), 143–52. Copyright © 1998 Ashgate Publishing. Reproduced by permission of Taylor & Francis Books UK.

Until now, the history of the German art market as well as eighteenth-century collecting and connoisseurship have been studied without recourse either to the auction catalogues of the time, nor for that matter to the catalogues of private art collections. This occurs in contrast to the study of eighteenth-century German literature where scholars have long profited from the information available from auction catalogues and other booklists.

Lugt's *Répertoire* (1938–87) provided the basis for [my] reappraisal of the German art auctions and research was extended to the holdings of further libraries and archives. In the space of two years it was possible to expand the list from the 114 catalogues known to Lugt to a grand total of 300. More important . . . is the sum of approximately 60,000 paintings put up at these sales. This should serve to correct a previous misconception and suggest the great importance of auctions for eighteenth-century art collecting. The material from the early German auction catalogues not only reveals details of the history of individual paintings, but also sheds much light on the development of the art market and its influence on collecting in Germany and other European countries. [. . .]

Auctions of paintings had already taken place in Germany in the seventeenth century: in 1690 the collection of Duke Rudolf Friedrich von Holstein-Norburg (1645–88) was sold by his heirs in Wolfenbüttel. . . . One of the earliest auctions of paintings that is recorded in a printed catalogue was held in Hanover-Neustadt during 1705 and consisted of the 'large and small paintings in the collection of Mr. Anton Lucio (Lucius) Hofrat of the Elector of Brunswick-Luneburg'. By the first half of the eighteenth century, auctions of art were being held in all larger cities: Dresden (1706), Hamburg (1710) or Leipzig (1714). [. . .] Before the beginning of the Seven Years' War in 1757, about thirty art auctions are documented in Germany by printed catalogues. As far as we currently know, auctions of paintings were isolated and irregular events except in case of Hamburg where a steady pattern of sales had already begun during the final quarter of the seventeenth century, even if most of these featured primarily books. Twenty auctions took place in Hamburg before the end of the Seven Years' War. To take advantage of the convenient location for transit trade, the Danish art dealer Gerhard Morell settled in Hamburg in order to sell paintings of the highest quality from Dutch auctions to the German nobility. Morell is probably the earliest art dealer to gain fame as a connoisseur. In 1757 he was called to the Royal Danish court in Copenhagen to fill the post of curator of the Danish royal collections. In [t]his capacity . . . he purchased more than two hundred paintings for the Danish court, including Rembrandt's *Christ at Emmaus.* [. . .]

The period of the Seven Years' War (1757–62/3) forms a watershed in the history of the art market. Only two auctions of paintings are known to have taken place in Hamburg during those years. Only after the end of this conflict did auctions resume spasmodically in Frankfurt, and to a lesser degree in Hamburg. Together with the painter Justus Juncker, the art dealer Johann Christian Kaller held a series of auctions of paintings in Frankfurt between 1763 and 1765 in quick succession. The French language of the printed catalogues recalls the period of the French occupation. Probably the most famous of the Frankfurt auctions of this period was that of the collection of the Baron von Häckel on 15 August 1764, recorded by Johann Wolfgang von Goethe in 'Dichtung und Wahrheit'. [. . .] As the catalogue of his own library shows, Goethe himself possessed an impressive number of catalogues of private art collections and of auctions.

It was the first time in the history of collecting that the auction came to assume such a central place for the private collector of the bourgeoisie as well as for the nobleman in the areas surrounding Frankfurt. For instance, the collector and dealer Johann Baptist Ehrenreich carefully informed Karoline Luise of Baden of the imminent auction of 'a Collection of Dutch Masters to be sold under the gavel of Messers Hl. Junkers and H. Kaller'. Ehrenreich had included the catalogue with a letter in which he assured the Countess: 'I have studied and examined them all [the paintings], also those items among them which I well know would appeal to the taste of Your Grace'. These paintings were marked by Ehrenreich in the catalogue with an asterisk, whereas one asterisk signified a 'good' picture, two a 'better' picture, and three asterisks 'impeccable'. [. . .] The Frankfurt art dealer Christian Benjamin Rauschner also maintained connections to the court at Karlsruhe. It emerges from his catalogue of 1765 that he had purchased paintings in Holland expressly to be auctioned in Frankfurt. Rauschner sent a list of paintings to Karlsruhe in the hope of selling some of these to the court. It has gone unnoticed that a large number of the pictures on this list had only the year before been auctioned among the holdings of the Elector Clemens August in Bonn. They had been bought by the Court Accountant Baruch. The art dealer Neveu had also bought a number of paintings at that sale in Bonn which he put up for sale in Paris in December of the same year. Other pictures from the Bonn collection ended up at the court in Copenhagen and others still in the collection of Frederick II of Prussia. The Clemens August sale at Bonn shows that even at larger German auctions pictures were being purchased for the sole purpose of being resold at a profit. Among the paintings auctioned at Frankfurt and originating in the Bonn sale are the *Interior of St Peter's Basilica in Rome*, and *The Piazza Navona in Rome* by Giovanni Pannini now in the Niedersächsisches Landesmuseum Hanover.

Nonetheless, a large number of the paintings auctioned in Frankfurt during the 1760s were purchased locally. Auction records include the names of all well-known local collectors: Städel, Boegner, Berger, Ettling, Uffenbach, Geyss, Pasquay, von der Lahr, Müller or Göring. Many of these collections were however themselves dissolved as soon as the early 1780s.

Unlike the Frankfurt and Cologne auctions, which at this time were most often held by public auctioneers domestically in the house in which the collector had died, those in Hamburg routinely took place at the stock exchange. That building, which had been built to the plans of the Dutch architect Jan Andresen in the sixteenth century (1578–81), formed the economic center of the city. A landmark was reached by the Hamburg art market in 1778 when twelve auctions of art were held in the building of the stock exchange, while Frankfurt, Berlin and Hanover only saw a single such auction during the entire year. But none of these catalogues indicated the owner of the respective collections. All the more pompously do the lavish title pages display the names of the brokers who had been in charge of such sales since the 1730s. By 1785 there were more than thirty such brokers registered in the Hamburg art trade, most prominent among them Packischefsky, Bostelmann and Texier. Most of the collections were probably brought to Hamburg from outside and destined to be sold again elsewhere. [. . .]

Beginning with the 1760s, published catalogues began to assume an important place in the development of connoisseurship. Experts were increasingly called in to appraise the paintings and compile these catalogues. An early example is the . . . catalogue of a collection from Brunswick of 1743, written by Anton Friedrich Harms, director of the local picture gallery at the court in Salzdahlum. [. . .]

It is striking that since the 1760s the entries of the Frankfurt catalogues increasingly resort to attributions qualified by epithets such as 'manner of', 'in the taste of', 'in the style of', 'school', or 'copy after'. Rauschner described Rembrandt's *Christ Before Pilate* in the following terms: 'Since this theme was often repeated by Rembrandt there are some who would question the authenticity of this version, but there is no evidence that this is a copy'. A further indication of the growing differentiation in the 'Handlungscursus', as Christian von Hagedorn described the activity of painting attribution, besides the more careful use of names is the increasing spectrum of pupils of the masters. The style of Rembrandt could be ever more clearly discerned once the work of Govert Flinck, Jan Victors, Gerbrand van den Eeckhout, or Aert de Gelder had been recognized. In dealing with a portrait by Jan Lievens, Rauschner notes: 'This master has much of Rembrandt's manner; this particular picture is not as warm in the tone, the ground too is deeply grey; on the whole though it is well drawn and painted, as any connoisseur will recognize'. One should not overgeneralise from the nature of such appraisals, but the role of the art market in the development of connoisseurship must also not be underestimated. The authors of these catalogues had earned their reputations. [. . .]

One result of the public auctions held in Frankfurt between 1779 and 1784 was the impulse given to the local art market. Sixteen catalogues of private painting collections are evidence of a second profound development in the art collections of Frankfurt. Sometimes the auctions were announced far ahead of time in newspapers, . . . as in the case of the Bernus collection reviewed by a connoisseur such as Christian Merk in the *Teutscher Merkur*. As with Hamburg, so too did Frankfurt by this time rejoice in a specific building directly equipped for the purpose of auctions, the 'Senckenbergisches Stiftungshaus'. [. . .] Auctions were usually held in the latter immediately following the Easter and the fall trade fairs. Visitors of the trade fairs and local collectors alike were able to view the paintings in advance during regular opening hours. In this way the city hosted a series of public painting exhibitions which could be seen to compete with the collections of the nobility, which were more difficult to access. The prefaces of the printed catalogues are unequivocally addressed to the connoisseur, who is invited to inspect the condition and aesthetic quality of the individual paintings and arrive at an opinion of their authorship.

In Leipzig since 1783, the auctions were scheduled in the 'Rostisches Kunsthaus', also during the spring and fall trade fairs. Like the Nuremberg art dealer Johann Friedrich Frauenholz (active since 1787) and the Artaria firm in Mannheim (active there since 1793), Rost dealt primarily in prints and drawings, and the number of paintings included in the Leipzig auctions rarely exceeded a hundred lots. Aside from the cities already mentioned, auctions of paintings were frequent in Freiburg, Würzburg, Augsburg, Bremen as well as in Flensburg. [. . .]

Frankfurt had been able to reassume its place as the busiest market for paintings in the early 1780s, ahead of Hamburg and Leipzig, but the political events in France contributed to the emergence of Hamburg once again. Whereas Hamburg hosted more than seventy art auctions between 1789 and 1800, Frankfurt is only known to have held four in the years before the French occupation in 1794 and completely to have stopped shortly thereafter. In Cologne also, the most important auctions of paintings, such as the Farina, Kox and Moureaux sales . . . occurred in rapid succession, but all before the Napoleonic army entered the city.

Besides German collections, an increasing number of foreign collections, particularly French, were [auctioned] in Hamburg in the years following 1789. The latter were either brought by their owners as refugees or else bought in France by German merchants to be sold for profit in Hamburg. The exchange rate had made the French market very lucrative for foreign investment. In January 1795 for instance, the Hamburg merchant Georg Heinrich Sieveking commissioned a friend in Paris to purchase luxury goods in the value of 50,000 to 100,000 Louis d'Or. [. . .] Sieveking seems to have had approximately six million Louis d'Or at his disposal for such purchases. Such exports were further facilitated by the French annexation of the Netherlands in 1795, so that nearly the entire Dutch trade was transferred to Hamburg. . . . Not all of the collections brought to Hamburg were immediately auctioned. In the preface to a catalogue of 1826 one finds the note that the present collection has been in Hamburg 'since the unhappy days of the French Revolution'. Until the city was occupied by the Napoleonic army in 1806, Hamburg remained the most active art market in Germany. As a result of such a flood of paintings, questions of attribution came to be neglected. Catalogues with more than eight hundred lots, often with no more than summary entries, low prices and the sale of entire collections of engravings soon gave art auctioneering in Hamburg a bad name. [. . .]

After the Napoleonic 'Wars of Liberation' (1814) most of the painting collections formed by the German bourgeoisie during the eighteenth century were broken up. This process itself engendered new and unexpected impulses in auctioneering and ultimately led to the institutionalization of the German art market, which had by this time attained . . . an international prestige.

II. SPAIN

The lack of cultural dominance of major Spanish cities such as Madrid and Seville can also partly be explained by geography: both cities were located inland and did not directly benefit from the maritime routes that replaced overland trading.

Moreover, the Spanish were more focused on expanding territory than investing in industry in the sixteenth and seventeenth centuries and waged wars on multiple fronts. As a result Spain was a major importer of European manufactured goods for its empire and military. It had become the richest country in Europe by the end of the sixteenth century, but much of its wealth (derived from mining precious metals, such as silver, in the New World) was used by the Spanish Crown to finance military protection of its European territories against the Ottoman Empire and for its wars with most of the major European powers. Revenues from its silver mines in the New World and from taxation, rather than trading profits, were used to pay for these imports, but at times these revenues fell short. The Spanish Crown went bankrupt in 1575, 1577, and 1596. By 1621, Spain's transatlantic trade with the New World also started to diminish. After the Dutch captured the Spanish treasure fleet in 1628, which contained much of its wealth in bullion, the country went into further decline.

Social factors played a major role in Spain's subsequent failure to establish major cultural centers and art markets in its cities. As the historian Henry Kamen (2007, xi) has pointed out, from the fifteenth century on Spaniards were faced with an uncomfortable choice between what was considered indigenous culture and what had been brought in from the outside. Continuing expulsions of large sections of the population, such as Jews and Protestants, produced a constant turnover of native elites, making it impossible to establish continuity in the formation of a Spanish cultural tradition. The expulsions also may explain why the Spanish lacked the type of prosperous bourgeoisie that drove demand for art in Italy, Flanders, and Holland. The Spanish merchants who did stay home preferred to buy land and titles with their wealth rather than invest in new commercial ventures. Over time, some of the most important Spanish artists established their careers on foreign soil—a practice that has persisted into the twenty-first century.

JONATHAN BROWN, *Painting in Spain, 1500–1700*

Excerpt (pp. 1–4) from "Introduction: The Frontiers of Spanish Art," in *Painting in Spain, 1500–1700* (New Haven, CT, and London: Yale University Press, 1999), 1–5. Copyright © 1999 Yale University Press.

The Golden Age of painting in Spain was founded on a contradiction. In the sixteenth and seventeenth centuries Spain was at the center of European politics and on the periphery of European art. As the leading political power for all but the last fifty years of the period, the monarchy was omnipresent and omnipotent in western Europe (and the New World). In Italy, Spanish viceroys governed the kingdom of Naples and Sicily and the duchy of Milan and, at least for some of the time, influenced the client states of Genoa, Mantua, and Tuscany. In the north, during the sixteenth century, Spanish governors ruled all of the Netherlands while maintaining the loyalty of the duke of Savoy. Even after the revolt of the northern Netherlands and the formation of the Dutch Republic in the later sixteenth century, Spain played a major role in the affairs of Northern Europe. [. . .]

Spain dominated the politics of Europe, only to be dominated itself by the cultures of Italy and Flanders. The agents and ambassadors who had fanned out across Europe to defend the interests of the monarchy provided a return flow of ideas, objects, and information that made an enormous impact on those who stayed at home, artists and patrons alike. Works of art produced in other parts of Europe abounded in the Iberian peninsula, adorning palaces, country houses, and, of course, ecclesiastical institutions of every sort. Foreign artists also came to Spain, frequently in the sixteenth century, rather less frequently in the seventeenth.

These historical circumstances are self-evident, but their artistic consequences are not so patently clear, as witnessed by the fact that almost every history of Golden Age Spanish painting is confined to the study of Spanish artists. The late seventeenth-century painter Antonio Palomino knew better. His fundamental series of biographies entitled "El Parnaso español pintoresco laureado," published in 1724, includes the lives of Titian, Rubens, and Luca Giordano, as well as those of Velázquez, Murillo, and Valdés Leal, despite the fact that Titian, for one, never set foot in Spain. It was obvious to Palomino, an eyewitness of the epoch, that neither these nor the other foreign artists patronized by the ruling classes could be excluded from the history of painting in his country.

Yet excluded they were, and merely on the adventitious grounds of nationality. The first serious accounts of Spanish art were written in the nineteenth century and reflected the rising importance of nationalism in contemporary political and cultural thought. Accordingly, the history of Spanish painting came to be understood as the history of

Spanish painters, of those artists who had spent all or most their lives working within what were in fact the political boundaries of the nineteenth- and twentieth-century state. Thus, it was easily forgotten that Rubens and Giordano, for example, had been subjects of the Spanish crown.

Once the political and geographical frontiers of the Spanish Habsburg monarchy are restored to their full extent, Spain's position on the periphery of artistic events becomes clearer. In this period, certain regions of Flanders and Italy were acknowledged as generative centers of the art of painting, and their connections with Spain facilitated the commerce of pictures in both the financial and the artistic sense. Waves of influence from these regions periodically washed over the country, but little was swept away with the tide. . . . Of course, in this respect, Spain was hardly unique among the artistic regions of Europe. It could even be argued that the Spanish experience was typical, since the evolution of painting in many parts of Europe depended on the transmission and absorption of ideas and fashions from Italy. [. . .]

The changes in artistic style and taste that occurred during the Golden Age may at first seem puzzling, if not arbitrary. However, beneath the confusing shifts of direction is a constant element—that of the relationship of patrons and painters. The influence of patronage on artistic production is, of course, a universal phenomenon in this period, but in Spain, as in many regions of Europe, the patrons were not the junior partners. On the contrary, their predominance resulted from the marked difference in their and the artists' social prestige and economic power, which operated to the artists' disadvantage. The case of Philip II provides the clearest instance of the exercise of political and economic strength in the field of art. Having decided that his needs could not be satisfied by the talent available in Spain, the king commissioned works from painters in Italy and Flanders and eventually brought practitioners from those lands to his peninsular realms. At the start of his reign, Philip employed Titian and Antonis Mor as his principal painters and later used only those Spaniards whose style had been shaped by the foreigners. [. . .]

Although individual members or the church and aristocracy never ceased to be important patrons, there is no doubt that they were surpassed by the monarchs who took a serious interest in the visual arts, notably Philip II and Philip IV. In addition, these two kings were responsible for fostering the extraordinary interest in art collecting, the significance of which has only recently been perceived. Yet even now it is apparent that the impressive collections gathered by the rulers, and also by high churchmen and aristocrats, greatly affected the development of Spanish painting.

These collections helped to broaden the horizons of Spanish painters who traveled abroad infrequently compared with the painters of Holland, France, Flanders, and even the German states. But the interest in collecting had a still more profound impact in that it imposed limits on the thematic repertory of Spanish painters. It has often been observed that Spanish painting of the Golden Age is largely restricted to religious subjects (mostly from the New Testament), portraiture, and still life, in that order. Absent, or nearly absent, are mythological and allegorical subjects, scenes of the daily activities of every class of society, and landscapes, townscapes, and seascapes. Although such paintings abounded in Spanish collections, they had been executed in Italy and Flanders. The preference on the part of collectors for versions of these subjects by foreigners, which began to emerge in the sixteenth century, effectively reduced the demand on local painters.

Thus, the home market was confined mainly to an ecclesiastical clientele, which, as ministers and guardians of the faith, was bound to give precedence to content over form. The churchmen, especially those in the provinces, tended to be both conservative and imitative in their artistic tastes. In this way, a curious situation came to pass, whereby the advanced sector of collectors indirectly strengthened the power of the conservative sector of patrons over the artists in their employ. The evidence of this power is readily found in contracts between painters and churchmen, for instance, in the 1628 contract between Francisco de Zurbarán and the prior of the Merced Calzada of Seville. The decisive clause, which is replicated in many similar documents, required the painter "to make twenty-two paintings of the story of St. Peter Nolasco to adorn the second cloister where the rectory is, putting in each one the figures and other things that the prior orders me to do, be they few or many." As a further control, the prior provided the artist with a set of engravings of scenes of the saint's life executed in Rome a few years earlier, which was to serve as a model.

This zealous if typical example of ecclesiastical patronage helps to explain the long duration of given stylistic modes within a particular center and the markedly different rhythm of artistic evolution in various parts of the peninsula. In addition, it illustrates an important characteristic of the working procedures of Spanish painters—their extensive use of prints as compositional sources. In the last forty years, scholars have identified a multitude of prints by northern and Italian artists that were appropriated with little if any variation by painters in Spain. Furthermore, the numerous publications of artists' inventories show that a print collection was a standard component of the atelier. When painters died and their possessions had to be sold, their prints were often snapped up by their colleagues.

This practice was followed by artists all over Europe and was by no means limited to Spain. It is fair to say, however, that its frequency among Spanish artists is truly phenomenal and cannot be taken for granted. The search for an explanation begins with the obvious: prints have traditionally served as vehicles for the transmission of artistic information, a purpose that was all the more important when painters were not accustomed to travel to other lands. During the sixteenth century, Spanish artists were on the move a great deal and foreign painters often came to work in the leading centers of the peninsula. But in the next century, the traffic dropped considerably and this made the print a necessity for discovering what was happening in the world outside. The use of prints could be promoted as much by the patrons as by the painters. As mentioned, church officials, with their overriding concern for orthodoxy, seem to have regarded the print as a kind of iconographical insurance policy which guarded them against unwelcome innovations or deviations from the doctrinal norm introduced by painters purely for artistic reasons. This control over composition in the name of orthodoxy was bound to have an influence on practice, albeit a subtle one. *Invenzione,* that quality of mental agility in composition praised by Italian theorists as a sign of the great artist, is also stressed by the major writers on art in the first half of the seventeenth century, Vicente Carducho and Francisco Pacheco. In practice, however, only a few artists were given scope to demonstrate their powers of invention in composition. The point is illustrated in the careers of two of the most inventive painters, Velázquez and Ribera. Velázquez left Seville for Madrid in search of an enlightened secular patron, while Ribera explicitly refused to return from Naples to his native Spain. The positive aspect of this situation was that the close relationships between the clergy and the painters contributed much to the ability of the Spanish artists to evoke with matchless power and sincerity the beliefs of the Catholic Church.

The reaction of the painters to the limiting conditions of the marketplace was decidedly ambivalent. A small, but articulate, sector resented its subordinate social and economic position and the lack of reliable support from the highest levels of secular patrons, who were often less encumbered by religious and moral considerations. Eugenio Cajés, a leading painter in Madrid during the first third of the seventeenth century, gave voice to this dissatisfaction in an encounter with an unidentified Italian painter called "Pedro Antonio," who was visiting Seville and Madrid. In a letter dated 5 May 1610 to a fellow painter in Rome . . . [he] reported his impressions of artistic life in Spain:

> And what most surprised me was to see how little Spaniards esteemed their own native painters. I was also disappointed to see how two very ordinary Flemish painters, whose works were all bright colors and nothing more, had acquired a great reputation, although in our country they would not have cast a shadow.

Puzzled by this situation, he sought an explanation from Cajés, who gave this revealing answer:

> Dear Sir, there are many reasons for it, and the first is the little confidence we have in ourselves, and in particular in this profession of drawing. To those who know little of the profession, it seems as if we are not apt in it. And because there are so few intelligent people among the masses, [our talent] never comes to be known. The second cause is that all the gentlemen [*señores*] who go abroad from Spain attempt to bring back great quantities of pictures from foreign provinces, but they take nothing with them when they leave, which, if it were done, would make the value of our talents known.

Here Cajés points a finger directly at the aristocratic preference for imported works of art . . . and the resulting, and now well-known, indifference of the foreign markets to works by Spanish artists. About twenty years later, a greater artist, Jusepe de Ribera, offered another perspective on the plight of Spanish painters in their society. When asked why he did not leave Naples and return to his native Spain he allegedly replied:

> My dear friend, I have a strong impulse to go, but judging from the experience of many well-informed and truthful persons I find this drawback. During the first year, I would be received as a great painter, but in the second year, no one would pay attention to me because when people know you are around they lose respect for you. This is confirmed because I have seen some works by excellent Spanish masters that were held in low esteem [in Spain]. Thus, I judge Spain to be a loving mother to foreigners and a very cruel stepmother to her own sons.

Even the greatest painter of them all, Velázquez, encountered the same bias and had to go to extraordinary lengths to achieve the social recognition and prestige he so earnestly desired and so greatly deserved.

NEIL DE MARCHI AND HANS J. VAN MIEGROET, *Exploring Markets in Spain and Nueva España*

Excerpts (pp. 81–83, 86–88, 90–94) from "Exploring Markets for Netherlandish Paintings in Spain and Nueva España," *Nederlands Kunsthistorisch Jaarboek* 50 (2000): 81–112. Copyright © 2000 Koninklijke Brill NV.

Editor's note: In this excerpt De Marchi and Van Miegroet examine the art export practices of Chrisostomo Van Immerseel and Marie de Fourmestraux, a Flemish husband-and-wife partnership, in the years 1621 to 1648. They base their observations on an analysis of contemporary archival records.

These Antwerp merchants were not ordinary dealers, but 'vertically integrated'. This means that they were involved with every phase of the business of art, from supplying materials to finding the artists to fulfill their orders, to distributing the product (shipping), to its final marketing abroad. Integrated trader-dealers necessarily influenced the kinds of images made. To describe their business practices is also to identify processes by which atelier production in the Spanish Netherlands, and its associated visual culture, was shaped. There were other influences too, outside those usually considered under artistic factors. One such was Spanish import legislation, which may have precipitated an artificial 'visual divide' between North and South. [. . .]

Dealing in images already had a long history in Antwerp by the late sixteenth century, but not till then was a sharp distinction made in the official records of the Antwerp Guild of St. Luke, the so-called *Liggeren*, between print sellers and dealers in paintings. This change came gradually. The Counter Reformation and the Jesuit emphasis on imagery contributed to an increased awareness of paintings. A concrete primary demand was realized via the needed restoration and refurbishment of damaged churches and a new building campaign for parish churches and church complexes associated with newly established reformist orders. We are not aware of vertically integrated traders in paintings comparable in size and intensity to Van Immerseel and Musson before 1620. But it would not be surprising to find experiments in that direction. After all, international traders in paintings were a natural counterpart to vertically integrated dealer-entrepreneurs in prints and tapestries in the sixteenth and early seventeenth centuries. Both print production and tapestry making required substantial capital and active involvement in various stages of the design, production, and distribution process. Merchants could supply some of this capital, as they did for Christoffel Plantijn's private book trade. Chrisostomo Van Immerseel's father Jan was similarly engaged with tapestry workshops.

But for vertically integrated traders in paintings to emerge two conditions were necessary: foreign offset, and production capability more than adequate to meet domestic demand. These conditions, especially the second, began to prevail in Antwerp towards the end of the 1620s, but not until then. Guild records distinguished specialist dealers in paintings much earlier, but when international traders emerged the guild did not separately acknowledge them. This was unnecessary since the distinction between a local dealer and a vertically integrated dealer or international trader turned on capital and firm organization, not on the article traded. New Guild membership in the last decade of the sixteenth and the first quarter of the seventeenth century reflects the spurt in church-stimulated demand for paintings and involved both makers and various sorts of marketers of paintings. [. . .]

Chrisostomo Van Immerseel and Marie de Fourmestraux were first and foremost merchants. . . . They relied little on Guild connections, and from the outset accepted that their ambit would be wider than the local Antwerp market. Chrisostomo learned the paintings trade in the 1620s, as Seville agent to, and perhaps at times as co-principal with, Peter and Antoon Goetkint, specialist dealers in paintings whom he knew through family connections. Earlier, Chrisostomo had experimented with textiles and high-end luxury goods such as tapestries, some valued at over 800 guilders. This was an outgrowth of the international trading business in textiles started by his father. Chrisostomo was schooled in this company, and succeeded his father, before heading the Seville branch of operations with Marie, his lifelong partner, from 1621.

The partners moved into paintings on their own towards the end of the 1620s. This was just as one of the conditions mentioned earlier was beginning to appear. For three decades there had been a strong growth in the numbers of new painters entering the guild. At the same time signs were appearing that church-related demand had passed its peak.

Buying in cheaply is always important to a dealer, but was especially so in this instance. Between 1623 and 1628, the Goetkints regularly shipped cases with paintings varying in quality and price to test the market in Seville. [. . .] Van Immerseel and de Fourmestraux sensed that local buyers, perhaps reflecting the gradual decline of the Americas trade and hence in the economy of Seville itself, were sacrificing quality for lower price. In 1629, Marie wrote from Seville to Chrisostomo in Antwerp, urging him to commission one hundred *waterverfdoeken*—water-based paintings on thin linen—with sieges and battles, but not to exceed six guilders a piece, since they would not sell above that price. From 1629, the numbers of inexpensive *waterverfdoeken* become prominent in their shipments, many for export to Spain and, via Seville, to Nueva España.

Exporting and importing was Van Immerseel's calling. Between 1623 and 1648, he shipped books, tapestries, prints and textiles to Spain, as well as cabinets with small attached paintings on copper. He and De Fourmestraux were not among Antwerp's largest merchants. . . . But after they had moved into paintings they sent what a first assessment indicates must be well over 6,000 in the period mentioned, excluding those on cabinets. . . . Their return imports to the Southern Netherlands included cochineal, expensive blue dyes, and leather from Havana.

Chrisostomo traveled regularly between Antwerp and Seville, the official point of exit and entry for the Americas trade, though he spent much time in Antwerp acquiring paintings and textiles. Marie stayed in Seville, where she was alternately his selling agent and a principal in acquiring return cargoes. Her letters contain detailed information on local taste and advice to Chrisostomo in 'neerlant', as to what paintings he should buy, or avoid.

Because of Marie's presence in Seville the partners possessed good firsthand knowledge of what buyers there wanted. Some of those buyers purchased for the Nueva España trade and large shipments went there. This is the case, for example, with a 1638 shipment of 504 paintings 'para yndias', sent together with a case of 50 paintings for Diego Coques, consul of the *Nación Flamenca* (Flemish trading nation) in Seville. For information on what buyers wanted in the Nueva España market, however, Van Immerseel and his wife had to rely to some degree on the reports of returning agents, their own and others. [. . .] There was no way of knowing just how good the information was until the next shipment was there and up for sale. The partnership therefore operated like any prudent investment manager working in the face of uncertainty: they spread their buying across paintings of different sorts to dilute the costs of error in any one direction. [. . .]

[. . .] They knew that there was a stable underlying demand for devotional paintings, and it is not surprising that these make up a substantial share of shipments both from 1629 and from the early 1640s. In the 1643 shipment, for example, 60% of the paintings were devotional. The percentages for the earlier shipments cannot be determined because the specification of subject or subject type is partial, but the *least* the share of devotionals could have been in the 1629 shipments was 26 and 30% for cases nr. 4 and nr. 5, respectively.

. . . Shipments for any single period . . . contained numerous paintings of recognizable themes, for which well-known models existed, especially in Antwerp and Mechelen. These include seascapes, landscapes, hunt scenes, battles and sieges, flower pieces, and series: *The Four Elements, The Five Senses,* and *The Times of the Year.* A well-formed taste for these subjects had developed in Spain, and we must assume had spread in some measure to Nueva España.

Sizes present problems that lie beyond the scope of this article, but on supports some shifting over time must be noted. Whereas the 1629 shipments comprised only linen and canvas, those of 1642 and 1643 contained a significant fraction of panels and copper plates (*laminas*). [. . .]

[. . .] Van Immerseel and De Fourmestraux, faced with uncertainty about the character of demand in Nueva España, kept to some standard themes. However, they varied the numbers for each type of support, size, and price range, in such a way that the overall cost remained roughly constant (though 'large' or 'small'), and the average cost price too was held to within a narrow range, shipment after shipment. This behavior is consistent with that of a mutual fund manager with various funds, though each either 'large' or 'small', who alters their composition according to what appear to be shifts in the market, so as to achieve a target rate of return on each. Assuming that the partners hoped for a constant average markup on selling prices over their cost prices (roughly stable across large and small shipments at any one time, as we have seen), we can interpret their aim too as the pursuit of a roughly constant target rate of return, shipment by shipment.

This sort of characterization of the Van Immerseel–De Fourmestraux business strategy may seem abstract and unrelated to the paintings they bought and sold, reflecting another set of considerations entirely. Not so. When trying to understand how different types of imagery became more or less prominent over time, grasping the business strategies of those involved in commissioning and selling paintings is anything but remote. In fact, for an integrated dealer-producer-marketer, the choice of an investment strategy is part of the very same processes that select imagery. And when the scale of operations is as substantial as that of the Van Immerseel–De Fourmestraux enterprise, the impact of their choices on the imagery produced in Mechelen and Antwerp seems undeniable. [. . .]

In Seville and Nueva España the challenge was to supply a mixed and uncertain demand with imagery from various painters and in different price ranges. Van Immerseel and De Fourmestraux—and other dealers operating in their league—could easily control subject matter, material and finish simply by bulk purchasing and commissioning. Through acquisitions attuned to Spanish demand, and, derivatively, those (they hoped) of buyers in Nueva España, they were in fact shaping a recognizable Antwerp and Mechelen product.

Local ateliers—the 'Brueghel enterprise' is an obvious but instructive instance—adjusted readily to their demand. They were well aware what kind of imagery international traders like Van Immerseel were buying. Such large-scale operations, often sustained over several decades, caused widespread visual adaptation and conformity. This, in turn, helped stabilize local sets of traditions and visual strategies for which there existed high demand. Greater homogeneity resulted, making workshop production from Mechelen (the home of the *waterverf* on linen technique) and Antwerp easier to identify. Given Spanish restrictions on imports from 'rebel' territories, to which we turn in a moment, recognizability was a definite benefit. [. . .]

If anticipating demand in markets in Seville and (especially) Nueva España was uncertain, the legal context of exporting to Spain was not. Not only did it reserve business in Spain and the Americas for Spanish citizens only, which led the pragmatic Chrisostomo and his partner to seek naturalization in 1629 (granted in 1631). But, from 1603 onwards, a new law even required notarized affirmation of the provenance of each product exported from the Southern Netherlands to Spain and Nueva España. Imagery imported into Spain had to be reliably certified (*Carta de certificación para España*) as not having been made by artists in Middelburg, Haarlem or Amsterdam, or elsewhere in what the Spanish considered 'rebel provinces'. Considering the sheer volume exported from Antwerp, such legislation supplied local painters with an incentive to differentiate their products from what Spanish customs officials at first glance might mistake for 'Dutch'. Tonal imagery from Adriaen van de Venne to Jan van Goyen, or the typically Haarlem *ontbijtjes* by Nicolaes Gillis, Floris Van Dyck or Pieter Claesz, would have fallen within this category. It is no surprise, then, that these, and similar types of paintings, were hardly traded to Spain.

This legal environment probably helped create an artificial divide between the visual cultures of the Northern and Southern Netherlands. Along with the focused acquisitions of international dealers like Van Immerseel, the legal restrictions contributed to defining mass-produced imagery as identifiably 'Southern Netherlandish', perhaps even as 'MECHELS' or 'Antwerps'.

MIGUEL A. HERNÁNDEZ NAVARRO, *Spanish Art and Global Discourse*

Excerpt (pp. 137–39) from "Contradictions in Time-Space: Spanish Art and Global Discourse," in *The Global Art World: Audiences, Markets, and Museums*, ed. H. Belting, A. Buddensieg, and E. Araújo (Ostfildern, Germany: Hatje Cantz, 2009), 136–53. Reprinted by kind permission of Miguel Ángel Hernández Navarro.

Over the last two decades, the center of several debates in Spain has pivoted on the scant presence of Spanish art in an international context, an issue that has also been taken up by Spanish critics. The Spanish art system (museums, galleries, magazines, universities) has evolved in recent years to the point where it is now on a par with European and international standards. Nevertheless, Spanish artists still remain inadequately represented in the global art world. Except for some single examples, such as Santiago Sierra (who, paradoxically, developed as an artist in Mexico), Spanish artists are not represented among the big global artistic events, the new biennialism, or the new collections of transnational museums.

Spanish critics, it would appear, have yet to reach a definite conclusion with respect to this lack of international presence. It cannot be attributed to the system being in poor repair, or due to a lack of knowledge about external realities—for there is sufficient contact with other places. Nor can it be entirely due to the problem of language, since knowledge of English as the *lingua franca* seems widespread among artists. Perhaps, the reason ought rather to be sought at a conceptual level.

I would like to suggest that this lack of global presence is linked to the absence of a kind of awareness that adapts to and coincides with the archetypal discourse of the global art world. Nevertheless, this system can still accommodate certain realities or contexts as easily identifiable as others within the Western system of art such as the Asian, African or South American. In Spain, a supposedly advanced European country, artists have not fully understood how to work with these multicultural codes, or the new globalized world. Today, while Spanish artists operate within artistic discourses that have little if anything to do with nationality or territorial identity, they do adjust to a different kind of discursive pattern at an international level—something which places artists in a very difficult position: since they have no obvious, recognizable identity and because they are not classified as other according to the system, their works are judged within the same parameters as those of any other international artist. Nevertheless . . . their internationalism is not complete. The power of a country like Spain to transmit and spread artistic discourses and narratives is very limited. Because we live in a global world, focal points of transmission or channels by which information is circulated remain in place. Spanish art receives information but cannot transmit it: however much art tries to find its voice, the channels in the world of global art are tuned in to a different station. [. . .]

While it cannot be said that Spanish art has enjoyed a prominent role over the last few decades, neither has it been excluded entirely. It has not assumed a role in which it is capable of speaking nor one of being spoken for. It has had little or no possibility of enunciation, at least not within the present global system. Oddly enough, the only prevailing narratives in contemporary Spanish art relate to the Spanish Civil War and to the Franco era, i.e. to the period during which Spanish art did indeed adapt to the hegemonic artistic imagination, those who felt the other to be in danger of yielding to the logic of the stereotype, of the controlled, the submissive and the dominated. Nevertheless, since the introduction of democracy in 1975, Spanish art has been unable to produce an image, to become a reference, or to think within a discourse other than that of emancipation. The so-called *movida madrileña* [the Madrid scene] at the beginning of the 1980s, worked with a concept of freedom which followed four decades of oppression. However, since then Spanish art has been incapable of generating powerful or articulate artistic dialogues, dialogues which, in any event, could respond to hegemonic influences.

7

LONDON

During the last quarter of the seventeenth century the Dutch economy went into a decline. The population had stopped growing, the pace of technological change slowed, and manufacturing stagnated. The industrial sector was partly dismantled, and growth in trade leveled off. By 1713, London had displaced Amsterdam as the new hub of the European world-economy and became the central entrepôt for European trade. After the Great Fire of 1666, new markets, quays, and wharves along the northern bank of the Thames had been built to improve London's ports. Geographically, the city was advantageously positioned for the increasingly profitable trade within the British Empire, especially with North America. While the economy initially was stymied by the wars with France and Spain in the eighteenth century, London's central position in the world of trade and its pioneering innovations in industrial production generated significant wealth for the upper classes.

London was slow to develop a primary art market and did not become a major center of art production—a phenomenon widely remarked upon at the time. As the British critic Tobias Smollett lamented in 1768: "England affords a great variety of geniuses in all the liberal arts, except in the sublime parts of painting. Portraits, it must be owned, are tolerably well executed, and drawing is well understood: but the spirit of invention, the grand composition, the enthusiasm of the art, seem wanting in this climate" (Gibson 2007, 22).

Yet a strong desire to own art permeated British high society. The passion of King Charles I (1600–1649) for collecting had been infectious among the aristocracy. The king and a number of his close associates, including the Duke of Buckingham, the Earl of Arundel, and the Duke of Hamilton, introduced a taste for Italian painting to England. Charles I's collection contained many works by what came to be known as Old Masters. The concept of the Old Master can be traced to Italy, where around 1700 the work of Renaissance artists—Raphael, Leonardo, Michelangelo, and others—came to be seen as holding a permanent and exceptionally high value (Haskell 2000). (The term itself did not appear until the late eighteenth century, when it came into use to refer to all works of art produced before the French Revolution.)

The execution of King Charles I in 1649 helped launch the British secondary art market. During the 1650s, the English Parliament sold the royal collection, which included an estimated 1,760 paintings. Thousands of important artworks suddenly went into circulation. While most of the works made their way back into the royal collection after the Restoration, in 1660, collecting continued to grow during the second half of the seventeenth century. By 1700 picture ownership had extended to the new social class associated with the expansion of trade in London (see Gibson-Wood 2002).

By the end of the eighteenth century Britain had solidified its dominant commercial power in the world marketplace. The importation of goods from British colonies and the exportation of these goods all over the world were the key to British prosperity. The invention of the steam engine in 1804 spurred the development of a rail network connecting London to every industrial city. Commerce drove the expansion of the shipbuilding industry, provided tens of thousands of jobs for laborers on the London docks, and spawned wholesale and retail trade everywhere.

In 1805 a circle of collectors formed the British Institution for Promoting the Fine Arts in the United Kingdom with the desire to promote the works of living British artists to the general public. The Institution, mostly known as Pall Mall Picture Galleries or the British Gallery, was dedicated to mounting two types of annual exhibitions. The first, open to the public, showcased and sold contemporary works by British artists (or artists resident in Britain). The second exhibition was limited to artists and students of the arts and featured Old Master works borrowed from the collections of the British Institution's subscribers. The exhibitions were a popular success and helped foster the development of the primary market in London in the nineteenth century.

CAROL GIBSON-WOOD, *Picture Consumption in London*

Excerpts (pp. 491–96) from "Picture Consumption in London at the End of the Seventeenth Century," *Art Bulletin* 84, no. 3 (2002): 491–500. Published by kind permission of the author.

Economic development in the late seventeenth century marked the beginning of the "consumer revolution" in England that witnessed an unprecedented range of people with the means and desire to acquire greater quantities and types of material possessions. Growing numbers of men and women from the middling ranks undertook business enterprises, for example, that gave them more disposable income to spend on the considerable variety of luxury goods becoming available in London, which by 1700, with about half a million inhabitants, was the largest city in Europe. The increased number of families engaged in trade or commerce comprised the core of a significant percentage (estimated at 20–25 percent) of London's population that, while less well off than the wealthy aristocracy (2–3 percent of the population), was nonetheless financially independent and largely self-employed, unlike the remaining 75 percent, consisting of waged laborers, servants, and the unemployed. This section of society, referred to in the eighteenth century as "the middle sort," "the middling classes," "the middle station," or "the trading classes," consisted not only of merchants, shopkeepers, tradesmen, and better-off artisans but also the growing numbers of professionals (including lawyers, physicians, surgeons, and apothecaries) who served their needs. [. . .]

. . . Inventories reveal that a surprisingly large number of middle-class London houses had pictures on their walls at the turn of the eighteenth century. Of the 100 households considered from the City of London, 62 included paintings, and the total number of pictures listed (excluding those identified as prints) was 773. Of the 110 examples from Westminster parishes, 30 had pictures, with a total number of about 360. [. . .]

The monetary values attached to most of these pictures indicate that they were not costly masterpieces. The inventories rarely assigned individual values to paintings and prints, normally giving subtotals only for the complete contents of each room. However, when a space such as a staircase contained little or nothing besides pictures, approximate values can be inferred. The value of paintings in these cases averaged between one and eight shillings each. [. . .] Even the pictures owned by contemporary painters (which must have included many by themselves) averaged only a few shillings each. [. . .]

[. . .] In any case, the figures indicate that pictures were affordable domestic embellishments for middle-class Londoners—much cheaper than clocks or mirrors, for example. Figures compiled by Gregory King in the 1690s for his "Scheme of the Income and Expense of the Several Famillies of England" suggest that the average expenditures of middle-class households for items besides food and clothing ranged between about £2 and £150 per year (depending on total incomes). At about ten shillings, a picture cost about the same as a woman's petticoat or a pewter dish.

Middle-class Londoners hung their pictures in many parts of their houses. While most commonly placed in the dining room (usually the main room for receiving visitors), they also regularly showed up in bedchambers, parlors, and staircases, and less frequently in garrets, nurseries, kitchens, and servants' rooms. They were also found in taverns and inns. In short, the evidence of the inventories suggests that by 1700 pictures were ubiquitous in London, a situation hence not dissimilar from that prevailing in the Netherlands some thirty years previously, when the Dutch had "their Houses full of Pictures, from the Highest to the Lowest" (Montias 1982). [. . .]

[. . .] We can probably assume that, unlike many of those adorning the grand homes of the British gentry, these pictures would not have been acquired abroad, since most middle-class Londoners would neither have traveled to the Continent nor employed agents there. Most of the pictures must have been bought in London. Some of them may have been portraits commissioned from London face painters—not masters like Godfrey Kneller or John Riley, whose prices would have been beyond the means of these house-holders, but less distinguished painters whose rates must have been relatively low, and about whom we unfortunately know very little. However, the majority of the pictures hanging in middle-class houses were probably decorative works acquired on the open market in London, from three possible sources: local artists who sold inexpensive, ready-made pictures; shops selling prints and paintings; and auction sales. [. . .]

Typical auction catalogues for the more common type of sale listed about three hundred pictures (although some had as many as seven hundred), including works identified as both originals and copies, "ancient and modern," and by "the best masters." Lists of artists that identify these "best masters" frequently appear on the title pages of the catalogues; they may include earlier artists such as Titian, Hans Holbein, or Peter Paul Rubens but correspond mainly to painters active in England in the late seventeenth century. . . . That these sales were directed at least partly toward buyers of domestic decor is also often indicated on the title pages, which regularly include announcements that the pictures offered include "large pieces fit for Halls," "small pieces for Ladies Closets," and others suitable for chimneys, overdoors, halls, and staircases. The subject matter of all paintings is briefly described, but artists are named for fewer than half.

As the Ogdens (1955) noted, the most popular types of subjects were landscapes (including "semi-landscapes" such as moonlight scenes and winter pieces) and historical themes, followed by portraits, genre, and still life. Pictures of animals and of battles also occur frequently. Historical subjects included a surprising number of religious paintings, given England's Protestantism: saints and Madonnas, as well as Old and New Testament scenes. Among the portraits, representations of royalty (especially William and Mary) figured largely. Genre themes were very much in keeping with Dutch taste: low-life scenes of smoking, drinking, and merrymaking, unspecified "drolls," "amorous pieces," and "smutty pieces." Still-life subjects included flowers, fruit, fish, game, and "vanities." [. . .]

If we can assume that auctioneers' descriptive terminology reflected consumer tastes and criteria, craftsmanship and finish seem to have been desirable qualities of paintings for middle-class buyers. Terms such as "finely done," "delicately painted," "neatly done," and "curiously painted" appear often, with other indications of style or quality limited to occasional characterizations of "well done," "well painted," or "extraordinary." Catalogues sometimes specified medium, if not oil on canvas ("on board," "on copper," "in water colours," or "in crions"), and gave the approximate dimensions of particularly large paint-ings. Others are simply called "large" or "little," or described as being suitable for a specific location in the home.

Approximately 24,000 paintings were offered for sale at London auctions in 1691. Henry and Margaret Ogden regarded this as an "extraordinary number" and suggested that there must have been a considerable amount of speculative buying and reselling, a conclusion that has been accepted by other scholars. [. . .] However, the number of pictures on the market does not seem so extraordinary when their popularity as house furnishings is taken into consideration. Although firm figures are not available, it has been estimated that London had about 25,000 middle-class households around 1700. Hence, if each household purchased one picture in 1691, the total of 24,000 paintings would be accounted for. Not every middling householder would actually have bought a painting in that year, of course; however, my probate inventory sample suggests that approximately 45 percent (hence, over 11,000) of these residences contained an average of 12 paintings each. This would mean that about 132,000 paintings were found in middle-class London homes around 1700, and statistics collected by Weatherill (1988) indicate that the percentage of households containing pictures in London increased markedly between 1675 and 1695 (from 54 percent to 79 percent of her sample, which used inventories from 1675, 1685, and 1695). Thus, although some picture owners no doubt sold as well as bought paintings, the total number of paintings being used as domestic furnishings was certainly and dramatically on the rise during this period. That more than 20,000 pictures were offered for sale at auctions in 1691 does not, in this context, seem unlikely. [. . .]

There is no evidence to suggest that the widespread picture buying in this early period represented a middle-class desire to cultivate "taste" as a means of gaining access to polite society. Rather, the emerging discourse on taste in the visual arts . . . was itself constructed as a response to the phenomenon of popular picture consumption. The elite's determination to differentiate between acceptable and unacceptable reasons for liking pictures, a feature absent from earlier English discussions of art, served to distance it from middle-class picture consumption. The success of this strategy led many upwardly mobile Londoners to adopt this discourse during the course of the eighteenth century by attempting to learn the new vocabulary of connoisseurship and adjusting the nature of their purchases accordingly. More importantly, and regrettably, the very writing of English art history also became, and remains, predicated on these distinctions.

IAIN PEARS, *The Art Market*

Excerpts (pp. 51–54, 67–68, 71–75, 89–92) from "The Art Market," in *The Discovery of Painting: The Growth of Interest in the Arts in England, 1680–1768* (New Haven, CT, and London: Yale University Press, 1988), 51–105. Copyright © 1988 Yale University Press.

The supply of paintings on the English market in the late seventeenth century came from two main sources. Firstly there was the production of new works by living artists, a separate and only partially commercialised sector. . . . The other, and more important, source was the resale of extant works, this latter section being numerically much larger. An Englishman would have found it fairly difficult to acquire a painting before the 1680s even if he had had both the money and the inclination to buy. Had he lived in London, he could perhaps have bought one at a print or book shop. . . . Alternatively, he could have commissioned a work from one of the many artists working in the city. However, problems would have begun to appear had he wanted a good painting as that, almost by definition, meant a foreign one. As most of the polemicists were forever complaining, there were few good paintings in England in the first place, and consequently many less on sale. Antwerp and Amsterdam were still the European centers for the art market and the few high quality paintings in England tended to be shipped there—remnants of the Arundel collection, for example, were sold in Amsterdam in 1684, as the bulk of the paintings from the Buckingham collection had been sold in Antwerp in the 1650s.

For an Englishman to build up a good collection of paintings in this early period meant, therefore, that he had to buy them abroad. It has been suggested that it was economic adjustments that made this a practical possibility, with the rapid advance in England's wealth and the slow decline of Italy's not only putting an increasing number of paintings on sale but also making the English more capable of outbidding competitors. Although this is undoubtedly true, such long-term changes in fact merely opened up the possibility that paintings would begin to flow northwards, rather than creating the certainty that they would do so. Before any large scale trading could begin to take advantage of economic change there were still many obstacles that needed to be overcome.

The first problem inhibiting the growth of a substantial art market in England was bureaucratic, in that it was technically illegal to import paintings into the country at all. Although the law was far from being enforced rigorously (one of the most notable seventeenth-century lawbreakers in this respect was Charles I), the government did remember it occasionally, and frequently enough to make importing pictures less than tempting. In the Restoration period, however, the relaxation of the law became as official as was possible without a statutory change. By 1672 the Treasury board was instructing the customs commissioners that 'as for pictures and gilt leather, where they are not brought in for sale, but only for the private use of gentlemen, you are to represent the particular cases unto us, so if we think fit, they may be permitted to pay customs *ad valorem*'. [. . .]

This alteration in official attitudes ultimately gained formal embodiment in 1695 with a law which for the first time permitted the importation of all paintings and which on its own signified a major shift in attitude towards the subject of art. The laws which had previously prevented the practice had been designed, it may safely be assumed, to protect the interests of the guild of the Painter-Stainers' Company. As such they reflect an attitude towards painting which was basically artisanal. Painting was a craft and the importation of paintings would have damaged the livelihood of English craftsmen in the same way that the importation of pottery would damage potters. [. . .]

Over the period 1695 to 1722 the reordering of official attitudes was completed, with the government moving by stages from banning importation to tolerating it and finally to making it as easy and as painless as possible. In sum, it seems to have come around to the idea that such imports were to be desired and encouraged rather than regretted. The act of 1695 laid an import duty of 20 percent on the value of all pictures coming into the country and this method was continued under Anne. Eventually, however, it was considered unsatisfactory and the law was changed again in 1721. . . . The problem with the original method of taxation was that the better the picture, the more it cost to bring into the country. The law of 14 February 1721 solved this by making the amount of duty dependent on the size of the painting, rather than on its original price. [. . .]

Clearing legal blockages and developing a sophisticated and flexible system of internal distribution for works of art were not in themselves sufficient for the full development of the English market in resold paintings. The final problem that had to be overcome was the initially small number of pictures in England, which necessitated heavy reliance on foreign stock, and consequently required an equal development of more sophisticated methods of importation. [. . .]

As a partial answer to this problem of bringing painting and buyer together there developed the professional agent working to commission, the supreme example of this type being William Petty, who worked for the Earl of Arundel in the 1630s. [. . .] The potential of the agent was, however, inevitably limited. On the one hand, if he worked for only one person then that buyer had to be prepared to spend on a lavish scale to make such an expensive employee worthwhile, and the number of people in the eighteenth century who were ready to lay out cash on the scale of an Arundel was decidedly limited. On the other hand, if the agent worked for two people simultaneously in order to cut costs then different but equally severe problems arose. When Thomas Roe acted for both Arundel and Buckingham in the Eastern Mediterranean in the 1620s, for example, the co-operative scheme fell apart because both employers began to suspect that the other was taking an unfair advantage in capturing the better works thus acquired.

If agents were to work for several clients at a time they had consequently to become more or less independent, taking responsibility for their purchases themselves and letting the distribution of the paintings be decided by that universal arbiter, the greatest willingness to pay. Such a scheme also offered the tempting prospect of greater rewards for those who chose works which sold well in the English market. Before this could happen, however, such traders had to be assured that there was a sufficient demand for paintings to provide a healthy profit. To buy a large number of paintings, even at bargain Italian prices, to ship them back to England and prepare them for sale, was far from being a cheap process and constituted a considerable entrepreneurial risk, especially as those people both prepared, and able, to perform these tasks were almost by definition unlikely to be independently wealthy.

The auctions of the 1680s and 1690s, however, demonstrated quite conclusively that the market for art was sufficiently buoyant for the agent to cut his links with his employer.

The first Englishman who can definitely be identified as having set up as an independent dealer was Thomas Manby, a landscape painter who studied for several years in Italy. During that period he acquired a large number of paintings (there were 168 in his sale) which he disposed of at an auction after his return to England in 1686. This sale moreover seems to have been a considerable success—Vertue noted that Manby was able to live comfortably on the profits for the remaining ten years of his life. [. . .]

The main importance of international dealers was that their existence took most of the pain and difficulty out of collecting. With such problematic areas as transport, insurance and laws governing exportation safely in the hands of the specialist, not only were the amounts of time and energy necessary for collecting reduced substantially but the element of risk involved was reduced to that inherent in the process of selection. In addition, although the appearance of the dealer was a result of the buoyancy of English demand for works of art, by ensuring that a steady flow of paintings arrived in England and were distributed efficiently, the dealers played a substantial role in maintaining and extending the development of that interest. The importance of paintings in the English social system increasingly came to rest on the significance engendered by their relative ubiquity, not in their exclusivity. For this to be possible it was essential that availability was subject only to taste and financial ability to purchase, not on arbitrary access due to having the appropriate contacts, or being in the right place at the right time. The concept of taste could not have gained its artistic and social significance if the evolution of an interest in the arts had been hindered by such practical and erratic barriers. The intervention of the dealers therefore played a major role in conditioning the English response to painting. In simple financial terms their emergence placed an additional level between buyer and work, while in social terms the enormous simplifications they permitted placed the buyer in close contact with the paintings and allowed much greater emphasis on the problem of choice.

Several types of dealer can be detected, although there was a gradual tendency for all to coalesce into one as the eighteenth century progressed. The two main categories were the shop dealer and the international dealer. Crossing over these two were the painter-dealer and the connoisseur-dealer who performed either of these main functions. [. . .]

From the 1740s onwards the prevailing distinction between the international and domestic dealers becomes increasingly blurred, the cause of which was partly the much greater integration of the market. [. . .] The costs of expeditions abroad meant that dealers increasingly acted through other dealers and were less inclined to travel in search of paintings themselves. Robert Bragge, for example, appears to have worked with the French dealer Rémy and Sam Glover had pictures bought for him in Holland in 1743 by Harsebroek, one of the largest Dutch dealers of the century. This is not to suggest that dealers no longer went abroad at all but rather that they went less often, as evidenced by the introductions to auction catalogues in which the description 'brought from abroad by . . .' is noticeably supplanted by the alternative 'sent from abroad . . .'.

The greater integration of the market meant that profit increasingly had to come from speculation rather than the more simple method of commercial supply. As a foreign expedition was necessarily expensive and as the expansion of the market meant that the supply of pictures in England was that much greater, international dealers increasingly began to act on the domestic market as well, joining shop-dealers in buying at auctions. This tendency developed rapidly from the mid-1740s onwards, producing a market of sufficient complexity for it to include an element of self-sustaining activity. In the 1758 van Haecken sale, for example, dealers bought 43 out of the 150 lots, i.e. nearly a third. This sale was a complicated one from the outset; it was a group effort put together by several dealers. . . . Most of the dealers involved in this sale on both sides conducted their main business through the auction, so we have the unusual spectacle of dealers getting together to hold an auction to sell pictures to other dealers to sell by auction. [. . .]

[. . .] This increasing complexity meant that the route from old to new owner became greatly lengthened. Instead of passing through one middleman, several pictures clearly went through many of them, going from one dealer to another, and occasionally even back to the first. A proportion of trade in the art market was thus artificially generated, with the result that, in part at least, art dealing became not only a market in the normal sense of the word, but even began to show distinct signs of the characteristics of a commodity market, where the article traded had its external value as a painting complemented by an abstracted value as a speculative asset. This should not of course be overestimated. It can be assumed that the overwhelming majority of paintings ended with 'genuine' owners, but there was nevertheless a growing stock of floating paintings in the limbo of the market and part of this was used for speculative purposes.

DAVID ORMROD, *England and the Netherlands Compared*

Excerpts (pp. 11–15, 17–19) from "The Art Trade and Its Urban Context: England and the Netherlands Compared, 1550–1750," in *Auctions, Agents and Dealers: Mechanisms of the Art Market 1660–1830*, ed. J. Warren and A. Turpin (London: Archaeopress, 2008), 11–19. Copyright © 2008 The Wallace Collection, London.

By 1713, London had displaced Amsterdam to become a world city and a new kind of *entrepôt*, a national *entrepôt* within an imperial trading system. It was, however, a late arrival as a major centre of art production and distribution, confirming Braudel's view that 'the cultural map and the economic map cannot simply be superimposed without anomaly'. Few historians nowadays recognize a close or simple relationship between economic conditions and periods of cultural efflorescence. But in the case of seventeenth-century Holland, the explosion of artistic creativity was matched by the emergence of an art market which appears to have been particularly sensitive to the economic climate. [. . .]

In post-Restoration England, the taste for painting developed relatively slowly, in spite of generally rising real incomes, and the scarcity of native artistic talent and training facilities persisted well into the early years of the eighteenth century. Although the early 1690s saw a short-lived boom in auction sales, the basic infrastructure of dealers, retail shops and regular picture sales was not established in London until the 1720s and 30s. With the exception of Bath, few English towns could lay claim to a resident artist until the closing years of the eighteenth century.

In comparison with Holland, England's art world was extremely small and concentrated in two adjacent areas of London around Covent Garden and Great Queen Street. By 1714, Sir Godfrey Kneller's newly established academy numbered 86 members, not all of whom were professional artists. Louise Lippincott (1983, 15, 32) estimates the total size of London's art world at this time at no more than 200, including students and apprentices, dealers, printsellers and auctioneers. At the height of the Golden Age, the number of painters working in the Dutch republic was somewhere between 650 and 750, or one painter for every 2,500 inhabitants—about twenty times the number found in Queen Anne's England. The Dutch market, indeed, suffered from 'structural overproduction', with disastrous consequences for many artists during the period of contraction after 1660. Nevertheless, the disparity is so striking that it seems appropriate to discuss the history of painting in England in terms of 'obstacles to growth'. To some extent, this is recognised in the only comprehensive account of the English art market available, Ian Pears's *Discovery of Painting* (1988), which was produced before the recent upsurge of writing on Northern European markets. . . . Unfortunately, Pears identifies the principal obstacle to market growth as an alleged prohibition on the import of paintings which, he claims, was only abandoned in 1695. At the same time, he sees the 'essentially artisanal guild' of the Painter-Stainers Company as necessarily inimical to innovation and assumes that it continued to exercise a baleful, though diminishing, influence on workshop practice until the early eighteenth century.

In fact, the late medieval and Tudor restraints on imports were a dead letter by the time of the Restoration (Ormrod 1998, 2002). The Treasury Books show that connoisseurs and collectors were freely importing paintings during the 1660s without inspection, and indeed without payment of customs. By that time, the Painter-Stainers Company was already a spent force and did little to control production. . . . Seen from a comparable northern European perspective, the most serious structural weakness affecting the development of painting in seventeenth-century England appeared to be the absence of a flexible and supportive guild structure of the type that existed in the Netherlands—or something like it. Furthermore the concentration of demand in London produced a situation in which commissions could be satisfied by relatively small groups of immigrant painters, catering for royal and aristocratic patrons. It may well be that 'achievement across several fields of endeavor tend to cluster within cities over relatively short periods of time', but a high concentration in the greatest single market may not necessarily be the most efficient means of developing and diffusing new craft skills. [. . .]

Recent research has revised the formerly negative view of craft guilds in early modern European industrial development, particularly by highlighting the way in which the emergence of new manufactures was often accompanied by a proliferation of specialised guilds. Epstein (1998), for example, emphasises the primary role of guilds in promoting the transfer of skills and contributing towards innovation by encouraging the clustering of producers and providing inventors with monopoly rents. He is careful, however, to distinguish between the normally beneficial 'technological spillovers' of craft activity, frequently unintentional, and the guilds' oligopolistic controls over output which were deliberate and often damaging. In the northern Netherlands, especially, a strong case has been made for the positive role of guilds in uniting previously unorganised artisans and shopkeepers, and promoting innovation in some sectors such as shipbuilding and wind-mill technology. [. . .] The craft of painting . . . required a uniquely rigorous and special-ised form of training, and there is little doubt that the guilds of St. Luke in the northern and southern Netherlands played a critical role in nurturing local talent and maintaining high standards of workmanship, particularly at the top end of the market. [. . .]

[. . .] In both Antwerp and the Dutch cities, guild attempts to exercise oligopolistic controls over output were resisted, and, by the middle of the seventeenth century, a number of guilds were dissolved. In their place—or sometimes alongside them—looser associations were formed, such as the *confrèries* of Amsterdam (1653) and The Hague (1656) or the 'College of Painters' in Utrecht (by 1644), which gave artists greater powers of self-management. In general the guilds and their successors failed to establish cartels in their local areas, and were powerless to prevent the collapse of the market during the 1660s and 70s. On the other hand, they maintained professional pride, facilitated the transfer of skills, and did much to nurture local talent. [. . .]

The positive aspects of these institutional arrangements, as Michael Montias (1982) has emphasised, depended substantially on the size and scale of the urban environment within which many Dutch artists worked. [. . .] Montias introduced the important notion of *critical mass* to explain how . . . communities maintained or lost their dynamic. . . . Specialisation and the proliferation of genres emerged naturally in the congeries of towns of central Holland, mutually accessible, but each sufficiently distinct to allow for the emergence of local schools. Guild regulations, by protecting local production at the expense of 'out of town' work, encouraged this diversity and thus accelerated the develop-ment of Dutch art as a whole. Hoogewerff (1947), indeed, went as far as to suggest that local particularities of style originated in contrasting patterns of guild regulation. [. . .]

The differences between the relative sizes of the Dutch provincial art centres were of course less significant than the contrast in population size between Amsterdam and the surrounding towns and cities of Holland. Amsterdam was more than twice the size of Leiden, the largest industrial city in Holland, but its dominance over its surrounding hinterland was much less pronounced than the corresponding position of London. . . . Instead, the whole western area of the province of post-medieval Holland may be considered as a 'decentralised metropolis'. Amsterdam never functioned as a primate city, or the hub in a central place system, as Dutch towns always tended to exercise complementary functions.

In relation to the art market, however, a division of functions arose between, on the one hand, Amsterdam as an international centre and a great export market (which also contained its own population of painters), and on the other, the smaller surrounding art centres producing a host of genres and specialities. The Haarlem Guild of St Luke, for example, described Amsterdam as a 'mercantile city', or one in which guilds could not expect to promote the interests of producers above those of merchants. Unlike the situation in the smaller centres, probate inventories record no disproportionately high percentage of work by local artists, and the city attracted the best artists from all over the United Provinces. Montias concludes that Amsterdam functioned as a relatively open market, and in this and other respects it increasingly resembled Antwerp in its golden age. Professional dealers became more numerous in the 1630s and 40s, especially in response to the increasing variegation of consumers' taste, with a minority, such as Kretzer and de Renialme, catering for a high-class clientele requiring work by Italian and Flemish as well as Dutch masters. Between 1675 and 1725, the demand for old master painting on the Amsterdam market rose sharply relative to that for contemporary art. During the first three-quarters of the eighteenth century, Amsterdam's position at the centre of the European art market was unrivalled, with sales conducted increasingly through public auction. Not until the last quarter of the century was it overtaken by Paris.

In the decentralised art world of the northern Netherlands, the movement of artists from one town to another was already common. As the market moved into recession during the 1660s and 70s, many artists went bankrupt, and places such as Utrecht lost the 'critical mass' necessary to sustain them as viable art centres. A fairly high elasticity of demand for art, the durability of easel paintings and the generally marginal character of art in the economy as a whole meant that collapse was rapid and the prospect of recovery remote. Several artists were drawn to Italy, while many emigrated to other parts of northern Europe where painting was less well developed, including Germany and England. London, in particular, was the favoured destination for several individuals. During the 1660s, the flow of painters and engravers arriving in London from the United Provinces was double the number recorded for the 1650s; during the 1670s numbers doubled yet again. This intense period of emigration represents a significant change in the long-term picture. The period from 1540 to 1620 saw a small outflow of painters from the southern Netherlands to England, mainly in response to invitations from the court, a flow which increased as the seventeenth century wore on. In the 1610s, however, artists from the northern Netherlands began to make their way to England, and soon outnumbered their Flemish and Brabantine colleagues. The upturn of the 1620s was mainly the result of Charles I's artistic aspirations, culminating in the arrival of van Dyck in 1632 for his second, definitive, stay in England. The influx of the post-Restoration decades, on the other hand, was a much more broadly-based phenomenon. As we have already noted, it resulted from 'structural overproduction' in Holland, and private patronage exercised a much more powerful influence than the court, although most patrons were well-connected aristocrats. Few members of this cohort found themselves painting for an anonymous market. [. . .]

[. . .] It would be . . . accurate to describe the London situation as operating in a post-guild environment, and one which was developing along similar lines to Amsterdam in the same period in terms of the growth of auctions and a rising demand for old rather than contemporary art. In two important respects, however, the London market differed from Amsterdam: the latter was export driven, whereas London relied on imports, and the British market was in some degree shaped by an increasingly assertive nation state, as taxes on imported art were substantially raised from 1695. [. . .]

Guild regulation was quintessentially a town- or city-based form of industrial control which, in early seventeenth-century England, was increasingly becoming a matter for central government, and a matter 'more of development and promotion than of simple regulation'. The crown tended to support extension of the jurisdiction of the craft guilds at this time. However in the case of the Painter-Stainers Company, Charles I's patronage of foreign painters undoubtedly undermined the company and the livelihood of English painters. [. . .]

In comparison with the situation in the Netherlands, the London painters' guild was weak and the strength of foreign competition was, by the 1620s, both overwhelming and demoralising. In 1627 the Painter-Stainers and their allies presented a list of more than fifteen foreign painters whom they wished to prosecute. . . . Whinney and Millar (1957) were doubtless right to argue that the arrival of van Dyck put an end to the possibility that 'a native school might flower under the influence of the sound craftsmanship of Mytens and Johnson', but the fact remains that the obstacles were of a deep, structural kind. Montias's conception of critical mass, as far as I am aware, has not been applied to London as an art-producing centre, and the possibility suggests itself that London's enormous size inhibited co-operation of the kind that existed in the Dutch towns between [residents] and newcomers. The Company's final effort to reassert its claims ended in 1641, and from this point onward, if not earlier, immigrant artists were free to work in the unregulated environment of an expanding metropolis.

Throughout the early modern period in England, the fine and decorative arts were heavily dependent on imported skills and craftsmanship, and the rate of borrowing greatly increased with the Huguenot diaspora of the 1680s and 90s. During the reigns of James II and William III, the proportion of foreign painters peaked. It was during the 1670s that the state gradually moved towards a policy of import substitution, directed in the first instance against the growing volume of luxury imports from France. By the 1710s Whig propagandists like Shaftesbury began to call for national control of a national culture involving, amongst other things, the establishment of academies of painting, sculpture and architecture. [. . .]

Charles II issued a declaration in March 1672, soon after the English declaration of war with Holland, welcoming immigrants from the Low Countries to settle where they pleased, with full liberty of conscience. Additionally, they had leave to bring their families, estates, goods and merchandise to England, without seizure or liability to customs normally paid by aliens. The crown's aim was a twofold one of encouraging both the influx of foreign craftsmen and their rapid denization, and the transfer of Dutch shipping to English ports through the migration of Dutch merchants to England. The 1672 declaration was part of Downing's blatant mercantilist strategy designed to undermine Dutch commercial advantage and to perpetuate a state of war. As we have seen, the collapse of the Dutch art market increased the pressure to emigrate, and many had already done so before the declaration was issued. The second set of measures involved substantial increases in import duties during the wars against Louis XIV. Pictures were singled out for heavy increase in 1695 and 1704, by which date they were liable to a duty of almost 60 per cent. Importers took elaborate steps to reduce the burden of duties, suggesting that the new taxes had more than marginal impact on London's growing trade in works of art.

In terms of both quality and quantity, it is clear that the substantial influx of Dutch and Flemish painters after 1660 made a crucial contribution to the growth of the London art market, by augmenting and raising the quality of domestic production, and by supplementing imports. The Ogdens (1955) suggested that over 35,000 paintings passed through the London auction sales during the boom years of the early 1690s, at a time when it was alleged that Dutch picture dealers in London 'imported large collections and disposed of them by auction'. During the 1680s and 90s, immigrant painters from the Netherlands were contributing the equivalent of over 400 working years per decade to English art production, and this was sufficient to furnish the London auction rooms with more than enough copies and originals to maintain a steady momentum of business. As we know, that momentum was lost after 1695, the point at which import duties were substantially increased, and by the early 1700s the centre of gravity in the European art market returned to Amsterdam. At the same time the flow of new immigrant painters tailed off, and English taste shifted further in the direction of Italian and classical art.

In broad terms . . . [the] characterisation of London as an unregulated market [is accurate]. A stronger guild structure might well have quickened the development of English art, and through competition encouraged the early development of a range of genres of a kind that arrived in the later seventeenth century. In practical terms, a relatively free labour market encouraged immigration, which English mercantilist practice incorporated into a developing strategy of import substitution. In this sense, we can describe the London art market as state-induced, a centralised national market in contrast to the guild-dominated markets found in the cities of the Low Countries.

TOBIAS SMOLLETT, *Engraving*

Reprint of "Article XI. Engraving," *Critical Review, or, Annals of Literature* 7 (1759): 375–77. Published online by Google Books.

Amidst the degeneracy, want of taste, trifling pursuits, and dissipation of the present age, we find many instances of uncommon genius, in all the different branches of liberal arts, shooting up as it were without culture, and even unheeded, like a number of delicate flowers on a common overgrown with weeds, heath, and brambles. Not to mention the progress which has lately been made by our countrymen in statuary, painting, and music, we can congratulate this age and island, upon having produced one of the best engravers that ever appeared in England. The reader of taste will immediately guess that we mean Mr. Strange, whose works have always excited the admiration of the public. This excellent artist, unlike his brethren, has never deviated from that respect which a man of extraordinary genius owes to his character. He has ever resisted the temptations of wealth when they were inconsistent with his reputation, and chosen rather to live on a moderate income, earned by the industry of his own hands, than acquire a large fortune, by prostituting his name and genius to the indiscriminating choice of ignorant employers, and the inaccuracy of hurried design. The subjects he has selected are some of the best pieces of the best masters, and these only; and every thing that comes from his hand is finished and perfect. The public has done justice to his merit, which stood entirely on its own foundation, unsupported by interest and cabal; and we doubt not that all lovers of the liberal arts will encourage that laudable ardour for improvement, which appears in his last proposals of subscription. He has already almost finished the three prints, which, in our opinion, are executed with a spirit and accuracy, that, if possible, exceeds those of his former productions.

One represents the choice of Hercules, and is engraved after a picture of the celebrated Nicholas Poussin, now in the possession of Henry Hoare, Esq.

The scene is laid as it were on the very boundary, between a fertile and a barren country. The hero may be said to stand on the confines, between the figures of Virtue and Pleasure, by whom he is alternately admonished and allured. On one side nothing is to be seen but barren hills, stunted trees, and rugged mountains; the other displays a charming paisage or landscape, adorned with verdure, shrubs, trees, and flowers in full blossom. Hercules, crowned with a garland of oak, and supported by his club, stands in an attitude of earnest suspense, between animating virtue and seducing pleasure. He appears in all the bloom of youth, with a mixture of delicacy, even in that robust composition of the bones and muscles, by which Alcides is always distinguished. On his countenance there is a fine expression of ingen'ous sensibility; a noble flush of features glowing with the dictates of honour; for he is already turned towards virtue, and his mind seems to be in the very act of triumphing over the allurements of pleasure.

Virtue is represented by a female figure modestly arrayed in a plain stole: her hair flows loose about her shoulders, without any other ornament but that of a fillet: her looks are composed, serene, and sensible; while she stands exhorting her pupil, pointing to a bare perpendicular rock, an emblem of the toil, danger, and difficulty that attend the pursuit of true glory. There is a simplicity in this figure, which, though it may disgust the eye of a common spectator, will, nevertheless, recommend it strongly to every person acquainted with the manner of the ancients.

On the other side, the eye is attracted powerfully by Pleasure, exhibited in the character of Venus, addressing the hero with all the blandishments of love and elocution. One hand is extended in the attitude of eloquence: with the other, she points to some scenes of effeminate pleasure, which, however, are concealed from the spectator's view: an infant Cupid holds his mother with one hand, and, in the other, presents a full blown rose to Hercules. In the figure of Pleasure, we find no glare of false, extravagant ornaments. The drapery consists of a loose robe and zone embroidered: her feet are cased in buskins: her hair is intertwined with a chaplet of flowers: part of it flows adown her neck: the rest is braided up in the Grecian manner.

The whole right leg, and part of the thigh, as well as arm, shoulder, and neck, on the same side, are naked: the head is in profile, and may be considered as a fine antique: for, although it be the work of Poussin, it is designed entirely in the antique manner.

The subject of Mr. Strange's second print, is Venus attired by the Graces, the picture by Guido Rheni in the royal collection at Kensington. We hazard nothing in affirming that this is one of the finest prints that ever attracted the public attention, whether we consider the design or the execution. Venus appears almost naked, reclining on a couch, displaying all the attractions of female beauty, with her eyes turned up, as if she were dissolved into all the languishment of pleasure. It is impossible for the spectator of sensibility to view this figure without admiration even to rapture; she is so fair, so soft, so tender, so elegant and alluring. Cupid stands between her knees playing with one of her trinkets, and exhibiting in his looks all that childish archness, by which he is usually characterised. The three graces are employed in attiring his mother. One stands behind her head, disposing a jewel in her hair, and is, herself, extremely elegant and beautiful, naked to the breast, with her own hair flowing in ringlets upon her neck and shoulder. She is contrasted in attitude by another tying a bracelet on the arm of Venus; and a third in a sitting posture, with the foot of the goddess on her knee, is employed in lacing on the buskin. Hard by is a casket of jewels on a dressing table: on the fore-ground lie the bow and quiver of Cupid; and behind we see another little love culling a nose-gay from a vase filled with flowers: perhaps there was never a finer group than in the composition of this picture, every figure of which is beautiful; but, that of Venus, altogether exquisite. The painter has displayed uncommon art in the conduct of the *chiaro oscuro*; for the whole is exhibited in a fine blaze or mass of light, that shews every figure to the best advantage. The third print is likewise taken from a picture of Guido at Kensington, and represents St. Agnes with her lamb, as the emblem of meekness and innocence. She appears standing with her hands clasped together, and her eyes lifted up in a transport of devotion. Her face discloses the unaffected graces of youth and beauty; all the mildness of humanity and benevolence, together with an unspeakable sweetness of expression, which denotes internal peace, the happy consequence of true piety and conscious virtue. Behind her, a Love is seen descending from the sky, with a crown of martyrdom in one hand, and a branch of palm in the other. On the fore-ground a second Love appears, playing with a lamb: and at one side, we see a magnificent vase and pillar, adorned with sculpture in *alto* and *basso relievo*, representing a sacrifice and other scenes of ancient superstition.

RONALD PAULSON, *Hogarth*

Excerpt (pp. 4–7) from "Patron and Public," in *Hogarth: His Life, Art, and Times*, vol. 2, *Hogarth: High Art and Low, 1732–1750* (New Brunswick, NJ: Rutgers University Press, 1992), 1–14. Reprinted by permission of Ronald Paulson.

By the autumn of 1732 [William] Hogarth had decided on another large print with which to follow up the success of the *Harlot's Progress*; too busy to produce a new painting, he turned to a conversation picture he had done a year or so before of a drinking club, titled it *A Midnight Modern Conversation*, added an inscription claiming disingenuously that no portraits were intended, and this time advertised his subscription in the newspapers—a distinct and bold step for a painter relying on a reputation for gentility.

The subscription was announced on 18 December. On 8 December the vintners of London had launched a full-scale attack on Sir Robert Walpole's proposed excise on wine and tobacco, which had become the most controversial issue in the career of the Great Man. The city of London was, to say the least, strongly against the Excise Bill. Hogarth must have dusted off and engraved this particular painting because it showed both tobacco and spirits being consumed with abandon.

In his advertisement of 18 December in the *Daily Advertiser* he emphasized the number of "characters" included (in the manner of his painted "conversations") and his worries about pirates:

> MR. Hogarth having engrav'd a large Copper Plate from a Picture of his own painting, representing a *Midnight Modern Conversation*, consisting of ten different Characters; in order to preserve his Property therein, and prevent the Printsellers from graving base Copies to his Prejudice, proposes to publish it by Subscription on the Terms following.
>
> The Price Five Shillings for each Print, to be paid at the Time of subscribing; for which the Author will give an etch'd Plate, with a Receipt to deliver the Print on the first of March next. But if the Number already printed be sooner subscrib'd for, then the Prints shall be sooner deliver'd, and Notice thereof given in the Papers. The Picture and Print to be seen next Door to the New Play-house in Covent Garden Piazza, where Subscriptions are taken in.

[Hogarth] not only advertised, he used his own name and gave his address (Rich's new playhouse had just opened). His advertisement was repeated in every issue of the *Daily Advertiser* through December and (with slight changes) January.

By 25 January he had come to another important decision: he deleted the last sentence of the second paragraph and replaced it with "after which Time they will be three Half Crowns each." He had probably discovered that his method of engraving-etching produced impressions by no means exhausted after some fifteen hundred had been printed. By this time it had occurred to him that he could increase the take by keeping both the profits of his subscription and all subsequent profits; so instead of limiting the printing to those subscribed for, he raised the price after the subscription and sold to the general public.

The painting was a long horizontal canvas of 31 × 64 inches (as opposed to the standard 25 × 30–inch canvas of these years), but he engraved it in the light of *A Harlot's Progress*, compressing the horizontal shape, enlarging the figures in relation to the picture space, and rendering, for such a crowded plate, a relatively balanced composition. Men are leaning back on opposite sides, like supporters on a coat of arms; a clock is balanced by a fireplace; and the two men in the foreground, one leaning back, the other precipitately forward, also balance each other. The bewigged figure is in the center of the table and only slightly off the exact center of the wall paneling. The result is what [Alexander] Pope would have called "harmoniously confused." [. . .]

The great popularity of *A Midnight Modern Conversation*—stimulated in part at least by the Excise Bill—was underlined by the piracies that immediately appeared and the infinite variety of copies and adaptations that followed on everything from snuffboxes and punch bowls to fan mounts. The print was presumably delivered (as promised) on 1 March. By the 12th a piracy had been advertised (*Daily Post*). Salt glaze ware mugs with rough approximations of Hogarth's design were available before the end of March; fan mounts were advertised in the *Daily Journal* for 24 May as sold at Mr. Chenevix's and other toy shops, with "a Description of each particular Person" attached "for the Entertainment of the Ladies."

MARCIA POINTON, *Portrait Painting as a Business Enterprise*

Excerpts (pp. 188–89, 191–92, 195, 200, 202–3) from "Portrait-Painting as a Business Enterprise in London in the 1780s." *Art History* 7, no. 2 (1984): 187–205. Copyright © 1984 Association of Art Historians. Reproduced with permission of Blackwell Publishing Ltd.

The centre of London artistic life in the 1780s was the Royal Academy. The annual exhibition of that institution was dominated by portraits, for all that its President, Sir Joshua Reynolds, insisted in his discourses on the supremacy of history painting in the hierarchy of the genres. Portraits comprised the largest percentage of works submitted to the Royal Academy between 1781 and 1785 with landscapes not far behind. In 1783 portraits made up 44.67 per cent of the exhibits at the Academy. If miniatures were taken into account this figure would be even higher. History painting, the most elevated and desirable of the genres as taught by Sir Joshua in England and by Diderot in France, made up only the smallest percentage of works exhibited. It is interesting to observe that whilst the number of exhibitors and the total number of exhibits fell in 1783, the number of portraits exhibited continued to rise in a spectacular way. Of all the genres, only portraiture lost no ground at all during the period 1781–5. [. . .]

The successful portrait painter was . . . at the centre of a flourishing industry, backed by a series of other crafts and businesses and he employed the Royal Academy as his chief publicity agent. Publicity was of great importance; the product of his studio was judged more by the recognised quality and status of the subject than by the inherent success of the painting as a work of art. Thus the struggling Gilbert Stuart was assisted in his career by a commission to paint two eminent men from the Quaker medical fraternity, Dr Lettsom and Mr Curtis. The same situation prevailed in the rest of Europe and particularly in Paris where a Salon critic complained in 1775 that if an artist had painted a beer sign featuring a group of renowned people it would immediately have taken pride of place in the exhibition.

Between the artist and the Academy lay a gulf that had to be bridged by personal contact, nepotism, patronage and determination. The studio practice itself was serviced by assistants, pupils, colour merchants and drapery painters. In turn the practice gave employment to carpenters and frame makers, engravers and carriers, wax modellers and miniature painters. [. . .]

Engravers worked in a particularly close and interdependent partnership with portrait painters. They enjoyed little recognition from the Academy where they were not accorded full membership rights until 1855. [. . .] Romney's sitters' book reveals a constant flow of pictures to and from leading London engravers. [. . .] This production line, for that was essentially what it was, also included copyists (though many copies were executed within the studio by the artist and his assistants) and artists specialising in miniatures. [. . .]

Assistants and pupils were in all likelihood particularly engaged with the copies that formed an important part of studio business. Modern day criteria of originality and individuality need to be set aside in this discussion for portraiture was the one genre in which copies increased rather than diminished the standing of the original. The portrait was a utilitarian object and was certainly regarded as such by most artists practising portraiture in this period. The virtuoso performance of a Reynolds or a Gainsborough launched by a sensational display at a Royal Academy exhibition was the exception rather than the rule. The Royal Academy catalogues make it a relatively simple matter for art historians to establish a chronology for an exhibition artist's work and to discuss the artist's reputation at any given time. But this gives undue weight to Royal Academy exhibits and fails to take into account the importance of copies. The multiplicity of residences used by royalty and by aristocratic families necessitated the replication of the families' leading members. With this in mind the French artist Nattier drew up a detailed list of all the royal portraits that he expected to be asked to repeat. A portrait commission from a distinguished or high-born patron obliged the artist willy-nilly to adopt the sort of pictorial conventions of pose, lighting and dress that could easily be repeated in oil or in engraved form. A commission of this kind, whilst it was constraining, also ensured publicity. In 1776 Romney was worrying about whether or not he would be able to please people but his success with the Duke of Richmond in profile was such that many of the Duke's friends ordered copies and the artist's reputation was ensured. Ten years later with a successful practice he evidently did not hesitate to continue to accept commissions for copies. [. . .]

Portrait prices were standardised according to size and format and artists, very conscious of the market, increased prices rarely and only according to demand and the comparative cost elsewhere. Reynolds's price for a three-quarter length portrait was twenty guineas in 1759 and rose to thirty five in 1764 and to fifty in 1766. Romney began by asking fifteen guineas in 1775 and raised his price to eighteen in 1776 and twenty in 1781. Competition came from provincial centres (though artists as distinguished as Gainsborough and Joseph Wright were rare) and from abroad. In the 1760s Pompeo Batoni, the Roman portrait painter favoured by Grand Tourists, received £25 for a full-length. Joseph Wright of Derby was charging £52 10s. and Gainsborough, in Bath, sixty guineas for the same size of work at that time whilst Allan Ramsay in Edinburgh was charging £84 and Reynolds in London £150. [. . .] In the 1780s when Reynolds, then in his sixties, was charging £200 for a full-length portrait, Batoni was charging only £50. [. . .]

The commissioned portrait was, to use Michael Levey's words, 'ordered almost as an article of utility (to provide a likeness)—not, however, from grocers or haberdashers but from artists' (1977, 3). Of course, it would be absurd to deny that many portraits from the period display originality in conception and execution. Nevertheless, if, as is often stated, portraiture is the image of society then it is not sufficient to look at individual portraits in search of reflections of types we believe to constitute society. Portrait painting in London in the 1780s was subject to social pressures and constituted a microcosm in which nationalism, commerce, class and all the pressures and conflicting tendencies of society at large are represented. Portrait painters were both used and abused and they constitute a particularly interesting group because they moved between class divisions. By virtue of their craft and their place in a complex system of production they belonged with artisans and craftsmen but the necessary intimacy of the portrait sitting and the conditions which dictated that the subject came to the artist placed the portrait painter within reach of his client's class. [. . .]

[. . .] The psychological *rapport* between artist and sitter is invariably recognised by art historians as a dimension to be taken seriously in the study of paintings. What is less often considered is the ambiguous nature of the class relationship between artist and subject. The artist talented enough to produce an effective image that reinforces the status of the subject is himself or herself in a position of power that is in direct opposition to the economic power relationship between artist and patron. Many of the difficulties encountered by portrait painters in the eighteenth century and discussed in this article are the immediate and tangible result of the necessity of constantly adjusting and readjusting within the economic structure. The demand for portraits generated a huge supply of artists glutting the market, if Northcote (1819) is to be believed. Thus while ideologically portraiture remained an inferior genre, actually it was the dominant art form for all classes of society. Whilst patrons paid little for portraits relative to the overall expenditure on household goods they created an extremely competitive market where reputations could be made and unmade overnight. This encouraged expansion, providing work for a wide range of craftsmen, but it also reinforced existing structures and dominant values. [. . .]

Reynolds's elevation of the portrait by an infusion of classical references was never a disinterested act motivated solely by devotion to theory and to the ideals of High Art. It was at least to some extent a response to the market. The aesthetic or iconographic character of an individual portrait, its meaning in social or political terms as well as the development of the individual portrait painter's style may be dictated by the conditions of production. Thus the fluid handling of paint (a feature of Romney's late work, for example) may evolve as a result of the need for speed of execution rather than as a latent tendency towards romantic sensibility; the disappearance of feet and hands behind drapery may be due as much to the lack of competence of studio assistants whose job it was to model them, and probably also to paint them, as to any overall aesthetic intention or adherence to fashion; the outdoor setting may be related to the fact that it is simpler to fill in an imaginary open-air landscape than to depict with accuracy an ideal or an actual interior, especially when sittings take place in the artist's studio. The highly competitive market and the dominance of the Royal Academy as a forum for display and publicity made it imperative for artists to develop an individual and readily identifiable visual formula as quickly as possible. Thus one might say that the more Reynolds succeeded with florid men, the more Gainsborough was impelled to produce depictions of ephemeral women. Portrait painting in the 1780s was, there is no doubt, a highly developed business in a buyer's market. If we are to understand the paintings both as material objects and as carriers of meanings we must address ourselves to the kinds of criteria appropriate to the subject and adopt some of the approaches of the business historian as well as those of the art historian.

THOMAS M. BAYER AND JOHN R. PAGE,
Christie's Auction House

Excerpts (pp. 143–49) from "The Formation of a Nexus: A Story of Christie's," in *The Development of the Art Market in England: Money as Muse, 1730–1900* (London: Pickering and Chatto, 2011), 143–51. Copyright © 2011 Pickering & Chatto. Reprinted by permission of Taylor & Francis Books UK.

Throughout most of the eighteenth century, the auction industry was characterized by the presence of numerous auctioneers disbursing collections generally assembled by middlemen to sell to the public. Liquidity sales appear to have been less frequent. The nineteenth-century scene, to the contrary, can be told as the story of one auction house—Christie's—primarily involved in the disposition of private estates to the trade.

This auction house alone conducted 92 per cent of all sales between 1840 and 1900 recorded by Graves; 90 per cent of all transactions involving Continental Old Masters; 92 per cent of sales of English Old Masters; 95 per cent of Contemporary Continental works and 93 per cent of Contemporary English paintings passed through Christie's. The remaining 8 per cent were spread across approximately thirty other firms. Since Graves recorded the top end of the market and only about 10 per cent of the estimated total volume of auction sales, we checked Graves's records against our records of the dealers Tooth and Agnew. Both data sets show that, indeed, Christie's was the overwhelmingly favoured auction house for these two dealers. In the years 1870 and 1871, the 150 paintings Tooth bought at auction all came from Christie's, while Agnew made over 90 per cent of its auction purchases between 1870 and 1880 at the same house. Comparing Graves's data from 1840–1900 to that from 1790–1840 shows that earlier on a much larger market share was taken up by Christie's competition. Only 62 per cent of all transactions involved the firm: 57 per cent of Continental Old Masters, 71 per cent of English Old Masters, 21 per cent of Contemporary Continental and 78 per cent of Contemporary English paintings with most of the overall growth occurring in the decades of the 1820s and 30s. The market had changed from one made up of many different 'exchanges' to one in which one exchange unmistakably dominated and became the nexus of the market. Sometime between 1840 and 1860, Christie's left its competition markedly behind. The rise to virtual supremacy over a nation's fine art auction industry by one firm and the maintenance of this position for well over sixty years and possibly beyond is remarkable and likely unprecedented. This near monopoly was among the favourable conditions behind the buoyancy and expansion of the art market, particularly of the market for contemporary paintings. [. . .]

For most of the eighteenth century, auction transactions were mainly limited to the Old Masters market, although occasionally the estates of recently deceased painters were also sold. Widespread trading in contemporary paintings did not occur until the second quarter of the nineteenth century and, increasingly, dealers were among the buyers at these auctions. To what extent occasional earlier sales of paintings by artists from the English School were associated with this trend remains conjecture. Our data list around thirty artist studio sales between 1770 and 1839 of which nearly two-thirds were conducted by Christie's. All were well attended by dealers. There must have been many more of these disbursements of painters' estates with the result of distributing progressively more works by artists of the modern English School among the trade and the public in general. The favourable publicity surrounding the 7 July, 1827 sale of the collection of contemporary English paintings formerly owned by Lord de Tabley certainly emphasized the profitability of buying modern pictures and may have helped to create the later pervasive aura of speculative potential in the market for modern paintings. Interestingly, J. W. M. Turner was present at this sale, most likely, as was his habit, to protect the value of his paintings. Of the six canvases by his hand he bought two, paying in one instance a record price of 515 guineas. [. . .]

. . . The much touted speculative aspect of contemporary paintings promoted the use of auctions as the exchange platform where profits could be realized. If the earlier description of the auctions as useful tools for market manipulation is correct as our discovery of at least one hundred sales at which consignor and buyer were identical suggests, then the absence of competition between different auction providers made such use of auctions simpler and more efficient. Competition would have benefited mostly the consignors in the form of lower commission rates. However, the presence of a large number of rivalling auction facilities would have made it more difficult for middlemen to oversee the market, undertake regulatory measures and gain the cooperation of auctioneers. [. . .]

Our data show that the majority of paintings offered at auctions during the Victorian period originated from estates of recently deceased individuals or, in some instances, business failures, personal debts and/or bankruptcies. Consignments in the form of liquidity trades, such as state liquidations, are by nature less suitable to competition as the likelihood of potential heirs or executors shopping for the best transaction costs is slim. The low number of individual repeat sellers also suggests . . . that the Victorian auction market was not an environment suitable for speculators—contrary to the pervasive aura. Indeed, buying and selling paintings through auction resulted during this period in an opportunity loss. Of course, on the positive side, this fact underscores the efficiency of this market. It should be noted that press reports, like Hall's financial accounting of the Bicknell sale, usually juxtaposed the amounts paid directly to artists and dealers with hammer prices. This stratagem promoted, although erroneously, contemporary painting as a good investment in general, and the use of artists and dealers as sources of supply, as well as the auction house as the exchange where profits can be realized.

While the above contention offers an explanation for the association between market growth and a prevailing near-monopoly condition, it gives no insight into the methods by which this market dominance was achieved. [. . .] However, scholarly research into the early business history of Christie's is still in its infancy. [. . .] Some observations, however, can be made already.

No doubt, Mr. Christie was in the right place at the right time. But that place was already occupied by well-established competitors. Major consignments from both Continental and English sources were sold in the 1770s by such houses as Cock and Langford, Squibb, Walsh and Peter Coxe. Langford handled, among others, the huge estate of the Duke of Argyle in the spring of 1771, that of the painter Jonathan Richardson in 1772, as well as the sale of the collection of the collector James West in 1773. Walsh landed the

Bertel consignment in 1775, in addition to several large collections from the Continent. Nonetheless, the recently arrived James Christie attracted a number of important accounts in the 1770s that sold in his newly established firm. Considering that his first picture sale did not take place until March 1766, this was a particularly impressive accomplishment. Among these consignors was the dealer Greenwood; Samuel Dickinson; M. Liotard, a relative of the painter J. S. Liotard and the banker Sir G. Colebrook who chaired the board of directors of the East India Company.

Beyond his ability to secure important consignments, James Christie also understood the importance of the media to the growth of his business. He became part owner of two London daily newspapers, the Whiggish *Morning Chronicle* in 1769 and its rival, the pro-Tory *Morning Post* in 1771. A prudent businessman, he covered both sides of the political spectrum and also reduced the firm's costs of frequent advertising.

Moreover, by whatever means, most likely through the employment of agents, Christie secured a number of the consignments that came on the market during the period leading up to the French Revolution. Christie's auction catalogues from this time list numerous Continental consignors such as the Biondi collection sale on 21 February 1777, or one described as 'property from abroad' on 16 April of the same year. Other notable foreign consignments came from the French (?) Count Schulenburg, the Hanoverian Count J. Got de Grote, the city of Rome, the Parma collection as well as property from the Calonna Palace. Christie also worked closely with the dealers Noel Desenfans, Gerard and Benjamin Vandergucht and Walsh Porter.

Besides collaborating with specific dealers, Christie may have also tried to promote his business by performing, in certain instances, private banking services. [Painter Joseph] Farington (1923, 265) recorded in his diary . . . that Christie, around 1799, had lent Chace Price the impressive sum of £14,000, evidently to cover some irregularities involving government funds. What motivated the auctioneer is not known. Price was a young man about town, and Christie may have thought him to be of some use in securing consignments. More telling, however, is the fact that he had such a large sum at his disposal. An auction 'business' usually keeps only a small percentage of revenues. However, to boost his income Christie may have taken equity positions in some of the consignments brought to him by the dealers with whom he worked on a regular basis. [. . .]

It may have also been at that time that James Christie began to provide advances on consignments to entice cash-strapped sellers from the Continent or the British Isles to favour his firm over rivalling companies. The practice of offering advances or loans, customarily around 50 percent of the pre-sale estimate and secured by the physical possession of the object(s) in question, is still used today to secure important consignments. However, such arrangements change the relationship of the auctioneer to the goods offered. The auction house is no longer merely an agent but instead becomes a stakeholder. Recent legislation requires that such financial interest be disclosed. There is also the inherent risk for auction firms that they might become owners of such properties if they fail to sell and consignors are unable to repay the loan. For James Christie, this practice would have required the availability of substantial capital in a notoriously cash-poor environment. Even though in the late 1790s, according to Farington (1923), Christie already took in commissions of between £10,000 and £16,000 annually, it would be no surprise if James Christie were to have had relationships with merchant banking houses and/or private venture capitalists. [. . .]

Christie also conducted the first major auction of modern paintings when [print publisher John] Boydell's bankruptcy released an unprecedented number of such works on the market in May 1805. Among the different aristocratic and middle-class buyers were also several dealers such as [Michael] Bryan, [William] Sequier, John Green and Gooden and most likely others whose identities as dealers we did not recognize. In the context of a developing secondary market in contemporary paintings, the Boydell sale and the later auction of the collection of Lord de Tabley were thus significant milestones. These sales together with studio sales may have given Christie a competitive advantage by establishing the firm as the best place to buy and sell modern works. While the firm after mid-century outperformed its competitors in all four painting categories, contemporary English and Continental paintings showed the steepest ascent. In sales of Continental Old Masters, Christie's moved slightly in front of its competition in the first decade of the century but did not surge ahead until around 1880; similarly, in the category of English Old Masters, the marginal lead advances noticeably in the 1870s.

From the 1840s onward, the earlier described patterns of the auction market became the norm and prevailed for the rest of the period. Christie's had become the nexus, dominating overwhelmingly the auction market for contemporary works and only slightly less so the market for older paintings; dealers were by far the largest group of buyers.

To what extent James Christie's business acumen was responsible for the demise of many of his competitors is impossible to say. Nonetheless, many of the larger auction firms discontinued their operations in the decades following the founding of Christie's. Our data show that Cock and Langford stopped in 1776; Walsh in 1777; Greenwood in 1794; Skinner's activity markedly declined after 1800. Coxe, one of the main competitors, ceased to do business in 1817, two years after Squibb had closed its doors. Competition, of course, still existed but experienced a steady decline throughout the entire Victorian period.

By the middle of the nineteenth century, the auction house was firmly entrenched as the leading art auctioneer in Europe and it maintained this position in part by closely cooperating with the retail trade. There are numerous examples of the use of auction catalogues to advertise and promote events staged by dealers. [. . .]

Besides collaborating with the trade, the company's management during this period showed also an understanding of the economics of auctions by providing longer, more factual and less hyperbolic descriptions of lots for sale. [. . .]

Image management of Christie's as a business and target marketing of the goods it sold may have been behind an arrangement under which several pre-sale views were held at the offices of the prestigious accounting firm of Price Waterhouse. Individuals who employed chartered accountants were, in terms of income, potential art buyers. Moreover, the implicit endorsement of contemporary paintings by financial specialists must have enhanced the works' perceptions as investments or, at the very least, as non-frivolous expenditures.

DIANNE SACHKO MACLEOD, *Art Collecting and Victorian Middle-Class Taste*

Excerpts (pp. 328–30, 336–37, 340–46) from "Art Collecting and Victorian Middle-Class Taste," *Art History* 10, no. 3 (1987): 328–50. Copyright © 1987 Association of Art Historians. Reproduced with permission of Blackwell Publishing Ltd.

The prosperity engendered by the Industrial Revolution created the requisite surplus capital for articles of luxury [in England], and the Reform Bill of 1832, which granted more recognition to the middle classes, gave them greater confidence in asserting their aesthetic preferences. [. . .]

While the nobility was preoccupied with the effects of the Reform Bill, the newly enfranchised middle class showed no hesitation about filling the role previously occupied by its social superiors in the realm of art patronage. To begin with, English parvenus may have wished to emulate the aristocracy by buying or building country houses and furnishing them with precious possessions, but they did not imitate the upper classes in bidding for pictures by the Old Masters. Like the merchant princes of Renaissance Italy and the burghers of seventeenth-century Holland, they hung their walls with freshly painted canvases by living artists. [. . .]

Although a few of the nobility supported the trend, most considered modern art inferior to the art of the past. One only has to glance through Gustav Waagen's four-volume description of the private collections of England written in the 1850s to see that the works of contemporary British artists were poorly represented in the major aristocratic collections. [. . .]

There were sound practical reasons for this class-based difference in artistic taste. The tradition of connoisseurship that had produced the British nobility's Old Master collections was fueled by extensive trips abroad where the cognoscenti could indulge in the leisurely contemplation of grand manner painting. Unlike the eighteenth-century connoisseur, however, the majority of Victorian collectors were men of business who had neither the time to make the Grand Tour nor the temperament required for deciphering European iconography. They preferred the familiar to the exotic: landscapes, scenes from daily life, or romantic costume pieces inspired by their favorite novels or historical characters.

The middle-class propensity for buying the more easily understandable art of living artists was nurtured by the leading art periodical of the period. The *Art-Union* (known after 1848 as the *Art Journal*) was founded in 1839 by Samuel Carter Hall who constantly tried to steer his readers away from the thriving market in Old Master fakes. Hall launched a campaign promoting contemporary art that was given a major boost in 1843 by the appearance of the first volume of John Ruskin's *Modern Painters*, in which Ruskin argued for the support of modern British artists in lieu of the ancients.

The general public quickly endorsed these pro-British sentiments in the same year, turning out in force (between 20,000 and 30,000 visitors a day) to see the exhibition of cartoons designed around British subjects for the new Houses of Parliament. More opportunities to see "works by living artists" were offered by the Great Exhibition of 1851 and the Manchester Art Treasures exhibition of 1857. [. . .]

Paintings, as well as engravings, were considered the helpmates of the disadvantaged as long as they were readily available to the public. For instance, when Robert Vernon, the middle-class collector of modern art, donated his collection to the nation in 1847, the *Art-Union* looked upon the paintings it contained as a means of rescuing the less fortunate from the hopelessness of poverty and drink:

> The salutary influence of Art on the universal mind requires no argument: it is impossible that a people can be coarse or vicious whose sources of enjoyment are refined and intellectual; a collection of pictures powerfully helps to thin our poorhouses and prisons; men to whom public galleries are open will be seldom found in public-houses; and that Government is prudent as well as wise, which directs the general mind into a wholesome and invigorating channel.

Thus the lessons of art were considered a means of aiding the low minded to rise above the temptations of the flesh. Similarly, when another early middle-class collector, John Sheepshanks, decided to make a gift of his collection, he requested that, if possible, the general public, 'and especially the working class,' be given access on Sunday afternoons. Because of this humanitarian emphasis, the donation of private art collections should be viewed in the context of the other socially ameliorating achievements of the Victorians, such as the Mechanics' Institutes, free libraries, and urban parks. And it follows that businessmen, whose investments depended on the productivity of their workers, should set a good example by recognizing the benefits of art, both in forming personal collections and in lending their support to public ventures. [. . .]

[. . .] The sale of the [Elhanan] Bicknell collection was one of the landmark events in establishing the economic viability of modern British art. It was living proof that an initial investment of approximately £25,000 could more than treble in value in thirty years. [. . .] The reaction in the popular press was amazement tinged with pride; for example, the reporter for the *Star* was moved to superlatives when he commented on his visit to the Bicknell sale:

> There took place last Saturday an event in London, such, as we venture to think, could scarcely in the same time and under the same conditions, have happened in any other city

in the world. It was not a great national event—a royal reception, or a popular demonstration . . . it was merely a sale of pictures. The collection of paintings thus sold had been
gathered together by a private Englishman, a man of comparatively obscure position, a
man engaged at one time in mere trade; a man not even pretending to resemble a Genoese
or Florentine merchant-prince, but simply and absolutely a Londoner of the middle-class,
actively occupied in business.

The *Star* reporter continued in this vein of wonderment, proudly proclaiming that
Bicknell's collection of modern art would have held its own in comparison with that of
Lorenzo the Magnificent. Clearly, contemporary art was now a force to be reckoned with,
and the star of British art was in the ascendant. Although the *Art Journal* had nudged its
readers in this direction for almost twenty-five years, those outside the limited spheres
of art publishing and collecting were convinced only by its monetary value that British
art had finally arrived.

Much to everyone's surprise it was not the Landseers or Websters in Bicknell's sale
that fetched the highest prices; that honor went to the landscapes—the Turners, Call-
cotts, and Stanfields. [. . .] Of course, many of Bicknell's landscapes contained figural
groupings that offered suitably elevating storylines, but he also owned a wide selection
of Turner's essays in color, in addition to the more realistic scenes of Thomas Creswick
and William Collins, and the topographical efforts of Clarkson Stanfield and David Rob-
erts. [. . .] While the presence of the Divinity could (and often was) read into natural
subjects, their simplicity also invited a more immediate and uncomplicated response
quite unlike that elicited by the sentimental anecdotes that formed a major part of other
important early Victorian collections. [. . .]

. . . Varied and complex motivations . . . shaped Victorian art collections. When we
add the discourses on morality and social amelioration to personal ambition and the
dawning realizations of the investment potential of contemporary art, we find that there
were a plethora of incentives for the private patronage of the period. John Ruskin, however, lectured that there was only one true motive for collecting art:

> those who are rich amongst us buy a painting or two, for mixed reasons, sometimes to fill
> the corner of a passage—sometimes to help the drawing room talk before dinner—
> sometimes because the painter is fashionable, occasionally because he is poor—not unfre-
> quently that we may have a collection of specimens of painting, as we have specimens of
> minerals or butterflies—and in the best and rarest case of all, because we have really as we
> call it, taken a fancy to the picture; meaning the same sort of fancy which we would take
> to a pretty arm-chair or a newly-shaped decanter. But as for real love of the picture, and joy
> of it when we have got it, I do not believe it is felt by one in a thousand.

[. . .] The new patriciate in the art world was comprised of the painters, critics, and
collectors of the Aesthetic movement. To them, art revolved around the appreciation and

enjoyment of beauty in its various guises, in contrast to the more entrenched members of the middle class who still demanded an inspirational message in art. To the collectors of the Aesthetic movement art was not a teacher but a source of personal gratification; it was not required to provide instruction to the entire family or to edify groups of visitors. The new patrons shared the outlook of critics like Walter Pater who argued that the goal of aesthetic contemplation was not to learn lessons, but to stimulate 'the desire of beauty, the love of art for art's sake.' [. . .]

Another collector who participated in the worship of beauty was William Graham, the Scottish jute manufacturer and Member of Parliament who was a major artistic benefactor of both Rossetti and Edward Burne-Jones. His daughter tells us that he was 'a passionate lover of beauty,' and Georgiana Burne-Jones, the artist's wife, relates a particularly striking instance of Graham's devotion to art: 'It was Graham who did a thing that surely no other man ever did, for Edward said that once when he showed him a picture, "it had a part of it painted so much to his mind that he went up to it and kissed the panel."' [. . .]

Like [Liverpool banker George] Rae, Graham reacted on a highly emotional and personal level to the images of beautiful women that he possessed. Just as Rae told Rossetti that he was in danger of falling in love with the central figure in *The Beloved*, Graham informed Burne-Jones that he must possess 'the Ladye I fell in love with at your Studio.' [. . .]

The insatiability of patrons like Graham made it financially possible for the painters of the Aesthetic movement to ignore the more unimaginative requirements of the majority of mid-Victorian middle-class collectors. For instance, it was William Graham, and the self-made Liverpool shipping millionaire, Frederick Leyland, who nurtured the talent of Burne-Jones during the critical middle years of his career. [. . .] Likewise, next to George Rae, Graham and Leyland were Rossetti's major benefactors from the mid-1860s until his death in 1882 and, as one acquaintance of the artist observed, 'without these patrons Rossetti would have been forced to adapt his powers to pleasing the popular taste, but by their help he was able to work out his own theories of Art. . . .'

Given their high regard for the artists they supported, it is only to be expected that Rae, Graham, and Leyland would take great pains to display their art to its best advantage. In keeping with the Aesthetic movement's credo that beauty must permeate life as well as art, these collectors created exquisite environments for their favorite painters in which they separated their canvases from the rest of the paintings they owned. [. . .]

Perhaps the most lavish setting of all was created by Frederick Leyland in his London house at 49 Prince's Gate, where he meticulously arranged his collection in rooms specially planned to accommodate paintings. The most dramatic feature of his home was the celebrated Peacock dining-room in which all decorative elements were designed to enhance James McNeill Whistler's *La Princesse du Pays de la Porcelaine*. [. . .]

The pattern developed by collectors in the 1880s and 1890s differs significantly from that of the early and mid-Victorian collectors. One witnesses the emergence of a group that was not personally associated with the artists of the Aesthetic movement but still subscribed to the form, if not the content, of its worship of beauty. A number of late Victorian industrialists assembled collections of mainstream genre and landscape painting and insisted upon displaying them with great pomp and circumstance in specially designed galleries that were extensions of the sanctuary idea created by the more avant-garde patrons of the 1860s and 1870s.

For instance, in 1882 Thomas Henry Ismay, the founder of the prosperous White Star Line, employed Norman Shaw, the architect responsible for transforming Leyland's home into a palace of art, to design a two-storey picture gallery for his palatial mansion near Birkenhead. Crowned by an enormous barrel vault, dignified by decorative friezes, and presided over by a massive altar-like chimneypiece, Ismay's gallery assumed the solemnity of a hallowed hall of worship. The art it contained was another matter. Instead of filling it with the hymns to beauty that characterized Leyland's collection, Ismay opted for pastoral landscapes by James Hook and narrative subjects by earlier British artists such as Daniel Maclise and David Wilkie. [. . .]

Motives of conspicuous consumption inspired a number of other builders of large-scale private art galleries in the 1880s and 1890s. George McCulloch, the Scot who made a fortune in the Australian gold and silver mines, is another example. When he returned to London in 1893, he set about building an extravagant house in South Kensington and filling it with modern art on which he is said to have spent more than £200,000.

The private art gallery in McCulloch's house on Queen's Gate was the last word in technical advances: overhead lighting, temperature control, and fireproof construction. In this carefully prepared environment, McCulloch placed an art collection that he hoped would warrant its museum-like setting: all of the canvases were gallery- rather than cabinet-sized, and the artists, as the *Art Journal* observed, 'summarised effectively the whole range of British art as we see it at the present moment'.

ANNE HELMREICH, *David Thomson and the Goupil Gallery*

Excerpt (pp. 33–43) from "The Art Dealer and Taste: The Case of David Croal Thomson and the Goupil Gallery, 1885–1897," *Visual Culture in Britain* 6, no. 2 (2005): 31–49. Reprinted with permission of the author and *Visual Culture in Britain*.

Editor's note: This section of the essay focuses on the activities of the art dealer David Croal Thomson (1855–1930), who managed the London branch of Goupil Maison from 1885 to 1897.

A significant number of factors converged to make London . . . a lucrative marketplace. As the first industrial nation, Britain experienced rapid population growth in its manufacturing and distributing centres. In 1801 the population of greater London was over one million; by the close of the century it was over six. Thus a substantial consumer base was born and, although historians disagree as to the extent to which the city was a source of great fortunes, it was nonetheless home, for at least the period of the London Season, to some of Britain's wealthiest citizens, drawn by the lure of politics, social prestige, luxury goods and entertainment. Urban technologies such as improvements in roads, railway networks, postal reform and the introduction of the telegraph and the telephone, all facilitated the exchange of goods. Moreover, London was well placed to take advantage of trade across the Channel and the Atlantic, providing a vital link between the United States and Europe. Indeed, the London branch of Goupil was a clear manifestation of the significance of London for the Atlantic economy and business flourished in the wake of improvements in communication (particularly the telegraph) that allowed the branch to respond quickly to client needs. [. . .]

Competition for patrons was stiff, given the multitude of art retail venues in London—artists' societies, auction houses, booksellers, printsellers, commercial (or what were referred to as 'private') galleries, and picture dealers and importers. In 1892 the London Trade Directory listed 19 private picture galleries and 88 picture dealers and importers. Yet, despite the increased opportunity for sales represented by such a rise in the number of dealers, artists did not universally embrace the middleman. [. . .] [Thus] a letter to the editor of *The Whirlwind* complained about 'rich dealers who absolutely control the art market', arguing that 'the monopoly which has been created is injurious to art and to artists, and should be broken up at any cost'.

The perception that wealthy dealers were exerting undue influence was enhanced by their consolidation in London's West End over the last half of the nineteenth century. The Goupil Gallery followed precisely this trajectory. When the London branch opened in 1857 under the name Adolphe Goupil and Co., it was located on 17 Southampton Street, near the Strand and Covent Garden, an area associated with printselling and publishing, and the firm was listed in trade directories as a bookseller. A marked shift in the branch's business occurred during Charles Obach's tenure. First, it expanded its range of goods to include paintings and drawings. Second, it began to hold exhibitions, shifting from its earlier practice of selling directly to art dealers. In 1875, at a larger space acquired at 25 Bedford Street, near the Strand, the first of several exhibitions of continental pictures and watercolours was held, drawn from the holdings of the Paris branch. Thus Obach established Goupil and Co.'s reputation as a publisher and dealer of foreign pictures and engravings and thereafter it was consistently listed in trade directories as such; although it also exhibited the work of contemporary British artists and sold a variety of prints, ranging from reproductions of works by Old Masters to the latest Royal Academy and Salon paintings. Its focus on 'foreign' art helped to distinguish Goupil and Co. from other London dealers and capitalized upon the gallery's connections with Paris, yet it was in keeping with the general rise in the importation of paintings from Europe into Britain during the 1880s and 1890s.

In 1884, Goupil and Co. made a strategic move when it changed premises, moving to New Bond Street, in closer proximity to other West End purveyors of luxury goods and the new upper-middle-class residences built around Kensington Park, St John's Wood and the surrounding wealthy suburbs. By the 1880s, the West End was London's leading retail centre, where . . . shops were compared to glittering jewels and museums, thus connoting both aristocratic and democratic values. Herbert Fry, when describing New Bond Street in his guidebook, promised that by frequenting the many art galleries that lined the street a man would learn to 'cultivate his taste'.

In February 1893, the London branch moved to 5 Lower Regent Street and 10 Charles Street, to a larger, more central space. The gallery was still in close proximity to other luxury goods retailers, including silk mercers, jewellers and wine merchants. Indeed, sumptuousness extended into the interior. Critic and painter D. S. MacColl, whose work was featured in the opening exhibition of the new gallery alongside that of Charles Conder, recalled the gallery as

> one of the pleasantest for proportions and lighting of the many belonging to dealers in those times, before a rise in rents drove most of them to poorly-lit back shops or attics and cellars. . . . Thomson hung his gallery with a rich crimson material highly approved by [Philip Wilson] Steer, who threatened never to set foot in the place when . . . it was proposed to substitute a lighter ground more the taste of the young.

[. . .] In keeping with its origins, the London branch's bread and butter was prints and illustrated books. Lists of engravings declared with the London Printsellers' Association reveal that between 1853 and 1894 the firm registered 432 prints, one of the largest numbers by any one gallery. The release of prints and the opening of exhibitions were often well timed: for example, twelve landscapes by James Maris, etched by Philip Zilcken, were published to coincide with the exhibition of Maris' paintings in June–July of 1888. The illustrated books and journals carried by the London branch, like the prints, were a mixture of works created for the British market and those carried over from Paris: examples of the former include illustrated catalogues to Royal Academy exhibitions and *English Art in the Public Galleries of London*; examples of the latter include illustrated catalogues to the Paris Salon and *Le Figaro-illustré*.

Thomson's distinctive contribution to the London branch was temporary exhibitions, and the annual schedule, like the print holdings, emphasized continental artists. . . . The programme indicates a preponderance of shows featuring travel views, such as Frederick Turner's watercolours of the Balmoral district in Scotland (1887) and a collection by the Institute of Water-Colour Painters entitled 'In and Out of Doors' (1888). But those that earned Thomson the most recognition were his important exhibitions of works by Corot, Daubigny, Diaz, and Troyon, and the modern Dutch painters and Whistler. He was one of the first dealers to recognize the merits of the English Impressionists, of Mr. Wilson Steer in particular. These artists reflect what was available to Thomson through his connections with the Parisian and Dutch branches of Maison Goupil as well as his ties to British artists who aligned themselves with contemporary French painting, particularly those affiliated with the New English Art Club. Indeed, the firm sought out the latter, according to John Brett, who noted in his studio log that Boussod, Valadon and Co. had visited and informed him they could 'sell Impressionist pictures'; in response Brett altered his style and exhibited under the pseudonym Trohbinet.

Indirect evidence suggests that Thomson was aware that these artists would appeal to a particular type of collector. [. . .] Whistler's atmospheric views would clearly not appeal to the 'taste of the ordinary British buyer'. But to whom they might appeal and why is suggested by a letter from the American iron-manufacturer Alfred Pope to the artist himself, reporting on a recent visit to London that included a stop at Thomson's gallery, where he considered the purchase of Whistler's *Yellow and Grey—Chelsea Snow*: 'We were real good to ourselves in gratifying our desires—but most fortunately our horizon was enlarged—taste refined, and love of the beautiful nourished by our good fortune in meeting the Whistlers—and other kindred souls.' The notion that Whistler's work indicated a shift in taste emerges in George Moore's essay 'Art for the Villa', which argued that art destined for the upper-middle-class villa was the age's definitive mode of expression. Rather than large subject pictures, such as those by Edwin Long or Elizabeth Butler, he insisted upon 'pleasant and agreeable art that will fit their rooms [of villa owners] and match their furniture'. As an example, he pointed to Whistler's work, which he praised for its 'rejection of subject' and embrace of 'harmonic arrangement of tints for effect'. Whistler, he believed, 'indefinitely enlarged the artistic horizon, and formulated the conditions of the modern movement in art—viz. the abolition of all interests except colour and line in painting'.

Moore's theory, however, did not take into account Whistler's rising prices. Moore recommended works priced between £10 to £50. This certainly applied to the prints and books carried by Boussod, Valadon and Co., as well as to paintings by contemporary British artists. For example, Philip Wilson Steer's *Girls Running (Walberswick Pier)* (1888–1894) was listed for £45 in his 1894 exhibition and Thomson reported that Hercules Brabazon Brabazon's drawings, priced between £10 and £25, 'sold remarkably'. But Whistler was keen to push his prices much higher and many of the continental artists Thomson handled commanded substantial prices. Thomson, for example, offered painter H. T. Wells £1,200 for a Daubigny he owned; Wells rejected the offer, explaining that 'ownership of the picture is almost, if not quite, worth that sum for the sake alone of engraving or etching'. [. . .]

The decisive exhibitions in Thomson's tenure at Goupil nonetheless largely supported the aesthetic described by Moore. A. D. Peppercorn, for example, who held solo exhibitions there in 1887 and 1889, executed relatively small-scale plein-air paintings reminiscent of Corot in their attention to atmospheric effects. In the accompanying essay to Peppercorn's 1889 exhibition, Thomson echoed Moore's sentiments when he explained, 'a landscape painting . . . should hang on the wall calmly and comfortably, so that it falls into its place in the decoration of the room without asserting itself too strongly. [. . .] In a word they are pictures to live with.' Finally, Thomson reeled in those buyers who sought distinction from the typical British buyer. He paradoxically suggested that Peppercorn's work was both 'accepted by the connoisseurs of England and the Continent' and 'debated in all the advanced studios in London'. Thus Peppercorn was both innovative and a safe investment. [. . .]

Having enticed a potential audience with such rhetoric, Thomson followed with a series of exhibitions beginning with a solo show of Corot in February–March 1889, Daubigny in February–March 1890, Diaz in March 1891 and a Barbizon School exhibition in 1896. These were given the prime slots in the gallery's schedule, coinciding with the start of the London Season when wealthy art buyers were likely to be in town. Thomson published accompanying catalogues, reprinting portions of his *Magazine of Art* essays, thus assisting both buyers and critics in digesting the shows, and, in turn, the exhibitions drew much attention from the art press. In terms of sales, the shows utilized an interesting strategy which Thomson adopted again for Whistler's 1892 exhibition. This was exhibitions of pictures loaned from major collectors, such as Alexander Young, James Staats Forbes and H. W. Mesdag, whose names lent prestige to Thomson's enterprise and might have encouraged emulative buying. The pictures were thus potentially on consignment, a practice that reduced the financial exposure of the dealer when compared with speculative buying. On the one hand, given that the paintings were already owned, customers were clearly being directed to purchase prints after the paintings, which were also available. On the other, exhibiting the works enhanced their value (as did publishing them), leading new patrons to solicit Thomson for paintings already owned and current owners keen to add to their collection. [. . .]

An account of the Goupil Gallery in 1895 singled out Whistler's one-man show of 1892 as 'one of the most notable exhibitions of modern art' held at the Bond Street location. The exhibition was extremely well attended and well received, largely because it was scheduled during what Thomson described as the 'cream of the season'. Thomson wrote proudly to Beatrice Whistler describing 'the most notable event that has taken place in London for many many years', adding that 'Mr. Whistler is becoming the fashion at least it is becoming the correct thing to pretend to admire him. What a dreadful thing it is that people *cannot* learn more quickly.'

To educate the gallery-going London public, Thomson orchestrated a marketing campaign, including a potential proposal for the National Gallery to buy a painting by Whistler. Whistler eagerly sought out publicity and assisted Thomson with designs for railway and street posters, sandwich men and notification cards. Advertisements appeared in '14 London, daily, weekly & evening papers' and Thomson was not above trying to manipulate the press. [. . .]

Thomson also attempted to shape taste and encourage sales by keeping a small stock of paintings, often by artists featured in exhibitions, as in the case of Whistler, Corot and Daubigny. Even before Whistler's exhibition, Thomson carried paintings by the artist, who approved of Thomson's practice of discreetly showing these works to 'special clients in a very choice and careful way' as opposed to exhibiting them openly. In general, however, Thomson did not follow the practice of building up a reserve of paintings and then releasing them when they had suitably increased in value. In a letter to Whistler, who was upset that Goupil had not bid more than £430 for his *Princess from the Land of Porcelain*, Thomson explained that he was authorized by Paris to spend only £400. He continued, 'the picture was too large for our sale & we want to buy only what we can sell readily. Had we been investors you might be certain we should have given double for it will be worth £1000 some day.' Goods bought 'on spec' needed to accord with a ready market.

Pricing was crucial in meeting market expectations. Thomson apparently took the unusual step of taking only a 10 per cent commission on Whistler's work whereas 20 per cent was more common. A more typical arrangement was the contract Thomson extended to Scottish painter Arthur Melville, which stipulated that the gallery would absorb the costs of the exhibition and take a 20 per cent commission on all pictures and advanced Melville '£200 on the work you have in hand or deliver to us'.

MARTHA TEDESCHI, *Whistler and the English Print Market*

Excerpts (pp. 15–16, 20–23, 25–27, 34–37) from "Whistler and the English Print Market," *Print Quarterly* 14, no. 1 (1997): 15–41. Reprinted by kind permission of *Print Quarterly*.

Although he frequently locked horns with the English art establishment, James McNeill Whistler nevertheless printed and marketed the majority of his 442 etchings and 179 lithographs in Britain. His activities and influence within the original print revivals in Britain and France are justly celebrated and have been thoroughly documented. Yet, because he was such a significant force in the arena of original printmaking, his career is seldom considered within the context of the British print market in general, which was dominated by an extremely lucrative trade in prints that reproduced paintings. The market for printed reproductions became increasingly accessible to a broad segment of the middle class with the advent of good-quality photo-mechanical prints in the 1870s. However, it simultaneously became a more confusing and undifferentiated market, as art dealers stretched their traditional marketing practices to integrate the new and often deceptive printmaking technologies. Not surprisingly, concern over such issues as authenticity, accurate terminology and the relationship of the art object to the artist date to this period.

Whistler had direct experience of the market for reproductive prints, and his work, at times, fell victim to the atmosphere of ambiguity surrounding the graphic arts. It is no coincidence that in the creation of his own *original* prints the artist increasingly grappled with the need to redefine the print as an art form, which included challenging prevailing notions not only about how prints should be made, but also about how they should be marketed and to whom. As discussed below, this process of redefinition is seen clearly in his evolving strategies for the marketing of his lithographs. Whistler's ambition to promote his prints as *drawings* may be seen as an impulse to reform a market moulded by popular patronage, a climate that he came increasingly to see as hostile to the production of great art.

Until recently, Victorian reproductive prints have been ignored—even despised—by art historians, curators and collectors. Large, costly engravings and cheap chromolithographs alike mirrored a style of painting that—with its emphasis on moralizing subject-matter and noble sentiment—has been largely dismissed as maudlin bad taste by critics writing in the twentieth century. The fact that such prints were also the first to be mass-produced using industrial technology has further separated them from the canon of fine art printmaking, which has come to be exemplified by the rare and highly personal expressions of such virtuoso painter-printmakers as Dürer, Rembrandt and, of course, Whistler. It should be noted, however, that reproductive prints were valued in Britain throughout much of the nineteenth century as objects of fine art, luxury commodities more affordable than paintings but still carrying the associations of high-art practice. Their function as reproductions, rather than undermining their status, as we now might suppose, allowed prints to appropriate the historical and artistic importance of the originals they interpreted. The mediating role of the print itself remained relatively transparent to viewers until photography gradually called attention to the separate identities of reproduction and original.

The boom in the market for reproductive prints after the paintings of Old Masters, but especially after living artists, reached its peak in the 1850s, the result of profound social and cultural transformation. The rise of a literate, newly wealthy middle class during the Industrial Revolution had vastly expanded the market for luxury products once associated only with the gentry and nobility. Unlike their social superiors, however, the new collectors tended to prefer pictures of familiar subjects by living British artists. Increased interest in modern painting in turn fuelled the print market, with reproductive engravings and mezzotints forming the largest and most lucrative component of the greatly expanded business of publishers and printsellers.

Subject-matter drawn from contemporary life reigned supreme, supported by Government committees on the arts, which praised 'the more homely scenes of common life' because 'they are oftentimes the only intelligible mode in which Art can speak to a large portion of the community' (quoted in Gillett 1990, 48). As their potential for mass communication became increasingly apparent, the graphic arts became an ever more powerful force within the art world because they furthered the national agenda of social improvement. As *The Art Union* declared in 1847, 'art should not be content to minister to the tastes of the few alone, to whom the possession of its best labours is a luxury; but its healthy influence should be felt among *the million*'. The idea that art should serve 'the many' took hold. In 1860, the critic F. G. Stephens echoed reformers of the two preceding decades when he wrote, 'Indeed a national service is rendered by the publication of really noble transcripts from noble pictures like these. Where the picture cannot go, the engravings penetrate'.

The hugely expanded audience for prints directly influenced the content and appearance of Victorian painting. Because the sale of copyrights for their paintings often yielded painters more than the outright sale of the canvases themselves, artists frequently altered their styles or shifted to more popular subject-matter to insure their success in the reproduction market. Likewise, to justify their large expenditures on copyrights, publishers favoured those artists and subjects with a track record of popularity on the print market; this, in turn, created a kind of artistic monopoly over both the painting and print markets. [. . .]

Through the organ of the print market, then, popular patronage wielded enormous aesthetic influence at the upper end of the art market, by determining which painters and which subjects would dominate. The intensifying demand for prints also spurred technological innovation, as unlimited quantities of impressions and more accurate copies became the objective of publishers. The Art Unions, which distributed prints annually to tens of thousands of subscribers, were instrumental in promoting new technologies for gross multiplication, such as engraving on steel plates, electrotyping, stereotyping, and eventually a vast array of photo-mechanical processes. Such industrial technologies permitted reproductive engravings to be disseminated in editions as large as 30,000 impressions, facilitating the new bond between the hitherto elite realm of art and the general public. In this period, a complex pricing structure for the sale of prints came to be widely and systematically adopted by dealers of reproductive prints. A fairly typical example of this hierarchical pricing structure is found in Ernst Gambart's plans for publishing Holman Hunt's *Christ in the Temple*: 'I propose to Print from 1,000 to 2,000 artist's proofs at 15 guineas; 1,000 Proofs before letters at 12 guineas, 1,000 proofs at 8 Guineas, and I hope 10,000 prints at 5 guineas'. Of course, this pricing structure trained the consumer to equate high prices with rarity and quality, while in actual fact, nearly all reproductive engravings, regardless of their price category, were mass-printed.

The marketing and acceptance of reproductive engravings as works of fine art in the Victorian period points to a cultural willingness to value translations in place of the real thing. However, by the early 1870s the perfection of both photography and photographic printmaking technologies began to pose a very real threat to the market for manual engraving, and simultaneously attracted public attention to issues surrounding the replication of art works. [. . .]

A new ideology of fine-art reproduction had begun to evolve, one in which absolute objectivity increasingly became the goal. [. . .]

No longer was the engraver's rôle virtually transparent to the viewer of a reproduction; no longer was the product of his labours—the reproductive engraving—seen as a glorious window on the original. Photography and its allied printmaking processes, by seeming to offer objective facsimiles of art objects, pointed to the subjectivity of human translations. [. . .]

This was an issue that concerned Whistler, who cared deeply about the quality of reproductions made from his work. Twice . . . he made attempts at reproducing them himself. In 1877 he etched two versions of *Arrangement in Black, No. 3—Sir Henry Irving as Philip II of Spain*. He tried again in 1894, this time creating two lithographs based on his recent portrait of Robert de Montesquiou. Whistler was dissatisfied with both his forays into reproductive printmaking, and following the latter attempt he declared in a letter to D. C. Thomson 'One *cannot* produce the same masterpiece twice over!! I had no inspiration—and not working at a new thing from nature, I found it impossible to copy *myself*'. Whistler, who began to use photographs to reproduce his paintings in 1876, ultimately came to favour photography for this purpose. [. . .]

Art dealers adopted a variety of strategies to establish for photo-mechanical reproductions a status within the art market, one of which was to issue artist's proofs of photogravures, applying the same hierarchical language of rarity used for engravings. Publishers also had their photogravures stamped by the Printsellers Association, the traditional method used to certify the authenticity of print publications. Also very effective was the publication of 'collections' of reproductions with titles like 'Portefeuille d'Amateur', which flattered both the contents and the buyer by using the language of high-art collecting. Whistler himself experimented with such strategies. In 1893, the year after his retrospective exhibition at the Goupil Gallery, the artist worked with the firm to issue a large portfolio of photographs reproducing the most important paintings from the exhibition. These were attractively mounted on heavy card stock, each was signed in pencil with the artist's butterfly monogram, and they were packaged in an attractive brown paper wrapper reflecting Whistler's simple, elegant taste in letterpress design.

Artists and art dealers sought to market photogravures as art, understanding that the less expensive technologies had the potential to reach a wide audience wishing to own objects of fine art. Yet, the ability of photography to report on the surfaces of works of art was simultaneously drawing attention to another desirable criterion in collecting: facture, or the evidence of the artist's touch. The ability to see, through photographs, the unique characteristics of an artist's draughtsmanship, for example, alerted the viewer to the separate characteristics of reproduction and original. Photo-mechanical reproductions engendered a hunger to see the original, and inevitably stimulated a market for art work that offered an unmediated link to the artist.

The emergence in the 1880s and 1890s of numerous hybrid print forms—part handwork, part technology—suggests the new and often conflicting demands on the print market in this period. [. . .]

[One] such hybrid was the reproductive etching, a method utilized for large, expensive reproductions well into the twentieth century. Faster and easier than line engraving, etching also had the appearance of greater freedom and spontaneity. At the same time, many reproductive etchings were combined with photogravure, so that minute details of the original painting could be transferred exactly. An interesting example is the large photogravure reproduction of Whistler's canvas *Symphony in White, No. 3*, painted in 1865–67. [. . .] Initially, the image was transferred photographically to the matrix; the plate was then entirely reworked in etching by Peter Halm. . . . Although a posthumous reproduction, the print was clearly intended to address the increasing market enthusiasm for works suggesting closeness to the artist. In the proofs of this print, a small *remarque* is sketched with the etching needle into the lower margin below the image, reproducing Whistler's own self-portrait. Ironically, while the use of etching—a medium closely associated with Whistler—and this small marginal motif were meant to personalize the print, the etcher also felt it necessary to reproduce as closely as possible the photographically transferred indications of the painting's surface. Etched lines delineate individual brushstrokes, as well as Whistler's correction of the '7' in the date.

These hybrid print processes summarize the market conflicts of the age: on the one hand, a greater desire for prints with a cachet of rarity, collectability and unmediated relationship to the artist; on the other hand, a desire for photographic accuracy, for information about the surface of the original and for speed and ease of execution. Ultimately, such hybrid creations must be understood as symptoms of the gradual separation of identities between reproductions and originals. [. . .]

The suggestion, increasingly, was that the true connoisseur would value a few inspired lines breathed onto the plate by a great genius far more than an enormous plate over which a commercial engraver had laboured for a year or more. [. . .]

[. . .] [Whistler] introduced yet another technique for distinguishing his etchings from the glut of images on the market. By manipulating surface ink on the plate during printing he could evoke different and subtle atmospheric effects. The printing process had become part of the act of creation, with the artist drawing directly on the plate. This approach was in stark contrast to the mass market, where the professional printer's goal was to obtain as many identical impressions of a given plate as possible. Many of Whistler's Venice etchings are essentially monotypes, unique works of art. They are prints in which the absence of labour on the plate was replaced with the personalization of each impression by the artist himself. The little tab he adopted for his butterfly signature at this time was another small indication of his presence in the creation of the object. In the marketing language of the etching revival, an artist-printed etching, like a master drawing, offered direct insight into the mind of the artist. [. . .]

Whistler's small editions and high prices were often criticized as an affectation. One could argue, however, that Whistler actually helped to foster a more truthful relationship between rarity and price than that which, as we have seen, governed the sale of expensive, but essentially mass-produced artists' proofs on the market. While artists' proofs of reproductive engravings were usually issued in 'limited' editions ranging from 250 to several thousand impressions, original etching plates were often destroyed after several dozen hand-printed impressions had been pulled. [. . .] In short, Whistler's production and marketing techniques had helped to put connoisseurship back into the activity of print collecting. [. . .]

In August and September of 1894 Whistler informed his print dealers in both London and New York that he was raising the prices of his lithographs. [. . .] The most telling letter of this period is the one he wrote to the New York art dealer Edward Kennedy:

Also I enclose new price list—you will see that any of the old proofs you have already in stock will benefit you as they will no longer be had at the ridiculous old prices, which were foolishly built upon the absurd representation that the 'masses' would rush in and buy by the scores, works that might be offered them at prices within their grasp—Bosh! I am happy to say Bosh!—You know now as well as I do that I have fallen no nearer popularity than before—and that only the same small circle of collectors who buy the etchings, ask for my lithographs—I do not therefore any longer propose to give these beautiful proofs on lovely old Dutch paper or rare Japanese at the absurd 'cheap' rate of 'prints for the people'.

The letter . . . confirms that Whistler originally had a more popular market in mind for his lithographs than for his etchings. . . . His use of quotation marks around the terms 'masses', 'cheap', and 'prints for the people' implies a deliberate and satirical reference to the popular print trade, which throughout the Victorian era had been hailed as a democratizing force. Finally, the letter demonstrates how aggressively Whistler involved himself in the marketing end of his printmaking. As we have seen, his dealers simultaneously handled his original prints, conventional reproductive engravings and photogravures, yet rather than be guided by their experience of the market, he set policy and expected them to cooperate.

ANNA GRUETZNER ROBINS, *Roger Fry's Commercial Exhibitions*

Excerpts (pp. 85, 89–94) from "Marketing Post-Impressionism: Roger Fry's Commercial Exhibitions," in *The Rise of the Modern Art Market in London, 1850–1939*, ed. A. Helmreich and P. Fletcher (Manchester: Manchester University Press, 2013), 85–97. Copyright © 2013 Manchester University Press. Reprinted by permission.

The dramatic impact of *Manet and the Post-Impressionists* (1910) and the *Second Post-Impressionist Exhibition* (1912) on the London art world, the two shows that the critic, painter Roger Fry devised, is well known. [. . .] Fry came up with the term Post-Impressionism as a last minute solution when looking for a way to describe the artists in the first exhibition. Fry certainly understood the power that a style of art described as an 'ism' had within the modern art world; however, the artists in his exhibitions were not the originating source for the term Post-Impressionism because they never formed a cohesive social network like the Impressionists, Fauves, Cubists, or Futurists. [. . .]

[. . .] Both exhibitions were modern art markets, and furthermore, most of the hundreds of works in each were offered for sale. When put this way the Post-Impressionist exhibitions were the Edwardian equivalent of an international contemporary art fair although admittedly only Paris dealers were represented. There were virtually no collections of

Post-Impressionist art in Britain in 1910 and the Paris dealers, artists, and European collectors were Fry's major ports of call for works of art. [. . .]

I have not located the account books for the Post-Impressionist exhibitions, and the catalogues do not list any prices. Desmond MacCarthy remembered that his 10 percent cut of the sales from *Manet and the Post-Impressionists* was £460, which means they sold nearly £15,000 of pictures. The £1,800 that the art gallery in Helsinki paid for Cézanne's *Viaduct at L'Estaque* for which Vollard asked 15,000 francs, accounts for nearly a fifth of this amount. The single Van Gogh, *Factories at Asnières*, that sold from the exhibition accounts for another large part of this percentage. [. . .]

Fry was not naive when it came to the art market. His agreement with the Metropolitan Museum of Art allowed him to take 'a commission of 5% on the paintings purchased for less than £5,000 and 3% on paintings above 15,000; and the liberty to propose to other buyers paintings refused by the Metropolitan Trustees.' [. . .]

Fry never underestimated the role that the art dealer played in creating the appetite for the work of a particular artist. He expressed this view most clearly in his 1917 review for the *Burlington Magazine* of Vollard's monograph *Paul Cézanne* where he wrote that: 'Vollard has played Vasari to Cézanne and done so with the same directness and simplicity, the same narrative ease, the same insatiable delight in the oddities and idiosyncrasies of his subject.' This linking of Vasari and Vollard, with the assumption that the modern art dealer could play the role of art historian in establishing an artist's legacy, is one example of the almost seamless transition between the marketplace and art history that Fry readily endorsed.

Fry cannily realized that he had his own role to play in the process of giving a mercantile transaction an aesthetic and historical importance. *Manet and the Post-Impressionists* had barely closed its doors for the final time when Fry began an active campaign to give Post-Impressionist art a greater credibility. He used his position as co-editor of the *Burlington Magazine*, which had built its reputation on its scholarly articles about old master painting, by writing an important notice on Cézanne, and publishing articles on Van Gogh by J. Meyer Riefstahl, and on the Post-Impressionists as a group in its illustrious pages.

Fry could have chosen to write about any one of the Cézanne pictures in *Manet and Post-Impressionists*, however, he chose the only one which sold from the exhibition, *The Viaduct at L' Estaque* (c.1883), acquired by the trustees of the National Gallery of Helsingfors . . . who also bought *Ulysses and Calypso* by Maurice Denis. Fry set out to canonize these two new works of art which had only just left the marketplace. He rightly tied Denis to 'the great classic tradition of France'. While he admired Denis's painting, Fry had a revelatory visual experience when looking at Cézanne and he sought to explain his perceptual reaction: 'To the inquiring eye new relations, unsuspected harmonies continually reveal themselves; and this is true no less of the subtle, pure and crystalline colour than of the linear construction of the pattern.' Fry continued: 'Cézanne is one of the most intensely and profoundly classic artists that even France has produced', before comparing his picture to the inexplicable mastery of Giorgione's *The Tempest*. This use of aesthetic and historical discourse in a highly respected journal devoted to the connoisseurship of old master painting gave a new importance to a picture that had only recently left the marketplace and secured Cézanne's lineage as a modern artist within an old master tradition. [. . .]

By the 1920s Fry had succeeded in giving Post-Impressionism a canonical status. The solo exhibitions of Van Gogh (1923), Gauguin (1924), and Cézanne (1925) at the Leicester Galleries, and the promotion of Post-Impressionist art at the Lefevre Gallery catered to collectors like Courtauld. In 1926, the year that Fry published his ruminations on the art market in *Art and Commerce . . .*, Courtauld purchased sixteen modern French paintings, including three works by Cézanne, *The Lac d'Annecy*, 1896 (Courtauld Institute Galleries) alone costing approximately £8,000, nearly a ten-fold increase over what the Helsinki museum paid in 1910. [. . .]

Many of the pictures in both Post-Impressionist exhibitions were sent to New York for the Armory Show in 1913. The term Post-Impressionism, which Fry used to describe the first exhibition, quickly gained currency within the Anglophone world especially after it crossed the Atlantic and appeared in Jerome K. Eddy's 1915 publication *Cubists and Post-Impressionists*. From this point on it became an established term within the canon of traditional modernism and it acquired a critical and historical meaning that stretched way beyond Fry's original term. Indeed Post-Impressionism—it was always hyphenated—has recently morphed into a new hybrid—Postimpressionism—which suggests that it has the same credibility as the so-called movements of Impressionism, Fauvism, Cubism, and Futurism.

Tracking the use of this term in early twentieth-century exhibitions catalogues, art writing, and other publications would cast light on the way in which the best known artists of Fry's exhibitions . . . became embedded in the discourse of modern art. [. . .] The competing and interdependent cultures of Post-Impressionism and commerce have not been studied and yet they had untold effect on twentieth-century museum cultures and academic art history.

8

PARIS

Since the Middle Ages, Paris had been the largest city in continental Europe and its major intellectual, religious, and artistic center. While France did not achieve dominance on the seas or function as a center of large-scale international trade during the sixteenth and seventeenth centuries, Paris was a vibrant and influential capital. The city's renown as a producer of luxury goods dates to the reign of Louis XIV, whose love of the arts, by some accounts, far surpassed his interest in politics or government. The dazzling royal court at Versailles, exquisitely furnished and fashionably attired, remains an icon of French elegance to this day. Under Louis XIV, the French state established new industries in the luxury sector, including the royal tapestry works at Beauvais; took over businesses such as the Gobelins tapestry works; protected inventors; recruited craftspeople from foreign countries; prohibited French craftspeople from emigrating; and in 1648 founded the Académie royale de peinture et de sculpture, modeled after the Accademia di San Luca in Rome, to elevate the status and professionalism of painters and sculptors.

After a prosperous interlude in the early eighteenth century, France's wars with Britain and Spain in the second half of the century put a significant strain on its economy. The French Revolution that followed, and the Napoleonic wars in the early nineteenth century, further depleted the nation's coffers. The 1830s, however, were a period of economic stability and relative calm. This changed once again when rural laborers, rendered redundant by technical improvements in agriculture, flooded into the capital to look for work. By 1846 Paris was home to more than one million people and had become desperately overcrowded. Poverty and squalid living conditions fed the revolution of 1848, which was a major turning point for the French economy.

Louis-Napoleon III, exiled in England for four years, had been deeply impressed by the economic transformation the Industrial Revolution had wrought there. After assuming the presidency of the French Republic in 1848 Napoleon directed his new government to take an active role in creating a similar infrastructure for economic growth: building railways, ports, canals, and roads; stimulating the stock market and investment banks (to provide credit); and providing training and education. He opened up French markets to foreign goods, forcing French industry to become competitive and thus more efficient. As a result, the French economy outperformed its rivals in short order—exports and imports tripled between 1850 and 1870. Stock prices increased almost 50 percent in just two years, along with a significant increase in the quantity of listed securities. The mushrooming in borrowing by the French state, towns and cities, banks, and French and foreign railway companies also attracted substantial foreign capital investment.

Establishing Paris as a world city was a major goal of Napoleon's economic stimulus program during the Second French Empire (1852–70). Paris was made the hub of a new railroad network that linked the capital to the major French ports. Napoleon tasked his prefect in Paris, Baron Haussmann, with modernizing the city itself. Large open spaces, including parks, were created to connect and unify the different urban areas into a cohesive whole. A network of wide boulevards was constructed to improve traffic flow and provide access to the new railroad stations. These lively thoroughfares, lined with shops and cafés, also served to promote sociability and consumer spending. Large department stores such as Le Bon Marché (founded in 1852), Printemps (1865), and La Samaritaine (1869) became centerpieces of Parisian commerce.

While London remained the undisputed center of the European world-economy, Paris was the financial center of continental Europe. France enjoyed a considerable surplus in its balance of payments, largely due to its invisible export surplus (tourism, profits from freight, insurance, and other services, income from capital). This made it possible for the French both to import large amounts of gold and to realize sustained exports of capital—the main factors enabling Paris to emerge as an international financial center by the end of the nineteenth century (Plessis 2005, 44).

The splendor of the newly proclaimed City of Light attracted visitors from all over the world—including many artists. Lured by the opportunities for training at the French national art academies and the city's numerous private schools, and for exhibiting work in the widely acclaimed international art exhibitions, young foreign artists with minimal or no domestic reputation flocked to Paris—to live, to make their art, to show and sell their work, all in the hope of gaining international recognition (Jensen 2013). This large group of émigré artists came to be known as the School of Paris. As Robert Jensen points out in this chapter, it was the first such international "school" in Western art history and came to dominate the historical narratives devoted to art of this period and place, to the point of eclipsing most of the prominent French artists of the time.

Excerpts (pp. 439, 444–46, 448–51) from "Watteau's Dealer: Gersaint and the Market-ing of Art in Eighteenth-Century Paris," *Art Bulletin* 78, no. 3 (1996): 439–53.
Reprinted by permission of Andrew McClellan, Tufts University.

In the course of the eighteenth century dealers became the essential middlemen in a rapidly expanding art market. As collecting increased as a form of recreation and means of distinction, so did the need for experts adept at evaluating paintings and managing the flow of art across national borders and through public auctions, which emerged as a crucial site of exchange. We know more about the role of dealers and patterns of consumption in England than in the rest of Europe, but with respect to France we might begin by examining the career of the best-known dealer in early eighteenth-century Paris, Edme-François Gersaint (1694–1750) [. . .]

At the height of his success in the 1730s and 1740s, Gersaint employed a variety of marketing tools to reach his public and bolster his reputation as a dealer.

To judge by advertisements placed in the *Mercure de France*, Gersaint moved away from fine art in the 1730s and became a dealer in luxury goods, which were in fact the province of the *marchand-mercier*. His expertise in paintings remained essential when it came to auctioning established collections . . . but his daily trade on the Pont Notre-Dame increasingly revolved around the decorative arts. [. . .] To modern eyes this shift from painting to the decorative arts might appear as a step down in prestige; the more normal progression would seem to work in the other direction, as it did for Lord Duveen (1869–1939), for example. The anomaly can best be explained by reference to the rise of the Rococo style during the 1720s and 1730s, arguably the one moment in post-medieval times when the decorative arts assumed an importance equal to that of fine art.

Through the 1730s, Gersaint and the other *marchands-merciers* were well placed to witness and foster the emergence of the Rococo style and the boom of the luxury trade. Acting as middlemen between foreign and domestic markets, between makers and consumers, and between craftsmen belonging to different guilds, the *marchands-merciers* have been credited with an active role in the genesis of Rococo taste and fashion. Gersaint himself dealt in all manner of luxury goods, natural and man-made, but his particular contribution seems to have been shells, which became immensely popular collector's items at this time as well as the leitmotif of Rococo decoration. To amass stock Gersaint traveled regularly to Holland, which, owing to its extensive trade network, became the primary source of shells and other exotica from the East. [. . .] From Holland, Gersaint also imported two marketing tools—the public auction and the sale catalogue—that he raised to new levels of sophistication. He was the first, in France at least, to realize the potential of auctions, which he organized as a kind of public spectacle and which he promoted as events both instructive and amusing. He was also the first and, during the thirties and forties, the only art dealer (apart from printsellers) to use the press, specifically the popular *Mercure de France,* to publicize his business. His advertisements appeared alongside other notices on the arts and to the extent that the *Mercure,* as a newspaper, contributed to the formation of a public sphere and an art world in the Habermasian sense, this juxtaposition served to legitimize the commerce of art. Gersaint's most important contribution to the art of dealing, however, was the sale catalogue, which in the 1740s took over from newspapers and public flyers as his primary mode of publicity. Through engraved frontispieces and elaborate texts, his catalogues carried on Watteau's task of crafting an image of the dealer.

The half-dozen major catalogues produced between 1736 and 1748 can be treated as a cohesive oeuvre, for each new one builds upon the last and Gersaint took it for granted that the reader had access to the ones that had gone before. They were intended as permanent reference works, as *objets de curiosité* in their own right. Each catalogue went beyond describing objects for sale and addressed the public on various aspects of collecting and connoisseurship: the social rewards of collecting, the origins and properties of porcelain, recent developments in compass technology, what to look for in shells and how and when to have them cleaned, and so on. We also find colorful asides, for example, on the difficulty of getting the Dutch to part with anything valuable or the English love of van de Velde's seascapes. Finally, we are given profiles of the men whose collections are for sale and the artists whose paintings are represented. This is how Watteau's life came to be written into the Lorangère catalogue of 1744. The long essay on Jacques Callot in the same catalogue, a model of scholarly connoisseurship, is no less interesting. But ultimately, this mass of information serves to tell us mostly about Gersaint himself. From one catalogue to the next the reader forms a cumulative impression of Gersaint's immense knowledge, extending from paintings and prints to porcelain and jewels; his social connections, at home and abroad; and last but not least, his conduct and ethics as a dealer, especially with regard to the attribution of paintings. [. . .]

Gersaint's major catalogues of the 1740s, comprising the Lorangère, Mosson, La Roque, Fonspertuis, and Godefroy sales, constitute a remarkable achievement, the fruit of many years of experience and much learning. Contemporaries were struck by their novelty, style, and erudition. In the time-honored language of the book review, the *Mercure de France* recommended the Lorangère catalogue as "a novel contribution to its genre," of interest to novices and experienced amateurs alike, and, in sum, necessary reading "for all those who possess a taste and a love for the arts of painting, drawing, and engraving." The catalogues still make fascinating reading, not least for the way in which Gersaint uses them to sustain his credentials as a scholar and a gentleman. [. . .]

In the rough and tumble of the eighteenth-century art market, where deception and dishonesty were already prevalent, Gersaint felt the need to insist on his own distinction, probity, and disinterestedness, and in the catalogues he spared no opportunity to enlarge on this topic. In the Godefroy catalogue of 1748, for example, an entry on a painting by

Carlo Maratta, made famous by an earlier scandal "too sinister to recall," provided the occasion for a long digression on the ethics of dealing. Dealers, Gersaint tells the reader, must be men of honor who take care not to abuse the authority they have over objects and those who collect. Buyers and sellers rely equally on the dealer's judgment, and he must at all times be consistent and impartial, keeping himself "within the strict bounds of the truth so as not to prejudice the interests of either party." The collector, meanwhile, should guard against the dealer whose self-interest might lead him to deliver false advice or a misleading opinion. In Gersaint's view, the dealer's authority extended from judgments of quality to determinations of condition, originality, and authorship.

In the Godefroy catalogue and others Gersaint sought to remain true to his word by shying away from firm attributions of paintings in cases where others were of two opinions or when he was himself in doubt. He acted on the principle that it was better to confess ignorance than to deceive a client. Furthermore, to quarrel openly over a painting with other connoisseurs would be bad form, a breach of convention that might jeopardize Gersaint's membership in polite society. More than deference was involved, however, for whenever he was faced with a painting of disputed attribution, he asserted his belief that it was the inherent quality of a painting that mattered more than its authorship. In the Fonspertuis catalogue of 1747, for example, Gersaint stated:

> A genuine *amateur*, or I should say, a true connoisseur is less concerned with a painter's name and the rarity of his paintings than with the quality of his work. . . . How many times one comes across pictures of quality, painted with artistry and intelligence and of indubitable merit, which the *curieux* scarcely acknowledge because the names of those who executed them are unknown to us. . . . It seems to me that one should devote one's attention to the painting itself rather than the name of the artist who made it. I will never tire of repeating this or of trying to persuade the *curieux* of its truth, despite much experience which leads me to think that my effort is in vain.

This passage, and others like it, was directly inspired by the writings of [Roger] de Piles and the Coypels [Antoine and his son Charles-Antoine], who for over fifty years had tried to define judgment and connoisseurship in terms of quality rather than attribution. To choose one characteristic example, witness this passage from Antoine Coypel's *Discours* of 1721:

> It is not a painting's reputation that determines its merit; rather its merit must determine its reputation, and I wish the *curieux* would address the question of what is good and bad instead of preoccupying themselves with authors, style, and originality. For the majority of them would not dare offer praise or blame until they had satisfied themselves in these matters.

The persistent effort of Coypel and others to define connoisseurship stemmed from a fear that privileging rarity and established names valorized the art of the past over the present and would prove prejudicial to living artists. Judgments of aesthetics and quality, on the other hand, made without reference to names and dates were egalitarian and disinterested. It was a worthy cause but a futile one, as the frustrated tone of Coypel's text acknowledges. The superior worth of the Old Masters had already become an article of faith among European collectors. The irony of Gersaint's attempt to ally himself with Coypel's cause and his disavowal of names in a sale catalogue would surely have been plain to many. For what was the dealer's purpose if not to classify and evaluate? Moreover, his professed indifference, his desire not to appear overly invested in the business of connoisseurship, ran counter to the detailed knowledge of artists and their works on display in every catalogue, not to mention his "rediscovery" of painters previously unknown in France. Gersaint and his fellow dealers were responsible above all others for fueling the growing demand for Old Master paintings across Northern Europe. [. . .]

The Fonspertuis catalogue of 1747 . . . employed a frontispiece by Charles-Nicolas Cochin that recalls Watteau and his shop sign [for Gersaint]. Like Watteau's painting— but this time as if through a keyhole—the engraving shows us the intimate sphere of privileged amateurs. Forms of dialogue, between art lovers and between eye and object, are once more presented as defining elements of connoisseurial conduct. The event represented is most probably a sale preview, a customary feature of Gersaint's auctions, but commercial implications are suppressed in favor of an image of sociability centered on art. During these previews Gersaint took over from the deceased collector and welcomed art lovers in an appropriate manner. "The disinterest and affability with which he receives those drawn to his premises by simple curiosity is well known," wrote the *Mercure* in 1739. Like Watteau's [shop sign], Cochin's frontispiece elides the distinction between private cabinet and commercial venue.

The most interesting digression in the Lorangère catalogue, apart from the essays on Watteau and Callot, is a passage describing the pleasures and social rewards of collecting. Collecting, Gersaint tells us, provides not only solace and recreation for the busy man of affairs after a hard day's work: it serves also as a vehicle for social integration and upward mobility. If a man tires of being home alone with his collection, his status as an amateur will give him:

> entrée into the most celebrated cabinets where he may also pursue recreation. As an *amateur*, he becomes by virtue of a common passion the equal of those superior in rank and condition; he is welcome at gatherings of theirs whose purpose is to share news of recent discoveries and acquisitions; he may partake of their pleasure as he profits from the discussion, increasing his knowledge and amusing himself all the while.

In this account, collecting secures a second, equally precious commodity, namely admission to elegant society and the freedom to converse with social superiors on matters of common interest. Gersaint's insistence on the communal as well as the private pleasures of collecting corresponds to the interpretation of consumption as ritual. In the words of

Mary Douglas and Baron Isherwood, "goods . . . are ritual adjuncts; consumption is a ritual process. . . . Enjoyment of physical consumption is only part of the service yielded by goods; the other part is the enjoyment of sharing names." Within the community described by Gersaint, sharing involved the exchange of information and opinion as well as, on occasion, gifts in the form of objects. Individual consumption, while beneficial in itself as a private amusement, ultimately derived meaning from the communal, public uses that stemmed from it. The purpose of this digression on collecting was to infuse his trade with the noble economy of immaterial exchange. The implication that one had to own, and therefore buy, before one could share went unspoken.

OSKAR BÄTSCHMANN, *David and the "Exposition Payante"*

Excerpt (pp. 45–47) from "The Exhibition as a Medium for the Presentation of Art," in *The Artist in the Modern World: The Conflict between Market and Self-Expression*, trans. E. Martin (Cologne: Dumont Buch Verlag, 1997), 12–57. Reprinted with kind permission of the author.

When exhibiting his painting *The Sabine Women* Jacques-Louis David had to give an elaborate defence of the "exposition payante", which was hated in France. David charged an entrance fee of 1.80 francs, and said that the best way to succeed was to catch the public eye, "captiver l'attention des spectateurs". If the artist failed to do that, the public stayed away, the exhibition was a financial failure, the artist lost his artistic freedom and the fire of genius died out. David very skillfully advertised his painting and invited offers for it in his text, but his tone was arrogant and didactic. He pointed out that exhibitions derived from a usage in Antiquity and were motivated not by the desire for profit but the need to maintain the independence of the artists; he lamented the sacrifice artists had to make and flattered the public. He also claimed that he was promoting young artists by indicating a source of income for them which could put an end to their impoverishment. But he destroyed any appearance of serving the general good the following year, when he added two versions of the equestrian portrait of Napoleon to his exhibition. Charles Paul Landon, who had defended the entrance charge in a preview of the exhibition of *The Sabine Women*, condemned the painter's speculative attempt to earn double by exhibiting two paintings that had been commissioned for an agreed fee. Landon accused David of using his palette, as the British artists did, for commercial ends; this was self-corruption. Jean-Baptiste Regnault and Louis Simon Boizot, who copied David's example and held exhibitions with an entrance charge, were not successful.

David called the American artists [Benjamin] West and [John Singleton] Copley, who were working in England, models of the "exposition payante". Henry Redhead Yorke comments in a letter written in 1802 that David's wife advised him to buy *The Sabine Women* for £5,000 and show it in London. Tischbein, in his review of the exhibition of David's *The Oath of the Horatii* in 1785, had noted the painter's intention of having the picture engraved in England. In 1788 David attempted to obtain a connection with the Royal Academy in order to show at its next exhibition, as Sir Brooke Boothby wrote to Joshua Reynolds. Boothby also reported that David was working on a new picture, *Brutus*. David probably wanted the English connection in order to hold a private exhibition there, which he could not do in France. It was not until 1822 that David exhibited the second version of *The Coronation of the Emperor and the Empress* in London; he had finished it during his exile in Brussels for a touring exhibition.

In his autobiography of 1793 David not only mentions the exhibition of *The Oath of the Horatii* in Rome in 1785, he actually says he owes his career and his reputation to the exhibitions. In 1776, while he was Director of the Académie de France à Rome, a post he held from 1775 to 1781, Joseph-Marie Vien had begun to show the works of the Rome scholars in S. Luigi dei Francesi and the Palazzo Mancini, before they were dispatched to Paris. In doing so he was following the Roman custom of publicly displaying works intended for export. In the exhibition of 1780 David showed the painting of St. Rochus, which had been commissioned by the military hospital at Marseille. In showing *The Oath of the Horatii* in 1785 David was combining this tradition with the studio exhibition. He prepared for his showing of *Brutus* in the Salon of 1789 by creating a press scandal.

The political events of 1789 put an end to David's plans for an exhibition in England. However, he did succeed in holding a private exhibition in Paris on the English model when he showed *The Sabine Women* in the Louvre from 1799 to 1805; he then held a one-man show in 1814. Unlike West and Copley, however, David had taken a subject from classical history painting. The relevance of the battle between the Romans and the Sabine Women lay in the pacifist message of the painting and the appeal to his native land to "stop sacrificing its children to this terrible war", which was published before the exhibition.

From the stylistic repertoire of the exhibition piece, *The Sabine Women* made use of shock and epic representation. The shock came from the nude male figures. Nude figures do not appear either in David's first idea on the subject, which he sketched in prison in 1793/94, or in a more detailed sketch or the drawings. In the composition sketch the men are wearing the breastplates usual in paintings on subjects from Roman history. It is evident from the brochure for the exhibition that David was fully aware that his nude heroes would both fascinate and shock the ladies, and that the offence to public morals was deliberate, as was his contravention of what was known of practices in Antiquity. Possibly he was hoping for a press scandal. As in the British exhibition pieces, David has focused attention on an emotional centre, by placing the women, with Herselia, between the aggressive males and allowing them to stand out against the background of figures in combat.

STEVEN R. ADAMS, *Noising Things Abroad*

Excerpts from "'Noising Things Abroad': Art, Commodity, and Commerce in Post-Revolutionary Paris," *Nineteenth-Century Art Worldwide* 12, no. 2 (2013): 1–28.

Reprinted by kind permission of Steven R. Adams and *Nineteenth-Century Art World-wide*. Available online at www.19thc-artworldwide.org.

During the ancien régime, history painting of the Italian school—the first of the "trois écoles"—took priority over the others on the basis that it was an intellectual, intrinsically noble art and the preserve of an educated social elite, the origins of which could be traced back to humanist writing on arts during the Renaissance. Italy's greatest painters typically took their subject matter from erudite sources and addressed the mind of the informed intellectual. In France, history painting's priority had been rehearsed in detail since the formation of the Académie Royale de Peinture et de Sculpture in 1648 and was subsequently restated in various scholarly histories of European art over the next 150 years. [. . .] Many of [Paris]'s most prominent dealers—Edmé-François Gersaint in the 1720s, Pierre Rémy and [François-Charles] Joullain a decade or so later—drew upon these systems of classification and broadly recognized Italian art's standing as the centerpiece of any collection. [. . .]

This vein of socially-exclusive art criticism disparaged the lower genres of the Flemish and Dutch Schools on the basis that their execution required only uninformed imitation and appealed to the senses. Art from the Low Countries typically depicted anecdotal scenes from everyday life, interiors, and landscapes. Meticulously finished, such pictures contained demonstrable evidence of an artist's labor and skills, artisanal aspects of painting that the untutored amateur could appreciate with ease. Genre paintings from the Dutch and Flemish Schools were consequently located at the end of a sale of works of art, again, often irrespective of their financial value, provenance, or historical importance. Despite the ubiquity of this method of classifying paintings, the hierarchy rarely troubled market forces, and there were numerous instances in which popular taste trumped academic dogma and the price paid for works by a well-known Dutch painter exceeded that paid for "nobler" works, especially during the last years of the ancien régime, when pictures from the Low Countries fetched astronomical sums. Adriaen van de Velde's *Landscape Divided by a River*, bought by Louis XVI for just under 20,100 livres at the Vaudreuil sale, fetched well in excess of the 15,100 livres Lebrun paid for Nicolas Poussin's *Fête en l'honneur du dieu Pan*, an ostensibly far nobler painting in the Italian tradition described in the catalogue as with an impeccable provenance and said to be one of the most beautiful works by France's most revered history painter. [. . .]

Over the next two decades, the stock of high quality, old-master paintings from Italy, the Low Countries and France circulating on the French market diminished. The Revolutionary and Imperial wars impeded the flow of pictures back and forth from Paris, London, and Amsterdam, and the Revolution itself decimated the educated class of patrons. . . . As a result, pictures of lesser cultural and financial value—typically old-master paintings of doubtful authenticity, works by minor masters, and eighteenth century French works—appeared in greater quantity on the art market. Particularly prominent were French genre and landscape paintings, small pictures depicting subjects that were easily accessible to a new class of largely untutored collectors. In the absence of traditional methods of validation—evidence of a work's provenance or the place of an artist in an historical canon—dealers exploited the market by constructing narratives known as *avertissements* set out in the preface to sales catalogues. These narratives called attention not to the work's place in history but to the person of the artist, his personal integrity, patience, and insight, highly subjective factors that a dealer might easily project onto the works of otherwise unstable cultural value. [. . .]

Many of the French painters whose works came up for auction during the late Empire and early Restoration had benefitted from the Académie's abolition and the National Assembly's reform of the Salon in 1791. No longer a privileged venue solely for the exhibition of work by academicians, the newly reformed Salon provided an important platform for all painters potentially to exhibit their work. [. . .] Invariably, they exhibited genre and landscape paintings that broadly followed Dutch models. [. . .]

[. . .] Few of the painters from the lower echelons of the profession who made their first appearance after 1791 enjoyed financial security. Indeed, the absence of patronage led some to be cast as "forgotten minor masters," isolated individuals sustained only by their personal insight and for whom recognition would come only later in more enlightened times, a critical trope that modernist criticism was to draw upon for the remainder of the nineteenth century. Furthermore, modernism's abiding concern with authorial conviction and the production of art for its own sake has largely repressed this vein of commercialized visual culture. When Jean Renoir recorded his father's reminiscences of decorating shop blinds and porcelain plates back in the 1850s while nursing the hopes of professional success as a painter at the Salon, he described a way of life that had first come about as a result of the 1791 reforms that gave rights to all artists to exhibit irrespective of their professional affiliation, a way of life that had been common among working-class Parisian artists for half a century. [. . .]

The making of art as a speculative commercial product without a patron in mind was seen by conservative critics to have had a potentially sclerotic effect on the profession and on French culture in general. [. . .] According to Quatremère, the arts were often now little more than an "aliment of curiosity," a commodity made to offer instant gratification to an ill-tutored middle class. Writing in the *Guide des amateurs*, Pierre-Marie Gault de Saint-Germain . . . conceded that the Revolution had brought to an end "the great reign of amateurs" and had compromised the nation's heritage accordingly. The production and consumption of art had become the preserve of the many rather than the few. Gault de Saint-Germain spoke of the feverish round of production and consumption, the "commercial circulation of an infinity of unknown objects; [that] ebb and flow through the hands of the many; often without merit or any use for the connoisseur whose role has been undertaken by an ill-informed class of men who buy and sell throughout the length and breadth of Paris." [. . .]

Perhaps one of the most historically significant examples of art's commodification—and the transubstantiation of unfettered cultural production into an embryonic form of modernist discourse—occurred at the posthumous sale of the collection of Robert de Saint-Victor, president of the Parliament of Rouen, in November 1822. The collection comprised some 450 Dutch and Flemish pictures, and 140 modern and contemporary works of which two thirds were landscapes. The catalogue also listed several landscapes by [Simon Mathurin] Lantara including a *Tempest* and a *Landscape by Moonlight*, along with a detailed account of the artist's life and work. While there was a precedent for narrative contextualization in the sale of works painted by artists of renown, the convention was rarely applied to modern French landscape and genre paintings, especially by those artists without a place in history. The account is of seminal importance. The idea of an autonomous art sustained by nothing other than an artist's personal integrity is typically first associated with art criticism in the early 1830s. During this period, for the first time, art was seen to have fulfilled no purpose other than to offer an insight into the soul of its creator; any attempt to harness the arts to some party's political, institutional or commercial ends was seen as tainting its essential purity. In Lantara's case, the same assertions of personal integrity are found, but they clearly have a commercial function. In the absence of a recognized place in history, Lantara's creative integrity was underscored as proof of the aesthetic and by extension the commercial value of his pictures.

FRANCIS HASKELL, *An Italian Patron of French Neo-Classic Art*

Excerpts (pp. 55–57, 61) from "An Italian Patron of French Neo-Classic Art," in *Past and Present in Art and Taste: Selected Essays* (New Haven, CT, and London: Yale University Press, 1987), 52–64. Copyright © 1987 Yale University Press.

Editor's note: The Italian politician and collector Giovanni Battista Sommariva had embraced Napoleon after the latter's conquest of Italy and enriched himself as Napoleon's representative in Milan. Sommariva moved to Paris in 1806.

Sommariva survived the downfall of Napoleon, as he survived most things, and it was indeed under the restored monarchy that he was able to commission a picture from the most famous of all living French artists, Jacques-Louis David, then an exile in Brussels—a large-scale mythological work, distinctly erotic in tone and harping on the theme of Psyche which appealed so much to Sommariva and his contemporaries.

But Sommariva's importance in the France of the first quarter of the nineteenth century did not lie only in the French paintings he commissioned . . . but also in his propagation—in France—of Italian sculpture, especially the sculpture of Canova. . . . [Pierre Paul] Prud'hon's great portrait deliberately depicted Sommariva with two of his statues by Canova, the flawed *Palamedes* and the *Terpsichore*. But the most famous object in his whole collection (though he had not actually commissioned it, but had bought it at second or third hand) was Canova's *Magdalene* for which he built a little altar described for us by a contemporary as half-chapel, half-boudoir, furnished in violet and lit only by an alabaster lamp hanging from the cupola. . . .

It would be hard to exaggerate the importance that this piece of sculpture had for French taste and the really astonishing enthusiasm with which it was greeted by artists, critics and connoisseurs—Stendhal was only one among many who thought of it as the greatest work of modern times—and for well over a generation its impact could be detected in French art of all kinds, for instance the figure of the Magdalene kneeling at Christ's feet in the pediment of the Madeleine in Paris. As so often happens, the Sommariva Magdalene, as it was often called, came to be associated at least as much with the owner as with the artist.

'You will have heard of the death of our good Canova. Now the value of his works will be doubled.' The words come from a letter written by Sommariva to his son, Luigi, in 1822. It is perhaps a little unfair to quote from such a source. Were it not for the survival of these letters, published, for private circulation only, by his daughter-in-law a generation after his death, Sommariva would have achieved his ambition and would have remained for those who bothered to remember him at all what he was for his French contemporaries: by far the greatest patron of his day and the sincerest of art lovers. But through these letters we can also see something else. We can see him systematically making use of his patronage and collection of art as an instrument of social prestige to establish himself in the best French and international company of the day. It was entirely through his art collection that the ex-barber's assistant, ex-revolutionary, ex-dictator of Milan, ex-Bonapartist now found himself, as the Marquis de Sommariva, receiving and visiting on equal terms the Duke of Devonshire, the Duc de Montmorency, Count Anatole Demidoff and the Duc de Blacas. . . . And he was aware of this. 'It is true', he wrote to his son, 'that it is an expensive business to cultivate the fine arts; but the capital always remains, and indeed sometimes increases. Besides, it does us a lot of honor. In fact I notice that abroad people talk about us even more favorably than they do at home.' To make sure that his *éclat* as an art lover would reach a wider public than could actually call on him in Paris or Milan he encouraged the engraving of his pictures, to be accompanied by suitable dedications, of course, and even had them copied in the form of enamel miniatures which could be conveniently carried around with him.

The theme that art collecting brings financial rewards and social prestige runs like a leit-motif through his correspondence. Of [Bertel] Thorvaldsen's marble frieze of the triumph of Alexander, which had been commissioned by Napoleon and which Sommariva had been able to buy for his villa after the Emperor's downfall, he wrote, 'I hope that this deal is the best that I have ever made in a matter of this kind, bearing in mind also the question of investment'—and I will only refer to one other instance of this attitude. In 1824 he was having a furious quarrel with a painter who was then well-known but is now barely remembered, Gautherot, about a picture of which only the preliminary sketch has so far been traced illustrating an allegory of vaccination—a strange subject, but one that was being much debated in medical circles at the time. It is incidentally, worth stressing Sommariva's particular insistence on a mythological treatment even for so prosaic a theme, for both his own letters and his surprised contemporaries reveal how close a control he aimed to exert on the artists he employed. [. . .]

[. . .] French and Italian art of the twenty-five years between 1789 and 1815 is inextricably linked in our minds with the dramatic events of the Revolution and the Napoleonic wars. But the tastes of Sommariva, whose sons both fought in Napoleon's armies, were very different. One of his earliest commissions, Luigi Acquisti's *Mars and Venus*, shows us a trembling Venus holding back a ferocious-looking Mars, and again and again the pictures and sculptures that he ordered dwell on the theme of peace and its delights. Guérin had barely painted *Napoleon Forgiving the Insurgents of Cairo* for Napoleon before he was at work on *Cephalus and Aurora* for Sommariva. It may be significant that Gros, the artist most closely identified with the Romantic style of portraiture and the military aspects of the Napoleonic epic, was never employed by him, despite the fact that his later work conforms to Sommariva's taste; and that Sommariva's own bust, by the Danish sculptor Thorvaldsen, shows him in the ancient manner rather than in the modern costume which Napoleon and the upstart society around him had brought into vogue.

The *Amour et Psyché* that David painted for him in 1817 springs directly from the pictures that he had been painting for the French aristocracy on the eve of the Revolution. It is, of course, true that David's style had evolved in the meantime. The picture for Sommariva is far harder, far more sensuous and shows a far bolder use of color than the earlier work, whose freshness and innocence it lacks. But looking at them together who would guess that the twenty-five years that separate them had been marked by the artist voting for the execution of the brother of the man for whom he had painted the first of them, by his own imprisonment and perilous proximity to the guillotine, by his glorification of Napoleon and by his exile?

NICHOLAS GREEN, *Circuits of Production, Circuits
of Consumption*

Excerpts (pp. 31–32) from "Circuits of Production, Circuits of Consumption: The Case of Mid-Nineteenth-Century French Art Dealing," *Art Journal* 48, no. 1 (1989): 29–34. Reprinted by kind permission of the Estate of Nicholas Green.

In the first half of the century dealer shops and luxury-goods businesses clustered more and more within the interlinked quarters of the Bourse, the banking sector of the chaussee d'Antin and rue Laffitte, the glamorous cafes and entertainments of the boulevard des Italiens, and the new residential quarters northwest of the center. The last, precipitated by the brief construction boom of the 1820s, set the standard for new housing, incorporating all the most up-to-date features of urban technology such as bitumen pavements, gas lighting, and new apartment block formats. Here was a modern city long predating Haussmannization, in which the new quarters were linked spatially and culturally as well as economically with finance capital and with the structures of entertainment and consumption from theaters and cafes to promenading and shopping. [. . .]

At the same time other moves were afoot; moves towards the individualization of the art object and towards a more active speculative strategy—by artists as well as dealers. On one level, the 1850s saw the intensification of metropolitan culture, now given the imperial stamp of approval. Riding on the economic boom following Napoleon III's seizure of power, a new generation of dealers set up shops that lacked the old artisanal ties to a secure trade. Another significant factor was the opening of the auction house, the hôtel Drouot, about 1853. Just up the road from the Bourse, it concentrated all public sales of art, antiquities, and bric-a-brac in one highly visible, even theatrical format. Established as a company back in the revolutionary era, the auctioneers had conducted sales in a number of premises, but their impact was dulled by internal dissension and some ambiguity about which auctions could legally take place in public. The hôtel Drouot swept all that away! A *pot-pourri* of every kind of collectible object from junk to "old masters," it offered continual surprises, spectacle, and entertainment—a staging post in the metropolitan parade.

Yet the hôtel Drouot also marked a shift in modes of consumption, with an increased emphasis on speculation and investment. Physical proximity to the stock exchange encouraged analogies with the fortunes of finance capital. By the 1860s, light-hearted accounts by Henri Rochefort and Champfleury were evoking a stock exchange of art objects and drawing comparisons to a gambling house with collectors as "roulette players." These jokey narratives made the most of the glamour, the dubious tricks of the trade, and, most insistently, Drouot's colorful cast of characters. First on stage was the auctioneer, a man of influence and fortune like the doyen of the company, maître Pillet, who "has found the secret of obtaining the most select clientele in Paris, and of selling for at least a third more than all the others." He was assisted by a so-called expert, who valued the objects on sale. This was a curiously fluid role. The continual errors and false attributions to be found in their catalogues had rendered the expert in "old masters" a character of almost universal derision. For just about anyone could become an expert, since "the auction house demands no diploma"—an ambiguity now to be exploited by modern-art dealers. Then, in the wings, lurked a host of other characters: dealers and middlemen, connoisseurs and speculative collectors.

Speculation—in building, then in railway shares—had been one of the recurring motifs in modern Paris from the 1820s. The boom conditions of the 1850s produced a dramatic expansion and diversification of speculative activity, and with it spawned whole new "families" of economic agents. This was equally true of the modern art circulating in the dealer shops. Up until the late 1840s, sales of contemporary collections carried little cachet, and shop dealers rarely became involved. Now, the most dynamic operators, like Alexis Febvre and Francis Petit, began to intervene as valuing experts. They also mounted sales of their own stock in the guise of anonymous collectors, brought in art historical experts to validate and publicize catalogues, and struck deals with auctioneers to fix prices up or down in their own interests. Of course, the possibility of this move was also set by other conditions, principally collectors' alarm at the number of "old-master" fakes on the market combined with a gradual reordering of aesthetic hierarchies that increasingly favored genre and landscape.

NICHOLAS GREEN, *Dealing in Temperaments*

Excerpts (pp. 68–72) from "Dealing in Temperaments: Economic Transformation of the Artistic Field in France during the Second Half of the Nineteenth Century," *Art History* 10, no. 1 (1987): 59–76. Copyright © 1987 Association of Art Historians. Reproduced with permission of Blackwell Publishing Ltd.

With the deaths of many of the romantic/Barbizon generation from the late 1860s biographies proliferated, ranging from detailed monographs to brief magazine vignettes. [Alfred] Sensier's *Souvenirs sur Théodore Rousseau*, 1872, was one early example. [. . .] The texts formed part of a two-way dialogue between art writers and the dealing market. Biographical activity was underpinned, at least in part, by commercial interest; likewise dealer and collector investment was stimulated by the writing of artists into history. In some instances, as between Sensier and [dealer Paul] Durand-Ruel, the objectives of the alliances were explicit. With one exception Sensier's 'loving' monographs were devoted to painters exclusively collected by the dealer—Rousseau, Millet and Georges Michel. Generally, the relationship was far less manipulative though equally fruitful to both parties, secured through informal contact in the auction house and through art reporting for newspapers and specialist journals.

Take the example of Philippe Burty, a noted habitué of the Hôtel Drouot, who edited the *Chronique des Arts* in the 1860s. A politically engaged art critic—he wrote for Gambetta's *La République française* from the 1870s—this did not inhibit enthusiastic participation in the commercial art world to which he contributed numerous sale catalogues. Simultaneously, he developed a reputation for art history, with special interests in contemporary, applied and Japanese art. His biographical writings on the Barbizon group complemented their commercial success at auction, while he was also prepared to back the 'futures' of risky trends like the impressionists. Eventually in 1881 his political loyalty was rewarded and his expertise recognized with an official position as inspector of fine arts, with special responsibility for lectures. That was a mark of the growing profile of art history as a definable professionalism. But what makes Burty's career worth investigating—and it was typical of many—is its elasticity. Part popular journalist, part political polemicist, part learned scholar, part financial broker; such institutional suppleness oiled the wheels of cultural exchanges between different agents in the circuit of cultural production.

Along with other forms of art historical writing biographies enriched the historical and aesthetic texture in which the cultural capital or the speculative commodity was grounded. But the widespread *production* of biographies does not in itself explain why nature art became so financially privileged. Rather, it was their *discursive organisation*, the particular interpretative framework that they established that supplied the vital ingredient. Here was a quite new formulation of creative individuality—one all too familiar today—which carried distinct implications not just for the meaning but also for the valuation of art products.

Look at any of the early biographies of Corot, Rousseau or Millet. There we find in varying proportions a kaleidoscope of personalized observation, anecdote and reminiscence juxtaposed with carefully gathered empirical documentation. Although the overall intention is to praise, unlike official obituaries of academicians which sternly eschewed the low ground of the personal, these texts revel in a detailed exposé of painters' lives. [. . .] Such different—even antithetical—devices point to structural and highly productive tensions in the particular mode of writing. For art biography and its conceptual repertoire currently hovered in a kind of no man's land, part popular journalism, part historical science. [. . .]

[. . .] Together, diversified anecdote and careful documentary 'fact' worked to evoke a graphic and sometimes complex picture of the life and character of the artist, while having little to say—apart from description—about the meaning and message of the art images. It was in nature biographies specifically that this formula took on the real force of explanation, for critical interpretation had traditionally concentrated on these artists' 'naive' and 'sincere' dialogue with the world in opposition to the academic (and noble) preoccupation with style. In other words, the given absence of stylistic analysis for nature painting—of a vocabulary which could engage with the formalist structure of the image—opened up space for the full-blooded entry of biographical explanation. Implicitly, the art works were to be read as the reflection of expression of the temperament descriptively explored in the written texts. Nature was the ground on which the plethora of creative individualities was inscribed. [. . .]

Aesthetic criteria deriving from the new discursive model had a direct input into contemporary dealing. Central to the market in 'old masters' was the rarity value of 'great' works. Through the specification of an individualized personality expressed in art the biographical approach transformed the means of measurement from the rarity of the object to the uniqueness of the artist. The market in modern art was reorientated around the buying and selling of individual *painters*. This was ideal for the promotion of nature painting where high productivity had been one of the mainstays of the earlier shop trade but a handicap in an investment market revolving around rarity. Now the great artist could be simultaneously prolific and unique. Traditional emphases on rarity were reconciled with large-scale commodity capitalism.

The principle was firmly grasped by those like Durand-Ruel who sought to corner certain artists' work and who actively encouraged art historical literature. But perhaps the tie-up could be most dramatically demonstrated in the changing attitudes to sketches. From mid-century sketches and studies had occasionally been sold to friends or on the open market, yet their value remained fixed by the status of the tools of the trade, the mechanical and artisanal aspect of artistic production. According to the biographical model, all kinds of sketches and unfinished work could be incorporated into the painter's *oeuvre*, reclassified as 'first thoughts', 'truly personal expressions', 'developing ideas'. Though smaller and more modest than exhibition machines they ceased to be qualitatively distinct. In staking out a claim over Rousseau, whose output of Salon pieces was limited but whose studio was littered with the debris of many years' experimentation, Durand-Ruel made full use of the redefinition of aesthetic priorities. Included in the studio sale of 1866 were many tiny oil sketches on paper dating from the painter's youth. Mounted on to board or canvas, cut down or even expanded to suitably attractive shapes, framed in rich gilt rococo frames, this material was now transformed into standard dealer stock. Similarly, in his 1873 catalogue, the *Recueil des estampes gravées à l'eau-forte*, no attention was drawn by the presentation of the text to massive differences in scale or function between small practice studies, memory notes, sizeable but unfinished canvases and worked up Salon/collector pictures. They all stood as representations of Rousseau's rich and complex individuality.

ANNE M. WAGNER, *Courbet's Landscapes and Their Market*

Excerpts (pp. 411–13, 416–18, 423–25) from "Courbet's Landscapes and Their Market," *Art History* 4, no. 4 (1981): 410–31. Copyright © 1987 Association of Art Historians. Reproduced with permission of Blackwell Publishing Ltd.

The fact that there was a market for Courbet's landscapes and that during his lifetime they attracted the critical approval denied his figure paintings has since worked effectively to block an adequate account of either subject, the landscapes or their market. It has seemed as if they both cannot be fitted as significant elements within one coherent construct of Courbet. Yet both Salon reviewers and a public of bourgeois collectors could come to terms with the landscapes as works by Courbet the revolutionary realist. Commercial and critical success in one genre did not stifle the controversy and threat of the other, nor was the converse true. The two aspects of the one artist were not held to be mutually exclusive. [. . .]

[Courbet scholar Klaus Herding's analysis of the landscapes has skirted] what remains their central characteristic, their production for a bourgeois market and their demonstrable appeal to it. Courbet may have despised patrons, as he avowed, but that scorn was qualified in practice. He rejected one kind of patron in favor of presenting his work directly to other purchasers, primarily an urban public, with both the price of entry to an exhibition in its pocket, and the cost of a picture within its command. Courbet's public was a segment of the population of European city dwellers, residents of Paris, Brussels, Munich, Lille, Amsterdam, London, Dijon, Vienna—cities where he put his work on show from the beginning of his career. His tactic of sending his work around the international exhibition circuit was meant to increase its exposure and expand its market in the urban milieu where it found purchasers. But this is only one strategy among Courbet's many manipulations of his work. Paintings are marshalled, deployed, recalled, lent, borrowed, given as hostage. The backbone of this small army was the landscapes, a force easily sold off and as easily replenished during a few weeks' excursion into the Saintonge.

The related facts of Courbet's execution of landscapes for sale to a particular market and their success in it must be understood as a defining condition of their production. [. . .] We need to ask what Courbet's landscapes offered their market. What did the owners and audience want? How did they see what the pictures provided? [. . .]

Champfleury was not the only one of Courbet's supporters to see his career in terms of his market and to doubt his ability to find purchasers for his work. The problem was in [Pierre Joseph] Proudhon's mind from the outset: 'A qui donc M. Courbet destinait-il ce tableau [the *Enterrement à Ornans*]?' All the usual depots for such monumental canvases, the parish church, a town hall, even a theatre, were closed to it. Rejected by church, state and commerce, 'il n'y a qu'un grand seigneur avide de curiosités qui puisse songer à le recueillier dans son grenier; il se gardera de le placer dans son salon.' [. . .] Throughout his career, no new class of patrons emerged. Courbet relied on rich, sometimes powerful supporters, as well as more modest members of the bourgeoisie, and it is worth noting that he saw his relationships with his benefactors as a liberating alternative to state patronage. No matter who the purchaser, it was necessary for the painter to sell his work. [. . .] He had to find, to convince a public and present it with works it wanted to buy.

From the beginning of his career, Courbet was perfectly well aware of that fact. He was endlessly demonstrating his concern, not just with living as an artist, but with making a living as an artist. His letters home report his fluctuating sales, the progress of commissions, and the activity of the Paris art market. From the outset, he recognized the necessity of the Salon exhibition to any artistic enterprise, even if he twice circumvented it with private shows. Throughout the 1840s he submitted canvases regularly, and suffered refusal until the second class medal awarded him in 1849 freed his work from jury scrutiny. His submissions were carefully selected, and he applied a traditional hierarchy of values to the presentation of various genres. Figure paintings came first; the rest, he wrote in 1854, was 'du remplissage,' the pictures—landscapes, portraits, still lifes—which filled in around them. A letter of 1861, written . . . to his friend Francis Wey, explains this valuation more clearly. The context is significant. Courbet is outlining the considerations involved in his choice of canvases for the 1861 Salon, the first year that he won a generally agreed success. Before the show opened, however, he had warned that he would be represented only by landscapes and animal pictures, and considered letting the *Cerfs à l'eau* stand as his sole entry. In the end, he sent five pictures, none of them figure paintings, and excused that decision in eminently practical terms: the added canvases were ready, a private purchaser could afford them, and he had to sell that year simply to keep on painting. [. . .] Independence meant two things: private patrons and freedom from state aid. The one purchased the other. [. . .]

The contacts with potential clients established through Courbet's relationships with dealers were extended by more informal arrangements. His public could see his work in dealers' showrooms, but they could also visit his studio on the rue Monsieur le Prince. If the painter was not in Paris, an assistant would show the works in stock. The visitor might conclude a deal on the spot or write to the painter a few days later. Or, had he never met Courbet, he might preface his request with an introduction from any one of several men who seem to have acted informally as the painter's agents both abroad and in France. [. . .]

Courbet's friends often showed themselves willing to promote certain types of his landscapes. Even the architect of the Pavillon du Réalisme, Léon Isabey, enlisted as Courbet's agent. He passed on a commission for a painting 'plus large que haut' and included a sketch should Courbet not at once grasp the idea. [. . .] Isabey's letter spelled out not only dimensions and general subject, *un paysage*, but more specific details: 'On désire une barque et un pêcheur, soit à l'épervier, soit à la ligne.' His prescriptions make it clear that the person who commissioned the painting was familiar with various types of Courbet's landscapes, and that they were distinguished not by color, for example, but by motif, size and price. In fact, the collector in question, M. Stumpf, who was also an admirer of Corot, later wrote Courbet directly to rescind the stipulation of the boat; its inclusion was left up to the painter. The letter resembles another enquiry from a patron impatiently asking when he could expect delivery of a seascape which he would accept with as many or as few rocks as Courbet felt like putting in.

With or without boats or rocks or fisher folk, such specifications suggest the ways in which Courbet's patrons saw and classified his landscapes. Elements which seem trivial to us take on decisive importance in their letters. It is significant that clients order a picture with a boat or a fisherman and make its presence a necessary condition for purchase, and equally important that the required fisherman could hold either a net or a line, with the final choice left to Courbet. It is significant that a friend could counsel the production of *paysages de matin* or a patron commission a *marine plein midi*. In these letters details are spelled out but the character of the landscape itself is most often left unstated. Accessories are specified but their landscape setting, the 'subject' of the picture, is identified only by a kind of verbal shorthand: a *paysage d'Ornans*, a *marine ciel léger*, perhaps, or in other letters, a *marine effet matin* or a *mer orageuse* or a *puits noir*. Phrases like these name individual types of Courbet's landscapes which collectors knew from having seen them on view in any one of the places I have described. They were asking for a variation or a repetition of a known model. [. . .]

Eventually, by the mid 1860s Courbet's titles reflect [a] change from the specific to the general view of nature. Names like *Paysage de neige, Marine, Le rocher,* even *Le ruisseau couvert* or *Ruisseau du puits noir* no longer identify a known, visitable spot so much as signal landscape types which Courbet had made familiar through exhibition. Courbet's public knew his landscapes by these titles; they were used by people like . . . Stumpf when they ordered pictures for their living rooms. They stand for canvases which, to recapitulate briefly, offer an image of nature meant to be perceived in ways very different from those provided by Courbet's earlier landscapes. Conventionally composed, the early pictures presented a viewer with a voyage into an imaginary terrain, knit together as a continuous fabric by visible passages which lead us into the illusionistic world. The act of looking is thus sustained and prolonged by both composition and handling. A *Marine,* a *Trombe,* or a *Puits noir,* on the other hand, create *effet,* a term which stands as a one-word summary for the process of looking at these pictures. [. . .] It is a word which should not have seemed unfamiliar to its users in the 1860s, since its history as a piece of critical terminology was at least a century old. But its earlier meaning, a precise, technical usage which described the unified relationship of planes of light and dark within a composition seems to have become submerged beneath a more general concept. As Courbet's critics used it, *effet* stands simultaneously for the overall impression a picture creates, no matter what technique causes it, and its audience's reading of the work. *Effet* does not suggest instantaneity alone (as it often will when used to describe landscape in the 1870s and later), but a range of impressions. The term might be used of a *Marine* from about 1870, one of the long series of paintings which utilize variations of the same simple motif. [. . .] [In *Marine*] the empty boats serve the function of the human figure. Horizontality is perfect. Touch is smooth, regular, rhythmic, with its only reflection the small bubbles and breaks in the icing of pig-ment it lays on. These suggest no priorities which might influence our reading of the scene. The illusion is immediate, complete, and it dissolves almost at once. When we have grasped the subject, we can read no further. All that is left to study is technique itself. [. . .]

[. . .] When the best known version of the type called the *Puits noir* was shown at the Salon of 1865, it bore a long descriptive title, which ended [with] *effet de crépuscule.* . . . But the *effet* of this title and that created by the picture and other, similar forest scenes are somewhat different. The one refers to a particular tonal cast, the other to an overall read-ing of the picture. In most of these scenes, especially their secondary versions, penetra-tion into the forest interior is almost defeated by a dense screen of branches, rocks and foliage. Each part is treated equally, drawn with the same generalizations, constructed with the same layered washes of pigment. The eye literally cannot penetrate the *effet;* the customary landscape reading is defeated.

This was the complaint of several of Courbet's critics. In 1866, Felix Jahyer wrote a rather peevish analysis of another forest scene, one of two pictures the painter had sent to the Salon. . . . In Jahyer's eyes, Courbet had broken the most basic rules of landscape composition—and he was right. Yet to another critic, Courbet's friend Théophile Thoré, the same picture secured Courbet's acceptance by a diverse public, not just true amateurs of good painting, but also society women, wealthy bourgeois, and the naive crowd. [. . .]

Are the two somehow connected, Courbet's impenetrable, simple composition[s] and their appeal to a wide market? The answer should be clear by now. But it was left to Courbet's erstwhile friend and supporter through the 1850s, Champfleury, to offer an explanation for the appeal that Thoré had noted with . . . sadness. [. . .]

According to [Champfleury], simplicity of motif assuages the jangled nerves of a particular audience, people who live shut up in cities. But Champfleury knows that this poor city-bound creature is not a worker camping in some squalid *logement* on the edge of Paris. The audience he describes is the *homme blasé*, the businessman 'burnt out from a day on the boulevards, chest seared by the dust rising from macadam, unnerved by the bold glances of painted women.' Undermined by the encroachments of 'le travail, l'invention, et la production de toute sorte,' he sinks down on his divan, heart and head empty. The drama is all Champfleury's, but his text suggests an antidote to this dire state of exhaustion: the sight of a landscape, a simple landscape, 'une matinée brumeuse de Corot, une roche portant ombre sur le gazon de Courbet.'

ROBERT JENSEN, *The Retrospective Exhibition*

Excerpts (pp. 107–12) from "The Retrospective," in *Marketing Modernism in Fin-de-Siècle Europe* (Princeton, NJ: Princeton University Press, 1997), 107–37. Copyright © 1994 Princeton University Press. Reprinted by permission.

For most of the nineteenth century the special exhibition held in the galleries of an art dealer, whether it was of a group or of an individual, carried the burden of appearing too commercial, its historical interest too insufficient to mask its self-interest. [. . .]

Despite social resistance to "expositions particulières" devoted to individual artists . . . they became perforce one of the dominant institutions of the fin de siècle. The Durand-Ruel/Cercle exhibition of Rousseau in fact signaled the inroads private exhibitions had already begun to make in the Paris cultural fabric by the 1860s. That Durand-Ruel was able with some success to exploit Rousseau's "apotheosis" at the 1867 Exposition Universelle, to show the work of a living artist held entirely in commercial hands for commercial purposes, was an important precedent for the one-man exhibitions of the 1880s. "Expositions particulières" also grew in eminence as the indirect result of both imperial and republican state policies that had pursued cultural consensus in the visual arts and had downplayed the role of écoles in French art in favor of the promotion of great individuals. These government efforts were inevitably undermined by the decline of the "la grande peinture" and the absence of heroes. But the evaporation of the academic tradition's ability to produce the genius of the future coincided with the discovery that the decorum prohibiting self-promotion within the context of a commercial gallery could be overridden if the notion of a one-man show was closely allied to group exhibitions that offered a single aesthetic and ideological front (e.g., the Impressionists). That is, the force of an école— . . . by virtue of theory's support of temperament—fulfilled the public expectation that a "school" or a "movement" naturally generates leaders, and that from leaders masters or "geniuses" emerge to carry on the canonical tradition of great art. While the original group exhibitions of the Impressionists were imbedded in the political, social, and cultural circumstances of their era, their eventual trajectory into one-man retrospectives represented an ahistorical, but institutionally comprehensible, turn in the construction of their careers and the careers of all artists who followed their example.

This recognition developed slowly. The one-person exhibition for a living artist could not readily command the political qualities of independence that helped the Impressionists' group shows overcome the appearance of commercialism. The right to such an exhibition had been traditionally conferred only when there existed some public consensus that the artist deserved this honor. So the historical process that validated the Impressionists as an "ism" institutionally coerced later artists to align themselves with a "movement." By the 1890s to be a member of a society, attached to some kind of aesthetic system, counted for more than the individual works of art displayed therein, and for much more than newspaper reviews of ephemeral influence. [. . .]

Although these large exhibitions gathered wide-spread public attention, the tendency was to create them, as Durand-Ruel says, as something akin to a museum, to look, but not to buy. Collectors, too, had to be educated away from the preference for the latest Salon painting, for the newest work, in fact, by any artist, over their older work. Realizing this fact "much too late," as Durand-Ruel says in his "Mémoires," the dealer had many notable failures with his exhibitions, the most prominent among them the 1878 exhibition of the École de 1830, held in conjunction with that year's Exposition Universelle—which received remarkably little critical attention and produced less in sales—and the 1905 exhibition of Impressionist paintings in London—equally ignored, and equally a commercial failure. Durand-Ruel appears to have forgotten that the great collection of Barbizon and Impressionist paintings that he took with him to New York in 1886 turned the tide on the commercial fortunes of the Impressionists. And the gallery's one-man retrospectives held in 1883 and the many more offered in the 1890s were well-received and resulted in significant sales. I would argue that if Durand-Ruel, even after witnessing the commercial triumph of the Barbizon painters and the Impressionists, still held reservations about the commercial viability of the independent, historically-minded exhibition, it was because the retrospective had grown up in the space between the competing forces of the markets for contemporary and old master art. [. . .]

Retrospectives were enabled by, were eventually unthinkable without, commercial galleries, particularly those such as Durand-Ruel's that had displayed a protracted commitment to an artist throughout their career (or conversely, as with Vollard, who made substantial lot purchases of an artist's work—e.g., Cézanne—which then could be exhibited as a survey of the oeuvre). These great dealer collections, backed by the archives and the personal relationship between dealers and their *amateurs*, made the planning of any significant retrospective after 1880 unimaginable without the active support of dealers. In turn, the dealers, who had usually long speculated on these artists in the auction houses, were only too eager to provide ample access to their art to the organizers of the retrospectives. In some cases, the retrospectives provided the occasion to assemble an ad hoc catalogue raisonné as an accompanying exhibition catalogue. The most ambitious of these shows, by virtue of their inclusiveness, served as the foundation for determining provenances and providing the stamp of authenticity on a work of art, a bench mark in the life of a painting's provenance, that in an age of rampant forgeries had significant commercial value.

In this way, the retrospectives were closely linked to the monograph, which, although not inherently a modernist phenomenon, played a significant role in elevating modernist artists over their popular rivals in the Salons. Biographical monographs had long been the customary formulae both for art historical writing and for contemporary notices for exhibitions and for auction catalogues. Modernism's special claim to the monograph lay in its discourse of martyrdom so frequently rehearsed and in the manner in which they codified the artist's role within a specific "evolution" of recent art. It began, as I believe Nicholas Green has correctly argued, with the linking of the personality or temperament of Barbizon landscape painters to nature itself. These biographies exploited the ubiquitous practice of combining anecdotal information, letters, diaries, and exhibition history. As art criticism, these monographs have an explanatory power that stands halfway between *Kunstwissenschaft* and hearsay. [. . .]

After 1900 the retrospective was widely and self-consciously employed as a weapon to redress the exclusions of the past, to rewrite history, to construct a canonical history of modernist artists as a sequence of great individuals in the evolution of modern art. In the process, retrospectives constructed their own genealogy, a tradition of vindicated masters, stretching back to Courbet's self-arranged retrospective at the Exposition Universelle of 1855. [. . .] The discourse of the retrospectives was in superlatives—could it be otherwise?—inevitably raising the artist from the ranks of realism or Impressionism or symbolism to transcendent master. Except for the authentication of works of art, the retrospectives were by nature uncritical, concerned only with laying out a biography of genius, punctuated by master works. In the process, retrospectives served, and continue to serve, to destroy the actual historicity of an artist's career. Works of art are treated in retrospectives in relation to each other rather than externally to other art, to the cultural, social, and political issues that helped to form the artist's horizon of beliefs.

The retrospectives operated on the principle of exclusion rather than inclusion, focusing attention only on the work of art as an isolated entity within the personal development of the artists. [. . .] The value of an artist's work could be measured by the internal progress of the master toward originality, while externally that same value could be measured against the development of modernism. In this way, the retrospectives historicized, but decontextualized, an artist's career; they created an oeuvre rather than a succession of single pictures or sculptures. They encouraged the construction of paradigmatic early, middle, and late "chapters" in an artist's life. Within this sensibility one also sees the fascination among fin-de-siècle art historians for the late work of artists. An artist's work ceased simply to be a succession of Rembrandts, but became an early, middle, or late Rembrandt, often with commercial values attached.

ALBERT BOIME, *Entrepreneurial Patronage in Nineteenth-Century France*

Excerpts (pp. 139–41, 144, 152–60) from "Entrepreneurial Patronage in Nineteenth-Century France," in *Enterprise and Entrepreneurs in Nineteenth and Twentieth Century France*, ed. E. C. Carter, R. Forster, and J. N. Moody (Baltimore: Johns Hopkins University Press, 1976), 137–207. Copyright © 1976 The Johns Hopkins University Press. Reprinted with permission of Johns Hopkins University Press.

The following conclusions may . . . be set forth: (1) the collecting of art was an urgent need for most entrepreneur-patrons; (2) entrepreneurs who amassed important collections were business leaders in their respective areas and helped set contemporary taste; (3) entrepreneurs who hired artists to design their industrial products likewise innovated in their field, and in cases where this practice was joined to a taste for collecting, entrepreneurs revolutionized their industries; and (4) the relationship of an entrepreneur's political and economic ideals to the character of his collection and patronage was highly variable. [. . .]

Insofar as patronage is a form of financial support, the method of dispensing it remains fairly stable; nevertheless, certain changes in the classic relationship between patron and beneficiary distinguish the nineteenth century from earlier epochs. For one thing, the entrepreneur-patron of the later period is the parvenu who springs from the undistinguished mass of mankind and stands in a different relationship to the artist from that of the old ruling classes. If he is called a *mécène*, in honor of Maecenas, the archtypal princely patron, this is often done with tongue-in-cheek irony. Both entrepreneur-patron and artist come from the same social background, and this identity of social and psychological dispositions essentially annuls any semblance to classic forms of patronage, where the artist was employed as a personal servant or otherwise dependent on an aristocratic class.

Another difference in the nineteenth century is the blurring of the categories of collector and patron. [. . .] In the nineteenth century, the patron . . . became far less important, since he was replaced by the collector of both old and new paintings. The two enthusiasms became fused, a change facilitated by the annual official exhibitions known as the Salons and by the emergence of dealers, as well as by the eclectic proclivities of the period. Then, too, by combining both types in his own person, the entrepreneur discovered another way to outshine the aristocratic models he had tried to emulate when he gained his fortune.

Among the various schools represented in the collections of entrepreneurs around mid-century, two stand out significantly from the rest: seventeenth-century Dutch and eighteenth-century French painting. The major private collections enumerated in the *Paris Guide* of 1867—the majority of them formed by such entrepreneurs as James de Rothschild, Casimir Périer *fils*, Achille Seillière, François Delessert, Eugène Schneider, and the brothers Péreire—conspicuously reflect this tendency. [. . .]

Not that the Dutch-picture cult was novel: it had enjoyed a vogue in the previous century and had never really gone out of fashion; but the early nineteenth-century entrepreneurs modeled themselves after the eighteenth-century aristocracy and adopted their status symbols. The later, more dynamic derivations coincide with a gradual displacement of the aristocratic model (and this includes the assimilation and modification of eighteenth-century art) and the self-assertive ideals of the later entrepreneurs. These demanded distinctive trappings to define their nonconformity, and the result was an anarchy of stylistic developments that has continued to the present day. This does not imply that the taste of the ruling classes is still not the generative factor: on the contrary, the taste for ever-increasing exoticism is the concomitant of status in the modern world. [. . .]

As a class of entrepreneurs, the department store magnates were usually enthusiastic, if conservative, art patrons. A department store is itself a kind of lively museum for spectators, and just as these pioneers delighted in surrounding themselves with sundry objects at work, so they enjoyed a home environment filled with a variety of art objects. The founders of La Samaritaine, Ernest Cognacq and Louise Jay, . . . attached their names in hyphenated perpetuity to fabulous collections of eighteenth-century art. [. . .]

It is probably not fortuitous that they named their firm after a work of art, since almost simultaneously with the inauguration of the new enterprise they began collecting art objects. Some pieces were earmarked for the decoration of the store, some were destined for their adjoining picture gallery, and some for their apartments. Initially, they bought Impressionist paintings, but they eventually sold them, save for a few precious examples by Monet, Boudin, and Degas. They preferred to concentrate on the eighteenth century, a period not only more suitable to their taste but perhaps more assuring as well. The rococo opulence of La Samaritaine de Luxe found an equivalent expression in the sumptuousness of their dwelling. [. . .]

Alfred Chauchard, the founder of the Galeries du Louvre, formed an exceptional collection of the Barbizon landscape painters, which he donated to the Louvre. [. . .] Chauchard began collecting only after retirement in the 1880s, when the prices of the Barbizon school were already inflated. [. . .] When he began collecting . . . he did so with great passion, even to the point of outbidding American millionaires to acquire Millet's famous *Angelus*. [. . .]

One exception to the generally conservative outlook of the department store chiefs was Ernest Hoschedé, an energetic entrepreneur who unflaggingly engaged in one enterprise after another. [. . .] In the decade of the 1870s he was involved in at least three department stores: Hoschedé, Tissier, Bourely, et Compagnie; Hoschedé, Blémont, et Compagnie . . . ; and Au Gagne petit on the avenue de l'Opéra. [. . .] Versatile and dynamic, he created in 1888 a periodical that made use of costly color illustrations, *L'art de la mode*, but this had only an ephemeral existence. [. . .]

Hoschedé has the honor of being one of the earliest and strongest champions of the Impressionists. Already in 1874, before the Impressionists had their first group exhibition, Hoschedé had accumulated a sufficient number of their works to hold a sale. Indeed, he bought paintings from the young artists as long as he had cash, but when one of his schemes failed, he sold them—much to the artists' chagrin—to pay off debts and finance a new undertaking. In 1878 he was forced to auction a remarkable collection of 117 tableaux—including 5 Manets, 12 Monets, 13 Sisleys and 9 Pissarros—at such ridiculously low prices that Pissarro moaned, "La vente Hoschedé m'a tué." [. . .]

[. . .] In fact, he was a genuine *mécène*, inviting artists regularly to his country estate . . . and occasionally giving them an original commission. [. . .] In Hoschedé's case, there seems to be a direct relationship between his bold entrepreneurial ventures and his active support of avant-garde and independent artists. His numerous enterprises attest to a total immersion in the contemporary world, and his restless, driving energy can be compared to the expressive character of Impressionist painting. [. . .]

Another group of fascinating entrepreneurs are those whose industry related intimately to the fine arts. They were patrons in a double sense: they employed artists in their business and also formed important collections. Jean Dollfus, director of the large textile center in Alsace, Dollfus Mieg et Compagnie, inherited a long artistic tradition: one of the founding ancestors of the firm was a painter who made the designs for its first cotton fabrics. Dollfus himself studied painting. . . . [He] carried over his aesthetic interests into his work, applying himself to the improvement of his printed fabrics through greater harmony of colors and fresh designs. To this end he employed a number of industrial artists, who made his fabrics among the most sought after in France.

Dollfus also consecrated a major part of his activity to amassing tableaux and art objects. . . . He assembled an impressive collection of fifteenth-century primitives and seventeenth-century Dutch painters. After the Franco-Prussian War, Dollfus moved to Paris, where he began buying Barbizon masters and the Impressionists. He gravitated especially toward Renoir, whom he met socially, ultimately earning a reputation for his small but choice representation of that artist, and also of Boudin, Sisley, and Pissarro.

Charles Haviland, the owner of the famous porcelain factory at Limoges, inherited the firm from his father David, an American who became a naturalized French Citizen. David planned from the outset to export his porcelains to the United States and, placing great emphasis on decoration, maintained an atelier of 100 apprentice painters and 4 art instructors. The Maison Haviland continued to expand this program, and out of a total of 500 employees in the 1860s, 165 were painters. [. . .]

The great fashion designers like Jacques Doucet, Paul Poiret, and Jeanne Lanvin provide another example of entrepreneurial involvement in the arts combined with active encouragement of fine artists. Not unexpectedly, creators of contemporary fashion styles reveal a taste for all things modern. [. . .] In addition to the Impressionists, Doucet purchased Douanier Rousseaus, van Goghs, Bonnards, van Dongens, Matisses, and Picassos. From Picasso he purchased a picture generally acknowledged to be the key work in the evolution of twentieth-century art, *Les demoiselles d'Avignon.* [. . .] Obsessed now with modernity, he constantly renewed his collection by selling off parts of it and then buying more contemporary works by the same artists or by supporting fresh talent. [. . .]

A fashion king for over twenty years, Paul Poiret also painted and plunged enthusiastically into the contemporary art world. [. . .] A close friend of many of the original Fauves and their followers, he purchased the work of Vlaminck, Matisse, Derain, Dufy, Marquet, Rouault, Utrillo, and Dunoyer de Segonzac. But his favorite artist was Dufy, whom he commissioned to sculpt wood-block designs for an exclusive line of Poiret's dresses. The success of this project inspired Poiret's competitors to take up the idea for their fabrics.

Poiret encouraged the commercialization of modern art, adapting it to fashion and cultural style. He wished to bridge the gap between art and industry and between art and the masses. He hoped to realize this in part by providing young girls from the working classes with art instruction. In 1912 he founded the Ecole d'art décoratif Martine and took over the responsibility of instruction himself, although Dufy and others participated in the project. [. . .]

Jeanne Lanvin (1867–1946) was the most successful female artisan in France. Incredibly energetic, she supervised a top team of designers and revolutionized the fashion industry. As an active collector she worshiped the Impressionists and Fauves. [. . .] Lanvin owned outstanding works by Degas, Sisley, and Renoir, but rather than treat the paintings as valuable objects, she studied them for ideas. Totally identifying herself with the artist, she once answered in response to the question, "How do you get your ideas?": "Si vous demandez à un peintre comment peignez vous? il serait fort embarrassé, il est possible qu'il vous dise simplement, 'mais avec des pinceaux, de la couleur, une toile, l'inspiration et cette force qui est en moi et qui m'oblige à m'exprimer.' Je vous dirai donc également que je crée avec des ciseaux, des étoffes, mon imagination et aussi mon inspiration." Thus the innovative entrepreneur and patron discovered a kinship between his activity and that of the group committed professionally to full-time creative pursuit.

PAUL GAUGUIN, *Ambroise Vollard Correspondence*

Excerpts (pp. 178–79, 188–92) from "Paul Gauguin—Letters to Ambroise Vollard," in John Rewald, *Studies in Post-Impressionism* (New York: Harry N. Abrams, 1986), 178–92. Reproduced by permission of Thames and Hudson Ltd., London.

[Tahiti, April 1897]

Dear Monsieur Vollard,

I have just received your letter with many requests, many propositions, but I find myself unable to discern its true meaning. [. . .]

You . . . want wood sculptures, models for bronze casts, etc. . . . For four years now all those things have been in Paris with no sales. Either they are bad, and then the new ones I might make would also be bad, and thus unsalable, or else they are works of art.—In that case why don't you sell them? Yet I believe that my large statue in ceramics, the *Tueuse* [*Oviri*], is an exceptional piece such as no ceramist has made until now and that, in addition, it would look very well cast in bronze (without retouching and without patina). In this way the buyer would not only have the ceramic piece itself, but also a bronze edition with which to make money. And the mask, *Head of a Savage*, what a beautiful bronze it would make, and not expensive. I am convinced that you could easily find thirty collectors who would pay 100 francs, which would mean 3,000 francs, or 2,000 after deduction of expenses. Why don't you consider this?

Hoping to hear from you soon, I am, with best regards,

P. Gauguin

.   .   .

[Paris, end of 1899]

Dear Monsieur Gauguin,

You will receive . . . two parcels containing about sixty sheets of Ingres paper and some watercolors. I am sending these in the hope that you will be good enough to make me some sketches in pencil washed with watercolor, covering the entire paper—something like the drawings you made in Brittany some time ago and afterward colored with pastels. I will buy all you make at the rate of 40 francs each. Then if you care to do some flower paintings for the price of the pictures I bought from Daniel [de Monfreid] I will take a whole series of them; in short I am willing to buy everything you do; the only stipulations are that we must come to an understanding with regard to prices and that the pictures must be painted on good canvas, which I could send you, and with good colors, which I could also have sent to you.

Needless to say, everything would be paid for in cash as soon as received. If I dwell so insistently on the question of price, it is because your work is so different from what people are accustomed to that nobody will buy it. [. . .]

Yours truly

Ambroise Vollard

.   .   .

[Tahiti] January 1900

[. . .] To start with, I am afraid your sheets of Ingres paper will not be of much use to me (very poor for watercolors). I am very finicky about paper; moreover, your requirement that the entire paper must be covered worries me so that I would never dare begin work. Now an artist (if you consider me such, and not a mere machine for turning out orders) can do well only what he feels, and to the devil with dimensions! I have tried all sorts of things in Brittany and throughout my life; I like to experiment, but if my work must be limited to watercolor, pastel, or anything else, all the spirit goes out of it. You would lose by it too, since it would look monotonous when exhibited. Patrons of art differ in taste: one likes vigorous work, another prefers it sweet as sugar. I have just done a series of experiments in drawings with which I am fairly well pleased, and I am sending you a tiny sample. It looks like a print, but it isn't. I used a thick ink instead of pencil, that's all.

You mention flower paintings. I really don't know which ones you mean, although I have done only a few, and that is because (as you have doubtless perceived) I do not copy nature—today even less than formerly. With me, everything happens in my exuberant imagination, and when I tire of painting figures (which I like best), I begin a still life and finish it without any model. Besides, this is not really a land of flowers. And you add (which seems contradictory) that you will take everything I paint. I should like to understand clearly. Do you mean flowers only, or figures and landscapes as well? [. . .]

You say that if you dwell on the question of price it is because my work is so different from that of other painters that nobody wants it. The statement is harsh, if not exaggerated. I am a little skeptical about it because, first, I saw pictures by Claude Monet sold for 20 francs about 1875 and bought a Renoir myself for 30 francs. Moreover, I made a collection of paintings by all the Impressionists which I bought at a very low figure when nobody would have them. [. . .]

Let us take up the question of prices. The last prices you paid Daniel were really astounding, unless they were a mistake; and if I had been there, or informed, I should have refused them at once. Prices only half as high as I received ten years ago!!! Therefore they cannot be allowed to serve as a precedent. But Daniel thought he was doing the right thing, so I had to agree with him and could do nothing but congratulate him on it, because he has much too noble a nature for it to be possible that we should ever have a misunderstanding.

Well, despite the fact that nobody wants my work because it is different from that of others (strange, illogical public which demands the greatest possible originality from a painter and yet will not accept him unless he resembles all the others and parenthetically, I do resemble those who resemble me, that is, those who imitate me), you want to do business with me—which is not easy at this distance—and you ask for an understanding with regard to prices. You know very well that if I had cared to make a business of my art I could have earned plenty of money by being shrewd, by exploiting Neine de Bretagne and other people devoid of talent; but I should not have become what I am and what I intend to be, a great artist. By this I mean to tell you that you must work in harmony with me and rely on my word.

I am willing to accept low prices (an average of 200 francs for each canvas, pictures such as I am accustomed to paint, of various subjects)—a maximum of 25 pictures a year. You will send me canvas and colors at your expense (according to the instructions I shall give Daniel). And for drawings, an average of 30 francs each, whatever their dimensions, whether in watercolor or not (the few small drawings of mine that Theo van Gogh sold at Goupil's cost an average of 60 francs and the lowest price for a picture was 300 francs, but people did want to buy them from him).

This is my final proposition, and I can assure you (with my word as an artist for guarantee) that I shall send you only art and not merchandise produced merely to earn money.

If you reject it, it will be useless to discuss the matter again.

There is another thing which is a *sine qua non*, as you will readily see. If I have no money I shall be obliged, as I told you, to find employment in Tahiti, and in that case I cannot devote myself wholly to art and fulfill my obligations to you. Therefore, if you accept my proposal, as soon as you receive this letter you will have to send me 300 francs every month, to be deducted from your payments for my work, which I shall be able to send you only from time to time as opportunities present themselves. However, I have enough pictures in storage [with Daniel de Monfreid] to cover these advances.

This is the *sine qua non*, which may upset you but which, as you must see, is absolutely essential to the arrangement, because obviously one must eat. And since you are a dealer, I do not imagine that you proposed this transaction without having considered it seriously; therefore it must be feasible. I have always said, and Theo van Gogh used to think so too, that a dealer could make a great deal of money out of my work. Because, first, I am fifty-one years old and have one of the best artistic reputations in France and other countries, and, having begun to paint very late in life, my pictures are very few in number, and most of them are owned in Denmark and Sweden. Hence there is no reason to fear in my case, as in that of other painters, the production of a tremendous number of pictures which must be continually repurchased. [. . .] I estimate the number of canvases I have done since I first began to paint at not more than three hundred, a hundred of which do not count because they were immature works. In this total are included about fifty pictures in foreign collections and a few in France belonging to people of real taste who will not sell them. As you see, there are only a few to be disposed of. That is a matter worth considering, especially since my average price of 200 francs is the price of a beginner, not of a man with a well-established reputation. [. . .]

Yours truly
Paul Gauguin

UNA JOHNSON, *Vollard's Bronzes*

Excerpt (pp. 40–42) from "Introduction," in *Ambroise Vollard, éditeur: Prints, Books, Bronzes* (New York: Museum of Modern Art, 1977), 18–43. Copyright © Una Johnson.

Early in his career, Vollard became interested in issuing editions of bronzes. About 1899 Aristide Maillol, poor and unknown, came to Paris from Banyuls, bringing with him a load of small terra-cotta statuettes. Edouard Vuillard saw them and excitedly brought Vollard to Maillol's quarters at Villeneuve-Saint-Georges. Ever on the watch for new or unknown artists whose work in his own judgment or in the judgment of his artist-friends seemed a profitable investment, Vollard saw possibilities in issuing bronze editions of the Maillol terra-cottas. He purchased a few pieces and had them cast in bronze.

The sale of these small figures provided Maillol with a modest living. But he still was unable to build a kiln necessary for the firing of his terra-cottas. Upon hearing of this, Vollard had one built for the sculptor at Villeneuve. With almost pathetic relief, Maillol remarked, "It is thanks to Vollard that I am able to live." In 1902 Vollard held an exhibition of Maillol's work, consisting of thirty pieces of sculpture and three of his earlier tapestries. [. . .] Critics and public alike welcomed the serenity and warmth of his sculpture. Maillol made a number of models for Vollard, always specifying that any bronze editions be limited to no more than ten casts. Often this stipulation by the artist was ignored, as Maillol observed with exasperation and finally with resignation: "Well, he made ten casts, all right, except that they turned out to be ten thousand!" There are occasionally slight irregularities and small changes in certain of the casts in which the sculptor perhaps had little or no part. Needless to say, this was the exception rather than the rule, and in the nine known Maillol bronzes issued by Vollard, the majority are well executed.

Vollard had attempted to interest Degas in his bronze editions, but the artist insisted that he was a painter and that his models were made only to facilitate his painting and for his own pleasure. [. . .]

Auguste Renoir was first inspired to work in sculpture when he posed for Maillol in 1907. It was after nearly a lifetime of painting that he was persuaded by Ambroise Vollard to consider working in sculpture. However, at the age of seventy-three he was in precarious health and gravely incapacitated by arthritis. It was Vollard who, on a visit to Cagnes, urged Renoir to work with a young assistant. Renoir was to supply the drawings and to supervise the work in plaster. First amused by such an idea, Renoir was soon involved in the plan. Vollard, amiable, witty, and nonchalant when artists were concerned, was adept at making his way into the most carefully guarded studios and persuading painters and sculptors to undertake his special projects. He also offered to bring them the necessary materials. With some dispatch, he brought the young sculptor Richard Guino to Renoir's studio. Guino had worked with Maillol and was unusually skilled in the various techniques of sculpture. He was also able and amenable to carrying out a style that was not necessarily his own. In the end Vollard's idea prevailed, with Vollard electing to pay Guino's expenses. This unusual arrangement proved to be uniquely successful, and the working relationship between Renoir and Guino was a happy and productive one. In fact, Guino's interpretations of Renoir's drawing, instructions, and wishes were so deft and expert that Renoir's bronzes and terra-cottas have always been accepted as originals. Perhaps Renoir's best-known sculptures are the modestly poised *La Laveuse*, or *Washerwoman*, and the stately *La Vénus triomphante*. Their method of working was carefully developed. Renoir would choose a figure from his paintings or drawings that he believed would lend itself to sculpture, then make a working sketch. Some of these sketches have been preserved. Guino in turn built up a small trial model in plaster. Occasionally he worked from a model who had formerly posed for Renoir. Vollard, a man of special taste and ingenuity, was always the astute businessman as well. Thus he managed to gain exclusive rights as agent for the Renoir sculptures. He obtained Renoir's permission to make bronze casts of some fourteen individual pieces. A letter from Renoir to Vollard, written at Cagnes, April 19, 1914 specifically states: "I authorize Monsieur Ambroise Vollard, picture-dealer, owner of my three sculpture models: small statue with base *Jugement de Paris*, large statue with base *Jugement de Paris* and the clock *Triomphe de l'amour*, to reproduce them in any material." The latter model, *Triomphe de l'amour*, was never cast in bronze for Vollard. It was cast for the first time in 1955–56 in an edition of eight by Alfred Daber of Paris. In several instances Vollard retained in his gallery the first casts of the larger bronzes by Renoir and Maillol with their bronze pegs and guides intact. Alfred H. Barr notes this procedure in The Museum of Modern Art's casts of Renoir's large *La Laveuse* or *Washerwoman*. [. . .]

In the twenty-odd bronzes that compose the Vollard editions only a few have cast numbers. It is doubtful that Vollard himself knew the total issue of each. His practice was to keep in his shop an example of each of the bronzes. When a collector or dealer wished to obtain one, Vollard would order a cast made. Being a good businessman, he never had more on hand than he could sell. The Maillol figures were probably the most popular and, accordingly, Vollard issued more bronzes by Maillol than by any other artist. Vollard's active interest in his bronze editions began early in the twentieth century and ended in 1917 with the series of six medallions by Renoir.

MICHAEL COWAN FITZGERALD, *La Peau De L'ours and Galerie Berthe Weill*

Excerpts (pp. 73–74, 76–78) from "Skin Games," *Art in America* 80, no. 2 (1992): 70–82, 139–41. Reprinted courtesy of Art Media Holdings, LLC.

Editor's note: La Peau de l'Ours was a consortium of thirteen Parisian art investors who acquired work by contemporary artists over a period of ten years.

From the beginning of La Peau de l'Ours in 1904, [collector and organizer André] Level sought to assemble a collection devoted to art of the *début,* rather than the fin de siècle in France. Although it included a few works by Post-Impressionist artists, most of the 88 paintings and 57 drawings that constituted La Peau de l'Ours were the work of 20th-century artists, and the largest concentrations were among the Fauves and Picasso. [. . .] While Level's emphasis on the Fauves (a year before they made headlines) probably reflects both his response to their paintings in the 1903 Salon d'Automne and his long-standing friendship with one of their minor associates, René Piot, his interest in Picasso's art could only have come from the rare gallery exhibitions that included it.

On weekly tours of Montmartre, Level exercised his skills as an astute *dénicheur* by assiduously cultivating the meager network of secondhand dealers, particularly Père Soulier, Clovis Sagot and the little-known Moline, as well as the galleries—such as they were. Unlike the plethora of outlets we know today, there were only two galleries in Paris that dealt in the work of artists of the new century. For Ambroise Vollard, Matisse and Picasso were only experiments outside his primary focus on the Impressionists and Post-Impressionists. In the first years of the century, only one gallery truly specialized in 20th-century art—the Galerie Berthe Weill. [. . .]

By 1900, Weill had opened her own antiques shop, but her specialization in contemporary art began when she opened the Galerie Berthe Weill on Dec. 1, 1901. As her business card stated, her gallery was a *"place aux jeunes."* And as a sign of her dedication and limited means, her working capital consisted of her dowry—4,000 francs. From the beginning, this independent woman presented the paintings of the French Fauves and Catalonian *modernistes* in group exhibitions that alternated with displays of more conventional prints. Weill may have been the first French dealer to sell works by Picasso—specifically, three bullfight scenes for which she paid a total of 100 francs and immediately resold for 150. She was also the first dealer to show Matisse's work (in a group show of February 1902) and the first to sell one of his paintings. . . . Weill's consistent adherence to very low commissions (whether or not for altruistic reasons) prevented her from ever providing the long-term support her artists sought, so as their reputations grew they left for better-capitalized galleries. Yet, she relished her gallery's position as an initial showcase of "new talent," and she persisted through the 1920s, when Picasso drew a stately portrait of her. As the only woman who showed the work of 20th-century artists and as the dealer who gave many of them their first shows, she deserves far more recognition than she has received.

In addition to Picasso's distrust of organizations, his alien status and poor grasp of the French language probably dissuaded him from exhibiting in the Salons. This left him particularly dependent on dealers to sell his work. His early reliance on Weill is recorded in a drawing he inscribed to her in 1901, and it appears that André Level's long-standing fascination with Picasso's work began at Berthe Weill's gallery that same year. [. . .] A list of her first dozen clients includes two collectors who would be the leading members of La Peau de l'Ours—Level and Ellissen. Moreover, Weill claimed that three-quarters of the items in the collection were purchased from her gallery. Even if this percentage is exaggerated, there is no doubt that Level bought from her on a regular basis.

Along with the Post-Impressionist works and three paintings by Matisse that Level acquired in the first year of La Peau de l'Ours, he bought from Weill's second Picasso show the first of 12 Picassos, *Intimacy* (1902–03), that would form the core of the collection. On Level's part, this choice of a sentimental scene of women and children in a domestic setting not only reflects his taste for Vuillard's interiors but also a cautious approach to entering the market for 20th-century art. This was exactly the type of buyer Picasso had in mind, since he admitted making the work to sell: "I was living on the Rue Champollion. I wanted to do something to make some money. I'm a little ashamed to admit it, but that's how it was. So I did this pastel. I rolled it up and carried it to Berthe Weill. She lived in Montmartre, at the other end of Paris. It was snowing. And me with my pastel under my arm. . . . She had no money. . . . So I went away . . . and left the pastel." A year passed before she hung it in a show and sold it to Level. [. . .]

By 1906, Picasso's reputation and financial condition were becoming more secure as he developed a group of collectors of his work that would convince Kahnweiler to become his dealer by 1909 and (so it seemed) end his financial worries. Late in 1905, Leo and Gertrude Stein had begun to collect his art, and probably in 1906 Sergei Shchukin made the first of his many purchases before the First World War. At this time, Level convinced his colleagues in La Peau de l'Ours to make a special commitment to Picasso, on whose work the majority of their budget for 1906 was to be spent. Culling Weill's stock and sending the dealer Clovis Sagot as his agent, Level assembled a group of six paintings and watercolors that he purchased for the collection. The works were primarily confined to the first years of the century. . . .

Also at this time, Vollard finally decided to buy a substantial amount of Picasso's art. Even though he had shown Picasso's work in 1901, Vollard did not make a major purchase until April 1906, when he acquired 20 canvases for 2,000 francs. Level's activities may shed light on Vollard's newfound confidence in Picasso's work. Quite uncharacteristically, Level claimed priority over Vollard in collecting Picasso's work, and it does appear likely that the clever but cautious dealer was responding to the purchases by Level, the Steins and others when he made this sizable investment. As Vollard surmised, he could now count on a market for Picasso's work. [. . .]

[. . .] Although Level chuckled over buying a still life by van Gogh from Vollard at a bargain price of 500 francs (*Flowers in a Vase*, 1890), the major purchase of the year was a single painting by Picasso, *The Family of Saltimbanques*. The picture had remained in Picasso's possession since it was finished in the fall of 1905 and appears to have been one of the few to have escaped Vollard's sweeps of his studio in 1906 and 1907, either because Picasso refused to sell it or because Vollard would not meet his price. [. . .]

By 1909, the market for contemporary art was developing rapidly. The activities of Level and other adventurous collectors had convinced prominent galleries and dealers with considerable capital to make commitments to the leading artists of the 20th-century avant-garde. Nearly a decade after their first exhibitions, Matisse, Picasso and their contemporaries began to be offered the substantial commercial support that Berthe Weill could not afford and Vollard refused to extend. Matisse signed a contract with Bernheim in September 1909, and Picasso accepted Kahnweiler as his dealer at about the same time, even though they did not have a written contract until 1912. The predictability of Kahnweiler's steadily escalating purchases enabled Picasso to move during the fall of 1909 from the tenement Bateau Lavoir to a spacious apartment with a separate studio on the Boulevard de Clichy and hire a maid to keep house and serve meals. [. . .]

When the appointed time came for the members of La Peau de l'Ours to [sell the collection], Level orchestrated a publicity campaign that turned the auction into a forum for the esthetic, political and economic estimation of the paintings and drawings in the collection. . . . Many observers saw the auction at the Hôtel Drouot as a vindication of Fauvism and Cubism. Economic success became an objective demonstration of the esthetic quality that many had doubted. This public achievement also placed avant-garde art in a broad social context that made it a focus of the political debate that would dominate the discussion of art during the First World War.

REBECCA RABINOW, *The Steins' Early Years in Paris*

Excerpts (pp. 21, 26–28, 32–35, 39–43) from "Discovering Modern Art: The Steins' Early Years in Paris, 1903–1907," in *The Steins Collect: Matisse, Picasso, and the Parisian Avant-Garde,* ed. J. Bishop, C. Debray, and R. Rabinow (San Francisco: San Francisco Museum of Modern Art; New Haven, CT, and London: Yale University Press, 2011), 21–47. Reprinted by permission of the San Francisco Museum of Modern Art. All rights reserved.

At the end of the nineteenth century, it seemed as if every wealthy American in France was hunting for art treasures. The Potter Palmers of Chicago, the H. O. Havemeyers of New York, and many others arrived in Paris with deep pockets, willing and able to purchase whatever caught their fancy. They filled their mansions in the States with thousands of contemporary paintings, ranging from canvases by medal winners at the annual Paris salon exhibitions (Alexandre Cabanel and Pierre Puvis de Chavannes, for example) to the controversial pictures of the Impressionists. During the first decade of the twentieth century, when the siblings Leo, Gertrude, and Michael Stein, together with Michael's wife, Sarah, began buying pictures by a younger generation of artists working in Paris, the Steins were assumed to be yet another millionaire family from America. But the

Steins were different. They were not particularly wealthy, and none of them had come to France with the goal of collecting paintings. Once they began purchasing contemporary art, they did not whisk the canvases back to America but instead chose to reside in Paris and open their apartments to anyone interested in seeing the pictures on their walls. Consequently their discovery of modern art—especially the work of Henri Matisse and Pablo Picasso—had an indelible impact on its development for years to come. [. . .]

On October 15, 1904, the second Salon d'Automne was inaugurated at the Grand Palais. Included were retrospectives of Paul Cézanne, Henri de Toulouse-Lautrec, Pierre Puvis de Chavannes, Odilon Redon, and Pierre-Auguste Renoir, who were considered to be among the most relevant artists for the younger generation of painters. Impressed, Leo and Gertrude stopped by Vollard's gallery two weeks later and spent 8,000 francs on seven colorful figurative canvases: two Cézannes, two Gauguins, two Renoirs, and a Maurice Denis. Both of the Cézannes were "bather" paintings, similar in composition and comparable in size to the one Matisse lent to the Salon d'Automne. (The Cézanne gallery at the Salon included two much larger Bathers as well.) The two works by Paul Gauguin chosen by the Steins had likely been included in Vollard's memorial tribute to the artist the previous November. [. . .]

Cynics questioned whether the Salon d'Automne retrospectives had been organized for the benefit of the rue Laffitte art dealers. Vollard's account books for 1904 reveal that he sold at least sixteen paintings by Cézanne, many at an enormous profit, between the time that the Salon opened in mid-October and the end of the year. The number of sales is all the more remarkable given that the artist was not yet particularly well known.

Vollard saw Michael, Leo, and Gertrude . . . in front of Cézanne's portrait of his wife every time he visited the Salon d'Automne. Surely he was not surprised when Leo and Gertrude turned up at his gallery a few weeks later determined to purchase a portrait by the artist. Gertrude recalled that they began with eight possibilities before narrowing the choice to two, one of a woman and one of a man (probably *Man with Crossed Arms* [ca. 1899]), both of which they would have acquired if they could have afforded to do so. They ultimately selected *Madame Cézanne with a Fan* (1878–88), which had just returned from the Grand Palais. It was an important painting with a price to match: 8,000 francs, exactly what they had spent the previous month on all seven of their pictures combined.

Leo and Gertrude considered their paintings to be investments, which explains why, during these years, they always pooled their funds. [. . .] The 16,000 francs that Leo and Gertrude spent at Vollard's gallery in October and November 1904 represented a princely sum for them. They would never again have the opportunity to spend so much money on paintings in such a short period. [. . .]

Impressed by the Toulouse-Lautrec display at the 1904 Salon d'Automne—which was immediately followed by an exhibition of the artist's graphic work at the Musée du

Luxembourg in December and a group show at Berthe Weill's gallery in late February 1905—Leo decided to add a Toulouse-Lautrec as well. [. . .]

The influence of Toulouse-Lautrec, who had died in 1901, was apparent in the work of many young artists. It certainly could be seen in the pictures that the Spanish teenager Pablo Picasso included in his first Paris exhibition. Unlike Matisse, Picasso did not participate in the annual salons; Leo supposed the reason was "partly diffidence, partly pride." Instead Picasso's work could be seen in group shows, including one held in February–March 1905 at Serrurier et Cie, a modern furniture store on boulevard Haussmann, behind the Opéra. This exhibition was organized by Charles Morice, the art critic for *Mercure de France*. It featured twenty-four watercolor scenes of Switzerland by Albert Trachsel, fifteen canvases by the painter and illustrator Auguste Gérardin, and thirty-four works by Picasso. It was reviewed by Morice himself, who did not seem bothered by the conflict of interest, and by Picasso's friend Guillaume Apollinaire. The exhibition was also mentioned in a recently launched British periodical, the *Burlington Magazine for Connoisseurs*, which noted Picasso's "extraordinary perfection of manner." Leo visited the exhibition. . . . The store's regular staff seems to have lacked the authority to sell the pictures on display, because Leo's request to purchase some of Picasso's drawings languished.

Undeterred, Leo returned to Clovis Sagot's nearby gallery—it was Sagot who had recommended that he stop by the Serrurier exhibition in the first place—and bought a sizable Picasso gouache, *The Acrobat Family* (1905). [. . .]

The 1905 Salon d'Automne . . . featured a large room devoted to retrospectives of Jean-Auguste-Dominique Ingres and Édouard Manet, who were presented as contradictory yet worthy role models. Anyone who spent significant time in front of Ingres's delicately modeled paintings and portrait drawings or Manet's pictures, especially his portrait of Berthe Morisot holding a fan (1874), would have been struck by Matisse's distortion of color and line in his depiction of his wife, Amélie, posing with a fan, *Woman with a Hat* (1905). Leo was not alone in thinking it "the nastiest smear of paint" that he had ever seen. After five weeks in front of the picture, he and Gertrude decided that it justified the asking price of 500 francs. [. . .]

The purchase of *Woman with a Hat* altered the direction of Leo and Gertrude's collection. They were shifting away from their earlier emphasis on modern French masters in favor of more affordable ultracontemporary work. Four days after the Salon d'Automne closed, Leo wrote a friend about the latest purchases: the provocative *Woman with a Hat* . . . and Bonnard's *Siesta* (1900), a large oil of a nude sprawled facedown on a bed. . . . Leo also boasted of earlier acquisitions, the two pictures "by a young Spaniard named Picasso whom I consider a genius of very considerable magnitude and one of the most notable draughtsmen living."

Picasso, savvy and in need of money, recognized that the Stein family—both the rue de Fleurus and rue Madame households—could be helpful to him. Not only had they purchased two of his large paintings, but they encouraged friends such as the wealthy Cone sisters of Baltimore to do so as well. Picasso presented casual portraits to the Steins, renderings of Leo (1906) and Allan (1906) painted in gouache on cardboard. Gertrude wanted something grander, and Picasso was happy to oblige. His companion Fernande Olivier noted that he had been "so attracted by Mlle Stein's physical presence that he suggested he should paint her portrait, without even waiting to get to know her better." Picasso used oils on a canvas almost identical in size to *Madame Cézanne*, by far the most valuable painting hanging on the walls of rue de Fleurus at that time. [. . .]

The walls of the rue de Fleurus studio . . . were covered with paintings by Cézanne, Gauguin, Manguin, Matisse, Picasso, Renoir, Toulouse-Lautrec, and Vallotton. The displays at the Musée du Luxembourg looked outdated in comparison. [. . .] Increasing requests to visit the collections led to frequent interruptions. Gertrude, who used the atelier as her writing studio, particularly resented the disturbances. A decision was made to consolidate the visits and open both apartments on Saturday evenings to anyone who arrived with a reference in hand. [. . .]

Guests often found Leo pacing the studio or reclining on a daybed while extolling the individual merits of the pictures. He claims to have convinced Vollard to reconsider the artists whose works hung on his walls. Certainly many factors influenced Vollard, not least of which was the avidity with which Druet was purchasing paintings by these artists. In the spring of 1906 Vollard made his move. On March 21 he paid Manguin 7,000 francs for 147 of his paintings and works on paper. One month later he acquired a group of twenty paintings and studies from Matisse for 2,200 francs, and in early May he offered Picasso 2,000 francs for twenty-seven of his paintings. Only a few months later Bernheim-Jeune & Cie hired the writer and art critic Félix Fénéon to head up its contemporary art division at rue Richepanse, a move widely interpreted as a direct challenge to all the dealers of contemporary art in Paris, especially Druet. Fénéon began wooing Matisse almost immediately and, on March 11, 1907, scooped the competition by sending him an agreement. In return for rights of first refusal and a commitment to purchase the majority of Matisse's work, Bernheim-Jeune received 25 percent of every painting sold, regardless of whether the gallery was directly involved in the transaction. The Steins could not have anticipated the consequences of their enthusiasm. Their promotion of modern art was rapidly contributing to their being priced out of the market. [. . .]

[. . .] On February 7, 1907, after much public debate, Manet's controversial *Olympia* was transferred from the Musée du Luxembourg to the bastion of high art, the Musée du Louvre, where it was installed as a pendant to Ingres's *Grande Odalisque* (1814). [. . .] It was against this backdrop that Matisse presented his rendition of the same motif, *Blue Nude: Memory of Biskra* (1907), at the spring Salon des Indépendants. Leo and Gertrude purchased Matisse's aggressive, edgy canvas as a replacement for Bonnard's *Siesta*, which they had sold two months earlier. A wide variety of bathers had appeared on the walls of the rue de Fleurus studio over the previous two and a half years. *Blue Nude* was the most provocative addition to date.

Picasso saw *Blue Nude* both at the Salon des Indépendants and on the Steins' wall. His response was immediate. He began drawing and painting the figure of a woman with a bent upraised elbow and crooked knee, as if the model for *Blue Nude* was holding her pose after being rotated to a standing position. The figure appears repeatedly in studies for *Les Demoiselles d'Avignon* (1907), *Nude with Drapery* (1907), and *Three Women* (1908). [. . .] Leo and Gertrude were delighted, and although they did not buy the painting, they acquired many of Picasso's studies for it. Michael and Sarah added one to their collection as well. [. . .]

When Apollinaire's article on Matisse was published in the December 15, 1907, issue of *La Phalange*, it was illustrated with the three major canvases that the artist had painted that summer—*Red Madras Headdress* (1907), *La Coiffure*, and *Le Luxe I*—as well as with his self-portrait (1906). Three of the four were hanging on the walls of Michael and Sarah's apartment; the fourth was acquired soon thereafter. With the exception of the artist's studio, there was no better place to see Matisse's most recent work. It was a short-lived moment. That month, December 1907, the Russian textile merchant Sergei Shchukin paid the Steins a visit. He soon began acquiring large and increasingly expensive paintings by Matisse. Unlike the Steins, with their modest budgets and small apartments, Shchukin had vast wealth and a palace in central Moscow. By the end of 1908 he had become the artist's most important patron, a role that he enjoyed until political conflict closed the borders in 1914.

MALCOLM GEE, *The Avant-Garde, Order, and the Art Market*

Excerpts (pp. 96–103) from "The Avant-Garde, Order and the Art Market, 1916–23," *Art History* 2, no. 1 (1979): 95–106. Copyright © 1979 Association of Art Historians. Reproduced with permission of Blackwell Publishing Ltd.

The Cubist 'Call to Order' which took place during the war under the leadership of [Juan] Gris and [Jean] Metzinger, had an important commercial dimension from the first. In the first two years of the war, the Parisian art market was stagnant. Consequently, the emergence of a group of artists with a disciplined and didactic approach to style, and who had the backing of a dealer, was bound to make a considerable impact on the art world. Léonce Rosenberg had the peculiarity that what attracted him in dealing was the possibility of promoting a movement—a collective whole transcending individual parts. When the continuation of the war made it clear that D.-H. Kahnweiler's arrangements with French artists would cease, Rosenberg acted quickly to secure their work. However, he appears to have been interested in other Cubist painters from the outset. Between 1916 and 1917 he made commercial arrangements with approximately twelve artists working in a Cubist mode. This support strengthened a tendency, already present amongst these artists, to emphasize group identity and, equally important, encouraged observers to perceive and even exaggerate such an identity. [. . .]

[. . .] For approximately a year—from mid-1917 to mid-1918—it seemed more likely than ever before that Cubism could be transformed into a 'style', in the sense of a system of artistic practice which was generally acknowledged to be valid for its place and time. The chief reason for this new cohesion was commercial: it was the patronage of Léonce Rosenberg which brought together, for the first time, the 'major' Cubists (including Picasso) and their 'minor' followers and interpreters, and consequently provided a powerful material basis for the theoretical aspirations of some of the group. [. . .] However, it was vulnerable in several respects: the market for this sort of art was unproven; the conformity of practice which it imposed came to be resented by some of the artists involved; and powerful elements in the Parisian art world opposed and undermined it.

When Léonce Rosenberg started buying up Cubist work systematically in 1915, he was one of very few dealers active in the market. . . . It was only in 1917 that the market showed real signs of coming to life again. [. . .] The decisive indication of buoyancy in the picture market . . . was the Degas auction, held in the spring of 1918. For avant-garde painting the difficulties were particularly acute. D.-H. Kahnweiler had relied on foreign markets for a livelihood before the war—two of these, Russia and Germany, were now entirely inaccessible, and there were serious obstacles to trade with countries like the USA and Sweden. In fact, Rosenberg did not really try to sell Cubism before 1918. Apart from anything else, he was mobilized: throughout 1916 and 1917 he was buying paintings largely *in absentia*. Consequently, the commercial 'thrust' of Cubism was to a certain extent illusory—at a time when the entire avant-garde seemed to have commercial backing, the dealer involved did not have a gallery in a formal sense. The *Galerie de 'L'Effort Moderne'* was only opened in March 1918. [. . .]

[Despite art critic Louis Vauxcelles's opposition to Cubism and criticism of Léonce Rosenberg], I do not wish to make him personally responsible for this victory of 'conservatism'. His attitudes and actions were symptomatic of general conditions in the art market which constituted a decisive obstacle to the 'Effort Moderne' as it was originally conceived. These can be resumed as follows: with some fluctuations, the market for modern painting developed rapidly from 1918 onwards; however, the demand for contemporary art had two fundamental characteristics—it was orientated towards individual originality as opposed to collective, disciplined, innovation, and it was unresponsive to art which inclined to non-figurative, 'pure' plastic values. This can be illustrated by looking at the strategy of two other art dealers—Paul Guillaume and Paul Rosenberg—and by considering the evidence of picture sales in the years after the war.

Paul Rosenberg and Paul Guillaume are directly comparable to Léonce Rosenberg in some respects: they emerged as prominent commercial backers of modern art at roughly the same time as he did, and they became interested in some of the same artists. Paul Guillaume, advised by Apollinaire, had also tried to engage the painters formerly attached to the *Galerie Kahnweiler*, while Paul Rosenberg, after the war, became the dealer of Picasso, Braque, and eventually Léger. However, neither of them supported Cubism as a movement, and in different ways the balance of their activity was anti-Cubist. Paul Guillaume had begun his career with a stock of *art-nègre* and some de Chiricos, but during the war he broadened the range of his commercial interests: on one hand he tried to buy work by the leaders of the pre-war avant-garde, and on the other he patronized younger artists working in the 'modern' figurative mode characterized by the paintings of Modigliani, whom he supported in 1915. The eclecticism of this policy is well reflected in an exhibition which marked the high point of his immediate post-war career—it was centred around six paintings by Derain, whose dealer he was to become, and included, notably, paintings by Matisse, Picasso, Kisling, Modigliani, de Chirico and Utrillo. Paul Rosenberg was more selective in his support for contemporary painting—he specialized in the 'masters' of the nineteenth century, whose work was now extremely valuable. This fact had the effect of emphasizing the lines of continuity between the modern artists he exhibited and the art of the past. It also inclined him towards painters in whose work such links were relatively easy to establish—although he was not apparently tempted by the archaism of Derain, he began buying from Picasso shortly after the development of his Ingresque style and from Braque at a time when echoes of Chardin and Corot became a prominent aspect of his work. The first modern artist Paul Rosenberg had supported was Marie Laurencin, whose painting combined elements of the modern 'primitive' with a style and subject matter reminiscent of the Rococo; in 1920 and 1921 he gave exhibitions to two painters making deliberate, and rather clumsy, efforts to reconcile the avant-garde with tradition—André Lhote and Bissière.

The significance of this comparison is that both Paul Rosenberg and Paul Guillaume were highly successful as dealers. Paul Guillaume, who had begun his career without either capital or an important stock of paintings, was a very wealthy man by the end of the 1920s, with a 'personal collection' worth millions of francs. Paul Rosenberg was, from the first, an 'Establishment' dealer and his support for a contemporary artist virtually guaranteed success—it is symptomatic of his influence that shortly after joining the gallery Braque had a large house and studio built for himself near the Parc Montsouris. Léonce Rosenberg, in contrast, was generally held to have failed in commercial terms. Certainly, his artistic policy was difficult to sustain on the market, as a consideration of the evidence shows. [. . .]

The most important body of evidence concerning the market response to Cubism . . . is constituted by the records of the Kahnweiler auctions, held between 1921 and 1923. These sales, the consequence of French government policy in respect of sequestered German property, placed just over 700 paintings by Braque, Derain, Gris, Léger, Picasso and Vlaminck on the market. Léonce Rosenberg was directly involved—he was the expert responsible for cataloguing and estimating the items, and he had backed the authorities' decision to hold the auctions, which was opposed by a significant section of the artistic community. He saw them as contributing to the victory of Cubism, but this interpretation was not justified by the results. [. . .]

[. . .] A number of important facts emerge from it: firstly, all the painters except Vlaminck saw their prices fall dramatically over the sequence of sales—this is a demonstration of the consequences of 'flooding' a specialist market, and also shows the influence of the economic depression of 1921–22; secondly, the market's estimation of Derain placed him in a different category from all other five artists; thirdly, in commercial terms, the four Cubist painters were not seen as a 'movement' but as four separate cases, each of which was judged differently; fourthly, the two painters who were still, in 1921, identified with a Cubist avant-garde—Léger and Gris—were more or less totally rejected. In addition, detailed analysis of the results indicates that buyers discriminated against 'difficult' work within the production of individual painters—paintings by Braque and Picasso of between 1910 and 1912 (incidentally, their most 'collective' phase) tended to obtain lower prices than others and the same was true of Fauve and proto-Cubist paintings by Derain.

There are three senses in which these auctions were important in relation to the Cubist 'Call to Order': they showed that the market refused to endorse this call; they made any attempt to sell Cubism in the future more difficult; and they brought out the extent to which the 'pioneers' of Cubism no longer identified with it. Almost all of the artists involved in the sales had publicly opposed them. They argued that the release of so many paintings at one time would lower their market 'rating', but underlying this, I believe, was resentment of Léonce Rosenberg's use of their old work to publicize a 'style' which they rejected. Only this, I think, can explain the violence of Braque's reaction in publicly striking Rosenberg at the first viewing session. Braque had left the *Galerie de 'L'Effort Moderne'* in 1920, and between 1919 and 1921 his work had evolved away from geometrical, abstract, composition, towards a 'painterly' exploitation of a simplified Cubist mode of representation. This change had been accompanied by an increase in his commercial success and in his reputation. Consequently, the sale *en masse* of his pre-war work represented a serious threat to the development of his career, and it is noticeable that between 1921 and 1924 he made a very clear attempt to distance his work from Cubism. For the other artists involved, the situation was less serious: the conflict of the old work with the new was less acute in the case of Derain and Vlaminck; Picasso had already established himself on the Parisian art market and did not feel threatened by the revelation of his earlier 'extremism'—although it is worth noting that Paul Rosenberg apparently dissimulated the Cubist side to his production in 1924; Léger remained attached to the *Galerie de 'L'Effort Moderne'* and seems to have accepted the marginal status which this involved—although, again, it is interesting to note that he produced his most 'traditional' paintings between 1920 and 1924.

MICHAEL C. FITZGERALD, *Galeries Georges Petit*

Excerpt (pp. 190–95) from "Lord of the Jealous Wood," in *Making Modernism: Picasso and the Creation of the Market for Twentieth-Century Art* (Berkeley: University of California Press, 1995), 190–204. Copyright © 1995 by Michael C. Fitzgerald. Reprinted by permission of Farrar, Straus and Giroux, LLC; Michael C. Fitzgerald; and the Watkins/Loomis Agency.

On June 16, 1932, a lavish retrospective of Picasso's work opened in Paris at the Galeries Georges Petit. [. . .]

Displaying 225 paintings, seven sculptures, and six illustrated books, the exhibition was a blockbuster. Apart from its sheer size, the show ranged across Picasso's career from 1900 to the early months of 1932. Yet, for all its similarity to the giant museum exhibitions that would follow, it did not include a single work lent by an institution and it was not organized by a cultural foundation. The lenders were the powerful financiers and industrialists of America, such as Chester Dale and Stephen Clark, whose collections would contribute so much to the holdings of the Museum of Modern Art and the National Gallery; the aristocrats of France, including Baron Gourgaud and the Viscount de Noailles, who would similarly enhance the Beaubourg's collections; and the cosseted Swiss collectors, such as G. F. Reber and Joseph Müller, whose works would grace the museums of Zurich and Basel, among others.

At the time, several of the institutions to which these lenders ultimately contributed did not yet exist, and very few of those in operation sought contemporary art, even that of Picasso. As the decade passed, they would begin to expand their collections and, in the process, take on the function of exhibition organization previously fulfilled primarily by the commercial galleries. Not only would the Georges Petit exhibition travel to the Zurich Kunsthaus, but it would serve as the model for the Picasso retrospectives staged at the Wadsworth Atheneum in 1934 and the Museum of Modern Art (in conjunction with the Art Institute of Chicago) in 1939–40.

As museums assumed the role of defining contemporary artists' careers for the public, dealers receded into the background, yet they continued to play essential roles. Curators frequently relied on dealers' knowledge of artists' work and sought their assistance in securing the loans of art and the substantial sums required to realize large retrospectives. Despite the dealer's lower profile, the great exhibitions of the 1930s were in many ways the culmination of the promotional program Picasso and Paul Rosenberg had initiated over ten years before.

In the early thirties, the market for contemporary art was still dominated by a handful of private collectors. Galleries that had seen ballooning numbers of buyers during the late twenties were left with vast oversupplies. Among the sixty-two lenders to the Petit exhibition, fourteen were dealers, who contributed the lion's share of works in the show from their bulging inventories. Without doubt, Paul Rosenberg led the group. But to the public eye, it was the prominent collectors, who swept into Paris for the celebratory dinners and opening party, that certified the vernissage as a gala event. Such scenes had been common at Picasso's openings since his inaugural show at Rosenberg's gallery, but this time the proceedings were on a grander scale. Shirking such glamour, Picasso confided to the American reporter that he planned to skip the opening and go to a movie.

Besides seeming odd for a man who was said to attend "every reception and elegant evening," his remark is particularly surprising since Picasso was the curator of the show. Not only had he played a large role in selecting the works but he had also installed them: "I've been hooking these things on the wall for six days now and I've had enough of them" is what he was reported as saying. Despite his evident fatigue, his dismissal of the opening is all too characteristic of the contradictory personas he had long cultivated. And according to Sidney Janis, Picasso indeed failed to appear. [. . .]

[. . .] The financial disasters spreading from the crash of the American stock market had overwhelmed the art market much as had the panic of the early 1920s. But this time it would not soon be reversed. In these extremely uncertain times, the dealers did indeed need to take the temperature of the Picasso market with great care because they could not count on the escalating prices that had fueled the profits and widening audience of the mid- and late twenties. Such difficult times required arrangements different from the freewheeling competition of the twenties, when the entrepreneurial dealers such as Paul Rosenberg, Paul Guillaume, and the Bernheims had prospered. The Galeries Georges Petit was a paradigm of the new relationships among dealers and collectors that formed in the early thirties.

Although bearing an illustrious name in the history of modern art, the gallery was far from its origins when the Picasso retrospective hung in its vast halls on the rue de Sèze. Founded in the late 1880s, it had by the 1890s wrested many of the Impressionists from their first dealer, Durand-Ruel, and presented such important exhibitions as Monet's *Mornings on the Seine* and Norman coast series. According to Emile Zola, who knew the Parisian art world inside out, Petit was the "apotheosis" of dealers when the Impressionist market soared and competition among *marchands*, including Paul Rosenberg's father, became intense. Yet despite a flamboyant sense of fashion, Petit did not follow the path of Rosenberg or the Bernheim brothers by renewing his stock with artists of the twentieth-century avant-garde. Characteristically, one of his last productions before his own death in 1921 was the estate sale of Degas's studio.

Petit's gallery passed into the hands of his more farsighted competitors. Having had a share in the business for decades, the Bernheims took control after his death and, in partnership with a colleague, Etienne Bignou, used the gallery primarily as an auction house throughout the twenties. Ironically, the crash of 1929 and its widening repercussions in Europe seemed to offer the opportunity to reinvigorate the aging institution.

Beginning in 1930, the Bernheims and Bignou responded to the hopeless state of the market by convincing their colleagues in the trade to band together to present exhibitions that, though no longer affordable for individual dealers, offered the possibility of generating sufficient publicity to make them worthwhile. Rather like the war period, the early years of the Depression shattered many old alliances between artists and dealers but forged new consortiums among former competitors. [. . .]

Instead of dividing the dealers, the Depression encouraged alliances between those who already dominated the market. While the lesser figures went broke, the Bernheims, Rosenbergs, and Wildensteins worked in greater concert than they ever had before. With the disappearance of most clients, their fierce competitiveness subsided into cooperation for self-preservation. [. . .]

Besides a truce among dealers, this period saw another development that seemed to overturn fundamental relationships: instead of keeping collectors at arm's length, dealers formed business partnerships with some of their best customers. In the early 1920s, Paul Rosenberg had fought bitterly to keep John Quinn from coming between him and Picasso; yet, by the end of the decade, Bernheim and Bignou allowed Chester Dale, a collector as important as Quinn, to buy a large block of stock in the Galeries Georges Petit. In later years, Dale was quite candid about his motives. Like Quinn, he wanted to gain quicker and more comprehensive knowledge of which pictures were available and to reduce the prices he paid by eliminating the dealer's markup. Perhaps the Bernheims and Bignou accepted him on the board of the gallery because they knew he was too skilled at business to be kept in the dark. Although Dale accused them of sometimes trying to exclude him from management decisions . . . he effectively became both a dealer and a client in the tradition of shifting alliances that characterizes the art market.

RAYMONDE MOULIN, *Painting as a Safe Investment*

Excerpt (pp. 20–22) from "Antecedents," in *The French Art Market: A Sociological View*, trans. Arthur Goldhammer (New Brunswick, NJ: Rutgers University Press, 1987), 19–24. Copyright © 1987 by Rutgers, the State University. Reprinted by permission of Rutgers University Press.

The market had just begun to recover from the Depression when war broke out. The economic function of painting as a hedge against inflation then became clear. Along with gold, foreign currency, stocks, and other scarce goods, painting was not only a good investment in times of inflation but a way of protecting one's fortune from government control. Paintings, easily concealed and readily traded, provide a means of evading the watchful eye of the fiscal authorities. More than a commodity, they could be used as a means of payment in international trade; a deed of sale for a painting could easily compensate a banker for handling an overseas financial transaction.

The nation's economic trials did not affect people in different walks of life in the same way. In hard times producers and merchants often profit as customers bid up the price of scarce goods. As consumption goods disappeared from the market, paintings became increasingly attractive to buyers. Illicit profits could be protected from confiscation by the tax authorities through investment in tapestries, rare books, stamps, or paintings. Black-marketeers looked to painting not only for financial safety but also for social prestige and personal satisfaction. They turned to dealers who offered them decorative paintings of relatively small size, suitable for hanging in relatively modest modern apartments. Still lifes, especially bouquets of flowers, proved particularly popular during the war, no matter when they were painted; this popularity continued even after the war was over. Landscapes were also popular, especially those by eighteenth-century Italian painters and by impressionists. Impressionist paintings and their byproducts became familiar and easy to comprehend; they combined the charm of nature and the outdoors with an air of easy living. [. . .]

Although the prices paid for old masters remained higher in general than those paid for the best modern paintings, the gap steadily diminished. Degas, Renoir, Cézanne, and Seurat were already "super values." But prices paid for twentieth-century masters were increasing just fast enough to offset the decrease in the value of the franc. By contrast, innovative modern painting from surrealism on was pacing the market. [. . .]

Apart from the unusual economic conditions, the political situation under the German occupation had direct repercussions on the art market. As part of their anti-Semitic policy the Germans confiscated paintings from private collectors . . . and dealers. . . . Old masters were simply confiscated when they belonged to Jews and purchased (sometimes by coercion, sometimes not) in other cases. [. . .]

While the "collaborationist" art market prospered, many Jewish-owned galleries were closed down. Before the war Jewish merchants played a prominent part in the sale of paintings as well as jewelry and furs. Some galleries survived under new names (the Kahnweiler Gallery became the Louise Leiris Gallery, for example) or in different countries (Georges Wildenstein and Paul Rosenberg left for the United States). Others, such as Bernheim-Jeune, Marcel Bernheim, Katia Granoff, Pierre Loeb, and Mouradian-Valloton, ceased operations until the liberation.

9

ART CONSUMPTION IN INDUSTRIAL AMERICA

During the second Industrial Revolution, the technological advances in transport and communications were adopted widely in Western Europe and, especially, in the United States. The accelerated rate of expansion of rail and telegraph lines after 1870 allowed unprecedented movement of people and ideas, while the invention of electrical power and telephones boosted industrial outputs. The sweeping changes created a new, wealthy class of American industrialists and bankers almost overnight. In the 1870s, there were one hundred millionaires in the United States; in 1892, more than four thousand. By 1916, that number had increased another tenfold (Cannadine 2014, 17). By 1929, according to Fernand Braudel (1992, 3:76), New York had taken over as the center of the Western European world-economy.

Yet the United States was slow to establish an artistic community. In the early nineteenth century, art had no "natural defenders in America, no establishment of professionals and connoisseurs" to encourage the making of art (Harris 1982, xi). By the 1860s Americans had started to recognize the value of artistic labor. However, cultural expectations had been shaped by a legacy of British values, including the preference for art that instructs the public rather than possessing pure "sensory appeals" (Harris 1982, xiii). The calls of clergy, conservatives, and moralizers for art to educate and improve American citizens constrained choice of subject matter—to the detriment of artistic excellence—and American art failed to achieve legitimacy in the nineteenth century. Collectors' preference for European art further inhibited art production in the United States.

The late nineteenth-century economic downturn in Britain prompted the selling off of many major art collections. Thanks to the activities of enterprising dealers, such as the (in)famous Joseph Duveen, a lively late nineteenth- and early twentieth-century transatlantic secondary art market emerged. Dealers competed to secure the most outstanding Old Masters and English portrait paintings and easily persuaded wealthy Americans that these were the pictures they needed to cement their new elite status.

Transatlantic voyages had become less costly and less time consuming with the advent of steamship lines. By the 1890s, travel time from New York to Britain was reduced to just over six days. Meanwhile, the new transatlantic cable installed in 1866 enabled more efficient communications between the continents. The free and rapid flow of information greatly benefited the secondary art markets in London and Paris. Wealthy Americans traveled to Paris regularly to purchase the latest fashions, luxury goods, and, especially by the 1890s, paintings produced by French artists.

American collectors also relied on dealers and advisers to locate works in Europe and present them (either through description, reproduction, or in person) for purchase. These American collector–adviser partnerships became famous in their own right: Bernard Berenson scouted for Isabella Stewart Gardner; Joseph Duveen scouted art and collectibles for J. P. Morgan; and John Carstairs of the New York–based Knoedler Gallery worked tirelessly on behalf of Henry Clay Frick. European art historians and curators, such as the Dutch and German museum directors Cornelis Hofstede de Groot and Wilhelm von Bode, also advised American collectors on what to purchase and, in addition, did not hesitate to authenticate Old Master paintings the Americans were especially keen to buy.

To compete with the French artists American collectors preferred, American artists left for Europe and enrolled in Paris's prestigious École des Beaux-Arts or one of the many private academies and studios in the city. The artists studied the masterworks collected in the Louvre and the avant-garde paintings on display in regular exhibitions. The Americans established their own professional credibility by showing their work at the Paris Salons, world's fairs, and other important exhibitions, such as the Salon d'Automne, that were open to foreigners.

The experience of Paris transformed American art. As Henry James remarked in 1887: "It sounds like a paradox, but it is a very simple truth, that when to-day we look for 'American art' we find it mainly in Paris. When we find it out of Paris, we at least find a great deal of Paris in it" (James 1887, 683).

MICHAEL LEJA, *Touching Pictures by William Harnett*

Excerpts (pp. 128, 140–42, 145–50) from "Touching Pictures by William Harnett," in *Looking Askance: Skepticism and American Art from Eakins to Duchamp* (Berkeley: University of California Press, 2007), 128–52. Copyright © 2007 University of California Press.

Trompe l'oeil painting was frequently described in [nineteenth-century] press reports as eliciting highly animated responses from its audiences. Viewers are said to have wagered whether the paintings presented illusions or the real things . . . ; or to have poked the pictures with canes and umbrellas; or to have tried to make off with the dead rabbit or pheasant, remove letters from the painted letter rack, or take down the violin to play it. William Harnett was the most prominent and influential painter of these illusions working in Philadelphia and New York in the late nineteenth century. Writers marveled at his paintings and sometimes praised them extravagantly as among "the most remarkable illusions ever produced by the brush of an artist." Such claims stand out even in the hyperbolic commentary on contemporary illusions. Newspaper articles discussing Harnett's work sometimes mentioned that a police guard had been stationed nearby to ensure that viewers kept their hands off. When his painting *The Old Violin* was exhibited at the Cincinnati Industrial Exposition in 1886, journalists wrote that spectators attempted with their fingernails to remove the newspaper clipping brilliantly rendered just below and to the left of the violin. One Cincinnati reporter even admitted having run his own hand over that clipping: "While the iron hinges, the ring and staple and the rest are marvelous, the newspaper clipping is simply a miracle. The writer being one of those doubting Thomases who are by no means disposed to believe their own eyes, was permitted to allay his conscientious scruples by feeling of it, and is prepared to kiss the book, and s'help me, it is painted." [. . .]

One of the features of Harnett's paintings much admired by early commentators was the strong impression of sensuous texture radiated by the still-life objects portrayed in them. The surfaces of familiar things acquired heightened tactility through Harnett's use of lighting and chiaroscuro as well as through his juxtaposition of contrasting materials. One period commentator was explicit on this point: "The artist shows the highest skill in the representation of textures. The wood is wood, the iron is iron, the brass is brass, the leather is leather. The fur of the rabbit and the feathers of the birds tempt the hand to feel their delicate softness." Another author, writing of the painting *Ease,* observed that "the table cover, a felt cloth of peacock blue with a rich figured border in several shades of brown, is painted so that the eye feels its texture. . . . [I]n every detail of the great variety of textures thus presented to the artist for his skill to reproduce, he has been sufficient to the task."

The tactile emphasis on surface and texture noted by these authors is magnified in the paintings by the signs of age and wear on the objects depicted. This is a quality the artist deliberately sought, as he said in a rare interview published in the *New York News* in 1889 or 1890: "The chief difficulty I have found has not been the grouping of my models, but their choice. To find a subject that paints well is not an easy task. As a rule, new things do not paint well. I want my models to have the mellowing effect of age. . . . [From older] pieces I can get the rich effect that age and usage gives to it—a soft tint that harmonizes well with the tone of the painting."

Not only the soft tint of these used objects appealed to Harnett, I would argue, but also the strong character and expressiveness they acquired from wear. Some of his paintings represent with extraordinary care the worn leather of book bindings: paper softened and creased from use, and wood smoothed by handling. As an index of sustained tactile contact—touching, holding, using—wear implies a residual human presence, which Harnett's paintings maximize and highlight. [. . .]

That the objects rendered so substantially and palpably in Harnett's still lifes are also endowed with the luster that comes from much handling enhances their tactile sensuousness for viewers. This feature merged with the rich variety of tactile sensations typically arrayed in his pictures to provoke an instinctive psychological response—a desire for tactile gratification. This desire may be compelling even if there is little or no deception in the illusion. The impulse to touch Harnett's paintings is not simply a check against the limited evidence provided by vision but a synesthetic response to a strong visual evocation of tactility. [. . .]

That Harnett's paintings develop a complex rhetorical apparatus for leading the viewer from seeing to touching situates them near the heart of turn-of-the-century visual culture in the United States. In the world of commercial visual amusements thriving in that culture, the provocation to bodily response met the standard of successful realism. [. . .] Although the sphere and importance of vision were expanding at this time, with the city and its inhabitants increasingly becoming aestheticized as picturesque and spectacular, visual experience was not becoming autonomous. In the realist aesthetic seeing was incomplete if it did not culminate in touching, which was implicitly more immediate, gratifying, and perhaps reliable than vision.

Another contemporary realm in which seeing led to touching comprised marketing, advertising, and commodity display, which were among the most dynamic spheres of turn-of-the-century visual culture. Inciting an impulse to touch and to hold through visual signs effectively stimulated a desire to have and to buy. The period's new experts on commodity display acknowledged that one reliable route from seeing to wanting passed through touching. For example, L. Frank Baum, now much better known as the author of many children's stories (including the *Wizard of Oz* series) but at the time a leading authority on the design of shop windows, published an important book on this subject in 1900. Baum's fundamental objective in *The Art of Decorating Dry Goods Windows* was to teach marketers effective techniques for displaying commodities.

The first step is to attract the look of the passerby with color and spectacle. Once that is accomplished, the display must lead from spectacle to desire, from looking to holding and having: it must "arouse in the observer cupidity and a longing to possess the goods you offer for sale." Baum's recommendations frequently acknowledged, albeit implicitly, that textural contrast could effect this progression. He extolled cheesecloth as background material over silks and satins, and he proposed combining linens with china and lamps. The book described elaborate styles of folding and draping cloth to maximize its weight and texture.

Textural variety figured prominently in Baum's discussion as an attribute of "attractive" displays. For example, the book pictures an "artistic" showcase to illustrate the progression Baum recounts from seeing to having: "The goods shown are laces, trimmings, handkerchiefs, and gloves, and the beauty of the display attracted the eye of many customers of the store and induced them to examine and purchase the goods."

The power of Harnett's paintings to arouse an impulse to touch the objects portrayed would probably have intrigued contemporary marketers of commodities, and many of his patrons in fact worked in the dry-goods trade. Prominent art collectors and art institutions at the time dismissed Harnett's paintings as mechanical and superficial, and as a result, his work circulated in idiosyncratic markets, outside normal channels for fine art. Once Harnett had established his reputation with some dry-goods merchants in Philadelphia in the late 1870s, it spread to others throughout the country, largely by word of mouth and personal contact. Moreover, dry-goods stores sometimes exhibited his paintings: in Philadelphia, Strawbridge and Clothier displayed one in its counting house, and Wanamaker's showed some in its windows. At Harnett's death, the *Dry Goods Economist* boasted of the support he had received from the trade: "It is gratifying to the dry goods trade that so many of his masterpieces should be in the hands of dry goods merchants of this country."

The powerful synesthetic effect was only one feature of Harnett's paintings that would have appealed to the dry-goods merchants who bought and exhibited them. Even more important, these paintings made manufactured objects represent so much that was desirable. I have noted already that Harnett's way of selecting, arranging, presenting, and painting objects made them powerful signifiers of fantasy worlds of comfort and leisure, of strong human presence, and of material fullness. Imbuing mass-produced commodities with such signifying power was becoming the core ambition of marketers at this moment, when a consumer economy was being born. They were learning to turn goods into signs as a means of generating consumer desire, even in the absence of a real practical need for the object. In the words of one contemporary expert, "People used to buy what they needed, now it's what they want; and that want is created by store display or advertising."

Harnett's paintings were masterly demonstrations of the possibilities in this realm. In them manufactured goods eloquently evoke worlds of comfort and ease, of pleasurable states of mind, of personal identity, and of interpersonal contact. Advertisers were developing representational strategies for producing similar effects at this very time. [. . .]

Karl Marx had already astutely described how through commodities a capitalist economy both conducted and obscured social relations. Under capitalism, he wrote, the dominant social relation is between individuals as possessors of commodities. Harnett's paintings gave a powerful form to this insight by leading viewers to infer an unseen individual whose cherished personal belongings were the medium for imaginary social communication.

To return for a moment to the theme of nostalgia in Harnett's art: much has been made of the suggestion, in the well-worn artifacts Harnett preferred, of artisanal products rather than mass-produced commodities. The objects may indeed call up "precommodity artifacts and eras," when the marketplace was communal and use value took priority over exchange value. [. . .] But if that is true, it cannot be the whole story. Objects are fetishized in these paintings: they are savored not for their practical utility but for their capacity to communicate mood and meaning. Their value no longer resides in their utility but in some imaginary history of past use. This imaginary history corresponds all too neatly to the imaginary future happiness stored in the commodity. Harnett's cherished models were objects that appeared to have made good on their promised satisfactions, indirectly verifying the claims of commodities. In fact, objects that on the surface elude the classification "commodity" are all the more effective for picturing the transformations involved in commodification. As less threatening carriers of such meanings, they could participate in a form of Freudian displacement.

For Marx, the root of the social content of a commodity was the human labor that produced it, which was effaced in the commodity's seemingly natural and intrinsic value. Harnett's paintings, however, construe the social character of goods as possession and prolonged use. The goods through which humans structure and conduct richly textured lives not only help individuals develop social identities but themselves become imprinted with the developing identity through extended physical contact in use and through association with other goods. This two-way process of identification gives goods a central place in social life. Harnett's paintings did not portray the stunning acquisitions of Gilded Age robber barons, which signaled certain features of identity (wealth, power, and taste) so assertively that they resisted reciprocal imprinting from their possessors. Harnett preferred to show less exalted goods involved in more complex processes of social representation. It is not Thorstein Veblen's notion of conspicuous consumption but Mary Douglas's (1979) theory of social communication through goods that seems most relevant to Harnett's still lifes. In them, goods generate (illusory) social relationships richer than mere competitiveness and serve as a nonverbal medium for creative communication.

KEVIN M. MURPHY, *Winslow Homer as Entrepreneur*

Excerpts (pp. 147–49, 154–55, 157–58) from "Painting for Money: Winslow Homer as Entrepreneur," *Winterthur Portfolio* 37, nos. 2–3 (2002): 147–60. Copyright © 2002 by The Henry Francis du Pont Winterthur Museum, Inc.

[Winslow] Homer used established exhibition methods that were available to late nineteenth-century American artists—art academies, private clubs, and expositions. Yet he did not take advantage of one common and time-honored method of selling art: commissions from patrons. [. . .] Homer clearly believed his best chance for financial reward lay in the open market rather than contracting with a patron on an arbitrary payment based on the size and potential quality of a painting. [. . .]

Homer's reliance on the open market rather than conventional forms of patronage creates an interesting parallel to his choice of subject matter. Indeed, it is fitting that an artist who specialized in painting scenes of modern American life—whether the reality of the Civil War, the latest fashions and games, new roles for women in education and industry, or technological advances in lifesaving—marketed these works using a mixture of traditional sales venues, including academies and private clubs, as well as those more recently available to American artists, such as expositions and dealers. Homer understood and embraced new forms of marketing, becoming not just a painter of modern America but a businessman in the modern mode. [. . .]

Homer exhibited consistently at the National Academy's annual exhibitions until 1880. . . . He stopped because . . . he felt that the academy's hanging committee poorly displayed his works, which were hung in a dark and narrow hallway where viewers—and potential buyers—could not view them in decent light or from a proper distance. [. . .] Even after Homer stopped showing annually at the National Academy . . . other public exhibition spaces—such as the Pennsylvania Academy of the Fine Arts, Chicago Art Institute, Carnegie Institute, Boston Art Club, and American Water Color Society— remained important venues for his work and allowed him to exhibit to a larger and more diverse audience than his dealers could reach.

Homer, like his peers, also exploited the popular world's fairs and expositions held throughout the late nineteenth and early twentieth centuries. He exhibited at many: the 1867 Exposition universelle in Paris; the Centennial International Exposition in Philadelphia in 1876; the World's Columbian Exposition in Chicago in 1893; the 1900 Exposition universelle in Paris (where the French government purchased *Summer Night*); the 1901 Pan-American Exposition in Buffalo, New York; and the Louisiana Purchase International Exposition in St. Louis, Missouri, in 1904. Although his participations yielded mixed financial returns, the expositions . . . allowed Homer to exhibit in national and international cities where he lacked dealer representation.

In addition, Homer exhibited and sold work at private social clubs in New York City. Several of these, such as the Union League, the Century Association, and the Lotos, held periodic art exhibitions where work was shown and sold to members. [. . .] Prominent, wealthy clubmen, including [Thomas] Clarke, William T. Evans, and George A. Hearn, were among the most important collectors of his work.

These men helped Homer's career beyond simply purchasing his works. Clarke, for example, subsequently exhibited paintings that he had bought from Homer at a variety of venues, including the social clubs he frequented. [. . .] An example of Clarke's positive, if indirect, role in Homer's success is the landmark and well-publicized sale of his extensive collection of American art, including thirty-one works by Homer, in 1899. [. . .] Homer understood the effect of Clarke's auction on his financial success and wrote to the collector soon after the auction, thanking him. [. . .]

[. . .] Homer sent practical advice [to his dealers] on how to display his works for maximum effect. In mid-1888, Homer asked [Boston dealer Eastman] Chase to display his etchings from December 1 until Christmas Day, prime holiday shopping time. Homer wrote that he would ask Clarke to lend him *Eight Bells*, one of the oil paintings that he had made into an etching, and directed Chase to place it in his show window to attract clients into the gallery. To facilitate sales, Homer further suggested that Chase equip the space "with a pretty girl at the desk to sell." In 1890 Homer agreed to a show at Reichard's Fifth Avenue gallery only if the dealer hung his paintings on one specific wall, and his letter included a detailed plan. In 1900 he instructed Clarke how to display three marines at an exhibition Clarke had arranged at the Union League Club. [. . .]

Homer understood the need to be responsive to market demands. Many of his major paintings . . . did not sell quickly. Although Homer believed his work should cost the same as a "$3000–6000" portrait, the invisible hand of the market dictated a lower price. Rather than becoming discouraged from painting such scenes, Homer adjusted his prices accordingly. He felt strongly enough about the merit of his work to be fluid about his pricing structure; indeed, he clearly believed that it was better to get his paintings into public and private collections at a lower price than not to sell them at all. He also realized that his dealers might try harder to sell paintings if they had a greater profit margin.

Homer assisted his dealers by paying for advertising, writing advertisements, and suggesting potential clients for his work. When Homer first sent watercolors of Cullercoats to Chase for an exhibition in 1882, he offered to pay for two weeks of advertising in a newspaper of Chase's choice. Eight years later, Homer advised Reichard, who was about to have an exhibition of Adirondack scenes, on the proper clients for the images, urging the dealer to get the membership list for the Adirondack Club and other sporting groups so that invitations could be targeted to specific individuals. [. . .] In this instance, Homer's savvy marketing paid off: Reichard sold twenty-seven out of thirty-two watercolor sporting scenes in February of 1890.

The most dramatic example of the effect of Homer's commercial concerns on his work is his altering of paintings after he had exhibited them. [. . .] Indeed, he seemed to alter paintings only after exhibiting them to poor critical reception and their failure to sell.

An early example of Homer reworking a painting is *The Coming Away of the Gale*, which he first sent to the National Academy in 1883. It carried the price tag of $2,500 and did not sell. Critics were not kind, complaining that "the principal figure is conspicuously out of proportion and ill drawn; the lines of drapery are neither graceful nor natural," and the painting next surfaced in 1893, substantially reworked. The original composition included a view of Life Brigade House and lifesavers at Cullercoats, but Homer removed these elements to focus on improving the female figure that had bothered the critics. After making the changes, he was able to sell the painting to Clarke in 1893, but for the much-reduced price of $750.

FLAMINIA GENNARI-SANTORI, *J. P. Morgan's*
Renaissance Bronzes

Excerpt (pp. 309–14) from "'I was to have all the finest': Renaissance Bronzes from J. Pierpont Morgan to Henry C. Frick," *Journal of the History of Collections* 22, no. 2 (2010): 307–24. Reprinted by permission of Oxford University Press.

The intrinsic connection between [J. P.] Morgan's collecting and the development of art-historical research was particularly evident in his collection of Renaissance bronzes which, according to [German art historian Wilhelm] Von Bode, was 'the most comprehensive and probably the most important collection of bronzes to be found in private possession'. Between the 1880s and the 1900s Von Bode established a 'modern' connoisseurship within this field, thanks to his acquisitions for the Kaiser Friederich Museum in Berlin and his advice to private collectors such as Oscar Hainauer. In the process, Von Bode greatly contributed to a dramatic increase in the exchange-value of Renaissance bronzes.

In 1907 Von Bode systematized his research in his *Italian Bronze Statuettes of the Renaissance*. Rather than constructing a history of bronze sculpture, Von Bode's landmark study assembled a series of new attributions for pieces in both public and private collections. He maintained that the collecting of Renaissance bronzes had preceded its art-historical interpretation and that in order to prepare his volume he had relied on dealers and private collectors as much as—if not more than—on fellow art historians or museum curators. Von Bode wrote his account with the assistance of Murray Marks, a partner in the London art dealers Durlacher Brothers, who had identified many of the pieces, while the collector Gustave Dreyfus had drawn his attention to otherwise unknown examples in French private collections. Durlacher was at the time the main dealer in *objets d'art* active in London, largely responsible for the making of the Wallace and Salting collections and later, of the Morgan collection of bronzes.

Von Bode attributed the immense appeal of Renaissance bronzes amongst private collectors to their having been originally produced for display in a private milieu, a fact that had allowed artists to represent free-standing, nude figures. Furthermore, in Von Bode's view, the variety of their finish and their small scale revealed 'the artistic ideas of their masters' more accurately than monumental sculptures. He recognized the importance of the emulation of antiquity in the production and appreciation of small bronzes during the Renaissance, although for him their utmost historical importance was that they provided quintessential evidence of 'Renaissance's artists' ability for composition and interpretation'. [. . .]

[. . .] Morgan acquired his first bronzes in 1901 when he purchased the collection of Renaissance *objets d'art* assembled by Charles Mannheim. The English connoisseur John Henry Fitzhenry . . . drew Morgan's attention to the collection and later he negotiated its acquisition and induced Morgan to lend the objects to the [Victoria and Albert Museum].

At about the same time, Fitzhenry also introduced Morgan to George Durlacher, and through Durlacher Brothers, a few weeks after the purchase of the Mannheim collection, Morgan bought the Pfungst collection: fifty-four pieces for approximately £9,000. Henry Pfungst . . . was an English connoisseur of German origin, closely linked to Von Bode, who had assembled a notable collection of mostly functional pieces. [. . .]

In 1902 Morgan purchased through Durlacher his first bronze ascribed to Riccio, the group of *Triton and Nereid*. Also in 1902, at one of the first public sales organized in London by the Florentine dealer Stefano Bardini, Durlacher secured for Morgan one of his most important acquisitions, the extraordinary *Hercules* by Antonio del Pollaiuolo. The dealer was pleased to inform Morgan that the prices at the sale were quite reasonable because, as he wrote, 'Mr. Bardini is evidently not popular'. The *Hercules* however was extremely expensive, even though it had a controversial reputation. Durlacher wrote to Morgan:

> As regards the figure not in the catalogue ascribed to Donatello or Pollaiuolo, there is a rumour spread about that it is not of the period, although its great artistic merit has not been questioned. I have several times carefully examined it, I absolutely believe it to be as described and I hope you will accept my opinion; Mr. Bardini has given me the origin and every possible guarantee and has shown me a letter from Dr. Bode of the Berlin Museum (the greatest authority on Bronzes) speaking of it in highest terms. Nevertheless I think it my duty to inform you of the rumour as the price is sure to be extremely high.

The sum of £6,000 was indeed a high price for the statuette described in the invoice as a sketch, but Durlacher's enthusiastic endorsement and the fact that Von Bode had authenticated it, persuaded Morgan to purchase it. Durlacher was profoundly involved in the creation of Morgan's collection of bronzes, and the correspondence between collector and dealer shows the extent to which the collection was as much a Durlacher as a Morgan project. [. . .]

In 1907, Von Bode published thirty-one pieces in Morgan's possession in his *Italian Bronze Statuettes* and in the introduction he acknowledged the collection as the most important in private ownership, after that of George Salting. Von Bode advanced some of the arguments in his text on the basis of Morgan pieces. He attributed to Bertoldo di Giovanni the so called *Wild Man*, which he linked to two similar figures in the collections of the Prince of Liechtenstein and the Museo Estense in Modena. He ascribed the *Susanna* to Riccio, and he attributed the *Neptune and Sea Monster*, an exquisite group coming from the Spitzer and the Hainauer collections, to Bartolomeo Bellano, shaping the interpretation of these two artists for decades. He also based his attributions to Francesco da Sant'Agata on the so called *St Sebastian*, linking the figure to the *Hercules* in boxwood signed by the artist in the Wallace Collection. However, the attribution of the *St Sebastian* to the 'Bolognese jeweller' had already been advanced by Durlacher and by Murray Marks in the 1903 invoice. This coincidence suggests that Marks provided Von

Bode not only with information about unknown pieces, but also with suggestions that Von Bode developed in his attributions. In other words, Marks's scouting of pieces, Durlacher's marketing of them and Von Bode's 'final' interpretation of the same, were aspects of a shared effort in the simultaneous establishment of the interpretation and exchange-value of Renaissance bronzes. In this dynamic, the role of Morgan was pivotal and, as usual, vigorous.

Once the *Italian Bronze Statuettes* was published, Durlacher, Marks and Von Bode concentrated on the catalogue of Morgan's collection. Of all those commissioned for his collections, the catalogue of Morgan's bronzes, entitled, *Collection of J. Pierpont Morgan. Bronzes of the Renaissance and Subsequent Periods*, was the most ambitious from a scholarly point of view and for the painstaking care taken with its illustrations. The catalogue was immediately and unanimously praised: the collection was in fact so wide that it provided material for a comprehensive history of bronze sculpture, not only Italian and not only of the Renaissance. With a text aimed at a readership not necessarily learned in the subject, written in a style less dry than that of *Italian Bronze Statuettes*, Von Bode confirmed the attributions advanced in his previous work, grouping around them several other pieces in the collection. In particular, he analysed in great detail the numerous functional pieces—like ink-stands and hand-bells—attributing many of them to Riccio or to his workshop. He also attributed several figures to Francesco da Sant'Agata, an artist that he described as typical of the quattrocento and yet 'characterized by a peculiar modern endeavour to develop a typical beauty of form, action and supple movement'.

The catalogue of Morgan's bronzes was a collective project, coordinated by George Durlacher. It was in fact Durlacher who determined the objective of the publication: to establish a new standard of quality for the reproduction of Renaissance bronzes, crucial for both the marketing and the analysis of the pieces. [. . .]

For Durlacher, the catalogue was a means to advertise his trade, and he personally distributed it to a selection of the major European museums and collectors.

Since 1901 Morgan had lent his collection to the V&A, where it was exhibited along[side] the Salting collection in a large octagonal gallery devoted to these two loans. Arthur Skinner, director between 1905 and 1908 . . . actively collaborated in the preparation of the Morgan catalogue, overseeing the photographs and the measurement of all the pieces. Therefore, while in London, the collection formed an integral part of the V&A, even if it was exhibited separately from the rest of the collections. [. . .]

At the time of their emigration to the United States, Morgan's bronzes were the centre of attention in the London art world. When they arrived in New York they found a much wider stage through the daily press and a large public that had been waiting for years to see the collection. At the end of 1910 Morgan had decided to remove the collection to the United States for a variety of financial reasons and also to fulfil his desire to see it exhibited at the Metropolitan Museum. Once again, he took his inspiration from the London art world and from the British tradition of loan exhibitions. One of the most important of these had been that of Sir Richard Wallace's collection, organized at the Bethnal Green branch of the then South Kensington Museum from 1872 to 1875, following the transfer of the collection from Paris to London. [. . .]

The exhibition opened at the Metropolitan Museum almost a year after Morgan's death, on 17 February 1914. Some 8,000 people visited it on the opening day and a million by the end of the year. The galleries in the new North Wing of the museum displayed more than 4,000 works of art that Morgan had kept in London until 1912, largely on loan to the V&A but partly in his private residence at Prince's Gate.

In 1914, with the exception of the Metropolitan Museum of Art, no American museum or private collector had acquired or displayed Renaissance bronzes, and before the Morgan loan exhibition few Americans, besides those familiar with European museums, had ever seen them. Nevertheless, or because of that, the 'truculent bronzes,' as Frank Jewett Mather, the art critic of the *Nation*, epitomized them, were the highlights of the collection. Before the opening, the *New York Herald* described several bronzes in a lavishly illustrated article. The critic Royal Cortissoz devoted most of his review in the *Tribune* to them, praising the collection as 'extraordinarily impressive'. According to the *Sun*, on the day of the opening 'most people kept their eyes lowered, upon the little bronzes of the Renaissance, which in this collection will practically begin our American education upon this subject'. [. . .]

. . . The size, variety and eccentricity of the collection raised a fundamental issue: was it the extravagance of a monopolist who compulsively amassed the world's wealth or a cultural project of public impact? No reviewer was able to give a definite answer, but rapidly a hierarchy of values was established within the overwhelming variety of the collection. Reviewers and critics agreed that, unlike other categories of objects, medieval ivories and enamels and Renaissance bronzes provided a thread by which the development of European art could be followed. On top of that, it was suggested that these objects were artistically and morally more relevant than the rest of the collection.

Frank Jewett Mather . . . was remarkably critical: 'we have to do', he wrote in the *Nation*, 'not with a collection, but with an impressive assemblage of fine objects, of which large collections are merely ingredients'. For more than a decade Mather had been calling, from the pages of the *Nation*, for the establishment of artistic and cultural hierarchies in the somehow anarchic American art market of the time. In the case of the Morgan collection he considered only the earlier works worthy of the critic or the art historian, while the later seventeenth- and eighteenth-century pieces were good for the dealer and the auctioneer. Such discrimination was made not merely on the grounds of historical relevance but also of wider cultural and ethical values. Mather wrote:

I do not mean to decry this sprightly and entrancing art of the eighteenth century when I say that no art which ministers narrowly to the caprices of a decadent aristocracy can be as important as the art that expresses the deeper ideals of an entire people. In the finest of the medieval ivories and enamels, in a score of the truculent bronzes of the Renaissance lie to me the interest of the exhibition. This is perhaps only to insist in the truism that to express Saint Dominic, Saint Francis, Saint Louis and Machiavelli is more import than to represent Louis XV and his Barrys and Pompadours.

However, Mather's account of the bronzes was not entirely positive. He placed them in a liminal position between works of art and curiosities. . . .

For reviewers compelled to make sense of a collection of staggering value, assembled by the most important and debated financier of the time, the Renaissance bronzes came to represent a standard of artistic quality and accessibility against which to consider the rest of the collection. Rather romantically, this quality consisted in their being objects made by 'artisans' rather than 'artists' and for 'common' cultivated people, rather than 'princes'; objects with a 'touch of human experience here and there to which we respond', and whose functional purpose could illustrate the culture of the Renaissance equally, if not more vividly than painting.

KATHERINE S. DREIER, *The Armory Show*

Excerpts (pp. 1–6, 10–11, 15–17) from "'Intrinsic Significance' in Modern Art," in *Three Lectures on Modern Art* (New York: Philosophical Library, 1949), 1–30. Reprinted by kind permission of Susan Dreier.

1913—The Armory Show!

That is more than a third of a Century. A long time for an Exhibition to be remembered and yet everyone interested in Art, whether as collector, student or artist, knows of it.

What happened that this exhibition should have made such a lasting impression? It was because a whole new World of Art was revealed there—an art which belonged to our twentieth century and not to the Renaissance or even to the "Impressionists"!

It was a large exhibition. Paintings from America, France and England, from Holland and Switzerland—from Germany, Russia and Sweden. Over a thousand paintings, sculpture, drawings and the various mediums of black and white could be studied—all forms of art—from the accepted to the rejected.

Europe was seething with new ideas and new forms in art and fortunately for us here in America there were two men who had been greatly aroused by this new stimulus to the eye. Arthur B. Davies, the painter, then at the height of his fame in America, and the brilliant Irish lawyer, John Quinn, together conceived the idea of bringing over all these new expressions in Art. To accomplish this Mr. Quinn first spent almost a year at Washington persuading Congress to remove all duty from all countries on original works of art. Until then France was the only country with a low tariff on her Art, for she had succeeded to win a trade-agreement with our country where the French duty on our pork was balanced with our duty on French Art. This arrangement left a deep impress on our American culture. [. . .]

We of today look upon Art with totally different eyes from those of 35 years ago, because our eyes have grown accustomed to a larger conception of vision. It is not only the physical eye which sees, but the mind or inner-eye. Few of us are conscious of the change which has taken place within all of us. No one today would think of an 'Impressionist' painting as being difficult to see and yet I have lived long enough to have experienced one of Child Hassam's paintings of a "Haystack" being hung upside down in an exhibition in Boston, while one of Monet's paintings of a similar subject met with the same treatment here in New York! To many of the people in the '90's the 'Impressionist' paintings were very difficult to visualize, for they were accustomed to such minute details that this innovation of painting "En plein-Air" especially seeking the moment in the sunlight, which eliminates all detail, caused a confusion it is hard for us to realize today. Through Mary Cassatt, a young American painter in Paris, the paintings by Manet were especially brought to America where they were bought, for she was the sister of the President of the Pennsylvania Railroad and had many rich and influential friends who saw through her eyes, the great contribution the Impressionists were making, especially through their color in shadow. I am speaking here from recollection—not from historical data. [. . .]

. . . I was . . . tremendously interested, as were many others, in studying these new forms of Art which were being shown at the Armory Show—for they had a quality of aliveness—of belonging to this century. They released an inner tension which was of tremendous importance, for at last the bonds had been broken which bound the artist to the past. This bondage had been a devastating force—especially the attitude so prevalent at the time and still in existence today, that Art had reached its climax with the Renaissance which climax had never been repeated. Yet here was a group of men of many nations, strong enough to assert their own individual expression. It was a great experience!

One can easily understand, therefore, why after twenty years of stagnation the cry of "charlatanism" went up. It seemed to me the only way to check on the truth of this accusation was to meet the artists personally, which I did. When I saw the price they were willing to pay to retain their freedom to paint their vision, which price certainly did not conform to our idea of the "American Standard of Life", I recognized that they were stirred by deep conviction to give expression to their ideas in Art which belonged to the century in which they were living.

After the Armory Show there appeared at first a great many small galleries, as well as small magazines. But as time went on, the novelty wore off, and the small galleries and magazines vanished. It then seemed as if New York would again sink back into a commonplace self-satisfaction. To those of us who had recognized that the new forms of art were giving expression to the new ideas which were stirring the century and were being developed along with mechanical inventions, it seemed a tragedy. It was then that Marcel Duchamp, Man Ray and I decided in 1920 to establish a modest center with a reference library, where people could come and study seriously good examples of this new form in art. Thus, the Société Anonyme Museum of Modern Art was born.

Since our desire was to promote art and not our own personalities, Man Ray conceived the amusing title of calling it the Société Anonyme, which is the French for 'incorporated', and as we incorporated, we became Incorporated Incorporated. This brought out the humor which we felt belonged to the modern expression. . . . Few people have realized what an important part humor played in all those early years before the dealers took up this new form of art. Our attitude was, that we also had a right to exist and so, we took as our emblem, the head of a laughing ass to show that we, too, could laugh at ourselves.

When I think of the anger which still continues towards us I am amazed. There are always people who wish to kill us off and so, from time to time, learned or amusing books have been written as to why we are degenerates and why we should be annihilated. In 1934 Thomas Craven, the well-known Art Critic, brought out his Book *Modern Art*. He condemned us and was hailed by the blind with enthusiasm. [. . .]

The tragedy is that many people in authority cannot see the Art of a painting, even when it is expressed in realistic form and therefore, naturally they cannot see it when it is expressed in the new forms. Hence they find it difficult to discriminate between the creative Abstract painters and the so-called 'camp-followers'. That is why they scold so. When it comes down to rock bottom they cannot see what makes the Art of a painting— regardless whether it is Realistic or Abstract in form.

We, as a nation in general, have a strange attitude towards art, based, it seems to me, on our unconscious Dadaistic-approach to life. I refer to the remark—I don't know anything about Art but I know what I like!!!!! [. . .]

It is well to remember while studying Art, that there exist two Schools of Thought current in relation to Art. The one School of Thought believes that Art has developed through the ages—and the second School of Thought to which most of the Modern Group belong— believe that there is only *ART* no matter when it was produced. There is no development in that which is Art. It is well to think this through clearly, and decide which School of Thought one wants to follow—for the effect on judgment in Art is very different.

In 1923 Picasso expressed it extremely well in an interview with De Zayas which Alfred Barr has reprinted in his book *Picasso: 50 Years of His Art*. To quote: "to me there is no past or future in Art. If a work cannot live always in the present it must not be considered at all. The Art of the Greeks, the Egyptians, the great painters who lived at other times, is not an Art of the past; perhaps it is more alive today than it ever was. Art does not evolve of itself, the ideas of people change and with them their mode of expression".

It is strange how the first School of Thought persists—for one does not find it in literature and the moment one translates it into that realm of Art one sees clearly its absurdity. For no one would claim that Shakespeare was greater than Sophocles or Aeschylus or that Wordsworth or Browning were greater than Dante. Neither would they say that literature had reached its height or climax at the time of Dante or Shakespeare and had receded never again to reach such heights. One is too conscious that *"the ideas of people change and their mode of expression"* to make any such statement.

To quote further from Picasso's interview: "They speak of naturalism in opposition to modern painting. I would like to know whether anyone has ever seen a natural work of Art. Nature and Art being two different things cannot be the same thing. Through Art we express our conception of what Nature is not. Velasquez left us his idea of the people of his epoch. Undoubtedly they were very different from what he painted them. . . . From the painters of the originals, the primitives, whose Work is obviously different from Nature down to those artists who like David, Ingres and even Bouguereau, believed in painting nature as it is—art has always been Art and not nature. And from the point of view of Art there are no concrete or abstract forms but only forms which are more or less convincing lies." Here I believe that the word *illusion* would make for greater clarity. But to continue—"Cubism is no different from any other School of painting. The same principle and the same elements are common to all. The fact that Cubism has not been understood for a long time and that even today there are people who cannot see anything in it means nothing. I do not read English, an English book is a blank to me. This does not mean that the English language does not exist and why should I blame anybody else but myself if I cannot understand what I know nothing about."

SARAH GREENOUGH, *Alfred Stieglitz*

Excerpt (pp. 26–33) from "Alfred Stieglitz, Rebellious Midwife to a Thousand Ideas," in *Modern Art and America: Alfred Stieglitz and His New York Galleries* (Washington, DC: National Gallery of Art, 2000), 23–53. Copyright © 2000 Board of Trustees, National Gallery of Art, Washington.

From 1902 through 1904 the Photo-Secession gradually took shape. Its members came to include many but by no means all of this country's leading artistic photographers: in addition to Edward Steichen, Frank Eugene, Gertrude Kasebier, Joseph T. Keiley, and Clarence H. White, later Alvin Langdon Coburn, Anne Brigman, and George Seeley joined its ranks. Stieglitz ran the Photo-Secession primarily as an exhibition society, mounting shows of members' work that were presented at camera clubs, as well as art museums, international fairs, and other venues in both the United States and Europe. Fully cognizant of the power of the written word, Stieglitz also knew that both he personally and the Photo-Secession in general needed a journal—a mouthpiece for their cause— to reproduce notable photographs, frame ideological issues, refute criticisms, and garner wider support. Thus, in January 1903 Stieglitz . . . published the first issue of *Camera Work*. Ensuring its independence, Stieglitz himself, not the Photo-Secession, edited and published *Camera Work*: it owed allegiance only to "the furtherance of modern photography," and to those with "faith in photography as a medium of individual expression." Devoting "all profits to the enlargement of the magazine's beauty and scope," Stieglitz expected that *Camera Work*'s "friends" would contribute both "moral and financial" support. Moreover, from its inception Stieglitz considered *Camera Work* as a forum where a variety of viewpoints would be discussed. Early issues included not only analyses of the work of the Photo-Secession but also articles on scientific and naturalistic photography, while later ones published both plaudits and harsh criticisms of the exhibitions Stieglitz organized.

By 1905, though, Stieglitz found himself in a difficult position. Although both the traveling exhibitions of the Photo-Secession and *Camera Work* had been received with great acclaim, his position of leadership within the photographic community had been seriously eroded. [. . .] [Stieglitz needed] to take a bold step to separate himself and the Photo-Secession from what he perceived to be the mediocrity and complacency that threatened artistic photography. With the spirited urging of his trusted young protégé, the photographer and painter Edward Steichen, Stieglitz rented three small rooms on the top floor of a building at 291 Fifth Avenue in New York to use as a gallery. [. . .] Because Stieglitz feared there would not be enough good photographic work to sustain a gallery, and because both men passionately believed in the need for photography to be seen in comparison with the other arts, they proposed to exhibit not only the "very best" photographs from around the world, but also other art. . . . They hoped that by exhibiting paintings, drawings, or sculpture they would draw artists and critics into their space and thus initiate a dialogue about the relationship between painting and photography. To further stimulate a spirit of shared community and encourage a lively exchange of ideas, they also envisioned that the rooms would serve as an educational facility, making available "art magazines and publications, foreign and American," and would become a meeting place for "all art lovers."

Stieglitz and Steichen also originally conceived of the gallery as a commercial space and proposed that it would "negotiate sales in behalf of the owners of the pictures exhibited, charging a commission of 15 percent for the benefit of the Photo-Secession treasury." This dual agenda would prove to be a major point of contention. With his dislike of commercialism and his distaste for financial discussions, coupled with his own personal income, Stieglitz came to see sales, at best, as a barometer of the American public's knowledge, appreciation, and commitment to modern photography or art (or lack thereof) and, at worst, as a form of prostitution. Understandably, both artists and their potential patrons were frequently baffled by his posture that pictures needed to "find homes instead of owners" and frustrated by his often wildly inconsistent prices. As his secretary Marie Rapp Boursault later recalled, if Stieglitz thought someone was treating a work of art as if it was a commodity, "he might double the price of the painting." [. . .]

After a year of exhibiting American and European photographs at 291, Stieglitz . . . came to believe that the ideas behind the fine art movement in photography were drying up. [. . .] To rattle this growing complacency, Stieglitz exhibited paintings and drawings by the symbolist artist Pamela Colman Smith at 291 in January 1907. Defending the exhibition, he defiantly proclaimed that neither he nor the "Secession Idea" were the "servant" of any one medium or group. While he initially showed Smith's work primarily to pique the Photo-Secession, he found it was indeed highly instructive to compare drawings and photographs in order to judge photography's "possibilities and limitations." In fact, the exhibition was so successful in his estimation that for the next ten years he continued to exhibit, with ever increasing frequency, paintings, drawings, prints, and sculpture.

The early exhibitions at 291 of non-photographic works were a varied mix. . . . Yet interspersed with these shows were exhibitions—often the first in this country—of Auguste Rodin (1908, 1910), Henri Matisse (1908, 1910, 1914), Henri Rousseau (1910), Paul Cézanne (1911), and Pablo Picasso (1911), as well as presentations of younger American artists, including John Marin (1909, 1910, 1911) and Marsden Hartley (1909, 1910). [. . .]

This odd mixture of exhibitions . . . was largely the result of Stieglitz's and Steichen's belief that they needed to rotate advanced work with what Steichen referred to as "understandable" or more conventional art, and photography. [. . .] Especially during the early years at 291, he and Steichen rotated "red rags" with exhibitions of both photographs and "understandable" art. Thus, for example, in 1907 and 1908 Stieglitz strategically opened the season at 291 with an exhibition of photographs by members of the Photo-Secession, followed by a highly provocative show of Rodin's spontaneous, minimal, and, at the time, shockingly sexually explicit drawings. [. . .] Stieglitz and Steichen's aim, though, was not simply to pace their shows or humor their audience to ensure their continued visitation and it was not merely to find what Steichen later referred to as "an antidote" for more radical work. Rather, both wanted to set up a dialogue that would enable 291 visitors to see, discuss, and ponder the differences and similarities between artists of all ranks and types: between painters, draftsmen, sculptors, and photographers; between European and American artists; between older or more established figures and younger, newer practitioners. While these 1907–1908 shows were photographic and non-photographic, conventional and controversial, commercial successes and failures, all shared a common theme: all included numerous depictions of the female figure, often nude. Thus, over the course of five months, visitors to 291—both artists and the public alike—could compare and contrast photographs, paintings, drawings, and prints, all depicting the female form, by such diverse artists as Rodin, Seeley, Smith, and Matisse. [. . .] In later years, as Stieglitz became increasingly fascinated with the ideas posed by modern art, he was less scrupulous about alternating between exhibitions of photographs and the other arts or between predictable and provocative work. [. . .]

During these years Stieglitz also grew increasingly sophisticated about the entire exhibition process. Through trial and error, he came to believe that it was highly important to focus an exhibition so that it either presented new ideas, what he called a "positive advance," or was "a summing up" and clearly elucidated the development of an artist's work. Otherwise, he concluded, a show was "nothing more than a market place for the mediocre or the parading-ground for the stupid vanities of the small mind." In addition, from Steichen's example he became increasingly sensitive to the role that design, installation, framing, sequence, and juxtaposition play in an exhibition. From his intimate, daily contact with an exhibition, he came to appreciate ever more keenly how these seemingly small details affected not just the look of a show, but also the ideas it engendered, and he discovered that these things alone could provoke new ideas and new associations far beyond those originally intended by the artist. Through his love for verbal gymnastics and Socratic dialogue, he became increasingly adept at dealing with both the press and the general public, and he realized that he could attract visitors who were as interested in hearing his unconventional, iconoclastic ideas and his highly unpredictable views of the world as they were in the art itself. Finally, from experience, Stieglitz learned that he could incite the most provocative discussions—those that addressed the broadest range of issues—by presenting the most radical art. Describing the 1908 Matisse exhibition, he tersely wrote, "here was the work of a new man, with new ideas—a very anarchist, it seemed, in art. The exhibition led to many heated controversies; it proved stimulating."

RENÉ GIMPEL, *Diary of an Art Dealer*

Excerpts (pp. 234–35, 373, 389) from *Journal d'un collectionneur, marchand de tableaux* (Paris: Calmann-Lévy, 1963). Translation © 2016 Gwen Wells. Reprinted by permission of René Gimpel, London.

May 26 [1923]—With Joe [Duveen]

His success comes from his taste, his audacity, and also from his talent for organization, of which the following is an example. For twenty-five years the best art critic in England was Humphrey Ward. Joe therefore had all his articles copied in triplicate, for his three branches, with an index, and when he wants to buy a picture or an object, he checks to see whether Humphrey Ward wrote about it and what he had to say.

He is currently having bound all the letters he has received from Berenson over the past fifteen years, again with an index. In them the expert speaks about all the fine Italian paintings in all the great European collections, and since this critic has only written two or three slight books, these letters, which run to many volumes, will be of great interest. I am advising Joe to bequeath them to the British Museum, along with his firm's business correspondence, and when he says it's too secret, I reply: "Have it remain sealed for one hundred years!"

In Austria this week Joe bought a Holbein for £40,000; last week, Lord Spencer's Hals for an enormous price, as well as a Mantegna; and at Christie's two weeks ago, Van Dyck's *Portrait of Alexander Triest*, for $146,000; a Cuyp for more than $90,000. At the William Salomon sale in New York a month and a half ago he bought three vases by Orlando Fontana for $100,000; a Fragonard, *Mademoiselle Colombe*, for $40,000. In two sessions he had run up a bill of $400,000. A month ago he was buying a Dürer. At the same time he was showing me a Fra Angelico and a Rembrandt, *Portrait of a Man in a Red Hat*. A few days ago, he was selling Lord Carnarvon's Lawrence *Mother and Child* for an enormous sum; and Turner's *Queen of the Adriatic* for $300,000.

Joe tells me that Nathan Wildenstein and Arnold Seligmann bought the thirteen gouaches by Joseph Bardac for $80,000.

To compensate for his lack of knowledge, Joe surrounds himself with all the great experts. Bode and Friedlaender cost him nothing but a few gifts to the Berlin museum, but Berenson is expensive: he takes a cut of twenty-five percent of the profits, whether he's negotiating a sale, giving his opinion, or bringing in a client. I pay this percentage too. Joe has made a number of gifts to France, to the Petit Palais, to the Louvre, to various propaganda societies, and has even just been awarded the rosette of the Legion of Honor. He hopes to receive a peerage in England one day.

.   .   .

November 30 [1928]—In the United States

I've been here for four weeks and have written nothing. Very bad. I've been extremely busy and have had a great many invitations.

The American collector is prey to the hugest swindle the world has ever seen: the certified swindle. Thirty years ago the American bought so many fake paintings that he later wanted authentications. Expressly for him, experts were created and canonized; the dealer handed off the responsibility to these irresponsible types, and the client no longer had anyone to whom he could appeal for justice. So, for example, I went to see Bache, who pays enormous prices, but he has a Bellini, a Botticelli, and a Vermeer of Delft— three old paintings that are not by the masters. At Ernest Rosenfeld's, a profile in marble by a sculptor like Rossellino, which is a fake. The Detroit museum also has a fake marble bust, bought by the deplorable expert Valentiner. All this stuff came from Italy. Over a short period, the American bought ten million dollars' worth of paintings whose certificates are indefensible.

Interest in modern art is now intense, and not just in the impressionists, but also in living artists, like Matisse, who is the most expensive. Derain, Modigliani, and Utrillo are highly sought after. Same furor over modern decorative art, but just for the last six months—as a result of the Paris exhibition.

.   .   .

March 4 [1929]—The fake certificates

The scandal of the fake marbles, which I mentioned at the beginning of this notebook, blew up this winter. The Italians sold the Americans two million dollars' worth of marbles by Dossena. A laughable sum compared to the all the money made off the certificates issued by German experts to German dealers every day. Just as there were paper marks, so there are paper canvases—an easy way of bringing dollars into Germany. This morning I went to Van Diemen's gallery, where there is a show of sixteen Venetians. Three of the paintings were good, apart from the Guardis and maybe the Longhi.

Last Sunday's *Times* devoted a full page to reproducing this scandalous show that gives only a faint idea of what's being brought in.

Bode, the director of the Berlin museum, died two or three days ago. The king is dead, long live the king! The Mayers, the Gronaus will replace him. The German title Doktor impresses the Americans.

The museums are even more bent than the collectors on defending their fakes or their phony attributions.

EDITH HALPERT, *Vollard*

Excerpt from an oral history interview with Edith Gregor Halpert, 1962–63. Archives of American Art, Smithsonian Institution.

All the things that [Ambroise] Vollard told me on how to peddle art—it was wonderful. It was really absolutely wonderful, and I remember every word he said to me. My French wasn't very good, but I understood everything he said: "Never own more than fifty percent and never invest a nickel."

It was the most beautiful hunk of advice, and it started with the Gaugin business. It all started with the Gaugin story—how he bought the Gaugins [*sic*], and how he sold fifty percent for the full investment, and he sat on his fifty percent until he sold it to ten dealers to distribute, so that ten dealers would have money invested and would knock themselves out to put this guy on the map. Vollard waited until they put him on the map to a degree where he was so expensive that his fifty percent was worth about five thousand percent, and that is the philosophy of merchandising which I haven't followed. It was too easy.

It certainly was not good for the artist. It was the worst possible method for the artist, including someone like Pascin. I saw contracts. It was the most—but the French artists were happy about it. The American artists won't take it. In that way the dealer remains the villain and the artist is the poor little helpless soul the dealer takes advantage of. Yeah! I'm still waiting after thirty-six years for the time I can take advantage of an artist. In my experience there are only two artists who have been honorable, two artists who haven't taken advantage of me, who haven't tried, and as I said previously, they were Stuart Davis and Charles Sheeler.

PRESS RELEASE, *Art of this Century*

"Peggy Guggenheim to Open Art Gallery 'Art of this Century,'" n.d. (ca. October 20, 1942). Pamphlet files in the Art and Architecture Collection, the Miriam and Ira D. Wallach Division of Art, Prints and Photographs, New York Public Library.

PEGGY GUGGENHEIM TO OPEN ART GALLERY "ART OF THIS CENTURY"

Peggy Guggenheim announces the opening of her Art Gallery "Art of this Century" on October 21st, 1942 at 30 West 57th Street, New York City.

In 19__ Miss Guggenheim established an Art Gallery in London and began to collect modern works of art. Towards the end of 1939 she went to Paris where she decided to save as many paintings and sculptures as possible from the threatening Germans and bring them to America. The collection, representing examples of all 20th Century Pioneer Art Movements, arrived in America in July and December of 1941 after an escape from Europe during which it had to be disguised at times as household-goods, was hidden in a chateau near Vichy and sheltered for six months by the Musée de Grenoble. Miss Guggenheim continued to add new important works to her collection here in America and it is today regarded as the finest collection of its kind. Artists from 16 countries, France, England, Spain, Czechoslovakia, U.S.A., Germany, Italy, Russia, Greece, Poland, Switzerland, Holland, Belgium, Chile, Argentina, and Roumania [*sic*] give ample evidence of the broad scope of the collection, which include [*sic*] such famous names as: Arp, Brancusi, Breton, Braque, Calder, Chagall, Chirico, Duchamp, Max Ernst, Gris, Kandinsky, Klee, Leger, Lipchitz, Magritte, Masson, Miro, Mondrian, Ozenfant, Picabia, Picasso, Tanguy and others.

After long and careful preparations and necessary research work the collection will now be shown at "Art of this Century" where it will serve as a basis as well as a background for changing exhibitions of individuals and groups. Frederick J. Kiesler designed the galleries in four distinct parts. The Cubist and abstract paintings and sculptures will be exhibited in Gallery 1 while the Surrealist paintings, sculptures and objects will be shown in Gallery 2 and 3. Gallery 4 has been reserved for changing exhibitions as well as a yearly salon of young artists creating in America and elsewhere. In designing the galleries Mr. Kiesler has executed his ideas and plans in an entirely new way of presenting paintings and sculpture. The paintings for example will be shown without frames and appear to be suspended in midair.

Miss Guggenheim hopes that "Art of this Century" will become a center where artists will be welcome and where they can feel that they are cooperating in establishing a research laboratory for new ideas. In an explanation in regard to the aims of her gallery Miss Guggenheim comments:

> Opening this gallery and its collection to the public during a time when people are fighting for their lives and freedom is a responsibility of which I am fully conscious. This undertaking will serve its purpose only if it succeeds in serving the future instead of recording the past.

Art of this Century will open on Wednesday, October 21st, 1942 and will be open to the public daily except Sundays from 10 A.M. to 6 P.M. and on Tuesdays from 10 A.M. to 10 P.M. Admission is free at all times.

JASPER SHARP, *The Exhibitions at Art of this Century*

Excerpt (pp. 288–89) from "Serving the Future: The Exhibitions at Art of this Century 1942–1947," in *Peggy Guggenheim and Frederick Kiesler: The Story of Art of This Century,*

ed. S. Davidson, P. Rylands, and D. Borg (New York: Guggenheim, 2004), 288–347.
Copyright © 2004 the Solomon R. Guggenheim Foundation. Used by permission.

Descriptions of Art of This Century, be they artistic or architectural, rarely stray beyond
the extraordinary series of galleries created by Frederick Kiesler for the display of Peggy's
own collection of abstract and Surrealist artworks. In doing so, however, they overlook
perhaps its greatest achievement. For past the concave walls, kinetic contraptions and
sinuous blue curtain lay two small, unremarkable white rooms inside which a significant
chapter in the story of twentieth century art was written.

Between the winter of 1942 and early summer of 1947, fifty-five temporary exhibitions featuring work by nearly one-hundred-and-fifty artists were mounted in the Day-
light Gallery of Art of This Century. Seen as a whole, they constitute a substantial artistic
legacy. [. . .]

[. . .] In an approach originally formulated for her proposed museum in London,
paintings and sculptures from Peggy's permanent collection were employed on occasion
as a convenient and inexpensive basis for certain exhibitions. They were most often
shown as part of important, museum-style retrospectives of established European artists,
among them Jean Arp, Giorgio de Chirico, Alberto Giacometti, Jean Hélion, Wolfgang
Paalen, Hans Richter, and Theo van Doesburg. Others for Marcel Duchamp and Max
Ernst were planned but not realized.

But it was to the future that Peggy and her gallery advisors most often looked. A succession of young, prodigiously gifted American artists, introduced in the seasonal group
shows for which the gallery quickly became known, were subsequently invited to exhibit
there alone. In close proximity to the works of established European masters, and very
often in their presence, several, including William Baziotes, Robert De Niro, David Hare,
Robert Motherwell, Jackson Pollock, and Charles Seliger, made important débuts. Their
work, like that of others such as Richard Pousette-Dart, Mark Rothko, and Clyfford Still,
who had previously exhibited in lesser-known galleries, was thrust firmly into the sights
of critics, curators, and collectors. In providing the opportunity, Peggy succeeded in
grooming almost the entire vanguard of a movement in American post-war art whose
impact is felt to this day.

"International modern art's newest movement filled those two little rooms with paintings that were scarcely dry and sculptures still warm from their molds," wrote Rudi Blesh
several years later. "Peggy Guggenheim's museum gave them a haven during the years
when the struggle was hardest. . . . Here trooped in, with canvases under their arms, a
dozen wild youths who had found the doors of other museums closed. They liked Peggy.
They found in her a fellow spirit as daring as they. For her, history was no post-mortem:
she lived it, as they were doing."

The art they exhibited in many respects mirrored the forces that contrived to shape
Peggy's own collecting. Surrealist and fantastic works, conspicuous in the opening season, were gradually replaced by more abstract compositions. Peggy herself became

increasingly estranged from the Surrealist milieu following her separation from Max Ernst, and the voices to which she had initially listened—among them Ernst, Duchamp, and André Breton—were themselves replaced by others more closely aligned with the emerging American tendency, such as Alfred H. Barr Jr., Howard Putzel, and James Johnson Sweeney.

Another significant factor in the gallery's activity, sometimes overlooked owing to the relative absence of their works from her collection today, is the leading role played by women. Two important group exhibitions in 1943 and 1945 and a dozen solo shows for artists such as Virginia Admiral, Alice Rahon Paalen, I. Rice Pereira, Sonja Sekula, and Isabelle Waldberg, contributed to a statistic remarkable even by contemporary standards; of the many artists, known and unknown, who exhibited at Art of This Century, almost forty percent were women. Their work, and that of their male contemporaries, was purchased from the gallery by more than thirty women collectors, and reviewed by a nucleus of progressive female critics led by Maude Riley. Furthermore, Peggy's efforts to extend the reach of her gallery's programming beyond New York led to collaborations with two spirited women of similar intention—Grace L. McCann Morley at the San Francisco Museum of Art and Rue Winterbotham Shaw at the Arts Club of Chicago—and exhibitions across the country of artists including van Doesburg, Motherwell, Pereira, Picasso, and Pollock.

Whether she realized it or not, Peggy's energy and commitment to the promotion of young, emerging artists during five seasons of exhibitions ensured that neither she, nor they, would ever be forgotten. "Her museum may well be remembered chiefly for those two plain, small rooms," wrote Blesh, "where she showed the new and the unknown and argued, cajoled and persuaded every visitor "'just to buy one picture.'"

10

NEW YORK

While the United States had, by all measures, achieved economic dominance in the Western world prior to World War II, the local primary art market was slow to develop. Wealthy Americans, as one prominent art journal editor lamented, were accustomed to purchasing art from the same source as their wines and gowns—Paris—and this inhibited the formation of the critical mass of artists and collectors needed for an American artistic culture to flourish.

World War II wrought dramatic changes, however. The explosion in industrial production and commerce during the four years of the war reignited the country's economic engine. By the late 1940s, New York had become the world's largest manufacturing center, with forty thousand factories and more than a million factory workers. The city had become the world's biggest port and continued in its position as the world's largest financial capital.

As war had loomed and then throughout the conflict, European artists had fled Paris, many of them to New York. This influx of an estimated seven hundred artists, including numerous prominent modern painters, played a large role in the cultural blossoming of postwar New York. In addition, the Federal Art Project (FAP), the artistic arm of the Works Progression Administration (WPA), had enabled American artists to continue working during the Depression years. The New York–based painters Jackson Pollock and Mark Rothko were among those artists free to create without artistic constraints while receiving a salary from the US government.

Over the course of the 1940s and 1950s, Americans came to embrace American art as worthy of investment. Reports on the investment returns on modern art sold at

auction—such as the 1952 sale of the collection amassed by the French department store
magnate Ernest Cognacq, which was attended by more than fifteen hundred people and
fetched a record 302 million francs—were widely publicized in general-interest magazines. Americans took note. By 1957, the arts writer of the *New York Times* was able to
report a "peak demand for pictures" and a fivefold increase in the number of New York
galleries (Dean 1957).

DORE ASHTON, *Artists and Dealers*

Excerpts (pp. 164–68, 170–73) from "Artists and Dealers," in *The New York School: A
Cultural Reckoning* (New York: Penguin, 1983), 164–73. Copyright © 1972 by Dore Ashton. Used by permission of Viking Books, an imprint of Penguin Publishing Group, a
division of Penguin Random House LLC.

Looking back in 1955, [Clement] Greenberg found that 1947 and 1948 constituted a turning point. He wrote that in 1947 there had been a great stride forward in general quality,
and that in 1948 'painters like Philip Guston and Bradley Walker Tomlin "joined up" to
be followed two years later by Franz Kline. Rothko abandoned his "surrealist" manner;
de Kooning had his first show; and Gorky died.' His slighting reference to those who
'joined up' indicates that the long-hoped-for constellation that could be called a New York
school was becoming visible, and also viable. There was unquestionably a surge of enthusiasm among painters all over the country as they began to hear of a real movement, and
they were drawn eastward. People down at the Waldorf Cafeteria were talking away, their
ranks swelling daily. Uptown there were new galleries opening; museums were beginning
to take notice. The myths that had supported the vanguard few were slowly being con-
troverted, although the decisive moment didn't arrive until several years later.

Greenberg took note of those myths in an article in *Horizon* in October 1947, writing
that

> The morale of that section of New York's Bohemia which is inhabited by striving young
> artists has declined in the last 20 years, but the level of its intelligence has risen, and it is
> still downtown, below 34th Street, that the fate of American art is being decided—by young
> people, few of them over forty, who live in cold-water flats and exist from hand to mouth.
> Now they all paint in the abstract vein, show rarely on 57th Street, and have no reputations
> that extend beyond a small circle of fanatics, art-fixated misfits who are isolated in the
> United States as if they were living in Paleolithic Europe.

And three months later in *Partisan Review* he again referred to fifth-floor cold-water
studios, poverty and the 'neurosis of alienation.' He maintained that the myth of bohemia
in nineteenth-century Paris was only an anticipation; it was in New York that it had
become completely fulfilled, and it was clear that he believed in the myth as a constructive

force. Having already reached an art-for-art's-sake position by 1945, Greenberg found it congenial, while lamenting the 'alienation'—a term that appeared not only in his own column in *Partisan Review* but also in the writing of almost everyone else's work published there in 1948—to take solace in the fierce individualism such alienation engendered. He was attracted, as intellectuals often are, to the Promethean violence of conviction many of the downtown artists displayed when times were hard. From this band who had touched spiritual bottom he expected to forge a movement, even though he pretended to see their plight as injurious, and asked plaintively in 1947, 'what can fifty do against a hundred and forty million?'

Greenberg's discernment showed when he grasped that the real fruits of the spiritual malaise of his *peintres maudits* were those large and daring paintings that led him to speak of 'The Crisis of the Easel Picture.' It is quite possible that he got this idea from Pollock, who early in 1947 wrote in his application for a Guggenheim grant that he intended to paint 'large, movable pictures that will function between the easel and mural,' and added: 'I believe easel painting to be a dying form, and the tendency of modern feeling is toward the wall picture or mural.' Thereafter, Greenberg raised the issue again and again, always suggesting that the easel painting would be replaced by the new 'polyphonic' modes suggested in Pollock's paintings. Curiously, his article in *Partisan Review* included a number of reproductions of the work of de Kooning, whose first exhibition had been a signal event that year, and who stubbornly persisted in easel painting.

De Kooning's myth was well established. He had been considered, as [Thomas] Hess understood, a 'painters' painter' since the thirties. He was, as [his biographer Edwin] Denby has said many times, absolutely incorruptible, a man who lived a life of total honesty, and who chose the uncomfortable rather than conform to anyone else's idea of what a painter's life should be. He had always lived as a 'loft rat' and at the same time had always been a cosmopolitan. [. . .] It was apparent in his tremendously knowledgeable conversation about painting and in his deep interest in the history of art and culture. He loved the complexity of the cosmopolis, and he found in its physical appearance an excitement and beauty that he consciously tried to reflect in his paintings.

Throughout the forties, those who gravitated to New York, or who painted by day and talked with each other by night, heard stories of de Kooning's courageous resistance to blandishments both from dealers and from occasional patrons. It was well known that he and Gorky chose poverty rather than to compromise in their work. De Kooning's reputation for working slowly, scraping out, starting all over again, and never really finishing a painting, was legendary already in 1943, when Denby recalls how conscientiously de Kooning sought to avoid the gratuitously beautiful, and how, despite the chance to exhibit in a good uptown gallery if he could only produce finished pictures, de Kooning waited and worked. It was Charles Egan who at last managed to get together de Kooning's first one-man show. Egan, who is fondly remembered to this day by many of the artists he once exhibited, had long been acquainted with downtown bohemia. He was intelligent, genuinely interested in painting, and had enough humor to be acceptable to the inner circle at the Waldorf, as well as in individual studios. His own idiosyncrasies and his bohemian temperament endeared him to many painters who, even when exasperated with his dilatory appearances at the gallery, never despised him as they did so many dealers who sprang up in the late forties and early fifties. [. . .]

Peggy Guggenheim relates that when she closed up shop she tried to find a dealer willing to take on Jackson Pollock. The only one courageous enough was Betty Parsons, who also fell heir to Rothko and Still. Her first show was arranged by Barnett Newman, whose judgment and humor Betty Parsons keenly appreciated. Thereafter, Newman was a considerable force in the decisions of the gallery and, for a time, Newman, Rothko, and Still formed a distinct trio in the gallery, with Pollock somewhat apart. [. . .] Both Still and Rothko had already begun to shield themselves from the encroachment of an affluent society by provocative gestures of refusal and statements of their incorruptibility. For a dealer trying to build a market, such behavior could be very trying, but Betty Parsons, herself an artist, was not only patient, but also supportive. In their efforts to control the 'life' of their paintings, Still, Rothko, and Newman seemed to have consulted with each other. Still, in his letters to Betty Parsons, was constantly arguing against group exhibitions and art appreciation in general, and he and Rothko refused to show at the Whitney Museum, proffering arguments that were phrased practically identically. This early quarrel with the establishment grew more acute as the fame of these artists grew, and their dealers' problems increased accordingly.

All the same, the new dealers were working effectively with the museums and the small sympathetic press, and mutual interest served to create an ever-widening interest. For instance, when *Life Magazine* (1948), with rather pompous pride, presented its first Round Table on Modern Art ('in which fifteen distinguished critics and connoisseurs undertake to clarify the strange art of today') the paintings of 'young American extremists' reproduced and discussed by the experts included de Kooning's 1948 *Painting*, which had just been acquired from Egan by the Museum of Modern Art; Baziotes' *The Dwarf,* warmly defended by the Museum's own James Thrall Soby (against Greenberg's assertion that it was bad art); Gottlieb's *Vigil*, shown by Kootz the year before; Stamos' *Sounds in the Rock*; and Pollock's *Cathedral*, which had just been shown that season at Betty Parsons to the predictable praise of Greenberg and Sweeney. Both the selection of paintings and the choice of experts indicate that the newly established galleries for American vanguard art were making headway in broadcasting the importance of their venture. That so many distinguished experts—among them Meyer Schapiro, Aldous Huxley, and Georges Duthuit—could be gathered together by *Life* to consider an absurdly posed question on modern art, was in itself a measure of the need postwar America was feeling for the modern art experience.

JAMES E. B. BRESLIN, *Mark Rothko and Betty Parsons*

Excerpt (pp. 247–53) from "An Art That Lives and Breathes," in *Mark Rothko: A Biography* (Chicago: University of Chicago Press, 1993), 231–70. Copyright © 1993 University of Chicago Press, Chicago and London. All rights reserved.

Rothko wanted to be understood; he wanted to be *recognized*, to be *seen*, in the deepest sense. Yet recognition entailed its own dangers: if he *were* understood, then he was no longer an outsider—he lost his edge. For the next twenty years, as his reputation grew and he became an internationally celebrated artist, he continued to insist that he was misunderstood. If someone praised the sensual beauty of his paintings, Rothko pointed to their spirituality; but if someone else hinted at spiritual properties, he defined himself as an earthy materialist. It is as if almost *any* verbal response, any *naming* of his work, made Rothko uneasy. He wished the self displayed in his works to remain elusive, free, hard to fix; and he wanted to feel that he was still, despite success, "resisting the suction of the shopkeeping mentalities," not to mention the critical, curatorial, and art historical mentalities. Wronged and deprived, he still needed consolation, comfort, encouragement. Embattled, fighting the absorptive power of the marketplace, he stayed angry. The "unfriendliness of society"—sometimes real, sometimes imagined—acted as a necessary lever toward creativity.

In the spring of 1949 Rothko could have comforted himself by considering that now at least there were reviews to wring his hands over. Or by reading the shrewd, sympathetic essay on his work that Douglas MacAgy—the first journal essay on Rothko's work—had published in the January issue of the *Magazine of Art*. Beginning with Rothko's own remark that "a painter commits himself by the nature of the space he uses," MacAgy distinguishes between a (Renaissance) space where "things may exist separately without necessity of interrelationship and the areas between things are defined as absences of contact" and a (Rothko) space where "objects and their environment seem to give way to each other so that dramatic emphasis cannot be fixed in a permanent unity." "Identities are elusive and roles enter a shifting relationship." Rather than trying to fix Rothko, MacAgy asserted his elusiveness, portraying him as an ambitious innovator.

Rothko damned the "shopkeeping mentalities." He railed against the "stinking mess" on 57th Street. Part purist, Rothko wished to protect his paintings from the mire of the marketplace. But Rothko needed money; he sought communication; he enjoyed self-display; he liked recognition. Part pragmatist, he shrewdly managed his career. For the early part of the summer of 1948 Rothko and his wife had rented a small house in East Hampton, Long Island. Rothko worked prolifically. At the end of the visit he invited several people—among them the critic Harold Rosenberg—to view the work, and, Rosenberg recalled, "he trotted out about, oh maybe fifty paintings he had done that summer." "And I thought they were marvelous, it was just one of the most exciting visits to an artist's studio that I have ever had. He took out one painting after another and set them down. They were just absolutely terrific." Rothko was bringing out paintings he had yet to exhibit publicly—the multiforms. But when Rosenberg visited Rothko's 1949 Parsons exhibit, "I found it very disappointing because all of those terrific paintings he had done in the summer weren't in the show. He went back to New York and painted a whole show," and the new paintings "didn't have any of the variety and surprise" of the ones he'd seen the summer before. "They were simplified versions of those paintings. Having done those paintings, he then studied them and made up a format based on them."

When Rothko called the day after the opening of his Parsons Gallery show to ask about Rosenberg's reaction, the critic bluntly told him, "I thought it was lousy." "What the hell happened to all those terrific paintings you did at Louse Point?" Rothko answered that "he had talked to a friend and they had decided there was too much variety and that he should do something more identifiable." The same Rothko who was trying to eliminate recognizable shapes from his painting "wanted a recognizable image." Before the end of 1949, after one final act of simplification—reducing the number of his rectangles to two or three and expanding their size—Rothko found in his empty, fluctuating rectangles an image that created the elusive yet recognizable presence he was after.

Speaking with his students at Brooklyn College, a few years later, Rothko stressed "somebody getting territory, this is your territory, you develop something and it's yours, it's your territory. Once a territory is taken, there's no reason for somebody else to take that territory. And to emulate one by imitation would be ridiculous." In the last few years of the 1940s Rothko, Jackson Pollock, Willem de Kooning, Franz Kline, Robert Motherwell, Barnett Newman, and Adolph Gottlieb were all evolving "signature styles," unique expressions marking the individuality of the painter, yet characteristic expressions marking that individual as recognizable—as *familiar*. Soon, it will make sense to speak of "a Rothko," a form of recognition with its own set of dangers. Like so many white settlers, the painters could turn unexplored inner territory into stylistic private property. Meanwhile, for Rothko, creating an image so identifiable that he didn't need to sign the painting—his identity being dispersed throughout the canvas—fulfilled not only personal but also marketing imperatives: a recognizable object, a "name" brand, a known value, can more easily be sold.

Rothko's dealer, Betty Parsons [née Pierson], was, for better *and* for worse, no shopkeeper. [. . .] Her father's family was old New York, wealthy and conservative; her mother's family was Southern and French, more lively and intellectual, though not artistic. [. . .] It was the Armory Show, in 1913, that awakened Betty Pierson to the possibility of art, "but my family disapproved highly of this." Her family also opposed college for women. Instead, after the revelations of the Armory Show, she was permitted to study sculpture with Gutzon Borglum, who gave us Mount Rushmore. At nineteen, however, Betty Pierson married Schuyler Livingston Parsons and seemed destined to become a Long Island socialite. Three years later, having determined that Parsons drank too much, she went to Paris for a divorce, then stayed for eleven years, living on the Left Bank, studying art (mostly sculpture), getting to know Alexander Calder and Man Ray, Hart Crane and Max Jacob, Gertrude Stein and Tristan Tzara, as if destined to become an expatriate artist.

But in 1933, left broke by the Depression, she returned to the United States, living first in Hollywood (where she got to know Marlene Dietrich and Greta Garbo) and then in Santa Barbara. Continuing to study sculpture, she supported herself by giving art lessons, painting portraits, and working in a liquor store. "I always wanted to get back to New York, though." After six years on the west coast, she sold the expensive engagement ring her husband had given her and used the money to return to New York. As a result of a successful showing of her work at the Midtown Gallery, she was asked to work for the gallery as a salesperson. She then worked, for a while, at a gallery owned by Mary Sullivan who, along with Abby Rockefeller and Lizzie Bliss, had been one of the three founders of the Museum of Modern Art. In early 1940, Betty Parsons started a gallery in the basement of the Wakefield Bookshop on East 55th Street, where she showed Joseph Cornell, Saul Steinberg, Hedda Sterne, Theodoros Stamos, and Adolph Gottlieb. Betty Parsons was adventurous.

When, in 1944, the Wakefield Bookshop moved, the Wakefield Gallery closed. Mortimer Brandt, until now a dealer in Old Masters, decided to try a modern section, which he hired Betty Parsons to run. Through Peggy Guggenheim, Parsons met Mark Rothko around this time, and she arranged an exhibit of his watercolors in the spring of 1946. Rothko called this "my most successful show," saying that he had sold enough to quit teaching at Center Academy and that "one person invested more than $1000 in the stuff. So maybe there is hope." But when Brandt examined the books after the 1946 season, he concluded that the cause of modern art was hopeless, moved to a new location, and left his space at 15 East 57th Street for Betty Parsons to use. She raised $5,000—$1,000 of her own and $1,000 each from four friends—and opened the Betty Parsons Gallery in the fall of 1946.

Provocatively, the gallery opened with an exhibit of Northwest Coast Indian art, curated by Barnett Newman, now a close friend and advisor of Parsons. Newman extolled the aesthetic value of the tribal objects he had assembled, but his catalogue essay mainly appealed to the authority of the primitive in order to justify the contemporary vanguard. [. . .] The essay establishes the intellectual closeness between Newman and Rothko in the mid-1940s; it also revealed the direction of the new Betty Parsons Gallery which, among "our modern American abstract artists," would soon acquire Jackson Pollock, Mark Rothko, Clyfford Still, Barnett Newman, Ad Reinhardt, and Theodoros Stamos.

"I realized that they were saying something that no European could say," Betty Parsons later remarked. "Europe is a walled city—at least, it's always seemed that way to me. Everything is within walls. Picasso could never have done what Pollock did." Too patrician to be a mere shopkeeper, too engaged with art to make her gallery a mere "plaything," and too adventurous to play it safe, Betty Parsons soon moved into and improved upon the space vacated by Art of This Century. Samuel Kootz's gallery showed young

Americans (William Baziotes, Robert Motherwell, Adolph Gottlieb); so did Charles Egan (Willem de Kooning, Franz Kline). But from 1947 to 1951, Betty Parsons ran the vanguard gallery. She *was* old New York Society, and that could create uneasiness with her proletarian painters. But as an artist herself turning to abstraction at this time and a collector who often bought the work of her artists, Parsons realized a painter's utopian fantasy of the humane dealer. Her gallery became a place for painters to meet, talk, hang each other's shows. "On Saturday afternoons, a dozen or more artists might gather in the back room and stay several hours, and then go out to dinner together." One painter described the gallery as more like an "artists' cooperative" than a business. Clement Greenberg found it "a place where art goes on and is not just shown and sold."

"I give them walls," she said. "They do the rest." In 1946, the decor of a 57th Street gallery, with lush wall-to-wall carpeting, potted plants, long elegant couches, ornamental molding, and walls (in one case) of *boiserie* and velour, denied its commercial character and reduced art to one among many luxuries in an opulent Victorian parlor. At Betty Parsons', the walls of her two gallery rooms were white, empty of decoration; the floors were plain, wooden. Parsons had invented the physical space of the modern avant-garde gallery, which denies commercial reality by seeming to focus solely and reverentially on Art. "It was the ideal environment for the big, single-image, visionary painting of the New York School." The more so, since Parsons *did* let the artists do the rest—select and hang their own shows, enlarge the size of their paintings without griping about the difficulty of selling such works. "Once Rothko wanted to hang more pictures than the walls would accommodate; he got Tony Smith and his other artist friends together the afternoon before the opening, and they stayed in the gallery overnight building a freestanding wall and installing the rest of the show."

Betty Parsons gave her artists walls and she gave them unusual freedom in filling them. But she didn't give them many sales. "Since 1940, Fifty-seventh Street has had an unprecedented boom," *Fortune* reported in 1946, just as the boom was about to expire, and just as Parsons was about to open. Due to a war-induced prosperity that made money available for "luxuries" such as works of art, sales by 57th Street galleries had increased by 300 percent between 1940 and 1946. The growth of the art market entailed, moreover, a shift in the social and economic identity of its clientele. A survey done by *Art News* in 1944 reported that one-third of the paintings sold the previous year had been bought by people purchasing their first painting. Collecting was no longer the prerogative of the tycoon (or his wife or heir). The "new collector," according to *Art News*, was under forty-five, upper-middle-class, a businessman, professional, or actor, and was inclined to buy Americans. "American paintings are cheaper; they are more plentiful; it is easier to find good ones; it is considered 'patriotic' to help by supporting American artists; there is a feeling, as one dealer put it, 'of getting in on the ground floor'."

Yet of the $6 million spent on art in 1945, only 15 percent went to Americans; in a market still dominated by the French, many American ground floors remained deserted. Certainly, for many years this "boom" did not benefit Mark Rothko, who, for instance, had sold only three paintings (for $265) through his 1945 Art of This Century exhibit. But Rothko did gradually increase his prices, so that *Gethsemane*, priced at $550 at Art of This Century in 1945, cost $750 in 1948 at Parsons, and his 1946 watercolor exhibit at Mortimer Brandt did generate substantial sales, including his first museum purchase, *Tentacles of Memory*, to the San Francisco Museum of Modern Art. Two works exhibited in this show, *Entombment I* and *Vessels of Magic*, were acquired the following year by the Whitney and Brooklyn museums. Among established collectors, Peggy Guggenheim bought *Immolation*.

But for the most part Rothko was selling to the "new collectors," for whom an inexpensive watercolor by a relatively unknown contemporary showing at an "old" 57th Street firm might make an ideal purchase. Of course, new collectors, like old ones, might be looking to establish an image of cultivation for themselves; they might be playing the art market as if it were the stock market. Or they might actually enjoy art, as seems to have been the case with Edward Wales Root, an upstate New Yorker, the son of Elihu Root, Theodore Roosevelt's secretary of state and himself a painter. Though he had started collecting many years earlier, E. W. Root concentrated on young American abstract artists after 1944, buying works by William Baziotes, Theodoros Stamos, Robert Motherwell, and Willem de Kooning. In the late 1940s Root bought two Rothko oil paintings.

A. DEIRDRE ROBSON, *The New York Art Market ca. 1960*

Excerpts (pp. 255–58, 260–63) from "The New York Art Market, circa 1960," in *Prestige, Profit, and Pleasure: The Market for Modern Art in New York in the 1940s and 1950s* (New York: Garland, 1995), 255–63. Copyright © 1999 Garland Publishing. Reproduced by permission of Taylor and Francis Group, LLC, a division of Informa plc.

By the end of the 1950s, there were signs of considerable change in the support system for modern art in New York. . . . The status of modern art museums had increased and was accompanied by much higher annual attendances, although the number of such institutions in New York had not grown since 1940 (the increase nationwide, however, had been considerable). At the same time, the number of galleries in New York had increased from some 70 establishments in 1940 to more than 115 in 1954 and about 275 in early 1960, with a concurrent expansion in the number of artists and variety of shows staged. The total volume of auction sales had also trebled, and those in private galleries had increased by a similarly substantial proportion, with a concomitant rise in general price levels. Finally, the number of collectors seemed to be burgeoning nationwide. [. . .]

[. . .] In the long term there was no substantive widening of the art market to include the middle class, as had seemed to be happening during the prosperous Second World War years. Instead, private collectors remained concentrated among the very wealthiest of the population and in the upper, and possibly upper-middle, classes (those who owned substantial property, inherited money, worked in the highest status occupations). [. . .]

The statistics of wealth distribution in the United States are particularly revealing on this point. There was, in statistical terms, almost no reallocation of wealth (liquid and convertible assets) from the richest to the less well-off: whereas in 1922, the top 0.5% of the population had owned 30% of all privately held assets, in the mid-1950s this tiny percentage still controlled 25% of the same wealth (although their share did fall briefly to only 19% and 20% in the 1940s). What little widening of the wealth base that did happen in the postwar years occurred in the 1950s, although this was basically an increase in the relatively small numbers of those in the uppermost income quintile (incomes of $10,000 and above) or with the greatest asset holdings. This slight shift in wealth allotment was undoubtedly helped by the personal and estate taxation reforms and reductions introduced by Republican-controlled Congresses in 1948 and 1954. These measures particularly encouraged reductions in the taxation liabilities of the more wealthy, and at the same time helped ensure that there was no real equalization of economic status between the richest and less well-off.

That the slight increase in the numbers of the most wealthy, those in the upper and possibly upper-middle classes, corresponded to the first real buoyancy in the art market since the war years seems to reinforce the linkage between personal income and art market potential, a linkage which appears to have persisted to the present day. For instance, in 1975, the National Research Center for the Arts found that 60% of those attending art museums had incomes in the uppermost income quintile, that consumers of high culture tended to come from the more highly paid professions or from business management, and that the more direct the consumption of art, the more financially elite the group.

But, as has already been seen, collecting is not merely a matter of economic potential. . . . The persistence of the link between class and art consumption can also be traced to the stubborn linkage between class and education. In particular, education at a relatively high level, of a type almost entirely restricted to the wealthy in the United States, has been proved to be vital if an individual is to have the kind of skills and experience needed to consume works of art, whether metaphorically (as in visiting exhibitions and reading books) or more directly in the sense of being purchasers of art works. Moreover, the association between certain educational experiences and arts consumption seems almost more significant than that between income and arts consumption, for in 1975 the same study by the National Research Center for the Arts noted that 78% of those going to art museums had a college degree.

Because of these factors, the tiny minority who made up the upper and upper-middle class were almost inevitably the only ones likely to be art collectors, to consume art directly as well as metaphorically. [. . .] On the rare occasion when individual collectors came from a different socioeconomic milieu, it is usually the case that they came from backgrounds which placed an unusual emphasis upon cultural values echoing those of the elite or upper classes. [. . .]

[. . .] But it must be said that American collectors of the postwar years showed distinguishing particularities which uniquely affected the development of New York as an art market centre. First, the continuing identification of direct art consumption, of art collecting, with the upper and upper-middle classes, had lingering consequences. Within the European context an important element of collecting motivation has been the attempts of elites to demark themselves not just by economic prestige, but by their patronage of artistic forms not yet appreciated by the majority. This has been seen as an attempt to delimit "aristocratic" taste from "bourgeois". It was certainly true of the Paris support system for modern art, where earlier in the twentieth century certain members of the social and aristocratic elite used their sponsorship of the avant-garde to distinguish themselves from the more mainstream taste of new entrants into the art market such as businessmen and professionals. This is thought to be a fundamental characteristic of taste formation and arts consumption in Europe to this day. But although it might have seemed in the early 1940s that this might occur in the United States too, it never actually happened. [. . .] There was never any real pressure for the upper class to distinguish itself by supporting the avant-garde (defined as Abstract Expressionism at this time). In these years, ownership of modern art as a whole remained sufficient to signify the distinction the elite was likely to desire. [. . .]

It must be stressed that, though the composition of the dealer sector changed constantly as galleries opened or closed, private commercial dealers of the kind found on Fifty-seventh Street remained the normal venues where art could be bought by collectors, despite attempts over the period to introduce alternatives. [. . .] During the early 1940s came the most important additional attempt to extend the private commercial network, one which received considerable publicity at the time, that of department stores such as Gimbel's and Macy's in New York. The former in particular held some newsworthy sales, such as the dispersal of Randolph Hearst's collection in the early 1940s. But despite the continuing presence of sales at department stores, there is no evidence that they affected the art market in New York in any profound way. The reason for this was that they did not attract people with the kind of background to be potential collectors. Moreover, stores merchandised art in a way which implied that it was a commodity little different from furniture or jewellery, an approach which, though in harmony with the democratising ethos of the early 1940s, did not fit in with the socioeconomic and cultural profile of the typical United States art consumer.

Perhaps the most striking way in which collecting patterns did change in the United States in the period under consideration was that the status of collecting among Americans began, though very slowly at first, to rise, as the arts were gradually thought of less in terms of being part of the "female" realm and more as an interest suitable for a hard-headed and successful businessman. Undoubtedly this change owed much to the market trends that we have already seen, more particularly the well-publicised auction sales of the 1950s, and the escalation of prices across the board from the early 1950s onward. [. . .]

So, finally, New York was transformed from a minor to a major art market centre by the end of the 1950s. The efforts of the elements of the support system already detailed must take much of the credit for this. Also, a certain strength in the support system is to be expected where there is a concentration of artists, and with the opening of educational opportunities and art education in the postwar years there was undoubtedly a considerable expansion in the number of artists living and working in New York. [. . .]

The key to the transformation of status of New York as art market centre was not just the greater willingness of Americans to buy art, but the changing prestige of American art in the 1950s. It was the greater openness of American collectors (particularly those crucial on-guard ones) to engage with the art of their own country, even developing an almost chauvinistic confidence in this regard, that was the last cue needed to make New York a cosmopolitan art market centre rather than a provincial one. What transpired in New York in the late 1950s is something similar to the situation in Paris in the early twentieth century, when this city's authority as *the* centre for modern art (in terms of production, presentation and consumption) had been unchallenged. Then Paris had been able to enforce its hegemony because, as Daniel-Henri Kahnweiler later noted, "a painter who does not live in Paris has very little chance of a success there." [. . .] Although the New York support system for modern art was never to go to the extremes of Paris in the 1920s of "believing unwaveringly in the superiority of its painters because it ignores any others," it seems that a cultural chauvinism was also a factor in New York becoming a major art market centre. [. . .]

Paradoxically, the key event in this transformation was not simply a greater support for American art at home, but rather the export of American art, and more particularly Abstract Expressionism, abroad. I say "paradoxical," because what signalled the end of a discrete period in the history of New York as an art market centre was in fact a late example of the cultural inferiority complex long characteristic of American collectors, the attitude that European art forms were necessarily superior to American and that "no American artist that would not be spoken about and collected in Europe was worth considering." [. . .]

[. . .] It is probably no coincidence that the final apotheosis of the Abstract Expressionist market, the final break through the glass ceiling which had until then held down the prices attained by American artists, came . . . when it became known that Europeans were starting to travel to New York to see what American artists were doing and to acquire their work, a reversal of the traditional flow of traffic.

ANDRÉ EMMERICH, *Clement Greenberg*

Excerpt (pp. 29–32) from "Recollections: Greenberg and Frankenthaler," *New Criterion* 12 (2004): 29–34. Reprinted by permission of Susanne Emmerich.

Much paper has been consumed by writing that falls into the category of art criticism. In my experience, the only critic who exerted an influence on artists was Clement Greenberg. He developed close relationships with painters and sculptors whose work he admired and championed in his writings and conversations. In turn, many of these artists highly valued his exceptional eye and his critique of their work. Many artists asked Greenberg to help them install their gallery shows.

For some, Greenberg became a one-man audience whose reaction to their new work was crucial to them. In the 1960s, word of mouth that an artist was well-regarded by Clement Greenberg often translated into commercial success. The world remembered that Greenberg had spotted Jackson Pollock early on as the great new master when he was still little understood, widely ignored, even ridiculed. Collectors, eager not to miss the next wave and to acquire work by a still unrecognized master before it became expensive, looked to him as an oracle, the Warren Buffett of the art world.

I had come to know Greenberg early in the 1950s when the world of contemporary art was still so small that everyone seemed to know everyone. Later on, my gallery came to represent artists whose work interested him, among them the painters Helen Frankenthaler, Morris Louis, Kenneth Noland, Jules Olitski, and Friedel Dzubas, and the sculptors Anthony Caro, Michael Steiner, and Anne Truitt. At the same time, the gallery also represented noted artists whose work did not have Greenberg's particular support, such as David Hockney, Sam Francis, Al Held, Beverly Pepper, and Pierre Alechinsky. Notwithstanding the gallery's broad spectrum, which reflected my own taste and interests, there were jealous tongues that claimed to know that, based on no evidence at all, I had financially subsidized Greenberg. From what I know of Greenberg, it would have been totally out of character for him to accept compensation from any dealer, although he did not disdain gifts of art from artists. As for me, I never gave him anything of value beyond including his name on the list of friends to whom I sent some decent red wine at Christmas.

In the wake of Morris Louis's death in September 1962, I began to work with Clement Greenberg in his role as art advisor to the Louis estate. Louis had left close to five hundred large paintings, all carefully rolled and stored in the basement of his and [his] wife's small house in Washington, D.C. As dealer for the estate, I was present when the paintings were unrolled and catalogued. Later on, after the canvases had been shipped to a New York warehouse, they needed to be looked at again periodically to select works for my gallery as well as galleries in other cities and abroad, and for museum exhibitions. Greenberg was present at these occasions and his critical comments were always carefully noted for future reference. It was fascinating to observe his perceptive, insightful eye at work.

Like many New York intellectuals of the time, Greenberg lived comfortably but modestly in a rent-controlled apartment on the then unfashionable Upper West Side. Greenberg liked to receive, much as in a nineteenth-century salon, the steady stream of visitors from all over the country and the globe, including artists, collectors, dealers, writers, and acolytes that clustered around him at the frequent cocktail hour gatherings at his apartment. It was from here that his ideas were first discussed and debated, and—during the later years of his life—from where they spread across the United States, Canada, England, and the Continent. These events included devoted old friends along with new pilgrims eager to meet the master. The visitors to this modern salon were treated to an aspect of Greenberg that could not come across in his writings, his exceptional charm.

But for all his brilliance, there was an aspect of Greenberg's personality that also drove away friends and followers, as well as some artists who owed much of their success to his embrace of their work. I made a deliberate effort to remain on good personal terms with him. At the same time, I kept a certain distance to avoid the possibility of a bitter break, as I witnessed happening to so many others. Greenberg's ideas as well as his acid tongue provoked a great deal of hostility, some of which was deflected onto the artists who were seen as his protégés and followers. In the late 1950s and the 1960s, his positive words about an artist's work translated rapidly into sales, but in the 1970s and 1980s his attention could easily turn into a handicap. The term "formalism" had become a pejorative and Greenberg's ideas were derided. Things had reached such a point that, after his death, when his friends wanted to organize a memorial service, no New York museum claimed to be able to make available a suitable locale for what had been the leading art critic of his generation. In the end, I arranged for appropriate space at the Century Association.

It is only now that a new generation, which never knew the man, but only his writing, is rediscovering his books and essays, and reading them with appreciation. I don't think it is a coincidence that, at the same time, there is a revival of interest in Color Field painting. I always suspected that Greenberg would find his proper place in the front rank of American art critics only after the generation which included the many he had alienated had largely left the stage.

In retrospect, it is remarkable how Greenberg achieved his status as the most influential and most discussed art critic of his time without a position of power and influence. He did not hold a professorship at any university or a curatorship at any museum. In 1939 his landmark essay "Avant-Garde and Kitsch" was published, and it lifted him from obscurity. From 1939 until 1942 he was an editor at *Partisan Review* and art critic for *The Nation* from 1942 to 1949. From 1959 to 1960 he served as consultant to the short-lived contemporary New York gallery, French & Co. He had no other formal affiliations. His fame was uniquely due to the force and persuasiveness of his ideas and his writing.

MIKE WALLACE INTERVIEWS MARCEL DUCHAMP

Mike Wallace Papers, Special Collections Research Center, Syracuse Libraries, New York. Reprinted by kind permission of Syracuse Libraries.

Original editor's note: The following interview with Marcel Duchamp was conducted by Mike Wallace on 12 December 1960 and aired on 18 January 1961 during the weekly television program *Mike Wallace—Interview & News.*

Wallace: *To all intents and purposes, you certainly left painting [in 1923] and never touched a brush. And I've heard it said that you quit because you believed that the art world was too commercial.*

Duchamp: That reason also comes in, absolutely. I felt that at that time, already *then* in 1923, there [were] a number of painters, of collectors, of dealers, in such a number that never was before the First World War. No, all there was before the war, around 1905, were very few collectors, very few dealers, very few painters, and they spoke an esoteric language that the layman would not understand. Today this is the opposite! *Everybody* speaks about painting, everybody *buys* painting if they can afford it, and it's a Wall Street *affair*, if you want to call it that way.

Wallace: *Painting is a Wall Street affair.*

Duchamp: I call it that way because money's attached to it.

Wallace: Well, what's wrong with money? Shouldn't an artist be permitted to make a living?

Duchamp: Nothing at all! But the difference is that the value of a painting is not in the amount of dollars or cents that are attached to it. In other words, a painting that was worth $50,000 in 1900 is worth $5,000 today, or *less*, or *nothing*. So, the value is absolutely artificial and of the moment, [and is] not really the actual value. Like a piece of metal is worth so much [today, which is not] the same [as] in 1815 [or in] 1950, according to the difference of the value of money.

Wallace: *Are you saying then, that Picasso or Braque or Rouault or whomever, they are in a sense . . . well, you have said that there is racketeering in modern art.*

Duchamp: Yes, yes.

Wallace: *And I believe that you said that anybody who makes money out of painting is a 'crook'.*

Duchamp: Yes. It's a sort of a *bon mot*, if you want to call it that way, to make my thought go over.

Wallace: *Well, not very bon. [Laugh]*

Duchamp: [Laugh] Not very *bon mot*, no. But 'crook' is a little exaggerated. But I mean, there is an element of racketeering in all this, admitted.

Wallace: *What is that?*

Duchamp: [By] racketeering I mean making money under false pretense. In other words, the painting you buy [for] 10 cents today may be worth 3 cents in twenty years. In other words, there is no actual final value attached to that painting, because the aesthetic value changes in money value. So there is racketeering when you profit [from] the moment, when you can make money with painting by making many paintings and much money. So that's where the racketeering idea comes from, you see.

Wallace: *Isn't it a question of simple supply and demand?*

Duchamp: Yes. *No.* But the supply and demand is not the same as copper or wheat, at all! At the moment if you want to say there's a man-in-offer, okay. But that's not enough. To me, is to excuse it. I've known young men of [today], age twenty, when they *want* to be an artist, they're *full* of ideals, never *thinking* of money, [and] mixing money with aesthetics.

Wallace: And you think that money and aesthetics cannot mix?

Duchamp: They hardly mix, to my taste. I mean they occasionally do, but it's not important whether they should mix or not.

Wallace: Did you, Marcel Duchamp, ever participate in this swindle, in this racket?

Duchamp: No, no. Because I can tell you what I ever got for my paintings; really funny, in prices. For example, that *Nude* of mine was sold for $240 in 1913.

Wallace: The Nude Descending?

Duchamp: Yes.

Wallace: The Nude Descending a Staircase *was sold for how much?*

Duchamp: $240; in francs 1,200 francs, at 5 francs [to] a dollar.

Wallace: This was in 1913?

Duchamp: 1913. Yes.

Wallace: And today it is worth?

Duchamp: Well, I couldn't tell because I [don't know] what [one would pay] for it. I know it has been insured in a show for $40,000.

Wallace: And this is hanging now in the Philadelphia Museum of Art in the Arensberg Collection. [. . .] If money disturbed you that much, if the whole swindle and crookedness of the art world offended you so, why could you not simply keep on painting and then not have shows, just paint for yourself?

Duchamp: It could have been done, but it didn't appeal to me because no matter what you are, if you live in your epoch, you cannot avoid it; and the epoch was full of this feeling of painting and selling paintings. You couldn't do it very well, and I don't know of anyone who has done it, in fact. I had other activities, like, as I said, those experiments with three-dimension[s] and sculpture. I can't explain very well all this. A life is a life, and it's all very well to say 'what did you do in 1932 at 10 o'clock in the morning?' It's too easy to say, and not easy to answer. It's a bit like that, and self-analysis is not my strong point either. [*Laugh*]

Wallace: I have here an advertisement from yesterday's New York Times: 'Exhibition and Sale. Thirty-One Small Paintings by Rouault'. Now here is a self-portrait by Monsieur Rouault. $3,000. Three-and-a-half inches by two-and-a-half inches. About this big. Does this offend you?

Duchamp: It does offend me a little. But the story is as an explanation—which is no explanation—that those paintings were made to illustrate a book, and as [such] would be reproduced in the book as illustration[s]. The book was never made by Ambroise Vollard, so the paintings have been sold, or are being sold now, as originals.

Wallace: *Would you pay?*

Duchamp: No, never. Not [ever] would [I] pay that money. I think it's *stupid.*

RICHARD BROWN BAKER, *The Leo Castelli Gallery*

Excerpt (pp. 180–84) from "The Days and Nights of a Collector," *Paris Review* 41, no. 152 (1999): 179–90.

New York, January 3, 1962

... [Castelli] and Ivan showed me a couple of new pictures, one of a turkey in a pot, another of skates, a third of an electrical cord and plug, by Roy Lichtenstein, the "unknown" whom they are about to explode upon the art scene. I learned that the background of tiny dots of my "Washing Machine" is applied by stencil. Ivan said that this picture of mine may soon be reproduced in the Milanese magazine *Metro.* Leo reported that quite a bit of interest in Lichtenstein's work has developed among Europeans. He also told me that a feature article has been written about him and Mr. Rosenquist, whom Dick Bellamy of the Green Gallery will soon exhibit, by a correspondent of the *St. Louis Dispatch.* Rosenquist, whose work excites Campbell, is also a painter in a rather flat billboard style of fragments of "real machine objects, of hands, etc." The *St. Louis Post-Dispatch* man has presented these two as rebels against abstract expressionism.

Ivan says they've now found out more about Lichtenstein, who is 36 years old and has already had seven exhibits, presumably in obscure galleries, having painted in various manners, among them abstract expressionism.

It is interesting to observe a career being launched. I presently have my "Washing Machine" on the wall. Campbell [Wylly, who had recently been put in charge of the Art Lending Service at MOMA] likes it, but few others have yet seen it, except Vernon Johnson [an old friend], who beheld it, predictably, with dismay and disapproval.

·   ·   ·

New York, January 16, 1962

Finished with shopping, I remembered that Ivan Karp had told me that new paintings by Roy Lichtenstein would arrive today at the gallery. I went there and was at once moved to admiration by the current exhibit of John Chamberlain's sculptures. There is one large magnificent piece I would love to own, but where could I ever put it? I asked to see the new Lichtensteins, and Leo Castelli told Karp he might show them to me as I was among the original enthusiasts for Lichtenstein. Ivan said they would just about knock me out.

The gallery's leading collector client, Bob Scull, has not responded well to Lichtenstein, I learn, but Chamberlain, on contrast, was so enthralled by these paintings that he wanted one of the largest hung on the gallery wall during his own sculpture show. Leo said Chamberlain was very insistent, but that of course it wasn't the thing to do. A visiting anthropologist from London, a collector, has also got very excited over Lichtenstein. His sole purchases in New York, if Leo is to be believed, are a Jim Dine and a Lichtenstein. He sent back an Alan Davie he had selected. But why, anyway, would a Londoner buy a Davie in New York?

Well, to get on to my confession, I was shown two very large new pictures, one of an air force officer kissing a girl, the other, wildly explosive, with WHAM [Baker later wrote in the margin "actually BLAM"] written on it, depicting the blazing destruction of a plane with the pilot being ejected from his doomed ship, his black figure rolling forth head over heels in the lower right corner. This painting, dynamic and bound to shock, had reached the gallery today only. Some of the flat blue paint looked uneven because it was not fully dry. Both Leo and Ivan were excited in their praise of it.

Another smaller picture of two clasped hands was carried in by Ivan with the cautionary remark, "Leo doesn't want to sell this, but I'll let you see it anyway." It took me only a split second to love it. To get a top small Lichtenstein to go with my large "Washing Machine" was what I had come for, and this was, to my eye, the best of his small pictures. But Leo cleverly was going to keep it.

The idea of acquiring the large exploding airplane picture then dawned upon me. As Leo remarked, its whirling violence is at the opposite extreme from the crisp calmness of "The Washing Machine." To have them both would be to acknowledge the two polarities of the artist's talent.

Leo had to go out. It was left with Ivan, to whom Leo had said to make me a favorable price if I wanted the picture. Ivan reduced it, he said, from $1,200 to one thousand dollars. "Four or five years from now you will be embarrassed by that low price," said Ivan. He and Leo make a slick sales team, I afterwards reflected, recalling all the steps of this transaction in which a dramatist could represent their words and actions as the calculated insincerities of two salesmen gulling an innocent. But of course I believe in the art of Lichtenstein, and therefore I believe in the genuineness of their enthusiasm.

I mentioned to Ivan that prompt payment couldn't be expected of me. "Do you know what this gallery is owed?" he confided. "$62,000."

That information makes me imagine a crash in art prices if the acquisition boom collapses and the many dealers who have accounts receivable are obliged to press for immediate payment. Anyway, having an excited admiration for Lichtenstein's WHAM painting, I decided to take the risk and buy it. Without the taking of risks, a great collection is not formed. Carried away, I even bought a small collage by Chamberlain.

ARTHUR DANTO, *Mr. Andy Warhol*

Excerpt (pp. 580–81) from "The Artworld," *Journal of Philosophy* 61, no. 19 (1964): 571–84. Estate of Arthur Danto. Reprinted by kind permission of the *Journal of Philosophy*.

Mr. Andy Warhol, the Pop artist, displays facsimiles of Brillo cartons, piled high, in neat stacks, as in the stockroom of the supermarket. They happen to be of wood, painted to look like cardboard, and why not? To paraphrase the critic of the *Times*, if one may make the facsimile of a human being out of bronze, why not the facsimile of a Brillo carton out of plywood? The cost of these boxes happens to be 2×10^3 that of their homely counterparts in real life—a differential hardly ascribable to their advantage in durability. In fact the Brillo people might, at some slight increase in cost, make their boxes out of plywood without these becoming artworks, and Warhol might make *his* out of cardboard without their ceasing to be art. So we may forget questions of intrinsic value, and ask why the Brillo people cannot manufacture art and why Warhol cannot *but* make artworks. Well, his are made by hand, to be sure. Which is like an insane reversal of Picasso's strategy in pasting the label from a bottle of Suze onto a drawing, saying as it were that the academic artist, concerned with exact imitation, must always fall short of the real thing: so why not just *use* the real thing? The Pop artist laboriously reproduces machine-made objects by hand, e.g., painting the labels on coffee cans (one can hear the familiar commendation "Entirely made by hand" falling painfully out of the guide's vocabulary when confronted by these objects). But the difference cannot consist in craft: a man who carved pebbles out of stones and carefully constructed a work called *Gravel Pile* might invoke the labor theory of value to account for the price he demands; but the question is, What makes it art? And why need Warhol make these things anyway? Why not just scrawl his signature across one? Or crush one up and display it as *Crushed Brillo Box* ("A protest against mechanization . . .") or simply display a Brillo carton as *Uncrushed Brillo Box* ("A bold affirmation of the plastic authenticity of industrial . . .")? Is this man a kind of Midas, turning whatever he touches into the gold of pure art? And the whole world consisting of latent artworks waiting, like the bread and wine of reality, to be transfigured, through some dark mystery, into the indiscernible flesh and blood of the sacrament? Never mind that the Brillo box may not be good, much less great art. The impressive thing is that it is art at all. But if it is, why are not the indiscernible Brillo boxes that are in the stockroom? Or *has* the whole distinction between art and reality broken down?

Suppose a man collects objects (ready-mades), including a Brillo carton; we praise the exhibit for variety, ingenuity, what you will. Next he exhibits nothing but Brillo cartons, and we criticize it as dull, repetitive, self-plagiarizing—or (more profoundly) claim that he is obsessed by regularity and repetition, as in *Marienbad*. Or he piles them high, leaving a narrow path; we tread our way through the smooth opaque stacks and find it an unsettling experience, and write it up as the closing in of consumer products, confining us as prisoners: or we say he is a modern pyramid builder. True, we don't say these things about the stockboy. But then a stockroom is not an art gallery, and we cannot readily separate the Brillo cartons from the gallery they are in, any more than we can separate the Rauschenberg bed from the paint upon it. Outside the gallery, they are pasteboard cartons. But then, scoured clean of paint, Rauschenberg's bed is a bed, just what it was before it was transformed into art. But then if we think this matter through, we discover that the artist has failed, really and of necessity, to produce a mere real object. He has produced an artwork, his use of real Brillo cartons being but an expansion of the resources available to artists, a contribution to *artists' materials*, as oil paint was, or *tuche*.

What in the end makes the difference between a Brillo box and a work of art consisting of a Brillo Box is a certain theory of art. It is the theory that takes it up into the world of art, and keeps it from collapsing into the real object which it is (in a sense of *is* other than that of artistic identification). Of course, without the theory, one is unlikely to see it as art, and in order to see it as part of the artworld, one must have mastered a good deal of artistic theory as well as a considerable amount of the history of recent New York painting. It could not have been art fifty years ago. But then there could not have been, everything being equal, flight insurance in the Middle Ages, or Etruscan typewriter erasers. The world has to be ready for certain things, the artworld no less than the real one. It is the role of artistic theories, these days as always, to make the artworld, and art, possible. It would, I should think, never have occurred to the painters of Lascaux that they were producing *art* on those walls. Not unless there were neolithic aestheticians.

MICHAEL BENEDIKT, *The Gutman Letter*

Excerpts (pp. viii–xi) from "Introduction," in *The Gutman Letter* (New York: Something Else Books, 1969), vii–xi. Reprinted with permission of Laura Boss.

[Walter Gutman] handled [a] modest role in the financial world well enough to be asked one day if he would like to try his hand at helping to write the weekly letter of stock advice which Goodbody published. What stock advice letters are supposed to do is, of course, to interest investors in the stock market, preferably by making profitable prophecies on the growth possibilities of different companies and firms. It is obviously a financial rather than a literary activity, but Gutman infused certain qualities of style into his letters here and there. More importantly, Gutman's prophecies turned out to be exceptionally effective examples of their genre. [. . .] By [1960] Gutman's peculiar combination of artistic sympathy and power of fiscal prophecy had won him such honors as a profile in the *New Yorker*, articles in *Vogue*, *Harper's Bazaar* and *Coronet*, and the offer from a major publisher to write a book on how to succeed in the stock-market (this became a compendium of hard-headed advice entitled "You Only Have to Get Rich Once"). More important here is the major bibliographical residue of those years. From our point of view the important factor is that it thus happened that starting in 1959, and running through until 1962, Walter Gutman, while continuing to live the life he liked, completed a series of Wall Street letters the like of which the stock-market had not seen before, has not seen since, and which it is not likely to see again in the foreseeable future.

The thing that Gutman obviously did differently from all other practitioners of the genre, was to pay a curiously great amount of attention to the art scene, both verbal and visual. Throughout, Gutman attempted to link the realms of creation and business analysis. On the referential level alone, the content is astonishing. There are references—natural enough since Gutman had continued his friendships with artists, initiated during the 1930s—to virtually the entire Abstract Expressionist generation (with stress on Willem de Kooning) and also to the entire generation of writers who were first advertised by the mass media as "Beat" (with stress on Allen Ginsberg). There is a stream of recommendations that art and business connections proliferate—an idea that we have seen take considerable root in recent years. The extreme of this tendency is the suggestion in one letter that maybe, to bolster the value of stocks, certificates be designed by the leading artists of the time, so that any sinking value of these documents as shares could be offset by their future worth as saleable "editions." Curiously enough, an equally extreme realm of reference is achieved in recommendations on promising stocks. Perhaps the best reason for recommending a company is its discovery or distribution of a new process or product. Frequently, Gutman discusses the conception and birth of the new synthetics, technologies or media which artists today consider it necessary as well as urgent to explore.

This kind of reference to art is, as we say, relatively direct. More interesting I think is the fact that Gutman wishes to link the realms of art and business not just by association, but by philosophy; and according to an esthetic. Like another businessman/artist, the poet Wallace Stevens (who was Vice President of the Hartford Accident and Indemnity Company), Gutman is concerned specifically with the necessity for fact to firmly engage fantasy, and fantasy, fact, for either field to be fertile in a lasting way. Invariably he finds such elements as intuition, taste or faith—all traditionally considered to be the peculiar province of artists—in full operation in the successful Wall Street mind—both his own and those of others. The difference between art and science seems, overall, to be resolved in favor of the artist, the poetic impulses containing all the scientific impulses; Gutman usually pictures his artist friends as being personally in possession of a sense of life which those in the so-called "exact sciences" might well heed. The extreme point in this vein is probably the connection of a falling (or, in the parlance of Wall Street, "bear") market with Allen Ginsberg's departure for Europe. On the other hand, credited at one time or another with being the cause of a rising or "bull" market are the new American dramatists, dancers, novelists, painters, sculptors, filmmakers, composers, and poets.

Still, Gutman's philosophy of art is relatively direct. For all the formality of the circumstances in which they were written, the letters are after all examples—remarkably searching ones, I feel—of a man attempting to explain his own life to himself. Autobiography is interesting as a genre; and Gutman's life happens to have been especially interesting. Still, what interests me about these letters most of all is that, whether or not they mention artists or art, whether esthetics is or is not their ostensible subject, these letters *are* art. [. . .]

Gutman's associates assure me that it is Gutman's more fanciful and seemingly fantastic attacks on the reality of reasoning which contained and perhaps still contain the greatest degree of insight. It begins, after all, to be a little like science fiction. Behind the sliding panel in his office the captain of industry has a collection of De Koonings. Behind the wall covered with De Koonings to which an occasional Ginsberg manuscript is clipped is another office wall which is the control panel of a computer and a space ship. Unique as is this visionary architecture of mine (I like to see Gutman's sensibility as possibly archetypal, obviously) a further bizarreness suddenly occurs to me. Is it possible that this captain of industry is concerned with the world of industry for reasons which are primarily esthetic, and the world of art for reasons which are primarily practical? Gutman's life interests me as a metaphor which resists all the clichés of industry lovers/art haters, art lovers/industry haters, and all the other classes of life-fearers, just that scrupulously and well.

AD REINHARDT, *Unpublished Notes*

Unpublished notes, ca. 1966. Reproduced with the permission of the Ad Reinhardt Estate. Copyright © Anna Reinhardt.

Things are lousy. The avant-garde is arrears. Artists are selling themselves like hot cakes. Art is a good thing. Art education is a holy-schmo business. Artists are jobbing. The lousy government is in this dirty war. One doesn't know what one can do about it. The art critics are all corrupt. The art critics are the art curators and they're also the art collectors and assistant art dealers too. The good old art words are dead. Things are awful. Artists don't know what to do, they're repeating themselves, they're making movies. Artists telephone directions for making art instead of making it themselves. Some people still think the mass media can explain things. Artists are like businessmen.

Things are great. The avant-garde is behind us. Artists are making out. Lots of money around. Art is a good thing, everywhere. You can do anything you want. Artists are free of expressionism. The old rackets, scumbling, fumbling, staining, straining, striping, stripping are all gone. The art critics are all corrupt. Artists are freer than they've ever been. There are bigger and nicer art books than ever before. Artists are working more and bigger and faster. Telephones have never been so busy. The mass media gives more space to artists who are working that gap between technology and life.

ANNA C. CHAVE, *Revaluing Minimalism*

Excerpts (pp. 466–71, 478–79) from "Revaluing Minimalism: Patronage, Aura, and Place," *Art Bulletin* 90, no. 3 (2008): 466–86. Reprinted by kind permission of the author.

Patronage studies are scarce in the literature on contemporary art for a reason: patrons have rarely exercised a decisive sway over the course of that art, broadly viewed. But the leading patrons of the Minimalist movement may be counted as an exception. The spiritualized view of Minimalism held by Count Giuseppe Panza di Biumo and the founders of the Dia Art Foundation, Heiner Friedrich and Philippa Pellizzi (née de Menil and later changed to Fariha Friedrich), led them to elevate certain artists within the Minimalist ambit and motivated them to underwrite particular forms of Minimalist production, especially site-specific forms, at times on an epic scale. These predilections would culminate in various initiatives—such as Walter De Maria's 1977 *Lightning Field* or the Dia:Beacon museum—that would often be likened by the press to pilgrimage sites or sanctuaries and would otherwise lead to an institutional framing of Minimalism putatively at odds with the movement's premises in their inception, for dominant critical accounts would have it that Minimalism is properly understood as an ineluctably secular, materialist undertaking.

Count Panza began collecting art by Dan Flavin and Robert Morris in 1967, followed by the work of Donald Judd, Carl Andre, James Turrell, Robert Irwin, and others, monopolizing the market for Minimalism over the course of a decade when prices were low and competition from fellow collectors scant. What he discerned in Minimalist initiatives generally was "the research of truth through simple forms," a quest for the "essential" that endued the work with auratic qualities. Over time, with his "taste for the metaphysical, [Panza] rewrote the Minimalist project to suit his own sensibilities," Rosalind Krauss charged in 1991. As for the founders of Dia, who largely succeeded Panza as the Minimalists' chief patrons, *Village Voice* critic Kim Levin inquired whether they were "propagating their own idealistic and somewhat mystical aesthetic" when they opened an exhibition space devoted to a limited number of outsize, long-term projects in an industrial building in New York's Chelsea neighborhood in 1987. Dia's establishment of stand-alone art projects in accordance with individual artists' designs was framed skeptically by Krauss in *October* in 1990, further, as the "reconsecrating [of] certain urban spaces to a detached contemplation of their own 'empty' presence," spaces that emanate an "inscrutable but suggestive sense of impersonal, corporate-like power to penetrate artworld locales and to rededicate them to another kind of nexus of control."

According to Dia's first annual report, of 1975, the foundation's aim was to "plan, realize and maintain public projects which cannot be easily produced, financed or owned by individual collectors because of their cost and magnitude." Heiner Friedrich chose the name Dia—Greek for "through"—to denote (albeit in a way arcane to most) the foundation's role as a "conduit." But *dia* is also said to mean "the godlike one," and the artists anointed by Dia as geniuses capable of "creat[ing] major works which would be gifts to mankind for all time," as Dia artist La Monte Young put it, were sometimes said by the press to have been "dia-fied," while the patrons themselves were slyly dubbed by Flavin the "dia-ties." In an age-old bargain, in short, artists and patrons each in a way affirmed the other as possessed of a superhuman spark. The press often compared the de Menil family generally to the Medici. And, for his part, Friedrich explicitly represented Dia's founding as a due response to a cultural moment of Renaissance-like dimensions: "We have artists of the magnitude of . . . Michelangelo, be it Dan Flavin; of the magnitude of Donatello, be it Walter De Maria."

Heiner Friedrich and Philippa Pellizzi welcomed Flavin, Judd, Turrell, De Maria, Young and his partner Marian Zazeela, and performance artist Robert Whitman into their founding Dia stable, promising to capitalize major projects by all of these figures. Like Panza before them, the Dia founders generally sought work that they perceived as auratic, and (like Panza, too) they embraced some of the leading California Minimalists equally with certain of their New York counterparts. [. . .]

Panza's initial forays as a collector of contemporary art proceeded in a fairly ordinary way, but rather than continue to acquire discrete objects that appealed to him, he developed an idealistic vision of the potential for public installations of contemporary art to "tak[e] the place of the cathedral." That vision came to be strongly shared by the founders of Dia, who in time established numerous permanent (and would-be permanent) sanctuary-like art installations, such as De Maria's 1979 *Broken Kilometer*, in New York's SoHo district. Though Panza could not afford to match Dia's costly initiatives, he was responsive to artists' interests in site-specific and environmental endeavors, and by the ways in which he commissioned, displayed, and dispersed elements of his own vast collection, he became a leading figure in driving such initiatives. For example, he commissioned Turrell and Flavin to mount installations at his villa in Varese, north of Milan—a place that long welcomed visitors and, more recently, became a public institution. Turrell completed his *Skyspace I* by 1975, and Flavin installed his *Varese corridor* in 1977. For years, Panza sought optimum sites to locate portions of his collection, beyond what his villa could continuously accommodate, as well as long-term housing for other projects by artists he supported, whether in historic buildings within Italy or elsewhere in Europe and the United States.

Among those who facilitated Panza's interest in site-specific work was Heiner Friedrich, who (prior to founding Dia) had established cutting-edge commercial galleries in Germany and New York. Friedrich opened his first gallery in Munich in 1963 with an erstwhile partner who recalls him as less a businessman than a would-be patron, one who revered artists as "the pinnacle of society" and art as "a system to build a new world." Born in 1938, Friedrich had grown up in war-torn Germany, the son of a man who became a wealthy industrialist following the war. Like Joseph Beuys—whose more Minimal-looking work Dia eventually acquired and showcased—Friedrich came to look to art as something that might afford a profound antidote to the shameful catastrophe of the war: "My early experience of total destruction made me want to create the permanence of indestructible properties, particularly the creative work of artists." Friedrich's galleries showed, among others, De Maria, Judd, Flavin, and Turrell, plus Young and Zazeela's jointly authored sound and light installations.

In 1968, Walter De Maria's *Earth Room* (as it came to be called) premiered at Friedrich's Munich gallery. . . . In 1977, De Maria installed his first New York *Earth Room*—110 tons of earth (including peat and bark), comprising 222 cubic yards, at a depth of 21 inches—in the 3,600-square-foot quarters occupied by Friedrich's first New York

City gallery (opened in 1973) at 141 Wooster Street, a project later made permanent. The necessary resources to achieve that and comparable projects—such as *The Broken Kilometer* (which overtook the space where Friedrich's New York gallery relocated, at 393 West Broadway)—came principally through the dealer's newfound connection to Philippa Pellizzi. Born in 1947, Philippa was the youngest child of Dominique and John de Menil, French-born, Houston-based heirs to the Schlumberger fortune. Known for their spiritually minded approach to art patronage . . . the de Menils commissioned the Rothko Chapel in Houston, close by where they later founded the Menil Collection museum. "It's in the desert that miracles happen," John de Menil once retorted to a friend who doubted the potential for successfully importing high culture to Houston; "Through art, God constantly clears a path to our hearts": so believed Dominique de Menil. [. . .]

Proving unique in our era for the aggressiveness with which they drove a certain course of development for a key movement, Dia's founders induced or encouraged certain artists to dream audaciously, as if money were no object and any given venue could be secured in perpetuity. "Heiner told me he wanted to establish a method of funding not seen since the Renaissance," Whitman recalled. "He wanted to make a Sistine chapel, create a Shakespeare." Avant-garde practices had been largely inimical to grandiosity until the advent in the later 1960s of the Earthworks movement and the contemporaneous emergence of Richard Serra's amplified iteration of the Minimalist vocabulary. The versatile De Maria may be counted a kind of pioneer in the Earthworks initiative, along with Robert Smithson and Michael Heizer, both of whom built importantly from the foundation of Minimalism, and whose work was more recently adopted by Dia, along with that of Serra. While outsize scale is an age-old mechanism for inspiring awe, in the event, Dia's spectacular plans tended to be executed with a distinctively understated aspect. The somewhat generic, industrial, or institutional spaces that Dia mostly acquired for the art projects it sponsored were evidently chosen and architecturally customized precisely to reciprocate the endemic reserve of the Minimalist aesthetic itself.

In general, the Minimalists' projects had not initially assumed an epic scale nor required great sums; rather, the (then impecunious) artists tended to use commonplace materials simply and on a moderate scale, exploiting resources at hand in the urban settings where the movement emerged. (The Californians mostly tended to master and deploy their chosen means of fabrication themselves, whereas the New Yorkers tended to be more removed, employing fabricators and more or less skilled assistants, or using ready-made materials.) Among the inaugural Minimalist sculptures, for example, was De Maria's untitled 1961 box, easily carpentered out of four standard-issue 4-by-8-foot plywood boards capped at either end by another such board cut in two—a decidedly plain, fairly portable artifact by comparison, say, with the five hundred meticulously machined, regularly polished, solid brass rods, 2 meters (6 1/2 feet) long by 2 inches in diameter, collectively weighing 37,500 pounds, permanently, precisely arrayed (one hundred to a line in five parallel lines) across a specially renovated and lighted 7,500-square-foot space: a summary description of *The Broken Kilometer* of 1979. While each individual rod remained loosely on a human scale—typical of Minimalism in its inception—the proliferation of those rods into a work that, in aggregate, constitutes a colossus attests to Dia's fostering of an epic, high-financed stage in the movement's development. [. . .]

The solemnity and quietness—at times, even secrecy—with which Dia would pursue its monumental projects, as well as the extreme solicitude it showed toward the mostly prominent artists it subsidized, generally helped insulate the foundation from pointed interrogation or critique concerning its unusually directive role. However, some came to question Dia's isolating of artists from the larger forces of society and the marketplace. "Dia monopolized some artists so completely that they almost disappeared from circulation," gallery owner Leo Castelli reportedly observed, and another New York dealer complained (anonymously), "It's absolutely crazy what they did. . . . You support artists by buying their work, not by making shrines to them." At issue here in part, arguably, was a conventionally American trust in the inherent rightness of the outcome of free market operations relative to contemporary art production (notwithstanding that Castelli was himself European in origin), versus an "old-world" ideal of art patronage as reanimated by Panza and the Dia founders. For that matter, in 2001 critic Dave Hickey (2002, 156) compared Judd and Flavin to certain "eighteenth-century neoclassical masters like Palladio . . . retained by old families who embodied the historical destiny of aristocratic European taste."

While acknowledging Heiner Friedrich's idealism, Dan Flavin himself reportedly asserted, in the mid-1980s, that his patron "really wanted control over a group of artists for his own ends." Yet such open disgruntlement had proven rare among Dia's chosen circle of artists prior to that moment—a moment when a financial crisis brought on by a collapse of oil prices caused the foundation to curtail and renege on numerous of its ambitious plans, after which Dia acquired a new administration, and Dia-affiliated artists were largely loosed from their "retained" status. [. . .]

Besides the facilities Dia underwrote in urban and small town enclaves along the East Coast, the foundation also sponsored certain Minimalists' initiatives in drawing the art public into untrammeled nature, following the path of gallery owner Virginia Dwan, patron (about 1970) of seminal earthworks by Heizer and Smithson. Friedrich recalled how "living in the countryside after the war in purest relation to nature, in great peace, made a huge impression on me—seeing the manifestation of the divine"—and Panza would share with Friedrich a sense of the particular gloriousness of the western United States. Dia's first such major undertaking, to which Panza contributed, was De Maria's *Lightning Field*, completed in the high desert of New Mexico in 1977. Soon after came the first phases of what came to be called the Chinati Foundation. At a disused military installation that Dia purchased in tiny, remote Marfa, Texas, in 1979, Judd assembled discrete bodies of work by himself and other artists and placed each in dedicated, renovated buildings. Journalists almost reflexively described visits to *The Lightning Field* and Chinati as pilgrimages, signaling the ordeal entailed in reaching such far-flung places as well as a perception of aura inhering in them. In a world where art is normally concentrated in urban centers, and in an era rife with flux and transposition, such outposts stood out by design for the stunning fact of their remoteness and permanence (with even photographic dissemination strictly controlled), radiating a sense of distance and uniqueness or authenticity—qualities that Walter Benjamin specified as endemic to aura. [. . .]

Minimalist projects typically entailed a paradoxical combination of humbleness and pretension, being ordinary in their forms and, seemingly, in their materials and means, yet grandiose in their claims to art status. In art, as in architecture—notably, including the spaces remade by Dia—the appearance of extreme simplicity can disguise great difficulty and expense, however. Once their patrons offered to capitalize ambitious schemes, the Minimalists devised projects that often appeared austere even as they occasioned hidden extravagance. For that matter, such a conjoining of simplicity and cost is deeply identified with a kind of patrician taste, a taste for which some members of the de Menil family happened to be particularly renowned.

VICTOR GINSBURGH AND A. F. PENDERS, *Land Artists and Art Markets*

Excerpts (pp. 219–26) from "Land Artists and Art Markets," *Journal of Cultural Economics* 21, no. 3 (1997): 219–28. Copyright © 1997 Kluwer Academic Publishers. With permission of Springer.

Since 1960, society has undergone major economic and social changes, which have substantially affected the artworld. The emergence of American art, and in particular Pop Art has recentered the visual arts and displaced both the creation and the trade of contemporary art to the United States. The first auctions of contemporary American art were held in New York in the early sixties, at about the same time as new "movements" (Minimal, Land and Conceptual Art) were born.

We chose to focus on Land Art, and compare it with Minimal and Conceptual Art, because we were interested in whether an art termed as "impossible" by Lipman (1970, 76) could or could not be marketed.

What has been called Land or Earth Art started in the mid-sixties, for the most part in the U.S. and in Great-Britain, at a time where some artists decided to leave their studio and work in "untouched" areas—at least not yet touched by art—such as deserts or industrial lots. Their purposes were diverse and sometimes contradictory but, by rethinking the art object, they tried to find new alternatives using time and space, remote places and large scale projects. The works took different forms, depending on the artist, from simple walks documented by photographs and/or drawings, to gigantic constructions using trucks and bulldozers in isolated deserts. This is why Land Art is hardly a movement with codes and a manifesto, but more a group of individuals working and finding their inspiration from similar ideas.

The type of works created by Land artists, and the timing at which they started to be produced (Vietnam war, May 68 in Paris, student protests in California, hippie movement, environmental concerns, etc.) often leads to think that Land artists were against or, at the very least, not interested in markets. Works by artists such as Robert Smithson or Dennis Oppenheim are often site specific. Though some earthworks have been financed by art galleries or private collectors who therefore own them, they can hardly be considered to have entered the traditional art market, since they cannot be moved. On the other hand, artists such as Richard Long, have produced ephemeral works (tracks left by walks in a mountain, circles of stones, etc.) which disappear naturally or are destroyed after some time by the artist himself.

All this apparently makes Land Art look different from other visual arts and generates several interesting questions. First, by working outdoors on large scale or on ephemeral projects, did Land artists intentionally place themselves outside of the system? Secondly, was and is there a market for Land Art and how did Land artists fare, compared with other contemporary artists? [. . .]

Even if conceptually—and in a social context where marxist theories were questioning the notions of consumption and productivity—creations may have been influenced by left-wing convictions, they were nevertheless, in many cases, presented at a very early stage through the usual channels.

Given the type of art produced by Land artists, what can be sold is seldom the "original" work but, in most cases, documents or sketches of the project and photographs. It is worth pointing out that though, originally, these were not necessarily considered as artworks by the artists, they eventually became artworks by themselves, and were shown in galleries, traded and bought by collectors as well as by museums.

The first show dealing exclusively with Land Art took place at the Dwan Gallery in New York in October 1968. It was followed, a few months later, by the first exhibition in a museum: "Earth Art" was held at the Andrew Dickson White Museum of Art, Cornell University, Ithaca. In March 1969, Harald Szeemann opened in Basel his (now considered as) mythical show "When Attitudes Become Form," where he presented what he thought of as being the most advanced art of the time. One month later, Gerry Schum ran his film "Land Art" on the German television. In July 1970, the Museum of Modern Art in New York presented "Information", an exhibition organized by K. L. McShine, which really launched Conceptual Art. This is followed by several site-specific shows all over the United States and Europe: "Pier 18" (New York, February–March 1971), "Sonsbeek 71" (Arnhem, the Netherlands, July–August 1971), "Prospekt 1971" (Düsseldorf, Germany, October 1971), to mention only the best known. From June to September 1972, Documenta V in Kassel put together the youngest figures of the Avant-Garde, while some of the best American galleries of the time—Castelli, Sonnabend, Emmerich and Weber, who were then sharing the same premises in New York—presented their artists in Spoleto, Italy.

Art historians and critics often insist on the importance of these shows, but do not pay enough attention to the role played (a) by artists themselves who initiated connections between young creators both in Europe and in the United States and (b) by galleries which showed artists who were still very young, and sometimes had not even finished their training. For instance, the German gallerist Konrad Fischer exhibited Richard Long as early as in 1968, two years after the artist had realized his first outdoors work, and before he left college. Moreover, many artists had rapidly one-man shows in foreign countries: among others, Smithson (U.S.A.) was shown at Fischer's in Düsseldorf in 1968, Long (U.K.) at the Dwan Gallery in New York in 1969, Oppenheim (U.S.A.) at Yvon Lambert, Paris in 1969, Dibbets (the Netherlands) at Castelli's New York in 1973.

Most Land artists were thus represented by important art dealers from the start. Therefore they cannot be thought of having rejected the "system," though their works were often questioning it. Moreover, the critical power of their works could only be understood by the initiated, i.e. by the members of this system. Finally, by integrating into the system at every level, Land artists were allowing their creations to be legitimated as artworks.

With the exception of Christo, whose works were already present at auctions, Land Art enters salerooms around 1969, with a collage by Dibbets. Though the number of works sold remains small (43 works sold between 1972 and 1977), it is worth pointing out that, just a few years after works by Land artists started to be shown and discussed internationally, both in exhibitions and in magazines, the "impossible" art is sold on secondary markets.

It seems clear that none of the artists would have refused to sell drawings or photographs. Therefore, we believe that the difficulty in selling, experienced by Land artists, was more due to the type of works than to their turning down trading. There may have been no intention to sell but this does not mean that there was a desire to keep the works away from the market. This has been beautifully expressed by Carl Andre (1976), one of the fathers of Minimal Art: "We always had the historical choice of either lying through or living through our contradictions. Now through the genius of the bourgeoisie, we have a chance to market them". [. . .]

Auctions are the only source of market indicators and one has to be careful not to consider them as representing the state of the market, especially when the art is very young and probably more often sold in galleries than at auction. To circumvent this issue, our conclusions will mainly be drawn from comparing three "movements" which started at about the same time and could therefore be thought to be subjected to similar factors. However, both the list of artists and the results we obtain have to be qualified for not being (and not aiming to be) exhaustive. We also have to take into account that several artists (Robert Morris, Walter De Maria, Robert Smithson among others) have actually been associated with two or even all three movements. This should not be of too much concern here, since what we are mainly interested in, is the attitude of Land artists, and not so much Land Art per se. Therefore, we distinguish three movements (Land, Minimal and Conceptual Art) by grouping artists according to their most used mode of expression for which they are best known and which made them well-known, and not necessarily to whether a specific work belongs to their Land Art, Minimal or Conceptual period.

Our results are based on some 2,000 observations. The sample includes sales by 51 artists, among the 65 artists whose names were chosen *a priori* (i.e. before collecting sales at auction) to represent Land, Minimal, and Conceptual Art. For Minimal and Conceptual Art, we chose well-known artists. For Land Art, we included those who initiated the movement: an important selection criterion was that each artist had to have worked outdoors with ephemeral materials.

[The results show] that Land artists have not been as successful as artists belonging to the two other movements. Forty per cent of the Land artists selected *a priori* never appear at auction. This is surprising for David Tremlett, Franz Erhard Walther or John Hilliard since they are well known, highly priced and frequently shown in international galleries and museums. Mary Miss, George Trakas, Andrew Leicester, Richard Fleischner or Nancy Holt work more in a Public Art scene; therefore, though some are represented by galleries, we did not expect them to show up at auction. For Minimal and Conceptual Art, most of the names chosen *a priori* appear at auction.

It is important to mention that more than half of the works sold by the group of Land artists did not belong to their Land Art period. This sheds light on the weakness of the impact of Land Art (at least in public auctions, since about one hundred works only were sold in twenty years). We think that it may also show that Land artists created other works for the market, once they realized that Land works were hard to sell.

The only artist sold each year since 1972 is, of course, Christo. But he himself told one of us that part of his works were sold directly (by him) through salesrooms, at least since the early eighties. What is more interesting is that, though the number of sales is very large (510 in twenty years), his works do not seem to be resold more than the works of any other artist.

Other Land artists appear later on the market and often more sporadically. Though they are younger than Christo, artists such as Dibbets and Oppenheim are sold quite early at auction. Others, like Fulton and Long had to wait longer, but in most cases, their appearance is obviously triggered by exhibitions and dealers. If one excludes Christo from the sample, the number of works sold is much smaller—though the number of selected artists is larger than for Minimal and Conceptual Art—and so are average prices over the period 1988–1992, some twenty five years after the inception of the three movements.

This may [be] due to the fact that Land Art offered at auction mainly consists of photographs, multiples, and documents, while many Minimal artworks are tridimensional and exist in one copy only. This leads us to conclude that, though it was shown in exhibitions and museums as frequently as the two other forms, Land artists did not reach the price level of their "competitors". [. . .]

Is there a specific market logic for Land Art? Though some works by Land artists show up relatively early on the secondary market (early seventies), they are not sold regularly before the second half of the eighties (with the exception of Christo). Their presence at auction seems to depend more on general trends of contemporary art markets than on characteristics specific to Land Art. This is confirmed by the fact that sales are concentrated in important salerooms such as Christie's and Sotheby's both in London and New York.

The hypothesis that Land artists worked in and on the nature to "avoid" markets, or because they were not interested in markets, is clearly not verified. The market for "pure" Land Art is small in comparison with Minimal and Conceptual Art. Both the number of sales and average prices are lower, but the evolution of prices obtained by Land artists is identical to what is obtained by other artists: They also produced works that the market "expects" with respect to size, technique, or materials. These are the most recent works which are often very far from the idea of Land Art itself. And though one may say that they were driven to create pieces that are easier to show and to sell, one has to point out that they did respond to what markets were expecting. They also relied on dealers, shows in galleries and museums in the same way as any artist tries to do it.

ALISON PEARLMAN, *Unpackaging Simulationism*

Excerpts (pp. 105–7, 109–10, 115–18, 121–22) from "Peter Halley, Jeff Koons, and the Art of Marketing- and Consumption-Analysis," in *Unpackaging Art of the 1980s* (Chicago: University of Chicago Press, 2003), 105–24. Copyright © 2003 University of Chicago Press, Chicago and London. All Rights Reserved.

By the summer of 1986, yet another artistic trend had risen. Simulationism—also known as Neo-Geo, Commodity Art, Neo-Conceptualism, and New Abstraction—was the most prominent trend to captivate the New York art world since Neo-Expressionism, Appropriation, and Graffiti Art. The hype culminated in a *New York Times* article of June 3, which trumpeted the trend's market success. The magazine *Arts* had already devoted a special section to Neo-Geo in March. The following month's issue featured "The Scene That Turned on a Dime," Robert Pincus-Witten's proclamation that this new phenomenon had displaced Neo-Expressionism. The *New York Times* article reported that the four primary practitioners of the new tendency—Peter Halley, Jeff Koons, Meyer Vaisman, and Ashley Bickerton—were moving from International with Monument, their young gallery in the East Village, to the Sonnabend Gallery, one of the most established and prestigious galleries in SoHo. "The Hot Four," as another article in *New York* magazine called the artists, were going to debut at Sonnabend in a group show in October–November 1986. The labeling of the trend, the spotlighting of a small number of representative artists, and the move to an established gallery all signaled its commoditization.

   . . . Polemics in response to the trend were defining it along one or more of the following axes: as a continuation of the aims of Appropriation Art (Donald Kuspit's emphasis), as an attempt to represent the simulation principle defined by neo-Marxist theorist

Jean Baudrillard (Hal Foster's emphasis), or as a cynically motivated exploitation of "retro" faddishness (Kay Larson's emphasis). [. . .]

Of all of the polemicists' definitions of the new trend, Kuspit's appropriation thesis was the most credible. Mainly since March 1986 (although beginning with isolated instances at least since June 1984), a number of articles reinforced the notion that there was continuity of purpose between the work of Halley and Koons and the work of Appropriation artists. An early instance was Halley's own 1984 essay for *Arts* magazine, "The Crisis in Geometry." Halley hailed the emergence of a new generation of artists exploring geometric abstraction. He included the established Appropriation artist Sherrie Levine in this group along with himself and Koons. He featured Levine's then most recent works, which were paintings that reproduced various generic features of modernist, abstract paintings. [. . .]

Halley was not the only one to link himself and his peers to the Appropriation artists. Critic Jeanne Siegel included Levine in her article on the work of Halley and his contemporaries, whom she grouped together because they were all using geometric abstraction. Ronald Jones compounded the association, although his article claimed that the artists were interested in hailing the death of modernism. The death of modernism had been central to polemicists' definitions of Appropriation in the early 1980s. [. . .] In addition, the gallery International with Monument, which helped to launch the reputations of the would-be Simulationists, itself did a lot to associate the two groups of artists. The gallery mounted exhibitions featuring the work of the so-called Appropriationists together with the work of would-be Simulationists during the early and mid-1980s. [. . .]

Despite being hyperbolic, Halley's Baudrillardian writings and statements in interviews from the period 1984–86 became the theoretical voice most often used to seriously explain the work of this group of artists in 1986. Halley's outspokenness, articulateness, ability to link himself and others to contemporary theory, and his opportunity to publish in widely circulated art magazines were surely catalysts. Although Halley's "The Crisis in Geometry" may have been read in 1984, people really began to take notice in 1986, when, for the first time, even the short reviews of Halley's exhibitions began to repeat the Baudrillardian vocabulary. Before 1986, however, it was rare at best for critics to discuss Halley's work in connection with Baudrillard, even though the "Geometry" article had been published as early as 1984.

A likely reason for this is that, in 1984, "The Crisis in Geometry" was written by someone who did not yet have significant status in the art world. That came later. Interviews were especially helpful in creating that status because interviews by nature reinforce the impression of the interviewee's authority. Some publications that helped to create recognition were Jeanne Siegel's "The Artist/Critic of the 80's: Peter Halley," in the September 1985 issue of *Arts*, and Michele Cone's "Peter Halley," in the February–March 1986 issue of *Flash Art*. In both interviews, Halley boldly pronounced his interest in Baudrillard. Because of Halley's association with Baudrillard's theory, Koons's and other artists' association with Halley prompted the extended association of Baudrillard with an entire group of artists, who were not then as outspoken as Halley or probably even familiar with Baudrillard. This view of Halley as group spokesman was popularized in print, including an article in the *New York Times*, John Russell's "Bright Young Talents: Six Artists with a Future." There Russell reinforced the common and inaccurate notion that Halley was the "theoretician of a group of painters." [. . .]

That a number of other artists associated with Simulationism were unconcerned with Baudrillard's theory is evident in their interviews and statements and in scattered individualized treatments of their work by critics. [. . .] In addition, the various artists considered in Jeanne Siegel's "Geometry Resurfacing: Ross Bleckner, Alan Belcher, Ellen Carey, Peter Halley, Sherrie Levine, Philip Taaffe, James Welling" were each featured in light of their individual agendas. Her separate treatment of each artist is prefaced by the statement: "Geometry has resurfaced, but is being put to new uses and given new meanings. Geometry's recurrence is broad and disparate." Such a focus on individuality occurred after the period of Simulationism's popularization in 1986. This process of re-individualization, however, belongs to a different phase—namely, the differentiation among well-known artists that takes place usually *after* a group trend has achieved recognition. [. . .]

By far the most well-developed early context for the work of both Halley and Koons was created by the writings and exhibitions of Collins & Milazzo. This was the signature used by Tricia Collins and Richard Milazzo for their collaborations from the time of their marriage in 1982 until 1994. The significance of Collins & Milazzo to the work of Halley and Koons, among numerous others, is twofold: First, in their roles as writers and exhibition organizers, Collins & Milazzo provided substantive and imaginative interpretative frameworks for the work; second, in their roles as friends, freelance dealers, and collectors, their active promotion of the work was crucial to the cultivation of its market.

C&M, as they were often called in the press, evolved their dual function as culture producers and brokers informally in the East Village, through friendships with artists and interest in writing about art at a time when the artists they were writing about were unfashionable. From 1982 to about 1984, the New York art world was still focused on the scars of Neo-Expressionist painting and Appropriation as well as Graffiti Art and other types of work associated with the Gracie Mansion, Fun, and related galleries in the East Village. What was in place for Collins & Milazzo, however, was the reputation of the East Village itself. By the time C&M moved to their apartment on Second Avenue and Saint Mark's Place in 1982, the area had already become New York's hottest new art neighborhood. [. . .]

By the end of 1982, C&M began holding informal get-togethers in the living room of their apartment, where artists would meet. Out of this environment came the idea to start a magazine as a forum for the art they were interested in, since articles they were submitting were getting little play in mainstream magazines. So from 1982 to 1984, they edited *Effects: Magazine for New Art Theory*, which contained reproductions of art works and brief writings by Collins & Milazzo, yet the bulk of the magazine consisted of writings by artists, short pieces of fiction or commentary on a variety of topics. It was low budget and limited in distribution. Its main audience was artists. Peter Nagy and his partner at Nature Morte, Alan Belcher, also an artist, did the typesetting and layout, respectively. The magazine featured many unheard-of artists, and for the first time placed them in the company of a small number of artists C&M had met from the slightly earlier generation at Metro Pictures, such as Jack Goldstein, Richard Prince, Michael Zwack, and Robert Longo.

In addition to editing the magazine, C&M began planning exhibitions. Their first two were held at Nature Morte and International with Monument, another young gallery in the East Village in which C&M took an interest. [. . .] It was not long until C&M exhibited the work of Halley and Koons for the first time—in December 1984 in their group show at White Columns, *The New Capital*.

Collins & Milazzo were doing much in the early 1980s to link older artists to younger galleries and younger artists to other younger artists. To Nature Morte and International and soon to another new gallery that opened in September 1983, Cash (later Cash/Newhouse), they brought older artists such as Vito Acconci, Michael Zwack, James Welling, Ross Bleckner, Sarah Charlesworth, Richard Prince, Allan McCollum, among others, who might not have otherwise exhibited at such little known venues. This helped draw attention to the younger galleries. In addition, C&M forged an immediate link between Nature Morte and International with Monument, made visible when Nagy and Belcher of Nature Morte were included in the first C&M show at International. That Nature Morte and International were the two principal launching pads of Simulationism in 1986 was due largely to the efforts of Collins & Milazzo.

Although C&M's efforts to give the artists exposure and to widen their social network were critical, it should be noted that they were not the only early supporters of these artists. However, C&M's sustained and dedicated intellectual involvement with the work was unique. For each of their exhibitions, C&M produced written statements—in themselves challenging objects—to accompany the shows. [. . .]

[. . .] C&M were in the forefront of the movement of independent curators working in commercial galleries. When a market for the work evolved, C&M began charging commissions on the art sold from their shows and fees from dealers. Were they art advisors, dealers, or curators? In the meantime, at first from gifts, and later through purchases, they accumulated an outstanding collection of over twelve hundred works. Perhaps they were mainly collectors. Adding to the confusion was their dense and mannered theoretical prose. [. . .]

In many ways, the theoretical, curatorial, and social framework Collins & Milazzo created for the work of Halley, Koons, and others had the makings of a successful artistic trend or package. C&M acted in an organized and consistent way, regularly exhibiting the work and writing statements for the shows over a sustained period. [. . .]

In addition to the extent of C&M's organization, their shows were recognized and brought much attention to these artists and galleries. *The New Capital* was publicized in the *Village Voice*, where Roberta Smith characterized it as a "dense and provocative" "theory show." Her notice of this work was key not only because she was writing for the *Voice* but also because she may have been the first to introduce Charles Saatchi, the mega-collector of the 1980s, to the work of Koons by bringing him to a show including Koons in mid-1985. Saatchi ended up buying the works of Halley, Koons, and others by the scores and determining the ultimate market and media success of Simulationism by stimulating a trend in the widespread collecting of this art.

11

THE GLOBAL ART MARKET

Major technological and geopolitical developments in the late twentieth century had a significant impact on the Western art market. First, the invention of the World Wide Web in 1991 revolutionized global communications by creating on the Internet a vast network of data publicly accessible throughout the world. Now rapid, nearly real-time dissemination of information was possible. Auction prices became readily available and art market analysis sites such as Artprice, Artnet, and Art Market Monitor found an instant following among art market participants. As a result, dealers and collectors are now able to obtain far more information, especially regarding the secondary market, than ever before.

Moreover, political changes in both the Soviet Union and China during the 1990s ushered in a new era, albeit slowly, for the European world-economy. With the lifting of national capital controls, the democratization of finance, technology, and information, as well as the end of the Cold War system (signaled by the fall of the Berlin Wall in 1989), a new global market emerged, attracting investors from many different countries. Financial institutions—major mutual and pension funds, hedge funds, insurance companies, commercial and investment banks—started moving capital globally. Large multinational corporations started investing in building new factories—or striking long-term deals with existing factories—around the world. The free flow of capital is one of the hallmarks of globalization. Globalization can also be described as a "communicational concept, which alternately masks and transmits cultural or economic meanings" (Jameson and Miyoshi 1998, 55–56). Fredric Jameson and Masao Miyoshi argue that the idea of a global network of communications has been translated into a popular—reductionist—

message about a new world culture that celebrates difference. Both concepts are reflected in an art world set in motion: the art trade is now conducted at far-flung locations at art fairs that draw collectors from around the world. Sixty countries sponsored 138 biennials in 2013 alone, and between 1992 and 2008, artists from 128 countries were represented at these international fairs.

In 1985 Mikhail Gorbachev, the new leader of the Soviet Union, introduced profound changes in Soviet economic practices and international relations. Within five years, his revolutionary program had swept Communist governments throughout Eastern Europe from power and brought an end to the political and economic rivalry between the Soviet Union and the United States and its allies, setting the stage for the Soviet Union's 1991 collapse. The ensuing privatization of the major industries in the former Soviet republics (mostly Russia and Ukraine) instantly created an oligarchy of powerful and wealthy business owners. In 2013, the number of billionaires in Moscow ranked just second after New York according to Wealth Insight. The new Russian riches contributed to the higher velocity and prices in the established art markets of New York and London.

At the same time, China began to unilaterally open its markets over the course of the 1990s. After joining the World Trade Organization in 2001, China further transitioned to a market economy. By 2013 it had become the world's biggest trading nation in goods, ending the postwar dominance of the United States. China surpassed the United States in 2015 as the leading destination for foreign capital. As the new locus for trade and investment, China, conforming to the patterns of this anthology's long narrative of the art market, was well positioned to become a major force in this realm. After the Chinese amended their constitution in 2004 to include guarantees regarding private property, Chinese demand for art exploded.

Artnet reported, for example, that in 2009, while most of the other major art markets were hit by the worst contraction in sales in nearly twenty years, the mainland Chinese auction market started an unprecedented boom, with sales values increasing by more than 170 percent. By 2014, the Chinese art auction market had become the largest worldwide by value and the focus of intense international attention, radically altering the global art market's hierarchy and threatening the hegemony of the Western art market.

The ranking of the world's top five auction markets in 2014 has New York in first place (accounting for 30.8 percent of all auction sales), London in second place (18.7 percent), and Paris fifth with 2.8 percent of sales. The Beijing and Hong Kong markets ranked third and fourth respectively, with shares of 18.6 percent and 6 percent of worldwide auction revenues. It remains too soon to tell what the effect of the emergence of this strong Chinese art market will have on Western markets. Considering the volume of Chinese art sold in the Chinese art market, it is not clear whether Beijing will become a dominant center in the global art trade in the twenty-first century as New York did in the twentieth and as Paris and London did in the nineteenth. Perhaps a different, bifurcated, model is emerging, in which the art market will revolve around the two major auction markets in existence at the time of this writing: New York (with a share of 30.8 percent) and China (accounting for 37.3 percent). This is reflected in the presentation of the above statistics in the annual market report, *The Art Market in 2014*, published by the website Artprice.com in association with the Art Market Monitor of Artron (AMMA), which is based in China. Unlike their previous reports, the 2014 report separated the two hemispheres and refrained from city-by-city comparisons. Major differences in the nature of the Western and Eastern art markets may account for this new approach. New York remains the center for sales of contemporary (American) art, while Chinese painting and calligraphy dominate the Chinese market. London has continued its dominant position in the Old Masters market. While Paris sales are less defined, the School of Paris painters continue to have a strong presence in the French auction market.

PAUL ARDENNE, *The Art Market in the 1980s*

Excerpts (pp. 106–13, 119–21) from "The Art Market in the 1980s," *International Journal of Political Economy* 25, no. 2 (1995): 100–128. Copyright © 1995 by Paul Ardenne. Reproduced by permission of Taylor & Francis LLC.

Like any village, that of the [art] market has a center, a periphery, and unfrequented zones. The incontestable center of this village is New York, a status that city acquired in the late 1940s, at first with a "patriotic" market, and later, by the mid-1960s, with an irreversibly international market. [. . .] In 1990, New York's dominance was impressive. The reason why New York has no contemporary art fair in the strict sense is obvious: *The fair goes on all year long.* More than 700 galleries for the most part serve the ultra-contemporary in art, missing no opportunity to take over from the museum as an institution or to better it, for instance, with buildings where one makes the rounds by electric cart on the famous SoHo (south of Houston Street in Manhattan, where there are approximately 300 galleries) Saturdays. [. . .] Even within the United States, Chicago and its fair carry little weight as a challenger, although they, too, are impressive by European standards. Without exception, the New York gallery owner travels little, though he or she is invited to all fairs. People usually come to him or her.

Europe has represented the periphery for more than thirty years now. The European continent suffered a decline in status in the early 1970s, Basel excepted. Basel was the only fair of any significance at that time, serving as a relay station between Germany and the United States. London was at the time first and foremost an American outpost, while France was utter torpor personified. Toward the end of the 1970s, the advent of several interrelated factors wrought a change in this depressing situation. First, the Europeans made an effort to legitimate their own avant-gardes. [. . .] Next, the actors on the market shifted to an offensive strategy and established themselves on American soil. Likewise, the establishment of Europe–U.S. links through the system of friendly galleries brought about a salutary delocalization. Accomplished within ten or so years, and marked by the emergence of fairs of every conceivable variety, the European revival nonetheless initially occurred on its own territory. Apart from a few privileged artists (Bacon, Baselitz, Yves

Klein for the *déjà-classiques*), European artists remained underrepresented across the Atlantic, where contemporary art suffered a fate comparable to that of European literature and film, held in little esteem by North American cultural chauvinism.

This is, of course, not a complete description of the periphery that is the West European continent. In fact, the old continent saw a fairly rapid relocalization on its own territory. All the established market places—Paris, London, Basel, Milan, Cologne, Düsseldorf—reinforced their positions. [. . .] The two most visible challengers are Madrid and Frankfurt, the future European business capital ("Bankfurt"). Both cities offer similar bait: Fairs are liberally subsidized by public or municipal authorities such as the famous ARCO in Madrid . . . (1982), and l'Art Frankfurt . . . (1989, at a cost of $2 million); the correlated establishment or programming of museums of international scope (e.g., the magnificent exhibition halls of Madrid's Centre Reina Sofia and Frankfurt's new museum for post-1945 art along the Main, opened in 1991). [. . .]

This reorganization of the internal European market, incomplete, bitterly contested, and resisted by the established centers, has made Europe a lively and more attractive neighborhood within the global village. The potential market seems promising to excess. Eventually, there will no doubt be a readjustment of the international market, to Europe's benefit. Thus, the future geography of the living art market will probably be represented by two competing top-class areas and a decline of the concept of the periphery—except for Japan. . . . It remains obstinately attached to classical art and has nothing to sell on the contemporary art market.

Although a market's structure and management play a role, its strength is ultimately sustained by the financial vitality of trade. In this regard, the 1980s were a decade of soaring prices, compounded by a revelation: Contemporary art, little esteemed by the eye and the pocketbook down to the end of the preceding decade, has created its own icons, its worthy artifacts, or to use the felicitous expression of Gérard Garouste, the value of the "gilded" has finally caught up with the value of the "sanctified." [. . .]

[. . .] The period 1980–90 is one of record setting for contemporary art as well as for the classic-modern or classic in art. [. . .] Until about 1987–88, the highest tenders were received in New York for the works of American artists. Such a situation had a dual effect. On the one hand, it confined the European artists to the old world market and shut the doors of New York to them (what was the point of hoping to sell something in New York that does not measure up to U.S. standards?). On the other, it enabled their dealers on the European side of the Atlantic to *work out* their list prices without competition. Finally, the recovery of prices was due not to the scarcity of works but to their abundance: On the contemporary art market, a scarce item is tantamount to no deal. A dealer who undertakes to launch an artist must have a number of significant works. Since a fad may be ephemeral, it is always important to satisfy demand promptly—unless the fame of the artist or the nature of the work permits him or her to curb production. [. . .]

More than the steadily rising sales figures or the ever-growing adulation of contemporary art, the rise of prices on this market has astonished the public. For the already consecrated assets, the now-famous classic moderns from Cubism to Pop art, the prices recorded during the preceding decade are not all that surprising: On the one hand, any reassessment of an artistic current translates into a rise in quoted prices; on an internationalized market, expanded demand bolsters the bid and can raise it astronomically. Classic works, marked with the aura of the "masterpiece" and embodying considerable symbolic capital, are rare. [. . .] Where prices are in fact surprising is in the market for more recent artistic products. Indeed, no one, the collector no less than the dealer, can ignore the fluctuation that now prevails in the contemporary art business. A price can crumble as easily as it can be set. As the product of many determining factors, not the least of which is fashion, it will vary in time and space in a more or less predictable manner. Price, however, is never an artifice but a truth—an instantaneous truth of a conflation, and translation into figures, at a given moment, of realities as disparate as desire, the particular art object's degree of consecration, financial liquidity, and competition in the bidding itself. [. . .]

[. . .] The frenzy observed on the marketplaces of New York and to a lesser degree in Western Europe before 1991 (when the market went into a perceptible slump) is beyond any doubt related to the collective perception of the 1980s: Triumphant free-marketism, producer of inflated fortunes and rapid accumulations of wealth—the "yuppification" of possessions and consciences, emblematic of a new relation to money—were accompanied by homage to the present and to *all* of its values of glorification, including art. Further, while price informs about the state of a social class in its relation to art, it also says something about art itself. The 1980s, because they failed to establish a principle, imposed the rule that it is less art that makes the price than it is the price that makes art. A work of art will have more aesthetic value if the price it fetches confirms that it has always been both coveted and well sold. Not only has the economic aspect reunited with the aesthetic, it also serves it as a prop. [. . .]

The abandonment of materiality as an evaluative criterion to the benefit of the sign (which by no means signifies its exile from the work of art, although there are premonitory signs pointing in that direction)—nothing new of course, but carried to its extreme by modernity—resulted in a double possible definition of contemporary art: Contemporary art is that which, by a sign, activates the networks of the art system in such a way that networks extrinsic to the work of art are able to establish its *signification*. But, by the same token, any offering that is able to defy the economic logic of assigning value is art. The exorbitant prices fetched by a number of works of art based on reputation, which may be no more than the effect of publicity, or on the capital importance attributed at the level of signification—an attribution that may be only partiality, even imposture—these prices, *a priori* and unlimited, are the best indication that such works do indeed belong to the sphere of art. The value attained sets the criterion of art, while at the same time it eclipses whatever aesthetic qualities a work of art may have. Ultimately, after a long historical process of substitution and simulation, art makes its mark via its commercial value, and not vice versa, as was once the case. Such an inversion of the code is one of the cardinal shifts of art at the contemporary end of the spectrum. In the premodern age, academic work was most in demand. In the era of modernity, a time of avant-gardes and ceaseless experimentation with the new, it is the best *glossed*, the best explained, and the most sanctified and sought-after work that can aspire to the highest value. In the so-called postmodern age, supposedly embodied by the 1980s, the best-sold work of art wore its price as a badge not just of its commercial value but also—and undoubtedly even more—of its aesthetic value.

The market's grip on art, and not the reverse, thus brought about its notorious de-sanctification. Where money is the sovereign value, art's initial value is as an equivalent of money. The artist is to that extent a producer of money. Picasso would sometimes pay his bill in a restaurant by drawing on the tablecloth. Joseph Beuys, following the same rationale, titled one installation *90,000 Marks*, thereby displaying the price in the work itself—but the work, already canonized, went for a sum far beyond the artist's price. To show that his work could not be dissociated from its relation to the market, the American simulationist Haim Steinbach included bank statements in some of his works. [. . .]

[. . .] The market necessarily requires works of art, capitalization in a material form of high symbolic and economic value, whose destiny, once the transaction is completed, is to be possessed. To be traded for hard cash, as an item of distinction and satisfaction, works must, quite simply, be produced and, at the same time, produced by *someone*. In the mechanism of the market, the artist so required by his works serves as a guarantee. He embodies a work's name and originality, he is the physical body attached to the work, which the buyer has not yet decided to allow to fade into oblivion. In these times of the ready-made, of widespread poor or second-rate art, nothing if not this sheer presence, this recognizable will that has acted in the still charismatic guise of the artist, enables the lowly object to be distinguished from the object of art. Three boards nailed together by Joel Shapiro constitute a sculpture, not the debris of a fence: The man is known, a diligent acknowledgment of his journey through the multiple agencies of legitimation justifies paying a high price for what would never even have been viewed without this legitimated presence. A work of art is a complex equation that does not suffer anonymity well. What it produces of aesthetic feeling, historic information, convention, or subversion demands, for the sake of credibility and value, to be attached to a body. The market therefore needs the artist as much as the work does; it knows how to outdo itself in exploiting the process of identification with the artist, or devotion to his production, a process always active in the act of acquisition of a work of art. [. . .]

This new kind of market has its organized hierarchy: the figure of the artist, obligatory point of passage in the act of acquisition, is at the service of the work; it alone is capable of producing its money equivalent. Selling a work is tantamount to selling an image of the artist *as well*, a portion of the fate accruing to its uniqueness. That is why, time after tedious time, the great artist is always presented as *different*—human, certainly, like each and every one flung into the chaos of contingency, but nonetheless other, an Olympian personage, a figure of sovereign Otherness. Difference being a need, the market must support it—and on occasion create it. It is the logic of *esse est percipi*, that constant by which one guarantees that an artist's quoted price is always in line with his overall influence. If the star system is classical in art more than elsewhere . . . it took on new proportions in the 1980s. By the time an artist put in his appearance on the art scene, he was effectively already formed. No sooner was the figure unveiled than his biography was written, and the critique of his work and the catalogue raisonné were in press. Such was the effect of an unbridled acceleration, in pace with an inflated demand and with the uncertainty surrounding the durability of the potential attraction for other projected works. An artist of the 1980s was almost invariably a creation of the market, reinforced by its traditional waystations of legitimation. Bolstered during the preceding decade, the decompartmentalization of the sales-critics-exhibits cycle further accelerated the process. A career was built quickly and on several intersecting planes. For a new figure, a price rise went hand-in-glove with a heightened interest among critics and curators. The actors in the system would then mobilize, often automatically—which was for that reason suspect, giving the impression of forces joined just for the occasion—to the benefit of the chosen artist, to further nudge him along his way. What was absolutely essential was the steadfast presence of the figure.

Like movie stars, the artist of the 1980s worked on location. As a producer of the visible, he had to pass a visibility test of his own. As a producer of meaning—or, supposedly, through the intercession and the authority of the criticism charged with producing in regular succession the necessarily *essential* signification of the work—he was condemned to presence. [. . .] This ever grander model of the artist as a self-promoting product or as a personality on the rebound—the artist plus his dealer, plus his selected critic, plus his group of appraisers and his groupies—gave rise to the system of privileged selection and overpresentation that sooner or later, strictly speaking, made the work *inevitable*. The example of a Jean-Michel Basquiat, a Keith Haring, or a Julian Schnabel—however edifying it may be—providing fuel to the argument that high-quality art is today very quickly recognized for its value—shows that aesthetic renown also depends on plain old renown, and on the networks able to promote, to impose, and to maintain it.

NOAH HOROWITZ, *Video Art*

Excerpts (pp. 58–68, 71–72) from "Video Art," in *The Art of the Deal: Contemporary Art in a Global Financial Market* (Princeton, NJ, and Oxford: Princeton University Press, 2014), 57–72. Copyright © 2011 by Princeton University Press. Reprinted by permission.

The video art market that began to take its form in the early 1990s is distinguished from its earlier manifestation of the 1960s and 1970s by the sophisticated management of both moving-image content and ancillary goods. This is in part technologically driven, in part due to growing familiarity with the capabilities of video art, and also a product of significant advances in the legal support structure of this market—most notably how an intellectual property regime is drawn upon to legitimize the practice's museological relevance and enhance the prestige value of ownership.

Christian Jankowski's *The Hunt* (1992), a seventy-one-second single-channel video, provides a good example of the new market. The work is sold as a two-tiered collectable: for €400 collectors can buy a VHS edition of two hundred for private consumption (to be screened on a television monitor); or for €10,000 they may purchase a DVD edition of six sold as an "exhibition version" (to be projected). While the content is identical, the VHS version represents a terminal sale in which the collector is not safeguarded from the inevitable degradation of content and is only allowed to present the artwork privately. The premium paid to acquire the higher-resolution DVD marks a long-term engagement with the artist and gallery to conserve and update the work as necessary and enables collectors to loan the work for public presentation. Elite collectors have thus been targeted by limiting supply, by enhancing image resolution, and by accommodating more sophisticated institutional preservation requisites; others benefit from their ability to attain a lower-grade version of the work at a cheaper price. Furthermore, five video stills, each in an edition of ten, are also sold in relation to this production. Jankowski's career has bloomed since the mid-1990s, and . . . both video versions have sold well and the stills have sold out.

[Matthew] Barney's *Cremaster Cycle* occupies a unique position within this history. This piece, unrolled in a series of chapters between 1994 and 2002, is the quintessential multidisciplinary contemporary artwork, spanning performance, sculpture, photography, drawing, video, orchestral composition, and a great number of art-historical, cult, and hermetic reference points. This proliferation of forms coincides with Barney's desired conflation of time- and object-based media. [. . .]

The breadth of saleable goods linked to his production stems from this symbiosis and is the project's most significant economic issue. The much heralded videos, for instance, are only one aspect of the overall production that comprises over 150 objects spanning flags, prosthetic limbs, and Vaseline-encased production stills, sold either independently or together as installations. When editioned, these account for the nearly one thousand items that compose the *Cremaster Cycle*, of which 70 percent are photographs.

Even more telling is how the content is parceled into bundles of material and immaterial properties, enabling the *Cremaster Cycle* to exist in the market in two states at once. For instance, the digital video footage that constitutes the source matter for each of the five *Cremaster* projects has also been transferred to 35mm film. This facilitates the projection of these works both in museums and movie theaters. This aspect of the *Cremaster Cycle* therefore mirrors that of the commercial film industry and constitutes one of the project's economic circuits. But a second, and arguably more important, circuit also persists: the *Cremaster* videos are sold to collectors in limited editions of ten as LDs and DVDs, encased in vitrines with accompanying props. Value is therefore strategically added to video content through the bifurcation of moving-image material as both 35mm film available for commercial rent and limited editioned art goods that can be exhibited both as sculpture (as vitrines) and as video art (by playing the LDs or DVDs).

This entrepreneurialism was evident from the project's outset. Seed funding for the first film, *Cremaster 4*, was secured through sales of a promotional photograph of Barney against a tartan backdrop as the Loughton Candidate. . . . The picture was taken in a New York studio during the earliest stages of filming; it was sold by Gladstone Gallery in an edition of thirty. At this juncture, the economic structure of the project was unclear. The gallery knew the work would ultimately be editioned though not precisely how, nor was it apparent who would fund its eventual exhibition and screening costs. The problem was solved first by raising money through sales of this photographic edition and second through an agreement with luxury goods multinational Cartier to cover outstanding expenses. [London gallery] Artangel was allowed to premiere *Cremaster 4* in British cinemas while Cartier obtained the rights to present a *Cremaster 4* exhibition in France in 1995, to screen the film in French cinemas, and to "secure some works [from Gladstone] at an advantageous price."

A much overlooked dimension of the *Cremaster Cycle* is that all but one of its productions (*Cremaster 1*) comprised similar large-scale editions. *Cremaster 2* included two photographic editions of forty, *Cremaster 3* included one photogravure in an edition of forty and two photographic editions of fifty, and *Cremaster 5* included one photographic edition of thirty; five etchings in an edition of forty were also sold at the close of the project. Tellingly, the photographic editions of both *Cremasters 3* and *5* were produced in the year prior to completion of the videos, the only objects associated with each of these works to have been fabricated as such. This underscores the strategic roles these editions played in securing income up front and highlights the extent to which *Cremaster*'s business strategy was correlated with the buoyancy of the contemporary photography market during this period. These factors were to become especially crucial as production values rose over the course of production, from approximately $120,000 for *Cremaster 4*, in 1994, and to more than $4 million for *Cremaster 3*, in 2002. [. . .]

Artists have for centuries bolstered the economic and prestige value of their work through limited editioning. Notable precedents include Albrecht Dürer's woodcuts and engravings of the early sixteenth century and Auguste Rodin's sculpture multiples from the late nineteenth century. The difference with artists like Barney is a fundamental lack of clarity concerning where the relevant "artistic" values reside: In the videos? Or in their physical manifestation as sculpture, photography, and ephemera? Judging from his emphasis on symbiosis, Barney may argue that all components be weighted with equal values. The danger is that against the gravitas of his moving-image work, sales of ancillary products can appear slight.

If Barney's economic success is exemplary, it is hardly unique. Numerous artists working in film and video command five- and six-figure prices for their work and complement such output with the sale of photographic editions and ephemera, often derived from or related to moving-image content. The mechanics of this are a practical resolution to monetizing the value of content that may otherwise be difficult to sell, and it has more in common with ordinary business enterprise than many artists and gallerists might be willing to admit. Shirin Neshat, who like Barney is represented by New York gallerist Barbara Gladstone, is one example. Neshat's *Rapture* (1999) is sold as a two-screen 16mm film installation in an edition of six, alongside twelve photographs in editions of ten. Tellingly, *all* of the nearly 350 works by Neshat sold at auction through 2009 have been photographs, many of which have links to her films and videos.

London-based Isaac Julien and his gallerist Victoria Miro offer another relevant example. Julien's *Paradise Omeros* (2002) was produced on a £160,000 budget. It was marketed as a three-screen version in an edition of four for £50,000 and as a single-screen version in an edition of ten at £10,000; fourteen photographs, comprising a mixture of triptychs, diptychs, and single works (all in editions of four), were also sold in prices between £8,000 and £20,000. Assuming an average cost of £14,000 per photograph, the seventy items produced for *Paradise Omeros* generate an aggregate list price of £1,084,000, or nearly seven times the project's cost. The rationale is classic venture capital: upfront financial risks are taken on by artist and dealer, and a sales strategy is implemented to net back costs, and ideally to turn a profit.

Julien's *True North* (2004), a fourteen-minute 16mm film (digitally transferred to DVD), is sold as a three-screen version in an edition of six at £60,000; as a two-screen version also in an edition of six at £50,000; and as a single-screen version in an edition of ten at £12,500. This is accompanied by a set of production photographs comprising four photographic triptychs at £12,000, nine single photographs at £6,000, and eight lightboxes priced between £15,000 and £25,000, each in editions of six. *True North* thus yields 148 saleable items at a combined list price of £2,357,000 against a production budget of roughly £336,000, also about seven times cost.

The buying audiences for these works reflect the . . . stratification of collectors: three of the three-screen works have been allocated to museums, one to a semipublic foundation, and two to private collectors; two of the two-screen works have gone to museums, one to a private foundation, and one to a private collector; all ten single-channel works have sold to private collectors; and the photographs have been evenly divided between private and institutional parties. Breaking down the market for *True North* as such illustrates its strategic economic nature.

Julien's prerogative is illuminating. He eloquently contends that the scaling up and scaling down of such pieces is a "version of versioning," something that filmmakers have been grappling with for decades. In his case, this is undertaken to distinguish output, to sanctify artistic production:

> For me, versioning or editioning is a way of valorizing a practice or medium that had been devalorized for so long. . . . There is an ethical aspect to it. . . . It's not to do with the market as such, but with the idea of placing value on a work, a way of establishing a certain autonomy within a framework. . . . I don't think the gallery is telling me to edition as such,

but it grows out of a multiplicity of interests spanning filmmaking, photography, and installation—a willingness to differentiate.

But the process is hardly haphazard, and its financial underpinnings are palpable. Julien acknowledges that the two-screen version of *True North*, for instance, is a "sponsor's edition" strategically fabricated to recompense the project's financiers. [. . .]

It is imperative to consider how artists and galleries have come to package video content in order to understand video art's marketization. The Lisson Gallery, which represents a number of artists working in video . . . accompanies many of their film and video sales with "presentation" or "collector" boxes. [. . .] The Lisson boxes cost approximately £200 to manufacture and offer collectors an attractive option for displaying their moving-image work. These typically contain one or multiple DVDs, a Digital Betacam submaster cassette, a certificate of authenticity, and installation instructions. The Lisson has furnished these to accompany work by nearly twenty of its artists, and they are becoming increasingly commonplace in the trade at large: Julien also produces such boxes, as does Zarina Bhimji, another successful artist working in video.

These developments are not limited to the literal packaging of this content: the production of immersive installations and increasingly high-definition film and video work is also significant. All of these qualities are acutely evident in Barney's *Cremaster Series*, of which the final two works (*Cremaster 2* and *3*) were shot on HD video, and in Julien's multiscreen audio/visual installations like *True North*, whose three-screen projection measures twelve by four meters and is shot with striking resolution against a picturesque tundra landscape. [. . .]

Three significant points must be raised in relation to this. The most critical from an institutional perspective is how the technical complexity and costs of these works have encouraged museums to begin coacquiring them. For instance, Viola's five-screen installation, *Five Angels for the Millennium* (2001), was jointly purchased by Tate, the Whitney, and the Pompidou in 2003. Another important example is *Cremaster 2*, coacquired by SFMoMA and the Walker Art Center, Minneapolis, in May 2000. These intricate acquisition/loan programs may be indicative of a genre of relationships set to burgeon as the prices to buy and the expenses to preserve such work increase. If so, they could have an important impact on editioning and pricing policies (will the dilution of one edition across three parties encourage dealers to charge more for it?), not to mention more basic issues such as how artists approach the fabrication of such work.

A second point concerns how advanced technological capabilities have enabled the presentation of video art to flourish in both institutional and private contexts. This has encouraged video art's migration beyond "black box" gallery display and offers expansive possibilities for artists to exhibit and sell their work. Aitken's *Sleepwalkers* (2007), projected nightly for three weeks onto eight different surfaces of MoMA's exterior in 2007, offers an excellent case in point. . . . Elsewhere, Michal Rovner collaborated with luxury goods multinational Chanel in 2005 to produce a work consisting of 200,000 computer-controlled LCD panels on the facade of the company's Hong Kong boutique. This transformation of walls into screens indicates new types of partnerships between art, architecture, design, and commerce that are likely to proliferate moving forward. It also indicates the instrumental role that technology-based arts in particular play in enabling cultural and corporate institutions to engage ever-wider audiences (through public presentations of art-as-advertising).

These features are not lost on private collectors. [For] Norman and Norah Stone, Aitken adapted his five-screen projection, *Electric Earth* (1999), which originally occupied 1,200 square feet of exhibition space, into a single-screen version that now resides in the couple's one-car garage-cum-installation space. [. . .]

In general, the most substantial extension of video art into private collections occurs in the form of LCD monitors and HD plasma screens. One therefore witnesses artists returning to monitors, though not as clunky props but as slick display devices. The ambitious manipulation of video content on such screens is central to the work of Paul Pfeiffer . . . and they have been readily appropriated as aesthetic supports by other video artists such as the Wilsons, and for much computer-generated art as well, including that of Julian Opie and Michael Bell-Smith. [. . .]

Growing use of wall-mounted plasma flat-screen televisions links up the third point concerning how present-day video art has come to occupy a reserve of sanctity and contemplation formerly dominated by painting. This reinforces comparisons between the video art and photography markets insofar as the large-scale dimensions and high-resolution finishes that have become characteristic of the latter have raised innumerable comparisons to the painterly tradition as well. Viola was referred to as simply "the Rembrandt of video" in a Christie's catalogue accompanying the sale of his 2001 video triptych, *Witness*, in 2005. This ensemble of three horizontal LCD flat panels was hammered down for $320,000, making it the sixth most expensive piece of video art ever sold at auction.

FRANCIS M. NAUMANN, *Money Is No Object*

Excerpts (pp. 476–80) from "Money Is No Object, Part II: The Art of Defying the Art Market," in *The Recurrent, Haunting Ghost: Essays on the Art, Life and Legacy of Marcel Duchamp* (New York: Readymade, 2012), 472–81. Reprinted with kind permission of the author.

For Duchamp, context is everything. A shovel in a hardware store is, after all, only a shovel; place it into a museum, and it is magically transformed into art. This is a concept that most collectors of classic European modernism would either fail to understand or flatly reject. Most collectors of contemporary art, on the other hand, accept the philosophical and aesthetic implications of the readymade as an important if not critical precedent to the underlying conceptual strategies of modernism. . . .

The [importance] of placing Duchamp's work within the context of vanguard art . . . was well understood by the organizers of a sale on May 13, 2002, of Contemporary Art at Phillips de Pury & Luxembourg in New York. The auction featured all fourteen of the readymades that had been issued by the Galleria Schwarz in 1964, these examples from the collection of Arturo Schwarz himself. The sale also included sculpture by Dan Flavin, Donald Judd, Carl Andre, Joseph Beuys, Jeff Koons, Rachel Whiteread and Maurizio Cattelan; photographs by Cindy Sherman, Andreas Gursky, Thomas Struth and Thomas Ruff; and paintings by Francis Bacon, Joan Mitchell, Agnes Martin, Gerhard Richter, Andy Warhol, Jean-Michel Basquiat, Damien Hirst, Neo Rauch and Ed Ruscha, whose untitled 1963 painting of the word "NOISE" in yellow against a dark blue ground graced the cover of the lavish, oversized catalogue, while Duchamp's *Bicycle Wheel* appeared on the back.

The sale was accompanied by as much advance publicity as the auction house could muster, including a regular run of advertisements in the *New York Times* reproducing the various readymades. The only newspaper to run a feature article about the sale, however, was the London *Daily Telegraph*. The *Bicycle Wheel* was reproduced, and the article was given the amusing title "Wheel of Fortune," for as its author Colin Gleadell remarked, it was "estimated to sell for up to $3 million." Gleadell also informed his readers that in contrast to the issuing of readymades in 1964, which were designed to be sold intact (as complete sets), these fourteen examples were being offered individually, so that collectors were at liberty to choose whichever one they wanted and could afford. He reminded readers that *Fountain* had sold a few years earlier for $1.7 million, and that, although this information could not be confirmed, an example of the *Bicycle Wheel* had "sold for more than $2 million on the private market." Moreover, when the evaluation assigned to all fourteen readymades is tallied, "the overall pre-sale estimate for the set is $8.5 million to $12.6 million," which, Gleadell informs his readers, falls short of the $15 million guarantee Schwarz was given. "Clearly Phillips has taken a gamble," Gleadell concluded, "one that Duchamp, who had a weakness for risk-taking when playing chess, might have enjoyed." [. . .]

[. . .] In the case of the Phillips auction . . . the owners and administrators did undertake a fairly serious financial risk, for it was later revealed that they issued Schwarz a guarantee of $10 million, an amount that fell in the middle of the low and high estimates. If the readymades sold for the low estimate of $8.5 million, the auction house stood to lose $1.5 million; if they sold for their high estimate, they would have made $2.5 million. Apparently, this was a risk the auction house was willing to take, drawing a certain degree of confidence, perhaps, from their recollection of the successful sale of *Fountain* two years earlier in a sale of Contemporary Art at Sotheby's. [. . .]

The sale began with Duchamp's *Paris Air*, one of the smallest and least known of the readymades, which was given an estimate of $200,000–300,000. Bidding was slow and halting. It eventually stopped at a hammer price of $150,000, short of the low estimate but still higher than the reserve, for, to everyone's surprise (probably even the successful bidders), the auctioneer announced that the work had been sold. A similar pattern continued for the remaining thirteen readymades: in most cases, prices only reached approximately half the low estimates, yet the works were repeatedly announced as having been sold. Only the *Bottle Rack* (estimated at $800,000–1.2 million) and snow shovel (estimated at $700,000–900,000) failed to meet their reserves. *Fountain*, which was given a conservative estimate of $1.5–2 million (a range that reflected the price it had attained two years earlier at Sotheby's), sold to José Mugrabi for a hammer price of just over $1 million, still nearly half a million dollars short of its low estimate. When the bidding stopped, a quick tally showed that the entire set of readymades sold for $5,370,000, exactly $4,630,000 short of the amount Schwarz was guaranteed, a substantial loss for the auction house, but a huge gain for Schwarz, who, in all likelihood, scurried back to Milan the next morning with a fat check in his pocket.

By contrast, the rest of the auction went rather well: eight artists had achieved record prices for their work, including the Ruscha cover-lot painting, which sold for over $2.5 million, and a Judd sculpture, which sold for over $1.3 million. The entire auction fetched $29,686,350, with 91% of the offerings sold by value. In a report issued by the auction house after the sale, these facts were of course emphasized and, in an effort to put a positive spin on the sale of readymades, it was even announced that Duchamp's "iconic *Bicycle Wheel* tied the record for any *Readymade*," which it did, since it sold for the same price as *Fountain* two years earlier at Sotheby's. Of course, there was no mention of the fact that Phillips lost over $4.5 million on its guarantee to Schwarz, which was perceived by many to have been a total disaster for the Duchamp market. [. . .]

So far as the sale of Duchamp's work is concerned, the failure of the readymades to attain their estimates may inhibit sales in the short term, but in the future, there will be little—if any—harm done to the general Duchamp market. To my way of thinking, there are two reasons why Duchamp's work continues to be assigned comparatively low evaluations: rarity, and, perhaps even more significantly, an unrelenting cerebral content.

Rarity is a factor that in most commercial markets causes an item gradually to escalate in value over time. Precisely the opposite occurs in Duchamp's work, for its rarity creates a situation in which reliable evaluations of comparable prior sales cannot be established. The best way to demonstrate this point is by citing a hypothetical example: Say that you own a work of art by a notable artist that you are interested in selling. When an attempt is made to evaluate the work, comparables are cited, earlier examples by the same artist from the same period that have sold—either at auction or privately—within the recent past (in the art market, up to five years is usually considered a fair indicator). If you should manage to find a comparable work that sold for X-number of dollars, naturally you want the work of art that you own to be evaluated at a somewhat higher figure, an amount that reflects the time passed since the comparable work was sold. When it comes to unique works by Duchamp, however, there are preciously few comparables. During his lifetime, he saw to it that his most important work was placed into important private collections (such as with Arensberg or Dreier), which he knew would one day be donated to museums. In the Duchamp market, then, the "snowball effect" that causes works of art to escalate in value over time is virtually nonexistent. As a result, one can ask whatever one wants for a unique work by Duchamp, but even here, the price must remain within reason, that is to say, controlled by some knowledge of prices that were paid for other works by the artist in the comparatively recent past.

Today, the most common way to check prices paid for an individual artist's work is on the Internet. A variety of sites offer postings of recent auction records, but it is virtually impossible to find any verifiable information pertaining to private sales. Of course, when a collector of means is matched with a work of art that he or she absolutely cannot live without, the question of comparable evaluations is of no relevance. In the André Breton sale that was held in Paris in April of 2003, for example, Duchamp's *Monte Carlo Bond* sold to the Principality of Monaco for 240,000 € (well above its pre-auction estimate of € 50,000–60,000). A similar situation occurred in the mid-1990s, when a collector and former art dealer living in Paris sold Duchamp's *Belle Haleine* perfume bottle to Yves Saint-Laurent for $5 million. The collector originally purchased the work some twenty-five years earlier from the Forcade-Droll Gallery in New York, and, at the same time, he also purchased the original *L.H.O.O.Q.*, which is still in his collection. [. . .]

When the prices paid for works by Duchamp are compared to the prices paid for the big names in contemporary art, there is no comparison. Even if the information pertaining to private sales were made public, I doubt that it would affect the comparatively depressed financial evaluation given to works by Duchamp. This, I believe, can be traced to a single overriding factor: the importance of vision over thought. Unlike more traditional works of art, which rely primarily upon visual comprehension for understanding their importance—and, thus, financial value—a work by Duchamp (particularly the readymades) relies upon more complicated processes of thought. We can look at a painting by Matisse, for example, and appreciate it on a purely visual level. Indeed, Matisse himself encouraged precisely this method of viewing when he stated that "an art of balance, of purity and serenity" is "something like a good armchair that provides relaxation from fatigue." By contrast, any viewer who looked at Duchamp's readymades in this same fashion would derive little or no aesthetic pleasure; no matter how long you look at a shovel—whether hanging in a museum or in a hardware store—it remains a shovel. In this case, viewers are forced to echo a strategy employed by the artist himself when selecting these objects, for he wanted the readymades to exhibit no exceptional visual interest; or, as he said, they are objects possessed of "visual indifference . . . a total absence of good or bad taste . . . a complete anesthesia."

If we apply this reasoning to the marketplace, then an art dealer or seller is placed in a somewhat unusual position. He or she can no longer present a work of art to his or her client and allow a purely visual response to convey its content. I have come to refer to this predicament as the triangle theory, where, under normal circumstances, three specific points must be identified and understood before a sale can take place: (1) the client's eyes; (2) the work of art; (3) the client's pocketbook. In trying to sell a work by Duchamp, one point in this triangle must be adjusted slightly, for in considering a readymade, one cannot rely solely upon a client's vision. Instead, the seller is obligated to move that point one or two inches back, to a position well within the client's gray matter. Only then can he hope to come anywhere near the client's pocketbook. If the person's intellect is not stimulated, then, as in the case of looking at a readymade like Duchamp's *In Advance of the Broken Arm*, a shovel remains a shovel, which in most hardware stores sells for about fifty dollars (not $600,000, which is the amount for which this item reportedly sold in a private sale to a European client a few days after the Phillips sale, although it could well sell today for as much as $6 million).

It is my belief that, in the future, works of art will be increasingly appreciated for their cerebral content, although for the present moment at least, vision is still required to comprehend the existence of the object. [. . .] Meanwhile, as was his habit, Duchamp seems to have timed things perfectly: if there is any correlation between the aesthetic value of a work of art and the amount of money that someone is willing to pay for it, at the very moment in our history when intellect and vision strive to achieve union, there are virtually no important works by Duchamp available to test the market. He was not only successful in thwarting attempts to commercialize his work in his lifetime, but his efforts continue to have an effect to this very day. Because he kept his production of unique works of art to a minimum, only replicas and works in edition remain within the marketplace today, and even these items come up only rarely. Some thirty-five years after his death—in both aesthetic and monetary terms—Duchamp remains securely one step ahead of the game.

ALAIN QUEMIN, *The Internationalization of the Contemporary Art World*

Excerpts (pp. 53–59, 61–68, 71) from "The Internationalization of the Contemporary Art World and Market: The Role of Nationality and Territory in a Supposedly 'Globalized' Sector," in *Contemporary Art and Its Commercial Markets*, ed. M. Lind and O. Velthuis (Berlin: Sternberg, 2012), 53–75. Reprinted by kind permission of the author.

Since the end of the 1960s, the international art trade has to a large extent been integrated into a world market, the *very heart* of which is constituted by international exchanges, and the main contemporary art institutions, including museums and art centers, have been part of a vast international network. The various actors on this scene often state that they consider geographical boundaries and nationalities, including those of the artists, to be negligible. Such a notion, which no doubt one would always find to be the majority view in the world of contemporary art (which in essence seems so obviously international, since, today, validation by space, by geographical distance, has replaced the validation by time characteristic of art in the past), has no doubt been reinforced by the current situation. Globalization, cultural mixing, and the questioning of the traditional frontiers and hierarchies between forms of artistic expression are all part of the zeitgeist, and extend well beyond contemporary art. [. . .] Since the beginning of the 2000s, globalization in the art world has been taken for granted so often that it is less regularly asserted now.

However, even if the actors on the international contemporary art scene are convinced that this planetary creative effervescence is a reality, along with the concomitant exchanges, and while they may often prove ardent upholders of the deepest cultural relativism by arguing that no country can claim greater artistic importance than any other, and that all this is a matter of talent and individual personality, it is also true that, paradoxically but imperturbably, they also often recognize the existence of a hierarchy of countries, a ranking that is familiar to all and is part of the world of contemporary art. [. . .]

When analyzing the hangings of the permanent collections in a number of the main international institutions, such as MoMA in New York City, Tate Modern in London, Centre Georges Pompidou in Paris, or the Hamburger Bahnhof in Berlin, a strikingly high proportion of national artists is evident, as well as a concentration on American artists, generally followed by German and British ones, then French and Italian. A similar tendency can be observed at the biggest and most prestigious art events, such as the major biennials, among them, the Venice Biennale.

The "Kunstkompass," which ranks artists in terms of institutional recognition, can synthetize artists' international visibility. It is based on solo shows and artists' participations in group hangings at the most prominent venues, and on their coverage in the main contemporary art publications. This ranking of the 100 most recognized artists has been published almost annually by German journals since 1970. . . . We can thus analyze the evolution of the different countries' positions over a considerable period in order to see which are the long-term leaders, how the ranking has evolved, and which new challengers have emerged. . . . The aim of the creator of the Kunstkompass, Willi Bongard, was to establish a scale for measuring artists' reputations, based on the rough assumption that this was an objective measure of their aesthetic value. An artist's rank in this classification is the result not of their prices on the contemporary art market but a set of judgments made by contemporary art "experts." [. . .] Whatever criticisms may have been made of the Kunstkompass as an instrument, the publication of the results obtained by Bongard and his successors has always had the effect of a *self-fulfilling prophecy*. Moreover, while one can certainly criticize the over-representation of Germany in the construction of this indicator . . . , the *evolution* of the countries' respective positions in this ranking is less open to debate, since it introduces much less bias.

As was mentioned earlier, the Kunstkompass takes the form of a ranking. The hundred best-known and esteemed artists are ranked in descending order of renown. In 2010, the rank of each artist for that year was followed by their rank in 2009 and then by their name, year of birth, country, main discipline . . . , the total number of points obtained, and other indications concerning, notably, the average price of a work, but also the artist's gallery.

In all, only twenty countries were represented in 2010 and in very unequal proportions: 29 artists were American and 29 were German, 13 were British, 4 were French and 4 were Swiss, 3 were Austrian, 2 were Italian, 2 were Belgian, 2 were Danish and 2 were Canadian. Ten other countries appeared in the ranking with only one artist each: The Netherlands, Greece, Serbia, Russia, South Africa, Iran, Mexico, Japan, Thailand, and India. It should be underlined that, although globalization is supposed to rule the contemporary art world today, national concentration is extremely strong and the West is clearly dominant when it comes to the most visible artists on the international art scene. [. . .]

[An analysis of the number of artists per country in the Kunstkompass shows that] while the United States has continued to dominate the rankings in terms of the number of artists, its position has nevertheless slipped. Still, this is only due to the fact that the Kunstkompass defines the countries of the artists in terms of passport. If country of residence were considered, most artists that appear in the ranking as nationals of minor or peripheral countries would prove to live in the United States, and the share of this country would literally jump. Germany's presence grew solidly during the 1980s and continues to gain prominence. In contrast, the United Kingdom's position slipped in relation to its position in the late 1970s, before its presence increased again recently. Belgium, which disappeared for a while from the list of the 100 most recognized artists, has re-entered it. Switzerland seems fairly stable, while the French and Italian positions have been eroded.

We may also note the disappearance of several countries from outside the Western world. These countries seem particularly vulnerable, in that they are each represented by a single artist. However, between the Kunstkompass of 1970 and that of 2010, a dozen new countries outside the Western European and North American ambit have produced artists who have entered the table—more than have slipped out of it.

If, in both 2005 and 2000, the 100 artists enjoying greatest international recognition were concentrated in twenty-two countries, it should be noted that in 1979, and even in 1997, they represented only fourteen countries. Recent years have therefore seen a diversification in the geographical origins of the most recognized artists, which clearly illustrates the phenomenon of multiculturalism. Still, in 2010, the number of countries represented in the ranking dropped to only twenty. That said, in 2005, ninety of the ranked artists still came from countries of Western Europe or North America (in 2000, the figure was eighty-eight); but in 2010, the number increased again to ninety-two, and while this still represents a decrease since 1979, when there were ninety-five, it clearly shows the overwhelming dominance of these two geographical ensembles when it comes to the most recognized contemporary art. [. . .]

Although constantly ignored or denied by the members of the art world, the weight of the nationality factor is nevertheless clearly perceptible and we can make out a recurrent opposition between a "center," a "semi-periphery," and a "periphery." The center clearly comprises the United States, or possibly the United States and Germany (if we decide to ignore the bias in favor of Germany), the semi-periphery comprises countries like the United Kingdom, France, Italy, or Switzerland; the periphery, all other countries. [. . .]

Territorial concentrations and a hierarchy of countries can also clearly be seen in both segments that constitute the art market, public sales at auctions on the one hand and private sales in galleries on the other.

The data published yearly by Artprice shows extreme concentration [in] the auction market. The repartition of fine art sales was extremely concentrated in 2010 as only three countries held just over 80% of all fine art auctions, with a share of 33% for China, 30% for the US, 19% for the UK, 5% for France, and the rest of the world sharing the remaining 13%! In just a few years, the rise of China on the auction market has been spectacular. [. . .] Although two western auctioneers, Christie's and Sotheby's, are still, by far, the world leaders, seven out of the ten most important auction houses are now Chinese. [. . .]

China's boom in the auction field and especially in the contemporary art sector is mostly due to the fact that Chinese collectors and investors, who are often relatively young (less than 50 years of age), are eager to buy works by contemporary Chinese artists, especially for reasons of social prestige. This pushes the prices of Chinese contemporary artists at auction to record highs. . . . Half of the top ten contemporary artists selling work at auction are now Chinese. Most of these Chinese artists are sold at auctions organized in China, and production is oriented toward Chinese buyers. It seems that only Chinese buyers are ready to hand over high sums for works by artists who are not equally supported by the most prestigious contemporary art institutions (who all happen to be located in the Western world), which might be because the Chinese are less conscious of the importance of institutional support to guarantee valuation of contemporary works in the long term; that they are culturally less afraid of gambling; or that they are sure enough of the durability of their prosperity and of the competition between national buyers for Chinese works of art, to be able to guarantee extremely high prices in the medium and long terms.

Sales in galleries tend to obey a different logic than at auctions. One of the ways to study the role played by territory and nationality in the gallery sales segment is through art fairs and gallery participation by country. The socio-scientific literature on art markets, so far, has largely ignored the role of galleries at international contemporary art fairs. . . . Participation at art fairs generates a major source of income for art galleries. Besides, they also provide a means of comparing the operations of different market sectors: the territorial dynamics of international contemporary art fairs with those of auction houses.

The national profiles of participating galleries at Art Basel, the most prestigious international art fair in the world, are exemplary in this regard: only 10% of exhibiting galleries are Swiss, whilst 23% are from the US, 17% are German, 10% are from the UK, 8% are French, and 7% are Italian. Although this example shows little national diversity given the small number of countries that each gallery represents, it is still the case that

Art Basel is truly international insofar as these countries are the most prestigious in art world terms and clearly are leading nations in the field.

With the help of data provided by Artprice, we identified all international contemporary art fairs held worldwide in 2008 and specialized in "contemporary" art. We then set up a selection criteria to include only those art fairs that featured (i) a significant number of foreign exhibitors; and (ii) galleries of sufficiently diversified nationality, in order to identify those fairs that exhibit an international dimension, and to determine how truly "international" this dimension is. [. . .] So while the world counts almost 200 countries in terms of distinct political units, [we found that] international contemporary art fairs—those that may be considered to exhibit genuinely contemporary art—are hosted in a mere twenty-one of these countries. Even though international contemporary art fairs have spread to other parts of the globe, entire regions—and even whole continents such as Africa—are completely unrepresented, and most regions are represented only marginally.

So what can be said now about the countries of origin of the galleries participating in international contemporary art fairs? The data produced by Artprice [show] the *total number of gallery participations* at international fairs in 2008 at 4,113 (many galleries participate in more than one fair), but also . . . that *the number of different galleries* involved in this social world is around 2,300 (2,322 galleries to be exact). The high number of galleries pertaining to the same country reinforces the previously noted concentration among a few countries and the uneven representation of these countries in the organization of art fairs. [. . .]

Not only are the locations of international contemporary art fairs limited to a very small geographical, and mainly Western, space, but the participating galleries come from just sixty-four Western countries, that is, one-third of the world's nations. The US, Germany, the UK, Italy, France, and Spain send no less than 55.5% of participating galleries: the US accounts for 20% while the five major European Union countries account for 35.5%. Australia (6.2%) and Japan (4.9%) have taken advantage of their physical distance from major international contemporary art market hubs and major international galleries to exercise a large measure of control over their domestic markets. The remarkable strides made by Chinese artists in terms of contemporary art auction sales (in just a few years) do not translate into an increased presence of Chinese art galleries at international contemporary art fairs, where they represent only 2.6% of participants. Even so, while these figures are indeed modest, Chinese galleries are already well ahead of other emerging economies such as Brazil (1.0%), India, or the Russian Federation (with 0.7% each). [. . .]

In spite of increasing internationalization, the different indicators that we have considered here make it quite clear that the territorial dimension certainly has not disappeared. Fashionable phenomena such as "globalization," mixing and cultural relativism, and the tremendous opening to other world cultures, touted in the world of contemporary art in recent years, are to a large extent illusory.

PACO BARRAGÁN, *Neo-modernity, Neo-biennalism,*
Neo-fairism

Excerpts (pp. 281–86) from "Neo-modernity, Neo-biennalism, Neo-fairism," in *2000
and Beyond: Contemporary Tendencies*, vol. 5 of The Art of the Twentieth Century series,
ed. V. Terraroli (Milan: Skira, 2010), 275–91. Copyright © 2010 Paco Barragán.
Reprinted by kind permission of Skira editore, Milan.

Art and its institutions cannot escape commodification, especially after the neo-liberalist
heyday. The relationship of the museum with consumption has become more than
natural. The spaces devoted to shopping are bigger and bigger, and at each visit the visitor has a wider array of articles available: from books, exhibition-related souvenirs to the
cafeteria. Some visitors even go straight to the restaurant, which is fine.

Museums are contexts that create signification and recognize artistic value. So do
biennials, which tend to act as temporary art museums. Art fairs, like galleries, don't—or
at least that is what we tended to believe until Larry Gagosian embarks on an artist he
particularly likes! Until the 1990s things were very clear and everyone knew his or her
place in the art system and in society; now the situation has become much more complex
and also much more confusing. [. . .]

. . . From the mid '90s on the globalization process, together with low cost travel, new
markets (China, India, Russia, Cuba, Puerto Rico, Dubai) and new players—hedge funds,
revolving funds, the newly rich—offered to new and not so new audiences a mobile,
cosmopolitan, multicultural and exotic art experience. Temporary events like biennials
and art fairs became the driving forces behind the art market. At different levels both
developed artistic strategies that reconciled local ambitions and international needs. As
was inevitable, globalization brought about homogenization. "You discover sometimes",
Robert Storr (2006, 52) writes, "that people are overwhelmed by the sense that there is a
sameness to international art and that their only choices are to join it or to be left out."

This has had a dual effect: on the audiences and on art production. Many art professionals have started to enjoy a limited tourist/nomadic version of contemporary art,
cemented in annual visits to an equally limited group of fairs and biennials. Like the
original eighteenth-century concept of the Grand Tour and its pristine effort to experience
"in its own flesh" remote places and to "catalogue its reality", the educated traveler today,
the same as the antihero of yesteryear, aspires to inform himself in his firm desire to be
the first one to discover, classify, and collect that "lost work of art". And this is exactly what
happened with the other *Grand Tour of the 21st Century*, which, as a result of once-in-ten-
year coincidence (according to the press release) that in turn resulted in a special and
practical synergy between the art fair and the biennials, took the sophisticated art crowds
in a marathon non-stop tour to Venice-Basel-Kassel-Münster in just 10 days.

The problem now is, and that brings us to the second point, that most of the art is
"biennial art" or "art fair art" that responds to a typical globalized canon. It's true that

much of this art responds to the nomadic curator's taste or thesis, who in turn interprets local demands. . . . "Art fair art" has simply to do with hectic production schedules that need to fuel an excessive number of art fairs, especially if the artist is in demand, and with art works that are sexy and arresting, as they are obliged to compete with many others for the attention of a potential collector/client.

Within the actual cultural industry, both the biennale and the art fair have become periodical and long awaited and at the same time foreseeable experiences. I agree with Michele Robecchi (2008, 13) when he states that "Comparing fairs and biennials in these terms is superficial but nevertheless useful for understanding two things: first, entertainment is becoming more and more of a decisive factor in this incestuous competition; and second, art fairs have now been unequivocally promoted to 'cultural event' status." The "biennalization" of art fairs and the "fairization" of biennials is not a recent trend, although it seems it has passed its apex. This parasitic or symbiotic behavior often tends to be related to our new world order, but much of its origins can be traced to the historical development of the art market itself.

It all started with the market in early modern Antwerp where the fair, from the ancient usage of the word *jaarmarkt* or annual trade fair, is its iconic metaphor. "This was an age [c. late 1500s]," writes Elizabeth Alice Honig (1998, 3–4), "when commerce overflowed the boundaries of the marketplace and penetrated all aspects of life: the market and its pictorial representation were crucial grounds for testing how ideas could be made to fit to what seemed reasonable patterns of belief and behavior." In the Middle Ages and the Renaissance the *coopman* or trader practiced a "policy of provision", in accordance with which as many goods as possible had to be attracted into towns for the benefit of consumers. The merchants started taking their wares from city to city and from trade fair to trade fair (maybe we can spot here a comparison with the contemporary gallery owner and his/her participation in art fairs in different cities). In the fifteenth century trade fairs like Antwerp, Bruges and Brabant rose in importance. In the course of the sixteenth century capitalism emerged as the dominant form of social organization of the economy. Painting and painters interacted with the markets as these were influenced by the changing roles played by merchants, church and city governments, and consumers. Some trade fairs are temporary and others are permanent, but both are awaited with impatience as the marketplace becomes a metaphor for social exchange and acquires its own alternative festive halo. With the unstoppable and constant development of capitalism, in which trade fair becomes synonymous with the dynamism of market commerce, it does not require great imagination to understand the later expansion that has ended up in the current "art fair age".

Biennials, triennials, and other international survey-type exhibitions like Documenta are inspired, on one hand, by the eighteenth-century salon, and on the other, by international trade shows, world fairs, and universal exhibitions that are also called "great exhibitions". These were very large public exhibitions held since the mid-nineteenth century, in which the national pavilions created by the participating countries were the main attractions and used as a way to promote their cultures, resources, industries, and products at that moment in history. The exhibition as such not only had an important informational, but also an educational component from the very beginning, and it was accessible to people of all classes and ages. The *Exposition Nationale des produits de l'industrie agricole et manufacturière*, held in Paris in 1844, in the footsteps of the French tradition of national exhibitions, and the *Great Exhibition of the Works of Industry of All Nations*, held in 1851, in the Crystal Palace built in Hyde Park, are clear examples on which many other contemporary international events have based themselves.

"The Venice Biennale," indicates the Biennale's web site, "arose from a resolution passed by the City Council on April 19, 1893, which proposed the founding of a 'biennial national artistic exhibition' to take place the following year to celebrate the silver anniversary of King Umberto and Margherita of Savoy." Thus a political decision underlay its origin as the Biennale represented a sort of acknowledgement to the monarchy for the recent unification of the country. Furthermore, the mayor of the city had other less political and more practical ideas in mind: "When in 1895 the mayor of Venice, Ricardo Selvatico, became involved in planning Venice's first biennial, he was clearly aware of the potential of the idea for positive promotion of his city. So he considered important the participation of international artists and their presence in order to emphasize international dialogue and the city as its meeting place," quotes Eivind Furnesvik (2003, 21).

The world's oldest biennale was held on April 30, 1895 and its trademarks of "international dialogue" and the "city as meeting place" heralded the birth of city marketing: it attracted 200,000 visitors! Like the great exhibitions of the century before, Venice started to build the first foreign pavilion in 1907, and since then the number of national pavilions has increased to 29. In 1951 the world's second-oldest art biennial, the Bienal de São Paulo, also opted for mix of international survey and national pavilions.

Documenta is held every 5 years, although until 1972 it was quadrennial. A curious but no less important anecdote is that Kassel had been chosen in 1955 to host the national garden show (BUGA) as "a collective undertaking through which", as the then Federal President Theodor Heuss put it, "a damaged or endangered community can make a recovery". Arnold Bode conceived *European Art of the Twentieth Century* as an exhibition to be integrated within the infrastructure of the garden show. German artists had to recover their contact with contemporary art and the nascent pro-European movement, and "the State of Hessen had to enhance the supra-local significance of the Garden Show in such way that it not only captured the attention of the experts, but also of those that were interested in culture". For his Documenta, Arnold Bode took the model of The Armory Show of 1913, a commercial show organized by the Association of American Painters and Sculptors. So, Documenta became a mix of tourist, economical, psychological, educational, and artistic elements. The 100 days of Documenta received 130,000 visitors. A little bit more than 50 years later Documenta is considered unanimously the most important international survey on contemporary art in the world.

This brief historical overview is symptomatic of the hybrid origins of and correspondences between art fairs and biennials. If art fairs deal overtly with the market, biennials in turn—especially Documenta and Venice—become a platform for sanctioning art trends and aesthetic attitudes by declaring what is particular, good or relevant art here and now. Whether we like it or not, these power structures, that report to both an international and local intelligentsia, and in which the curator performs a key role, create their own exhibition requirements and economic efficiency because they are oriented towards an international elite and the construction of value, be it symbolic or real.

To quote [Boris] Groys (2008, 51): "It can of course be stated that the independent curator, as the museum curator before him, cannot but depend on the art market, even lay the groundwork for it. An art work's value increases when it is presented in a museum, or through its frequent appearance in the diverse temporary exhibitions organized by independent curators."

The curator, whether independent or associated to an institution, has taken on a predominant role in contemporary art in his profane activity of detecting, contextualizing and narrativizing works of art. The '90s witnessed the banalization/biennalization of biennales. This has also resulted, especially in the last 5 years, in a greater presence of the curator at art fairs, which "resort to the curator to act as an enabler or facilitator of positioning via projects that are specifically created for the fair." . . . More curators have started to work as artistic directors for art fairs, are conceiving special exhibitions—see Neville Wakefield, who curated the *FRIEZE Projects*—or are finding their ways into the selection committees. Curators that by definition conceive shows for institutions or biennials have arrived recently in the world of art fairs; although it is maybe more precise to put it the other way around: art fairs have attracted the intellectual capital of curators in a move to distinguish themselves among the mass of art fair proposals. In short, this means that the curator has started to become even more central to contemporary art practices. Here he works directly with/for the market; in the case of biennials it's more elliptical and subtle but still very obvious. It should be seen in a bigger and more structural context: the worldwide shift from museum-style management centered on the conservation and acquisition of a permanent collection towards a thematic or monographic exhibition policy, which prioritizes objectives of media coverage and increasing visitor numbers, in which the curator becomes a mediator between the institution and the public.

ACKNOWLEDGMENTS

I am indebted to all the authors in this volume who graciously allowed me to excerpt and reprint portions of their texts.

Thank you, Gwen Wells, Darcy Tells, Nadine Little, and Karen Levine, for shepherding this project from cradle to press. Thank you, George Baker, Aruna d'Souza, Eric Jan Sluijter, and Jonathan Brown, for pointing the way. Thank you, Frances Cohen and Christine MacMillan, for making it possible. Thank you, Barbara Mundy and Betsy Lunt, for wisdom and friendship.

I am grateful to Michael Lobel and Véronique Chagnon-Burke for their early and instrumental support in the conception of this book.

Adams, Steven R. 2013. "'Noising Things Abroad': Art, Commodity, and Commerce in Post-Revolutionary Paris." *Nineteenth-Century Art Worldwide* 12 (2): 1–28.

Adorno, Theodor W. 2001. "Culture Industry Reconsidered" (1975). In *The Culture Industry: Selected Essays on Mass Culture*, 98–106. London: Routledge.

Ainsworth, Maryan W. 1998. "The Business of Art: Patrons, Clients, and Art Markets." In *From Van Eyck to Bruegel: Early Netherlandish Painting in the Metropolitan Museum of Art*, edited by M. W. Ainsworth and K. Christiansen, 23–37. New York: Metropolitan Museum of Art.

Alpers, Svetlana. 1988. "Freedom, Art, and Money." In *Rembrandt's Enterprise: The Studio and the Market*, 88–122. Chicago: University of Chicago Press.

Anderson, Robert. 1974. "Paintings as an Investment." *Economic Inquiry* 12 (1): 13–26.

Andre, Carl, with J. Gilbert-Rolfe. 1976. "Commodity and Contradiction, or Contradiction and Commodity." *October* 2: 100–104.

Ardenne, Paul. 1995. "The Art Market in the 1980s." *International Journal of Political Economy* 25 (2): 100–128.

Ashton, Dore. 1983. "Artists and Dealers." In *The New York School: A Cultural Reckoning*, 164–73. New York: Penguin.

Baker, Richard Brown. 1999. "The Days and Nights of a Collector." *Paris Review* 41 (152): 179–90.

Barragán, Paco. 2010. "Neo-modernity, Neo-biennalism, Neo-fairism." In *2000 and Beyond: Contemporary Tendencies*, vol. 5 of The Art of the Twentieth Century series, edited by V. Terraroli, 275–91. Milan: Skira.

Bätschmann, Oskar. 1997. "The Exhibition as a Medium for the Presentation of Art." In *The Artist in the Modern World: The Conflict between Market and Self-Expression*, translated by E. Martin, 12–57. Cologne: Dumont Buch Verlag.

Baudrillard, Jean. 2003/2005. "Art . . . Contemporary of Itself" (2004). In *The Conspiracy of Art*, edited by S. Lotringer, translated by A. Hodges, 89–97. New York and Los Angeles: Semiotext(e).

Baxandall, Michael. 1988. "Conditions of Trade." In *Painting and Experience in Fifteenth-Century Italy*, 1–28. 2nd ed. Oxford: Oxford University Press.

Bayer, Thomas M., and John R. Page. 2011. "The Formation of a Nexus: A Story of Christie's." In *The Development of the Art Market in England: Money as Muse, 1730–1900*, 143–51. London: Pickering and Chatto.

Becker, Howard S. 1982. *Art Worlds*. Berkeley: University of California Press.

———. 1988. *Les Mondes de l'Art*. Paris: Flammarion.

Belk, Russell W. 1994. "Collectors and Collecting" (1988). In *Interpreting Objects and Collections*, edited by S. M. Pearce, 317–26. London: Routledge.

Benedikt, Michael. 1969. "Introduction." In *The Gutman Letter*, vii–xi. New York: Something Else Books.

Benjamin, Walter. 1969. "The Work of Art in the Age of Mechanical Reproduction" (1935). In *Illuminations: Essays and Reflections*, edited by H. Arendt, translated by Harry Zohn, 217–51. New York: Schocken.

Bernié-Boissard, C., L. Dreyfuss, and N. Le Strat. 1999. *Ville et employ culturel, le travail 'créatif-intellectuel' dans les agglomerations de Nimes et Montpellier*. Montpellier, France: Université Paul Valéry, ARPES.

Boime, Albert. 1976. "Entrepreneurial Patronage in Nineteenth-Century France." In *Enterprise and Entrepreneurs in Nineteenth and Twentieth Century France*, edited by E. C. Carter, R. Forster, and J. N. Moody, 137–207. Baltimore: Johns Hopkins University Press.

Bok, Marten Jan. 1998. "Pricing the Unpriced: How Dutch Seventeenth-Century Painters Determined the Selling Price of their Work." In *Art Markets in Europe, 1400–1800*, edited by M. North and D. Ormrod, 103–11. Aldershot, England: Ashgate.

———. 2001. "The Rise of Amsterdam as a Cultural Centre: The Market for Paintings, 1580–1960." In *Urban Achievement in Early Modern Europe: Golden Ages in Antwerp, Amsterdam and London*, edited by P. O'Brien, D. Keene, M. 't Hart, and H. van der Wee, 186–209. Cambridge, England: Cambridge University Press.

Bourdieu, Pierre. 1993. "The Production of Belief" (1980). In *The Field of Cultural Production*, edited by R. Johnson, 74–111. New York: Columbia University Press.

Braudel, Fernand. 1992 [original French edition 1984]. *Civilization and Capitalism, 15th–18th Century*. 3 vols. Translated by S. Reynolds. Berkeley: University of California Press.

Breslin, James E. B. 1993. "An Art That Lives and Breathes." In *Mark Rothko: A Biography*, 231–70. Chicago: University of Chicago Press.

Brown, Jonathan. 1995. "The Prestige of Painting." In *Kings and Connoisseurs: Collecting Art in Seventeenth-Century Europe*, 227–53. Princeton, NJ: Princeton University Press.

———. 1999. "Introduction: The Frontiers of Spanish Art." In *Painting in Spain, 1500–1700*, 1–5. New Haven, CT, and London: Yale University Press.

Bryan, Michael F. 1985. "Beauty and the Bulls: The Investment Characteristics of Paintings." *Economic Review* (Federal Reserve Bank of Cleveland), first quarter: 2–10.

Cannadine, David. 2014. "Pictures across the Pond: Perspectives and Retrospectives." In *Reflections across the Pond: British Models of Art Collecting and the American Response*, edited by I. J. Reist, 9–18. London: Ashgate.

Carriera, Rosalba. 1985. *Rosalba Carriera: lettere, diari, framment.* Edited by B. Sani. 2 vols. Florence: L. S. Olschki.

Chave, Anna C. 2008. "Revaluing Minimalism: Patronage, Aura, and Place." *Art Bulletin* 90 (3): 466–86.

Christensen, Carl C. 1973. "The Reformation and the Decline of German Art." *Central European History* 6 (3): 207–32.

Clark, T. J. 1999. *Image of the People: Gustave Courbet and the 1848 Revolution.* Berkeley: University of California Press.

Danet, Brenda, and Tamara Katriel. 1986. "Books, Butterflies, Botticellis: A Life-span Perspective on Collecting." Paper presented at the Sixth International Conference on Culture and Communication, Philadelphia.

Danto, Arthur. 1964. "The Artworld." *Journal of Philosophy* 61 (19): 571–84.

Dean, Clarence. 1957. "Peak Demand for Pictures." *New York Times,* February 25.

De Marchi, Neil, and Hans J. Van Miegroet. 2000. "Exploring Markets for Netherlandish Paintings in Spain and Nueva España." *Nederlands Kunsthistorisch Jaarboek* 50: 81–112.

Denby, Edward. 1988. *Willem de Kooning.* New York: Hanuman.

Douglas, Mary, and Baron Isherwood. 1979. *The World of Goods.* New York: Basic Books.

Dreier, Katherine S. 1949. "'Intrinsic Significance' in Modern Art." In *Three Lectures on Modern Art,* 1–30. New York: Philosophical Library.

Durkheim, Emile. 1912/1915. *The Elementary Forms of Religious Life.* London: George Allen and Unwin.

Emmerich, André. 2004. "Recollections: Greenberg and Frankenthaler." *New Criterion* 12: 29–34.

Epstein, S. R. 1998. "Craft Guilds, Apprenticeship, and Technological Change in Preindustrial Europe." *Journal of Economic History* 58: 684–713.

Etro, Federico, and Laura Pagani. 2012. "The Market for Paintings in Italy during the Seventeenth Century." *Journal of Economic History* 72 (2): 423–47.

Ewing, Dan. 1990. "Marketing Art in Antwerp, 1460–1560: Our Lady's *Pand.*" *Art Bulletin* 72 (4): 558–84.

———. 2015. "Jan De Beer's Lifetime Reputation and Posthumous Fate." *Journal of Historians of Netherlandish Art* 7 (2): 1–23.

Fantoni, Marcello, Louisa C. Matthew, and Sarah F. Matthews-Grieco, eds. 2003. *The Art Market in Italy, 15th–17th Centuries.* Ferrara, Italy: Panini.

Farington, Joseph. 1923. *The Farington Diary.* Edited by William Greig. London: Hutchison and Co.

Feigenbaum, Gail. 1993. "Practice in the Carracci Academy." In *The Artist's Workshop,* edited by P. Lukehart, 59–76. Studies in the History of Art 37, Center for Advanced Study in the Visual Arts, Symposium Papers 22. Washington, DC.

Fitzgerald, Michael C. 1995. "Lord of the Jealous Wood." In *Making Modernism: Picasso and the Creation of the Market for Twentieth-Century Art,* 190–204. Berkeley: University of California Press.

Fitzgerald, Michael Cowan. 1992. "Skin Games." *Art in America* 80 (2): 70–82, 139–41.

Freedberg, David. 1986. "Art and Iconoclasm, 1525–1580: The Case of the North Netherlands." In *Kunst voor de Beeldenstorm. Noordnederlandse Kunst 1525–1580,* edited by J. P. Filedt Kok, W. Th. Kloek, and W. Halsema-Kubes, 69–84. Amsterdam: Rijksmuseum.

Furnesvik, Eivind. 2003. "Phantom Pains." In *Verksted #1: New Institutionalism*. Oslo: OCA.

Gee, Malcolm. 1979. "The Avant-Garde, Order and the Art Market, 1916–23." *Art History* 2 (1): 95–106.

———. 1981. *Dealers, Critics, and Collectors of Modern Painting: Aspects of the Parisian Art Market between 1910 and 1930*. New York: Garland.

Gelderblom, Oscar. 2012. "The Golden Age of the Dutch Republic." In *The Invention of Enterprise: Entrepreneurship from Ancient Mesopotamia to Modern Times*, edited by D. S. Landes, J. Mokyr, and W. J. Baumol, 156–82. Princeton, NJ: Princeton University Press.

Gennari-Santori, Flaminia. 2010. "'I was to have all the finest': Renaissance Bronzes from J. Pierpont Morgan to Henry C. Frick." *Journal of the History of Collections* 22 (2): 307–24.

Gérin-Jean, Pierre. 2003. "Prices of Works of Art and Hierarchy of Artistic Value on the Italian Market (1400–1700)." In *The Art Market in Italy*, edited by M. Fantoni, L. C. Matthew, and S. F. Matthews-Grieco, 181–94. Ferrara, Italy: Panini.

Gibson, William. 2007. *Art and Money in the Writings of Tobias Smollett*. Lewisburg, PA: Bucknell University Press.

Gibson-Wood, Carol. 2002. "Picture Consumption in London at the End of the Seventeenth Century." *Art Bulletin* 84 (3): 491–500.

Gillett, Paula. 1990. *The Victorian Painter's World*. Gloucester, England: Sutton.

Gimpel, René. 1963. *Journal d'un collectionneur, marchand de tableaux*. Paris: Calmann-Lévy.

———. 1966. *Diary of an Art Dealer*. Translated by J. Rosenberg. New York: Farrar, Straus and Giroux.

Ginsburgh, Victor, and A. F. Penders. 1997. "Land Artists and Art Markets." *Journal of Cultural Economics* 21 (3): 219–28.

Goddard, Steven. 1985. "Brocade Patterns in the Shop of the Master of Frankfurt, an Accessory to Stylistic Analysis." *Art Bulletin* 67 (3): 401–17.

Goetzmann, William N. 1995. "The Informational Efficiency of the Art Market." *Managerial Finance* 21 (6): 25–34.

Golahny, Amy. 2013. "Italian Paintings in Amsterdam around 1635: Additions to the Familiar." *Journal of Historians of Netherlandish Art* 5 (2).

Goldthwaite, Richard A. 1993. "The Culture of Consumption." In *Wealth and the Demand for Art in Italy, 1300–1600*, 212–55. Baltimore: Johns Hopkins University Press.

Grampp, William D. 1989. *Pricing the Priceless: Art, Artists and Economics*. New York: Basic Books.

Green, Nicholas. 1987. "Dealing in Temperaments: Economic Transformation of the Artistic Field in France during the Second Half of the Nineteenth Century." *Art History* 10 (1): 59–76.

———. 1989. "Circuits of Production, Circuits of Consumption: The Case of Mid-Nineteenth-Century French Art Dealing." *Art Journal* 48 (1): 29–34.

Greenberg, Clement. 1939/1986. "Avant-Garde and Kitsch." In *The Collected Essays and Criticism*. Vol. 1, *Perceptions and Judgments, 1939–1944*, edited by John O'Brian, 5–22. Chicago: University of Chicago Press.

Greenough, Sarah. 2000. "Alfred Stieglitz, Rebellious Midwife to a Thousand Ideas." In *Modern Art and America: Alfred Stieglitz and His New York Galleries*, 23–53. Washington, DC: National Gallery of Art.

Greffe, Xavier. 2002. "The Artist as an Entrepreneur of His Talents." In *Arts and Artists from an Economic Perspective*, 107–35. London: Unesco.

Groys, Boris. 2008. *Art Power.* Cambridge, MA: MIT Press.

Hadley, R. van N., ed. 1987. *The Letters of Bernard Berenson and Isabella Stewart Gardner, 1887–1924.* Boston: Northeastern University Press.

Harris, Neil. 1982. *The Artist in American Society: The Formative Years 1790–1860.* Chicago and London: University of Chicago Press.

Haskell, Francis. 1980. *Patrons and Painters: A Study in the Relations between Italian Art and Society in the Age of the Baroque.* New Haven, CT, and London: Yale University Press.

———. 1987. "An Italian Patron of French Neo-Classic Art." In *Past and Present in Art and Taste: Selected Essays*, 52–64. New Haven, CT, and London: Yale University Press.

———. 2000. *The Ephemeral Museum: Old Master Paintings and the Rise of the Art Exhibition.* New Haven, CT, and London: Yale University Press.

Haverkamp-Begemann, Egbert. 2006. "Remembrance." In *In His Milieu: Essays on Netherlandish Art in Memory of John Michael Montias*, edited by A. Golahny, M. M. Mochizuki, and L. Vergara, 13–15. Amsterdam: Amsterdam University Press.

Heilbrun, James, and Charles M. Gray. 2006. "Arts Markets." In *The Economics of Art and Culture*, 165–86. Cambridge, England: Cambridge University Press.

Hellmanzik, Christiane. 2010. "Location Matters: Estimating Cluster Premiums for Prominent Modern Artists." *European Economic Review* 54 (2): 199–218.

Helmreich, Anne. 2005. "The Art Dealer and Taste: the Case of David Croal Thomson and the Goupil Gallery, 1885–1897." *Visual Culture in Britain* 6 (2): 31–49.

Hernández Navarro, Miguel A. 2009. "Contradictions in Time-Space: Spanish Art and Global Discourse." In *The Global Art World: Audiences, Markets, and Museums*, edited by H. Belting, A. Buddensieg, and E. Araújo, 136–53. Ostfildern, Germany: Hatje Cantz.

Hickey, Dave. 2002. "The Luminous Body: Sourceless Illumination as a Metaphor for Grace." In *Light in Architecture and Art: The Work of Dan Flavin*, 147–48, 153–54. Marfa, TX: Chinati Foundation.

Hirschman, A. O. 1977. *The Passions and the Interests.* Princeton, NJ: Princeton University Press.

Hoffman, Barbara. 1990. "Whose Image Is It?" *College Art Association News* 15 (5): 5–6.

Hoftijzer, Paul. 2008. "Metropolis of Print: The Amsterdam Book Trade in the Seventeenth Century." In *Urban Achievement in Early Modern Europe: Golden Ages in Antwerp, Amsterdam and London*, edited by P. O'Brien, D. Keene, M. 't Hart, and H. van der Wee, 249–63. Cambridge, England: Cambridge University Press.

Hollanda, Francisco da. 1928. *Four Dialogues on Painting.* Translated by A. F. G. Bell. London: Oxford University Press.

Honig, Elizabeth. 2008. "Art, Honor, and Excellence in Early Modern Europe." In *Beyond Price: Value in Culture, Economics, and the Arts*, edited by M. Hutter and D. Throsby, 89–105. Cambridge, England: Cambridge University Press.

Honig, Elizabeth Alice. 1998. "Trade and Art in Seventeenth-Century Antwerp." In *Painting and the Market in Early Modern Antwerp*, 110–14. New Haven, CT, and London: Yale University Press.

Hoogewerff, G. J. 1947. *De Geschiedenis van de St Lucasgilden in Nederland.* Amsterdam: Van Kampen en Zoon.

Horowitz, Noah. 2014. "Video Art." In *The Art of the Deal: Contemporary Art in a Global Financial Market*, 57–72. Princeton, NJ, and Oxford: Princeton University Press.

Houghton, Charlotte. 2004. "This Was Tomorrow: Pieter Aertsen's *Meat Stall* as Contemporary Art." *Art Bulletin* 86 (2): 277–300.

Hutchison, Jane Campbell. 1990. *Albrecht Dürer: A Biography*. Princeton, NJ: Princeton University Press.

Hutter, Michael, and Richard Shusterman. 2006. "Value and the Valuation of Art in Economic and Aesthetic Theory." In *Handbook of the Economics of Art and Culture*. Vol. 1, edited by V. A. Ginsburgh and D. Throsby, 171–208. Amsterdam: Elsevier.

Jacobs, Lynn F. 1998. *Early Netherlandish Carved Altarpieces, 1380–1550: Medieval Tastes and Mass Marketing*. Cambridge, England: Cambridge University Press.

James, Henry. 1887. "John S. Sargent." *Harper's Magazine* 75 (449): 683–91.

Jameson, Fredric, and Masao Miyoshi, eds. 1998. *The Cultures of Globalization*. Durham, NC: Duke University Press.

Jensen, Robert. 1997. "The Retrospective." In *Marketing Modernism in Fin-de-Siècle Europe*, 107–37. Princeton, NJ: Princeton University Press.

———. 2013. "Why the School of Paris Is Not French." *Artl@s Bulletin* 2 (1): article 5, http://docs.lib.purdue.edu/artlas/vol2/iss1/5/.

Johnson, Una. 1977. "Introduction." In *Ambroise Vollard, éditeur: Prints, Books, Bronzes*, 18–43. New York: Museum of Modern Art.

Jonckheere, Koenraad. 2008a. "The 'Solliciteur-Culturel': Some Notes on Dutch Agents and International Trade in Art and Applied Arts." *De Zeventiende Eeuw* 24: 162–80.

———. 2008b. "Supply and Demand: Some Notes on the Economy of Seventeenth Century Connoisseurship." In *A Closer Look at Paintings by Rembrandt, Rubens and Their Contemporaries*, edited by K. Jonckheere and A. Tummers, 82–109. Amsterdam: Amsterdam University Press.

Kamen, Henry. 2007. *The Disinherited: Exile and the Making of Spanish Culture, 1492–1975*. New York: HarperCollins.

Kant, Immanuel. 1790/1987. *Critique of Judgement*. Translated by W. S. Pluhar. Indianapolis: Hackett.

Kaufmann, Thomas DaCosta. 2004. *Toward a Geography of Art*. Chicago: University of Chicago Press.

Kemp, Martin. 1997. *Behind the Picture: Art and Evidence in the Italian Renaissance*. New Haven, CT, and London: Yale University Press.

———. 2006. *Leonardo da Vinci: The Marvellous Works of Nature and Man*. Oxford: Oxford University Press.

Ketelsen, Thomas. 1998. "Art Auctions in Germany during the Eighteenth Century." In *Art Markets in Europe, 1400–1800*, edited by M. North and D. Ormrod, 143–52. Aldershot, England: Ashgate.

Kopytoff, Igor. 1982. "Slavery." *Annual Review of Anthropology* 11: 207–30.

———. 1986. "The Cultural Biography of Things: Commoditization as Process." In *The Social Life of Things: Commodities in Cultural Perspective*, edited by A. Appadurai, 64–91. Cambridge, England: Cambridge University Press.

Krauss, Rosalind E. 1990. "The Cultural Logic of the Late Capitalist Museum." *October* 54: 3–17.

————. 1991. "Overcoming the Limits of Matter: On Revising Minimalism." In *American Art in the Sixties: Studies in Modern Art*, edited by J. Elderfield, 123–41. New York: Museum of Modern Art.

Lee, Susan. 1988. "Greed Is Not Just for Profit." *Forbes*, April 18.

Lehmann, Ulrich. 2002. "The Trademark Tracey Emin." In *The Art of Tracey Emin*, edited by M. Merck and C. Townsend, 60–78. London: Thames and Hudson.

Leja, Michael. 2007. "Touching Pictures by William Harnett." In *Looking Askance: Skepticism and American Art from Eakins to Duchamp*, 128–52. Berkeley: University of California Press.

Levey, Michael. 1977. *A Royal Subject: Portraits of Queen Charlotte*. London: National Gallery.

Lindberg, Erik. 2008. "The Rise of Hamburg as a Global Marketplace in the Seventeenth Century: A Comparative Political Economy Perspective." *Comparative Studies in Society and History* 50 (3): 641–62.

Lipman, J. 1970. "Money for Money's Sake." *Art in America* 58: 76–83.

Lippincott, Louise. 1983. *Selling Art in Georgian London: The Rise of Arthur Pond*. New Haven, CT: Yale University Press.

Lugt, Fritz. 1938/1953/1964/1987. *Répertoire des catalogues de ventes publiques intéressant l'art ou la curiosité*. 4 vols. The Hague: Martinus Nijhoff.

MacLeod, Dianne Sachko. 1987. "Art Collecting and Victorian Middle-Class Taste." *Art History* 10 (3): 328–50.

Mainardi, Patricia. 2000. "The 19th-Century Art Trade: Copies, Variations, Replicas." *Van Gogh Museum Journal*: 63–74.

Malvasia, Carlo Cesare. 1678/1841. *Felsina Pittrice*. Edited by A. Arfelli. 2 vols. Bologna: Per l'erede di Domenico Barbieri.

————. 1678/1980. *The Life of Guido Reni*. Translated by C. and R. Enggass. University Park: Pennsylvania State University Press.

Mancini, Giulio. 1956–57. *Considerazioni sulla Pittura*. Edited by A. Marucchi. 2 vols. Rome: Accademia Nazionale dei Lincei.

Mattick, Paul. 2003. "Illusions of Disinterest." In *Art in Its Time: Theories and Practices of Modern Aesthetics*, 39–46. London: Routledge.

Mauro, Frederic. 1993. "Merchant Communities, 1350–1750." In *The Rise of Merchant Empires: Long Distance Trade in the Early Modern World 1350–1750*, edited by J. Tracy, 255–86. Cambridge, England: Cambridge University Press.

McAfee, R. P., and John McMillan. 1987. "Auctions and Bidding." *Journal of Economic Literature* 25 (2): 699–738.

McClellan, Andrew. 1996. "Watteau's Dealer: Gersaint and the Marketing of Art in Eighteenth-Century Paris." *Art Bulletin* 78 (3): 439–53.

McMillan, John. 2002. *Reinventing the Bazaar: A Natural History of Markets*. New York: Norton.

Meijer, Bert W. 2000. "Italian Paintings in 17th Century Holland: Art Market, Art Works and Art Collections." In *L'Europa e l'arte italiana*, edited by M. Seidel, 377–417. Venice: Marsilio Editori.

Merryman, John Henry. 1993. "The Wrath of Robert Rauschenberg." *American Journal of Comparative Law* 41 (1): 103–27.

Montias, John Michael. 1982. *Artists and Artisans in Delft: A Socio-Economic Study of the Seventeenth Century*. Princeton, NJ: Princeton University Press.

———. 1987. "Cost and Value in Seventeenth-Century Dutch Art." *Art History* 10 (4): 455–66.

———. 1988. "Art Dealers in the Seventeenth-Century Netherlands." *Simiolus: Netherlands Quarterly for the History of Art* 18 (4): 244–56.

———. 2002. *Art at Auction in 17th Century Amsterdam.* Amsterdam: Amsterdam University Press.

Moulin, Raymonde. 1987. "Antecedents." In *The French Art Market: A Sociological View*, translated by Arthur Goldhammer, 19–24. New Brunswick, NJ: Rutgers University Press.

———. 2011. "The Genesis of the Rarity of Art." *Art in Translation* 3 (4): 441–71.

Murphy, Kevin M. 2002. "Painting for Money: Winslow Homer as Entrepreneur." *Winterthur Portfolio* 37 (2–3): 147–60.

Naumann, Francis M. 2012. "Money Is No Object, Part II: The Art of Defying the Art Market." In *The Recurrent, Haunting Ghost: Essays on the Art, Life and Legacy of Marcel Duchamp*, 472–81. New York: Readymade.

Northcote, J. 1819. *The Life of Sir Joshua Reynolds.* Vol. 2. London: Henry Coburn.

Ogden, Henry V. S., and Margaret S. Ogden. 1955. *English Taste in Landscape in the Seventeenth Century.* Ann Arbor: University of Michigan Press.

Ormrod, David. 1998. "The Origins of the London Art Market, 1660–1730." In *Art Markets in Europe, 1400–1800*, edited by M. North and D. Ormrod, 167–86. Aldershot, England: Ashgate.

———. 2002. "The Rise of the London Art Market, 1660–1760." In *Economia e arte. Secc. XVII–XVII*, edited by S. Cavaciocchi, 303–29. Prato, Italy: Datini Institute.

———. 2008. "The Art Trade and Its Urban Context: England and the Netherlands Compared, 1550–1750." In *Auctions, Agents and Dealers: Mechanisms of the Art Market 1660–1830*, edited by J. Warren and A. Turpin, 11–19. London: Archaeopress.

Osten, Gert von der, and Horst Vey. 1969. *Painting and Sculpture in Germany and the Netherlands, 1500 to 1600.* Translated by M. Hottinger. Harmondsworth, England: Penguin.

Paulson, Ronald. 1992. "Patron and Public." In *Hogarth: His Life, Art, and Times.* Vol. 2, *Hogarth: High Art and Low, 1732–1750*, 1–14. New Brunswick, NJ: Rutgers University Press.

Pearlman, Alison. 2003. "Peter Halley, Jeff Koons, and the Art of Marketing- and Consumption-Analysis." In *Unpackaging Art of the 1980s*, 105–24. Chicago: University of Chicago Press.

Pears, Iain. 1988. "The Art Market." In *The Discovery of Painting: The Growth of Interest in the Arts in England, 1680–1768*, 51–105. New Haven, CT, and London: Yale University Press.

"Peggy Guggenheim to Open Art Gallery 'Art of This Century.'" n.d. (ca. October 20, 1942). Pamphlet files in the Art and Architecture Collection, the Miriam and Ira D. Wallach Division of Art, Prints and Photographs, New York Public Library.

Pepper, D. Stephen. 1984. *Guido Reni.* New York: New York University Press.

Pesando, James E. 1993. "Art as an Investment: The Market for Modern Prints." *American Economic Review* 83 (5): 1075–89.

Piper, Adrian. 1999. "Notes on the Mythic Being I–III 1974–1976." In *Out of Order, Out of Sight.* Vol. 1, *Selected Writings in Meta-Art 1968–1992*, 120–21. Cambridge, MA: MIT Press.

Plessis, Alain. 2005. "When Paris Dreamed of Competing with the City . . ." In *London and Paris as International Financial Centres in the Twentieth Century*, edited by Y. Cassis and E. Bussière, 42–56. Oxford and New York: Oxford University Press.

Pointon, Marcia. 1984. "Portrait-Painting as a Business Enterprise in London in the 1780s." *Art History* 7 (2): 187–205.

———. 1997a. "Pricing or Prizing Potential in the 1990s." *Art Bulletin* 79 (1): 17–20.

———. 1997b. *Strategies for Showing: Women, Possession and Representation in English Visual Culture.* Oxford: Oxford University Press.

Pollock, Griselda. 1993. "Reference, Deference and Difference." In *Avant-Garde Gambits 1888–1893: Gender and the Color of Art History*, 12–35. New York: Thames and Hudson.

Quemin, Alain. 2012. "The Internationalization of the Contemporary Art World and Market: The Role of Nationality and Territory in a Supposedly 'Globalized' Sector." In *Contemporary Art and Its Commercial Markets*, edited by M. Lind and O. Velthuis, 53–75. Berlin: Sternberg.

Rabinow, Rebecca. 2011. "Discovering Modern Art: The Steins' Early Years in Paris, 1903–1907." In *The Steins Collect: Matisse, Picasso, and the Parisian Avant-Garde*, edited by J. Bishop, C. Debray, and R. Rabinow, 21–47. San Francisco: San Francisco Museum of Modern Art; New Haven, CT, and London: Yale University Press.

Reitlinger, Gerald. 1961–1970. *The Economics of Taste.* Vols. 1–3. London: Barries and Jenkins.

Rembrandt. *Die Urkunden über Rembrandt.* Edited by C. Hofstede de Groot. The Hague: Martinus Nijhoff, 1906.

Rewald, John. 1986. "Paul Gauguin—Letters to Ambroise Vollard." In *Studies in Post-Impressionism*, 178–92. New York: Harry N. Abrams.

Robecchi, Michele. 2008. "Let Me Entertain You: The Never-Ending Debate around Art Fairs and Biennials." Preface to *The Art Fair Age*, edited by P. Barragán, 10–13. Milan: Charta.

Robins, Anna Gruetzner. 2013. "Marketing Post-Impressionism: Roger Fry's Commercial Exhibitions." In *The Rise of the Modern Art Market in London, 1850–1939*, edited by A. Helmreich and P. Fletcher, 85–97. Manchester: Manchester University Press.

Robson, A. Deirdre. 1995. "The New York Art Market, circa 1960." *Prestige, Profit, and Pleasure: The Market for Modern Art in New York in the 1940s and 1950s*, 255–63. New York: Garland.

Santagata, Walter. 1995. "Institutional Anomalies in the Contemporary Art Market." *Journal of Cultural Economics* 19 (2): 187–97.

Schiller, Friedrich. 1794/1986. *On the Aesthetic Education of Man.* Edited and translated by E. Wilkinson and L. A. Willoughby. Oxford: Clarendon Press.

Schneider, Friedrich, and Werner Pommerehne. 1983. "Analyzing the Market of Works of Contemporary Fine Arts: An Exploratory Study." *Journal of Cultural Economics* 7 (2): 41–67.

Schwartz, Gary. 2002. "The Structure of Patronage Networks in Rome, the Hague and Amsterdam in the XVIIth Century." *Economia ed Arte*, secc. xiii–xviii: Atti della xxxiii Settimana di Study dell'Instituto Internazionale di Storia Economica.

Scott, Allen J. 1997. "The Cultural Economy of Cities." *International Journal of Urban and Regional Research* 21 (2): 323–39.

Seymour Jr., Charles. 1968. "'Fatto di sua mano': Another Look at the Fonte Gaia Drawing Fragments in London and New York." In *Festschrift Ulrich Middeldorf*, edited by A. Kosegarten, P. Tigler, and U. Middeldorf, 93–105. Berlin: W. de Gruyter.

Sharp, Jasper. 2004. "Serving the Future: The Exhibitions at Art of This Century 1942–1947." In *Peggy Guggenheim and Frederick Kiesler: The Story of Art of This Century*, edited by S. Davidson, P. Rylands, and D. Borg, 288–347. New York: Guggenheim Museum.

Sicca, Cinzia Maria. 2013. "Vasari's *Vite* and Italian Artists in Sixteenth-Century England." *Journal of Art Historiography* 9: 1–18.

Silver, Larry. 2000. "Second Bosch: Family Resemblance and the Marketing of Art." *Nederlands Kunsthistorisch Jaarboek* 50: 31–56.

Simmel, Georg. 1900/2004. "Economic Value as the Objectification of Subjective Values." In *The Philosophy of Money*, 61–139. London and New York: Routledge.

Sluijter, Eric Jan. 2008. "Determining Value on the Art Market in the Golden Age: An Introduction." In *Art Market and Connoisseurship: A Closer Look at Paintings by Rembrandt, Rubens and Their Contemporaries*, edited by A. Tummers and K. Jonckheere, 7–28. Amsterdam: Amsterdam University Press.

———. 2009. "On Brabant Rubbish, Economic Competition, Artistic Rivalry, and the Growth of the Market for Paintings in the First Decades of the Seventeenth Century." *Journal of Historians of Netherlandish Art* 1 (2): 1–32.

Smollett, Tobias. "Article XI. Engraving." *Critical Review, or, Annals of Literature* 7 (1759): 375–77.

Spear, Richard E. 1997. "Marketing" and "Di Sua Mano." In *The "Divine" Guido: Religion, Sex, Money and Art in the World of Guido Reni*, 210–75. New Haven, CT, and London: Yale University Press.

Spear, Richard E., and Philip Sohm. 2010. *Painting for Profit: The Economic Lives of Seventeenth-Century Italian Painters*. New Haven, CT, and London: Yale University Press.

Stewart, Larry. 2001. "Philosophers in the Counting Houses: Commerce, Coffeehouses and Experiment in Early Modern London." In *Urban Achievement in Early Modern Europe: Golden Ages in Antwerp, Amsterdam and London*, edited by P. O'Brien, D. Keene, M. 't Hart, and H. van der Wee, 326–45. Cambridge, England: Cambridge University Press.

Storr, Robert. 2006. "The Biennale: Art Forum or Global Salon." Madrid: Fundación ICO.

Syson, Luke. 2007. "Leonardo and Leonardism in Sforza Milan." In *Artists at Court: Image-Making and Identity 1300–1550*, edited by S. J. Campbell, 106–23. Boston: Isabella Stewart Gardner Museum.

Tedeschi, Martha. 1997. "Whistler and the English Print Market." *Print Quarterly* 14 (1): 15–41.

Tracy, James D. 1993. "Introduction." In *The Rise of Merchant Empires: Long-Distance Trade in the Early Modern World, 1350–1750*, edited by J. Tracy, 1–13. Cambridge, England: Cambridge University Press.

van der Woude, Ad M. 1991. "The Volume and Value of Paintings in Holland at the Time of the Dutch Republic." In *Art in History, History in Art: Studies in Seventeenth-Century Dutch Culture*, edited by D. Freedberg and J. de Vries, 285–329. Santa Monica, CA: Getty Center for the History of Art and the Humanities.

Vasari, Giorgio. 1568. *Lives of the Most Excellent Painters, Sculptors, and Architects, from Cimabue to Our Times*, or *Le Vite de' più eccellenti pittori, scultori, e architettori da Cimabue insino a' tempi nostril*. http://vasari.sns.it/vasari/consultazione/Vasari/indice.html.

Veblen, Thorstein. 1881/1912. "Conspicuous Consumption" and "Pecuniary Canons of Taste." In *The Theory of the Leisure Class: An Economic Study of Institutions*, 68–101, 115–67. New York and London: Macmillan.

Velthuis, Olav. 2007. "Symbolic Meanings of Prices." In *Talking Prices: Symbolic Meanings of Prices on the Market for Contemporary Art*, 158–78. Princeton, NJ: Princeton University Press.

Vermeylen, Filip. 2000. "Exporting Art across the Globe: The Antwerp Art Market in the Sixteenth Century." *Nederlands Kunsthistorisch Jaarboek* 50: 13–29.

Vlieghe, Hans. 1977. "Erasmus Quellinus and Rubens's Studio Practice." *Burlington Magazine* 119 (894): 636–43.

de Vries, Jan. 1996. "Art History." In *Art in History, History in Art: Studies in Seventeenth Century Dutch Culture*, edited by David Freedberg and Jan de Vries, 249–82. Santa Monica, CA: Getty Center for the History of Art and the Humanities.

Wagner, Anne M. 1981. "Courbet's Landscapes and Their Market." *Art History* 4 (4): 410–31.

Warhol, Andy. 1977. *The Philosophy of Andy Warhol*. Orlando, FL: Harcourt Harvest.

Warnke, Martin. 1993. *The Court Artist: On the Ancestry of the Modern Artist*. Translated by D. McLintock. Cambridge, England: Cambridge University Press.

Weatherill, Lorna. 1988. *Consumer Behaviour and Material Culture in Britain 1660–1760*. London: Routledge.

Wee, H. van der. 1963. *The Growth of the Antwerp Market and the European Economy*. 3 vols. The Hague: Martinus Nijhoff.

Welch, Evelyn S. 1995. *Art and Authority in Renaissance Milan*. New Haven, CT, and London: Yale University Press.

Werckmeister, O. K. 1973. "Marx on Ideology and Art." *New Literary History* 4 (3): 501–19.

West, Shearer. 2011. "Gender and Internationalism: The Case of Rosalba Carriera." In *Italian Culture in Northern Europe in the Eighteenth Century*, edited by S. West, 46–66. Cambridge, England: Cambridge University Press.

Whinney, Margaret, and Oliver Millar. 1957. *English Art, 1625–1714*. Oxford: Clarendon Press.

Wilson, J. 1986. *Painting in Bruges at Close of the Middle Ages*. University Park: Pennsylvania University Press.

Winckelmann, J. J. 1755/1987. *Reflections on the Imitation of Greek Works in Painting and Sculpture*. Translated by E. Heyer and R. C. Norton. La Salle: Open Court.

291 (New York gallery), 308–10

Abrégé de la vie des peintres (de Piles), 79

Abstract Expressionism, 317–19, 326–27, 336; signature "styles" within, 321

abstraction, 305, 347; at Art of This Century, 312–15; Greenberg on, 317–18

academicism in art, 14, 25, 133, 253, 261, 334, 356; kitsch and, 25, 26; waning of influence of, 254, 266–67

Académie royale de peinture et de sculpture (Paris), 132–33, 246, 254, 255; classification system of, 254, 263; Salons of, *see* Salon (Académie, Paris)

academies of art, 15, 24, 127, 175, 216; in England, 213, 222; in France, 247, 272, 293; guilds and, *see* guild(s); in U.S., 293, 297, 298. *See also* academicism in art; entries for specific academies

Accademia di San Luca (Rome), 132, 246

Adams, Steven R., 253–56

Adolphe Goupil: *see* Goupil and Co.

Adorno, Theodor, 14, 30–32

advertising, 221, 237, 299, 362; by artists, 220–21; display and, 295, 296; Gersaint and, 248, 249

advisors, art. *See* experts

Aertsen, Pieter, 142–45, 150

Aesthetic movement, 231–33

aesthetic value, 2, 41, 70–71, 77, 95, 96, 192, 244, 245, 256, 262; artists' success as measure of, 357, 367; Duchamp on, 330–32; price and, 128, 129, 355–56, 366; in video art, 359–60

aesthetics, 261, 267, 295, 374; connoisseurship and, *see* connoisseurs and connoisseurship; culture industry and, 32, 355; idealist, 19, 22, 23, 338, 339; Kant on, 15–17; portraiture and, 223–24; ready-mades and, 365–66; theories of, 14, 41; of uselessness, 55–56, 70–71

agent(s), 112, 186, 194, 200, 210; Dutch *solliciteurs* as, 181–83. *See also* auctions and auction market; dealer(s), art

Agnew, (London dealer), 225

Ainsworth, Maryan W., 137–39

Aitken, [Doug], 361, 362

art market(s): for American art, 323–24; China in, 352; for Courbet landscapes, 262–66; flooding of, 159–60; for Harnett's work, 296; historical, *see* art markets (historical); identified by city, 10; internationally based, *see* international art markets (historical); Land Art and, 343–46; masterpieces on, 106–7; Minimalism and, 341; nationalism having impact on, 194, 223; as open market, *see* open market(s); *panden* as, 139–40; preference for genre and landscape painting, 254, 263; for print reproductions of paintings, *see* reproductive prints; for prints, *see* prints and printmaking; profit from, Duchamp on, 330–32; purchaser preferences, 200–201; Rembrandt's approach to, 172–76; secondary, *see* secondary art market; stock market compared to, 103–6; supply and demand in, *see* supply and demand; for video art, 357–62. *See also* fair(s), art

Art Market Monitor of Atron (AMMA), 351, 353

art markets (historical): Amsterdam (17th/18th cents.), 6, 158–62, 215; Antwerp, *see* Antwerp; for Cubism (early 20th cent.), 284–87; Delft (17th-cent.), 1, 158; the Depression and (1930s), 289–90; early Spanish (16th-cent.), ecclesiastical nature of, 195–96; English (17th/18th-cents.), 204–5, 213, 216; for Flemish art (16th cent.), 149–51; in Frankfurt (18th-cent.), 190–92; in Golden Age Netherlands, 86–88; Italian–English, Vasari on (16th cent.), 118–20; Italy (17th cent.), 127–30; in London (18th-cent.), 204–5; merchants and, 10; in post-war New York, 323–24; during World War II, 290–91

Art News (periodical), 323

Art of This Century (New York), 312–13, 322, 324

art production. *See* production

Art Rogers v. Jeff Koons and Sonnabend Gallery, Inc., 96, 98

Art Unions (England), 240

Artangel (London), 359

Artaria (Mannheim), 192

artisanship. *See* craft and craftsmanship

artist(s): advertising by, 220–21; aesthetic logo of, 92, 93, 95; alienation of, 317–18; appropriation in work of, 96–98; assistants to, 129, 154–55, 222; authentication by, 78, 79; buying own work at auction, 226; critical mass of, 8, 9, 214–16, 327; collaboration among, 122, 125, 156, 163; competition among, 138, 160–61, 165; copy work by, see copies/copying of artwork(s); creative *vs.* commercial needs of, 14–15, 96; creative integrity of, commercial value of, 256; dealers and, 44–46; employed by dealers, 166–68; from England, *see* English School; as entrepreneur, Rembrandt's example and, 173–74; female, *see* women artists; financial benefit for, 16–19; French biographies of, 259–60; in gift-exchange relationship, 83–85, 124–25; P. Guggenheim and, 313–15; guilds for, *see* guild(s); hierarchy of, in global art market, 367–68; interviews of, 347; Land Art made by, 342–46; legitimation of, 355–57; marketing by, 173–74, 237–38; Minimalists, Dia's relationship with, 339–41; mobility of, 127, 129; museums defining careers of, 288; patrons of, *see* patrons and patronage; price decrease and reputation of, 51, 53–54, 226; productivity of, 158, 165, 224; profession of, 175–76, 246; profit motive of, Duchamp on, 330–32; property rights sold by, 99–102; public identity of, 90, 356; publicity for, *see* publicity; pupils of, 191, 222; ranking of, by Kunstkompass, 367–68; Reinhardt on (1960s), 337; relationship to art market of, 4, 7, 57, 356; relationship between patron and, 82–85, 87, 116–18, 121, 123, 125, 223–24; in Renaissance Italy, status of, 115–16, 118; retrospectives of work by, 267–69; secondary art market and, 5; self-promotion by, 266–67; sexuality in work of, 93–95; signatures on work of, *see* signature(s), artists'; solo exhibitions at galleries of, 266; from Spain, 194, 197–98, 202–3; studios/workshops of, *see* studio(s), artists'; style-based social networks formed by, 243; styles of, in Renaissance Italy, 121–22; in teams (Renaissance Lombardy), 121, 122,

artist(s) *(continued)*
124; touch of (facture), 241; trademarks *(poncifs)* of, 92–94; training of, *see* training of artists; use of prints by, as compositional sources, 196; as value producer, 43–44, 355–56; wages of, 153, 154; work of, defining, 58–60, 154–55

artistic cult value, 42

Artnet, 351, 352

Artprice, 351, 353, 369, 370

art production: educational purpose of, 239; industrial, 48, 269, 271; Kant on nature of, 15–16; labor as anathema to, 16–17; mimesis in, 27; as useless, 55

ArtQuest, Inc., 105

Arts (periodical), 346, 347

Art-Union (British, later *Art Journal*), 229, 230, 239

artwork(s): appreciation of, 231–32; as assets, 63–65; attribution of, 168, 179–81, 191, 193, 250; authentication of, 78–79; authenticity of, *see* authenticity (of art); autograph status of, 85, 121, 126; autonomy of, 31; avant-garde, 41; "biography" of, 33; cerebral content of, 365–66; commissions for, *see* commissioned artworks; communicative power of, 40–41; contemporary to sales, *see* primary art market; as domestic decor, 206–8; export of, 149–51; genres of, affecting prices, 88; hybrid forms of, 241–42; iconoclastic destruction of, 164–65; interpretative writing on, 261; as investment, *see* investment; legitimation of artist and, 355–57; movable, trade in, 136–37; multidisciplinary, 358; Old Masters, *see* old-master paintings; pricing of, *see* prices and pricing; property rights and, 99–101; public, architecture as, 111; reciprocal gifts of, 82–83, 124–25; reproduction of, 39; resale of, *see* secondary art market; in retrospective exhibitions, 268–69; searches for, by dealers, 166; as secular object, 112–14; signification established for, 355; size of affecting pricing, 51, 52, 87–88, 331–32; sourcing of, by dealers, 166; studies for, *see* drawing(s); utility and, 70–71, value of, *see* value of art. *See also* engraving(s) and engravers; fakes and forgeries; object(s); painting(s); sculpture(s)

Arundel collection, 80, 171–72, 204–5, 209

Ashton, Dore, 317–19

asset(s), 63, 212, 325; art as, 63, 175, 354–55; demand, theory of, 63; in efficient market hypothesis, 103–4; information gathering on, 105–6; speculative, art as, 62, 208, 212

ateliers. *See* studio(s), artists'

auctions and auction market, 3, 161, 227–28, 251, 344; advances paid on consignments to, 227–28; in Amsterdam (17th-cent.), 6, 161, 216; of avant-garde art, 280, 345–46, 360; catalogues from, *see* catalogues, auction; in China, 352–53, 369, 370; of commodities, 157; of contemporary American art, 342, 363–64; in Germany (18th-cent.), 189–93; Land Art at, 344–46; in London (17th/18th cents.), 207–8, 210–11, 216; modern prints at, 106–8; price information from, 104, 105; primary market affected by, 5–6, 61; public, Gersaint and, 248–49; Rembrandt's buying at, 174–76; risks associated with, 227, 363; in secondary market, 5, 62, 106. *See also* Christie's; Sotheby's Auction House

audience (for art), 1; for Courbet's paintings, 263–64, 266; for prints based on paintings, 239–40; purchasers, *see* collectors, art; technological innovation and, 362; as value creators, 45, 52

aura, 12, 30, 32, 38–39, 42, 55, 86, 355; of Minimalist art, 338, 339, 341–42

authenticity (of art), 15, 39, 79; certificates of, 80; market value and, 86; prints, 238; role of museums, 293; Reni on, 126; Rubens's approach to, 174. *See also* appraisal(s) of artworks; connoisseurs and connoisseurship; museum(s)

Aux Quatre Vents (Antwerp), 136–37, 146

avant-garde art and avant-gardism, 14, 271; Collins & Milazzo and, 348–50; Conceptual art and, 6, 47; Cubism and, *see* Cubism; European (1980s), 353–54; kitsch and, 24–26; La Peau de l'Ours and, 277–80; Land Art and, 4, 342–46; Minimalism and, *see* Minimalist art; in Paris, 326, 354; strategies in, 89–91; Reinhardt on, 337. *See also* contemporary art

Chamberlain, John, 332–33

Champfleury, 259, 263, 266

Chanel [S.A.], 361–62

Charles I, king of England, 78, 209, 215, 216; collections of, 204–5

Charles II, king of England, 87, 216–17

Charles V, Holy Roman emperor, 187

Chauchard, Alfred, 270

Chave, Anna C., 337–42

Chicago, 298, 353

China, 351, 352, 371; art fair participation by, 370; arts of, market for, 353; auction market in, 369, 370

Chinati Foundation, 341–42

Christensen, Carl C., 9, 186–89

Christie, James, 227–28

Christie's, 62, 77, 310, 346, 362, 369; contemporary works sold by, 225; establishment of, 226–27; old-master paintings sold by, 225; pricing by, 107–9

Christo, 344–45, 346

Christus, Petrus, 138

Cincinnati Industrial Exposition (1886), 294

cities: art markets identified with, 10; innovators clustering in, 8–9, 58, 157, 214; as mercantile centers, 68; modernization of, 234, 238, 259. *See also* specific cities

Claesz, Pieter, 165, 202

Clark, T. J., 1

Clarke, Thomas, 298, 299

classical art. *See* antiquity; Greek art

classics (field of study). *See* antiquity

clustering, 213–14; of artists, 8, 9, 185; guilds and, 213, 214; of merchants, 10, 137, 258; of urban professionals, 157

Cochin, Charles-Nicolas, 251

Cock, Hieronymus, 136–37, 146–47

Cock and Langford (London), 226, 228

Cognacq, Ernest, 270, 317

collecting, 195; addictive nature of, 75–76; in England (17th/18th cents.), 205, 209; Gersaint on rewards of, 249, 251–52; international dealers and, 211; motivations for, 76, 231, 233, 248, 251, 326; in Netherlands (17th cent.), 175–76; patterns of (U.S.), 326–27; in Renaissance, 115; sacralization of objects in, 76–77; and sense of self, 77–78; as social-class leveler,

251, 257–58; taste and, *see* taste; in Victorian period, 231–33

collectors, art, 76, 296; advice to, 106, 267; advisors to, *see* experts; as agents in art market, 57, 96; American, in Europe, 1, 7, 293; attribution and, 180–81, 191; of avant-garde art, 338–42, 343, 360–62; of Boschian prints and paintings, 146–48; British, 205, 208–9; catalogues published by, 80, 190; community among, 251–52; as connoisseurs, *see* connoisseurs and connoisseurship; dealers and, 45, 250, 290; galleries in homes of, 233; P. Guggenheim and, 312–15; inventories of, *see* inventories; of middle class England, 229–33; the "new," in post-war U.S., 323, 324; of photography, 48; property rights to art and, 99–101; psychology of pricing for, 51–54; Rembrandt as, 175–76; in Renaissance Italy, 112–13; reselling by, 64, 271, 272; swindles of, 311; taste of, *see* taste; wealth profile of, in U.S., 324–25; women as, 313–15

College of Painters (Utrecht), 214

Collins, Tricia, 348–50

Collins & Milazzo (C&M), 348–50

Cologne, 151, 190, 192, 354

Color Field painting. *See* Abstract Expressionism

The Coming Away of the Gale (Homer), 299

commercial culture(s), 25, 43; art as separate from, 18, 252; art critics in, 327; art exploited by, 31, 266; Cubist art and, 284–87; denial of, in exhibitions, 251, 266–67; in England, 205, 208; in Europe, 133, 187; Homer and, 297, 299; modernism in, 255, 272; spheres of exchange values in, 34–35; value of art in, *see* value (of art). *See also* culture; dealer(s), art; galleries; industry

commissioned artworks, 117, 161, 195, 210; altarpieces as, 117, 118, 122, 127, 130, 139; in Baroque-period Venice, 129–30; by Charles V, 187; copies and, 153–54, 222–23; from Courbet, 263–64; for dealers, 153, 168; frescoes as, 117, 122, 130; Homer's refusal of, 297–99; legal aspects of, 127–28; from Minimalist artists, 339–40; patron requirements for, 69, 111–12, 121, 128;

commissioned artworks *(continued)*
portraits as, 62, 164, 207, 222–24; by
religious entities, 125–26, 186, 187; in
Renaissance Italy, 118, 138–39; taste of
patron and, 138, 187, 256–58
commissions (payments), 5, 161, 226; for
advisors and agents, 243, 311, 349; at
auction houses, 61, 108–9, 228; from
dealers and galleries, 5, 238, 278, 308
commodification, 33–38; of art, 147–48, 154,
256, 371–74; of artists, 90, 94, 346; as
marketing strategy, 94–95; singularization
and, 35–38, 76–77
commodities, 33–34, 308; artworks as, 18, 90,
154, 212, 255–56, 371–74; artists as, 261–62;
culture industry and, 30–32; kitsch as,
24–26; marketing of, 295; nostalgia and,
296, 297; religious, 164; Rembrandt and,
173–74; singularity and, 35–38
common-value auctions, 109
communication, 32; globalization of, 351–52;
improvements in, 234, 293; social, theory
of, 252, 297
communism, aesthetics and, 19; art production
under, 21, 23; artists under, 14, 22; collapse
of, in Europe, 351–352. *See also* Marx, Karl
computer-generated art, 55, 362
Conceptual art, 6, 47; Land Art compared to,
342–46 *passim*
confrèries (Amsterdam), 214
connoisseur(s) and connoisseurship, 168; in
17th-century Europe, 78–80; art commodification and, 255–56; attribution and,
179–80, 191, 249; catalogues and, 191–92,
249; Coypel's ideas on, 250–51; early
publications on, 79–80; Gersaint as, 249,
250–51; museum personnel as, 48, 50;
old-masters paintings preferred by, 229,
251; and painting prices, 160–61; in
photography, 48, 49; and social status,
208. *See also* appraisal(s) of artworks
consignment(s): to Christie's, 226–27; to
dealers, 167, 237
conspicuous consumption, 6, 69, 72, 131, 233,
297
consumer revolution, British, 205–6
consumerism and consumption, 111, 115, 133,
205–6; art and, 101–2, 145, 208, 255,

324–25, 358; collecting as form of, 75,
114–15; cultural identity and, 10, 25, 30, 113;
culture industry and, 30–32, 371–74; kitsch
and, 24–26; of luxury goods, 71–72, 187;
marketing and, *see* marketing; museums'
relationship to, 371; in Paris (19th cent.),
258–59; ritual aspects of, 251–52; Veblen
on, 71–74. *See also* commercial culture(s)
contemporary art: American interest in, 311,
323, 353; art fairs specializing in, 369–70;
auctions of, 316–17, 369; in Bicknell sale,
230–31; biographies of artists and, 261,
268; by Chinese artists, 369; by continental
artists, London shows of, 235; dealers in
(early 20th cent.), 284–87; by Dutch
painters, 235; Guggenheim and, 313;
middle class purchasing, 229–30; Parisian
market for, 259–60, 327; retrospectives
and, 268; upper-class support for, in U.S.
vs. Europe, 326; during World War II,
market for, 291. *See also* avant-garde art
and avant-gardism; Cubism; primary art
market
contract(s), 166; between churchmen and
painters, 196; for commissioned paintings,
127–29; between dealers, 168; from Goupil
and Co., 238; between master and pupil,
148–49
Copley, John Singleton, 252, 253
copies/copying of artwork(s), 2, 57, 79; and
appropriation, 96–97; by artists and their
studios, 91, 126, 156, 222; at auction, 180,
191, 207, 217; commissioned by dealers,
145–48, 153–54, 167; demand for, 114,149,
221; impact on original, 39; trade in, 141,
149, 153, 154, 223. *See also* fakes and
forgeries; reproduction(s)
copyright: Dürer's monogram, 186; on
engravings, 174; exhibition right and,
101–2; property rights and, 100, 101; on
Victorian paintings, 239–40; on works of
art, 96–98
Corot, [Jean-Baptiste Camille], 260, 264, 286; at
Goupil and Co., 235–37
corporation(s): demand for artworks by, 63;
multinational, 351
Corporation of Image Makers (Antwerp), 138
Correggio, 131, 132, 152, 153, 171

Whistler and, 238–43; Restoration period in, 205, 209; social improvement fostered in, 231–32, 239; taste in, 213, 217; Victorian period in, *see* Victorian period; war with Dutch Republic, 216–17; war with France, 217, 246. *See also* United Kingdom (U.K.)

English School, 205, 225, 229, 293; at Goupil, 234, 235–36; impressionism by, 235–36; portraiture and, 221–24

engraving(s) and engravers, 49–51, 193, 222, 235, 239, 257; artist's proofs of, 242; copyright and, 174; in England, Smollett on, 218–20; painters executing, 155–56; Quellinus's work as, 155–56; Rembrandt's work on, 173; of Rubens's work, 154–55, 174; technological advancement and, 240. *See also* etching(s); prints and printmaking; reproductive prints

entertainment: art as, 41; art fairs as, 371–72; visual, as commercial, 295. *See also* kitsch

entrepreneur(s), artist as, Rembrandt, 173–74; patrons of art as, 269–72

Ernst, Max, 313, 314, 315

eroticism in art, 131, 132, 256

etching(s): in *Cremaster Cycle* editions, 359; Homer's sales techniques for, 299; Rembrandt's reworking of, 173; reproductive (technique), 241; Whistler's techniques for, 242–43. *See also* engraving(s) and engravers; prints and printmaking

Etro, Federico, 3, 127–30

Europe, 65, 131, 234; art prices in, 108; avant-garde art (1980s) in, 353–54; growth of consumerism in, 115–16; Western, as world economy, 7, 8, 9, 110

Ewing, Dan, 139–42, 148–49

exchange value, 2–3, 38, 301; spheres of, 34–35, 37; use value *vs.*, 297

exchanges, 34, 109; art, *see* auctions and auction market; commodities on, 33–34; of currencies (Antwerp), 141–42

exhibition(s): art fairs and, *see* fair(s), art; biennial, *see* biennial exhibitions; biographical approach to, 261–62; of British artists, 205, 230; catalogues for, 235, 237, 244, 268; by Collins & Milazzo, 348–49; conceptualization and design of, 309–10; curator's role in, 374; dealers' role

in, 267–68; by Durand-Ruel, 89, 267; of film and video art, 358–59; by Fry, 243–45; by Goupil (London), 234–38; of Impressionism, 90, 267, 271, 289; of Land artists' work, 343–45; loans of art to, 302–3; by Minimalists, 337–39; national/international (expositions), 372–73; in Paris, 89–91, 247; of Post-Impressionism (London), 243–45; right to present, 99–103 *passim;* at Royal Academy (London), 221–22; at Salons (Paris), *see* Salon (Académie, Paris); of Simulationists' work, 347, 349; of single artist's work, 266–67; sites for, 89, 282, 297–99; site-specific, 338, 339, 343; as source of artist income, 252–53; Stieglitz's ideas about, 307–10; survey, rise of, 372–73; temporary, 101, 235; of video art, 358–59, 362

exoticism in art, 91, 270

experts, 103; C&M as, 349; collectors reliant on, 65, 79, 293; on contemporary art, judgment of, 319, 367; Duveen seeks out, 310–11; on photography, 50; valuation by, 57, 78, 85, 105, 259–60. *See also* art historian(s); connoisseurs and connoisseurship

export(s): from Amsterdam, 216; from Antwerp, 149–52, 159–60, 198; from New York, 327. *See also* import(s)

expositions particulières, 266

expositions payantes, 252–53

Expositions Universelles (Paris), 91, 266–68, 298

Eyck, Jan van, 7, 137–38, 143, 150

facsimile(s), 29

facture, see production

fair(s), art, 6–7, 60; in Antwerp and Bruges, 136, 138, 139–41, 150; at Basel, 353, 369–70; biennials competing with, 372; Chinese galleries' participation at, 370; curators at, 374; in Europe, subsidization of, 354; galleries at, 369–70; Germany and, 185; globalization and, 352, 371–74; London Post-Impressionism exhibitions as, 243–44; New York dealers and, 353; territory/nationality affecting, 369–70; trade fairs and, 8, 110, 192, 372

fair use, doctrine of, 97–98

fakes and forgeries, 2, 39, 77–79, 160, 221; on
    Antwerp market, 141, 145–46; on Parisian
    art market, 260; in U.S., 311. *See also*
    reproduction(s)
fame, 114, 133; as determinant of value, 50, 70
Farington, Joseph, 227, 228
fashion: in artists' trademark-*poncif*, 92, 94;
    designers as patrons, 272
Fauvism, 29, 243, 245; collectors of, 272, 278,
    280
Federal Arts Project (U.S.), 316
Fénéon, Félix, 283
Fête en l'honneur du dieu Pan (Poussin), 254
fetishism: of commodities, 38, 90; of objects, in
    Harnett paintings, 297; religious art and, 21
film: culture industry and, 31; horror genre, 146;
    property rights and, 101; versioning in,
    360–61. *See also* video art
Fitzgerald, Michael C., 277–80, 288–90
Fitzhenry, John Henry, 300–301
Flanders, 10; artists of, in Germany, 186; dealers
    in, 198–202; demand for art in, 193;
    Holland and, 157, painting in, *see* Flemish
    School; Spain and, 150, 194–96 *See also*
    Antwerp; Bruges; Netherlands
Flavin, Dan, 338–39, 341, 363
Flemish School, 169, 171, 254; markets for art
    of, 114, 149–51
Florence, 10, 68, 120, 127, 150; as artistic center,
    8–9; arts in, Vasari on, 119–20; in
    Renaissance, 110–11
folk culture, 25–26
Fonspertuis sale, 249, 250, 251
forgeries. *See* fakes and forgeries
Fortune (periodical), 323
Fountain (Duchamp), 363, 364
Fourmestraux, Marie de, 198–202
France, 65, 66, 69, 133, 246, 291, 304, 353; art
    fair participation by, 369, 370; art from,
    American preference for, 293; auction
    market in, 369; contemporary artists
    in, 367–69; monarchy of, monopoly
    enterprises by, 116; Napoleonic wars and,
    246–47, 254, 258; national exhibitions in,
    372; as republic, 247; Revolution in, *see*
    French Revolution; sculpture from,
    256–58; Second Empire in, 247, 255; Third
    Republic, 90. *See also* Paris

Francesco da Sant'Agata, 301, 302
Frankfurt am Main, 186; art market in, 354;
    auctions in, 190–92
free markets, 133, 139, 176, 341, 355
Freedberg, David, 164
French Revolution, 205, 246, 258; effect on art
    trade of, 254; effect on connoisseurship of,
    255
Friedrich, Fariha, 338, 340
Friedrich, Heiner, 338–42
Fry, Herbert, 235
Fry, Roger, 29; exhibitions mounted by, 243–45
Furnesvik, Eivind, 373
Futurism, 243, 245

Gainsborough, [Thomas], 222, 223, 224
Galerie Berthe Weill, 278, 282. *See also* Weill,
    Berthe
Galerie de "L'Effort Moderne" (Paris), 285, 287
Galerie Druet (Paris), 283
Galeries Georges Petit (Paris), 288–90
Gallerani, Cecilia, 123–24
Galleria Schwarz (Milan), 363
galleries, 47, 96, 291, 369; at art fairs, 369–70;
    avant-garde art in, 338–42, 343; in China,
    370; cooperation among, in 1930s Paris,
    289–90; in department stores, *see*
    department stores; in East Village (New
    York), 348–50; exhibitions at, 53, 102,
    267; Guggenheim and, 312–15; in London's
    West End, 234–35; in New York, 305, 323,
    324, 348–50, 353; Our Lady's *Pand* as first,
    140–41; photography in, 48, 307–10;
    pricing strategies of, 51–54; retrospective
    solo shows at, 266–68. *See also* dealer(s),
    art
Gambart, Ernst, 240
Gardner, Isabella Stewart, 135, 293
Gauguin, Paul, 29, 89–91, 245, 281, 283;
    Vollard and, 272–76, 312
Gault de Saint-Germain, Pierre-Marie de, 255
Gautherot, [Claude], 257–58
Gee, Malcolm, 284–87
Gelderblom, Oscar, 157
Gennari-Santori, Flaminia, 300–304
Genoa, 68, 110, 150, 194
genre scenes, 142, 158, 260, 916; in England,
    207, 233; of Flemish and Dutch Schools,

254, 255; by French artists, 255, 256;
Victorian taste for, 229, 233, 239
gentry, 66–68; leisure class and, 71–74
geography, 193; art markets and, 10, 107, 185,
193, 204, 354; auction results and, 108–9;
international art trade and, 366–68
geometry, 47, 287; Simulationists' use of, 346–48
German Expressionism, 107, 108
German Ideology, The (Marx and Engels), 22–24
Germany, 10, 133; art auctions in, 189–93; art
fair participation by, 369, 370; art market
in, 9, 48, 108, 151, 353, 369; artists'
reputations in, 367–69; Dutch artists in,
159, 215; financial crisis (16th cent.) in,
187–88; merchant economy of, 185–86;
Minimalism in, 339; Napoleonic army in,
192, 193; primary art market in, 185–86
Gersaint, Edme-François, 248–52, 254;
catalogues by, 248, 249–50; on dealers'
ethical responsibility, 249–50
Gibson-Wood, Carol, 205–8
gift economy: Dürer and, 82–83; Reni and,
124–25
Gimpel, René, 310–12
Ginsburg, Allen, 336, 337
Ginsburgh, Victor, 4, 342–46
Giordano, Luca, 194, 195
Giorgione, 170, 171, 245
Gladstone Gallery (New York), 359, 360
Gleadell, Colin, 363
global art market (21st cent.): art fairs in,
369–70; China and, 352–53, 369;
contemporary art fairs in, 369–70; in
Europe *vs.* America, 353–57; makeup of, in
nationality, 367–69; multiculturalism in,
368. *See also* international art markets
(historical)
Godefroy sale, 249–50
Goethe, Johann Wolfgang von, 190
Goetkint, Peter, 151, 199
Goetzmann, William, 58, 103–6
Golden Age(s): Dutch, *see* Netherlands; Spanish,
193–95
Goldthwaite, Richard A., 111–16
Gonzaga court (Mantua), 114, 121
Gonzaga family, 134
Gorky, [Arshile], 317, 318
Gottlieb, [Adolph], 319, 321, 322, 323

Goupil and Co. (London), 233, 234–38, 275
government: academic art supported by, 266;
art-related regulations imposed by, 209–10;
duties and tariffs on art by, *see* duty (import
and export); economic development by, in
Renaissance, 115–16; in French Republic,
247; guild regulation by, 160, 216;
Kahnweiler auctions mandated by, 286–87;
taxation and, *see* taxes and taxation; Third
Republic French, 90. *See also* legal system
and art
Goyen, Jan van, 88, 162, 163, 202
Graffiti Art, 346, 348
Graham, William, 232
Grand Tour, 131, 133, 134; contemporary art
market compared to, 371; portraiture for,
223; in Victorian period, 229
Grand Tour of the 21st Century, 371
graphic arts. *See* prints and printmaking
Graves (auction records), 225
Gray, Charles M., 57, 60–65
Great Britain. *See* England; United Kingdom
(U.K.)
Great Depression, 289–290, 316
Great Exhibition (1851, London), 230
Greek art: Marx on, 19–21, 23; Winckelmann
on, 14–15
Green, Nicholas, 258–62, 268
Greenberg, Clement, 14, 24–27, 317–18, 319,
323; Emmerich on, 327–29
Greenough, Sarah, 307–10
Greenwood (London), 227, 228
Greffe, Xavier, 57, 58–60
Gris, Juan, 284, 286, 287, 313
Gros, [Antoine-Jean], 258
Groys, Boris, 374
Guercino, 125, 129
Guérin, [Pierre-Narcisse], 258
Guggenheim, Peggy, 312–15, 319, 322, 324
Guicciardini, Ludovico, 147
Guicciardini, Piero, 112–13
guild(s), 175, 214; in Amsterdam, 160, 164, 167,
215; in Antwerp, 9, 14–45, 140, 155, 199,
214; in Bruges, 138; in Brussels, 140; for
craftspeople, 209, 213–14; in Delft, 1, 164;
in Dutch Golden Age, 88, 160, 164, 213,
214; in England, 213, 217; in Florence, 118;
in Italy (17th cent.), 127; regulation of, 216

Guild of Saint Luke, 9, 155, 172, 198, 199, 214
Guillaume, Paul, 285–86, 289
Guino, Richard, 277
Gutenberg, Johannes, 185
Gutman, Walter, 335–37

Haarlem, 159, 168, 169, 202, 215
Habsburg Empire, 137, 151, 195
Häckel collection sale, 190
Hagedorn, Christian van, 191
The Hague, 163, 164, 170, 214
Hall, Samuel Carter, 226, 229–30
Halley, Peter, 346–50
Halpert, Edith Gregor, 312
Hals, Mathijs, 168
Hamburg: art auctions in, 186, 189–93; art
    market activity in, 191, 193
A Harlot's Progress (Hogarth), 220, 221
Harnett, William, 294–97
*Harper and Row Publishers v. Nation
    Enterprises,* 98
Haskell, Francis, 256–58
Haviland, David, 271
Hearst, Randolph, auction of collection of, 326
Hegel, Georg Wilhelm Friedrich, 19, 21, 23
Heilbrun, James, 57, 60–65
Heinauer, Oscar, 300, 301
Heizer, Michael, 340, 341
Helmreich, Anne, 233–38
Helsinki art gallery, 244, 245
Hercules (Pollaiuolo), 301
Herding, Klaus, 262–63
Hernández-Navarro, Miguel A., 202–3
Het Loo paintings sale, 170
Hickey, Dave, 341
history painting(s), 159, 164; David and, 252–53;
    in England, 151, 207, 221–22; in Golden
    Age Spain, 195–96; in hierarchy of genres,
    221, 254; political messages in, 253; pricing
    of, 87–88. *See also* religious art
Hoffman, Barbara, 58, 96–98
Hogarth, William, 220–21
Holbein, Hans, 171, 172, 207, 310
Holland. *See* Netherlands
Hollanda, Francesco da, 85
Hollar, Wenceslaus, 80
Homer (Rembrandt), 173
Homer, Winslow, 4, 297–99

Hong Kong auction market, 352
Honig, Elizabeth, 57, 81–85, 152–54, 372
Hooch, Pieter de, 163, 164
Hoogstraten, Samuel van, 88, 162
Horizon (periodical), 317
Horowitz, Noah, 357–62
Hoschedé, Ernest, 270–71
Houbraken, Arnold, 87, 88; on Rembrandt,
    172, 173
Houghton, Charlotte, 142–45
Howard, Aletheia, Lady Arundel, 171
Howard, Thomas, Earl of Arundel, 171, 204–5,
    210
humanism and humanists, 79, 111–12, 254;
    culture of, 67; interest in antiquities of, 115;
    on patronage of artists, 114
The Hunt (Jankowski), 358
Hutter, Michael, 14, 40–42
Huygens, Constantijn, 88; Rembrandt's
    correspondence with, 176–79

iconoclasm, 158, 164, 188
idealism in art, 19, 22, 23, 338, 339
imitation in art, 27; Netherlandish painting
    disparaged for, 254; theory of, 28–29;
    trompe l'oeil painting and, 294–97
Immerseel, Chrisostomo van, 153, 154, 198–202
immigrant artists: in England, 216–17; in New
    York, 9, 316; in Paris, 246, 247; in
    post-Restoration England, 213, 215, 216–17;
    from the Spanish Netherlands to
    Amsterdam, 159–60
import(s), 198, 201; duty paid on, 209, 210; into
    England, 209–10, 213, 216–17; regulations
    for, 198. *See also* export(s)
Impressionism, 9, 90, 243, 245, 278, 289;
    collectors of, 270, 271, 272, 274, 280, 291,
    311; Durand-Ruel and, 267; English artists
    and, 235–36; group shows of, 267, 271;
    U.S. reception of, 305
India, 35–36, 182, 368, 370, 371
Industrial Revolution (19th cent.): kitsch and,
    25; Louis-Napoleon III inspired by, 246;
    prosperity engendered by (England), 229,
    238
Industrial Revolution, "Second" (20th cent.),
    292–93
industry: art and, Gutman on, 337; culture,

30–32, 371–74; in French Republic, 247;
globalization of, 351–53; photography and,
49; privatization of, 352
information in art markets: auction records
and, 103–4; collectors' sources of, 64–65;
flow of, 185; innovation enhanced by,
163–64; internet as source, 351, 365; price
forecasting and, 104, 364–65; price risk
decreased by, 106; primary *vs.* secondary
markets using, 61; Spanish artists and,
203. *See also* catalogue(s); inventories
Ingres, Jean-Auguste-Dominique, 282, 283
innovation: in Dutch art (17th-cent.), 165, 173,
174; guilds fostering, 214; information flow
assisting, 163–64; in painting, 9, 41, 47,
162, 163, 165, 305; patents and, 162, 165;
product *vs.* process types of, 161–65 *passim*;
urban clustering and, 8–9, 58, 157, 214;
Veblen on, 71, 74
Institute of Water-Colour Painters, 235
institution(s), cultural. *See* museum(s)
insurance, 211, 247
interior space(s), 111; of bedchamber (Renaissance Italy), 112; furnishings in, 111–13; in
middle-class England, 206, 207, 236; of
modern avant-garde gallery, 323; paintings
in, 112–13, 291; price of paintings affected
by position in, 128, 130; in Victorian
houses, pictures arranged in, 232; of villas,
art for, 236
international art markets (historical): Cubism
on, 285; dealers/agents in, 211; development of, 6; exportation of art and, 149–51.
See also art markets (historical); global art
market (21st cent.)
International with Monument (New York), 346,
347, 349
inventories, 141, 144, 170, 180, 206; of artists'
own work, 62, 196; attributions in, 168,
180; of auction houses, 108; of Dutch
collections, 87, 166; as indicative of
demand for art, 115, 158; of Italian
collections, 112–13; of Netherlandish art
dealers, 152, 153, 167, 168; of Rembrandt's
collections, 175; as source of historical
information, 88, 164, 169
investment, 44, 51, 53, 95–96, 103; American art
becomes, 316–17; Bicknell sale and, 230–31;

for Chinese collectors, 369; contemporary
sales and, 226, 229–32; dealers advice to
collectors about, 106; by foreign princes,
solliciteurs making, 182–84; Gutman on,
335–37; as hedge against inflation, 290;
market efficiency and, 103–5, 226; in
masterpieces, 106, 107, 261; in modern art,
261–62; research for, 105; risk and, 60–61,
64, 104–6, 140, 210–11, 333; Steins'
purposeful, 281; value *vs.* aesthetic value,
95–96; Vollard's interest in, 276–77
Isabella of Aragon, 122, 123
Isabey, Léon, 264
Ismay, Thomas Henry, 233
Italy, 8, 65, 111, 135; art fair participation by,
369, 370; contemporary artists in, 367–69;
cultural dominance of, 194, 195; English
collectors' interest in, 205, 217; landscape
paintings (18th cent.) from, 291; as market
for Flemish art, 150–51; merchants from,
in Antwerp, 137; Netherlandish artists
working in, 150, 215; northern Europeans
collecting art from, 169–72; old-master
paintings from, 6, 205; patrons from, 138;
during Renaissance, *see* Renaissance Italy;
schools (styles) of art in, 122, 124, 127;
sculpture of, Sommariva and, 256–58;
secular art's ascendancy in, 113–14. *See also*
Florence; Rome; Venice

Jabach, Eberhard von, 78, 80, 172
Jahyer, Felix, 265–66
James, Henry, 293
Jankowski, Christian, 358
Japan, 48, 64, 354, 368, 369; art of, 91
Jegher, Christoffel, 155, 156
Jensen, Robert, 247, 266–69
Johnson, Una, 276–77
Jonckheere, Koenraad, 179–84
journalism. *See* critics and criticism; press
Judd, Donald, 338–39, 341, 363, 364
judiciary (U.S.): on fair use, 97; nobility
conferred through, 66–67. *See also* legal
system and art
Julien, Isaac, 360–61

Kahnweiler, [Daniel-Henry], 279, 280, 284, 291,
327; auctions of collection of, 286–87

Kamen, Henry, 193

Kandinsky, [Vassily], 27, 313

Kant, Immanuel, 13, 14, 15–17, 21, 40; on
    fairness, 99, 100

Karp, Ivan, 332–33

Kassel, 343, 371, 372, 373

Kemp, Martin, 121

Kennedy, Edward, 242–43

Ketelsen, Thomas, 189–93

Kiesler, Frederick J., 313, 314

kinetic art, 47, 314

King, Gregory, 206

Kippfigur(en), 92–93

Kisch v. Ammirati and Paris, Inc., 97

kitsch, 25–26. *See also* entertainment

Kline, Franz, 317, 321, 323

Kneller, Godfrey, 207, 213

Knoedler Gallery (New York), 293

Koegel, John, 98

Koons, Jeff, 363; legal actions against, 96–98;
    work by, 346–50

Kootz, Samuel, 319, 322–23

Kopytoff, Igor, 14, 32–38, 76–77

Krauss, Rosalind, 338

Kretzer, Marten, 166, 215

Kunstkompass, 367–68

Kuspit, Donald, 346–47

labor, 13, 82; art price based on, 4, 85, 87, 88,
    96, 125; artists', recognition of, 4, 172, 173,
    292; commodities and, 2, 21, 297; division
    of, 16, 22, 31, 163; fine art distinguished
    from craft by, 13, 15–16, 254, 334; by hand,
    73–74; in painting techniques, 157, 160;
    theory of value, 2–3, 35, 44, 334

Land Art, 4, 342–46

Landon, Charles Paul, 252

landscape painting(s), 236, 268; artists'
    specialization in, 158, 161, 163, 173; in
    Bicknell sale, 231; by Courbet, 262–66;
    effet in, 264, 265; in England, 207, 221,
    231; French market for, 255, 256, 291; in
    hierarchy of genres, 127, 129, 260, 263;
    from Holland, 159, 165, 201, 254;
    popularity of, 161, 168, 196, 207, 229,
    291; pricing of, 88, 165; Victorian taste
    for, 229, 231, 233

Lanfranco, Giovanni, 125–26

Lantara, Simon Mathurin, 256

Lanvin, Jeanne, 272

Latin America, 136, 150

Laurencin, Marie, 286

Le Strat, Nicolas, 60

legal system and art: Chinese demand and,
    352; copyright and, *see* copyright; property
    rights and, 99–101; trademarks and, 96;
    video art and, 358. *See also* judiciary (U.S.);
    taxes and taxation

Léger, [Fernand], 286, 287, 313

Lehmann, Ulrich, 58, 91–95

Leiden, 159, 160, 163, 169, 214

Leipzig, 189, 192

leisure class, 71–74; gentry and, 66–68

Leja, Michael, 293–97

Leo Castelli Gallery, *see* Castelli, Leo

Leonardo da Vinci, 42, 171, 205; at the Sforza
    court, 121, 122–24

Level, André, 277–80

Levey, Michael, 223

Levin, Kim, 338

Levine, Sherrie, 347

Leyland, Frederick, 232, 233

Lichtenstein, Roy, 47, 332–33

Liesaert, Suzanna, 152

Lievens, Jan, 169, 191

Life Magazine, 319

Lightning Field (De Maria), 338, 341

Limborch, Hendrick van, 87

Limoges porcelain, 78, 271

Lippincott, Louise, 213

Lisson Gallery, 361

literacy, universal, 24

literature, 44; avant-garde, 25, 26; on change in
    art, 306–7

*Lives of the Most Excellent Painters, Sculptors, and
    Architects* (Vasari), 78, 84, 118–20

Lombardy: art from, in Cosimo III de' Medici's
    collection, 170–71; painting style of, 122,
    124; team painting in, 121, 122, 124

London, 5, 8, 48, 206, 214, 254; art prices in,
    108, 223, 226, 240; as artistic center, 9,
    10, 213, 354; auction market in, 207–8,
    226–27, 346, 352, 353; David exhibiting
    in, 252–53; as European world-economy
    center, 204–5, 247; exhibitions at, 230, 234,
    236–37, 243–45, 252–53; guild structure in,

nature: Barbizon painters and, 268; Courbet's
landscapes and, 264–65; writing about, 261
Nature Morte (New York), 349
Naumann, Francis M., 362–66
Neo-Expressionism, 346, 348
Neo-Geo, 346–50, 356
Neshat, Shirin, 360
Netherlands, 10, 69, 81, 150, 192, 202, 368;
accumulation of goods in, 175, 206; art
markets in, *see* art markets (historical);
artists trained in, 159, 213; Dürer in, 81–84;
Dutch paintings, 270, 354; as European
world-economy, 157, 304; Flemish
paintings, *see* Flemish School; Gersaint
exporting from, 248–49; guilds in, *see*
guild(s); iconoclastic destruction of art in,
164–65; immigrants in, 159–60; Italian art
collected in, 169–71; paintings market in,
158–62, 229; Spanish domination of, 194,
198. *See also* Dutch Republic; Flanders
network(s), artists', 58, 59, 89, 243, 349. *See also*
clustering
The New Capital (New York), 349, 350
New York (city), 5, 8, 298, 302, 324; Abstract
Expressionism in, 317–19; American art in,
316–17, 321–24, 327; as artistic center, 9, 11,
326–27, 353; auction market in, 108–9,
346, 352–53; avant-garde art in, 343, 348,
353; as center of western-European world
economy, 292, 316; East Village art scene
in, 348–49; European art in, 316, 354; Minimalist artists and, 338–42
New York Herald, 303
New York Sun, 303
New York Times, 317, 331, 334, 346, 348, 363
Newman, Barnett, 319, 321, 322
nobility: avant-garde and, 24–25; in England,
229; hierarchies within, 67–68; ostentation by, 68, 69; painters serving, 78, 269;
social mobility toward, 65–67. *See also*
aristocracy
Nude Descending a Staircase (Duchamp), 331
Nueva España, 200–202
Nuremberg, 186

Obach, Charles, 234
object(s): consumption of, in Renaissance, 112,
113; in court system, significance of, 83;

fetishizing, 38, 296–97; in medieval
Europe, collecting of, 114–15; owning,
psychology of, 70–71; photographs as,
48–50; Pop art use of, 334–35; as readymades, 55; sacralization of, by collector,
76–77; sales catalogues as, 249; in still
lifes, *see* still life painting(s). *See also*
artwork(s)
objectification: of the body, 92–93; of cultural
values, 30, 115; as development from utility
to aesthetic value, 70–71
Officina Plantiniana (Antwerp), 136, 155
Ogden, Henry V. S., and Margaret S., 207, 208,
217
The Old Violin (Harnett), 294
old-master paintings, 205, 207, 251, 259, 355; on
Amsterdam market, 215; Christie's sales of,
225, 228; commissions for, 129–30; fakes
of, 230, 260; on French market, 251, 254,
261, 291; from Italy, 6, 205; in London,
demand for, 216, 225, 229, 353; modern
artists within tradition of, 244–45; prints
after, 239
Olivier, Fernande, 283
Olympia (Manet), 91, 283
open market(s): Amsterdam and, 162, 174;
Antwerp as, 145, 147; artists selling on, 133,
297–98; London as, 207, 215
Oppenheim, Dennis, 343, 344, 345
Ormrod, David, 212–17
Ostade, Adriaen van, 167
Ostade, Isaac van, 167
Our Lady's *Pand* (Antwerp), 140–42

Paets, Adriaen, collection of, 182, 183
Pagani, Laura, 3, 127–30
Page, John R., 224–28
Painter-Stainers Company, 209, 213, 216
painting(s), 49–50, 88, 232, 318; artisanal
attitude and, 209, 254, 262; for ceilings,
130, 132, 155; classification system by genre,
254, 263; contracts for, *see* contract(s);
copying of, *see* copies/copying of
artwork(s); in Dutch homes (17th-cent.),
158–62; engravings of, *see* engraving(s)
and engravers; guilds' impact on, 213, 214;
nature, French market for, 261–62;
patron-client relationship reflected in,

Poiret, Paul, 272

Poland, 81, 133, 313

Pollock, Griselda, 57–58, 89–91

Pollock, Jackson, 314, 315, 316, 318, 319, 320, 322, 328

poncif of artist, 92–95

Pop art, 4, 6, 324–35

Pope, Alfred, 236

Porta, Tommaso della, 120

portfolio(s): of masterpieces, 106–7; of photographs, 241; print collections sold as, 241

portrait(s) and portraiture, 159. 195, 258, 281, 283; by Cézanne, 281, 283; commissions for, 62, 164; copies increasing standing of, 222–23; early Netherlandish, 138, 139; in England, popularity of, 204, 207, 221–24; iconographic import of, 223–24; Milanese, Leonardo's influence on, 123–24; as old-master paintings, American taste for, 293; profile formula for, 122; sculpted, 120–21, 258; self-, 114, 241–42; sitters' renown and artists' success, 120, 222; utilitarian aspects of, 222–23

Portugal, 150, 157

Post-Impressionism, 278; imitation theory of art and, 28–29; London exhibitions of, 243–45

postmodern society, 14, 356

Poussin, Nicholas, 218, 219, 254

press (journalism), 237, 267, 294, 302, 367; on Bicknell sale, 6, 226, 230–31; Gersaint's use of, 248–49; Minimalism covered by, 338, 341–42. *See also* critics and criticism

press (printing). *See* prints and printmaking; reproductive prints

prestige, 27, 37, 144, 291; of buying contemporary art, in China, 369; as motivation, 326; of painting ownership, 257, 291, 358; value of art and, 43, 44, 112

Price Waterhouse, 228–29

prices and pricing: in Amsterdam art market, 159–60; in Antwerp art market, 141, 152–53; appraisal to set, 51–54, 106, 179–81, 191; for avant-garde art, 354–57; in Baroque Venetian Republic, 129–30; client determining, 124–25; of commissioned works, 128–30, 153; comparables used in,

364–65; contracts and, 127–28; discounts and, *see* discount(s) and discounting; Duchamp on, 330–32; elasticity of, 51, 63; of English portraiture (18th cent.), 223, 224; figure-count and, 125, 128–29, 130; fixed price method, 125, 133–34; at Goupil and competitors, 236, 238; Homer's approach to, 299; information on, access to, 4–5, 61, 104, 105; for Land Art, 345, 346; legitimation of artist and, 355–57; as market signals, 51–54; of photographs, 49–50; piece rates and, 166–67; predicting, market efficiency and, 103–4; in primary *vs.* secondary art markets, 61, 62; process innovation and, 162; production of art and, 44, 86–87, 324; rarity and, 50, 240, 242; Rembrandt's approach to, 176–79; reserve, 61, 364; by size, 52, 87–88, 117, 125, 128, 130; by time artist spends, 86–88, 125; of video art, 358; Vollard–Gauguin correspondence about, 273–75; Whistler setting, 242–43. *See also* auctions and auction market; value (of art)

primary art market(s), 5–6, 60–62; Christie's 19th-century sales in, 225, 226, 228; in Germany, 185–86; in London, 204–5; in post-war U.S., 316–17

La Princesse du Pays de la Porcelaine (Whistler), 232, 238

print run(s), 49, 50, 240

prints and printmaking: in 16th century, 82–83; Antwerp as center of, 136, 186; as art form, Whistler and, 238–39; audience for, expansion of, 239–40; of Boschian imagery, 147–48; as compositional source for Spanish artists, 196–97; Dürer and, 186; editions in, 49, 53, 242; hybrid forms of, 241–42; lithography for, 238–40, 242–43; market for, 49, 238, 240, 241; modern, auction market for, 106–9; patrons using, 196–97; publishers of, 80, 137, 234, 240; rarity and market value for, 50, 240; by Rubens's workshop, 155–56; sold by Goupil, 234, 235, 237; sold by subscription, 218, 220–21, 240; by Whistler, 238–41, 242–43. *See also* engraving(s) and engravers; reproductive prints

theories in art, 24, 236, 335; artistic value in,
  40–42; Baudrillard's, *see* Baudrillard, Jean;
  of effective rarity, 48–49; Halley's, 347–48;
  imitation (IT) in, 28–29; Kantian, *see* Kant,
  Immanuel; Marxist, 21, 22, 343; reality (RT)
  in, 29, 334; in Simulationism, 346–47;
  socratic, 27–29
Thomson, David Croal, 233–38, 241
Thoré, Théophile, 266
Thorvaldsen, Bertel, 257, 258
Times (London), 311
Tischbein, [Johann Heinrich Wilhelm], 252–53
Titian, 152, 153, 154, 170, 186, 207; paintings for
  Spanish monarchy by, 194, 195
Tooth (London dealer), 225
Toulouse-Lautrec, Henri de, 281–82, 283
trade: fairs, 8, 110, 192, 372; impact of
  technology on, 234, 239; international, 145,
  157–58, 205, 290; maritime, 8, 10, 111, 186,
  193; overland, 8, 185, 186, 193; retail, 141,
  145, 205, 213, 228, 235; wholesale, 61, 66,
  142, 205
trademark, Emin's, *poncif,* 92–94, 96–98;
  Whistler's motif, 242
training of artists, 159; in England, 213, 222; in
  Paris, 247, 272, 293
transportation, 8, 87, 127, 164; in France, 247;
  of household goods, 113; international art
  market and, 211; technological advances
  in, 292
travel, 247, 371; mobility of artists and, 127,
  129
Triomphe de l'amour (Renoir), 277
trompe l'oeil painting, 294–97
True North (Julien), 360–61
Turner, J. W. M., 226, 231, 310
Turrell, James, 338–39
Tuscany, 115, 194

Uffelen, Lucas van, 6
Union League Club (New York), 298, 299
United Feature Syndicate v. Jeff Koons, 96, 98
United Kingdom (U.K.), 102; art fair participa-
  tion by, 369, 370; artists from, 367–69. *See
  also* England
United States (U.S.), 234, 327; art fair participa-
  tion by, 369, 370; artists in, 108, 314–15,

367–69; attitude toward art in, 292—93,
  306; auction market in, 324, 326, 342,
  369; China and, 352; collectors from, in
  Europe, 1, 7, 293, 324–25; copyright in, *see*
  copyright; photography market in, 48–51,
  307–10; post-war art of, Guggenheim and,
  314–15; primary art market in, 316–17;
  visual culture of (turn-of-century), 295;
  wealth in, art collecting and, 292, 324–25.
  See also New York (city)
upper class. *See* aristocracy
urban society. *See* cities
use value, 2–3, 34, 297
utility, 72–73; of art, 55–56; value, 2, 3, 4, 70–71,
  297
Utrecht, 164, 214, 215
Utrillo, [Maurice], 272, 286, 311
Uylenburgh, Gerrit, 167–68

valorization (of art), 90, 102, 250–51, 360
value (of art), 85, 181, 334; aesthetic, *see* aesthetic
  value; authenticity affecting, *see* authenticity (of art); beauty and, 70–71, 73; belief
  supporting, 43–46; commodification
  affecting, 33–37; Duchamp on, 330–32;
  editioning and, 360–61; establishing, 2–3,
  6, 38; exhibitions affecting, 237, 374; fame
  of artist affecting, 50, 70; in gift-exchange
  system, 82–85; in honor system, 83–85;
  market dictating, 355–57; nonmonetary, 37,
  40–42, 86–87, 124–25; rarity contributing
  to, *see* rarity and scarcity; Rembrandt's
  approach to, 172–76; "true" *vs.* market,
  105–6; in video art, 358–59. *See also*
  exchange value; prices and pricing
value(s), 14, 36, 43, 70, 79; art historical, 2,
  41–42; of commodities, 2–4, 34, 37;
  cultural, 5, 25, 34–35, 43–44, 115; social,
  83–85; as subjective, 70–71; taste and,
  17–18; use, 2–3, 34, 55, 73, 297; utility, 2, 3,
  4, 70–71, 297; value equivalence of, 34, 35,
  100, 128–29, 355, 356
Van Dyck, Anthony, 152, 155, 184, 310; in
  London, 215, 216
Van Gogh, Theo, 275
Van Gogh, Vincent, 29, 244, 245, 272, 279
van Haecken sale (1758), 212

Printed in the USA
CPSIA information can be obtained
at www.ICGtesting.com
LVHW080609191223
766839LV00007B/165